ASTD Handbook for Workplace Learning Professionals

Elaine Biech, Editor

Alexandria, Virginia

ASTD Press is an internationally renowned source of insightful and practical information on workplace learning and performance topics, including training basics, evaluation and return-on-investment, instructional systems development, e-learning, leadership, and career development.

Ordering information: Books published by ASTD Press can be purchased by visiting our website at store.astd.org or by calling 800.628.2783 or 703.683.8100.

Library of Congress Control Number: 2007939270

ISBN-10: 1-56286-512-9
ISBN-13: 978-1-56286-512-2

ASTD Press Editorial Staff

Director: Cat Russo
Manager, Acquisitions & Author Relations: Mark Morrow
Editorial Manager: Jacqueline Edlund-Braun
Senior Associate Editor: Tora Estep
Editorial Assistant: Maureen Soyars
Retail Trade Manager: Yelba Quinn

Pillar sidebar authors: Justin Brusino and Maureen Soyars
Copyeditor: Phyllis Jask
Indexer: April Michelle Davis
Proofreader: Kris Patenaude
Interior Design and Production: Kathleen Schaner
Cover Design: Alizah Epstein

Printed by United Book Press, Inc., Baltimore, Maryland

ᕫ Contents

✑ Foreword

The American Society for Training & Development (ASTD) is the world's largest professional association dedicated to the workplace learning and performance (WLP) profession. Trainers, designers, facilitators, human resource practitioners, consultants, and other WLP professionals turn to ASTD for the world's most comprehensive and powerful network of people, tools, and information.

The *ASTD Handbook for Workplace Learning Professionals* is a great example of ASTD's commitment to delivering relevant tools and information to the profession. It has been compiled for learning professionals at all levels of expertise: those new to the profession who are trying to understand the nuances of the field, as well as experts in the profession who need a reference guide or information on a specific topic.

The *ASTD Handbook for Workplace Learning Professionals* is the culmination of the efforts of many of the most influential and respected leaders in the field, whose work continues to shape the profession. I hope you find it a valuable resource for many years to come.

Tony Bingham
President and CEO, ASTD
May 2008

✍ Introduction to the *ASTD Handbook for Workplace Learning Professionals*

Any book with the word *handbook* in the title suggests a tremendous amount of work was required to produce it. The *ASTD Handbook for Workplace Learning Professionals* is no exception. Certainly its more than 60 contributors and dozen or so editors, designers, and ASTD staff members have put in thousands of hours to produce this volume. All this effort has led to a book—which is substantial both in form and in content—that will serve as a reference and a go-to guide, bringing together in one volume methodologies, practices, processes, theories, and other key information for workplace learning professionals.

This *Handbook* brings together many of the best practitioners in the field to present professionals like you with authoritative and critical information. It summarizes and integrates many areas of the broad field known today as *workplace learning and performance.* It is a standard reference guide for definitive answers, as well as a source of practical ideas. Need a refresher on Bloom's taxonomy? It's here. Need implementable ideas for how to make your training session more interactive? It's here. Want more information on distance learning or performance models? It's here.

How Did the Contents of the *Handbook* Transpire?

The word *handbook* suggests an exhaustive and comprehensive document, but, in actuality, the field of workplace learning and performance is so broad as to make it impossible to include everything the profession touches. An editorial advisory board, which consisted of John Coné, Tora Estep, Pat Galagan, Pat McLagan, Mark Morrow, Nancy Olson, Dana Gaines Robinson, Cat Russo, Marc Rosenberg, and myself, did a laudable job of narrowing down an expansive list of topics that could have filled many volumes into the single volume you are holding.

We started by identifying a list of everything you ever wanted to know about training, development, and workplace learning and performance. But because we were writing a handbook, not an encyclopedia, we needed to narrow the scope. Topics were combined, some were eliminated, and others changed focus. As you can imagine, we had several lively discussions. And in the end, a table of contents emerged that we thought would resonate with our audience—you.

The next task was to identify authors who are experts in the identified chapter topic. We decided early on that we wanted only the best of the best and were delighted when the authors agreed to write the selected chapters based on their areas of expertise.

Tora Estep did a yeoman's job of coordinating the contributions from the authors. The advisory board read and edited the chapters as well as the pillar sidebars. The result is a handbook that meets the needs of the WLP professional.

What Are the Components of the *Handbook*?

The *Handbook* is divided into nine sections, and although there may be a slight amount of overlap, in general, each section represents a major area of the profession:

- Learning in the Workplace
- Assessing and Analyzing Needs
- Designing and Developing Effective Learning
- Face-to-Face Delivery—As Important as Ever
- Delivering Technology-Enabled Learning
- Measuring and Evaluating Impact
- Organizational Level Applications
- Managing the Learning and Performance Function
- The WLP Professional.

Each section is introduced by a luminary—an individual who has reached legendary stature in the profession. These are individuals who are leaders in the field and have achieved prominence as philosophical practitioners, including

- Geary Rummler, author; performance analysis, design, and management consultant; past president of the International Society for Performance Improvement (ISPI); former member of the ASTD Board of Directors; Distinguished Contribution to WLP Award recipient; and member of the HRD Hall of Fame
- Robert Mager, author and originator of the criterion-referenced instruction (CRI) methodology, currently applied worldwide; and Distinguished Contribution to HRD Award recipient

- Elliott Masie, chair of the Learning CONSORTIUM, CEO of the MASIE Center, author, internationally recognized futurist, e-learning guru, and Distinguished Contribution to WLP Award recipient
- Don Kirkpatrick, former national ASTD volunteer president, Gordon Bliss Award and Lifetime Achievement in WLP Award recipient, member of the HRD Hall of Fame, author, and creator of the four levels of evaluation.

The other luminaries represent corporate leaders:

- Bill Wiggenhorn, originator of Motorola University, acknowledged expert in various WLP arenas, senior executive at Xerox, chief learning officer at Motorola and Cigna, and currently on the Board of Governors for the Center for Creative Leadership
- Bill Byham, cofounder, chairman, and CEO of Development Dimensions International (DDI), an internationally renowned human resource training and consulting company with more than 1,200 associates around the world, author of 22 books, and Distinguished Contribution to HRD Award recipient
- John Coné, one of the founders of Motorola University, vice president of human resources and chief learning officer for Sequent, vice president of Dell Learning, interim CEO of ASTD, named by *Training* magazine as a visionary in organizational learning, former chair of the ASTD Board of Directors, and Gordon Bliss Award recipient
- Donnee Ramelli, current vice president and chief learning officer for Fannie Mae, past president of General Motors University, vice president of learning and organization development for Allied Signal/Honeywell, and member of the ASTD Board of Directors
- Tony Bingham, current president and CEO of ASTD.

All these individuals are seen as authorities in the sections that they introduce. It's easy to see why we are honoring them with a "luminary" designation. You will enjoy reading their particular perspective on the section topics they introduce.

These sections are made up of a collection of 49 chapters, written by an elite team of experts, all writing in their area of expertise. The names of these authors read like a billboard list of who's who in the field of WLP. So who are they? These are individuals who have influenced the profession for many years and have more than 2,000 years of experience among them.

I am humbled by what these WLP professionals have accomplished. If you read the short biographies after each chapter, you will be amazed at what they have done—and in most cases are still doing. They have written and edited hundreds of books—and counting; they have written a couple thousand articles and chapters. They are members of the HRD Hall of Fame and former members of the ASTD Board of Directors. They have received hundreds of awards and have been honored by ASTD and well-known magazines, journals, and organizations. They have advised some of the largest private and public organizations in the world, trained millions of participants, presented at thousands of conferences, and led *Fortune* 100 businesses. Truly, the chapter contributors represent the best, most experienced practitioners in the world.

These are names you know. Names you rely on every day. Here's a sample:

- Dana Gaines Robinson, performance consulting leader, Distinguished Contribution to WLP Award recipient, and former member of the ASTD Board of Directors
- Rita Bailey, former chair of the ASTD Board of Directors and leader of Southwest Airlines University for People
- Pat McLagan, author, consultant, WLP expert, Gordon Bliss Award recipient, and former member of the ASTD Board of Directors
- Harold Stolovitch, author of the wildly successful *Telling Ain't Training*
- Bob Pike, trainer extraordinaire, model for most trainers around the world, and former member of the ASTD Board of Directors
- Mel Silberman, scholar, author, and authority on active learning
- Marv Weisbord, OD Network Lifetime Achievement Award recipient and author
- Thiagi, facilitation master of games and simulations
- Jean Barbazette, train-the-trainer expert and author
- Allison Rossett, expert on job aids and performance support, Distinguished Contribution to WLP Award recipient, and former member of the ASTD Board of Directors
- Chris Argyris, author, Harvard University professor, and recipient of 13 honorary degrees and the Lifetime Achievement in WLP Award
- Peter Senge, senior lecturer at MIT, founding chair of the Society for Organizational Learning Council, author of *The Fifth Discipline*, and Distinguished Contribution to WLP Award recipient
- Geoff Bellman, wise and warm consultant and author.

Within the mind-expanding chapters by these renowned authors are sidebars that feature distinguished professional leaders, or "pillars," who have influenced the content of the chapter in which they appear. These pillar sidebars describe some of their accomplishments and contributions to the field of WLP. Of course, some of these pillars have had a far-reaching effect on the profession and could quite conceivably appear in several chapters.

How Do You Get the Most Out of the *Handbook*?

This *Handbook* is not meant to be read from cover to cover. The editorial advisory board repeatedly brought up the need for a practical, go-to resource—a source where practitioners, students, librarians, or experts can find the information they require when they need it.

If you need general information about a subject, such as web-based learning or data collection, use the table of contents to locate a section or a specific chapter. If you require information about specific topics such as Bloom's taxonomy or copyright guidance, turn to the comprehensive index in the back of the book. Likewise, if you need information about a leader in the profession—for example, Malcolm Knowles, Thomas Gilbert, Robert Gagné, or Ned Herrmann—the index will lead you to a pillar sidebar that provides a synopsis of that individual's accomplishments. A glossary in the back of the book provides definitions to key words you may encounter in the *Handbook.*

In addition, the CD-ROM provides additional tools, such as worksheets, checklists, activities, case studies, and more.

And the *Handbook* Would Not Have Been Possible Without . . .

- The editorial advisory board. You created the vision and ensured that we stayed true to it throughout. You and Rhonda Munford also gave your time to review the chapters to ensure that they support the overall intent of the project; contribute to the profession; and deliver worthwhile, accurate content. Thank you.
- The luminary guest contributors. You skillfully introduced each section, which is just another example of why you are the leaders in our profession. Thank you.
- Authors. Your contribution of time and expertise has turned an exciting ASTD project into a tool that will be used globally. Thank you.
- Justin Brusino and Maureen Soyars. You researched and wrote about the pillars of the WLP profession. Thank you.
- ASTD staff. You envisioned a handbook, a resource for WLP professionals at all stages in their careers. Thank you for the opportunity to be a part of this worthwhile project.

Elaine Biech
May 2008

Section I

Learning in the Workplace

 **Section I**

Learning in the Workplace

Luminary Perspective

A. William (Bill) Wiggenhorn

In This Chapter

- ➢ Learn five keys to learning
- ➢ Understand how to learn from those around you

My mentor, Robert W. Galvin, former chairman of Motorola, is well-known for his unconventional wisdom, innovation, curiosity, and modeling of lifelong learning. Bob taught us to use "scouts" to chart the way to new territories. Back in the days when only one executive in our company had a passport and everyone knew where he was, Bob continuously challenged us to learn more about the world, to scout out new geographies, new global partnerships, potential products. The company grew and times changed. Suddenly it seemed that everyone in the company had a passport, and no one knew where anyone was. We were making history, however, as scouts in developing countries, charting new territories for our rapidly expanding business model. The global thrust of our company forced us to expand and refine our development efforts.

Bob gave me a mantra that changed my life for the better. I have carried his teaching with me throughout my career, and I am pleased to share it with you in the context of learning and performance.

"Bill," he would admonish, "be sure you always travel with two suitcases—one filled with everything you know and a second empty one to fill with what you will learn from others along the way."

This introductory chapter gives me the opportunity to share less of what I alone know—and more of what I've learned from the thousands of people I've met and hundreds of locations to which I've traveled. Over the years, my empty suitcase has overflowed with the following learnings:

- The world turns quickly.
- Adapt to the future or fail.
- Honor Harry Potter's generation.
- Learning is the ultimate antioxidant.
- Frequently take stock of your leadership legacy.

The World Turns Quickly

In this section of the book, we are reminded of the evolution of workplace learning and human performance improvement. It's been quite a ride. Think of the basics of telling employees that they were our most important assets and, because of that, we were going to nurture them and grow them. Consider how that has changed to the model of giving people learning experiences during their moments within our companies, knowing that they will likely travel on and accrue additional learning at other firms. We've moved from lifelong employment to the whim of Wall Street and an ebbing and flowing competitive landscape.

I've seen telegraphs segue into fax machines and brick-sized cell phones evolve to those the size of candy bars, and I've experienced the wonder of how wired and wireless the world really is.

I spent considerable time last year winging the world—from Michigan to Moscow, from São Paulo to Santa Clara, from Shanghai to Sydney to Cairo to South Bend. In these varied geographies, I have continued to fill my suitcase. In each client location, I've learned even more about the importance of assessment; how to engage the younger, slicker learner; why "face" still matters; and how critical leadership development and skills enhancement continue to be.

Adapt to the Future or Fail

My personal commitment to lifelong learning has resulted in experiences and opportunities that have evolved from the days of classroom training and purely instructor-led experiences to the richness of blended learning and morphing technology.

We've come a long way from the days of flip charts, chalk, overheads, and extension cords. The workplace of tomorrow is here, and it houses many faces, languages, and ages. Baby Boomers interact with Generation X, Generation Y, and Generation Next. Learning is offered in blogs, podcasts, portals, and Skype.

Honor Harry Potter's Generation

You might be asking yourselves, what's an old guy like him know about Skype? Well, someone put it in my suitcase—about three weeks before Moscow. It's called just-in-time learning. The someone who introduced me to this new communication technology is actually a mature colleague (whom I am convinced learned it from one of his very with-it kids). For most things technological, I rely on the Harry Potter generation.

My nephew Robert was born the same year as Harry Potter. Being a combination CEO-wannabe and engineer, Robert has been leading me kicking and screaming through technology for the past several years. Robert programs me, wires me, wirelesses me, and challenges me to keep up with technology. He once (almost) complimented my wife, Pat, by telling her that she was one of the most technologically astute older people he had ever met. She's still mulling that one over.

Seriously, in the age of emerging learning systems, global interaction, compressed time-frames for learning, record-breaking changes in technology, I've learned that it would be easy to become a dinosaur if I didn't keep up and connect every day. My connectivity secret is my nephew.

The business case for learning, which you will read about in chapter 3, is rock solid. My client organizations and I have seen absolute proof that learning drives performance. We know that if we don't continuously adjust our thinking and provide buzz and click and blog and pods to our toolkits, we lose.

By the way, Pat and I got back at Robert in an unusual way. For his high school graduation gift, I took him with me to Beijing for the sole purpose of introducing him to the competition he will face for the big jobs of the future. He got the message.

Learning Is the Ultimate Antioxidant

The most critical—and exciting—learning from my suitcase is that the more you learn, the younger you stay. There's an energy and an excitement to continuing in the game of learning and teaching and stretching and flexing. There's a lethargy that sets in when learning no longer matters. I've seen people drop out and drift off too early in life. It's important to remember that when you hang up your shoes and opt out, you are out of the

---

The Legend of the Divine Dr. M

I've learned over the years that to survive in our industry, one must be, if nothing else, flexible and willing to adapt to the next new thing. Here's how I was reminded of that during a recent program I ran in Moscow.

Tuesday evening, a call came in from the company coordinating our travel. "Dr. M," our facilitator for the critical Wednesday and Thursday portions of our program had a visa problem and would not be allowed into Russia. Instead, Dr. M was put on a plane and flown back to North Carolina. How in the world would we save the day?

It didn't hurt that Dr. M is a young, intelligent, resourceful, and energetic professor. With the flick of a switch we, with our laptop camera and Dr. M with another, Skyped across the ocean for one-and-a-half days.

Was it crystal clear, in sync video? No. Was it pretty darn good? Yes. Was it on a par with the level of teleconferencing we did years ago? It was much, much better.

So, flexibility, technology, and solving the problem in real time were key.

Our audience of 30-something high potentials loved the experience. We saved face, and that is another important learning. At the end of the day, the reason Dr. M engaged and captivated our audience is that, filled with pixels though it was, the delivery was definitely "face to face." Live, energized facilitation remains at the center of learning differentiation and effectiveness—even when it's "virtual."

---

game. I've found that keeping in touch with my older mentors and listening to my younger clients is enriching and, in deference to my late father and father-in-law, much more fun than golf.

As learning professionals, you wield enormous power. It is your job to show those around you how and why learning matters. Think of the political currency you have at your fingertips:

- You align and integrate learning in support of your organization's strategy.
- You create leadership bench strength for growth and succession.
- You enable the introduction of new products and services.
- You educate your customers and your community.
- You improve processes.
- You model the way.
- You scout.

Frequently Take Stock of Your Leadership Legacy

At this stage in my life, I am living the wisdom of Steven Covey's advice to "begin with the end in mind." James Kouzes and Barry Posner (2006) write about *A Leader's Legacy*. This is critical advice. It is important to leave our mark and pull others up behind us. It is up to each of us, individually and collectively, to live and learn and grow and model and teach—and share our suitcases. For therein lies our legacy: giving what we know and gleaning what we don't in order to lead others to greatness. What a privilege!

∞

About the Author

As principal of the Main-Captiva consulting business, A. William (Bill) Wiggenhorn partners with corporate clients to develop customized executive development, talent management, retention, and strategy programs. An acknowledged expert in the fields of training and development, leadership development, e-learning, marketing, and global business strategy, Wiggenhorn currently serves on the board of governors of the Center for Creative Leadership.

Best known for establishing Motorola University (MU) as the benchmark corporate university, he expanded MU's international reach to encompass 101 education offices in 24 countries. Wiggenhorn served as a senior learning and development executive at Xerox, as CLO (chief learning officer) at Motorola and Cigna, and on several for-profit and nonprofit boards.

Reference

Kouzes, James, and Barry Posner. 2006. *A leader's legacy.* San Francisco: John Wiley & Sons.

The Evolution of the Training Profession

Tora Estep

In This Chapter

➢ Learn how the training profession has developed over time

➢ Understand the roots of training practices in use today

The training profession has changed dramatically over the last 15 years. Today the profession receives more of the respect it deserves as a partner in the ultimate success of organizations around the world. This development is welcomed by training professionals. However, change is not without cost or, well, change—much of it good and some of it questionable. The good part—increased respect for the contribution of learning and participation at the highest levels in strategic and financial decisions—is undeniably positive. The unfortunate part of this positive development is that the term that most identifies the profession—*training*—has taken a back seat. Taking its place are other broader, more strategic terms: workplace learning professional, performance consultant, workplace learning and performance (WLP) professional. Even the title of this book represents part of this ongoing transition.

These changes are not necessarily wrong, or even reversible. They represent the most recent development in a profession that must continually change to stay relevant and vital.

In its history, the training profession has changed many times from its initial focus on skills training to individual development to systems theory and organization development to learning and, most recently, to performance. However, a good part of the profession considers the term *trainer* to be as complete a description as needed. So with that as an introduction, what follows is a brief and inclusive history of the training profession, from its roots in medieval history to modern-day online training.

Early Learning Models and Practices

Learning is as critical to human life as breathing. Without it we can't feed ourselves, talk to each other, protect ourselves from heat and cold, and raise healthy offspring, let alone achieve great results as individuals and organizations. Thus the history of training and learning begins with the very beginning of humankind with elders teaching the young how to find and recognize edible plants, hunt and process game, care for children, and make weapons and tools from local materials. But these are basic skills that people need to survive. When and how did training first develop as a profession?

The advent of agriculture enabled societies to create a surplus of food, which in turn allowed people to become more specialized in their job roles. As a result, the need to train individuals in specific trades became more pressing. To meet this need, on-the-job training, apprenticeships, guilds, vocational and manual schools, factory schools, and vestibule training arose (see Figure 1-1 for a time line of early training and learning practices).

On-the-Job Training

The earliest form of training was on-the-job training, which is one-to-one training in which an experienced craftsperson shows a novice how to do a task (Sleight, 1993). On-the-job training is still common today, in part because of its simplicity; all that an organization needs to do is assign an experienced employee to show a new employee how to do the job. Furthermore, on-the-job training obviates any problems with transfer because training takes place in the job setting, so the learner has no problem in understanding how the learning applies to the work. However, some drawbacks of on-the-job training are that the experienced employee is unable to accomplish any productive work while he or she is providing training and that any equipment and resources in use during training will be out of commission for production. In addition, being experienced at one's job is not necessarily an indicator of ability to teach or train well.

Apprenticeships

While on-the-job training was the earliest form of training, it was typically informal in nature. A more formal arrangement arose with the apprenticeship system. Although

Figure 1-1. Time Line of Early Learning and Training Practices

Training formats and theories

Antiquity	The Middle Ages and the Renaissance	The Industrial Revolution	WWI	1920s	1930s
On-the-job training	Apprenticeships	Vocational or manual training schools; factory schools; vestibule training; gaming situations; case method; role-play method	Show-tell-do-check method (Charles B. Allen)	Eduard C. Lindeman challenges idea of teaching adults with pedagogical methods; sales training; Hawthorne studies	U.S. government-instigated training programs

Societal influences

Antiquity	The Middle Ages and the Renaissance	The Industrial Revolution	WWI	1920s	1930s
	Formation of guilds; invention of the printing press	Emergence of factories and mass production	Scientific management (Frederick Winslow Taylor); assembly lines	The post-war boom discourages the application of training to industry	The Great Depression

Source: Compiled by Tora Estep, ASTD.

Steinmetz (1976) notes that rules governing apprenticeships appeared in the code of Hammurabi in 2100 B.C., apprenticeships really took root in the Middle Ages when jobs became too complex to master with just a few days of on-the-job training (Sleight, 1993).

Apprenticeships typically took several years. In exchange for work, the master trained a beginner in a craft. The beginner, who lived with the master and got no pay, became increasingly proficient in a particular craft and eventually became a journeyman or a yeoman. Although apprenticeships are generally thought of as applying only to artisanal crafts, they were not restricted to such jobs but could apply to medicine, law, and education (Steinmetz, 1976). Apprenticeships still exist today. In the United States, where apprenticeships are less common, apprentices are safeguarded by the U.S. Department of Labor, which ensures equality of access to apprenticeship programs and provides employment and training information to sponsors and the employment and training community.

In Asia and Europe, however, modern apprenticeship programs are more common. In Germany, they are an important part of the successful dual education system, which combines apprenticeships with vocational education. In India, the Apprenticeship Act, enacted in 1961, regulates the way that apprentices are trained so that their training conforms with Central Apprenticeship Council standards and meets industry needs. The United Kingdom has more than 160 apprenticeship frameworks—including National Vocational Qualifications—which now extend beyond craft and skilled trades to other areas of the service sector without an apprenticeship tradition. Although apprenticeship declined in the United Kingdom in the early 2000s, the percentage of young people completing apprenticeships began to increase again in 2004 after the government established the Modern Apprenticeships Advisory Committee to make recommendations on the apprenticeship system.

Guilds

The guild system also developed in the Middle Ages, in England before the Norman invasion of 1066. Guilds were "associations of people whose interests or pursuits were the same or similar. The basic purpose was mutual protection, assistance, and advantage" (Steinmetz, 1976). The guild system controlled the quality of products by establishing standards and regulating the people who were authorized to produce them. This also meant that apprenticeships came under the authority of the guild, which determined when a worker had reached a certain level of proficiency. Within the guild there were three levels of workers: the master, who owned the materials and directed the work; the journeyman, who worked for the master in return for pay; and finally the apprentice. Guild guidelines determined when a worker had reached a certain level of proficiency and was able to graduate to journeyman or master level.

Guilds also strictly regulated workers' hours, tools, prices, and wages and required that all workers have the same privileges and pursue the same methods. These conditions coupled with the ever-growing capital investment required to start a workshop and the increasingly high standards set by masters made it so difficult for journeymen to attain master status that they banded together in yeomanry guilds, which became the forerunners for today's labor unions (Steinmetz, 1976).

Vocational and Manual Schools

The guild and apprenticeship systems continued to dominate training and learning until the Industrial Revolution, which began in England, spread to France and Belgium, and then to Germany and the United States (Miller, 2008). However, the onset of industrialism started the acceleration of change in business that we see today as well as changes in training and learning practices. One of the new forms that learning took at this time was vocational and manual schools. These schools were intended to provide training in skills related to specific jobs. One of the earliest vocational schools was established by the Masonic Grand Lodge of New York in 1809; in 1824, Rensselaer Polytechnic Institute in Troy, New York, became the first technical college; and in 1828, the Ohio Mechanics Institute opened in Cincinnati, Ohio (Miller, 2008; Steinmetz, 1976).

Vocational schools—which lost popularity in the United States and have only recently begun to resurge—have continued to be an important force in training especially in Europe, which has included vocational training in the draft Constitutional Treaty establishing the European Community. To establish a vocational training policy that would apply to all members of the European Community, "two important schemes were devised: Europass-Training, which described skills acquired by training abroad, and Europass, which combines five documents aimed at providing a clear and simple picture of the qualifications and skills of citizens throughout Europe" (European Communities, 2007). Germany's successful vocational training program has also served as a model for Australia's vocational training program.

Manual training started in the United States around 1825. It started primarily as a correctional tool based on the idea that it was better to give idle hands something productive to do but then became widely established by the late 1880s. One of the greatest leaps forward in learning in the United States at this time was the passing of the Land Grant Act of 1862. In signing this act, Abraham Lincoln provided a way for average people to get an education, which had previously been restricted to the wealthy.

Factory Schools

By the time that Hoe and Company in New York City started its factory school in 1872, classroom training had become the norm in education. The innovation was to attach the school directly to the factory and to develop the curricula based on tasks that were carried out in the factory. Sleight (1993) explains why factories turned to classroom training at this time:

> The machines of the Industrial Revolution greatly increased the ability of the factory to produce concrete goods quickly and cheaply, so more workers were needed to run the machines. The factory owners wanted the workers trained quickly because there was a large demand for the produced goods. Since the machines were much more complicated than the tools of the agrarian society of the past, and training needed to be accomplished quickly, the training methods of the past were inadequate.

The benefits of classroom training, compared with on-the-job training and apprenticeships, were that many workers could be trained at once and that fewer trainers were required. Also, learning was taken off the factory floor, minimizing distractions and leaving equipment in production. However, classroom training had some downsides as well. Learners needed to remember what they had learned until they got to work, and they also needed to transfer what they had learned back to the workplace. Furthermore, learners now had to learn at the trainer's pace and did not get the same level of feedback that they would have with on-the-job training and apprenticeships.

Vestibule Training

Around the turn of the 20th century, an innovation came about that addressed some of the problems of classroom training, namely vestibule training. Also called "near-the-job" training, vestibule training took place as close to the factory floor as feasible and contained the same equipment that the worker would use on the job. The trainer was an experienced employee in the company and would train six to 10 people at a time. This combined the benefits of classroom training (economy of scale, minimal distractions on the floor, equipment kept in production) with the benefits of on-the-job training (more hands-on, more feedback, fewer problems with transfer, fewer accidents). It did have some downsides, however. It was expensive, requiring duplication of the production line and full-time instructors, so it was restricted to situations in which many workers needed to be trained at once on unskilled or semiskilled tasks. Nonetheless, this form of training was popular through both world wars (Sleight, 1993).

The World Wars—Systematic Training

The world wars—especially World War II—saw the profession of training and learning really start to take off. The wars brought on a massive surge in demand for products, at the same time that large numbers of experienced workers were enlisting. As a result, industry needed workers not only to fill positions left empty but also to fill new positions. Zuboff (1984), as quoted in Sleight (1993), summarizes the situation, "With the growing complexity and size of factories, expanding markets that exerted a strong demand for an increase in the volume of production, and a rising engineering profession, there emerged a new and pressing concern to systematize the administration, control, coordination, and planning of factory work."

In response to these conditions, Frederick Winslow Taylor proposed a method to shorten the amount of time that it took to complete a task by studying workers and eliminating nonproductive time, which is referred to as scientific management. Another innovation conceived to speed up production was the assembly line. Training methods also had to be developed to train workers faster and more thoroughly than before. During World War I, Charles R. Allen put forward the show–tell–do–check method of training to train shipbuilders, which he adapted from the 18th century German philosopher, psychologist, and educator Johann Friedrich Herbart's five-step framework for pedagogy. Herbart's framework included preparing the students, presenting the lesson, associating the lesson with ideas previously studied, using examples to illustrate, and testing pupils to ensure they learned (Clark, 1999).

Allen's work and Army research gave rise to several training principles. Sleight (1993) summarizes these principles:

- Training should be done within industry by supervisors who should be trained how to teach.
- Training should be done in groups of nine to 11 workers.
- The job should be analyzed before training.
- Break-in time is reduced when training is done on the job.
- When given personal attention in training, the worker develops a feeling of loyalty.

Although these principles were used in training, a systematic approach to training did not develop until World War II. At this point large numbers of women and men over the age of 40 were entering the workforce to replace the men who had been called up for the war. These people needed training, but the supply of vocational school instructors ran out before the need was fully met (Shaw, 1994; Steinmetz, 1976). To supply much-needed trainers, the Training Within Industry Service of the War Manpower Commission developed the Job Instructor Program, or JIT. The JIT's purpose was to teach first- and second-line supervisors how to teach their skills to others. These train-the-trainer programs came to be known as J programs and expanded to include topics such as human relations, job methods, safety, and program development. Influences on these topics included Abraham Maslow's "A Theory of Human Motivation" (1943) and Kurt Lewin's first experiments with group dynamics (1948).

In concert with systematic training came a systematic approach to instructional design. During World War II, the military applied a systems approach to learning design, which became the forerunner for today's instructional systems design (ISD). The research and theories of B.F. Skinner on operant conditioning affected the design of these training programs, which focused on observable behaviors. Training designers created learning goals by breaking tasks into subtasks, and training was designed to reward correct behaviors and remediate incorrect behaviors.

During the war, industry also came to recognize how important the training of supervisors had become. As Steinmetz (1976) puts it, "management found that without training skill, supervisors were unable to adequately produce for the defense or war effort. With it, new production methods were being established by the aged, the handicapped, and industrially inexperienced women." The need for leadership in training had become obvious, and so the title of training director became increasingly common in management hierarchies. In 1942, the American Society of Training Directors (ASTD) formed during a meeting of the American Petroleum Institute in New Orleans, Louisiana (for more on the history of ASTD, see the sidebar later in this chapter).

In addition to the development of leadership in the training function came the recognition of the need for development in leadership more generally, which led to the emergence of the first management development programs. According to Steinmetz (1976), these programs were sponsored and guided by universities and colleges, which offered college-level courses in management and technology.

The 1950s

After World War II, the economy boomed as the efficiencies that had been gained in industry to accommodate the demands of war production were harnessed for peacetime reconstruction. However, some of the methods that had been used to achieve those efficiencies—specifically, scientific management—were beginning to prove demotivating to employees. As a result, human relations training grew increasingly popular, and supervisors were often trained in psychology (Shaw, 1994).

Training departments had become widely established during the war. Businesses wanted to continue training their workers but at the same time lower the costs of training and increase its efficiency. In 1953, B.F. Skinner's book *Science and Human Behavior* was

❧ B.F. Skinner ❧

B.F. Skinner was a renowned behavioral psychologist and a major proponent of behaviorism, an influential school of psychological thought that was popular between World War I and World War II. Skinner, who is categorized as a neobehaviorist, believed that the best way to learn about human nature was to explore how an organism responds to stimuli, both from the external environment and from internal biological processes, in a controlled, scientific study. Skinner's scholarly interests were influenced by psychologists such as Ivan Petrovich Pavlov; Bertrand Russell; and the founder of behaviorism, John B. Watson. Skinner's major works include The Behavior of Organisms *(1938),* Walden Two *(1948), and* Science and Human Behavior *(1953).*

As a professor of psychology at Harvard University, Skinner devised experimental equipment to train laboratory animals to perform specific acts as tests of his behaviorist theories. One of his most famous experiments was teaching pigeons how to play table tennis.

These experiments led to the development of Skinner's principles of programmed learning. Skinner discovered that in most disciplines, learning can be most effectively accomplished when it is taught through incremental steps with instantaneous reinforcement, also known as reward, given to the learner for acceptable performance. Programmed learning should be implemented using teaching machines, which present the user with a question, allow the user to answer, and then immediately provide the user with the correct answer. Programmed learning as an educational technique has two major types: linear programming and branching. Linear programming rewards student responses that lead toward the learning goal; other responses go unrewarded. A correct response also moves the learner along through the program.

The branching technique uses an electronic program that provides the learner with information, asks a question based on the information, and then responds to the learner based on the answer. A correct answer results in a screen that reinforces the right answer then and moves the learner along in the program toward the learning goal. A wrong answer returns the learner to the original information or provides further tutorial.

published, introducing behaviorism, which was built on the work he had done during the war. Behaviorism and the concept of job analysis formed the basis for a new form of training—individualized instruction—which would answer business's need for cheaper and more efficient training. Sleight (1993) describes the practice:

> Individualized instruction in essence replaces the teacher with systematic or programmed materials. Programmed materials are instruction that has been divided into small steps which are easily understood by the learner. After each

step is required an active response by the learner in the form of answering a question, drawing a graph, solving a problem, and so on. Immediate feedback is given after each response.

Individualized instruction was later automated through the use of teaching machines in the 1960s and also formed the basis for early computer-based training. It had the advantages of enabling learners to learn at their own pace, giving them privacy to correct mistakes, and reducing training time and error rates when back on the job. However, it could be expensive to produce, included only what the designer put into it, and required the learner to transfer knowledge back to the workplace.

Another development in ISD that occurred during the 1950s was the introduction of Bloom's taxonomy of educational objectives. In 1956, Benjamin Bloom presented this classification of learning objectives, which describes cognitive, psychomotor, and affective outcomes. Cognitive outcomes, or knowledge, refer to the development of intellectual skills. Psychomotor outcomes, or skills, refer to the physical movement, coordination, and use of motor skills to accomplish a task. Affective outcomes, or attitudes, refer to how people deal with things emotionally (ASTD, 2006). These categories are often referred to as KSAs (knowledge, skills, attitudes) and relate to the way that learning objectives are written to specify the types of learning to be accomplished. For example, a knowledge objective might be to describe how the increased production needs of World War II affected the field of training and learning.

At the end of the decade, ASTD published Donald Kirkpatrick's articles about four levels of evaluation in *The Journal of the American Society of Training Director* (later *T+D*), which introduced a new theme into the field: *measurement.*

The 1960s

The introduction of measurement into the field of training tied closely with another theme that started to emerge in the 1960s: the need to understand the business. Already during the 1950s more and more articles had appeared noting the importance of involving top management in training, and in 1960 Gordon M. Bliss, then executive director of ASTD, urged members to seek "wider responsibilities" and to understand "the vernacular which is used to report profits" (Shaw, 1994). To reflect this broader focus, ASTD changed its name to include the word *development* in 1964.

Another sign that the training profession was beginning to broaden its horizons at this time was the adoption of organization development (OD). According to the Organization Development Network, a professional organization for OD practitioners, "Organization

Time Line of ASTD's History

1942: The American Society of Training Directors (ASTD) is formed on April 2, 1942, at a meeting of the American Petroleum Institute, in New Orleans, Louisiana. Fifteen training directors hold their first meeting on January 12, 1943, in Baton Rouge.

1945: ASTD publishes the first issue of *Industrial Training News,* a quarterly publication that is eventually to become *T+D* magazine. ASTD also holds its first national conference, on September 27 and 28, in Chicago, Illinois.

1947: *Industrial Training News* changes its name to *Journal of Industrial Training* and becomes a bimonthly periodical.

1951: ASTD opens its first permanent office in Madison, Wisconsin, the hometown of Russell Moberly, the secretary-treasurer who keeps all the records at the time.

1952: Membership reaches 1,517. There are 32 chapters across the country.

1954: *Journal of Industrial Training* changes its name to *The Journal of the American Society of Training Directors.*

1959: *The Journal of the American Society of Training Directors* publishes Donald L. Kirkpatrick's article establishing four levels of evaluation for training: reaction, learning, behavior, and results.

1961: ASTD begins publication of *Training Research Abstracts,* later incorporated into *Training & Development Journal.*

1963: *The Journal of the American Society of Training Directors* changes its name to *Training Directors Journal.*

1964: ASTD changes its name to the American Society for Training and Development.

1966: *Training Directors Journal* changes its name to *Training and Development Journal.*

1967: McGraw-Hill publishes the first edition of *Training and Development Handbook.*

1968: Membership reaches 7,422. There are 65 chapters.

1972: ASTD and the U.S. State Department sponsor the first international training and development conference in Geneva, Switzerland. Two hundred people from six continents attend.

1975: ASTD opens a branch office in Washington, D.C.

1976: ASTD holds White House Conference on HRD in the World of Work in Washington, D.C.

1978: In Washington, D.C., ASTD hosts the seventh annual conference of the International Federation of Training and Development Organizations. Membership reaches 15,323; chapters number 110. Following ASTD's efforts in Congress, the Employee Education Assistance IRS exemption is approved. ASTD's publishes its first competency study, *A Study of Professional Training and Development Roles and Competencies,* by Pinto and Walker.

1979: ASTD elects its first woman volunteer president, Jan Margolis.

1980: Kenneth James Kukla becomes the 20,000th member of ASTD.

1981: ASTD moves its headquarters from Madison, Wisconsin, to Washington, D.C.

1983: ASTD publishes its second competency study, *Models for Excellence,* by Patricia McLagan.

(continued on next page)

Time Line of ASTD's History (continued)

1984: ASTD implements a new governance structure, resulting in a new leadership direction for the Board of Directors and the creation of a Board of Governors to look to the future. ASTD also launches *INFO-LINE,* a monthly publication designed to train the trainer in a broad array of topics.

1987: ASTD establishes a research function and receives a $750,000 grant from the U.S. Department of Labor. Research grants will reach almost $3 million by 1993. ASTD launches its second annual conference: National Conference on Technical and Skills Training.

1988: Membership reaches 24,451. There are 153 chapters.

1989: ASTD publishes its third competency model, *Models for HRD Practice,* by Patricia McLagan.

1990: ASTD and the U.S. Department of Labor publish *The Learning Enterprise* by Anthony P. Carnevale and Leila J. Gainer, as well as the more comprehensive *Training in America: The Organization and the Strategic Role of Training* by Carnevale, Gainer, and Janice Villet. Both publications establish the size and scope of the training enterprise in the United States. ASTD also launches a new magazine, *Technical & Skills Training.*

1991: ASTD publishes *America and the New Economy* by ASTD's chief economist, Anthony P. Carnevale, establishing the economic link between learning and performance. *Training & Development Journal* becomes *Training & Development.* The Benchmarking Forum is launched to benchmark learning and performance improvement processes, practices, and outcomes against the accomplishments of Forum members and to engage a worldwide network of high-level professionals and organizations.

1994: ASTD launches ASTD On-Line, an electronic information access service, and turns up on the Internet, where trainers are discussing the formation of a "cyberchapter" of ASTD. In addition, ASTD holds its 50th annual and first international conference in Anaheim, California.

1996: ASTD publishes its fourth competency study, *ASTD Models for Human Performance Improvement,* by William Rothwell.

1998: ASTD publishes its fifth competency model, *ASTD Models for Learning Technologies,* by George Piskurich and Ethan Sanders. The first Excellence in Practice Awards are given to recognize results achieved through the use of practices from the entire scope of workplace learning and performance. The first certificate program in human performance improvement is held. By 2007, ASTD offers 25 certificates. ASTD publishes the first annual State of the Industry report.

1999: ASTD publishes its sixth competency model, *ASTD Models for Workplace Learning and Performance,* by William Rothwell, Ethan Sanders, and Jeffery Soper. ASTD holds its first annual ASTD TechKnowledge Conference.

2000: ASTD starts a program to build a global community of practice, combined with local presence and action. By 2007, ASTD has 25 global networks. ASTD also launches its first online magazine, *Learning Circuits,* which covers topics related to e-learning.

2001: The ASTD Job Bank—a job site exclusively for workplace learning professionals—is launched. *Training & Development* magazine changes its name to *T+D.* The ASTD Certification Institute is established to govern certification and will launch certification for e-learning courseware in 2002.

2003: The first annual BEST Awards are held to recognize organizations that demonstrate enterprise-wide success as a result of employee learning and development.

2004: ASTD publishes its seventh competency model, *ASTD 2004 Competency Study: Mapping the Future,* by Paul Bernthal and others. This model forms the basis for certification.

2005: The ASTD Certification Institute launches the pilot of its certification program for individuals.

2006: The ASTD Certification Institute formally launches its individual certification program.

2007: In September, ASTD launches its first magazine directed exclusively to the learning executive audience, *Learning Executive.*

Development is a values-based approach to systems change in organizations and communities; it strives to build the capacity to achieve and sustain a new desired state that benefits the organization or community and the world around them." Its roots lie in the behavioral sciences, using theories about organization change, systems, teams, and individuals based on the work of Kurt Lewin, Douglas McGregor, Rensis Likert, Richard Beckhard, Wilfred Bion, Ed Schein, Warren Bennis, and Chris Argyris (Haneberg, 2005). For more on OD, see the sidebar.

The wider focus on business results also related to the emerging field of human performance improvement (HPI) or human performance technology (HPT). Performance improvement is a systematic, systemic, results-based approach to helping organizations meet their goals through the work of people. The work of Thomas Gilbert, Geary Rummler, Donald Tosti, and Dale Brethower moved the field of workplace learning from a singular focus on training to a wide variety of activities that improve business results. For more on the history of HPI, see chapter 2.

However, the general attitude toward business remained "let the adding-machine jockeys worry about the business." More popular were topics such as the psychology of influence, motivation, and attitude change. Topics related to the emerging American civil rights movement, such as workplace diversity, were also becoming more common.

In the areas of learning theory and design, the 1960s saw Jean Piaget, a Swiss developmental psychologist, create a model of cognitive development with four stages: the sensorimotor stage (birth to two years), the preoperational stage (age two to seven), the concrete operational stage (ages seven to 11), and the formal operational stage (11 and up). His theories form the foundation for the development of constructivism, which began to appear in the 1970s and 1980s.

Organization Development

Organization development work is, at its core, a purposeful and systemic body of work that improves how people and processes perform. Activities and initiatives represent a conscious and planned process to align the various aspects of the organization to meet its goals. Organization development professionals seek to improve the organization's capabilities as measured by its efficiency, effectiveness, health, culture, and business results. They do this by facilitating, consulting, coaching, analyzing, training, and designing.

There is some disagreement within the field about which practices and tools fit in OD. Some adopt a narrow interpretation that focuses on organization alignment and change intervention. Others see OD as a broader set of practices that includes leadership, diversity, and team training. There is some overlap of skills and practices among OD, training, human resources, project management, and quality improvement. To muddy the definition further, each company interprets these functional boundaries differently.

Warner Burke, an OD pioneer, said "Most people in the field agree that OD involves consultants who try to help clients improve their organizations by applying knowledge from the behavior sciences—psychology, sociology, cultural anthropology, and certain related disciplines. Most would also agree that OD implies change and, if we accept that improvement in organizational functioning means that change has occurred, then, broadly defined, OD means organizational change."

This definition, as well as the Organization Development Network's definition, share the notion that OD focuses on helping organizations get from point A to point B using a systemic approach based on knowledge of the behavioral sciences. The definitions also emphasize that OD work involves managing and implementing change.

Source: Haneberg (2005).

Meanwhile, Robert F. Mager proposed his model for instructional objectives in his 1962 book, *Preparing Objectives for Programmed Instruction.* This model indicates that objectives should have three components: behavior, condition, and standard. That is to say that the objective should describe the specific, observable behavior that the training should accomplish; indicate the conditions under which the behavior should be completed; and state the desirable level of performance. This type of objective is alternatively known as behavioral, performance, or criterion-reference objectives (ASTD, 2006).

Mager's theory of objectives was originally developed for use in programmed instruction. In the 1960s, programmed instruction became increasingly automated through the briefly popular use of teaching machines, which were electromechanical devices for delivering programmed instruction. Another development in technology at this time was the increasingly wide availability of minicomputers starting in 1965.

The 1970s

Sociotechnical-systems theory became widespread in the 1970s (Shaw, 1994). The theory indicates that the interaction of both social and technical factors support or hinder the successful functioning of an organization. As Pasmore (1988) describes it,

> The sociotechnical systems perspective considers every organization to be made up of people (the social system) using tools, techniques, and knowledge (the technical system) to produce goods or services valued by customers (who are part of the organization's external environment). How well the social and technical systems are designed *with respect to one another and with respect to the demands of the external environment* determines to a large extent how effective the organization will be. [emphasis in original]

Thus trainers began to understand that to achieve peak performance, both the technical and the social aspects of organizations had to be considered and optimized together. This aligned with the broader focus for the field that OD and HPI had begun to establish in the 1960s.

At the same time, social movements, such as feminism, environmentalism, and the gay rights movement were having an effect on society as well as on how training took place in organizations. As a result, trainers increasingly turned their attention to social issues, such as pollution, racism, and discrimination against women.

Another popular training topic during the 1970s was sensitivity training—also known as the laboratory method—which was a form of human relations training that took place in groups and was designed to raise the attendees' self-awareness and understanding of group dynamics and enable them to modify their own behavior appropriately. The method was attacked by George Odiorne and others, who did not think it was appropriate for training to help "managers achieve authenticity and develop self-esteem," but its principal defender was Chris Argyris of the National Training Laboratories (Shaw, 1994).

Chief among new forms of training that developed during the 1970s was the case method, which had been used in business schools prior to this time but not in training programs. The case method involves the use of a case study to explore a topic. Trainers also begin to teach management by objective, introducing expectancy theory as a way to predict employee behavior (Shaw, 1994).

The area of learning theory saw several developments. Malcolm Knowles's book *The Adult Learner: A Neglected Species* was published in 1973, which introduced adult learning theory. Although not the first to suggest that adults learn differently from children (already back in 1926 Eduard C. Lindeman challenged the notion that pedagogy was appropriate for adults in *The Meaning of Adult Education*), Knowles coined the term *andragogy* and presented five key principles that affect the way that adults learn:

- Adult learners have a need for self-direction and learn best when they have some control over what they learn.
- Linking learners' prior experience to learning is an important way to create powerful learning.
- Learners' readiness to learn is linked to their perception of its importance in filling their roles.
- Adult learners seek knowledge they can use immediately to solve a problem or complete a task.
- Adult learners are motivated to learn by internal incentives and curiosity (ASTD, 2006).

At about the same time, the nine events of instruction were presented for the first time in the 1974 book *Principles of Instructional Design,* by Robert M. Gagné and Leslie J. Briggs. Although Gagné originated from the behaviorist school of learning, the nine events represented a new theory in learning: cognitivism. While behaviorism focuses on outward behaviors, cognitivism focuses on how information is processed, stored, and retrieved in the mind.

Another learning theory that emerged in the 1970s is constructivism. With its roots in Piaget's theories about cognitive development, constructivism indicates that learning is a process of constructing new knowledge. Another important theorist related to constructivism, Jerome Bruner, saw learning as "a social process, whereby students construct new concepts based on current knowledge. The student selects information, constructs hypotheses, and makes decisions, with the aim of integrating new experiences into his existing mental constructs" (Thanasoulas, 2002). With the constructivist learning theory, the impetus in learning design is to create learning experiences that enable learners to discover and construct learning for themselves.

The 1980s

In the 1980s, productivity in the United States slowed down, while global economic competition became the biggest business challenge. Organizations in the United States underwent large downsizings, and many managers found themselves without jobs (Shaw, 1994). These events led organizations to look more closely at their training budgets, causing many training and development executives to focus more on training budgets and the

---

❧ **Malcolm Knowles** ❧

Malcolm Knowles is a key figure in adult education and is often regarded as the father of adult learning. Knowles made numerous contributions to the theory and practice of human resource development, but is best known for popularizing the term andragogy, *which is the art and science of teaching adults. Andragogy recognizes that adults learn differently than children and as a result need to be treated differently in the classroom. In 1973, Knowles defined four assumptions about adult learning in his book* The Adult Learner: A Neglected Species. *These were expanded to the six listed below in a subsequent edition (1984):*

- *Adults need to know why it is important to learn something before they learn it.*
- *Adults have a concept of self and do not like others imposing their will on them.*
- *Adults have a wealth of knowledge and experience and want that knowledge to be recognized.*
- *Adults become ready to learn when they know that the learning will help them with real problems.*
- *Adults want to know how the learning will help them in their personal lives.*
- *Adults respond to external motivations, such as the prospect of a promotion or an increase in salary.*

---

bottom line and on proving the value that training brings to organizations. For this reason and others, cost-benefit analysis and the concept of return-on-investment (ROI) became increasingly hot topics.

At the same time, women entered the field of training and development at an unprecedented rate. By 1989, women made up 47 percent of ASTD's members. Assertiveness training flourished. Other popular training topics were behavior modeling, teamwork, empowerment, diversity, adventure learning, feedback, corporate culture, and trainers' competencies (Shaw, 1994).

The latter—trainers' competencies—were the topic of two competency models published in the 1980s that increasingly positioned the field of training and development as part of the broader field of human resources work. The first modern attempt to define training and development—*Models for Excellence: The Conclusions and Recommendations of the ASTD Training and Development Study*—captured this expansion of the role of training (McLagan, 1983). By 1989, career development and organization development had been added to the repertoire of training and development work, and the report titled *Models for HRD Practice* (McLagan, 1989) captured this new development by using Leonard Nadler's term for the field: *human resource development* (HRD). This report defined HRD as "the integrated use of training and development, organization development, and career development to improve individual, group, and organizational effectiveness." (For more on HRD, see the sidebar.)

In technology, the first electronic workstations came on the market in 1981. By 1986, PC-compatible laptop computers had also become available. The rise of these technologies was about to change much of how learning was designed, delivered, and managed in organizations.

The 1990s

In the 1990s, technology exploded. Proponents of e-learning, computer-based training, and online learning proclaimed that classroom learning was over. Early e-learning followed the same behaviorist model that informed the programmed instruction of the 1950s and the learning machines of the 1960s in which a learner went through a sequence of steps, after which he or she responded correctly (or incorrectly) and then continued to the next learning element or doubled back as required.

The benefits were also similar: learners could learn at their own pace, make mistakes and get feedback without being embarrassed, and repeat sections until they had mastered them. E-learning had the additional benefit of more branching capabilities than the old programmed instruction and learning machines, which allowed learners to automatically bypass sections they already knew and focus more on problem areas. Multimedia capabilities also made e-learning more effective by stimulating more of the senses and appealing to different types of learners. And finally, e-learning allowed greater accessibility to training by minimizing costs associated with travel to training, time off of work to attend, and facilities.

However, e-learning did have some drawbacks. For one thing, it was hard to keep learners involved. Without the interactivity of a classroom, learners frequently tuned out of e-learning programs. Also, e-learning did not work as well for training interpersonal skills as live training. Another problem was that it could be costly and difficult to maintain and keep up-to-date. Thus blended learning, which combines e-learning with live classroom elements, became an increasingly viable option. One way to use blended learning was for learners to use e-learning elements to complete any prerequisite training so that all participants in a classroom session started from the same point, thus minimizing time spent to get everyone up to speed and maximizing time on the new skills and knowledge to be learned.

Definition of HRD

HRD is the integrated use of training and development, organization development, and career development to improve individual, group, and organizational effectiveness.

- *Integrated* means that HRD is more than the sum of its parts. It's more than training and development, or organization development, or career development in isolation. It's the combined use of all developmental practices to accomplish higher levels of individual and organizational effectiveness than would be possible with a narrower approach.

- *Training and development* focuses on identifying, assuring, and helping develop, through planning learning, the key competencies that enable individuals to perform current or future jobs. Training and development's primary emphasis is on individuals in their work roles. The primary training and development solution is planning individual learning, whether accomplished through training, on-the-job learning, coaching, or other means of fostering individual learning.

- *Organization development* focuses on assuring healthy inter- and intra-unit relationships and helping groups initiate and manage change. Organization development's primary emphasis is on relationships and processes between and among individuals and groups. Its primary intervention is influence on the relationship of individuals and groups to affect the organization as a system.

- *Career development* focuses on assuring an alignment of individual career planning and organizational career management processes to achieve an optimal match of individual and organizational needs. Career development's primary emphasis is on the person as an individual who performs and shapes his or her various work roles. Its major solution is influence on self-knowledge and on processes that affect individuals' and organizations' abilities to create optimal matches of people and work.

- *To improve individual, group, and organizational effectiveness* means that HRD is purposeful. It is instrumental to the achievement of higher goals. Because of HRD, people and organizations are more effective and contribute more value to products and services: the cost-benefit equation improves.

Source: McLagan (1989).

An alternate use for e-learning technologies that gained popularity at this time was their use as a performance support tool. Performance support tools in the form of job aids had been around since World War II in the form of printed cards with step-by-step instructions (Sleight, 1994), but technology allowed performance support to become integrated into the work.

Another development in HRD in the 1990s was the introduction of the concept of the learning enterprise. In 1990, Peter Senge published his book *The Fifth Discipline*, which presented this concept. A learning organization commits itself to disciplines that will allow it to develop its learning capacity to create its future. Ideas underlying the learning organization are systems thinking, mental models, personal mastery, and shared vision and dialogue.

These last two topics—performance support and learning organizations—were popular training topics in the 1990s. Other popular topics included "reengineering, reorganization and transformation of work, customer focus, global organizations, 'visioning,' and balancing work and family" (Shaw, 1994).

This decade also saw training gain legitimacy in the public sector. President Bill Clinton was elected on a platform that endorsed training. Robert Reich, a strong proponent of training, became U.S. secretary of labor and established the Office of Work-Based Learning (Shaw, 1994).

The 2000s

Since World War II, learning has evolved in many directions (see Figure 1-2 for a summary). In learning theory, behaviorism continues to have a strong influence on learning design, but cognitive and constructivist learning theories also have their effects through the use of Gagné's nine events of learning and discovery learning. Malcolm Knowles's theory of adult learning informs most training by emphasizing making learning relevant, using learners' experience as a platform for learning, and giving learners some say in how or what they learn.

In learning design, the basic ISD model has evolved; new models have developed that are applicable to different situations and have different emphases, such as rapid prototyping and learning modules. However, Bloom's taxonomy and Mager's model for learning objectives continue to influence the way that learning objectives are written today by specifying first the type of learning—knowledge, skill, or attitude—and then the behavior, condition, and degree.

Measurement is another strong theme in the field of training and development. Kirkpatrick's classic four levels of evaluation—reaction, learning, behavior, and results— and the work of people such as Jack Phillips and others in ROI still dominate the ways that learning is measured and reported. Measurement plays a big part in the drive to understand the business and to make the learning and performance function a strategic part of organizations. New in this area is the launch of the ASTD WLP Scorecard, which is an online real-time benchmarking and decision support tool that enables organizations to

- Monitor and benchmark a broad range of learning function indicators
- Compare the quality of the learning function with other organizations

Figure 1-2. Learning and Development Time Line, World Wars to Present

Training

	WWII	1950s	1960s	1970s	1980s	1990s	Present
	Systematic training: train-the-trainer (J) programs; management training; foundation of ISD	Programmed instruction (chunking subject matter): Bloom's taxonomy; Kirkpatrick's four levels of evaluation	HPI/HPT; OD; Mager's model for training objectives; teaching machines	Case method; sensitivity training/laboratory method (Chris Argyris)	Assertiveness training; cost-benefit analysis; electronic workstations and laptops; cross-cultural training; competency-based training	E-learning; the learning enterprise, learning organizations (Peter Senge)	Just-in-time learning; m-learning; skills gap; certification

Theoretical underpinnings

	WWII	1950s	1960s	1970s	1980s	1990s	Present
	Maslow's theory of human motivation; Lewin's group dynamics	B.F. Skinner; behaviorism; motivation theory	John Piaget's cognitive development; cognitivism; Richard Beckhard coins the term *organization development*	Malcolm Knowles's *The Adult Learner* (andragogy); Gagné's nine events of instruction (behaviorism); Jerome Bruner (constructivism)			

Societal influences

	WWII	1950s	1960s	1970s	1980s	1990s	Present
	Industry shifts to war production; entry of massive numbers of women and men over the age of 40 into the workplace	Emergence of the idea of involving top management in training	Emergence of the civil rights movement	Sociotechnical systems; feminism; environmentalism; the gay rights movement	Large numbers of women enter the workforce; global economic competition; globalization		Rapid proliferation of new technologies: games, MP3 players, Web 2.0

Source: Compiled by Tora Estep, ASTD.

- Diagnose strengths and weaknesses in the learning function
- Make decisions about all aspects of learning.

On the international stage, the explosive growth of China and India is having an increasing effect on business as well as on training and development worldwide. Chinese companies are beginning to see the importance of developing managerial and professional talent, which ties in to another trend in the field: talent management (Law, 2006). Pressure to grow and change organizations is causing executives to become more concerned about current and future shortages of talent in the workforce. Consequently, the field of learning and performance is evolving toward a focus on managing talent across the enterprise by integrating functions that often exist in isolation even though they all concern the development of human capital. These are some of the elements that companies may include in talent management:

- Leadership development
- Career planning
- Succession planning
- Learning and training
- Competency management
- Retention
- Professional development.

This shift in thinking presents an opportunity for learning professionals who are well equipped to play leading roles in managing talent across an organization. Many see this as one more sign of the increasing relevance for the profession.

The dominant learning-related trend in India is growth in developing custom e-learning content (Harris, 2006). India's dominance in the area of providing custom e-learning content relates to the overall way that technology continues to grow and branch at an ever-increasing rate and the ways that training professionals continue to find new ways to put it to use for learning. For example, iPods and cell phones are harnessed for mobile learning (m-learning); Web 2.0 technologies allow people to connect to each other to enhance collaborative learning; and wikis, knowledge management systems, and more allow workers to find the knowledge and learning they need, when they need it.

Despite the growth in these technologies, traditional classroom learning continues to be a strong and excellent way to improve people's skills and knowledge. The exuberance over e-learning in the 1990s has been tempered by experience; the understanding now is that each form has its best uses and that one does not replace the other but instead complements it.

In Closing

Also complementary are the fields of training and development and performance. This feature lies behind the most recent term for this profession: workplace learning and performance. Training focuses on the business results to be achieved as an outcome of the training, while performance has much of its roots in the same behaviorism that has informed training. Although *training* remains the word that most people in the field identify with, the term *workplace learning and performance* reflects the ways that WLP professionals are trying to contribute more to their organizations by encompassing technology, applying business acumen, demonstrating bottom-line value, and managing talent in organizations. This broader definition of the profession informs the contents of this book and lies at the heart of the most recent ASTD competency study (Bernthal et al., 2004) and the certification program that is based on it. The history of training and learning reveals a recurring theme in the profession: expansion and growth. It shouldn't really be a surprise that the profession has continually expanded over the years—from training to HRD to WLP—when considering that the focus of the work has been on learning and growth for individuals as well as for organizations.

The author would like to thank Carol Chulew for her invaluable assistance in preparing the Time Line of ASTD's History sidebar.

About the Author

Tora Estep is a senior associate editor at ASTD, where she has been a staff editor and writer for more than five years. She edited *Infoline,* ASTD's monthly publication dedicated to training workplace learning and performance professionals in a wide variety of topics and wrote several issues, including "Be a Better Manager," "Meetings That Work!," "Basics of Stand-Up Training," and "Managing Difficult Participants." She has also contributed several articles to *T+D* and was part of the editorial and writing team that produced the *ASTD Learning System,* a 10-volume study guide for practitioners preparing to take the CPLP knowledge exam. Prior to ASTD, she worked as an editor for International Communications Inc., editing books and magazines for the World Bank, the International Development Bank, the U.S. Southern Command, and more.

References

ASTD. 2006. *Designing learning.* Module 1 of the *ASTD Learning System.* Alexandria, VA.

Bernthal, Paul R., et al. *ASTD 2004 competency study: Mapping the future.* Alexandria, VA: ASTD Press.

Clark, Donald. 1999. World War I—show, tell, do, and check. *Knowledge, performance, training, & learning.* Available at http://www.nwlink.com/~donclark/hrd/history/war1.html.

European Communities. 2007. Vocational training. *Europa glossary.* Available at http://europa.eu/scadplus/glossary/training_en.htm.

Gagné, Robert M., and Leslie J. Briggs. 1974. *Principles of instructional design.* New York: Holt, Rinehart, and Winston.

Haneberg, Lisa. 2005. *Organization development basics.* Alexandria, VA: ASTD Press.

Harris, Paul. 2006. India Inc. Supplement to *T+D* 60(11): 14-18.

Knowles, Malcolm S. 1973. *The adult learner: A neglected species.* Houston, TX: Gulf Publishing.

Law, Alice. 2006. High-flying dragons in China. Supplement to *T+D* 60(11): 10-12.

Lindeman, Eduard C. 1926. *The meaning of adult education.* New York: New Republic.

Lewin, Kurt. 1948. *Resolving social conflicts; selected papers on group dynamics.* Ed. Gertrude W. Lewin. New York: Harper & Row.

Mager, Robert F. 1962. *Preparing objectives for programmed instruction.* Belmont, CA: Fearon Publishers.

Maslow, Abraham H. 1943. A theory of human motivation. *Psychological review* 50(4): 370-396.

McLagan, Patricia A. 1983. *Models for excellence: The conclusions and recommendations of the ASTD training and development study.* Alexandria, VA: ASTD.

McLagan, Patricia A. 1989. *Models for HRD practice.* Alexandria, VA: ASTD.

Miller, Vincent A. 2008. Training and ASTD: An historical review. In *The 2008 Pfeiffer annual training,* ed., E. Biech. San Francisco: Pfeiffer.

Pasmore, William A. 1988. *Designing effective organizations.* New York: John Wiley & Sons.

Shaw, H. Walter. 1994. The coming of age of workplace learning: A time line. *Training & Development* 48(5): S4-S12.

Skinner, B.F. 1953. *Science and human behavior.* New York: The Macmillan Company.

Sleight, Deborah A. 1993. A developmental history of training in the United States and Europe. Available at http://www.msu.edu/~sleightd/trainhst.html.

Steinmetz, Cloyd S. 1976. The evolution of training. In *Training and development handbook,* eds., R.L. Craig and L.R. Bittel. Sponsored by the American Society for Training and Development. New York: McGraw-Hill.

Thanasoulas, Dimitrios. 2002, November. Constructivist learning. *Karen's Linguistic Issues,* available at http://www3.telus.net/linguisticsissues/constructivist.html.

Zuboff, Shoshana. 1984. *In the age of the smart machine: The future of work and power.* New York: Basic Books.

Chapter 2

The Evolution of Human Performance Improvement

Joe Willmore

In This Chapter

- ➤ Understand the terminology of performance
- ➤ Learn about the disciplines that have influenced performance
- ➤ Learn how human performance technology or human performance improvement has developed over the decades

---

As the study and practice of human performance improvement (HPI), also known as human performance technology (HPT), becomes more widespread, it is natural for those new to the field to wonder how it started and for potential clients to question if this is a recent fad or a practice based on decades of strong research and a proven track record of successful application. Consequently, a basic understanding of how HPT or HPI came to be as well as recognition of some of the major contributors and developments in the field is useful in helping to address those questions.

The field of performance improvement has emerged and evolved over the past 45 years. It has a strong theoretical and research foundation, has borrowed from several recognized fields, has created original concepts, and continues to evolve today. Because many of the leading figures within performance were practitioners or consultants (and thus busier doing than publishing), the time line and credit for particular achievements is sometimes a matter of perspective (see the sidebar for more on this).

Caveats

Any effort to examine the foundations and evolution of performance improvement must start with some initial warnings. First, even in talking with or reading the works of the original pathfinders and developers of HPT, perceptions differ about some aspects of the field regarding who originated a particular concept or deserves credit for a specific approach. A classic case that illustrates this point in a related field is the disagreement over credit regarding the development and early application of Six Sigma (Ramias, 2005). Simply put, some of the earlier pathfinders and creators of what came to be called HPT have different perceptions of who deserves credit for what. In part this happened because so much of HPT evolved in a short timeframe and in parallel. This evolution also happened at a time when many of the critical figures in the performance arena were consultants and seeking to brand particular models or tools. Naturally, some perspectives therefore differ as to who did what first or how similar or different particular approaches may be.

Second, using publication dates to establish a time line is deceptive regarding HPT. For starters, some of those who contributed greatly to the field were prolific writers whereas others were barely published despite their heavy involvement as consultants or academics. Additionally, the introduction of most concepts does not correspond with the date that they were published in many instances (Rummler, 2003). Relying on publication dates (or even publication itself) to establish a history is inherently flawed when it comes to HPT—there are numerous examples of concepts that were in use in workshops and presented at conferences years, or in some cases decades, before they were formally published (Rummler, 2003). There are also practitioners who are regarded by their peers as key figures in the development of HPT, such as Don Tosti and Dale Brethower, who did not publish frequently in the early stages of their HPT careers when they were both contributing significant intellectual capital to the field. Consequently, the written and academic record is at best an incomplete basis for identifying major contributors and establishing credit for key HPT concepts.

Finally, this chapter should not be regarded as a detailed list of the major contributors to the performance field. As mentioned earlier, in some cases it would be very difficult to reach agreement on whom to credit for some developments or concepts. Additionally, in a field that has gone through such explosive growth and development, any attempt at such a comprehensive list would be certain to omit useful contributors. Thus, individuals are credited at various times just to illustrate the nature of their involvement or to provide a sense of how interrelated some of the evolution of HPT has been and continues to be.

Terminology and the Performance Field

Before examining the evolution of performance improvement, it is important to clarify some terminology. Thomas Gilbert is generally credited with first coining the term *human performance technology* in reference to the body of knowledge and practice that make up this field (Gilbert, 1992). Since that time, the literature has consistently referred to HPT, or human performance technology, and practitioners have often referred to themselves as *human performance technologists*. James and Dana Robinson helped to popularize the terms *performance consultant* and *performance consulting* in part to clarify the role of working with (or consulting with) the client (Robinson and Robinson, 1995). ASTD advocates the term *human performance improvement*, arguing that this terminology is clearer to clients and more accurately reflects the role (consultant) that needs to be played by the practitioner. Some practitioners see little practical difference among these three terms (HPT, HPI, and performance consulting), whereas others draw significant distinctions, arguing that "Performance consultants are what we are, human performance technology is what we do, and human performance improvement is what we seek." For the purposes of this chapter, these terms will be used interchangeably. Regardless of one's belief about the merits of any of these positions, such differences in linguistics do exist; they are important to many senior practitioners in this profession; and historically, the literature has referred to HPT.

Generally speaking, performance improvement can be defined as a systematic, systemic, results-based approach to helping organizations meet their goals through the work of people. An understanding of the words that make up HPI or HPT is helpful. The word *human* acknowledges that the focus is on how people influence the organization. Therefore, the focus is not on the performance of financial investments or computer functions—except to the extent that these are influenced by humans. The word *performance* indicates a focus on the behavior and especially the accomplishments or results that are valuable to the organization.

Technology is often perceived as referring to machinery. But technology in this context refers to a system that applies techniques and science to a subject matter (Gilbert, 1992). For instance, the field of organization development (OD) refers to outdoor team-building activities (such as ropes courses or white water rafting) as challenge technology. For many performance professionals, the word *technology* is important because it implies that HPT is more than a collection of tools and techniques but is indeed a discipline. And the word *improvement* refers to measurable results in human performance that benefit the organization.

The Foundation

The foundation for HPT was laid decades before it ever existed in name or practice. And this foundation consists of several diverse fields of study with strong research and practical background. These fields provided some of the background that led to the creation and synthesis of HPT, or they served as resources as performance became more sophisticated. Some of these fields developed concurrently with performance, and HPT work also made contributions to them (Ramias, 2005). The foundation disciplines for performance include behaviorism, systems theory, OD, instructional systems design (ISD), ergonomics and human factors, and the management sciences. Although all of these fields provided significant contributions to what became known as HPT, behavioral psychology and systems theory were the critical sources (Brethower, 2004).

Behaviorism

Behaviorism, especially regarding the study of learning and performance, was a major contributing discipline to the field of performance. The work of B.F. Skinner and others played a key role in the work of many early human performance technologists (although performance as a field had yet to emerge and no consensus label for it existed at this point). Applied behavior analysis and operant conditioning research helped drive some of the initial thinking that led to the development of the performance field. Several critical contributors to HPT, such as Dale Brethower, Thomas Gilbert, Joe Harless, Susan Markle, Geary Rummler, and Donald Tosti, worked with or studied under Skinner or Fred Keller. It would be practically impossible to overstate the impact that applied behavior analysis had in shaping the thinking of many HPT pathfinders (Brethower, 2004).

Systems Theory

Systems theory involves studying various parts of an organization and identifying interrelationships and patterns to understand how the organization functions. Systems theory takes a holistic approach to analysis and is an essential component of HPI, partially because the performance field integrates so many disciplines. But some of the very earliest contributions to HPT came from the insights gained by using a systems approach. For instance, Rummler, with the help of Brethower and George Geis, developed the Human Performance System Model in 1964 (Rummler, 2003).

OD

OD deals in part with understanding organizations, looking beyond just skills and knowledge, and dealing with change. For a discipline such as HPT, which recognizes that training is not the answer to all ills and that analysis requires examining more than just individual performers, OD is a natural resource. OD has served as an area of cross-fertilization for developing and continually refining the performance field. Generally speaking, the more solution-focused and less precise approach of OD and the more systematic, measurement-focused approach of HPT appear to have limited the degree to which OD has served as a building block, instead contributing pieces, tools, or concepts (Rosenberg, Coscarelli, and Hutchison, 1992).

ISD

ISD as a discipline evolved and intermingled with HPT in several ways. The systematic approach of ISD lent itself well to performance. Most of the early key pathfinders in HPT had strong roots in ISD. As ISD developed in the 1950s, the importance of task analysis grew as well as an awareness of the need to identify the outcomes of training—both insights that would later be incorporated into HPT. Many of the critical pathfinders in HPT, such as Bob Mager, also played similar roles in the ISD field.

Scientific Management

Management sciences can be interpreted as a mixture of different disciplines that all provided some insights later useful in forming HPT. Frederick Taylor wrote in 1911 about categorizing a workforce into thinkers or doers, standardized production processes, and looked closely at job design issues that helped to create scientific management. This con-tributed greatly to the discipline of ergonomics and human factors research. Although a psychologist, Kurt Lewin contributed greatly to the management sciences with his work on participative management and also forcefield analysis. Peter Drucker's insights shaped how people saw the nature of organizations and provided a better understanding of the role and function of management. Douglas MacGregor developed theories of manage-ment styles and raised organizational awareness of motivational issues (Sanders and Ruggles, 2000).

Other Contributing Fields

Additionally, other fields contributed insights in various ways to either the formation of HPT or its subsequent evolution. Work in the evaluation and measurement fields has been a source of inspiration for many performance consultants. The quality field pro-duced a range of tools that were later modified or incorporated by various HPT practi-tioners. Cognitive engineering and information technology (IT) have also provided insights that have been integrated into performance work. This is not an exhaustive list of the fields that have contributed in some fashion to the study and practice of performance. Ironically, at a time when many professionals are becoming more specialized, the job of performance consultant benefits from a multidisciplinary approach and a breadth of knowledge. HPI practitioners have pulled lessons from many disciplines in the past to grow the field and are likely to continue doing so in the future.

The Formation of HPT

Starting in the 1950s and 1960s, key HPT pathfinders were beginning to describe the emerging body of knowledge that would come to be known as HPT. The 1960s and 1970s proved to be a very fertile time for HPT, and then the discipline took on a more public face in the 1980s and 1990s. Finally, the mid-1990s to 2007 have seen the performance field continue to evolve and grow, incorporating new technologies and responding to new conditions in the world of work, such as globalization, increased speed, greater emphasis on accountability, and more.

The Late 1950s and Early 1960s

In the late 1950s and early 1960s several researchers had begun study in applied behavior analysis and focused on programmed instruction. Some of these individuals, such as Rummler, Tosti, and Brethower, began to realize that multiple factors influenced performance. Gilbert had formed his consulting firm, TOR, at this point, and a former student—Harless—was one of his associates. Rummler and Brethower were leading workshops at the University of Michigan's Center of Programmed Learning for business in which they taught performance analysis and a three-level framework (organization, process, and job/performer), which would be published 25 years later in the book *Improving Performance* (Rummler, 2003). It was also about this time that Gilbert offered a workshop on what he called *human performance technology* (Gilbert, 1992).

The Mid-1960s to the Mid-1970s

The period from the mid-1960s to the mid-1970s was a very fertile time for the field of HPT. Many of the key innovators were crossing paths professionally and had developed much more active consulting practices. Concepts and tools that had been developed earlier were now being implemented and revised rapidly in the consulting world. The emergence of HPT was not orderly. Much of the work during this period involved intense competition among key pathfinders seeking to brand particular tools and concepts before the competition was able to do so (Rummler, 2003). Gilbert and Rummler had formed Praxis Corporation with Irving Goldberg in 1969. Praxis formalized its Performance Audit methodology, which used Gilbert's now famous Worth concept, which relates to measuring the worth of a performer. Mager and Peter Pipe's book *Analyzing Performance Problems* was published in 1970. And in 1972, Gilbert began work on the HPT book that would be published in 1978: *Human Competence*.

By this point, a synthesis from other fields as well as original insight from a key group of players had produced a definable body of knowledge. It had a name—human performance technology. Despite several competing consulting firms' claims to unique approaches to the work, there were enough shared elements to identify common HPT principles. These principles included a strong focus on results and a recognition that many factors contributed to performance—not just knowledge and skills. The concept of measuring performance by using accomplishments rather than behavior and the importance of focusing on closing performance gaps had also been identified as key principles of the discipline. Whether it was Mager's analysis of performance problems, Praxis's performance audit, or Harless's front-end analysis (which all shared some similarities), systemic and systematic analytical approaches had been developed and were being used within organizations (Rummler, 2003). A growing body of case studies and publications documented the work being done and allowed more efficient sharing of knowledge among practitioners.

Since HPT was formed, there was always a heavy emphasis on analytical and diagnostic tools and systems (Rosenberg, Coscarelli, and Hutchison, 1992). This period saw a series of approaches developed (Rummler, 2003), but it is also fair to say that an ongoing theme in future years for HPT would be the continual development and refinement of analytical tools and approaches as practitioners sought better ways to do this work.

By the early to mid-1970s, HPT had a robust body of knowledge with a definable and distinct field of practice, depth in concepts and models, many successful case studies, and some visible practitioners with outstanding reputations. Although many deserve credit for the formation, initial use, and then branding of HPT, several individuals truly deserve the reputation as pathfinders for this discipline, including Brethower, Gilbert, Harless, Mager, Rummler, and Tosti.

The Mid-1970s to the Mid-1990s

From the mid-1970s to the mid-1990s, the field of HPT began a more public evolution. More specifically, the previous decade had seen a frantic and competitive development of models, concepts, and tools driven by client demands. Very little of this work was research driven, and many important elements of this discipline were not publicly accessible because they resided in the heads of consultants or clients or perhaps at workshops and conferences (Rummler, 2003). In 1975, Harless was interviewed by *Training* magazine and talked about front-end analysis. Although he had used the term before, this interview

Thomas F. Gilbert

Thomas F. Gilbert is widely considered to be the father of human performance technology (HPT). Although close friends with B.F. Skinner, he came to believe that people should be judged by their accomplishments, not by the behavior they exhibit.

In his seminal book, Human Competence: Engineering Worthy Performance *(1978), Gilbert developed a behavior engineering model that sought to define the barriers between individual and organizational performance. The model identifies three environmental factors—data, resources, motivation—and three human behavior factors—knowledge, capacity, and motives. Each of these factors can either contribute to or hinder an employee's productivity. Gilbert's model is significant because it identifies factors outside of the individual that affect performance.*

Another of Gilbert's major contributions to the field is his performance equation; he reasoned that "worthy" performance (W) *is a function of the ratio between valuable accomplishment* (A) *and costly behavior* (B). *The function reads* W = A/B.

In 1996, the International Society for Performance Improvement named an award after Gilbert, the "Thomas F. Gilbert Distinguished Professional Achievement Award," which recognizes significant contributions to the field of human performance.

helped to increase the exposure and awareness of the concept as well as brand his approach. Gilbert's 1978 book *Human Competence* proved to be a landmark publication for the field because it shared his insights about HPT and captured many of the key concepts and approaches that consultants (especially those at Praxis) had been using. It also was a platform for Gilbert to discuss his Behavior Engineering Model, which became a standard in the field and has been used by many others as a starting point in developing tools for understanding performance variables (Chevalier, 2003).

Two other books published during this period were also significant for performance. The 1990 Rummler-Brache book *Improving Performance* covered concepts and models that in some cases had been developed as much as 25 years earlier, making Rummler's work much more accessible. The idea that performance analysis required a systems perspective and that potential solutions needed an integrated approach was consistent with decades of Rummler's work, but the book served to clarify key points about systems theory and HPT that are now commonly accepted principles in the field (Rummler, 2003).

In 1995, the Robinsons' book *Performance Consulting* was published. This book introduced performance to an entirely new audience, thus raising the visibility of HPT. The

Robinsons' model emphasized the role of client engagement. This book also helped to popularize the term *performance consultant,* which many people found preferable to *human performance technologist.*

Collectively, these three books and the Harless interview increased the exposure and accessibility of HPT and provided branding or labels that made it easier or more attractive for the next generation of potential performance professionals. For a discipline in which so many of the key figures had been busy doing rather than writing, these publications (all of which provided strong exposure for the field) allowed critical concepts to be captured. They also expanded the visibility of the discipline. These were by no means the only HPT-related publications during this timeframe but these four in particular provided a unique role in publicizing the discipline, clarifying what it was, and making it accessible to new entrants.

This timeframe was also a period of significant refinement of HPT. A new generation of performance consultants entered the field and began to make their contributions either through work, research, or publication. In some cases the contributions involved new models or tools; in other cases they involved refinement of previously existing approaches. In still other instances contributions involved clarifying or reemphasizing principles from HPT's early days in ways that made those principles more preeminent.

From 1960 to the mid-1970s, formal research in the field had suffered, but now HPT began to benefit from dedicated research, documentation of results, and more formalized sharing of information (Stolovitch, 2000). New tools, concepts, and approaches were added or existing ones were clarified or sophisticated. For instance, variations of Gilbert's Behavior Engineering Model were proliferating (Chevalier, 2003). Rummler and Panza added Organizational Maps (Rummler, 2003). Mary Broad and the Robinsons helped build the case for partnering as a critical stage in HPT work. Jim Fuller, Roger Kaufman, and others emphasized the need to both understand the business and focus on organizational goals to drive HPT projects rather than just existing performance gaps. Although many of his publications came after this period, Tosti was making important contributions about feedback, culture, and performance. New insights into evaluation were occurring with work by Robert Brinkerhoff, Jack Zigon, and Jack Phillips leading the way. The range of possible projects available to performance consultants continued to expand. Harless and then Allison Rossett both improved the understanding of the value and use of job aids. Action learning, coaching, large group solutions, electronic performance support systems (EPSSs), and much of the work led by Sivasailam Thiagarajan around games are examples of just some of the solutions that either emerged in this era or were further refined.

Although both Gilbert and Harless had emphasized the role of the exemplar, this period also saw a greater awareness of the original wisdom of identifying key performers with work by Paul Elliott and others, which helped to further systematize this approach. Finally, as the role of IT and computing exploded within organizations and society, HPT acquired tools for both analyzing the effect of IT and also tapping it for solutions. Gloria Gery was one of the leaders in this area with her work involving electronic performance support systems (EPSSs). Distance learning was also an area of innovation—programmed instruction had been one of the precursor fields to HPT and many of those original insights gave birth to new applications.

Up to this point, the discipline was known as HPT. The publication of *Performance Consulting* led to many practitioners labeling themselves performance consultants (Robinson and Robinson, 1995). Additionally, ASTD concluded that the term *human performance improvement* was clearer to potential clients and began referring to the discipline in this manner.

The Mid-1990s to the Present

The mid-1990s to 2007 has seen the performance field continue to evolve and grow. The roles and competencies of a performance consultant became clearer as William Rothwell and others' work was published in this area (Rothwell, 1996) and included movement from behavior-based competencies to outcome-based competencies. The International Society for Performance Improvement (ISPI) began to certify performance professionals with the Certified Performance Technologist (CPT) designation, and ASTD later offered the Certified Professional in Learning and Performance (CPLP) certification. The result of this work (clarifying competencies, providing certification) serves to further professionalize the performance field.

From the beginning, systems theory has played a significant role in understanding performance, and there have been continual insights in this area as HPI has evolved. Harless's approach to analysis has been refined since the 1990s to reflect a less linear approach. Klaus Wittkuhn and others continued to rethink the understanding of cause analysis with performance—especially from a system's perspective (Wittkuhn, 2004). Although research into HPI that both validates elements of the discipline and expands the field continues to grow, there is a need for additional work to build credibility in a field that is focused on results (Huglin, Johnsen, and Marker, 2007).

Technology has played a role in how HPI has evolved. It continues to lead to new insights about performance support (Rossett, 2007). Performance diagnostic models and tools have been converted to software such as the Performance DNA Desktop, a set of electronic tools—guides, checklists, and templates—to conduct a comprehensive analysis of human performance. The prevalence of matrix or virtual work settings has created new challenges for performance consultants. PDAs, wikis, blogs, websites, and miniaturized technology have revolutionized the job aid, information, and communication options available to the HPI field.

Outreach and education have accelerated within performance. Starting with Rossett's graduate level course in 1992, several schools now offer graduate degrees in performance improvement. Online HPI degree credit courses and a degree are available. Both ISPI and ASTD offer extensive training in the principles and tools of performance work at levels that weren't available 15 years ago. For instance, more than 11,000 individuals worldwide have taken ASTD's HPI certificate courses. As a result of this expansion in performance resources, acquiring skills in HPI is much easier now, and the numbers of performance consultants continue to grow.

Science fiction novelist William Gibson once wrote "the future is already here—it's just unevenly distributed." There are several organizational developments that have significant implications for HPI. Some of these developments have been present for decades, but all of them have become more relevant to HPI since the mid-1990s. There is much more pressure from clients for fast results. This has always been an issue to some extent, and Rossett was one of those who acknowledged this with her book *First Things Fast* (1998). But competitive pressures and faster business cycles have resulted in clients who are demanding even quicker performance analysis (Willmore, 2004). As a result, HPI is looking for ways to remain rigorous, systemic, true to its principles, yet able to speed up analysis.

Another trend that has major implications for performance consultants is the growing emphasis on accountability. Executives are increasingly being held accountable for producing results, and this accountability is spilling down throughout the organization. Although this is another trend that has been happening for decades, it has accelerated since the mid-1990s. It has significant implications for HPI because this creates an organizational climate in which performance consulting has more perceived value by potential clients. HPI has also begun to migrate in some instances from human resources to other departments in the organization (such as operations), or internal performance consultants are co-located to be close to their internal clients.

Since 2000, there has been a significant interest in the practice of Six Sigma. Ironically, Rummler helped provide much of the insight to Motorola where Six Sigma evolved (Ramias, 2005). In a very short time Six Sigma has gained tremendous visibility and executive support, sometimes at the expense of HPI. So two questions for the future will be how effectively performance consultants can both explain to clients why Six Sigma is not a competitor with HPI and also effectively partner with Black Belts to further organizational goals.

Additionally, the nature of work is changing, which also has implications for HPI. More work is being automated, and some have argued that this potentially results in less value that performance consultants can provide organizations (Nickols, 2003). Others, however, take the position that the jobs that remain require more decision making or discretion and therefore are more variable in terms of how the work can be done correctly (Pepitone, 2000). Because HPI focuses first on the results rather than the behavior, performance consultants should become more valuable as older models that rely on evaluating employees through behavior become less relevant.

Finally, the nature of the workforce and competition is changing. Most markets are truly global. Many workforces (certainly in North America and Western Europe and in many other regions as well) are much more diverse and multicultural. This has had a significant effect on HPI in that the discipline has become more international—there are now many more performance consultants outside of North America. This may create cultural challenges to some elements of the performance analysis approach, such as a need to couch the performance gap in terms of a different concept. For the performance consultant, the presence of a less homogenous workforce with different languages and cultures has always been an organizational challenge, but it is much more prevalent today. Combine this with global markets where businesses work across hemispheres and with different cultures, and it is obvious that organizations will face new challenges as they compete internationally. As a result, performance consultants will face more performance issues that are fully or partially a function of challenges presented by a balkanized workforce and multiple markets.

Summary

HPI has grown significantly since the formation of the performance field in the early 1960s. One sign of a vibrant and healthy discipline is the ability to tap into new developments, innovate, and also capture insights from other fields. HPI continues to do exactly that. The last decade has seen a tremendous expansion in the number of performance consultants as well as new ways in which the performance field has evolved.

The author would like to give special thanks to Geary Rummler and Don Tosti for their assistance in preparing this chapter.

About the Author

Joe Willmore is president of the Willmore Consulting Group, a performance consulting firm located in Northern Virginia in the United States. He is a former member of ASTD's board of directors and the author of *Managing Virtual Teams*, *Performance Basics*, and *Job Aid Basics*. He is also a facilitator for ASTD's HPI program. He has consulted for a range of clients around the world for the past 26 years.

References

Brethower, Dale. 2004, September. *Yes, we can,* available at www.ispi.org/services/Glossary /YesWeCan.pdf.

Chevalier, Roger. 2003, May/June. Updating the behavior engineering model. *Performance Improvement,* 8-14.

Gilbert, Thomas. 1978. *Human competence: Engineering worthy performance.* New York: McGraw-Hill.

Gilbert, Thomas. 1992. Foreword. In *Handbook of human performance technology,* eds., H.D. Stolovitch and E.J. Keeps. San Francisco: Jossey-Bass.

An Interview with Joe Harless. 1975, March. *Training,* 43-45.

Huglin, Linda, Elizabeth Johnsen, and Anthony Marker. 2007, 1st quarter. Research priorities in performance technology. *Performance Improvement Quarterly,* 79-96.

Mager, Robert F., and Peter Pipe. 1970. *Analyzing performance problems or 'you really oughta wanna.'* Belmont, CA: Fearon.

Nickols, Fred. 2003. *Human performance technology: The end of an era,* available at http://home.att.net/~OPSINC/end_of_era.pdf.

Pepitone, James. 2000. *Human performance consulting.* 1st ed. Houston, TX: Gulf Publishing.

Ramias, Alan. 2005, October. *The mists of Six Sigma,* available at www.bptrends.com/publication-files/10-05%20WP%20The%20Mists%20of%20Six%20Sigma%20-%20Ramas1.pdf.

Robinson, Dana Gaines, and James Robinson. 1995. *Performance consulting.* San Francisco: Berrett-Koehler.

Rosenberg, Marc J., William C. Coscarelli, and Cathleen S. Hutchison. 1992. The origins and evolution of the field. In *Handbook of human performance technology,* eds., H.D. Stolovitch and E.J. Keeps. San Francisco: Jossey-Bass.

Rossett, Allison. 1998. *First things fast: A handbook for performance analysis.* San Francisco: Jossey-Bass/Pfeiffer.

Rossett, Allison. 2007. *Performance support yesterday and today,* available at http://it.coe.uga .edu/itforum/paper99/ITForum_rossett.pdf.

Rothwell, William J. 1996. *ASTD models for human performance improvement.* Alexandria, VA: ASTD Press.

Rummler, Geary. 2003, August. *The perils of writing and reading histories of HPT,* available at www.performancedesignlab.com.

Rummler, Geary, and Alan Brache. 1990. *Improving performance: How to manage the white space on the organization chart.* San Francisco: Jossey-Bass.

Sanders, Ethan S., and Julie L. Ruggles. 2000, January. HPI soup. *Training & Development,* 27-36.

Stolovitch, Harold D. 2000, April. HPT: Research and theory to practice. *Performance Improvement,* 7-25.

Willmore, Joe. 2004, August. The future of performance. *T+D,* 26-31.

Wittkuhn, Klaus. 2004, March. Systems, nontrivial machines, circular causality, and other ghosts haunting HPT. *Performance Improvement,* 33-38.

For Further Reading

Dean, Peter, and David Ripley. 1997. *Performance improvement pathfinders.* Washington, D.C.: ISPI Press.

Elliott, Paul, Elena Galbraith, and Al Folsom. 2005, June. Making the exemplary normal. *T+D,* 41-51.

Harless, Joseph. 1989, May. Wasted behavior: A confession. *Training,* 35-38.

Rummler, Geary. 2004, April. Reader's forum. *Performance Improvement,* 5.

The Business Case for Learning

Rita Bailey

In This Chapter

- ➤ Understand the key business issues that organizations face

- ➤ Learn how the learning function can become a strategic partner in supporting organizational needs

- ➤ Learn a model to make the learning function more strategically oriented

---

Why is there a need to present a business case for learning? Because a significant number of organizations profess that their workforces are not adequately prepared to meet future plans. The focus on learning ebbs and flows with the changing tides of business, but there has never been a better time for workplace learning professionals to establish a permanent seat at the table as strategic business partners. The value and proof are demonstrated through the positive effect that learning has on every facet of a business.

Talent management is the buzz in every organization whether profit or nonprofit, domestic or international, large or small. Chief executive officers and boards realize that it is more critical than ever to have an integrated approach to talent management and to ensure that they focus on aligning their workforce with organizational goals. The learning function can play a significant role in providing people with solutions that address critical business drivers such as retention, leadership development, operational effectiveness, employee motivation, and workforce performance. Aligning employees with the goals of the organization leads to individual commitment, improved culture, and positive financial results.

By reviewing key business issues, learning trends and indicators, and best practice examples, I will present a provocative case for leveraging the learning function in your organization. I will also provide a framework for you to evaluate your current plan or develop a strategic learning plan.

Training Versus Learning

The cover story in the December 2003 issue of *T+D* magazine concerned the future of the profession formerly known as training (Galagan, 2003). When asked how the profession should be identified, 32.4 percent of the respondents included the word *training* in their answers, whereas *workplace learning and performance* was the largest single answer at 31.9 percent. Since that time, ASTD has been very deliberate in driving the industry toward learning for performance. There really is no debate, because training and learning go hand in hand.

Whether you consider yourself a trainer or workplace learning professional, the focus should be on the intended outcome and result of the training. For the purpose of making a case for learning, it is important to define how the two concepts coexist. Although many people use the words interchangeably, there are fundamental differences. Training (something an organization provides for employees) focuses on the event, whereas learning puts the emphasis on the learner to apply the new information. Training is about what I, the trainer, am providing for you; whereas learning (something an individual accomplishes with possible assistance from the organization) is more self-directed and about how I, the learning professional, can collaborate to help you get what you need to be successful. Training events are rooted in instruction and drill and are focused on specific skills that are not always transferable to other job responsibilities. Training is essential for performing critical skills and processes.

Creating a learning environment and preparing people to adopt and apply knowledge and new behaviors require much more than instruction or drill. It is an ongoing commitment for people to develop deeper understanding and thoughts that drive the right action for different situations beyond specific events. It's important to increase the value quotient for applying learning as an outcome, versus training events that may or may not motivate, engage, or change participant behaviors, thoughts, or skills. By shifting this perception, the chances of being at the top of the cut list can be considerably reduced, because the learning function is no longer viewed as just a series of training events.

Table 3-1 illustrates the difference between training in a skill and focusing on intended business outcomes.

Table 3-1. Differences Between Training and Learning

Training	Learning
Classrooms, labs, lectures, demonstrations, seminars, conferences, shadowing, job aids, presentations, etc.	Discussions, simulations, role plays, experimentation, mentoring, coaching, case studies, games, interactivity, support, etc.
Management techniques	Leadership
Technical operation	Strategic planning
Sales techniques	Successful selling
Six Sigma (quality) tools	Six Sigma (process improvement)
Order processing	Customer service
Project management tools	Effective project management
Performance appraisal	Performance management
Product features and functions	Technical troubleshooting
Report writing	Communications

Not Training as Usual

I once visited with a CEO who desired to change the culture of his organization. He suggested that everyone in the organization needed customer service training to address the decline in customer satisfaction scores. He wanted a blended learning approach where all 300 employees would attend a four-hour class with an online module as a follow-up. This had been the model for the previous five years and seemed to have satisfactory results. I asked several questions to determine the real business issue before recommending additional solutions:

- What business are you in?
- What differentiates you from the competition?

- Why are people resisting change?
- Are they saying, why should I or how can I?
- Is the issue that they don't know how to or they don't want to?
- Does the work environment support different ways of learning?
- How tightly are your culture and business results linked?

After a few more questions like these, he finally agreed that training was not the only answer. This was a perfect opportunity for the training department to elevate its value by not just taking the order to deliver customer service training, but recommending and developing a strategic solution to address the business need. By involving senior leaders and customers in interactive discussions with employees, everyone in the organization was involved in contributing ways to increase customer satisfaction that went beyond training classes. Whether you are a trainer, organization development or learning professional, consultant, or coach, the effect on the bottom line depends on what happens as a result of your recommendations or actions. Too often, trainers and workplace learning professionals are relegated to the role of order taker versus strategic partner. This will change only when we learning professionals start to think like the CEO and position the learning function as a catalyst for change. Executives realize that to stay ahead of the competition and consistently grow the business they must have a high-performing, engaged workforce.

The Value Proposition

Identifying business needs and problems and coming up with appropriate solutions are the way to deliver valuable results. Value is defined by the receiver, not the giver, so establishing collaborative relationships and partnerships inside and outside the organization is paramount for successful outcomes.

Until the organization embraces the notion of learning as a strategic advantage, the requests will still focus on "doing training." The response should be yes, thus opening the door to turn training requests into opportunities to add value and to change the perception of the training function.

Following are examples of how traditional training events were leveraged to create additional value and benefits:

- Level 1 initiative: Turn a training request into an opportunity to create value and have an effect.
- Level 2 initiative: Identify opportunities to partner with clients on strategic initiatives.

- Level 3 initiative: Recommend new opportunities to add value or affect clients or executives.
- Level 4 initiative: Use long-term tracking to evaluate sustainability.

In today's dynamic environment, organizations must find innovative ways to leverage talent and connect people to the business. Providing development opportunities for employees can be a competitive advantage. It's no coincidence that we're seeing a movement toward training that speaks to the whole person. Many companies are offering courses that focus on personal and family issues such as "how to talk to your teenager" or "how to be a great single parent" or "finding your creativity." Although some executives consider this insignificant and fluffy, savvy organizations know that better human beings make better employees. Many organizations treat their people like human doings instead of human beings. Organizations on the *Fortune* 100 list of best companies to work for and other lists that highlight great places to work consistently invest in developing the whole person. SAS offers a work-life center with programs that address the issues its people are most concerned about, from raising children and taking care of aging parents to financial planning for the future. By getting the help they need, employees are less burdened and can be more effective on the job. As a result, voluntary turnover is about 3 percent. The Container Store, a national retail chain, has purposefully created a people-centric culture that stands out from other retailers. New full-time employees receive 235 hours of training, compared with the industry average of seven hours.

The learning philosophy at Southwest Airlines is to support the company customer service mission by providing all employees equal opportunity for growth and development and ensuring that they are treated with the same respect and care that they are expected to show the customer. This philosophy provides a lot of latitude for the trainers and learning professionals to design, develop, and deliver the most effective learning initiatives. In addition to the standard technical training and leadership development offerings, the University for People at Southwest also provides career development sessions and optional career coaching, leadership briefings for directors and vice presidents, an annual Message to the Field road show, and countless partnership initiatives with various departments.

In the long run, the best companies win with highly talented, highly committed employees. General Mills recruits people with great potential and provides the tools and experiences to bring that potential to life. Commitment to perform is based on working for terrific leadership, getting meaningful development, and having empowering jobs where you can make a difference. At General Mills, the CEO is committed to supporting learning as an enabler for the business strategy.

At Tyco Fire and Securities the focus is on business results, not course content per se. Learning is integrated into the fabric of work. Content must be tied to current and future job requirements. The organization provides a road map of courses that, given level, tenure, and function, clearly defines what skills are required for an employee to succeed.

North Shore–Long Island Jewish Health System (LIJ) is a 17-hospital network with some 35,000 employees to educate annually. To meet the challenge of educating and synthesizing such a large and diverse medical system, the organization created a comprehensive learning strategy to help the health system culture emerge, transfer knowledge and best practices, and implement learning initiatives that support North Shore–LIJ's strategic business goals and objectives. The Center for Learning and Innovation (CLI) was launched in January 2002 using a "leader as teacher" model that places senior executives at the helm of classroom instruction. Their job is to encourage mutual learning between the front line and executive leadership. Outcome measures are developed in alignment with learning initiatives. Learning initiatives include separate tracks for different levels of management: middle management, senior management, senior executives, and executive education for nurse and physician leadership. There are enrichment classes like stress and time management, leadership concepts, and team building, which are available to all employees to enhance personal and professional development. In addition, every Monday morning, Michael J. Dowling, president and CEO of North Shore–LIJ, hosts a foundations course for all new employees.

Keep in mind that not all training has an immediate effect on the bottom line, so considering strategic and tactical initiatives in the plan is important. Although compliance and regulatory training do not have the same appeal as other offerings, they are an important part of the integrated strategy. If not implemented, there can be a negative financial effect on the organization. It is the role of the learning function to determine the priorities linked to the business goals and decide what to focus on and why.

How ready for change is the average person in your organization? How would people define the organization (a learning organization or learning community)? Can you change direction quickly to stay competitive? Do people see changes that could benefit the organization, but they aren't speaking up? What signals alert you to the need for change? What have you missed in past years that should have been a signal for change? How do organizations like Southwest Airlines, Four Seasons Hotels, Nordstrom, SAS, TDIndustries, Timberland, W.L. Gore, and Goldman Sachs maintain long-term success and stability and continue to invest in people development during the tough times? The organizations that achieve the best results in building forward-thinking, adaptable practices that transcend the "stagnant quo" have little to do with implementing various change models. They maintain the leading position because they have been successful in intricately connecting people to their business. The learning function is perfectly positioned to affect the bottom line by building trusting relations, providing relevant learning solutions, challenging and changing inefficient and ineffective processes and systems, and developing inspiring leaders to reshape the workplace of the future.

A Model for Developing a Strategic Learning Plan

If you ever had a BHAG (Big Hairy Audacious Goal) but just didn't know how to get there, the following model will serve as a map to develop an extraordinary strategic learning plan that links people to the business (see Figure 3-1). It divides the thinking process into four continuous phases that are linked sequentially to provide a unique route to improved performance.

Awareness

Awareness involves creating a compelling picture that everyone can see.

The fundamental outcome of awareness is focus. Where do you want to be? How relevant is the learning function? Why should the organization not outsource the entire function? What needs to change if you are going to gain trust and respect at the executive level? How are employees involved in providing input and feedback? What do you offer or do better than anyone else, and how is this communicated throughout the organization?

Figure 3-1. The 4-A Model

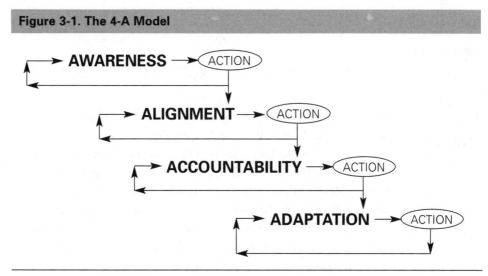

Source: Cawood and Bailey (2006). Used with permission.

Once you've identified the business need and determined opportunities to create value and positively affect the bottom line, it is important to communicate throughout the organization the purpose and role that the learning function has in solving a problem or contributing to the overall strategy. Even though the titles vary by organization (training, performance improvement, human capital management, and organizational effectiveness), the typical expectation of this role is that people will have the skills to do their jobs, leaders are developed to carry the organization forward, and overall productivity and performance continue to improve. In addition to these fundamental needs, the goal is to expand the expectations to include involvement in broader business objectives like improving core business processes, assisting with entering new markets faster, improving cycle time for product introduction, increasing customer satisfaction, and helping to reshape the culture.

Every learning strategy should answer the "what" and "how" questions at an intellectual and emotional level, so that employees will be more likely to take an active role in the learning experience. Needs first, solutions second!

Six traits of a highly effective learning organization include

- Learning aligned to business goals
- Measures that indicate the overall business effect of the learning function
- Learning outside the walls of the organization
- Focus on competencies that support most critical organizational needs
- Blended delivery approaches
- Mature design and delivery of leadership development.

Alignment

You have alignment when all the dots are connecting (people, processes, systems, and so forth).

Is everything and everyone focused on the business results? Balancing priorities, eliminating contradictions, removing constraints, and designing systems that support the learning goals can be a powerful contribution to the organization and can eliminate many internal and external customer frustrations. The learning function can play a significant role in eliminating silos. Many of the best practices inside organizations are not shared and, therefore, cause duplication of efforts, unnecessary outsourcing, conflicting messages, and lost revenue. Knowledge sharing and access to content are key factors in establishing a foundation for participatory learning. When people have information, resources, and support, it increases their capability to perform at peak levels.

Accountability

Are the right behaviors being reinforced? Is there accountability in your organization?

Having a shared purpose for learning is what motivates people to actively participate and contribute because they want to, not because they have to. Whether for individual development, team building, or leadership advancement, learning is everyone's business. Creating a culture that promotes, acknowledges, and rewards learning results in committed engagement and high performance rather than compliant apathy.

Adaptation

Are ongoing adjustments made to keep the learning strategy on course?

The way we communicate is changing, technology is constantly changing at warp speed, learners are changing, and our role as learning professionals is changing. Learning is about change, but it doesn't have to be painful. When done well, people change for the better. Relationships change. Organizations change. It's about making appropriate small adjustments as the business evolves and monitoring results. It's deciding what to start, stop, and continue doing. The learning function can assume the scout role in monitoring competitive, trend, and benchmark data that help keep your organization out in front of the competition. What is your organization doing to enable employees to create the ideal customer experience? How does learning help to influence innovative thinking?

Summary

Aligning the workforce with organizational goals leads to individual commitment, an improved organizational culture, and positive financial results. One way to do this is to create a learning environment and prepare people to adopt and apply knowledge and new behaviors, which requires more than the traditional, order-taker approach to training. One way to elevate the learning function beyond this traditional approach is to apply the 4-A model, which combines awareness, alignment, accountability, and adaptation to create a compelling picture of what the learning organization could achieve; connect the dots among people, processes, and systems; reinforce the right behaviors; and make adjustments to keep the learning strategy on course.

About the Author

Rita Bailey, CEO of QVF Partners, consults with organizations that want to develop people-centric cultures. Bailey served for 25 years at Southwest Airlines in several leadership positions, including head of Southwest Airlines University for People. She now travels the world, speaking and consulting on topics such as organizational culture, leadership, service, innovation, and branding. She is the coauthor of *Destination Profit: Creating People-Profit Opportunities in Your Organization* and has been a featured guest on radio talk shows across the United States. Bailey serves on several advisory boards and committees and was the 2005 chair of the ASTD Board of Directors. When asked what business she's in, the answer is simply, "The People Business."

References

Cawood, Scott, and Rita Bailey. 2006. *Destination profit: Creating people-profit opportunities in your organization.* Mountain View, CA: Davies Black.

Galagan, Pat. 2003. The future of the profession formerly known as training. *T+D* 57(12): 27-38.

For Further Reading

Bingham, Tony, and Tony Jeary. 2007. *Presenting learning.* Alexandria, VA: ASTD Press.

Elkeles, Tamar, and Jack Phillips. 2007. *The chief learning officer: Driving value within a changing organization through learning and development.* Burlington, MA: Butterworth-Heinemann.

Sloman, Martyn. 2007. *The changing world of the trainer.* Burlington, MA: Butterworth-Heinemann.

Chapter 4

Performance Consulting: A Process to Ensure Skill Becomes Performance

Dana Gaines Robinson

In This Chapter

- ➢ Understand why skills don't necessarily mean performance
- ➢ Learn common reasons why people don't use their skills
- ➢ Learn how performance consulting helps employees use their skills for enhanced performance

---

Too frequently, the results that occur from the training and development investments made by organizations are disappointing. People attend workshops or participate in a technology-enabled learning program, acquiring the skills and knowledge focused upon in the training. However, when returning to the workplace, these individuals often apply little of what they have learned. The reasons for this lack of skill transfer often can be found within the work environment of the employees. As a workplace learning and performance (WLP) professional, you have a responsibility to ensure the work environment supports the skills acquired by those who attend a learning experience you manage.

In this chapter you will learn the eight most common reasons why people do not use skills they acquire in learning programs. You will also learn how the performance consulting process is used to ensure that skills developed by employees do result in enhanced performance in the workplace.

As WLP professionals, we frequently receive these kinds of requests:

Safety is a primary goal for our manufacturing organization. Unfortunately, we are experiencing an increasing number of preventable accidents. What kind of safety training can we offer operators and supervisors?

We need to improve how we manage customer problems. I'd like to discuss what training programs you have that would help with this need.

In each instance the assumption is that some type of learning experience by itself will yield enhanced performance. It is as though skill and performance are identical. Unfortunately, this is not the case. Beginning with the seminal work of Thomas Gilbert (2007), *Human Competence: Engineering Worthy Performance,* and continuing through to the work of contemporary authors such as Harold Stolovitch and Erica Keeps (1999, 2004), we have irrefutable evidence that learning, by itself, rarely changes performance. In the 1980s various studies reported the rate of transfer of skills acquired in a training program to the job to be between 10 and 40 percent; in research reported since 2000, transfer rates from training as a single solution have not increased—the current range is from 10 to 30 percent, with most on the low end (Broad, 2005). Clearly developing skill, while important, does not ensure that enhanced performance will result.

In actuality skills and performance are not identical. Skill is a cognitive or behavioral capability; most learning experiences are designed to enhance the skills of those who participate in that experience. Performance is behavior people use on the job to produce accomplishments. Accomplishments are the outcomes of behavior. For example, writing is a behavior, whereas producing a book is an accomplishment. Running is a behavior; winning a marathon an accomplishment. Figure 4-1 illustrates the relationship among skills, behaviors, and performance for a sales representative.

Why is it that people acquire skills through some type of learning experience and then use only 10 to 30 percent of the skills in their jobs? Assuming the learning experience was well designed and implemented, the reasons for this transfer rate most likely lie within the work environment of employees. And this is where the process of performance consulting comes in.

What Is Performance Consulting?

Performance consulting is a process that requires WLP professionals to focus on results (that is, on performance change and business impact) and not only on solutions (that is, training). I define *performance consulting* as a process in which clients and WLP professionals partner to achieve the strategic outcome of enhanced workplace performance in support of business goals.

Figure 4-1. Relationship of Skills to Performance

Skills	Performance	
	Behaviors ⟶	**Accomplishment**
Questioning Skills	• Ask questions to identify the customer's requirements	• Meet or exceed revenue goals agreed upon with manager
Influencing Skills	• Link customer requirements to features and benefits of service	
	• Seek to understand and overcome objections the customer may have about the service	

The words in this definition have been selected purposely, so let me explain the rationale behind key words and phrases.

Process. Performance consulting is a flow of steps with an entry and an exit; this process is discussed later in this chapter. It is a systematic and data-driven process that helps WLP professionals and business managers make sound decisions regarding people and their performance within the organization.

Client and *WLP professional.* These are the two roles for people working within the process. The client role is filled by the individual or team of people who are accountable for achieving the business goals and who manage the people supporting those goals. The WLP professional role refers to the individual or team of people who work with the client to identify and implement solutions needed for the given situation. This individual must influence and guide the client throughout the performance consulting process. The WLP professional may also complete some of the tasks involved, such as any performance assessment necessary.

Partner. The dynamic of the relationship between client and WLP professional is that of partnership. Performance and business results cannot be obtained by the WLP professional alone; the client who ultimately benefits from these results must play an active role. The goal is to work synergistically and collaboratively so the results that occur are greater than would have been the case if either the client or the WLP professional had worked independently.

Strategic outcome. Achieving business goals and improving workgroup performance *are* the strategic outcomes that the WLP professional and client share—a strategic (not tactical) outcome. Linking business results to the performance accomplishments required of people is a key concept. It is insufficient that people attend a training program and acquire skills; what is ultimately important is that these individuals apply the skills on the job so their performance is enhanced and the organization benefits.

Enhanced workplace performance in support of business goals. This is a shared outcome for the WLP professional and the client. The outcome is solution neutral. Nowhere in my definition of performance consulting does it indicate the goal is to increase skills or to provide a more efficient work process; these are tactical, solution-focused outcomes. The ultimate goal is to enhance performance of people to the betterment of the business, which is a strategic result. To do this requires a systemic and holistic approach, viewing organizations and the people who work within them as interrelated. A change in one factor within the organization will have ripples in other areas; the goal of performance consulting is to create alignment among all internal factors that affect workplace performance, ensuring that results do occur from investments made in learning.

What does it take to "do" performance consulting? Performance consulting requires that you, as a WLP professional, practice two things in *your* day-to-day performance:

- Operate from a mental model that supports a holistic and systemic view of any request or situation in which you are involved. This mental model requires that you seek root causes for a given problem or situation, using a learning solution only when lack of skill and knowledge is a root cause.
- Partner with clients as you follow the four-phased performance consulting process.

Let's look closer at each of these, beginning with the mental model.

The Mental Model for Performance Consulting

A mental model is the cognitive map within your mind that guides your behavior. It is similar to a map you use when setting out on a road trip to a new destination. That map guides you in making decisions regarding both your destination and the path to take to reach it. So, too, a mental model influences how you approach your work and the many requests you obtain from your clients. It will influence the questions you ask, the goals you agree to support, and the solutions you recommend for getting there. When working from a learning framework, your focus is to identify and address capability needs. When working from a performance perspective, your focus enlarges to include identifying and aligning four needs: business, performance, work environment, and capability. Referred to as the need hierarchy and illustrated in Figure 4-2, these four needs nest like boxes in a box, with business being the highest level of need.

Figure 4-2. The Need Hierarchy

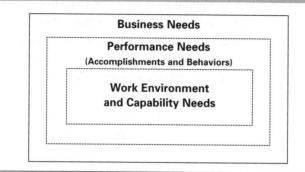

Source: Partners in Change, © 1995, 2007. Used with permission.

Business needs describe the operational and strategic goals for an organization or some unit or department within it. These needs are what the organization must accomplish if it is to be successful over the long term. Business needs are measured quantifiably. Growing market share is an example of a business need; it can be measured in terms of the percentage of market share, the number of new customers, and the revenue generated. Other examples of business needs are to increase customer satisfaction, increase operational efficiency, retain talent, decrease operational costs, and increase profit. Each of these is a goal for an organization or business unit and has one or more numeric measures that can be used to establish the goal and to assess current results.

Business needs are the highest order need in this hierarchy because all other needs *should* emanate from them. If business needs go unmet for some protracted period of time, the future of the enterprise is threatened. The term *business need* is typically used within for-profit organizations. In a nonprofit organization, the term is often changed to *organization* or *operational need.* A governmental organization may use the term *agency need.* Note use of the term *need* rather than *goal* or *problem.* This is a term that is broad enough to encompass all types of situations from a business shortfall to a business opportunity. Likewise, performance need is broad enough to include desired performance, a performance problem, or a performance gap.

Performance needs describe on-the-job accomplishments and behaviors required of individuals who are performing within a specific job or role *and* who contribute to achieving the business goals through their performance. Performance needs identify what individuals must do more, better, or differently if business goals are to be achieved; these needs are described in behavioral terms. Examples of a performance accomplishment and behaviors for customer service representatives are that they must successfully resolve customer complaints (accomplishment) by asking questions, evidencing empathy, and taking responsibility for ensuring the problem is addressed (behaviors).

Work environment and capability needs are in the center box of the need hierarchy. These factors have a direct effect upon the performance of people in workgroups. Work environment needs refer to the infrastructure in an organization, including the work processes, information, and incentive systems that are present. Capability needs refer to the skills and knowledge people must have if they are to perform as required. Any of these factors can work as a barrier or an enhancer to desired performance. The factor will be an enhancer if it both encourages the on-the-job performance and supports business results that are desired. The same factor can be a barrier if it discourages the required behavior and business results. For example, if coaching is done effectively, it is an enabler to performance; if absent, it is a barrier.

Identifying causes for business and performance gaps is key to success when working as a performance consultant. To assist people in identifying causes, James Robinson and I created a tool called the Gap Zapper. It is displayed in Figure 4-3.

The Gap Zapper begins with the box labeled "successful on-the-job performance." This references the performance box in the need hierarchy. It is this performance that will facilitate achieving business results. As you can see, successful on-the-job performance is resting on a three-legged stool, so to speak, with each leg acting as a cause category. These categories are buckets, organizing barriers of a similar nature together. Let's look at these categories in more detail beginning on the right with capability needs.

Factors internal to individuals refer to capability needs. These are factors within individuals enabling them to perform effectively. Although these factors reside within the individual, actions taken by the organization will affect these factors:

- *Skill and knowledge* is a factor for which some type of structured learning experience is an appropriate solution. People cannot perform successfully on the job if they do not know how.
- *Inherent capability* refers to the raw ingredient that is within each of us, making each of us unique. It includes our previous education and work experience, as well as attributes and traits. Inherent capability develops over time. It is influenced by our DNA and our life experiences. It is very difficult to change. It is, therefore, more efficient to use a process that identifies, at the time of selection, people with the required inherent capabilities for the position.

As noted earlier, and more clearly shown in Figure 4-3, skill is not performance. For example, if a manager called and asked you to develop the negotiating skills of a work team, this manager has provided you with a capability need, not a performance need. To qualify as a performance need, the manager must describe what people are expected to actually *do* on the job with the negotiating skills they acquire.

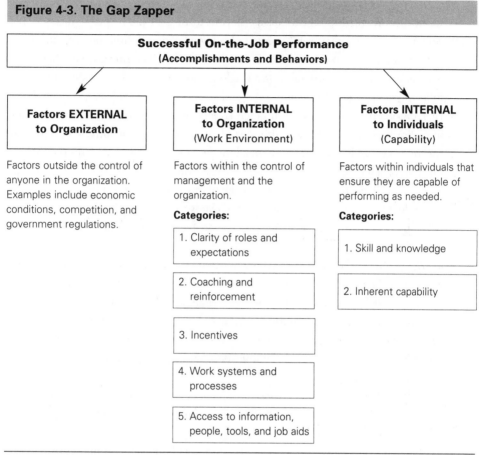

Figure 4-3. The Gap Zapper

Successful On-the-Job Performance
(Accomplishments and Behaviors)

Factors EXTERNAL to Organization	**Factors INTERNAL to Organization** (Work Environment)	**Factors INTERNAL to Individuals** (Capability)
Factors outside the control of anyone in the organization. Examples include economic conditions, competition, and government regulations.	Factors within the control of management and the organization.	Factors within individuals that ensure they are capable of performing as needed.
	Categories:	**Categories:**
	1. Clarity of roles and expectations	1. Skill and knowledge
	2. Coaching and reinforcement	2. Inherent capability
	3. Incentives	
	4. Work systems and processes	
	5. Access to information, people, tools, and job aids	

Source: Partners in Change, © 1995, 2007. Used with permission.

In the center of the Gap Zapper are *factors internal to the organization,* which are the work environment needs. When these factors are present in a positive manner, they enable performance. They will hinder performance when absent. Note, however, that management can change these factors because they are all within the control of the organization. These factors are discussed below.

- *Clarity of roles and expectations* focuses on employees knowing specifically what their roles and responsibilities are relative to their job goals and accountabilities. This means that people know how their responsibilities differ from others who are supporting the same business goal. Role confusion is a frequent barrier to performance. Another common problem is unclear expectations such as telling people to be more customer-oriented and proactive. These statements qualify as examples of fuzzy requirements.

- *Coaching and reinforcement* include the system in place to ensure coaching support is provided to individuals as they perform their job responsibilities. This factor also involves reinforcing and acknowledging desired performance and providing developmental feedback when needed. The presence of coaching and reinforcement on the job is the single greatest contributor to skill transfer following a learning experience.

- *Incentives* are the rewards, both tangible and intangible, that encourage people to perform as needed. Financial bonus plans are tangible incentives; opportunities to grow and learn are nonfinancial incentives. This category requires that a positive balance of consequences exists within the organization for the performance that is expected. When there is lack of any consequence, performance often does not change. It is easy for employees to maintain the status quo when there are no consequences, positive or negative, for changing on-the-job performance.

- *Work systems and processes* are the workflow and organizational systems within which individuals perform. These can make work performance easier and more efficient; they can also make desired performance difficult or even impossible. Geary Rummler (1995), co-author of the book *Improving Performance: How to Manage the White Space on the Organization Chart*, stated it quite succinctly when he said, "If you pit a good employee against a bad system, the system will win almost every time."

- *Access to information, people, tools, and job aids* is a category of work environment needs that continues to grow in importance because people are expected to perform effectively in complex environments without a lot of day-to-day guidance. How can people perform effectively without accurate and current information or access to the type of tools required to do the job?

Factors external to the organization are yet a third category of causes to be identified. This category refers to factors that are outside the control of any organization. Examples include competitive pressures, economic conditions, and regulatory requirements within which the organization must operate. No individual or group within an organization can change these factors; rather, leaders must form strategies that minimize the effects of external barriers and optimize those external factors that are favorable. For example, when oil prices are high, companies and organizations in the transportation industry, such as airlines, must find ways to succeed and meet profit goals despite this challenge. Of course, there are times when these factors can support an organization's business needs, as when there is a growing economy. During robust times businesses with products valued in the marketplace benefit.

You may have noted that nowhere in the list of causes is listed "lack of time" or "low morale." Why is that? It is because each of these is a symptom of a problem and not a root cause. Using the mental model of performance consulting, if people indicate either of these as reasons for a problem, it is important to probe more deeply. What is preventing people from having the time to perform as needed? Perhaps staffing levels are low and people need to perform more than one job, or perhaps too much administrative work is making it difficult to take time to be with customers. And why is morale low? Perhaps people in the job are not acknowledged for their accomplishments so they have stopped caring about the job. Or maybe those in the position are bored by the type of work they are doing so they show little interest in it. Probing below symptoms is an important skill set when working as a performance consultant. Only when root causes have been identified can the appropriate solutions be selected and implemented so the performance gaps are closed.

Take a look at the Gap Zapper one more time. There are a total of eight categories of root causes (two capability factors, five work environment factors, and the external factor category). For how many of these eight root cause categories is learning a good solution? The answer is one! Learning solutions, of any type or modality, are appropriate when lack of skill or knowledge is a root cause for performance that is not at desired levels. All other root causes will most likely require different solutions. And we know that performance of people is the result of multiple factors—it would be rare for lack of skill to be the *only* reason a group of people is not performing as needed. Now the research findings that indicate 30 percent or less of what is acquired through learning solutions is applied to the job becomes more understandable. The work environment is a powerful influence on skill transfer.

In summary, the need hierarchy and Gap Zapper are critical elements in the mental model that guides your thinking and behavior when working as a performance consultant. The mental model will influence the type of information you seek and the solutions you recommend.

You Try It!

As noted, a mental model is a cognitive approach to your work. To operate from a performance perspective, it is vital that you can discriminate between and among the four types of needs within the need hierarchy. Performance consultants seek to partner with clients to define and align these four needs. The requests you receive to do your work will, most likely, not come with all four needs identified; therefore, it is important that you can determine what needs are known and what needs are unidentified. It is these unidentified needs for which information must be obtained before proceeding with learning and nonlearning solutions.

Below is an exercise. Take a moment to test your skills to discriminate among the four needs. Imagine that each of the following statements is a request from a manager you support. Using only the information in the manager's statement, determine what need or needs in the hierarchy the manager is describing. Make no assumptions or inferences when selecting your answers.

BN = Business Need. The statement refers to the goals or strategies of the business or organization. The statement may or may not contain numerical measures; however, that information could be obtained through questions you ask.

PN = Performance Need. The statement defines what people must do on the job to support the business goals. It may also refer to what people are doing now. The descriptors may be vague, but on-the-job behavior and accomplishments are clearly the focus.

WN/S = Work Environment Need/Solution. The statement identifies one or more of the five categories of work environment needs described in the Gap Zapper, or it provides a solution that addresses one of these needs.

CN/S = Capability Need/Solution. This is a statement that identifies the skill, knowledge, or inherent capability required of people. The statement may also provide a solution to address this category of cause.

Each statement can be one, or a combination of these four needs. After you have made your selections, compare your responses to the ones that appear following the exercise.

	BN	PN	WN/S	CN/S	
1.	☐	☐	☐	☐	There is an increasing amount of conflict in my group. What kind of conflict resolution training can we deliver to help build their skills in this area?
2.	☐	☐	☐	☐	We need to build market share for our new product. The trouble is that our account representatives lack in-depth knowledge about the product. How can we develop their product knowledge quickly?
3.	☐	☐	☐	☐	I need some technical training for my operators. When can you get started?
4.	☐	☐	☐	☐	The work people have to do in my area is changing. I'd like your help in building an electronic tool kit that will assist people in performing the new tasks they are being asked to do.

Answers to Exercise

1. **PN, CS:** Conflict is a behavior that is occurring on the job within an employee group, so this is a performance need. The request for conflict resolution training is a capability solution.

2. **BN, CN/CS:** Building market share is a business need; this is a goal for an operational unit and can be measured numerically. Account representatives lacking product knowledge is a capability need; building their knowledge would be a capability solution.

3. **CS**: This is a request for training; so it is a capability solution only.

4. **PN, WS:** There are really two performance needs expressed in this statement: work that people do is changing and they must now perform new tasks. Each of these describes, in a vague manner, something people are going to do on the job. The electronic tool kit is a work environment solution.

Performance Consulting Process

As a WLP professional, you are familiar with many work processes that assist you in designing and developing quality learning solutions. For example, instructional systems design and the ADDIE (assess, design, develop, implement, and evaluate) model are two of the many processes and models that instructional designers use. Each of these processes is helpful once a decision to provide a learning solution has been made. The performance consulting process is a solution-neutral process. It begins when a client's need or request is forming and continues through completion of the work done in support of that need. Figure 4-4 illustrates the major phases within the performance consulting process.

Entry Phase

How do you typically learn of a potential need for support? Perhaps a manager contacts you directly. Or you may be contacted by a colleague in human resources. In this phase of work, people who use a performance consulting approach learn of opportunities both reactively (when the manager calls) and proactively (through their own initiatives). The key to managing this phase of work effectively is to maintain a solution-neutral perspective even though the requesting manager may be asking for a training program. Let's look at an example of how this is done. Perhaps a manager has called, requesting that you deliver a leadership workshop to supervisors in the business unit. To obtain more information, you ask questions. But how do you ask questions that are solution neutral? Consider these two questions—which is solution neutral?

- What is it you would like your supervisors to do more, better, or differently once they have completed the leadership training?
- What is it you would like your supervisors to do more, better, or differently?

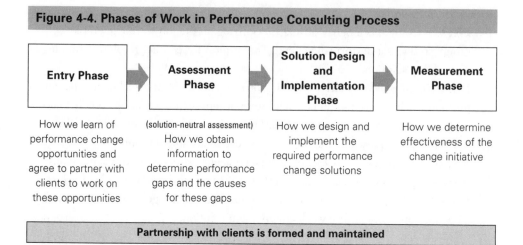

Figure 4-4. Phases of Work in Performance Consulting Process

Entry Phase	Assessment Phase	Solution Design and Implementation Phase	Measurement Phase
How we learn of performance change opportunities and agree to partner with clients to work on these opportunities	(solution-neutral assessment) How we obtain information to determine performance gaps and the causes for these gaps	How we design and implement the required performance change solutions	How we determine effectiveness of the change initiative

Partnership with clients is formed and maintained

The first question assumes a training program will be delivered; your goal with this question is to ascertain what performance is desired following the training. But how do we know that lack of skill is the reason the supervisors are not performing as required? Better to ask a solution-neutral question, such as the second example, to begin the discussion. Then, of course, you'll want to ask questions to identify the causes for why supervisors are not performing in this manner. (For more examples of questions that you can use to explore a manager's request, see Tool 4-1 on the accompanying CD-ROM.)

Another important activity in the entry phase is to identify the "true" client for the need, gaining agreement to partner with that person on the project. A true client is the person who

- Owns the business and performance needs supported by the project
- Has the most to gain or lose from these needs being addressed
- Has the authority to make and implement decisions, garnering resources associated with the solutions required to achieve the business needs focused upon.

A problem occurs when WLP professionals confuse contacts with clients. A contact is the person who requests that a learning solution be provided. This person may or may not be the client. By asking probing questions during the entry phase, it becomes possible to identify who the client is and gain access to that individual. Until you partner with the true client, it is not possible to do the work of a performance consultant. This is because you need to influence the thinking and decisions of the client; without access to that person, your opportunity to influence is greatly reduced. Desired outcome from the entry phase:

Gain agreement with the client on the results desired from the initiative and what, if any, information must be obtained to ensure appropriate solutions can be identified.

Assessment Phase

The assessment completed as part of the performance consulting process is also solution neutral. The focus of the assessment is to identify, as specifically as possible, the gaps that exist between what people should be doing on the job and what they are currently doing. In other words, we are identifying the performance needs within the need hierarchy. In this phase of work, we also want to determine the root causes for gaps—why are people not performing on the job as we need them to do if the business goals are to be realized? Is there role confusion among the employees? Perhaps there is an incentive system that is rewarding a different performance than what we require in the future. It is also possible that people lack the skills needed to perform as we wish them to do. The Gap Zapper is an important tool to use during this assessment phase of work. The probability is very great that there are multiple root causes for why people are not performing as needed, with insufficient skill being only one of those reasons. Desired outcome from the assessment phase: *Gain agreement with the client on the root causes for the problem, the goals for success, and the solutions needed to achieve those goals.*

Solution Design and Implementation Phase

Again, note the use of the neutral term *solution*—not learning or training. When working from a performance consulting framework, it is probable that multiple solutions will be required. As a WLP professional, your role may be to focus on designing and implementing the learning solution only, with the client accountable for ensuring that the other solutions are also implemented. In this phase of work, you may be purchasing or designing a learning solution, piloting it if necessary, and rolling it out to the target groups. Although you, as a WLP professional, are managing this part of the process, there will be others (we hope) who are working on the additional solutions that were identified. Updating the client on progress being made and any problems you are encountering also is a part of this phase of work. Desired outcome from the solution implementation phase: *Design and implement all solutions as agreed upon with the client.*

Measurement Phase

When we measure results from learning solutions we often answer the questions, "Did people like the learning experience?" and "Did people acquire the intended skill and knowledge?" In other words, the focus is on Level 1 (reaction evaluation) and Level 2 (learning evaluation), the two levels first identified by Donald Kirkpatrick.

When we focus on performance, these two evaluation levels are important but insufficient. We now want to know "Are people using the skills on the job?" (Level 3—performance change) and "In using the skills, how is the business benefiting?" (Level 4—operational effect). We may even want to determine Level 5, the cost-benefit ratio, that Jack and Patricia Phillips have described in their work. Cost-benefit analysis determines the cost of the solutions and compares that cost to the benefits that were derived to ascertain if there is a positive or negative return-on-investment (ROI) from the entire initiative. In measuring performance and business results, it is also important to identify what capability and work environment factors may be contributing to any deficiencies still present. Only when causes for performance gaps are known, is it possible to determine what additional solutions or actions will be required to ensure a successful outcome. Desired outcome from the measurement phase: *Determine performance and business results that have been obtained from the solutions; identify any additional solutions that are required to ensure ultimate success.*

As you reflect upon work that is done within the performance consulting process, you may note that this is a front-loaded process. By that I mean that much of the work occurs *before* solutions are designed and implemented. The partnership with the true client(s) is key to success. Only clients can take the actions needed to address work environment barriers. That is why you see the statement "client relationships formed and maintained" appearing across the entire performance consulting process. With actively involved clients, you share accountability with them for results, so the learning solutions you provide will have sustained and long-lasting business impact.

The Performance Consulting Process in Action

Let's look at an example of how one WLP professional worked through the four phases of the performance consulting process to address a client's request.

Entry Phase

Daniel received a request from sales management to provide training to several hundred sales representatives in a large consumer products company. These representatives called upon, and worked with, retail stores with a goal to increase the volume of the organization's products that these stores were purchasing and to ensure that the many product promotions were implemented successfully. Daniel's client, a member of the sales management team, asked that the sales representatives be trained in how to execute advanced spreadsheet functions to analyze and interpret the data contained in sales reports.

Daniel met with his client to discuss the drivers for the requested training, including what management had observed that indicated training was needed. Management was concerned that the sales representatives were not using the sales data to set priorities for product promotions and to establish purposes for store visits. The client acknowledged that there were a few sales representatives who were using data effectively and were meeting, or exceeding, the sales volume goals for which they were responsible. However, the client could not answer the question, "What are these sales representatives doing more, better, or differently than others to achieve these results?" The client thought it would be helpful to obtain an answer to that question. So, Daniel moved ahead to gather more information; the training request was put on hold until that information could be obtained.

Assessment Phase

Daniel interviewed the high-performing sales representatives (often referred to as stars); he also interviewed some of the more typical sales representatives so he could determine what it was that the stars were doing differently. Finally, he interviewed some of the area sales managers who were the leaders to whom sales representatives reported. This information yielded many significant findings including the following:

- The accountabilities, as understood by sales representatives, were that the area sales managers were to analyze the data; provide representatives with the strategic direction; and prioritize store visits, product placement, and promotional activities. The sales representatives were then to execute these strategies. Sales representatives did not know they were to do the analysis themselves—although the client thought this was a clearly understood expectation.
- The area sales managers were not analyzing the sales data and were not providing the type of guidance the sales representatives expected and needed. The sales managers also provided limited coaching regarding territory and product priorities.
- The sales reports were data rich but very difficult to analyze.

Solution Design and Implementation Phase

In the meeting with Daniel's client, at which the results from interviews were discussed, several solutions were agreed upon. One of these was a decision to have the sales reports restructured so they were easier to sort, analyze, and draw conclusions from. Included in the redesigned reports was creation of automated functions to facilitate analysis. An example was building capability of the software to automatically recognize and report key trends within each territory. Daniel created a self-guided manual for the sales representatives enabling them to more effectively use the sales reports and the automated spreadsheet functions. The accountabilities of sales managers and sales representatives regarding analysis of sales reports were clarified and the role of sales manager as a coach was reinforced as a key performance requirements.

Measurement Phase

Several hundred sales representatives and approximately 50 area sales managers reduced their weekly administrative time by many hours. Daniel's efforts also resulted in the learning organization *not* delivering advanced spreadsheet training to several hundred sales representatives, which was the original request. Clearly the original request would have required substantial resources and provided minimal results. Several months after implementing the selected solutions, the client indicated that these solutions were one of three contributing factors that led to record-breaking sales for the fiscal year.

What You Can Do

As you see, there is much to consider when using a performance consulting approach. When you work as a performance consultant, you are ensuring that investments made in skill building *do* result in performance change and business impact. Specifically you are using a performance consulting approach each time you

- Partner with clients to implement solutions rather than work independently of these managers
- Ask questions of clients to determine the linkage between any solution you are being asked to implement and the performance and business results the client seeks
- Determine the root causes for what prevents people from performing as needed on the job
- Use learning as a solution only when lack of skill or knowledge is one of the root causes identified for the current situation.

The need to adopt a performance consulting framework in your work is growing. We know that the amount of time and money invested in learning is on the increase within organizations. According to ASTD, as reported in the December 2006 issue of *T+D* (Ketter, 2006), this investment is currently at $109 billion for the United States; the investment globally would, obviously, be even greater. And we know that when this investment is made in a strategic manner, and not just executed as a learning activity, the benefits to the business are significant. Consider a study of 740 organizations that found that firms with the greatest intensity of human resource practices that reinforce and support performance had the highest market value per employee (Becker and Huselid, 1998). You are a key player to ensure that learning investments yield results—remember to "think performance" as you work.

Adapted with permission from *Performance Consulting* by Dana Gaines and James Robinson (Berrett-Koehler, 2008).

About the Author

Dana Gaines Robinson is a recognized leader in the area of performance consulting. She supports human resource and learning functions in their transition to a performance focus; she also helps to enhance the capabilities of people within these functions to work more strategically with organizational managers and leaders. She is the coauthor of six books, including *Strategic Business Partner: Aligning People with Business Goals* (Robinson and Robinson, 2005) and *Performance Consulting: A Practical Guide for HR and Learning Professionals* (second edition), (Robinson and Robinson, 2008). Together with her husband, James Robinson, she was presented with ASTD's Distinguished Contribution to Workplace Learning and Performance Award in 1998. She is also a former member of the ASTD Board of Directors.

References

Becker, Brian E., and Mark A. Huselid. 1998. High performance work systems and firm performance: A synthesis of research and managerial implications. In *Research in personnel and human resources management,* ed., G.R. Ferris. Greenwich, CT: JAI Press.

Broad, Mary L. 2005. *Beyond transfer of training: Engaging systems to improve performance.* San Francisco: Pfeiffer.

Gilbert, Thomas. 2007. *Human competence: Engineering worthy performance.* Washington, D.C.: ISPI Press.

Ketter, Paula. 2006. Investing in learning; looking for performance. *T+D* 60(12): 30-33.

Robinson, Dana Gaines, and James C. Robinson. 2008. *Performance consulting: A practical guide for HR and learning professionals.* 2d ed. San Francisco: Berrett-Koehler.

Rummler, Geary A., and Alan P. Brache. 1995. *Improving performance: How to manage the white space on the organization chart.* 2nd ed. San Francisco: Jossey-Bass.

Stolovitch, Harold D., and Erica J. Keeps. 1999. *Handbook of human performance technology: Improving individual and organizational performance worldwide.* 2d ed. San Francisco: Pfeiffer.

Stolovitch, Harold D., and Erica J. Keeps. 2004. *Training ain't performance.* Alexandria, VA: ASTD Press.

For Further Reading

Gilbert, Thomas F. 1996. *Human competence: Engineering worthy performance* (ISPI tribute edition). Silver Spring, MD, and Amherst, MA: ISPI/HRD Press.

Kirkpatrick, Donald L., and James D. Kirkpatrick. 2006. *Evaluating training programs: The four levels.* 3d ed. San Francisco: Berrett-Koehler.

Phillips, Jack J., and Patricia P. Phillips. 2008. *Costs and ROI: Evaluating at the ultimate level.* Measurement in Action series. San Francisco: Pfeiffer.

❧ Section II

Assessing and Analyzing Needs

Some Important Questions Regarding Needs Assessment and Analysis

Luminary Perspective

Geary A. Rummler

In This Chapter

➢ Understand why effective needs assessment and analysis should be the starting point for WLP professionals

➢ Learn the role of needs assessment and analysis

➢ Understand the responsibilities of WLP professionals

Three important questions frame this introduction to needs assessment and analysis:

■ Why bother?
■ What needs are we talking about, anyway?
■ What is the major pitfall in needs assessment and analysis?

Why Bother?

Why emphasize needs assessment and analysis? The answer is twofold: first, these processes are integral to workplace learning and performance (WLP), and, second, the

WLP professional is employed by an institution that expects the professional to ensure that its employees can perform the value-add work required for business-level success. Needs assessment and analysis are the only means of measuring a results gap and demonstrating whether a WLP intervention has closed the identified gap.

Role of Needs Assessment and Analysis in WLP

Figure A is a model—an output chain—for understanding the relationship between workplace learning and workplace performance. Following the chain from the left to right, you see the following:

- Knowledge or skill (K/S) input (1) is provided to the performer (2).
- The performer uses the K/S input to produce certain behaviors (3) in the workplace.
- Such behaviors contribute to execution of relevant job tasks (4).
- The accumulated job tasks produce desired job outputs (5).
- Job outputs lead to business process outputs (6). (All jobs in an organization are part of and contribute to work processes.)
- Process outputs contribute to organizational outputs (7).

Let's take another look at the model from a performance perspective. The organizational output (7) in this example is profits. Several processes in the organization contribute to this output, but this example relates to the sales process (6), which produces customer orders and sales revenue. The sales process, in turn, is executed by a sales representative performing his or her job and producing job outputs (5) required for the sales process. The sales job consists of a sequence of job outputs, as shown: qualified leads, appointments made, opportunities identified, proposals requested, and proposals generated. When successful, these five job outputs should result in the process output of customer order most of the time. Exemplary sales representatives perform five tasks (4) to identify potential opportunities for the product or service they are selling. Such exemplary performers exhibit several likely behaviors (3) as they undertake the task of information gathering. The pivotal link in the chain is the performer (2), a sales representative who exhibits critical behaviors integral to the performance of tasks that lead to job outputs; to process outputs; and, finally, to organizational outputs. The first link in the output chain is the K/S (1) required for the performer to produce the desired behaviors.

This model shows clearly the business context for WLP. What, then, is the role of the WLP professional?

Figure A. Output Chain

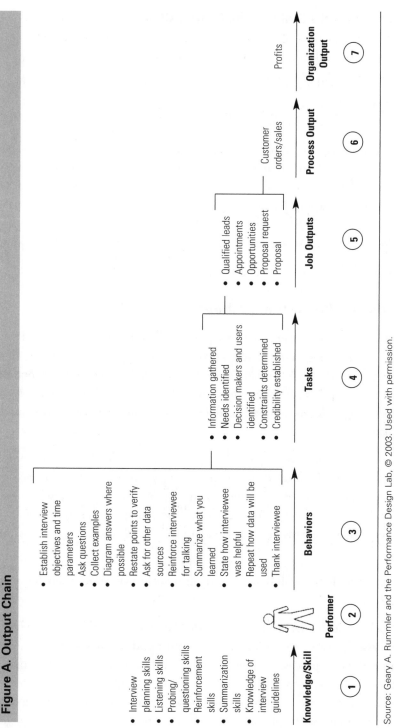

Source: Geary A. Rummler and the Performance Design Lab. © 2003. Used with permission.

The WLP Professional's Stake in the Output Chain

In the context of the model in Figure A, the WLP professional has responsibility for two essential requirements in the organization:

- Correctly identify the value-add work that must be performed in the workplace
- Prepare workers or employees at any level in the organizational hierarchy to competently perform that value-add work.

To meet these challenges, the WLP professional must understand the institution's goals and outputs, the value-add work required to accomplish organizational goals, job outputs involved in performing the value-add work, and the K/S and performance support necessary to produce the job outputs. The only way a WLP professional can pinpoint the value-add work required and help the worker become competent in performing that work is through an effective needs assessment and analysis, which brings us to the second question opening this chapter.

What Needs Are We Talking About, Anyway?

In the context of the output chain, exactly what needs does the WLP professional assess and analyze? Looking at Figure A, should the WLP professional be concerned with the learning needs represented by K/S inputs (1) to the left of the performer or the performance output needs (3, 4, 5, 6, and 7) to the right of the performer? The answer to that question makes a *big* difference in what is done in the name of needs assessment and analysis and how!

In a perfect world, WLP professionals should do both, but they should identify the workplace *learning* needs in the context of workplace *performance* needs. Workplace performance needs must underlie the understanding of workplace learning needs. Whenever possible, a workplace performance needs assessment and analysis should take priority over and serve as a basis for a subsequent workplace learning needs assessment and analysis.

To understand the factors that influence workplace performance, consider the model presented in Figure B.

The premise behind the model is this: Every performer in an organization is in a human performance system (HPS), consisting of five interdependent components. The performer (1) is required to process a variety of inputs (2), such as a form, sales opportunity, or a phone call. For each such input, there is a desired output (3), such as an inquiry answered, form processed, or decision made. For every output produced (as well as the action required to produce an output), a resultant set of consequences

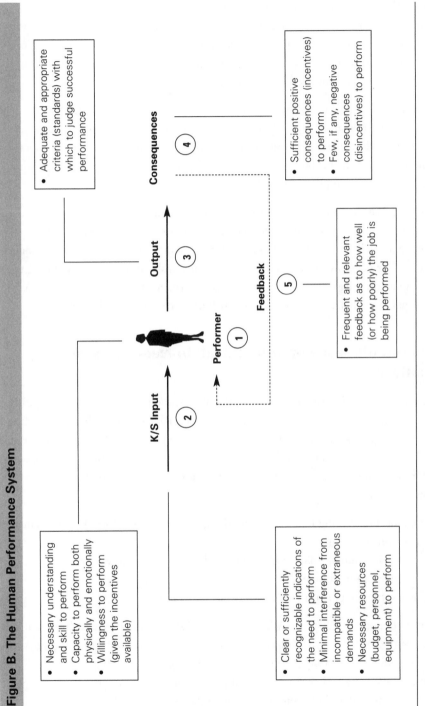

Figure B. The Human Performance System

Consequences

- Adequate and appropriate criteria (standards) with which to judge successful performance

- Sufficient positive consequences (incentives) to perform
- Few, if any, negative consequences (disincentives) to perform

Output ③

Feedback ⑤

- Frequent and relevant feedback as to how well (or how poorly) the job is being performed

Performer ①

K/S Input ②

- Necessary understanding and skill to perform
- Capacity to perform both physically and emotionally
- Willingness to perform (given the incentives available)

- Clear or sufficiently recognizable indications of the need to perform
- Minimal interference from incompatible or extraneous demands
- Necessary resources (budget, personnel, equipment) to perform

Source: Geary A. Rummler and the Performance Design Lab, © 2003. Used with permission.

(4) affects the performer. These consequences are interpreted uniquely by the performer as either positive or negative. People will do things that lead to positive consequences and avoid things that lead to negative consequences. The last component of the performance system is feedback (5) to the performer on the consequences of the output. To be effective, this feedback must be specific and timely.

If there is a breakdown in any one of the components, the desired output will not be forthcoming. A particular HPS is only as good as its weakest component. For a person to consistently provide a particular output, each component in the HPS must meet the requirements shown in the boxes in Figure B. If performers are not clear on what is expected, chances are slim they will produce it.

As a practical matter, the WLP professional could transform the HPS into the poor-performance troubleshooting template shown in Figure C. The template shows that knowledge and skill constitute just one factor in achieving workplace performance; at least five other factors—performance specifications, task support, consequences, feed-back, and individual capacity—in the workplace performance environment or system must be at par if workplace learning is to contribute to organizational results.

What Is the Biggest Potential Pitfall in Needs Assessment and Analysis?

Workplace learning and performance professionals put themselves in a perilous position when they attempt a learning needs assessment and analysis without first conducting a performance needs assessment and analysis. The consequence of doing so is a training program built on a quicksand foundation of management's impressions. If both learning and performance needs assessments and analyses are not done, the WLP professional faces risks, such as

- Squandering training money on something that has no significant performance impact on the business
- Developing training that is not supported by the real-world workplace performance environment
- Wasting trainee/performer time on irrelevant training.

All too often, the challenge for the WLP professional starts with a request from manage-ment for training of some group of employees. Usually, in the context of Figure A, the requestor specifies the K/S input to the trainee ("Please train the employees in X") but seldom mentions a desired performance output or job result. At this point, the WLP professional has to choose between two divergent paths.

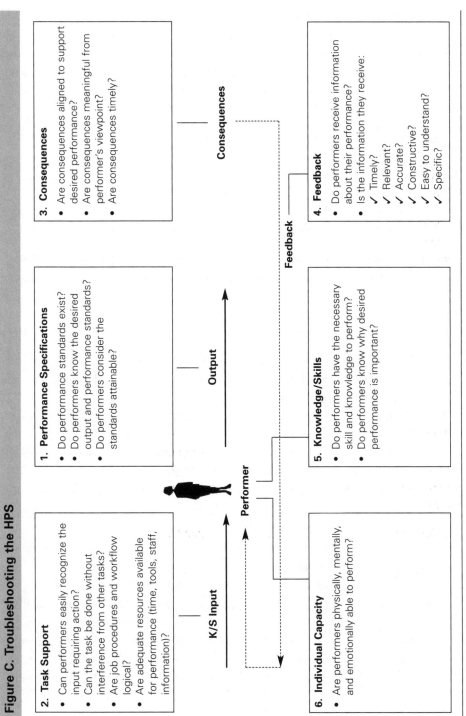

Figure C. Troubleshooting the HPS

2. Task Support
- Can performers easily recognize the input requiring action?
- Can the task be done without interference from other tasks?
- Are job procedures and workflow logical?
- Are adequate resources available for performance (time, tools, staff, information)?

1. Performance Specifications
- Do performance standards exist?
- Do performers know the desired output and performance standards?
- Do performers consider the standards attainable?

3. Consequences
- Are consequences aligned to support desired performance?
- Are consequences meaningful from performer's viewpoint?
- Are consequences timely?

6. Individual Capacity
- Are performers physically, mentally, and emotionally able to perform?

5. Knowledge/Skills
- Do performers have the necessary skill and knowledge to perform?
- Do performers know why desired performance is important?

4. Feedback
- Do performers receive information about their performance?
- Is the information they receive:
  ✓ Timely?
  ✓ Relevant?
  ✓ Accurate?
  ✓ Constructive?
  ✓ Easy to understand?
  ✓ Specific?

K/S Input

Performer

Output

Consequences

Feedback

Source: Geary A. Rummler and the Performance Design Lab, © 2003. Used with permission.

Path A (followed by many novice WLP professionals or those in the uncomfortable situation of having to acquiesce to management's ill-founded request for training) is to immediately focus on the learning needs and elect to operate on the input side of the performer (Figure A). They will respond to the request as presented and deliver the training as requested, or they might attempt to validate the requested need for training and K/S content by surveying other supervisors or managers to ascertain what K/S they *think* the targeted group of employees require or organizing a focus group of the targeted population of employees and asking them what K/S input they *think* they need.

Although various techniques can be used to try to gather such data on workplace learning needs, they are of little value because this approach to determining learning needs is fundamentally flawed. The WLP professional is heading down the path of attempting to identify workplace *learning* needs with no connection to workplace *performance* needs.

Although more challenging, Path B is the way followed by WLP professionals. Paths A and B both start with the same request from management ("Please train the employees in X"), but Path B proceeds differently from there. WLP professionals realize that, although the request begins on the input side of the performer, they must move around to the output side to determine the gap in results to be closed by the proposed training input. The performance *and* learning needs assessment and analysis work like this:

- The WLP professional listens to the request and responds to the requestor with some combination of the following statements and questions:
  - "Can you tell me what is happening or not happening in the workplace that leads you to conclude that this particular training is required?"
  - "If we were to deliver the training you are requesting, how will you know if it has been effective? What will you look at to determine if it made a difference?"
  - "For me to design a cost-effective training intervention, I need to observe and question the targeted employees in their workplace. Do you have any problems with my taking a few days to do that?"
- Assuming that the requestor of the training agrees to this request, the WLP professional will then take certain steps, such as
  - Use hard performance data to identify exemplary performing individuals, processes, or organizational units (districts, regions, offices, plants, or shifts).
  - Closely observe, interview, and analyze what these exemplary performers do, in contrast with nonexemplars. The objective is to ascertain if a gap exists with respect to job, process, or organizational results. If so, what are the possible causes of the gap, as discerned by using the adapted HPS template in Figure C?

— Based on these data, the WLP professional begins the design of a training intervention that will contribute to closing the identified gap and show the initial requestor of the training what additional workplace performance support would be required if the training is to be successful in helping to close the results gap.

Is the Path B scenario a stretch? It is not beyond the expertise for the WLP professional who meets the parameters defined earlier. Recall that the role of the WLP professional requires an understanding of *all* the following:

- The institution's goals/outputs
- The value-add work required to accomplish organizational goals
- The job outputs required to perform the value-add work
- The K/S and performance support required to produce the job outputs.

To recap, the biggest potential pitfall in performing needs assessment and analysis stems from the failure to start with Path B's performance needs assessment and analysis. Of course, Path B is challenging and requires that the WLP professional be cognizant of various organizational realities and be persuasive and flexible. When confronted with a request for training, the WLP professional should pursue Path B only if there is an opportunity to significantly affect workplace performance through training or another HPS intervention. Following Path B seldom is worth the effort if the request is for a one-time event such as a special program, or if the training is mandated by senior management or a regulatory entity.

If the WLP professional is successful in converting a Path A training request into a Path B needs assessment and analysis, it is important for him or her to use professional judgment. Path B should be pursued as far as feasible, but it is possible that management will run out of time and tolerance for a complete performance needs assessment and analysis before all the work is completed. It is also possible that, in the course of conducting a complete assessment and analysis, no real results gap can be identified. In this case, the WLP professional should try to convince the requestor to drop the project. If this is not possible, the best course is to jump onto Path A and deliver the requested training as efficiently as possible.

It is conceivable that the performance needs assessment and analysis will show the need for *both* training and performance support interventions if workplace performance is to be improved. It is also possible that the requestor of the training will not want to address the deficient HPS components; in this circumstance, it's probably best for the WLP professional to just deliver the training and then figure out how to leverage his or her HPS knowledge of the workplace for responding effectively to the next request for training.

Every trip down Path B, even if only moderately successful, is another step up the WLP professional's learning curve and a step closer to becoming a strategic partner in the organization.

Conclusion

The foundation, the starting point of everything discussed in this handbook, is *effective* needs assessment and analysis. The ultimate success of WLP professionals; their programs; and, most likely, their employers depends on the accuracy of the needs analysis they conduct.

About the Author

Geary A. Rummler is the founder and chairman of the Performance Design Lab, a Tucson, Arizona–based research and consulting firm specializing in the design of performance systems for organizations in the United States and abroad. His research and consulting in the areas of performance analysis, design, and management have taken him around the globe.

His most recent book is *Serious Performance Consulting According to Rummler* (2007). He is also co-author of *Improving Performance: Managing the White Space on the Organization Chart* (1990, 1995, with A.P. Brache). He received his MBA and PhD from the University of Michigan and has served as the president of the International Society for Performance Improvement (ISPI) and as a member of the ASTD Board of Directors. He was inducted into the Human Resource Development Hall of Fame in 1986, received ISPI's Distinguished Professional Achievement Award in 1992, was awarded the Distinguished Contribution to Workplace Learning and Performance Award from ASTD in 1999, and received the Presidential Citation for Intellectual Leadership from ISPI in 2000.

Data Collection and Assessment—Finding the Right Tool for the Job

Ethan S. Sanders

In This Chapter

- ➢ Learn the fundamental rules of data collection
- ➢ Understand the whos, whats, and hows of measurement

The subject of data collection can best be captured in a very old joke:

> *6th Grader: "Mommy, I got a 100 on my math test."*
> *Mom: "That's wonderful."*
> *6th Grader: "Unfortunately, there were 200 questions on the test."*
> *Mom: "Oh, I'm sorry to hear that."*
> *6th Grader: "But it was the second highest score in the class."*
> *Mom: "That's wonderful."*
> *6th Grader: "But only two people were able to take the test that day."*

As with most things in life, children often exemplify what we see in the workplace. It is not uncommon to see "corporate statistics" that lack the type of relativity necessary to render a sound judgment on what the data mean. The first (and most important) rule of data collection is to only collect information that has a clear purpose and helps the organization to answer fundamental questions about its operation. The second rule is to always have a data collection plan that encompasses a sound data collection strategy. This chapter will explore some of the fundamental rules of data collection and will highlight some of the principal considerations that must go into a data collection strategy. To effectively collect data, workplace learning and performance (WLP) practitioners must know what they are measuring, who they are measuring, the pros and cons of different tools used for measuring, and how to analyze and present the data. Each of these topics is discussed in this chapter.

Know What You Are Measuring

"A strong conviction that something must be done
is the parent of many bad measures."

—Daniel Webster

The Research Question

All good research begins with a fundamental question that the researcher (or organization) is trying to answer. The research question describes the who, what, where, why, when, and how of the investigation. In the social sciences, a research question might be, "Will low-income housing residents gain employment faster if they are provided additional education?" In the physical sciences, the research question might be "Will the manipulation of proteins on the DNA molecule reduce the incidence of cancer cells forming?" When addressing WLP issues, the type of research being conducted is generally based in the social sciences. Therefore, the research questions tend to look like the former example. In addition, because organizations are complex economic and social systems, the more specific the research question is, the more focused the data collection effort will become. There are several components to a research question that must be covered:

- The *subject* of the assessment (that is, what relationship between two or more variables is being assessed?)
- The *source* of the data that will be used to measure the subject of the assessment (that is, according to what set or sets of data?)
- The *standard* for evaluating the subject (that is, by when, by how much, or by what quality measure is success being measured?).

One example of a good WLP research question is, "Does the new pay for performance system increase the number of loans processed by employees by 15 percent or more, as measured by the loan application reports?"

✍ **Joe Harless** ✍

Joe Harless, one of the early pioneers of human performance technology (HPT) and a student of Thomas F. Gilbert, followed Gilbert's diagnostic approach to performance, believing that the best way to find a solution is to first uncover the cause of the problem. Harless found that most projects would benefit if analysis was done up front rather than at a project's end; he is credited with being the first person to coin the term front-end analysis. Like Gilbert, Harless derived his own performance equation. Harless's equation states that performance (P) equals an employee's inherent capabilities (ic), skills and knowledge (s, k), motivation and incentives (m, i), and environmental supports (e); the equation is represented as P = ic + (s, k) + (m, i) + e. Harless was also one of the first to speak out about the power of job aids and was a proponent of using them as a training solution.

Harless's book An Ounce of Analysis (Is Worth a Pound of Objectives) *(1975) outlined his performance improvement process, which stresses the importance of organizational alignment and continually measures training solutions to gauge their effectiveness in addressing performance gaps. The performance improvement process gave trainers what they needed to truly address performance issues.*

In this example, notice that the subject of the research question is the effect that the "pay for performance system" is having on employees' productivity. The standard is "increase the number of loans processed by 15 percent" and the data source is "loan application reports."

Consider for a moment how much would change in data collection efforts if the research question were "Does the new pay for performance system increase the morale of the employees by 15 percent or more, as measured by the yearly employee satisfaction survey?"

Although the standard (15 percent) of the research question has not changed, and part of the subject remains the same (that is, it is still examining the effects of the new pay for performance system), there are considerable differences in these research questions. The latter research question focuses on the effects of the pay for performance system on employee morale rather than on productivity. The data source is an annual employee satisfaction survey. The difference will drastically affect the data collection strategy. The focus of the data collection effort now centers on validating employee opinions and attempts to link changes in perception to the pay for performance system. In general, the WLP professional will now address far more subjective and relative information than would be examined with the first research question. Although crafting clear and succinct research questions can be challenging, the data collection effort will be lost without a clear vision of what is being studied.

The Level of Performance

Goals within an organization are a funny thing. They tend to be multilayered and often float according to the perspective of the person examining the goals. As Geary Rummler (1990) highlights in his seminal work *Improving Performance,* there are three levels of goals within an organization: organizational, process, and individual. To achieve optimal performance, these three levels of goals must be aligned (see Figure 5-1). For example, if an organization's goal is to "achieve 90 percent customer satisfaction," a fulfillment process goal might be "all products ready for shipping within 24 hours of receipt." An individual goal might be "complete form 1712 with 98 percent accuracy before shipping date occurs."

When conducting a data collection effort, it is essential that one gives careful consideration to which level is initially being measured and perhaps how many levels are being measured. For example, if the goal of a WLP project is to decrease the cycle time it takes to deliver a course to a customer, this would be a process level goal (because what is being examined is an instructional design process). The types of measures that would typically be used are (1) time to create the course outline, (2) time it takes to gain approval for outline, (3) time it takes to develop the course, and (4) number of pilot sessions necessary to refine the course. In other words, the data collection effort would center on mapping out all steps in the design process and calculating how long each step takes. Conversely, if customer

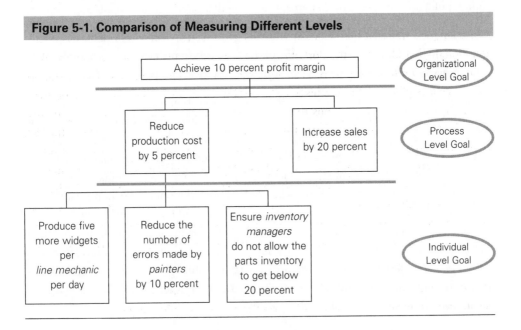

Figure 5-1. Comparison of Measuring Different Levels

satisfaction or profits from a course are being examined (which is an organizational level goal), the types of measures would be (1) actual versus projected design budget for course, (2) level 1 and level 2 evaluation results, and (3) gross sales of course materials. Table 5-1 highlights these distinctions.

If the project involves aligning individual, process, and organizational goals, the number of variables (and the number of data sets) will increase.

Standards and Measures

Once the WLP professional has a clear idea of the subject matter at hand and a general sense of which level of performance he or she is assessing (that is, individual, process, or organizational), the next step is to clearly define how the subject will be assessed. There are two elements that factor into this assessment: standards and measures. Measures describe how high the bar is being set; standards describe the bar itself. Table 5-2 describes the difference between absolute and relative standards, the differences between objective and subjective measures, and the intersection between measures and standards.

A helpful way to think about standards and measures is to equate them to the legal concept of burden of proof. In the legal system, the burden of proof varies depending on the crime: in a criminal trial, the burden of proof is beyond a reasonable doubt; and in a civil trial, the burden of proof is a preponderance of evidence. As the seriousness of the crime increases, the burden of proof also increases. In WLP data collection, the same holds true depending on the ultimate decision that will be based on the data collection results. Remember that all data collection efforts are either trying to assess "did A cause B" or "does A have a relationship to B." The assessment is trying to determine if some solution (or even a lack of a solution) has had the desired effect on some aspect of human performance. Depending on how serious the human performance issues are (or how expensive the solution is), the burden of proof will increase accordingly. For example, if the data collection effort is focused solely on determining employee satisfaction, relative standards and subjective measures will normally suffice. The data collection instruments may ask questions such as, "Are you happier working for this company today compared with a year ago?" This question is asking for a subjective measure of happiness and asking the respondent to make a relative comparison to a year ago. It may also ask for a relative comparison to other employees (for example, "Are you happier working here than most of your other colleagues?").

If the ultimate intent of this data collection is to help the human resource manager decide if certain solutions aimed at improving morale should continue, the employee's

Table 5-1. Sample Types of Measurement and Data Collection Techniques

	Goal Statement	Typical Types of Measures	Data Collection Techniques
Organizational	"Solve World Hunger"	• Number of people who do not have adequate food • Volume of food required to feed people • Number of organizations that currently provide food to feed the population • Tons of food required versus food available for population.	• Examination of historical data related to food tonnage • Examination of operational capacity of various relief organizations • News articles, UN reports, etc., on food needs for the target population.
Process	"All food inventories filled within one week of request."	• Number of steps currently in the process • Amount of time each step takes • Most time-consuming steps • Perspectives of team members on which steps are ripe for improvement.	• Examination of operational manuals • Interviews with relief agency workers • Observation of various process steps • Examination of performance records • Focus groups with relief agency workers.
Individual	"Reduce number of damaged goods during handling by dock workers by 50 percent."	• Damage rates by region, location, or individual • Perspectives of team members on causes for damage • Difficulty of tasks rating.	• Examination of damage reports • Observations of exemplary versus average dock workers • Examination of damaged shipments • Conduct a job-task analysis.

Table 5-2. Sample Absolute and Relative Standards and Objective and Subjective Measures

	Absolute Standards *Example: "I want to build 10 widgets."*	Relative Standards *Example: "I want to build more widgets than my co-worker Bob."*
Objective Measures *Example: Average number of widgets built per hour.*	*Examples:* • Build 10 widgets per hour. • Call detachments within 24 hours of receiving coaching assignment. • Complete all HPI projects by deadline.	*Examples:* • Build 10 more widgets than Bill. • Call detachments at least one hour faster on average than all the other coaches. • Complete projects faster than detachment average for a "5."
Subjective Measures *Example: Average customer satisfaction score on a survey.*	*Examples:* • Have 90 percent of Acme customers agree that they like our widgets. • Receive 80 percent approval rating from detachments related to coaching assignments. • Supervisor "strongly agrees" that all HPI projects are accurate.	*Examples:* • Acme customers are at least 15 percent happier than competitor customers. • Receive the highest satisfaction rating among all coaches to get a "5." • Receive the highest supervisor accuracy assessment among all detachments.

subjective and relative responses are probably ample. However, if the intent is to determine the reason for excessive employee turnover, which is costing the company millions of dollars a year, simply capturing these subjective, relative responses will probably not suffice. The "burden of proof" has just increased and therefore a compelling case for change will require more absolute standards coupled with more objective measures. This might include actual turnover rates today versus those of last year (absolute standard, objective measure), a wage analysis to see how fairly the company is compensating employees (absolute/objective data), and then exit interview data (subjective data that tend to be more relative) to help triangulate the data.

Although it is impossible to have a measurement system that relies solely on absolute standards and objective measures, the aim should be to have a good mixture and to always attempt to find as much absolute and objective data as possible (see Figure 5-2).

Figure 5-2. Ideal Mix of Standards and Measures

Burden of Proof		Absolute Standards	Relative Standards
High	Objective Measures	#1 Choice	#3 Choice
Low	Subjective Measures	#2 Choice	#4 Choice

Know Who You Are Measuring

"I will prescribe regimen for the good of my patients according to my ability and my judgment and never do harm to anyone."

—The Hippocratic Oath

These words have endured in the medical community for thousands of years. Although WLP practitioners are not normally making life-and-death decisions with their data collection, the same principles must hold true. Collecting data on human performance issues requires a careful assessment of how much trauma the act of inquiry might have on the target population. For example, surveys are rarely seen as intrusive because the respondent always has the option of not participating in a survey. Likewise, requests for interviews and focus groups are normally not met with anxiety on the part of the respondent because respondents control what responses are given.

On the opposite end of the anxiety spectrum, however, observations and document analysis can have a profoundly traumatic effect if they are not handled properly. The act of being watched always carries with it some undertones of being spied on (even if the subject was notified that they were selected to be observed because they were identified as an exemplary performer). Likewise, the act of rooting around in a performer's file cabinet looking for empirical evidence on a performance issue is sure to elicit some anxiety. In general, data collection efforts should always seek to gather the information in the least intrusive manner possible. This is not to say WLP practitioners should avoid observations and document analysis, just that great care must be taken when doing so.

The Target Population

There are numerous factors related to the target population that should be considered when creating the collection strategy. These include the demographics of the target population, the respondent's experience with similar data collection efforts in the past, the degree of anonymity required, the geographic dispersion of the target population, the particular sensitivities of the respondents around certain topics, and the logistical or technological realities. Table 5-3 summarizes some of the primary considerations.

Business Type

Just as every target population varies in terms of preferences, so too do different industries prefer certain types of data collection approaches. Highly regulated businesses such as financial services, transportation, and pharmaceuticals are usually driven by hard data. Over time WLP practitioners learn that these clients will never accept recommendations that are based on an aggregate of options. Some types of businesses are very fast paced and have little patience for data collection efforts that take months to complete. These types of businesses tend to go for less than perfect analysis, preferring to generate an educated opinion on the performance issue and then refine the solution as the implementation unfolds. Typically this approach is found in high-tech companies, research and development firms, and military establishments. By contrast, many nonprofit, federal government, and educational institutions are more interested in having rich, qualitative data that may take more time to gather and analyze. Of course, these are all generalizations, and it is imperative that a WLP practitioner gets to know the specifics of each organization for which he or she works.

The Client

Clients are no different in terms of various preferences. There are many questions that should be addressed with a client before a data collection effort begins:

- What is the deadline for completing the effort?
- What resources will be available?
- Who is the advocate for this effort?
- Will he or she be able to help get access to the required data?
- What are the client's expectations in terms of the final report (for example, a presentation, a report, or a database)?
- What are the primary decisions that will be made based on the data?
- Will they be releasing the final analysis to the target population?
- If yes, how and when?
- What level of involvement will the client have in the data collection effort?
- How frequently does the client want status updates?
- What are some expected barriers to collecting the data or getting stakeholders to accept the recommended solutions?

Table 5-3. Primary Considerations for Target Populations

Factors	Questions to Consider	Comments
Demographics	• Is there a large range of ages in the target population? • If so, does this make a difference in how the data should be collected? • Is it necessary to distinguish supervisor, manager, executive, or individual contributor data? • Is it necessary to consider differences in race, experience, gender, or educational background?	Normally a simple set of demographic questions at the beginning of the data collection instruments will suffice. Do not ask questions about race, gender, experience, etc., unless this information is needed for the analysis. Providing this information should be voluntary, and the instrument should explain why this information is necessary. Also consider a privacy act statement at the bottom of the instrument that specifically describes who will have access to the information.
Past Experiences	• What similar types of data collection efforts have occurred in recent years? • What became of those data (i.e., were there ever any recommendations, did the respondents ever see the results, etc.)? • Was the data collection process itself seen as valid, user friendly, and efficient? • Are the people who did the previous data collection still in the picture? • If yes, will they be receptive to the current data collection effort? • What were the client's perceptions of previous data collection efforts? • If negative, what are the specific things that should be avoided or changed this time?	Most data collection efforts fail due to inappropriate expectations being set with the client or the target population. Unfortunately, subsequent data collection efforts will experience guilt by association. It is essential to be aware of past attempts at data collection and to carefully plot a strategy that will serve to distinguish surveys.

Anonymity Required	• How important will anonymity of responses be to the target population? • Can all respondents be guaranteed anonymity? • If not, how will the data collection effort ensure that individual responses that might embarrass the respondent are not inadvertently provided to the customer?	Anonymity is a make or break issue for data collection. If the WLP practitioner is perceived at any point during the process as compromising confidentiality, participation in the effort will wane immediately. If they want to know the identity of each respondent and specifics on what they said, the WLP practitioner must convey to the respondents that all comments will be on the record.
Geographic Dispersion	• In how many locations does the target population reside? • Does it make more sense to gather the respondents in one location, or have the WLP practitioner travel to the various locations?	As the target population becomes more dispersed, the data collection effort will need to become more reliant on surveys and document analysis rather than observations, focus groups, and interviews. Remember that disruptions to productivity are normally not well received, so minimize the amount of travel time that participants will need.
Sensitivity	• Are there issues or topics within the organization (that are related to the data collection effort) that are taboo? • Are there any labor relations issues currently occurring that could affect the data collection effort (e.g., wage negotiations, EEO complaints, negative publicity about the company, etc.)?	Normally a list of these issues can be generated by talking with the client or with an appropriate HR person. Although it is advisable to tread lightly on these subjects, they should not be avoided if they appear to be central to the larger issue being examined.
Logistics/ Technologies	• What are the working hours of the target population (i.e., do they all roughly work the same hours or are there different shifts)? • Is there travel money available? • Do the various locations have private spaces for interviews or focus groups? • Do the respondents have access to computers, networks, or the Internet? • What policies does the organization have regarding storage of confidential data?	Modern technology has made data collection a lot easier and more efficient. Think carefully about the ultimate database that will be used to house the data (e.g., MS Excel, MS Access, SPSS, SAS, etc.). Try to find a way to collect survey data electronically, but make sure it is compatible with the chosen database. Be very careful about where the data is stored and who has access to it. In general, avoid putting data on portable devices such as laptops, PDAs, flash drives, etc.

This is a short list of questions to consider when determining the best way to work with the client. It is also helpful to ask the client if there are any questions that should have been asked but weren't.

Know the Pros and Cons of Different Tools

"Any tool is a weapon if you hold it right."

—Ani DiFranco

The tools used for data collection in a workplace setting are neither unique nor particularly modern. They are, however, the main interface between the data collection strategy and the target population. The most visible element to the respondent is the physical survey, the interview questions, the focus group format, or the test he or she is asked to take. If these tools are not well designed, thought provoking, aesthetically pleasing, and clearly written, the entire process will be called into question. Two of the most vital factors to consider when building or buying data collection tools are validity and reliability. To say a data collection tool is valid means that it is testing for what it is designed to test for. For example, if a teacher in a French language course gave a test to the students in German, it would not be valid.

To say a tool is reliable means that the results of the data collection using that tool should be repeatable. For example, if the French students received the same test on Monday morning and then again on Monday afternoon, the results should be about the same (assuming additional instruction was not provided in between the tests). It is essential to remember that a tool could be reliable but not valid. For example, for the students taking French who took the test in German, the result would be reliable (that is, the students would fail the exam over and over again) until they were taught German. Table 5-4 details the pros and cons of the various tools, as well as provides some tips for ensuring validity and reliability.

Know How to Process the Data

"The only thing that counts is if you know how to prepare your ingredients. Even if with the best and freshest ingredients in the world, if your dish is tasteless or burnt, it's ruined."

—Martin Yan

Collecting data is similar to grocery shopping. The process begins with a definition of the central ingredients. When grocery shopping, this takes the form of a recipe and then a

Table 5-4. Pros and Cons of Data Collection Tools

Tool Type	Pros	Cons	Tips on Validity and Reliability
Interview	• Collects rich, qualitative data. • Allows follow-on questions. • Allows observation of body language.	• Is time consuming. • Requires a lot of data synthesis. • Because data are very subjective, normally requires corroboration of information from other sources.	• Write clear interview guide in advance. • Have a subject matter expert review and revise the form. • Tell the interviewee in advance what the purpose of the interview is and provide a general description of what types of information will be examined.
Observation	• Is the best way to see how work gets done. • Can often detect self-created job aids and other distinct advantages that exemplary performers possess. • Is the only method that allows the WLP practitioner to truly see the barriers that are present on the front line.	• The people being observed may adjust their behavior while being observed. • The people being observed may feel uncomfortable being observed. • It is a time-consuming method that will require a lot of data analysis later.	• Make sure the people being observed know in advance why they were selected and what information is sought. • Don't be perceived as a "spy" by standing over people while observing them. • The best way to get a feel for the job while observing is for the WLP practitioner to ask to try to do the job (assuming it is safe to do so).
Focus Group	• Allows respondents to build on each other's ideas. • Enables the consolidation of individual responses.	• It can easily deteriorate into a "whining session." • If working with an organization that has low trust, participants may refuse to speak in front of others. • It does not work well if participants feel intimidated by other participants (e.g., the "big boss" is in the room and no one wants to speak).	• Carefully choose participants according to a set of criteria. • Avoid mixing individual contributors with their supervisors. • Advise participants in advance about the ground rules (especially on confidentiality). • Record session and use private room. • Have a recorder to take notes. • Use a structured approach, such as nominal group technique.

(continued on next page)

Table 5-4. Pros and Cons of Data Collection Tools (continued)

Survey	• Reaches a large population. • Automates data collection if online survey tools are used. • Tests assumptions over a large population.	• It is very difficult to predict how the respondent will interpret questions. • It does not allow a lot of follow-on, probing questions. • It tends to have very low response rates.	• Buy whenever possible. • Pilot test, review, revise, and test again. • Use a simple split-half reliability check.*
Test	• Is the best way to determine learning gains. • Is quick and easy to administer. • Carries a lot of weight when studying learning systems.	• It requires considerable skill to build a valid and reliable test. • Test anxiety may skew the results. • It is difficult to administer in situations where language is a barrier.	• Buy whenever possible. • Pilot test, review, revise, and test again. • Use a simple split-half reliability check.*
Document Review	• Is normally the only method for gathering hard data on performance issues. • Is difficult to argue with if the data come from valid performance records. • Is quick compared with more qualitative forms of data generation. • Is less subject to interpretation.	• Documents can be hard to access. • Documents must be true and accurate. • Review of some documents may be perceived as a violation of privacy.	• Only review documents that are directly linked to the research question. • Get written permission to review any sensitive documents. • Gather data on how much confidence the client and stakeholders have in the accuracy of these documents (e.g., ask employees if they believe that the standard operating procedure is accurate).

*A split-half reliability check allows the researcher to determine if the phrasing of the question has an influence on how the respondent answers the question. Two versions of the survey or test are provided. In one version, the questions are phrased in the affirmative, while in the other version the questions are phrased in the negative. The responses are then compared to see if the way the questions were worded affected the response.

shopping list. When collecting data, this takes the form of a data collection plan. But imagine spending the entire day shopping in the most exclusive grocery stores, driving to farmer's markets, and getting fresh milk from a dairy farm to throw all of the ingredients into a microwave for a few minutes and see what comes out. The act of data collection has not met its pinnacle until the ingredients are properly prepared through a process of examination and contemplation.

The beginning of this process is normally intimidating. The sheer amount of data can often be overwhelming, and, regardless of how much focus has been placed on the original research questions, extraneous data have a way of creeping in. Being able to address ambiguity early in the process of sifting through data is a key competency for WLP practitioners. It is not uncommon for the data to appear fuzzy early in the process. Processing data involves three distinct and important steps: synthesizing, displaying, and presenting.

Synthesizing Data

Depending on the type of research being conducted, synthesizing data can be done several ways. In general, the process involves the following steps. The first step is to become familiar with the data. This normally involves some initial frequency distributions to see if the data have initial face validity. To do so often means the data need to be coded. For example, if the research involved interviews, focus groups, or observations, the notes from these events must be placed into categories to spot trends. Table 5-5 provides an example of what this might look like.

Table 5-5. Sample Results of Employee Focus Group: Why Are Customers Unhappy with Our Service?

Code	Response
R1	"My phone set doesn't work consistently, so the customers can't hear me."
K1	"I don't know how to use the customer database."
R1	"Phone sets do not work properly."
R2	"Shrinking budgets do not allow us to develop new products that the customer wants."
P1	"The fulfillment process is a mess. There are no standardized steps to follow."

Key:

R = Resource barriers
K = Knowledge barriers
P = Process barriers

In this example, notice that there are two nearly identical responses related to the broken phone system. Both responses are coded as R1. There is also another resource issue related to budgets that is coded R2. This coding will allow the WLP practitioner to understand how common these perceptions are and to place them into categories that potential solutions can be aligned to. Once the WLP practitioner is familiar with the data, the next step is to draw meaning from this information. It is essential to revisit the research questions and begin to run tests to see what answers the data provide. In the above example, the original research question might have been "What are the primary causes for low customer retention rates?" The data set in Table 5-5 might provide part of the answer from the employee's perspective. Of course, employees can only see elements of the problem.

The next perspective the WLP practitioner collects might be from company records on customer complaints. These data would provide the specific reasons that customers are unhappy. If these data also showed that customers were complaining about difficulty in hearing the employees over the phone, a much stronger case for changing the phone system would be made. Another source of data might be the number and type of product returns that have occurred. What's vital when synthesizing data is that a clear focus remains on telling a compelling story. Remember that the goal of all data collection is to provide the client and stakeholders with the right information to use to make sound decisions. If they are not armed with persuasive data, the case for change will be very difficult to make. Spend an appropriate amount of time determining which research questions can be answered with confidence, which ones seem to have some data to support the original hypothesis, and which ones really have no data to support or reject the original assumption. Remember that no data are data. If an important organizational issue is not being tracked in any meaningful way, this is a very revealing element of the problem. In general, organizations track issues that are important to them.

Displaying Data

All clients have preferences when it comes to the look and feel of a presentation or report. It is important to establish the report guidelines up front. Some clients only want an executive summary and the supporting information in an appendix. Others expect to be walked through the entire set of findings. Some clients are very visual and enjoy charts, graphics, and pictures of the performance environment. The following are some important guidelines to consider when drafting the report or presentation of the findings:

- Begin by walking the client through the methodology used for the data collection. Keep the description simple, but make sure there is enough information so that the client has confidence in the approach that was used.
- Point out strengths and limitations of the data collection approach.

- Do not drown the client in data.
- Summarize the data first without interjecting any interpretation of the data. Just stick to the facts.
- Next, highlight the data that clearly provide answers to the central questions. Do not give personal opinions of what the data say.
- Try to anticipate questions that the client may have and address them in the presentation.
- Include a distinct section that provides recommendations for change.
- Tie these recommendations to the data. Never stop using the data to justify the conclusions.
- Provide menus of options rather than a single approach toward addressing barriers.
- Include a section on "next steps," which might include a cost-benefit analysis or risk assessment.
- End with a very strong set of conclusions. The client pays the most attention to the first and last page of the report (or first and last slides of the presentation).
- Use appendixes to back up the report and provide a clear table of contents for finding the information.

Presenting Data

Just as there are numerous ways to display data, there are numerous ways to present the data. Again, a lot depends on the client's preferences and the WLP practitioner's own comfort level with writing and speaking. A formal report carries a lot more weight than just a presentation. Even if the customer only requests a presentation, having a report to leave behind is advisable. Another possibility is to provide the report several weeks before the scheduled presentation, and then use the report as context during the presentation. During presentations, it is best to generate a discussion rather than give a lecture. If the customer has been provided with continuous status reports as the data collection effort was under way, there should not be any big surprises during the presentation. Instead, the presentation should provide a framework where learning occurs by reviewing the issues and collaborating on the ideas for moving forward. It is essential that the presentation of the data is not seen as a discrete event. There should be a lot of instances both before and after the formal presentation of the findings where the client is being educated. Also consider having multiple presenters if a formal presentation is given. It is quite powerful to have members of the target population help present the data. Their involvement can often be the most compelling testimony on the barriers, and their perspectives carry with them a certain credibility that the WLP practitioner can never have.

Conclusion

> *"You have to understand, my dears, that the shortest distance*
> *between truth and a human being is a story."*
>
> —Anthony de Mello, from *One Minute Wisdom*

Collecting and presenting data is a dance that combines solid reasoning, comprehensive research, and thoughtful conclusions. It is also a process of weaving a good tale. The most technically proficient data collection will still fail if it does not find a central message that resonates with the decision makers who are depending on it. Great storytelling is a process of finding authentic information that carries the true colors and flavor of the subject being described. Movies, books, and even songs feel contrived when they attempt to describe something that the author or musician does not really understand. A great literature professor once said "If you are having trouble describing something in words, it is probably because you do not understand what you are trying to describe." When he or she crafts the final report, it will soon become apparent how well the WLP practitioner really understands the data. If the outline takes shape quickly and the words begin to flow, the story that needs to be told is probably there. If, however, there are fruitless starts and stops, the story is still hidden in the workplace. A great picture always begins with a blank canvas and a great idea. Use data collection as a process for discovering the elements that will be needed to paint that picture, and the customer will be captivated by the findings.

✍

About the Author

Ethan S. Sanders is a fellow with ICF International's Human Capital Strategies Group. He is former president of Sundial Learning Systems and former director of organization development for the U.S. Navy's Human Performance Center. Before founding Sundial Learning Systems, he was manager of instructional design for ASTD, where he led the research and writing of two major competency studies, redesigned several of ASTD's courses, and participated in high-profile research studies on the profession. Before joining ASTD, he worked as an internal consultant in the publishing and banking industry and was a training manager in the transportation industry. He is the co-author of *ASTD Models for Learning Technologies, ASTD Models for Workplace Learning and Performance, Performance Intervention Maps: 36 Strategies for Solving Your Organization's Problems, HPI Essentials,* and the ASTD courses on "Human Performance Improvement in the Workplace." He also teaches several of ASTD's courses offered through public and corporate seminars. He holds a master's degree in applied behavior science from Johns Hopkins University.

Reference

Rummler, Geary A., and Alan P. Brache. 1990. *Improving performance: How to manage the white space on the organization chart.* San Francisco: Jossey-Bass.

For Further Reading

Kranzler, Gerald, Janet Moursund, and John H. Kranzler. 1995. *Statistics for the terrified.* Upper Saddle River, NJ: Prentice-Hall.

Mager, Robert F., and Peter Pipe. 1997. *Analyzing performance problems or you really oughta wanna.* 3d ed. Atlanta, GA: Center for Effective Performance.

Rossett, Allison. 1998. *First things fast: A handbook for performance analysis.* San Francisco: Jossey-Bass.

Weisbord, Marvin Ross. 1978. *Organizational diagnosis: A workbook of theory and practice.* Reading, MA: Addison Wesley.

Zemke, Ron, and Thomas Kramlinger. 1982. *Figuring things out: A trainer's guide to task, needs, and organizational analysis.* New York: Addison Wesley.

Identifying Performance and Learning Gaps

Paul H. Elliott

------------------------------------ **In This Chapter** ------------------------------------

➢ Learn an approach for and the benefits of identifying performance gaps

➢ Identify exemplary workers

➢ Learn to use performance analysis for continuous improvement

---

If you asked your chief operating officer (COO) or divisional vice president which of the following he or she values most in an employee, what do you believe would be the response?

1. Employees who knew more, had greater skills and competencies, and scored higher on relevant tests
2. Employees who were busy all the time
3. Employees who consistently produced outstanding results that supported corporate initiatives.

My experience indicates that across industries and levels, from senior manager to the COO, response three is consistently the dominant choice. It makes sense that business leaders would care more about actual business results than they would about the potential to perform. People need to have the capability to perform (skills, knowledge, and so forth) in order to excel at their work, but having the capability does not correlate directly with superior results. If you doubt this, simply ask yourself this question: Do I know a highly capable person who is, at best, an average performer?

Identifying performance gaps allows you to clearly define what business results matter, how those results are judged or measured, and how exemplary performers produce outstanding results on a consistent basis. Once you have clearly defined the performance gaps, you can then identify the learning gaps (knowledge and skills) that can be addressed via training or performance support. You will also be able to identify additional interventions that are required to drive the greatest improvement in actual business performance.

This chapter will describe an approach to identifying performance and learning gaps that will allow you to target your support where it will have the greatest measurable effect on your client's business results. Benefits can include

- Improved business results through enhanced performance—accomplishing more with the team you have in place
- Increased customer satisfaction by providing customer-facing personnel, from sales to consulting to customer service, with best practices proven to increase desired results
- Reduced turnover by providing the support required to develop a high-performing workforce that understands the "worth of their work"
- Reduced training costs and time by focusing only on the tasks and accomplishments that directly affect business achievement
- More strategic positioning for you and your team with the business leaders you are supporting.

The model advocated in this chapter has been heavily influenced by Thomas Gilbert's classic work, *Human Competence* (Gilbert, 2007). His focus on results versus activity has illuminated our field for 30 years. This approach serves as the basis for ASTD's human performance improvement workshop titled Analyzing Human Performance. This workshop uses an analysis toolset, the Performance DNA Toolkit, which is a complete, flexible set of tools—guides, checklists, and templates—for conducting a comprehensive analysis of human performance (ASTD, 2007).

The Performance Analysis Process

Performance technology is a systematic approach to improving human performance in the workplace through the use of solutions such as skills or knowledge training, work environment improvements, and worker incentives. The critical tool that drives human performance improvement is performance analysis. Gilbert (2007) identified two distinctions that are essential to effective performance analysis. First, you need to focus on what people produce in the work environment and not simply on what they do. It's the contrast between accomplishments or results and the tasks or behaviors that produce those results. Helping workers perform the wrong tasks more efficiently does not improve a company's performance. You must identify up front what a worker's major accomplishments are and how those accomplishments contribute to the company's business goals. Only then can you determine the tasks and support systems needed for workers to produce those accomplishments with a high level of competence.

Table 6-1 illustrates this accomplishment-based approach to improving human performance. The organization provides support systems (interventions) so that the performers do work (tasks) and execute processes. The effective work produces tangible results (accomplishments) that support the business goal. It is important to notice that costs are incurred in the left two columns and value is produced in the right two columns. That is to say, no matter how elaborate the interventions and how busy the people are, if no accomplishments are produced, then no value has accrued to the organization!

Gilbert's second distinction points out that you can best identify what workers produce and what they do to produce it by interviewing and observing exemplary performers. That is, observe workers whose accomplishments exceed standards. For example, how does a high-performing loan officer select borrowers with a high percentage of paybacks? Understanding how exemplary performers work can reveal ways to improve the performance of other workers. Not all of their high performance will be transferable; however, you can capture facets of their performance that can be easily transferred to others and have a significant effect on the success of the company. This idea is in stark contrast to asking managers, policy makers, or subject matter experts what they believe workers should be doing or what they need to know.

Table 6-1. Accomplishment-Based Approach to Project Management

Interventions	Tasks	Accomplishment	Business Goal
• Training in cost analysis • Cash incentive for projects completed at or above targeted margin	• Prepare work breakdown • Assign project staff • Write proposal • Negotiate proposal	• Project plan	• Increased profits

The Role of Exemplary Performers

Within every role in your organization, there are individuals who routinely and consistently produce greater results than do their peers. These are your exemplary performers. They may or may not be the brightest people on the team. They may or may not have the longest tenure. They may or may not have a degree from a prestigious university. The important differentiator is their ability to produce outstanding, measurable, and consistent business results. In Figure 6-1, notice that the horizontal axis is labeled Level of Performance. To identify true stars, you must first identify the key business results or accomplishments that your client wants to achieve. Then you select people on the far right of the curve—those who are producing those results at an exceptional level on a consistent basis.

The difference between stars and standard performers is significant, and it increases as the complexity of the work increases. For example, in high complexity, nonsales roles, exemplary performers outperform their peers by 50 percent or more. In sales roles, they outperform their peers by more than 100 percent.

Often these stars are unconsciously competent—they are unaware of how they produce exceptional results or are unable to explicate what they do and how they do it. The role

Figure 6-1. Typical Performance Distribution

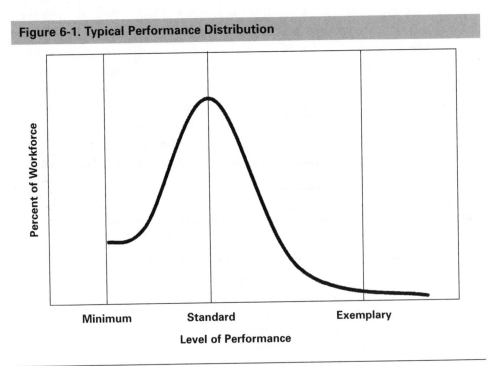

Source: Exemplary Performance, LLC, © 2006, 2007. Used with permission.

of the analyst is to capture and document the high performance system that allows the worker to be successful. The documentation is referred to as the role profile. It includes data such as the results produced, the success criteria for those results, the key activities or tasks used to produce the results with their success criteria, and system facilitators and barriers that the stars have discovered. The data in the role profile provide the design basis for the performance architecture—an integrated set of solutions designed to maximize the performance of everyone in the targeted role (see Figure 6-2).

Figure 6-3 shows the desired result of implementing the performance architecture. Standard performers who are meeting current expectations start to produce greater results, skewing the curve to the right. The organization begins to produce more results with the current workforce and cost structure. This return-on-investment (ROI) is indicated by the solid area in the figure.

The economic implications are significant. When you produce greater results (sales, customer satisfaction and retention, quality, reliability, and so forth) with the incumbent workforce, the great majority of the difference between the old and the new standard will go directly to the bottom line. For example, let's say that you have a salesforce of 400 people carrying a quota of $1 million. Your best people are generating $2 million to $2.5 million in revenue. By implementing a performance architecture based on the current stars, you close the gap by 20 percent ($200,000), skewing the curve to the right. The solid area in

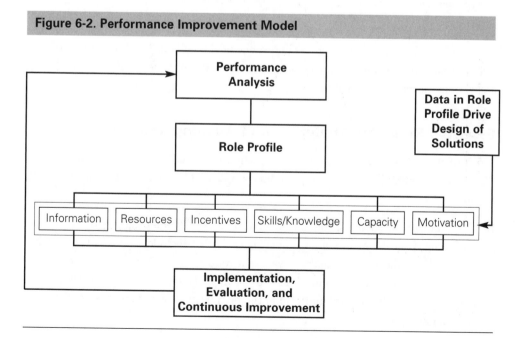

Figure 6-2. Performance Improvement Model

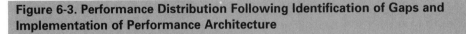

Figure 6-3. Performance Distribution Following Identification of Gaps and Implementation of Performance Architecture

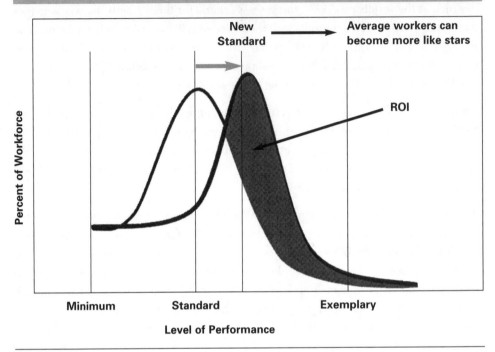

Figure 6-3 would equate to an increase in revenue of $80 million. This is the power of analyzing exemplary performers and helping the standard performers with a performance architecture or integrated solution set.

Essential Steps for Analyzing and Aligning Your Business

Much of the rest of this chapter is an adaptation of my chapter entitled "Analysis" in *Moving from Training to Performance*, edited by Dana Gaines Robinson and James C. Robinson (1998).

Before you begin any analysis, you must align the purpose of the project with the organization's business goals. A formal alignment meeting that includes the client, key stakeholders, and members of the analysis team is a requirement. During this process, you want to verify and clarify the request that led to this specific project. You might ask what situation prompted the request and who in the organization would be affected the most by the proposed project.

You want to verify the organization's basic business goal. My experience indicates that consensus is rare between the client and his or her stakeholders regarding a project's purpose, the business goal it is to support, and how project success should be measured. Is the goal improved customer satisfaction or enhanced profits? It is important that you spend time reviewing internal documentation to see how the goal is stated formally prior to the meeting.

It is even more important that you work through the goal with the team to ensure that you have captured the real operational indicators of the goal. That is, how do the client and the stakeholders visualize and assess organizational performance on a day-to-day basis? During the business analysis process, you also want to capture parameters and constraints of the project. When does the client require the results? How many sites need to be visited? Are there any budget and travel constraints? It is also essential to determine roles within the project and to identify who will be the final authority on determining the accuracy of the results and usefulness of the recommendations.

Perhaps the most important part of a business analysis is the clarification and representation of the organization's goals. This is true for two reasons. First, it determines how the results of the analysis are evaluated. Ultimately, the client wants any data and recommendations coming out of the analysis to directly affect the achievement of organizational goals. Second, workers perform best when they know what their company is trying to accomplish and how they fit into the big picture. Goals must not only be clearly stated but also clearly communicated to workers. Unfortunately, many workers don't understand the relationship between their work and their company's goals, and this is one of the most significant inhibitors in achieving optimal performance. For example, a colleague of mine recently visited a manufacturing facility on a day that a 30-year employee was retiring. Managers asked the employee how he would like to spend his last day on the job. He said that he wanted a tour of the entire plant; he had never seen the entire operation. Consequently, he probably never understood his role in it or the value or worth of his work.

Capturing the Data from the Exemplary Performers

There are four critical steps involved in conducting a performance analysis:

- Determine the key accomplishments or results that the exemplary performers produce.
- Collect data on those accomplishments.
- Produce a task list for each accomplishment.
- Collect key data on each of the tasks.

✒ **Geary A. Rummler** ✒

Geary A. Rummler is a management and performance consultant who coauthored Improving Performance: How to Manage the White Space in the Organization Chart *(1990) with Alan Brache, which was the first book that sought to bridge the gap between organizational strategy and the individual. The book identifies environmental factors as having a major effect on workers' performance, stating that "[i]f you pit a good performer against a bad system, the system will win almost every time." This idea is further developed in the book's performance improvement model, which identifies nine performance variables. The model determines organizational effectiveness by looking at three levels of performance in an organization: the organizational level, the process level, and the job level. These three levels of performance are then combined with three performance needs: goals, design, and management, thus creating nine performance variables (see figure).*

The Nine Performance Variables

THE THREE PERFORMANCE NEEDS

	Goals	Design	Management
Organization Level	Organization Goals	Organization Design	Organization Management
Process Level	Process Goals	Process Design	Process Management
Job/Performer Level	Job Goals	Job Design	Job Management

(left axis label: THE THREE LEVELS OF PERFORMANCE)

Source: Geary A. Rummler and Alan P. Brache (Jossey-Bass, 1995). *Improving Performance: How to Manage the White Space on the Organization Chart.* 2nd ed. Used with permission.

Rummler is also widely credited with contributing to the development of Six Sigma, a performance improvement process created in the 1980s at Motorola. Six Sigma seeks to eliminate defects and mistakes in manufacturing and business and is widely used in many organizations.

Determine Key Accomplishments

In an ideal environment, you will collect data on accomplishments and tasks by interviewing and observing exemplary performers. You cannot rely simply on a task force or focus group to get reliable and valid information. Often some of the characteristics or behaviors that differentiate the exemplary from the standard performer are subtle and intuitive and will not be self-reported through an interview process alone. It requires observation combined with debriefing following performance to "get inside the skin" of the star. If actual observation is not possible or is impractical, case-based interviews are a good alternative.

If an exemplary performer is not available within your organization, you may attempt to find one in an organization that will allow you to benchmark. For example, if the new performance is in support of new technology, you may work with the technology provider to find noncompetitive organizations that have already implemented the technology. If the performance analysis is being done in support of a new job, you may find that some of the accomplishments of the new job were produced in existing positions. You may spend time with exemplary performers who are currently only performing parts of the new job, and your analysis for the new job will be a composite based on multiple stars. When you do not have access to an exemplary performer either inside or outside of your organization, you will have to rely on other data sources. Documentation that supports the new technology can serve as a source. A task force of people performing similar work from within your company can be used. Interviewing the process or technology designer can also be a source of data. None of these alternative sources will provide the quality of data you'll get from an exemplary performer, but they will provide close approximations.

Develop a summary statement that captures the overall purpose of the job. You might ask questions like "What overall accomplishment, result, or output summarizes this job?" or "What is the main thing that you produce?" Once you have developed your job summary, begin to create a list of the key accomplishments that routinely make up the job. You might ask questions like "What is produced during a day, week, or a month?" You would then probe further to identify those accomplishments that are not routinely produced, paying particular attention to those nonroutine accomplishments that carry a high consequence of error. Table 6-2 shows a sample job summary and major accomplishments for a project manager.

Accomplishments Versus Competencies

I'm often asked about the relationship between accomplishments and competencies. Many organizations have invested significant resources in capturing the competencies required to perform various jobs. They've established human resource development systems that are based on providing these competencies to people either for their current positions or as a way of preparing them for future positions within the organization.

Table 6-2. Sample Job Summary and Major Accomplishments

Project Manager Job Summary: Manage projects to budget and at or above projected gross profit.	
Routine Accomplishments	• Project plans • Deliverables produced on time and to standard
Nonroutine Accomplishments	• Troubleshooting client complaints to produce maximum client satisfaction and minimum negative effect on project profitability and company reputation

Although this may be a useful model and is certainly a popular one, my concern is that competency does not correlate directly with performance.

Imagine a situation where an athlete practiced all week long and developed competence in each basic skill required to play on a basketball team, but at game time chose to sit on the bench. In this environment, you wouldn't consider the individual's capability to play as competence. Instead, you would focus on how the person actually performed during the game. A competent basketball player is one who applies his or her skills to pass, defend, and score during the actual game. Accomplishments are the passing, defending, and scoring within the organizational environment. Developing capable employees who don't contribute to the organization is not a valuable goal.

The other concern with competencies that are not tied to results or accomplishments is the inability of individuals to ascertain where to focus their priorities. The competency list for a particular position can be long and complex and not tied directly to day-to-day performance. The work in competency models is valuable, but it can be leveraged and extended by having the competencies tied to accomplishments and by measuring the ability of the individual to produce the outputs and not simply be satisfied by being competent.

Collect Data on Accomplishments

Once you have determined the job's major accomplishments, you need to collect data on each accomplishment. First, identify the criteria or standards for the accomplishment. As a rule, these criteria can fall under the categories of accuracy, time, productivity, or safety. Once you have identified the criteria, look for any anticipated changes that could affect the accomplishment in the near future. These changes might include reorganizations; new equipment or technology; and changes in policy, regulations, or procedures.

Next, you need to determine what percentage of time is spent producing this accomplishment in a typical week or month. Finally, you would identify the interactions required to produce the accomplishment, that is, with whom or with what does the worker interact while producing this result.

Table 6-3 is an example of data collected on one major accomplishment of a project manager—a project plan.

Produce a Task List for Each Accomplishment

The task list is the basis for almost all subsequent work in your analysis, so it is worth the time to be rigorous here. At this point, the analysis of human performance is identical to traditional models of job and task analysis. It may be useful here to further define what is meant by a task. A task is a unit of behavior that has a clear beginning, a process composed of two or more steps, and an output that contributes to the desired accomplishment. For example, if late one night you were caught in a downpour and discovered that you had a flat tire, you might call for assistance. When the tow truck showed up, the desired accomplishment would be a car ready to drive. To achieve that accomplishment, several tasks would need to be performed: jack the car, loosen the wheel, remove the wheel, replace the wheel, and lower the car. Each of those tasks has a clear beginning, a series of steps, and a result. For example, the result of jacking up the car is a wheel that can be removed. However, as a customer, you will not pay for the wheel being removed in isolation from the desired accomplishment, which is a car ready to drive.

Table 6-3. Data Collected on Project Plan

Major Accomplishment	• Project plan
Percentage of Project Time	• Five percent
Major Criteria	• Plan clearly describes scope of work, deliverables, work breakdown, staffing, schedule, cost, assumptions
Anticipated Changes	• No changes likely in overall approach to project planning; however, each project requires specific tailoring of planning steps
Interactions	• Project director, project staff, peers who may be involved with similar projects

If a draft task list is available, work with an exemplary performer to identify tasks that should not be or are not currently done. See if any of the tasks should be part of another job or another accomplishment. See if there are any tasks that are missing and review the wording of each task to make sure the terminology is accurate.

If a draft task list is not available, you will achieve the best results by observing the exemplary performer doing the actual work and generating a task list in real time. If the task takes too long for you to observe, ask the exemplary performer to simulate the process of producing the accomplishment while you observe him or her.

This process works effectively even when the work is cognitive in nature. For example, suppose you need to analyze the process of a loan officer reaching a decision concerning whether or not to grant a loan to an applicant. To get the best results, place individuals in their actual work environment and ask them to simulate how they go about making such a decision. You'll see them spending some time reviewing the application, perhaps turning to a policy and procedures manual, and maybe interacting with a colleague. Make extensive notes of the observable behavior as they go through the simulated activity and then go into extensive debriefing and ask them questions such as "When reviewing the application, what are the key things you look for?" Suppose their response is "I review the application to determine the credit worthiness of the applicant." Your response might be "What data do you use to determine if the applicant is credit worthy?" Next you may ask how they think about the various pieces of data. There are a series of tools that are available within Performance DNA, a new performance-analysis approach that combines sophisticated analytical methods and diagnostic tools, that can be very useful at this point. They were developed to support the capture of the cognitive performance of exemplary performers. Table 6-4 is a task list for producing a project plan.

Table 6-4. Task List for Producing a Project Plan

Major Accomplishment	Project plan
Tasks	• Prepare work breakdown • Assign project staff • Complete project pricing proposal • Write proposal • Negotiate proposal and obtain purchase order • Set up project baseline • Write detailed project plan

Collect Key Data on Each Task

Once you have created a draft task list and confirmed its accuracy with the exemplary performer, determine the criteria for each task. You might ask the exemplary performer "How do you know when the task is complete?" or "How would you judge that the task has been done correctly?" Examine any available documentation with the exemplary performer to capture some critical data on each task that you have analyzed. These data will be used to make important decisions in the design of interventions.

Determine if speed is a factor in performing the task. Do seconds count? Look at the work environment in which each task takes place. Are there any characteristics of the environment that are particularly noteworthy? For example, would it be difficult for a worker to use a job aid? Determine the frequency of performance for each task. In addition, determine what the possible consequence of error is if the task were performed incorrectly or below standard. Might it result in loss of life or injury? Could it cause intolerable economic costs?

Find out the complexity of each task in terms of number of steps or difficulty in doing any of the steps. Finally, determine what the probability is that the task will change in any significant way within the foreseeable future.

When you have determined the major accomplishments of a job, generated accurate and valid task lists, and captured critical data on each task, you have the data necessary to make critical decisions about how to support exemplary performance. It is important that you validate the data that you have in hand before proceeding. There are several options for doing this. You may take the data to exemplary performers in other parts of the organization to verify and validate. You may also have them reviewed by technical experts and people familiar with organizational policies, procedures, and safety regulations. Finally, the ultimate validation comes from the client and key stakeholders.

Performance Analysis Case Study

The following case study illustrates how performance analysis can significantly accelerate the launch of new technology, new work processes, or new organizational designs. A refinery decided to enter the asphalt market, so it began by conducting a detailed human performance analysis. The goal was to process an asphalt delivery truck safely in less than 30 minutes from the time it arrived at the refinery's gate.

To ensure a successful market entry, a performance analyst worked with management to identify company goals based on the needs of potential customers. The analyst then scrutinized every facet of human performance that would be involved, including blending, testing, certifying, loading, and handling paperwork. The analyst also identified the major accomplishments and tasks required to meet the goal of processing the truck quickly and safely. Finally, the analyst translated these accomplishments and tasks into training, work procedures, and job aids to ensure high performance for all workers involved in the process—from the operators blending the asphalt to the security force controlling truck traffic. The asphalt facility showed a 75 percent return-on-investment in the first year of operation and part of this success was attributed to the targeted analysis that had been performed.

Performance Analysis as a Continuous Improvement Tool

Rather than analyzing an entire role or process, you may be requested to support an improvement initiative. Basically you will be asked to find out what your client's problems are, the reason why the problems exist, and what the solutions are. The steps of this type of analysis include the following:

- Identify the deficient accomplishment that led to the request.
- Define the tasks of the deficient accomplishment.
- Determine where inadequate human performance is causing the deficient accomplishment.
- Generate cause hypotheses.
- Collect evidence to support or deny hypotheses.
- Identify probable causes and make recommendations.

Identify the Deficient Accomplishment(s)

Often the request from the client comes in with a specific solution in mind. The client didn't ask for help in improving performance, but requested training on some topic instead. The recommended response to a solution request is to state "Yes, I can help you with that. Can you tell me more about the situation that led you to this request?" With most requests for training, you need to identify what is not being achieved in the client's organization. You might ask questions like "If this intervention was successful, what would you see changed in your organization?" "Is there some current goal or product that your team produces that is currently being produced below standard?"

Be sure to identify any current measurements within the client's organization that deal with the deficient accomplishment. Review the data on historic performance and compare them with expected performance. If hard data are not available, explore with the client what anecdotal data would be acceptable to him or her. It is essential that you achieve consensus with the client at the beginning of the project on what needs to be measured, what data will be acceptable, and how your efforts in analysis and later intervention design will be assessed in relationship to any improvements. You can never give credible results to the client at the end of the project unless you have achieved consensus on how to measure those results at the beginning of the project.

Be sure that you and the client have clearly defined the gap between current performance and desired performance and tied it directly to business goals. Also determine the potential value to the company—in dollar terms if possible—of resolving the problem.

Define the Tasks of the Deficient Accomplishment

Once you have identified the deficient major accomplishment, you need to obtain or generate a task list. Then have the exemplary performer produce or simulate the production of the major accomplishment while you observe with the task list. Revise your list as needed.

Determine Inadequate Human Performance

Distinguish between those tasks that are being performed adequately and those that are being performed below standard. You can determine this by reviewing existing data; observing exemplary performance and comparing it with average performance; and interviewing incumbents, managers, and technical experts. Look for the following:

- Tasks that are not being performed at all
- Tasks that are not being performed fast enough
- Tasks in which errors are made in some of the steps
- Tasks that are not being performed safely
- Tasks in which steps are performed out of order
- Tasks in which steps have been added that are not required.

Also try to ascertain whether the deficient performance of tasks occurs at a particular time or place. After identifying the deficient tasks, you can generate cause hypotheses for why the tasks are not performed adequately.

Generate Cause Hypotheses

It is useful to cluster possible cause hypotheses into three categories: skill or knowledge, work environment, and incentives. For the first category, consider whether workers know how to perform the task, when to perform the task, and what the task standard is.

For the second category, examine work conditions and the type of equipment workers use. For the third category, consider whether workers are rewarded for performing the task correctly.

Collect Evidence to Support or Deny Hypotheses

Use the following diagnostic questions to help you collect evidence on which hypotheses are valid and which are not.

Skill or knowledge questions

- Do deficient workers ever perform the task correctly?
- Have deficient workers ever been trained?
- Are job aids available? If so, are they used?

Work environment questions

- Do workers receive all the needed inputs?
- Is the workload too heavy? Do workers have enough time?
- Does emphasis on quantity cause quality to suffer?
- Are there any performance criteria?
- Are the criteria too high? Does anyone meet the criteria?
- Are workers and supervisors using the same criteria?
- Are tools and equipment adequate to do the task?
- Are the physical working conditions adequate?
- Is the work well designed?
- Are processes and procedures for performing effective?
- Do workers have control over the variables influencing the work?
- Are elements needed to do the work easily obtained?
- Do workers have adequate authority to make decisions?
- Are there any other factors that interfere with the correct performance?

Motivation and incentive questions

- Is the task aversive (dangerous, unsafe, difficult, boring, and so forth)?
- Do workers get any feedback on the accomplishment of the task? If so, is it adequate?
- What are the consequences of performance?
- Is there an absence of consequences?
- Is there a positive consequence for incorrect behavior?
- Is there a negative consequence for correct behavior?

- Is effort greater than positive consequences (not worth it)?
- Does the task lack value (no purpose in doing it)?
- Do workers disagree about how it should be done (I know better)?
- Do workers think someone else should be doing it (not my job)?

Data from multiple sources support the fact that when workers are not performing to standard, 80 percent of the time it's not due to a lack of skill or knowledge, but rather to a poor work environment or a lack of incentives. Interestingly, these data align with much of the data from the quality movement, which state that 85 percent of the problems reside in the system and not in the individual job performer.

Identify Probable Causes and Make Recommendations

Based on the answers to your diagnostic questions, identify probable causes for the deficiencies and make general recommendations to your client. I would recommend pulling together the client and the stakeholders who participated in the alignment process for this presentation. The tone of the meeting should be to validate and verify the information, not to simply present your results to be accepted or rejected.

Continuous Improvement Case Study Based on Performance Analysis

A performance analyst working for a large manufacturer faced the challenge of having department managers who historically exceeded their budgets by 7 to 23 percent annually start to keep costs within budget. A performance analysis revealed that managers prepared their budgets without help and then submitted them to their vice presidents for approval. Many of the managers did not know how to estimate costs accurately or justify their numbers to their superiors. The analysis also found that managers were given feedback on how much money they spent only twice a year and managers who overspent their budgets were "rewarded" by having their monies increased the next year.

The performance analyst for this project recommended several interventions. Managers were given training on projecting costs and preparing budgets based on those costs. They could request technical assistance from the financial department during budget preparation, and they received training in how to justify their numbers to their superiors. Monthly reports were adjusted to show actual versus projected spending on each line item, significantly reducing the delay in feedback concerning performance. In addition, the company established a policy that overspending would negatively affect a manager's performance evaluation.

Evaluating the Success of Your Analysis

The success of your analysis depends on whether the major accomplishments of the job now meet the company's standards of quantity, quality, and cost. If at the end of the project the accomplishments still don't meet standards, you should assess which interventions were inadequate and make changes where necessary. Only through this rigorous analysis of human performance within the workplace can you select appropriate interventions to help workers produce the major accomplishments needed to meet a company's business goals.

⤸

About the Author

Paul H. Elliott is the president of Exemplary Performance, LLC (EP), based in Annapolis, Maryland. His expertise is in the analysis of human performance, the design of interventions that optimize human performance, and organizational strategies for transitioning from training to performance models. Prior to starting EP, he was a fellow with Saba Software of Redwood Shores, California.

From 1995 through 2001, Elliott was president of Human Performance Technologies, LLC, a leading provider of methodologies and training for performance consultants. He served on the board of directors of ASTD from 1993 to 1995. In 1996, he served as executive-in-residence for ASTD, where his focus was on the paradigm shift from training to performance.

References

ASTD. 2007, July 7. *HPI certificates—Course descriptions*, available at www.astd.org/astd/Education/HPI/HPI+Certificate+Course+Descriptions#Analyzing.

Elliott, Paul. 1998. Assessment phase: Building models and defining gaps. In *Moving from training to performance*, eds., D.G. Robinson and J.C. Robinson. San Francisco: Berrett-Koehler.

Gilbert, Thomas. 2007. *Human competence: Engineering worthy performance*. ISPI Tribute edition. San Francisco: Pfeiffer.

For Further Reading

Robinson, Dana G., and James C. Robinson. 2005. *Strategic business partner: Aligning people strategies with business goals*. San Francisco: Berrett-Koehler.

Robinson, Dana G., and James C. Robinson. 2008. *Performance consulting: A practical guide for HR and learning professionals*. 2d ed. San Francisco: Berrett-Koehler.

Rummler, Geary A. 2007. *Serious performance consulting according to Rummler.* San Francisco: Pfeiffer.

Rummler, Geary A., and Alan P. Brache. 1995. *Improving performance: How to manage the white space on the organization chart.* 2nd ed. San Francisco: Jossey-Bass.

Swanson, Richard A. 2007. *Analysis for improving performance: Tools for diagnosing organizations and documenting workplace expertise.* San Francisco: Berrett-Koehler.

Chapter 7

Competencies and the Changing World of Work

Patricia A. McLagan

In This Chapter

➤ Learn what competencies are and why they matter

➤ Understand what competency models and menus are

➤ Use competencies in today's workplace

➤ Understand the future of competency models

Organizations today are looking for better ways to describe the capabilities people must have to do the variety of knowledge work associated with the information age. Old forms of job descriptions that focused on tasks and routine work are not good enough. Many of today's most critical work requirements relate to making judgments, taking creative action, and handling exceptions. Thus, descriptions of roles and jobs must focus more on the qualities that enable people to handle job uncertainties and exceptions.

Competency models and menus have moved in to fill this need. In the United States, the initial competency surge of the 1970s focused on leadership. It was driven partly by business's accelerating interest in strategic management and global competitiveness. Then the competency focus spread to the professions (many professional associations now create and fund models to guide professional performance and accreditation). Today, competency models and menus are applied to practically every realm of human performance and provide the content for a variety of electronic human resource and management applications.

Countries in Africa, Asia, and Europe started their competency journeys by focusing primarily on technical skills. Their concern was creating the technical skills base that is so essential to global competitiveness.

Regardless of global location or initial focus, it makes sense that organizations everywhere are beginning to care about their human competency base and how it is developing. Market values rely increasingly on intangibles—knowledge, the loyal customer base, patents, and other expressions of knowledge capital. Until now, the hard assets of the organization and how they deployed and acquired capital dominated the value of most organizations. But today the wealth of nations depends on the knowledge and skills of their people.

In this chapter, I provide a big picture view of the world of competencies. First, I'll review the state of the practice, noting the variety of definitions of terms and methods. Then I turn attention to the emerging requirements of the new world of work and how they are changing our views of people and jobs. Finally, I talk about how we can and must move the competency field forward.

The Traditional Competency Response: Where We Are and Where We've Been

Competencies have been around as a concept for centuries. We can trace them at least back to the medieval guilds, where apprentices worked with masters to learn specific skills. Then, beginning with John Dewey early in the 20th century, educators created long lists of knowledge and skills to guide school curriculum development. Taxonomies of objectives for the cognitive, behavioral, and affective domain (knowledge, skills, and attitudes/values, or KSAs) have been built and revised for years. More recently, organizations have brought competency analysis into the mainstream for use in various human resource management and development applications. There are many differences in competency definition, approach, and outcomes, however. To make an informed and optimal choice among options, managers and human resource professionals must be aware of the uniquenesses, advantages, and disadvantages of the various methods and approaches.

There are eight key questions to ask to understand any particular competency methodology and its current uses in organizations:

- Why develop competency models?
- What's the definition of competency?
- What is a competency model? A menu?
- How detailed are competency definitions?
- What is the analysis process?
- Who does the work of competency identification and model development and how long does it take?
- What are competencies used for?
- How do we ensure validity?

Why Develop Competency Models?

In the late 1970s—when organizations began to take an interest in competency models as we know them today—I got a call from a CEO in a large manufacturing company. He had read an article I wrote about competencies and said, "We need to do this." I asked him, "Why?" He had a hard time articulating the answer. The concept made sense to him, but he hadn't articulated what he would do with a competency model if he had one.

He was a forward-thinking leader who viscerally and intuitively felt the need for something better than the job descriptions available to him. Today, we know that competency models and their competency menu relatives provide important frameworks for a variety of selection, performance, and development decisions and actions in any organization:

- *Selection applications.* Competency models provide the framework for recruitment strategies, selection and promotion decisions, and succession planning.
- *Performance-related applications.* Competency models help guide organization design, job design, goal-setting, appraisal, job evaluation, reward, and other performance categorization and management actions.
- *Development applications.* Competency models provide the basis for individual and organizational needs assessments, individual development plans, organization training plans, and a variety of organization assessment and development activities (for example, "What prevents people from using competency X and how do we address it?").
- *Reward applications.* Competency models can also help focus reward and recognition systems on critical contribution areas.

It is vitally important to know how the organization will use competency models before deciding on the competency type and model characteristics (see Table 7-1).

What's the Definition of Competency?

In the job world, competencies may take one of three major forms. The first focuses on the work (task, result, and output competencies). The second describes characteristics of the people doing the work (KSAs). Finally, there is a hybrid form that often mixes the two, which I call an attribute bundle.

Competencies describing the work. These include task, result, and output competencies. For some people the tasks and activities of a job—what people *do*—are competencies. Regardless of the terminology used, job descriptions and many approaches to

Table 7-1. Competency Model Features X Uses

	Primary Uses			
	Selection	**Performance**	**Development**	**Rewards**
	(Recruitment, interviewing, selection, promotion, succession planning)	(Organization design, job design, performance goals, appraisal, business reviews)	(Individual and organization needs analysis, forecasting, individual development plans, organization training plans)	(Recognition, bonuses, other tangible rewards)
Contents of Competency Model or Menu				
The work (outputs, tasks, results)		X		X
The people (knowledge, skill, affect)	X		X	
Attribute bundle	X			X
Breadth of Competency List				
Job or role (a model, possibly drawn from a menu)	X	X	X	X
Function, profession, industry, organization, business unit (a menu)			X	X

competency today take a task approach (for example, sweeps the floor, analyzes survey data following the manual guidelines, develops organizational strategy).

Results competencies are a bit rarer, but by adding the phrase "ability to" to a result (ability to produce profits, ability to raise customer satisfaction), some methodologies create what they call competencies.

An output or deliverable is something a person or team produces, provides, or delivers. Adding "ability to" to an output makes it a competency for some people (for example, ability to produce engineering designs, ability to create brochures).

Competencies describing characteristics of the person. These may be knowledge, skill, or attitude/value (affective) competencies. Here, subject matter like engineering knowledge; process capabilities like listening skill; or attitudes, values, or orientations like integrity or achievement orientation are all called competencies.

Attribute bundles. Many models blend some or all of the above, creating bundles of attributes. A bundle of attributes is a large concept or label that is really a collection of KSAs or values and/or tasks, outputs, and results. Examples are leadership, entrepreneurship, and management competence. These are all attribute bundles that contain several or many elements. Even apparently simple concepts like problem solving or decision making are really attribute bundles. Take problem solving, for example. It is really made up of some knowledge (the technical knowledge needed to solve the problem, knowledge of problem-solving methods), some conceptual skills (analytical skill, lateral thinking skill), and some attitudes/values (achievement orientation, service orientation). In other words, problem solving is an attribute bundle, whose components could appear in many other bundles.

The decision regarding what version of competency to choose should be based on the nature of the work and on how the competencies will be used. However, decisions frequently reflect the orientation or paradigm of the analyst. Industrial psychologists tend to stress bundles of attributes and selected KSAs. Educators focus on KSAs. Personnel staff tend to use task-based systems (see the sidebar Competency Approaches Through History).

What Are Competency Models and Menus?

A competency model is a group of competencies believed to be relevant to successful work performance. However, there are differences in breadth, in time orientation, and in inclusion.

Competency Approaches Through History

Three main schools of competency research and practice have been popular in the workplace since the Second World War: the differential psychology approach, the educational and behavioral psychology approach, and the management sciences approach. Each grew out of its own philosophical framework and has its own language and application focus. Here are brief descriptions of each and what distinguishes them:

The Differential Psychology Approach

This approach focuses on human differences, especially capabilities that are harder to develop. People who practice this approach tend to have psychology training. They emphasize intelligence, cognitive capabilities, hard-to-develop physical abilities, values, personality traits, motives, interests, and emotional qualities. That is, they focus on process capabilities and drives versus subject matter or knowledge. They also tend to single out those qualities that distinguish superior performers from average or typical performers. The bell-shaped curve is an important concept here, because the underlying belief is that human talents are distributed in a bell curve, with very few people at the top and bottom ends of the curve. Daniel Goleman, David McClelland, Richard Herrnstein, and Milton Rokeach are some thought leaders for this approach.

The Educational and Behavioral Psychology Approach

Although the differential approach emphasizes the unique and more innate abilities that people bring to work, the educational-behavioral approach is driven by the desire to shape and develop people so that they can be successful. The differential proponents also have this concern, but it is not their main focus. People who practice the educational-behavioral approach tend to have an education and training background. Their models and menus include subject matter and knowledge areas as well as some of the process and affective areas of the differential approach. Also, their models usually include *all* the competencies that are important to quality performance, whether they distinguish superior performance or not. Often, proponents of this approach also focus on the performance environment. They believe that the environment (including education) is often a more powerful determinant of behavior than genetics. For the differential practitioners, the emphasis would be reversed. Albert Bandura, B.F. Skinner, Thomas Gilbert, Geary Rummler, Benjamin Bloom, and David Krathwohl are chief proponents of aspects of this approach.

The Management Sciences Approach

This approach produces job descriptions and job evaluations. So, it mainly defines the *work to be done,* often spending a lot of time on work and task analysis and documentation. The models that emerge from this process include task and activity lists, and descriptions of tools and processes needed for effective performance. Knowledge, skills, and other personal characteristics needed to do the work may be added to the description, but are usually a secondary emphasis. Job evaluation consultants, personnel administrators and compensation specialists, reengineering and total quality experts, and task analysts are the major purveyors of this approach. Frederick Winslow Taylor, Michael Hammer, and Elliott Jaques are some of the key thought leaders here.

Regarding breadth, a competency model may be broad or narrow, listing competencies associated with work in an entire industry, organization, unit, profession, functional area, team, role, or job. Initial models followed the precedent of traditional job descriptions, focusing on individual jobs or roles. The advantage was and is that they help clarify individual work requirements. The disadvantage is that creating such models requires a very time-consuming job-by-job analysis that often requires months, or even years, to complete. Also, focusing on individual jobs ignores the fact that job requirements change as individuals join new task forces or as strategies change.

Besides differing in breadth, models vary in time orientation. The intent is always to guide various management, performance, and human resource decisions today and tomorrow. However, when competencies are derived from analyses of current work requirements or are based solely or primarily on studies of what people do *today*, the real-time orientation of the model (despite any intent to guide future decisions) is the past. Any future-oriented model takes into account emerging and new strategic requirements. This means the analytical process must include valid attempts to bring the implications of the future (strategy, competitive analyses, trend assessments) into the modeling process. This happens by articulating the future assumptions and inferring the competencies that relate to them.

Models also vary in what they include. Some include all competencies related to doing the work. Others only incorporate those competencies that distinguish superior performers from average performers. In other words, if a good salesperson needs product knowledge as a competency, but product knowledge is common across both average and superior performers, then it will not be included in a salesperson model. (Later you will see that the more restricted model is fine for selection purposes, but not so good for training purposes.)

A competency menu is a list of all the major competencies related to a function (including leadership/management), profession, industry, and organization. It provides a list from which people can assemble a role, team, or job profile. Menus provide the building blocks for most electronic systems—providing a common language to use across jobs and applications. Menus are faster and more cost effective to develop than specific job or role models, and support the role flexibility that today's organizations require. Because specific job and role requirements must be flexible and are increasingly defined by the people in them, rigid job-focused models add less value today than creating more comprehensive menus focused on larger units (industries, organizations, business units, professions, functional areas, generic roles like salesperson or leader).

How Detailed Are Competency Definitions?

For the moment, let's assume that any of the three definitions of competency (related to the work, the person, or an attribute bundle) is acceptable. How detailed, then, should definitions and descriptions be? To answer this question you must first address the question: How can you further define each type of competency?

Defining task competencies. To further define tasks, we break them into subtasks or provide the range of situations in which the tasks will be done. Breaking tasks into subtasks helps reduce behavior variability, but it can also inhibit creativity and improvements. For example:

Task: Sweep the floor

Subtasks

- Select the appropriate broom.
  — Sub-subtask: Determine benefits of broom X.
  — Sub-subtask: Determine the benefits of broom Y.
  — Sub-subtask: Choose the broom with the most benefits for the application.
- Sweep in forward motions in direction with the prevailing air current.
  — Sub-subtask: Test prevailing air current.
  — Sub-subtask: Test several sweeping directions and determine the one with the least wayward dust.
- Push piles of dust and rubbish toward door or into dustpans.
- Dispose of collected dirt in bins; close top.
- Retrieve any potential items of value and bring to lost and found.

Range of situations

- Most complex: hospital operating room
- Least complex: hospital entrance

Defining results competencies. Break them into subcomponents: cascade so that the total contributions to results equal the grand result desired.

Result: Deliver 15 percent pretax profit (up from 10 percent).

- Subresult: Increase margin on product X from 60 percent to 80 percent.
- Subresult: Increase staff or line productivity ratios from 1/200 to 1/300.
- Subresult: Implement empowerment program to achieve 10 percent greater productivity per person in the manufacturing operation.

Defining output competencies. Identify what deliverables internal and external receivers or customers get and either break the deliverables into subcomponents or create quality requirements or standards to further define them.

Output: A Product Design

- Suboutput: Engineering blueprint
- Suboutput: Customer requirements list
- Suboutput: A visual replica of the product.

Quality requirements for product design

- Meets specific customer needs (specify)
- Ensures long-term, high-profit payback to the company
- Incorporates appropriate state-of-the-art technical options
- Ensures a cost-of-goods of 20 percent to revenue
- Is scalable.

Range of situations

- Most complex: a multicomponent product that is very sensitive to environmental conditions and will be used in dangerous situations
- Least complex: a single component product that has no safety or environmental implications.

Defining KSA competencies. These can be defined either by behavioral examples, by tests, or by visible results or indicators related to the competency. For example, for the affect competency, achievement orientation:

Sample behaviors

- Sets stretch goals that are achievable
- Finds ways to deal with seemingly insurmountable problems to achieve a goal
- Uses goals as a guide to prioritizing work every day.

Sample tests

- Motivation assessment instrument.

Indicators/results

- Consistently achieves stretch goals.

Defining attribute bundles. Behaviors and results are commonly used to further define attribute bundles. For example, a behavior for leadership might be "gets people who must implement actions motivated to do so." A result would be "teams consistently achieve desired results." Attribute bundles tend to be less useful for assessment and development applications, however. Why? Because they can only be developed by focusing on the specific tasks, knowledge, skills, or attitudes/values that make up the bundle.

◈ Howard Gardner ◈

Howard Gardner is best known for his multiple intelligence theory, a reappraisal of the long-held belief that there is one single human intelligence by which everyone processes information. Gardner claims that each person has a unique, multifaceted blend of intelligences that traditional psychometric instruments, such as intelligence quotient (IQ) tests, cannot accurately gauge. In his groundbreaking book, Frames of Mind: The Theory of Multiple Intelligences *(1983), Gardner initially formulated a list of seven intelligences: verbal-linguistic, logical-mathematical, visual-spatial, bodily-kinesthetic, musical-rhythmic, interpersonal, and intrapersonal. Since publication of the book, Gardner expanded the list of intelligences to include emotional, naturalistic, and existential. Gardner's research suggests that most learners are comfortable with three to four intelligences and are likely to avoid the other intelligences, greatly affecting knowledge acquisition. Although multiple intelligence theory was not immediately accepted by the psychological community, educators have embraced it, integrating the theory into curricula ranging from nursery school to adult education.*

Gardner is the John H. and Elisabeth A. Hobbs Professor in Cognition and Education at the Harvard Graduate School of Education. For the past 20 years, he and colleagues at Harvard University's Project Zero have been working on the design of performance-based assessments, education for understanding, and the use of multiple intelligences to achieve more personalized curriculum, instruction, and assessment.

In the leadership example above, a person may not be successful in leading teams to consistently achieve desired results. But, assuming that the leader and not something else in the system is the problem, what is missing? Listening skill? Empathy? Self-awareness? Business knowledge? Skill in team process? Some combination of these? Bundles of attributes are more useful in selection and other processes where behavioral and results definitions may be sufficient to support management and human resource decisions. Attribute bundles are less useful for development applications that require more focused definitions (for example, KSAs or tasks).

It is important to realize that every time you break competencies down to the next level of detail, the precision of the model may increase, but so does the amount of data: it increases exponentially. In most cases, I prefer to train or guide users to have the conversations and do the deeper thinking that can balance the lack of precision of simpler models. The more detailed the model, the more formidable it is to users and the less likely it is to be used.

What Is the Competency Analysis Process?

How do we arrive at the competencies? There are three popular approaches:

Do a work analysis. Watch people do the work and record their results and what they do to achieve them. You can focus on the best performers or job experts and ask them to help define the competencies related to doing the work. The competency model or menu that results will be one that documents *all* the major tasks, outputs, or KSAs they describe.

Do a critical incident interview with current performers. Ask them what situations they have been in and what challenges they have faced. Ask them what they thought, did, felt, and caused to happen in those situations. Then describe the tasks and outputs or infer the KSAs (KSAs can't be directly observed, but only inferred through behavior or test performance).

Do separate sets of critical incident interviews with average and with superior performers. List the competencies of each. Eliminate any competencies that both average and superior performers express. What is left are the differentiators of current superior performance.

The above three approaches draw on learning from past behavior. Because the environment and strategies are changing at a rapid pace, there is a danger that what worked in the past will be insufficient—and maybe even detrimental—in the future. This leads to several other approaches:

Create assumptions about the future work and work environment. Draw from trend information, industry forecasts, and the business's own strategy. Ask knowledgeable people to infer from the assumptions and forecast what the work and competency requirements will be. Create models or menus that incorporate the future requirements as well as today's best practices.

Train the workforce and management in competency thinking. Provide questionnaires, worksheets, and planning documents that help them think through the implications of strategy and environment changes for their work. Give them a menu or set of competency cards and let them select the competencies relevant to their work. In other words, don't develop competency models for people, but provide them with a process where they must continually define their own requirements (teach people to fish rather than giving them the fish).

Who Does the Work?

Job analysis, and its more recent derivative, competency analysis, has usually been done by third parties: human resource or personnel staff and consultants. Managers and workers may participate, but mainly to give input that is later analyzed and turned into models by someone else. Traditionally, this occurs in a job-by-job fashion—with occasional studies focusing on job families. Each job modeling effort usually requires hours of focus groups, expert analysis, validation, and communication and selling. It is not uncommon for an organization-wide job reevaluation or competency analysis to take months and even years—and to cost in the millions of dollars for the analysis phase only, excluding application!

Recent advances in facilitation methodologies make faster processes possible. Given competent facilitation and a rigorous process, large groups consisting of strategists, job and role experts, customers, and others can help create competency menus and models in one- or two-day meetings. When these are accompanied by postmeeting validation processes, valid and useful models and menus can be ready for use within weeks rather than months or years.

What Are Competencies Used For?

The most common uses for competency models in the United States have been assessment, selection, promotion, and selectively focused training and development programs. This is probably why the superior performer differentiator method has been so popular in the United States.

In countries struggling to participate in the competitive race by reaching parity in technical areas, the task and KSA approaches are the favorite, and models and menus tend to cover all important aspects of the work (whether or not they differentiate superior performers from average performers). These nations need a broad base of technical and literacy competence. Individual superiority is not a key concern when the national baseline is the issue.

What Is the Source of Validity?

Let's first look at what validity is. Something is valid when it actually relates to what we say it relates to. Our search for validity is a search for truth. Validity in the social sciences often requires more inferences than in the hard sciences. When we say a test result relates to or expresses a competency, we are making a construct validity statement. When we say that a competency is needed in the real world of work, we are making a content validity statement. When we say that a competency, used at one point in time, is associated with superior performance at that time, we are making a concurrent validity statement. When we say that a competency someone possesses today will make her effective in future work, we are making a predictive validity statement. Finally, we may use a valid process—one that is consistent and has either convergent, or face, validity. For example, if a trained manager and team work together to identify competencies, using a worksheet and a menu of competencies, and they agree on the competencies, then they have produced a model that has convergent validity. It also has face validity because the people involved accept the logic behind the selection of competencies.

When we define work and the competencies required to do it, we want those definitions to be valid. Business success and fairness (as well as legal compliance) depend on this. One generally accepted way to ensure validity is to have job experts pool their expertise to define the work and competencies. Another, more complex way to ensure validity is to continually compare people's behavior and qualities with real performance measures. In the past, we have ensured validity by observing or asking what superior performers do, creating models of their performance, assessing people, and predicting their likelihood of success, and (in a few heroic cases) actually tracking the relationships between competencies and performance or the hit rate of our predictions.

Validity is more of an issue for competency models that focus on characteristics of the person versus descriptions of the work. It's easy to see why this is true: the work (tasks, deliverables, results) is its own source of validation. However, descriptions of personal characteristics involve inferences, and these inferences are what need additional validation.

Competencies and the New World of Work

Creating value for an organization or a nation depends on its competencies. This is the primary reason that line and human resource people from public and private sectors are flocking to competency conferences and traveling the world to find best practice benchmarks. But there are other reasons why the competency field is burgeoning and re-creating itself today. Here are some of the main ones.

New Ways to Integrate People Practices

Organizations realize that past selection, development, work design and evaluation, performance management, succession and career practices, and pay systems often delivered discrepant messages about desired performance and values. It is not unusual for some processes to be open and others closed, for some to involve customers and others to be internally driven, for some to tout quality whereas others allow and even encourage minimum standards (for example, those appraisal systems that reward people who exceed objectives, thus promoting low goals).

These practices should deliver common messages and reinforce the same virtues. They also should draw on a common language about work that can be used across all practices. Competencies can provide this common language. But if competencies are to be an integration mechanism, they need to include both work descriptors and person descriptors. Why? Because some people practices, like work evaluation, multiskilling, work design, and performance management, must focus primarily on the work. Others, like career development, learning, and selection, require us to specify KSA requirements. All people practices can benefit from both. It is a matter of emphasis.

Ways to Quickly Link People Requirements to the Business Strategy

Strategies continue to outpace our ability to achieve them. Human resource plans, workforce plans, and succession plans are among the most important responses to this issue. The trouble is, human resource processes are too often mired in bureaucracy and tied to models of the past. Integrating a competency review and projections into the strategic planning process can help ensure and speed the realignment of people requirements to the strategic goals of the business.

A Lot of Talk About Empowerment, but No Daily Practice

The U.S. Department of Labor estimates that only about 7 percent of U.S. businesses are implementing enough high-involvement people practices to be included in the high-performance or high-involvement category. And that figure is not growing at a rapid pace. In the meantime, the need to bring accountability and power to everyone in the organization is increasing in urgency. It takes a self-managing person to respond to and anticipate customer needs, to care about quality and see opportunities for improvements and breakthroughs, and to protect the company's resources as though they were his or her own. Organizations today ask people to do all these things without providing them with sufficient tools and support for success. Systematically implemented competency menus and models and the application tools that give them life can help transfer the people management role from human resources to management and ultimately to the people themselves. Competency systems can and should provide the language, structure, and tools for empowerment.

Changes in the Role of the Human Resource Function

In the past, many human resource people spent their time on administrative tasks like record keeping, payroll administration, and policy enforcement. Or they spent time doing work that managers and the people themselves should be doing: managing conflicts and discipline, guiding careers, doing personal counseling, and picking up the pieces when teams can't cooperate or managers are not leading. Today, with human resource staff ratios decreasing and technology taking over the administrative tasks, human resource people no longer have to do many of these things. Nor should they. There are major strategic people challenges related to such things as reorganizations, mergers, technology changes, and globalization that require a strategic human resource perspective. There's also the massive culture shift going on as organizations move from deep hierarchies to networks and cross-functional teams as their modus operandi. These are the issues that human resource staff should be addressing, but they are still pulled back into the administrative and day-to-day people work of the past. Well-constructed competency practices and application tools (for selection, training, development, work design, pay decisions, and so forth) allow the best human resource practices to move into the hands of managers and the people themselves. With human resource expertise living inside the models, tools, and materials that managers and the people themselves use, human resource staff is freed to do more strategic work and to focus on the massive strategic and culture changes required today.

The Diminishing Job as the Unit of Work

We all know that traditional job descriptions are inadequate in many organizations. They just aren't flexible enough for the constantly changing world. New strategies, memberships on multiple teams, continually shifting and nuanced customer requirements, and competitive maneuvers all demand constant change in what an individual is responsible for. We need processes and language that support performance flexibility. Competency-based approaches are the answer. Competencies can and should be organized into menus that people and teams can draw from to describe their work and do the variety of people practices listed in Table 7-1.

New Initiatives, Shifting Views of Best Practices, and Ongoing Organizational Disturbances

The high-performance organization, reengineering, customer focus, total quality management, the learning organization, mergers and divestitures, outsourcing, and so forth—every time a new philosophy or initiative hits the organization, it changes the competency requirements and the roles that people must play in future success. People are bound to ask, "Do I have to start all over again? Are there any competencies I can carry forward into the organization we are creating?" A new era competency system has inbuilt flexibility to quickly adapt to and help communicate changing requirements.

All of these changes in the global and local context of work make it both more important to use competency approaches *and* critical to ensure that the methods we use are right for today's needs and environment.

No matter which of the above issues or combinations of issues faces us, questions arise for individuals: Where do I fit? What is the work? What competencies do I need? How can I prepare for the future? For organizations, it's a question of having the competencies to thrive today and tomorrow. Competency-based approaches that go beyond the models and practices of the past can help address these issues. A competency response is a powerful answer to the problems individuals and organizations face as we move into the next century.

The New Direction for Competencies: Aligning to the New World of Work

As we move into the future, our methods of defining the relationship between people and work must change. Here is what I believe are the main changes that must occur in the competency and work analysis field.

Shift the Focus from the Job to the Organization

In the past we have analyzed jobs. This often takes weeks and years; job models are obsolete before they are even used. Today we can identify competencies for the entire organization—using modern large system meeting processes. We can do this in several days and then provide individuals and teams with tools and processes for customizing or creating valid models for their current work and for adjusting them quickly when conditions, customer requirements, and strategies change. This means we create more menus and fewer models. The models themselves can then be constructed real time by the users, guided by worksheets and tools.

Speed Up the Analysis

Spend less time analyzing and more time on applications. The analysis process, whether it focuses on a role, job, team, unit, function, profession, or an entire organization or industry, should and can be very quick—almost "just in time." On an ongoing basis, competency analysis should become part of the strategic planning process of the business, finally enabling us to quickly connect the people requirements to the business. Then most of our time and effort can go into the applications themselves. Practically every people practice of the business can be transformed by a modern competency approach. But the focus must shift from months and years of analysis to time and money spent on applications. That is where the payoff is. The era of months and years and thousands and even millions of dollars of analysis is over, and good riddance. Competency menus and models of the future will be commodities, with the real added value in the applications.

Stop Depending on Experts

Internal staff, managers, and the people themselves, with proper tools and training, can create and use models for themselves. If they don't develop these skills and have access to these tools, the organization will be endlessly dependent on outside experts because models must continually flex to meet changing requirements, team configurations, and continuous improvement brainstorms. Outside experts have a duty to make the organization able to do its own competency work.

Use Both the Language of Work and the Language of People

We don't have to choose whether menus and models list the work to be done or the people requirements to do it. The most valuable menus and models will include both. I prefer to use outputs as the language for work and KSAs as the language related to people. Outputs are the language of the customer—they want deliverables, not activities and tasks. Outputs are also more durable than tasks. In a quality and continuous improvement environment, we want tasks to continually improve and change. KSAs are the enabling resources that people bring to the work, enabling them to produce, provide, and deliver outputs. Both outputs and KSAs are also useful building blocks for menus and easy for people to use in constructing job models, selection profiles, development and career plans, team designs, and other things.

Be Simple

Models of the past have tended to be long, very detailed, filled with jargon, and generally not very user friendly. Certainly, many have been very accurate and insightful. But many potential users think they are too complicated, bureaucratic, and hard to use; they don't use them. We can have rigor and validity and still keep things simple. To do this we need to discipline ourselves to models and menus that users want to use when they see them. We must make our application tools very simple and short. We must encourage conversation and assessments among customers, workers, teams, managers—the real work experts—as our real source of validity. The bonus we get is mutual clarity about the work and greater commitment by all stakeholders to get it done—with quality! Electronic applications can help make competency-based practices accessible and easy. It's possible to create competency-based selection profiles, development plans, needs analyses, and many other processes online. A caveat is to ensure that conversations occur among managers, teams, and individuals to establish mutual clarity and intent.

Democratize the Process

Besides involving large numbers and all segments of the organization's people in developing models and menus, bring the menus and modeling process to everyone—especially to people in the main value stream of the work. They face the paying customers. They are where the work that adds value to the product and service is done every day. They are where quality lives and dies. This does not diminish the importance of managerial and staff work. Done well, this support work can have vast leverage for present and future performance. Both leadership and technical competencies are important for performance success. The competency processes should, therefore, involve and affect everyone and all work.

On a related note, we must see the new generation of competency approaches as one of the most powerful tools at our disposal for bringing accountable participation into every corner of the organization. Competency approaches are transparent. When we say, "here are the tasks/outputs/results, KSAs, or attribute bundles that are important in this company," and "here are the tasks/outputs/results, KSAs, attribute bundle profiles for this team or job," then we are being open about requirements. Anyone can and should question managers' integrity if they hire people who operate to a different profile or if they create an organization that contradicts their competency descriptions.

Summary

We are living and working in a new world of work. It is global, fast-paced, and customer driven; expects quality; and is intolerant of delays and excuses. At the same time, people and their competencies—their very passion for work—are becoming a source of unbeatable advantage.

In this context, companies are pursuing several related goals: how to integrate and simplify their people practices, how to get a faster translation of their strategies into action, how to create conditions where people take the risks and have the trust needed to innovate and go the extra mile with the customer, how to free the shrinking cadre of human resource professionals to do more strategic work and less administration and handholding, how to provide structure and guidance in a world where the job is disappearing and all our people practices that focus on the job seem irrelevant, and how to keep one's sanity in the face of constantly shifting views of what is world class.

Organizations have been dabbling in competency models and systems for generations. There has been a surge in the last 30 years, and the movement has taken unique directions in the United States and other highly developed first-world nations. It's taken other directions in third-world and emerging nations. Most methods have been job focused and concentrated on a few human resource applications. They have been developed and driven by consultants and human resource experts. All of these efforts have helped us make gigantic strides in understanding work and how to define it and the people who do it.

But it is time to make some greater leaps forward. We can move away from the job as our focal unit. We can make the process of work design and competency definition a far more participative process. We can vastly simplify and, at the same time, link many human resource and people practices so that managers, teams, and individuals actually *want* to use competencies and find them helpful. We can use the next generation of competency systems as a major vehicle for clarifying and implementing strategy.

To do this, we will draw on what we have learned from the past; let go of practices and assumptions that no longer serve us; and innovate for better ways to connect people to work.

❧

About the Author

Patricia A. McLagan is the author of the 1983 and 1989 ASTD competency studies, the author of *Change Is Everybody's Business,* and the coauthor of *The Age of Participation: New Governance for the Workplace and the World* and *On-the-Level: Performance Communication That Works.* She has received many professional leadership awards, including ASTD's Gordon Bliss Award, and is known internationally for her pioneering work in competency model and menu development, competency-based people practices, and organization transformation. She is also a former member of the ASTD Board of Directors.

For Further Reading

Bandura, Albert. 1969. *Principles of behavior modification.* New York: Holt, Rinehart, and Winston.

Bloom, Benjamin S. 1956. *Taxonomy of behavioral objectives, handbook I: Cognitive domain.* Boston: Addison-Wesley.

Fishbein, Martin, and Icek Ajzun. 1975. *Belief, attitude, intention, and behavior.* Boston: Addison Wesley.

Gilbert, Thomas. 2007. *Human competence: Engineering worthy performance.* ISPI Tribute edition. San Francisco: Pfeiffer.

Goleman, Daniel. 1997. *Emotional intelligence: Why it is more important than IQ.* New York: Bantam.

Hammer, Michael, and James Champy. 2006. *Reengineering the corporation: A manifesto for business revolution.* New York: Harper Collins.

Herrnstein, Richard J., and Charles Murray. 1996. *Intelligence and class structure in the United States.* New York: Free Press.

Krathwohl, David R., Benjamin S. Bloom, and Bertram B. Masia. 1999. *Taxonomy of behavioral objectives, handbook II: Affective domain.* New York: Longman Publishing.

Jaques, Elliott. 1989. *Requisite organization.* Arlington, VA: Cason Hall, McClelland.

McLagan, Patricia A. 1989. *Models of HRD practice.* Alexandria, VA: ASTD Press.

Quinn, James B. 1992. *Intelligent enterprise.* New York: Free Press.

Rokeach, Milton. 2000. *Understanding human values.* New York: Free Press.

Taylor, Frederick W. 1919. *The principles of scientific management.* London: Dover Publications, 1997.

Rummler, Geary. 2007. *Serious performance consulting according to Rummler.* San Francisco: Pfeiffer.

Skinner, B.F. 1976. *About behaviorism.* New York: Vintage.

Spencer, Lyle. 1993. *Competence at work: Models for superior performance.* New York: John Wiley & Sons.

Selecting Solutions to Improve Workplace Performance

Harold D. Stolovitch and Erica J. Keeps

In This Chapter

- ➢ Learn to establish yourself as a credible partner to your client
- ➢ Get useful tools to help determine learning and performance solutions
- ➢ Learn about useful solutions for WLP professionals

As a workplace learning and performance (WLP) professional, you have probably been faced with a scenario in which a client comes to you for help with a performance problem and then asks for a specific solution. Then, when the requested solution doesn't work because it doesn't adequately address the problem, you are the one left looking like you don't know what you are doing.

What a bleak way to open a chapter on selecting learning and other solutions to achieve desired performance success! Nevertheless, many years of experience in a wide variety of organizational settings have built a sad database of poorly selected solution examples. Too many of these have generated flurries of activity resulting in little, if any, demonstrably significant relief from the performance pains our clients suffer. This chapter offers a means for alleviating some of the agonies WLP professionals are forced to endure when faced with the type of situation described in the opening scenario. It lays out a comprehensive approach for presenting information about the true causes of unattained performance, provides a means for matching information gathered during needs or front-end analyses with appropriate solutions, and describes several alternative interventions from which you can select to meet your clients' needs.

Let's Get Started

First, let us begin with a note of caution. In your initial meetings with clients, *never* discuss whatever solution he or she proposes. No matter how much the client presses for a training program; a motivational event; an informative, awareness webcast; or anything else, your first words must be, "I can help you solve your problem." Let's quickly analyze this.

When you say, "I can help you solve your problem," do you... (check off your selection for each):

Yes   No

☐   ☐   Agree to provide training (or whatever solution was requested)?

☐   ☐   Offer your support?

☐   ☐   Create a launch pad for conducting more in-depth discussion and analysis?

☐   ☐   Act arrogantly or aggressively to put your client down?

Here is how you should have replied: 1—No; 2—Yes; 3—Yes; 4—No. With this simple sentence, you establish yourself as a collaborative partner, ready to provide assistance—the emphasis is on partner and assistance. You offer no solution.

You then follow up with a dialogue, one that elicits concrete answers to these four questions:

- "What triggered this request? Please give me more background to truly understand the issues."
- "In an ideal world, what would you love to see happening? Please share with me what it's supposed to be like when everything is working perfectly."
- "Compared to this ideal state, what specifically is happening now? It's OK to repeat earlier statements, but please focus on the difference between ideal and current performance."
- "What will put a smile on your face based on clear evidence that things are now right? Let's list key success criteria and, for each one, let's also select a measure (or metric) that will concretely demonstrate desired performance has been achieved."

Through the dialogue centered on these four key questions, you achieve two major results. You separate the client from the preconceived solution (whether it was appropriate or not). You also focus your client on the bottom line results, not on the means for achieving them. You have accomplished an enormous amount during this interaction and have set the stage for what may end up as a selection of surprising solutions.

From Dialogue to Action

Now, you have your work cut out for you. This chapter addresses solution selection and not the activities related to data collection and analysis. Nevertheless, solution selection is, in a sense, the easy part once the data have been gathered. Here are some brief guidelines and suggestions for collecting information upon which to base your solution selections:

1. Document the true business need based on continued dialogue with your client and other relevant stakeholders. Keep your eye firmly fixed on the success criteria and metrics, but gather information or data to verify and refine these.

2. Investigate to obtain specific information on desired and current performance. Tap into the following sources of information: existing data, documentation experts, management, customers, and members of the target populations. Use a variety of information collection techniques. The most common and useful ones are observation, surveys and questionnaires, structured interviews, focus groups, critical incident method, performance testing, documentation analysis, and existing data analysis. Although this may sound onerous, you select your techniques based on appropriateness, time, and resources. Gather enough credible information to present the true story to your stakeholders. Overkill is unnecessary.

3. Pull together all the information you obtain using the front-end analysis synthesis tool shown in Table 8-1 (a copy of this tool is presented in Tool 8-1 on the accom- panying CD-ROM). This tool offers a comprehensive means for linking what you have learned with recommended actions to close the gap between current and desired performance. Its power lies in the linkage. This is what you found—based on credible evidence—so this is what should be done. Using this tool, you lay out a basket of appropriate solutions.

4. Select a workable set of solutions. Often a large number of recommended actions emerge. An important role for you as a WLP professional is to help identify appropriate solutions, not necessarily create and deliver all of them. For example, suppose equipment to do the work is inadequate. You are not expected to replace equipment. Your job is to identify the inadequacy as a contributing factor to substandard performance. How extensively you become involved in the solutions

Table 8-1. Front-End Analysis Synthesis Tool

Question	Findings	Gap Factor	Recommended Actions
Information			

1. Are expectations clearly communicated?
— Clearly sent
— Clearly received
		☐ Lack of clarity
		  ☐ In transmission
		  ☐ In reception
			☐ Clarify communication of expectations

2. Is there any conflict over expectations? — Conflicting expectations — Conflicting priorities		☐ Conflicting expectations ☐ Conflicting priorities	☐ Resolve or eliminate expectation conflicts
3. Are expectations achievable given capabilities, resources, and constraints? — Acceptable — Attainable		☐ Expectations unacceptable ☐ Expectations unattainable	☐ Modify expectations
4. Are there adequate role models of desired performance? — Appropriate or credible models — Accessible models		☐ Lack of appropriate models ☐ Inaccessible role models	☐ Provide role models

5. Are there performance standards?
— Clear and measurable
— Reasonable and attainable
		☐ Lack of clear, measurable performance standards
		  ☐ Immeasurable standards
		  ☐ Unreasonable standards
			☐ Specify or modify performance standards

Question	Findings	Gap Factor	Recommended Actions
Information (continued)			
6. Do workers receive feedback? — Timely — Specific — Confirming or corrective — Work-related, not personal		☐ Lack of feedback that is ☐ Timely ☐ Specific ☐ Confirming or corrective ☐ Task focused	☐ Develop a feedback system
7. Do workers have access to required information? — Easy to access — Timely — Accurate and up to date — Clear and comprehensible		☐ Lack of access to required information ☐ Hard to access ☐ Not timely ☐ Inaccurate or out of date ☐ Unclear	☐ Provide access to required information
Tools and Resources			
1. Are required equipment and tools readily available? — Reliable — Efficient — Safe		☐ Equipment or tools unavailable ☐ Unreliable ☐ Inefficient ☐ Unsafe	☐ Provide adequate equipment or tools
2. Are materials and supplies available? — Quantity — Quality		☐ Lack of materials or supplies ☐ Quantity ☐ Quality	☐ Provide adequate materials or supplies

(continued on next page)

Table 8-1. Front-End Analysis Synthesis Tool (continued)

Question	Findings	Gap Factor	Recommended Actions
Tools and Resources (continued)			

3. Is there time to perform correctly?
— Amount
— Timing
		☐ Lack of sufficient time
		  ☐ Amount
		  ☐ Timing
			☐ Provide sufficient time or scheduling

4. Are there adequate job aids, performance-support tools, or reference materials to facilitate performance?		☐ Lack of support materials to facilitate performance	☐ Provide job aids, performance-support systems, or reference materials

5. Is the environment supportive of desired performance?
— Physical
— Administrative
— Emotional
		☐ Lack of supportive environment
		  ☐ Physical
		  ☐ Administrative
		  ☐ Emotional
			☐ Redesign the environment

6. Is there adequate human support to monitor and encourage desired performance?
— Management or supervisory
— Specialists
— Co-workers
		☐ Lack of human support
		  ☐ Management or supervisory
		  ☐ Specialists
		  ☐ Co-workers
			☐ Provide human support

Question	Findings	Gap Factor	Recommended Actions
Tools and Resources (continued)			

7. Are policies, processes, or procedures supportive of desired performance?
— Available
— Based on sound logic and efficiency
— Clear and comprehensible
		☐ Lack of supportive policies, processes, or procedures
		  ☐ Not available
		  ☐ Not sound
		  ☐ Not clear
			☐ Provide or redesign supportive policies, processes, or procedures

Incentives/Consequences			

1. Is compensation adequate for desired performance?
— Competitive
— Fair
		☐ Inadequate compensation
		  ☐ Not competitive
		  ☐ Perceived as unfair
			☐ Adjust compensation

2. Are there appropriate financial rewards for desired performance?
— Perceived as fair
— Perceived as fairly distributed
— Efficiently administered
		☐ Lack of appropriate financial rewards
		  ☐ Unfair
		  ☐ Unfairly distributed
		  ☐ Poorly administered
			☐ Provide appropriate financial rewards

3. Are there meaningful nonpay incentives or recognition for desired performance?
— Valued by recipients
— Perceived as fair
		☐ Lack of meaningful nonpay incentives
		  ☐ Insufficient or nonexistent
		  ☐ Not valued
		  ☐ Unfair
			☐ Provide meaningful nonpay incentives or recognition

(continued on next page)

Table 8-1. Front-End Analysis Synthesis Tool (continued)

Question	Findings	Gap Factor	Recommended Actions
Incentives/Consequences (continued)			
4. Do workers see a relationship between superior performance and career advancement? — Perceived as adequate — Perceived as fair		☐ Lack of relationship between performance and career advancement ☐ Inadequate ☐ Unfair	☐ Link career-advancement opportunities with performance
5. Are incentives and rewards scheduled appropriately?		☐ Poor timing of incentives and rewards	☐ Redesign timing of incentives or rewards
6. Are workers punished for per-forming correctly? — By management or supervisors — By co-workers — By customers		☐ Punishment for desirable performance ☐ By management ☐ By co-workers ☐ By customers	☐ Eliminate punishments for desired performance
7. Are workers rewarded for per-forming incorrectly? — By management — By co-workers — By customers		☐ Rewards for undesirable performance ☐ By management ☐ By co-workers ☐ By customers	☐ Eliminate rewards for poor performance

Question	Findings	Gap Factor	Recommended Actions
Knowledge and Skills			

1. Do workers possess the essential skills and knowledge to perform adequately?
— Basic skills and knowledge
— Advanced or technical skills and knowledge
— Skills and knowledge for specific tasks
		☐ Lack of essential skills and knowledge
		  ☐ Basic
		  ☐ Advanced or technical
		  ☐ Task specific
			☐ Provide training

2. Are workers able to discriminate between good and poor performance?
— In others
— In themselves
		☐ Lack of discrimination between good and poor performance
		  ☐ Others
		  ☐ Self
			☐ Provide performance discrimination training with feedback

3. Are workers smooth and "fluent" in their performance?
— Speed
— Smoothness
		☐ Lack of performance fluency
		  ☐ Slow
		  ☐ Hesitant
			☐ Provide practice with feedback

4. Do workers have sufficient opportunities to apply skills and knowledge to maintain proficiency?
— Frequency
— Variety
		☐ Lack of opportunity to maintain proficiency
		  ☐ Lack of frequency
		  ☐ Lack of variety
			☐ Provide periodic practice with feedback

(continued on next page)

Table 8-1. Front-End Analysis Synthesis Tool (continued)

Question	Findings	Gap Factor	Recommended Actions
Capacity			
1. Do workers have the required capacity to perform correctly? — Personal characteristics and values — Intellectual — Emotional — Interpersonal — Management or organizational — Physical, perceptual, or psychomotor		☐ Lack of capacity to perform ☐ Personal traits ☐ Intellectual ☐ Emotional ☐ Interpersonal ☐ Management ☐ Physical	☐ Revise selection criteria and procedures; shift personnel or tasks to match capacity with job requirements
2. Do workers possess required prerequisites to perform correctly? — Education or training — Technical — Experience		☐ Lack of prerequisites ☐ Educational ☐ Technical ☐ Experiential	☐ Select prerequisites; train or provide seasoning experience
3. Do workers possess appropriate political, cultural, or linguistic capacity to perform correctly?		☐ Lack of political, cultural, or linguistic capacity	☐ Select appropriate political, cultural, or linguistic requirements

Question	Findings	Gap Factor	Recommended Actions
Capacity (continued)			
4. Do workers have personal limitations that prevent them from performing as desired? — Family — Health or disabilities — Education — Other		☐ Personal limitations that inhibit desired performance ☐ Family ☐ Health or disabilities ☐ Education ☐ Other	☐ Provide accommodation or resources to overcome limitations
Motivation			
1. Do workers value the required performance? — Initially — Over time		☐ Lack of value for desired performance ☐ Initially ☐ Over time	☐ Demonstrate value
2. Are workers confident they can perform as desired? — Underconfident — Overconfident		☐ Lack of appropriate level of confidence ☐ Underconfident ☐ Overconfident	☐ Provide credible models and support; provide examples of consequences due to overconfidence
3. Do workers feel threatened in their work? — By management or supervisors — By co-workers — By their work environment		☐ Threatening work conditions ☐ Management ☐ Co-workers ☐ Environment	☐ Eliminate threats and threatening conditions

(continued on next page)

157

Table 8-1. Front-End Analysis Synthesis Tool (continued)

Question	Findings	Gap Factor	Recommended Actions
Motivation (continued)			

4. Do workers perceive that they are treated fairly?
— In work assignments
— In career advancement
— In compensation
— In hiring practices
		☐ Perceived lack of fairness
		  ☐ Work assignments
		  ☐ Career advancement
		  ☐ Equity
			☐ Eliminate discriminatory practices; demonstrate fairness and equity practices

Task Interferences			

1. Do workers perform tasks that interfere with desired performance?
— Tasks interfere
— Conditions interfere
		☐ Interferences
		  ☐ Tasks
		  ☐ Conditions
			☐ Eliminate interfering conditions; eliminate or reassign interfering tasks

External Forces			

1. Are there factors outside the workplace that affect attainment of desired performance?
— Economic
— Cultural, political, or social
— Physical
— Health related
		☐ External factors that inhibit desired performance
		  ☐ Economic
		  ☐ Cultural, political, or social
		  ☐ Physical
		  ☐ Health related
			☐ Counter or accommodate for external factors

Question	Findings	Gap Factor	Recommended Actions
External Forces (continued)			
2. Are there competitive factors that affect attainment of desired performance?		☐ Competitive factors	☐ Counter or accommodate for competitive factors
3. Are there events occurring that affect attainment of desired results?		☐ External events	☐ Exploit or accommodate for external events

themselves depends on what you are capable of doing. WLP professionals can usually deal with the learning and job aid solutions. They can assist with many others, such as developing feedback systems, participating in expectations clarification, finding ways around task interferences, or redefining selection criteria and improving performer's perceptions of job value. However, the primary responsibilities for these reside with management. Solutions related to environmental redesign, inadequate compensation, or faulty equipment, once identified, become the responsibility of other specialists.

Of immediate concern, at this point, is selecting solutions the stakeholders require to move forward. To accomplish this, the WLP professional can use the performance intervention selection rating in Tool 8-2 on the CD-ROM. Table 8-2 shows what a completed chart might look like. It narrows down the basket of solutions proposed for achieving performance success.

Learning and Performance Solutions

We have always been somewhat concerned about the word *solution*. It gives the impression that whatever we offer will, in fact, solve a performance problem. We wish it were so. More modestly, we prefer the term *intervention*. This is analogous to medicine in which something specific is done with the expectation that positive results will be forthcoming. No guarantees.

Let's, then, do some rapid defining in this part of the chapter and present an array of some of the most powerful performance interventions in the WLP professional's arsenal. We begin with the term *intervention*, which sounds somewhat cold or clinical. It's a frequently used term in the performance literature denoting something specifically designed to bridge the gap between current and desired states. It can be a stand-alone option or part of an integrated set of interventions. It is anything you, as a WLP professional, either strategically introduce into or remove from a given situation to achieve a specified performance outcome.

We can conveniently divide interventions into two categories: learning and nonlearning. Nonlearning interventions subdivide into three clusters: performance aids, environmental, and emotional. The learning interventions focus on improving the skills and knowledge of workplace performers. Performance aids take the form of materials, equipment, tools, and systems that, through their application, help the performer achieve near-expert results. Environmental interventions address manipulating or changing conditions in the environment that inhibit optimal performance. Finally, emotional interventions, as the name suggests, zero in on the feelings of performers, in some cases removing elements

Table 8-2. Performance Intervention Selection Rating Example

Interventions	Selection Criteria				Total	Rank	Retain (✓)
	Appropriateness	Economics	Feasibility	Acceptability			
Elimination of task interferences	4	3	2	3	12	3	✓
Job redesign	3	1	1	3	8	4	
Environmental redesign	3	0	0	2	5	5	
Process redesign	4	4	3	3	14	2	✓
Provision of resources	4	3	4	4	15	1	✓

that cause negative attitudes that, in turn, lower performance, and in other instances adding something that incites and encourages performers to work in desirable ways. We now examine the interventions at our disposal more concretely and in greater depth.

Learning Interventions

If, as a result of our analyses, we determine that the people who must perform in a particular way cannot do so because they lack required skills or knowledge, then some form of learning intervention is probably necessary. Training is one option. Tool 8-3 offers a variety of learning alternatives you may apply individually or in concert with others.

On the basis of your investigations, if you discover a lack of knowledge or skills and you checked off recommended actions involving training or learning in the front-end analysis tool (see Table 8-1), then use Tool 8-3 to select appropriate and feasible means to build the missing skills or knowledge. The ones to select are those that you and your team or stakeholders check off as both appropriate and feasible, given your performers, work context, resources, and constraints.

Performance Aid Interventions

You are having trouble filling out a tax form. You phone a help line and a customer agent answers. You explain your problem. She poses a series of questions. You respond to each. After several questions, she says, "Go to line 14 and subtract the amount you entered there from line 72. Place this on line 73. If this exceeds $2,000, complete the rest of the form. If not, skip everything that follows and enter the amount on the last page, line 144. That's what you have to pay."

"Wow!" you exclaim after hanging up. She was quick, efficient, and very expert. Right? Probably not. Most of these customer agents are nonexperts. However, armed with job aids and performance support tools, they can often act like one.

Performance aids are external memories. They provide information that allows a novice to produce correct answers (although there are highly sophisticated ones designed for expert use only). Two common performance aids are job aids and performance support systems (often computer-driven). Some are static and provide use-formatted information, fill-in forms, or figures and pictures to guide performance. There are also highly dynamic ones that facilitate calculations, allow try-out of what-ifs, and offer multiple comparisons (for example, one type of car versus a series of others along dimensions you choose). They can help forecast weather patterns. All do the same thing in the end:

provide the necessary support for you to answer correctly, make the right decision, or take the appropriate action. Performance aid users require very little *content* learning. Their primary task is to be able to use the tool.

If during your investigations, you found that people lacked expertise to perform, but with appropriate guidance from reference materials, help screens, or aids that present expert advice they could achieve success, and you indicated this in the front-end analysis synthesis tool (you checked off "Provide job aids, performance support systems, or reference materials"), then examine Tool 8-4. This tool describes what a job aid is, with seven different variations and sample applications. As in Tool 8-3, there are two columns labeled *appropriate* and *feasible* (taking into account time, funds, resources, and constraints). With your team or stakeholders, check off each item as appropriate or feasible. If you place two checkmarks beside an item, select this intervention.

Environmental Interventions

This category of nonlearning performance interventions covers a vast territory. Many authors—Dean (1994), Gilbert (1996), Rummler (2004)—have noted that people's performance in the workplace is far more frequently influenced by environmental than individual factors, but we keep trying to fix individuals rather than the environment. As a WLP professional, manager, organization development specialist, or any other person charged with achieving results through people, you must first examine the workplace environment to discover what is inhibiting attainment of valued accomplishments.

If through your investigations you discovered factors in the list that follows and noted these in your front-end analysis synthesis tool, then you will be selecting environmental interventions. Here is the list:

- Unclear expectations
- Insufficient or inadequate role models
- Unclear, inconsistent performance standards
- Poor feedback
- Inaccessible required information
- Inadequate tools
- Insufficient materials or supplies
- Insufficient time to perform
- Unsupportive environment
- Inadequate or insufficient human support
- Unsupportive policies, processes, and procedures
- Counterproductive consequences for performance

- Poorly selected people to do the job
- Task interferences
- Inhibiting external events.

Impressive list, isn't it?

What to do about these? The good news is that in discovering the problem you frequently also identify the appropriate intervention. Imagine that you discover expectations to be unclear and counterproductive consequences for performance to be present. Identifying these along with credible, documented evidence (for example, clear-cut cases and examples) generally suggests what must be done. This means that although painful, particularly if these have existed for a long time, the solution-interventions are somewhat easy to recommend. Implementation, of course, is another matter.

Tool 8-5, although incomplete, nevertheless presents a number of frequently found environmental elements that negatively affect performance. Use this to refine your analyses. Review findings with stakeholders to make decisions on what should be done.

Three of the most common factors affecting workplace performance are lack of clarity of expectations, lack of timely and specific feedback, and task interferences. We have written extensively on each of these. You can find summaries of the key points on our website at www.hsa-lps.com. Select "Publications" and then "Articles" if any of these three factors appeared in your investigations; Stolovitch and Keeps (2006) also provide guidelines for overcoming each of these performance inhibitors.

To close out this section, Tool 8-6 presents a job aid for helping you overcome environmental performance barriers. Examine each item in light of your investigations, what you checked off as recommended actions in the front-end analysis synthesis tool, and what you retained from your ratings. If any intervention garners two checkmarks, one for appropriateness and the second for feasibility, select it.

Emotional Interventions

Of all the factors affecting workplace performance, the ones most difficult to get our arms around are those of an emotional nature. Most WLP professionals—and this is also true for managers—are familiar with work-related content and practices. For the WLP person, training or learning and general human resources issues are more or less known territory. For managers, specific content or workplace experience plus management practices are areas of familiarity and comfort. In addition, much of what is written on incentives, motivation, and their relationship to workplace performance springs from personally held beliefs, opinions, experiences, testimonials, and myths masquerading as fact. For most interactions, two types of emotional interventions are relevant: incentives and motivation systems. "Incentives are stimulus elements the environment provides that, when perceived as meaningful and valued, increase [desire] to perform" (Stolovitch and Keeps, 2004). An incentive system offers appropriate potential rewards that performers value and monitors the proper use and effect of such rewards.

Motivation is what drives us to do things. Although it is an internal feeling, it is almost always triggered by external circumstances. Three major influences affect motivation: value—the more a person values a performance, the greater the motivation to engage and succeed at it; confidence—how strongly a person thinks he or she can succeed at the performance affects motivation to engage in it (underconfidence and overconfidence lower motivation); and mood—positive, upbeat feelings increase motivation, whereas negative feelings decrease it. In workplace settings, mood is often affected by workplace conditions.

Tool 8-7 offers two types of emotional interventions along with descriptions and sample applications. As before, if either of these align with what you have discovered in your investigations and you check off both appropriateness and feasibility, select the checked off items as part of your overall basket of performance improvement solutions.

Putting It All Together

This chapter has focused on selecting relevant, applicable solutions to attain desired performance from people. It has explored both learning and nonlearning interventions—those a WLP professional can recommend based on analyzing a performance gap, and identifying causes or factors affecting the gap—and has provided not only extensive intervention menus, but also means for making selection decisions. Table 8-3 summarizes all of the key elements this chapter contains. Use it to review your selections to ensure you have covered the key factors affecting performance.

As a concluding note, please remember that selection must occur based on credible information and data obtained during analysis. It should also involve key stakeholders in the process. The more clients, managers, unions, performers, and other affected parties contribute to solution selection, the more likely they will support the design, implementation, and monitoring of all the components of that solution. This is critical to ultimate performance success.

Table 8-3. Performance Interventions: Putting It All Together

If your analysis indicates that performers cannot achieve desired results because they...	Then select...	Such as...	That offers...
do not have the necessary skills and knowledge	a learning intervention	natural experience	real-life trial-and-error learning.
		experiential learning	real-life learning with structured reflection.
		on-the-job training	informal learning guided by co-workers.
		structured on-the-job training	organized and certified learning guided by trained lead workers.
		simulation	learning through realistic, but not real practice.
		role play	emotional learning (how it feels) through intense participation in realistic scenarios.
		laboratory training	learning from hands-on practice with real objectives and equipment.
		classroom training	learning from an instructor and peers with some practice as feasible.
		self-study	learning on one's own from structured resources.
do not have the necessary skills and knowledge, but must still produce immediate, near-expert performance	a nonlearning intervention that acts as an external memory or expert guide	job aids	immediate performance of a highly specific nature once use of the job aid has been mastered. Predictable results.

If your analysis indicates that performers cannot achieve desired results because they...	Then select...	Such as...	That offers...
do not have the necessary skills and knowledge, but must still produce immediate, near-expert performance (continued)	a nonlearning intervention that acts as an external memory or expert guide	performance support system	sophisticated, expert, or near expert performance once use of the performance support system has been mastered.
have a work environment that lacks facilitating elements or presents barriers to achieving desired performance	a nonlearning environmental intervention	provision of information	clear expectations, feedback, and access to unambiguous, required data and guidelines.
		provision of resources	tools, procedures, processes, time, and support needed to perform.
		work environment redesign	supportive physical, administrative, management, communication, and work-task structures that enhance performance.
		elimination of task interferences	clear focus on priority tasks and results and suppression or reassignment of nonessential activities.
		selection	the right performers for the job in terms of competencies, characteristics, and values.
		provision of support	people, systems, and structures that foster increasingly greater performance through encouragement, monitoring, feedback, and reward.

Table 8-3. Performance Interventions: Putting It All Together (continued)

If your analysis indicates that performers cannot achieve desired results because they...	Then select...	Such as...	That offers...
have a work environment that does not stimulate, encourage, or reward desired performance or in which performers do not demonstrate an interest to perform as desired	a nonlearning emotional intervention to build commitment, engagement, and perseverance to perform	provision of incentives or consequences	tangible monetary or nonmonetary rewards that performers value for performing as desired or recognition for valued rewards.
		enhancement of motivation	increased perception of value with respect to desired performance, appropriate level of confidence to succeed, and positive feelings toward achievements of valued results.

About the Authors

Harold D. Stolovitch and Erica J. Keeps share a common passion—developing people. They have devoted a combined total of more than 80 years to make workplace learning and performance both enjoyable and effective. Their research and consulting activities have involved them in numerous projects with major corporations, such as Alcan, Bell Canada, Canadian Pacific Railway, The Coffee Bean & Tea Leaf, DaimlerChrysler Academy, General Motors, Hewlett-Packard, Merck, Prudential, and Sun Microsystems.

Stolovitch and Keeps are the principals of HSA Learning & Performance Solutions, specialists in the application of instructional technology and human performance technology to business, industry, government, and the military.

Together, they edited the first two editions of the award-winning *Handbook of Human Performance Technology: A Comprehensive Guide for Analyzing and Solving Performance Problems in Organizations* and *Improving Individual and Organizational Performance Worldwide.* They are also the authors of the award-winning bestsellers *Telling Ain't Training* and *Training Ain't Performance* and of the *Beyond Telling Ain't Training Fieldbook* and *Beyond Training Ain't Performance Fieldbook,* all published by ASTD Press. Stolovitch and Keeps are co-editors and co-authors of the Learning & Performance Toolkit series published by Pfeiffer.

References

Dean, Peter J. 1994. *Performance engineering at work.* Silver Spring, MD: ISPI Press.

Gilbert, Thomas F. 1996. *Human competence: Engineering worthy performance.* Washington, D.C.: ISPI Press.

Rummler, Geary A. 2004. *Serious performance consulting.* Silver Spring, MD: ISPI Press.

Stolovitch, Harold D., and Erica J. Keeps. 2004. *Training ain't performance.* Alexandria, VA: ASTD Press.

Stolovitch, Harold D., and Erica J. Keeps. 2006. *Beyond training ain't performance fieldbook.* Alexandria, VA: ASTD Press.

Section III

Designing and Developing Effective Learning

Designing and Developing Effective Learning

Luminary Perspective

Robert F. Mager

In This Chapter

> ➤ Understand the purpose of instructional design
> ➤ Develop learner-efficient instruction

---

ontinual learning is essential for survival in the workplace—instruction in the form of training is not. For workers who are already able to do what is expected of them, but are not performing to expectations, training is not the answer.

As you have already learned, inadequate performance is often caused by lack of tools, equipment, authority to perform as desired, and other obstacles, rather than by workers' lack of requisite skills and knowledge. Just as often, they don't perform as expected because they are punished if they do, rewarded if they don't, or ignored *regardless* of the quality of their performance.

This reality highlights the critical importance of conducting an analysis before settling on a mix of remedies for a particular performance gap. The absence of analysis usually results in instruction that misses the mark, wastes time and money, and destroys trainee motivation to learn more. (This may explain why managers often wonder why they allocate so much money to developing courses that don't affect the problem they were intended to solve.)

Caution: Deadwood Ahead

When approaching the tasks of designing and developing instruction, it is useful to remember that this field is strewn with wasteful, ineffective practices (for example, hosing down a group of trainees with the same information for a fixed amount of time without regard for the individual trainee's needs, grading on a "curve," using multiple-choice questions as a tool for assessing accomplishment of performance objectives). Unfortunately, these questionable practices are so tightly woven into the mythology of what constitutes "good" practice, it is often impossible to dislodge them with more effective and efficient practices derived from wisdom and sound research.

With this in mind, it might be useful to consider the topics of instructional design and development.

Design

Instructional design is a planning and structuring process that creates a blueprint (that is, specifications) that developers can use as a guide for drafting the instructional components, along with the methodology by which these will be delivered to trainees.

There are many ways to design instruction, many ways to create the required components, and many possible environments in which to deliver the resulting instruction to the learners. But regardless of the component mix selected, the purpose remains the same: *to prescribe instruction that will teach the learner to perform as the objectives require, and at the same time, to adjust to the needs of the individual trainee.*

In effect, this means the training will provide instruction and practice *only* in those skills and tasks not yet mastered, but only as much as needed to accomplish the level of competence required, while at the same time enhancing trainees' motivation to apply what was learned to the world of work. Then the instruction will stop. In other words, however the instruction is designed, it should guarantee to produce graduates able to perform as desired and be flexible enough to avoid the enormous waste associated with a one-size-fits-all delivery format.

A design for effective and efficient instruction will, at the very least, include answers to these questions:

- Who is the instruction for? Write a description of the target audience. This will be useful for selecting examples and vocabulary most meaningful to the trainees.
- What must trainees be able to do when they leave the instruction that they couldn't do when they arrived? Derive clear statements—objectives—describing

the performance outcomes to be accomplished. These will facilitate derivation of instructional content, evaluation plans, and practice formats.

- How will you know when a trainee can perform as desired? Create an evaluation plan through which trainee performance will be compared with the performance specified by the objectives.

- Do materials already exist that will prevent reinventing the wheel? Search for, and collect, existing materials potentially useful for reducing the need to create original material.

- How will trainees know which instructional units they are qualified to attempt? Draft course maps depicting the path trainees might follow while working their way through the instruction.

- How will trainees learn the rules and procedures by which the instruction will be governed? Write a description of course procedures for trainees, instructors, and facilitators that embodies as many learning principles as the learning environment will allow.

Development

Just as a blueprint (that is, design) describes the dimensional details of a desired structure (for example, a building), the development process involves collection, creation, and stitching together of the bricks and mortar resulting in the structure itself (that is, the instruction). In addition to items created during the design phase (such as objectives), the development process of learner-efficient instruction usually results in at least these items:

- A brief unit outlining an introduction or orientation period acquainting learners with the location of available materials and equipment, course procedures, and other housekeeping details.

- Skill checks providing the means by which accomplishment of the objectives (competence) will be measured.

- Performance guides (job aids) useful in smoothing the path of the learner, during both the learning process and on the job.

- The means by which relevant practice exercises and feedback will be provided to ensure accomplishment of the desired performance levels.

- Prescription of the media mix through which instruction will be delivered to the trainees.

- Instructional units (for example, modules, lessons) containing the information and practice designed to lead the trainee to competence. These include both the trainee materials and the guides for the instructor, facilitator, or coach.

- Tryout and revision of the draft materials and procedures.

These components are intended to ensure that the finished instruction will

- Focus on the desired performance described by the objectives
- Provide practice and feedback in the skills to be mastered
- Impose as few learning obstacles as circumstances allow
- Prevent trainees from having to study what they already know.

In short, the package will guarantee that trainees will leave the training environment able to perform as desired and leave willing and eager to apply what they have learned.

Although instructional development procedures are often made to appear (unnecessarily) ponderous and formal, these procedures are not followed like lemmings marching over a cliff; there is great variability in their application. After all, one ought not be wedded to the development dance when simpler, more direct avenues for facilitating desired performance are available. For example, interventions such as job aids, well-designed operation manuals, intelligent labeling on machinery, and simple permission to perform all can facilitate desired performance without resorting to formal training.

The mission is to guide trainees to competence with as little intrusion into their lives as possible. That, rather than perpetuation of needless, clumsily assembled instruction is the goal of intelligent, learner-centered design and development.

᠀

About the Author

Robert F. Mager has been active in the human performance field since 1954, has held various teaching posts, and has established and managed behavioral research laboratories for two corporations. His significant contributions include his criterion-referenced instruction (CRI) methodology, currently applied world-wide through his successful workshops: Criterion-Referenced Instruction (with Peter Pipe), Instructional Module Development, and The Training Director Workshop. He is widely known for his books *Preparing Instructional Objectives, Analyzing Performance Problems* (with Peter Pipe), *What Every Manager Should Know About Training,* and others. His published novels include *Killer In Our Midst,* (2003), *Dying for Jade* (2006), *The Reluctant Miracle Man* (2006), and *The Price of a Miracle* (2007). He is also a Distinguished Contribution to Human Resource Development Award recipient.

For Further Reading

Mager, Robert F. 2000. *Instructional module development.* Atlanta: Center for Effective Performance.
Mager, Robert F. 1999. *What every manager should know about training.* Atlanta: Center for Effective Performance.

Mager, Robert F. 1997. *Making instruction work.* Atlanta: Center for Effective Performance.

Mager, Robert F., and Peter Pipe. 1997. *Analyzing performance problems.* Atlanta: Center for Effective Performance.

Mager, Robert F., and Peter Pipe. 1994. *Criterion-referenced instruction: Practical skills for designing instruction that works.* Atlanta: Center for Effective Performance.

Chapter 9

Research in Learning: What We Know for Sure

Wellesley R. (Rob) Foshay

In This Chapter

- ➢ Learn the difference between declarative and procedural knowledge

- ➢ Learn how learners learn best and solve problems

- ➢ Recognize what cognitive load is and why it's important

I won't tell you to forget what you think you know about learning. But I would like to challenge some of your habits of practice and help you grow and change your understanding of what learning is and how it happens. The key theme of this chapter is that because of the revolutionary advances in cognitive science now in progress, learning theory has advanced considerably, and it's time for these advances in theory to guide practice in training.

To help you, I will present 11 rules of learning, based on current cognitive learning research and theory. These principles are *not* derived from adult learning theory (Knowles, Holton, and Swanson, 2005) or from constructivist theory (Duffy and Cunningham, 1996 or Jonassen, 2000) or from behaviorist theory (Skinner, 1965)—

although they are not inconsistent with many ideas from those theories. A full understanding of the processes of learning and motivation requires an understanding of these relationships. A useful resource is *How People Learn: Bridging Research and Practice* (National Research Council, 1999). The rules I present use the terms and concepts of cognitive theory because there is actual research data (beyond just nice theories) to show that everything in this chapter actually reflects current research evidence about how people learn and how to improve it. At the end is a list of key references that will lead you to the research, further development of these rules, and applications of these rules to instructional practice.

The bottom line: if you teach the way you were taught, there is a good chance your methods don't reflect current learning theory. Applying these principles of cognitive learning theory will give you new insights and new strategies for training.

Rule 1: Job Tasks Include Declarative and Procedural Knowledge

Declarative knowledge is "knowing what"; procedural knowledge is "knowing how." If you know how to use a copier, you have procedural knowledge. If you know how a copier works, you have declarative knowledge. Even if your knowledge of how it works does not extend beyond where to put the paper and what buttons to push, you still have a *mental model* of how a copier works, but it's a simple one. Declarative knowledge has been called passive because you use it to describe, to state, or perhaps to understand something. Procedural knowledge is active because you use it to do things, such as solve problems.

There is good evidence that declarative knowledge is different from procedural knowledge. You can learn everything there is to know about a subject but still not be able to use that knowledge to do anything. For example, learning the rules of Italian grammar (declarative knowledge) may help you learn the language, but being able to state the rules does not mean you can speak the language (and many native speakers can't articulate the rules, even though they can apply them—they just say what "sounds right"). That requires procedural knowledge.

This distinction is not widely understood in the training community. Trainers often describe rather than show, and they often ask learners to state or describe rather than to do; that is, they focus both their teaching and testing on declarative knowledge, whereas the intended learning outcomes of most training focus on procedural knowledge to be used on the job.

But while declarative knowledge often receives too much attention in training, it does not follow that you can or should ignore it. Declarative knowledge is a necessary part of any complete knowledge structure. In fact, you might think of declarative knowledge as the "framework" upon which procedural knowledge is built. For example, to operate that copier, you have to know where the paper bins are, which buttons tell it what to do, where the output is, where the original goes and how it has to be oriented, and so on. You also need to know how these parts interact. Once you know these parts of many copiers, then you can learn a generalized form of the procedure for copying. If you have this general understanding of how all copiers work, then it's very easy to learn to use a new one—often with no additional training at all. By contrast, if we train you to memorize a procedure by rote, without teaching the declarative knowledge, then it is likely you will need retraining whenever something changes (such as an upgrade to a newer model of copier).

Rule 2: Knowledge Is Learned in Structures

All knowledge is learned in structures, which are related to the logic of the knowledge, what you already know, and how to use the knowledge. I already said that declarative knowledge (such as the parts of the copier and their functional relationships) fits together in a mental model (as in a mental model of how the copier works). Although no one has ever seen a mental model, research is clear that we organize the things we learn into structures (sometimes also called schemas or scripts) to make it possible to store and retrieve them from our memories. And the research is clear that what the model looks like differs in different people—we build those models when we learn by adding new knowledge onto mental models we already have (hence the importance discussed in chapter 11 of knowing about the learner). Mental models differ based on what we already know about related content, how we are going to use the content, and how much we already know about the content. Thus, experts' mental models are different from those of novices.

If your training teaches the parts of the copier in isolation, without explaining how they work together and what the trainee will be doing with them, you make it difficult for the trainee to build the most useful mental model for operating a copier. For the model to make sense, you should help the trainee link the new mental model to what the trainee already knows (perhaps about other copiers, fax machines, scanners, and so forth). The mental model also is structured according to the way the trainee will use it, so the mental model of someone who will only copy is different from the mental model of someone who will use the collator and stapler, make two-sided copies, clear jams, and refill toner. That has important implications for design issues, such as how much and what kind of detail to include in diagrams.

❧ **Benjamin Bloom** ❧

Benjamin Bloom was a noted educational psychology scholar who transformed the field with his influential Taxonomy of Educational Objectives, also known simply as Bloom's taxonomy. As head of a committee of cognitive psychologists at the University of Chicago, Bloom developed the idea of three learning outcomes based on three domains: cognitive (knowledge), psychomotor (skills), and affective (attitude) and published his findings in the book Taxonomy of Educational Objectives: Handbook 1, The Cognitive Domain *(1956). The three domains are the goals of the learning process. Trainers sometimes refer to the three domains as KSAs.*

Bloom and his colleagues then created a hierarchical ordering of learning outcomes by subdividing the cognitive and affective domains beginning with the simplest behavior and working up to the most complex: knowledge, comprehension, application, analysis, synthesis, and evaluation. Each level builds on the previous level, which means that the learner must possess knowledge before comprehension, comprehension before application, and so on. This principle is used throughout the education community to assist in preparation of curricula and evaluation materials.

Bloom developed another influential educational philosophy in his book Developing Talent in Young People *(1985) in which he explores the influence that environment exerts on human performance. Bloom proposes that attention and guidance from parents and educators as well as opportunity and effort on the part of the young person play a greater role in achieving goals than genetics. It is the mission of educators, therefore, to provide students with an environment where their natural aptitudes can be discovered and then supported and cultivated.*

Some highlights of Bloom's distinguished career include serving as the Charles H. Swift Distinguished Service Professor at the University of Chicago and as educational advisor to the governments of India and Israel among others, aiding in the creation of the International Association for the Evaluation of Educational Achievement (IEA), chairing committees on the College Entrance Examinations Board, and serving a stint as president of the American Educational Research Association.

Rule 3: You Learn Each Type of Declarative Knowledge in a Different Way

Although psychologists differ in their terminology, most agree that there are different types of declarative knowledge. (Learn more about alternative terminology structure in *A Taxonomy for Learning, Teaching, and Assessing;* Anderson, Krathwohl, and Bloom, 2001.) A common distinction is among facts, concepts, and principles. Let's look at each of them in more detail—what each is and how you learn it.

Facts

A fact is something you remember word for word. Your phone number is a fact. So are the names and definitions of the parts of the copier. Research is clear that it is easier to learn facts that are related to one another in a structure (see Rule 2) than random isolated facts. If you think back to high school, you memorized Lincoln's Gettysburg Address and the periodic table of elements (both structures containing lots of facts) more easily than you learned all those isolated dates in history class. You learn facts by memorization, but often the learning happens spontaneously as you use the facts, and no explicit training is required: just give the trainee a job aid to look up the facts until they are remembered.

Concepts

You can think of a concept as a way of grouping similar things or ideas and giving them a common name. For example, "chair" and "photocopier" are concepts because there are many different kinds of each, but when we see one, we recognize it as a member of the larger group. Because we can see and touch them, we call concepts like these concrete. "Leadership" and "freedom" are also concepts and work the same way in our minds, but because we cannot see or touch them, we call them abstract or defined concepts. Concepts are important because they are the basic building blocks of all other knowledge types. If learners don't understand concepts, they will not understand any of the other things they try to learn about the concepts.

The way we know someone has learned a concept is to show that person some items he or she has never seen before, and ask him or her if they fit within the concept or not. So we might show you a computer printer/scanner/copier that looks very different from a large photocopier most of us are familiar with. Or, we might ask a trainee to construct a novel example of a concept.

Most training gets concept learning wrong. It asks the learner for the definition of the concept instead of giving new examples to classify or asking the trainee to generate new ones. The key test for deciding if a given piece of knowledge is a fact or a concept is this: if the trainee has to recall literally from memory, it's a fact. If the trainee has to identify, classify, or construct new examples, then it's a concept. This can be tricky, because we often use the same name to apply to facts and concepts (and principles—see below). For example, if you ask your trainee, "What's your computer's password?" then the answer is a fact. If you ask, "What's an acceptable password for your computer?" then the answer is a concept definition.

Principles

A principle is the reason why something works: it states a causal relationship between two or more concepts. It allows trainees to explain situations and predict what might happen in a situation. We could not get through the day without using principles. If you look outside the window and see that it is dark during the day, you see dark clouds instead of sun, and you feel high humidity, you predict that it might rain and you take an umbrella—that is using a principle. Often you can think of a principle as an "if... then" statement. For example, you can predict that if the paper supply bin in your copier is loaded, then the copier will work. Knowing that principle automatically equips you to explain one reason why a copier isn't working (no paper supply), and it prepares you to diagnose a problem in copier operation (out of paper condition)—often with no further training on troubleshooting. By contrast, if you don't understand this principle, then you might be able to follow explicit instructions on when and how to reload paper on this copier (from an expert, or from a job aid built into the machine), but it won't make sense until you figure out the principle. On the next copier you try, you will need the same training or help.

Just as we find it difficult to distinguish between facts and concepts, we also often confuse concepts with principles and mental models. As stated previously, it's particularly confusing because people often use the same word to refer to a fact, a concept, and a principle (for further discussion of this point, see Foshay, Silber, and Stelnicki, 2003).

Training frequently gets principle learning wrong also. Most teaching and testing focuses on learning or remembering the words of the principle, but that is only fact learning. For principle learning to occur, you must be able to explain why something happened or predict what would happen in a new situation. For example, every time we get a new boss, we use principles we have learned based on past experience to predict what we might expect (reorganization, new mission, new measures on our performance reviews, and so forth).

Rule 4: Concepts and Principles Are Best Learned from a Combination of Examples and Definitions

We used to think that when we had learned things, what we remembered were the abstract definitions or statements of concepts and principles. But research says something different and important. What you remember are idealized *prototype examples* of concepts and principles, and they are often related to the first examples you encounter (I'm showing my age, but for me it's hard to think of rock and roll without an Elvis tune coming to mind. But if you are younger than me, then your prototype example might be a Beatles, Phish, or Snoop Dog song.) Examples can be what a concept or principle *is* (positive examples) or what it *is not* (negative examples or contrasts between examples of concepts, such as car versus truck versus bus). From those examples, we actually construct, *not* remember, the definitions.

Therefore, although abstract definitions of concepts and principles often are useful in learning, they should always be used with an appropriate set and sequence of examples. Effective training usually involves identification, classification, and construction of examples—not memorization and recitation of definitions. Some psychologists believe that this rule also applies to procedural knowledge (see below). For procedural knowledge, the examples are problem solutions, particularly when they include an account of the decision making involved.

Rule 5: Learners Learn Best When They Learn the Whole Knowledge Structure at Once

The research evidence all points in the same direction: teach all the related parts of a knowledge structure together. Even though it may seem like more to learn at once, it's easier for the learner to start with a view of the "forest" and then go into detail on the "trees." When the overall knowledge structure and the relationships among its facts, concepts, and principles are presented along with the prototype examples, learners can more easily understand how the concepts relate to each other, and to the job on which they will apply the concepts. For example, if you are teaching software operation, it makes sense to start with an overview of the logic of the user interface's organization and relationship to function (perhaps accompanied by a wall chart showing the menu hierarchy).

Rule 6: Procedural Knowledge Is How to Do

As compared with declarative knowledge (see Rule 3), procedural knowledge is "know how." It is some sequence of actions you take to solve a problem. For example, when you make a copy, you use your procedural knowledge of copier operation: First you load the paper. Then you put the original in the tray. Then you select the number of copies. Then you push the "copy" button, and so on.

What makes this procedural knowledge, not declarative knowledge? Remember that declarative knowledge is your knowledge of the parts of a copier, what they do, and how they work together. Procedural knowledge is your knowledge of the *sequence of decisions and actions* to perform to solve a problem, such as making a copy. To operate the copier, you need both the declarative and procedural knowledge.

The way you know if a trainee has learned procedural knowledge is the most simple and obvious of all we have discussed so far: ask the trainee to do it. Note that training gets this wrong often—either asking only to describe the procedure or select the correct steps in the procedure. The only valid way to see if you have learned the procedure is to ask you to do it.

Rule 7: Procedural Knowledge Varies According to Its Structure

There is a continuum from well-structured problems to ill-structured problems (Newell and Simon, 1972). It's sometimes useful to also consider an in-between class of moderately structured problems (Jonassen, 1997). Making copies is an example of a well-structured procedural knowledge, because you know completely when to use the procedure, you always do it the same way (it's an algorithm you could flowchart), and the goal is completely defined (having copies).

Moderately structured procedures usually have a clear goal, but often the starting conditions aren't fully known, and the trainee has to figure out how to solve the problem. Examples include most kinds of troubleshooting, whether it's of a piece of equipment, a process, or even some aspects of organizational performance. Note that there may be more than one acceptable goal, as well as many ways to reach the goal.

Ill-structured procedures typically do not have well-defined goals, and often the starting conditions and ways to get there aren't fully defined, either. There are usually many acceptable solutions and many ways of getting to them, and information needed to solve the problem is often incomplete. Examples include many design and creative tasks, strategic planning, and some management and organizational development tasks. Solving ill-structured problems typically involves figuring out the properties of an acceptable solution and developing a strategy to get to a solution that falls within the class of acceptable ones.

I believe that a common error in training is to try to treat all procedural knowledge as if it were well structured. The optimum instructional strategies are quite different at the well- and ill-structured ends of the procedural knowledge continuum. Also, note that this error causes trainers often to overlook (or fail to understand) the kinds of expertise that are often most valuable in a company.

Another common error, in my view, derives from our use of conventional job task analysis (JTA) as a design tool for training. JTA, as often practiced, omits or obscures critical parts of the procedural knowledge structure. For that reason, a family of analytical techniques called *cognitive task analysis* (CTA) has emerged (Jonassen, Hannum, and Tessmer, 1989).

Another common error in training is to fail to recognize that the first step in any procedure is to decide to use the procedure. Often, training fails to include opportunities to decide to use a procedure or how to select among alternative procedures.

Rule 8: Procedural Knowledge Involves Manipulating the Relevant Mental Model

Although declarative and procedural knowledge are different types of knowledge, they are *not* independent. When you solve problems of any type, you use the declarative knowledge (facts, concepts, and principles—synthesized into a mental model) along with your procedural knowledge. To solve a problem, you have to recall or generate appropriate procedural knowledge and apply it to solve the problem. Declarative knowledge is what allows you to understand the problem and decide which procedural knowledge to apply.

For you to solve a problem, you have to look at the problem, recall the appropriate mental model related to the problem, and then restructure and "run" your mental model to figure out what needs to change and to predict what any proposed solution to solve the problem would be. For example, if the copy machine is broken, you have to recall your mental model of how the machine works, and then add possible faults (such as no paper, no toner, paper jam, no power, software glitch) to decide what actions to take and what effects they might have (adding paper won't help if the problem is that the paper is jammed).

Thus, you have to develop a mental model with the right kind of structure for solving a particular class of problems to be successful at problem solving. Manipulating your mental model is a key step in problem solving because it helps you predict the effects of various possible actions and select the action that will move you closer to the solution.

I believe the importance of mental models, their development, and their manipulation has been underemphasized in the training literature and in practice. Because developing problem-solving skills depends upon learning an effective mental model, I believe you should teach learners to develop and manipulate appropriate mental models as the main prerequisite for learning to solve problems—especially moderately structured and ill-structured problems. Instruction on the mental model can occur before the actual procedural knowledge instruction begins, or can occur as a part of the procedural knowledge instruction. But it must occur.

Research says that development and manipulation of mental models usually doesn't happen incidentally; there is only weak evidence to support the assumption that learners are able to develop their own mental models that are adequate, with relatively little support and no direct instruction. Therefore one of your key responsibilities in training development is to help learners develop mental models, through lessons designed to develop a deep understanding of how things work and how they are related.

Rule 9: People Solve Unfamiliar Problems Inductively

To do problem solving, the trainee has to go through a number of steps. Although different experts define the steps differently (for example, Jonassen, 1997), most authors would probably agree with the seven-step process below.

1. Form an *initial representation* of the problem, called a "problem space," including all the elements of a problem (as described above).
2. Recall declarative knowledge (in the form of a mental model) and procedural knowledge (in the form of similar problems solved) appropriate to the problem space just created.
3. If the learner has previously solved a similar problem, he or she will probably just recall the procedure used last time and follow it as a rote procedure. This is the case for well-structured procedures and for *familiar* moderately structured to ill-structured problems.
4. If the learner doesn't see a match to something previously encountered, then he or she has to generate a new solution. Note that this is *always* the case for moderately structured and ill-structured problems, if they are recognized as being new or unique in some ways. He or she uses one or more strategies, both general problem-solving strategies (called *domain independent*) and strategies specific to the content of the problem (called *domain specific*), to plan to solve the problem—to get from the initial state to the goal state. He or she integrates the mental model, prior procedural knowledge, and these strategies to generate an algorithm or a heuristic for solving the problem.
5. The learner then implements the algorithm just created.
6. The learner then checks the results of the problem-solving efforts against the goal state to see if they match. If so, then the problem is solved.
7. If the problem is solved, be happy and quit; if not, the learner goes back to either

   - Step 1, to reformulate the problem
   - Step 2, to recall other declarative and procedural knowledge
   - Step 3, to plan to solve the problem using a different strategy.

Many variations of this basic strategy have been identified for various types of problems, so this is *not* a general strategy for solving all problems; the research of the past 20 years is generally inconsistent with the idea there is a single strategy for problem solving, for all domains, and for all degrees of problem structure.

If you think carefully about these seven steps and the rules in this chapter, you will realize how different the preferred strategies are for teaching well-structured, moderately structured, and ill-structured problem solving. For example, well-structured problem solving stops at Step 3, and involves

- Presenting an algorithm for solving the problem
- Teaching declarative knowledge
- Teaching when and how to follow the algorithm.

By contrast, moderately structured problem solving spends most time on steps 4–7.

The goal is clear, but the key task is to invent a way to get to the goal. So training should focus on:

- Formulating a problem-solving strategy, based on past experience and considering model examples of similar problem solving
- Using declarative knowledge (how things work)
- Testing problem-solving strategies against the goal.

Ill-structured problem solving also uses steps 4–7, but with the added complication that the first task is to define the goal: what would be the characteristics of a good solution? Once these characteristics are defined, then the problem has become moderately structured, and the focus of the training changes to those described above.

You should also realize that a specific problem is moderately structured to ill structured only once for each trainee. The next time the identical problem occurs, the trainee can simply recall how it was solved and do so using steps 1–3. That's why it's generally true that teaching moderately structured to ill-structured problem solving is important for problems that don't happen the same way twice, or for problems that have volatile content and would otherwise require constant retraining, or problems you can't anticipate. These are often the most important problems in the company, at every level.

Also, remember that many problems can't be solved using a single strategy. They have to be broken down into component subproblems, which usually have clearer goals and more structure than the whole problem. For example, to perform a moderately structured electronic troubleshooting task, you have to be able to do the well-structured procedures for performing circuit tests. Training for the complete job task of troubleshooting a type of electronic device includes performing the well-structured tests and replacement procedures and the moderately structured logical task of troubleshooting—together with an appropriately detailed mental model of the device.

Rule 10: An Expert Problem Solver Knows Different Things Than Does a Novice

Experts aren't just faster and more accurate than novices, they know more and different things about the problem, and they have insights that a novice cannot yet understand. Six major differences between novices and experts are summarized below.

- In general, experts do have more declarative knowledge, but of a specific kind. They have more principles in their problems spaces, at a higher level of automaticity. This allows them to synthesize the declarative knowledge they have and bring it to bear more systematically on problems.
- Experts have better links between the declarative knowledge structures (mental models) and their procedural knowledge structures (if...then statements) in their problem spaces. These links allow them to bring principles and procedures together to solve problems more efficiently. The structures resulting from these links are sometimes called mental models of the problem space.
- Experts are really great at organizing their problem spaces. Recall that solving a problem (except when blindly following a rote procedure) involves constructing and manipulating the mental model of the system within the problem space. Experts do it so there are more associations among the declarative and procedural knowledge structures in the problem space. These allow the experts to get around in those problem spaces more quickly and efficiently bring the needed knowledge to bear on the problem. It provides them with what others see as "mental shortcuts," which make the experts efficient. Note that these mental shortcuts often involve insights about the problem space that novices could not possibly understand because they don't have the supporting knowledge structure.
- Experts categorize and group problems differently from novices. Whereas novices look at surface, perceptual issues in putting problems in the same category, experts extract the abstract problem features (underlying meaning) from the problems and categorize them based on their deep structure—making it easier to bring the right existing declarative and procedural knowledge structures to bear on solving them.
- Experts sometimes generate heuristics (strategies) for solving problems by "working forward" from the initial state, generating hypotheses, and then carrying them through to see if they lead to the goal. Novices, however, try to

generate them "working backward" from the goal state, generating operations that include the goal and a path to get there (Jonassen, et al., 1977).

■ Complicating the issue of novice versus expert are the issues of situational and individual differences. They are believed to affect processing capacity, thus making cognitive load and automaticity a huge issue. For example, an expert is more likely to persist if the first strategy doesn't work, but a novice may give up.

Based on these issues, our challenge in training, then, is to assist (but not tell) learners to categorize problems the way experts do and to build (but not just memorize) an appropriate "working" mental model of the system that contains the right components, in the right relationships, with the right operating principles, to enable the kinds of problem solving needed—but without needless additional details (so, for example, don't use a schematic diagram when a block diagram will do).

Rule 11: Cognitive Load Is Important in Training and in Performance

Cognitive load is the amount of cognitive processing, or "brain power," a particular task requires of you. The more familiar the information or problem presented, the more familiar the task required, and the smaller the size of the information and the task, the lower the cognitive load. In training situations, however, the reverse is usually true: the amount and newness of the information and task required typically means that cognitive loads are high for trainees. You certainly remember being in training when the instructor just poured information out at you until you just felt "this is too much" and you shut down or you said "my brain is on overload." You were exactly correct. That's one of the many reasons all those endless "brain dump" lectures are practically worthless.

Other things can happen that reduce your cognitive processing capacity, thereby effectively increasing your cognitive load. These include stress, fatigue, lack of confidence, distraction, and even "lack of focus" on the problem at hand (often called *motivation*).

That's why to maximize learning, it's important for you to (1) present new knowledge to be learned in organized and properly sized "chunks" that do not create overload and (2) create a learning environment that is free of distraction and that helps the learner to be refreshed, relaxed, confident, and focused.

Managing cognitive load is a key issue for trainers. Carefully presenting the right kinds of hints, controlling the rate of presentation of content new to the learner, and allowing time for the learner to reflect on new content all reduce cognitive load. Another technique is to teach some subskills or knowledge as prerequisites, so they only need to be recalled when teaching the whole problem-solving skill. This is especially effective if the prerequisites are practiced to a high state of automaticity (fluency) so the learner can "do them without thinking about it" (Clark, Nguyen, and Sweller, 2006).

Summary

The cognitive view of learning is quite a bit different from the theory in use by much training. You have seen how well- and ill-structured problem solving differs, the types of declarative and procedural knowledge needed, and how expert and novice problem solvers differ. You also should conclude that problem solving is mostly a context-bound skill: there is no such thing as a generally expert problem solver.

In conclusion, I encourage you to think about when the apparent inefficiency of ill-structured problem solving is worth it. If a goal is for transfer (to new or unpredictable problems) or reduction of repetitive training and re-training, then you should define the training goals to include moderately structured to ill-structured problem solving. In the opposite cases, treating problems as well-structured may be more efficient.

⌖

About the Author

Wellesley R. "Rob" Foshay is director of research for the Education Technology Group of Texas Instruments and president of the Foshay Group. For 15 years, he was the chief instructional architect of the PLATO Learning System, one of the oldest and largest e-learning systems. His doctorate is in instructional design from Indiana University. He has contributed more than 70 major articles to research journals and book chapters on a wide variety of topics in instructional design, technology, and education, and speaks frequently before educators and trainers worldwide. He is co-author of the award-winning textbook, *Writing Training That Works: How to Teach Anyone to Do Anything.* He is a fellow of the International Board of Standards for Training, Performance, and Instruction; was cited by ISPI with honorary life membership and the distinguished service award; and is a certified performance technologist.

References

Anderson, Lorin W., David R. Krathwohl, and Benjamin S. Bloom. 2001. *A taxonomy for learning, teaching, and assessing: A revision of Bloom's taxonomy of educational objectives.* New York: Longman.

Clark, Ruth Colvin, Frank Nguyen, and John Sweller. 2006. *Efficiency in learning: Evidence-based guidelines to manage cognitive load.* San Francisco: Jossey-Bass.

Duffy, Thomas M., and D.J. Cunningham. 1996. Constructivism: Implications for the design and delivery of instruction. In *Handbook of research on educational communications and technology,* ed., D.H. Jonassen. New York: Macmillan.

Foshay, Wellesley R., Kenneth H. Silber, and Michael Stelnicki. 2003. *Writing training that works: How to teach anything to anybody.* San Francisco: Jossey-Bass/Pfeiffer.

Jonassen, David H. 1997. Instructional design models for well-structured and ill-structured problem-solving learning outcomes. *Educational Technology Research and Development* 45(1): 65-94.

Jonassen, David H. 2000. Toward a design theory of problem solving. *Educational Technology Research and Development* 48(4): 63-85.

Jonassen, David H., and University of North Carolina at Greensboro, Library Science/Educational Technology Division. 1977. *Taxonomic analysis of behavioral objectives: An instructional program.* Greensboro, NC: Library Science/Educational Technology Division School of Education University of North Carolina.

Jonassen, David H., Wallace H. Hannum, and Martin Tessmer. 1989. *Handbook of task analysis procedures.* New York: Praeger.

Knowles, Malcolm S., Elwood F. Holton, and Richard A. Swanson. 2005. *The adult learner, sixth edition: The definitive classic in adult education and human resource development.* Burlington, MA: Elsevier.

National Research Council (U.S.). Committee on Learning Research and Educational Practice, J. Bransford, et al. 1999. *How people learn: Bridging research and practice.* Washington, D.C.: National Academy Press.

Newell, Allen, and Herbert A. Simon. 1972. *Human problem solving.* Englewood Cliffs, NJ: Prentice Hall.

Skinner, B.F. 1965. *Science and human behavior.* New York: The Free Press.

**Chapter 10**

Instructional Design Models and Learning Theories

Darryl L. Sink

In This Chapter

- ➤ Use and expand models to meet your needs

- ➤ Understand different learning theories and make them work for you

- ➤ Understand how to integrate ISD models and learning theories for effective instruction

---

The best place to start when deciding an organization needs training solutions is to understand the business and individual needs that underlie the training initiative. This requires defining the business drivers for training program development and the organizational results needed or desired.

Once that initial, critical first step has been taken, instructional design models and learning theories enter the picture to provide a systematic approach (or plan) to help instructional designers craft effective and efficient training solutions that meet organizational and individual needs. These plans are referred to as instructional systems design (ISD) models.

Learning theories and the strategies and tactics (that is, lesson designs) derived from ISD models can help practitioners develop optimal instructional designs for learning—designs that support the learners as they acquire the knowledge, skills, experience, and motivation needed to produce results for themselves and their organizations.

The design phase of ISD models is the point where learning theories and their resulting strategies and tactics primarily come into play. This chapter will discuss ISD with emphasis on two popular approaches—ADDIE and the Dick and Carey model. It will focus on learning theories and their influence on the ISD model design phase.

ISD Models

ISD models are based on the systems approach; the output from one model phase provides the input for the next phase. ISD model origins can be traced to the application of a systems approach by the military starting in World War II. After the war, the military applied the systems approach to the development of training materials and programs.

During the 1960s, the systems approach began to appear in procedural models of instructional design in U.S. higher education and became widely taught through a college consortium including Syracuse, Michigan State, U.S. International University, and USC (later joined by Indiana University). This work culminated in a joint project known as the Instructional Development Institute (IDI).

In 1973, the U.S. Department of Defense commissioned the Center for Performance Technology at Florida State University to develop procedures to substantially improve Army training. These procedures evolved into a model that was adopted by the Army, Navy, Air Force, and Marines called Interservice Procedures for Instructional Systems Development (IPISD).

The phases of this ISD model included analysis, design, development, implementation, and control. The *control* phase was later renamed *evaluation* and gave rise to the well-known acronym ADDIE. For a more complete history of ISD, see Molenda and Boling (2007).

The ADDIE Model

ADDIE remains one of the most popular ISD models and continues to be updated and used in many large organizations. The phases for the ADDIE model can be seen in Figure 10-1. The arrows illustrate the interactive nature of a systems approach model.

Figure 10-1. The ADDIE Model

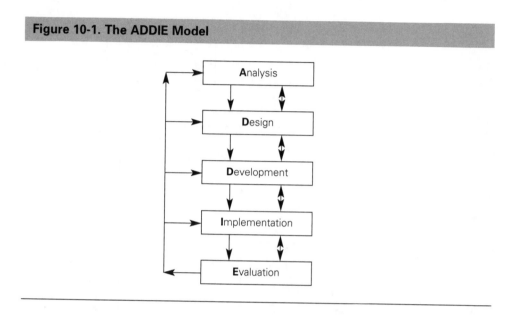

Each phase of the model is made up of different procedural steps. For example, analysis typically includes needs analysis, learner analysis, context analysis, and content analysis. The output of the analysis phase is learning objectives, which serve as the input to the design phase. For an expansion of basic ADDIE phases into a more detailed procedural guide, see Gagné, Wager, Golas, and Keller (2005).

The Dick and Carey Model

The Dick and Carey model is shown in Figure 10-2. Named for its developers, it is the most widely known and used ADDIE-type model (Dick, Carey, and Carey, 2005).

The Dick and Carey model is taught in most introductory college and university instructional design courses. Two of its characteristics are particularly noteworthy in our discussion of ISD models.

The model suggests creating assessments for learning objectives *before* designing and developing the instruction. This departure from the basic ADDIE model helps ensure alignment of learning objectives with the evaluation of success in achieving those objectives early in the development process. This sequence often results in an iteration revising the objectives to better align with how they will be measured.

The Dick and Carey model also places increased emphasis on formative evaluation—the evaluation of materials and approaches as they are being formed. Revision information

Figure 10-2. Dick and Carey Model of ISD

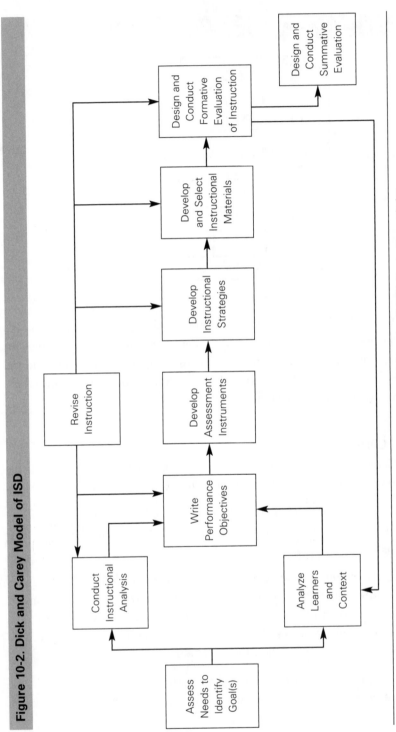

Source: Dick, Carey, and Carey (2005). *The Systematic Design of Instruction*. Pearson Education, © 2005. Used with permission.

gained from early try-outs of instructional materials is fed forward in the training development process, rather than waiting and facing the possibility of revising an entire program after it has been fully developed.

ISD Models, in General

Many ISD models have been developed and used over the last few decades. Models differ in terms of the number of steps, the names of the steps, and the recommended sequence of functions. Gustafson and Branch's (1997) *Survey of Instructional Development Models* includes 18 models. Their list is not intended to be exhaustive; rather it illustrates the various ways of implementing a systems approach.

Organizations typically use their own uniquely customized ISD model, often adapting or combining concepts from other models.

Expanding Models to Meet New Delivery Systems

Expanding, modifying, and combining instructional design models with other models and considerations is often necessary when a particular medium or delivery system is chosen. Figure 10-3 shows one such adaptation for teaching e-learning training development (Sink, 2002).

The first part of the model depicts the basics of ISD, beginning with needs analysis to determine workforce training needs and matching solutions. If analysis confirms some sort of training is needed, the front-end analysis continues with audience, context, and content considerations. The results of these analyses enable a decision as to whether e-learning is an appropriate delivery system choice.

Next, the model expands into three distinct paths that function simultaneously. The three paths are a programming model, an ISD model, and a model for project management. The programming portion of the model is needed to guide software development. An ISD model is needed to guide instructional program development. A model to guide project management is also needed due to increased project management responsibilities given the complexities of a delivery system that may involve so many different media, software programming, user-interface testing, and learning design strategies. Fairly large design and development teams may be required to provide all the different types of expertise needed.

The instructional design path in Figure 10-3 illustrates the basic components of a typical instructional design process. Additionally, the three-path model shows how and where the programming path and the instructional design or development path interact, and the checkpoints for project management and evaluation.

Figure 10-3. ISD for E-Learning

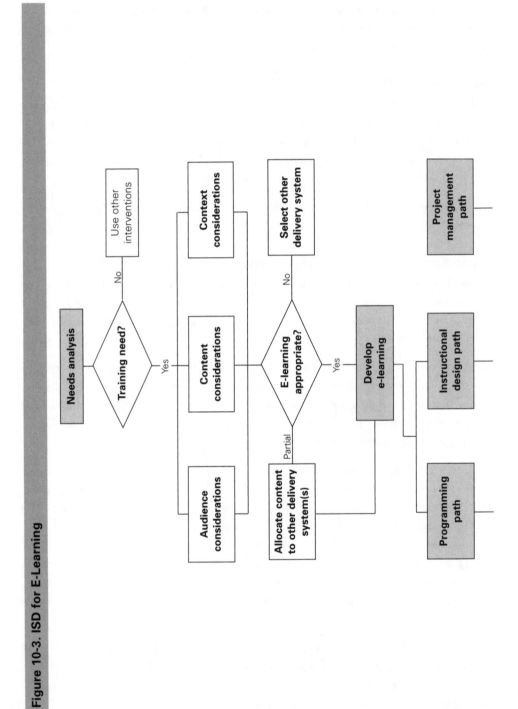

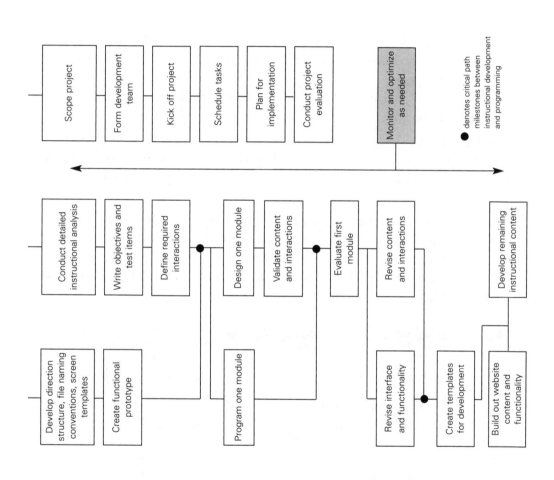

Scope project

Form development team

Kick off project

Schedule tasks

Plan for implementation

Conduct project evaluation

Monitor and optimize as needed

● denotes critical path milestones between instructional development and programming

Conduct detailed instructional analysis

Write objectives and test items

Define required interactions

Design one module

Validate content and interactions

Evaluate first module

Revise content and interactions

Develop remaining instructional content

Develop direction structure, file naming conventions, screen templates

Create functional prototype

Program one module

Revise interface and functionality

Create templates for development

Build out website content and functionality

All these ISD models provide a road map or process for a systems approach with the goal of training outcomes that are results oriented. ISD models systematically strive to deliver the results individuals and organizations need and desire.

Learning Theories

Learning theories attempt to describe what is going on when people learn. Gagné (1997) puts it this way:

> [Learning theories] try to provide conceptual structures involved in the process of taking in information and getting it transformed so that it is stored in long term memory and later recalled as an observable human performance. This entire process, or set of processes, forms the basis of what I refer to when I speak of learning theory.

Learning theories give rise to learning strategies, tactics, experiences, and learning environments that support theory. Given the ISD models, instructional designers make the most use of learning theories and their resulting learning strategies in the design phase (see Figure 10-4).

The different ways training courses may be structured and designed (as well as the structure and design of individual lessons, modules, or units of instruction within the course) usually have their origins in one or more learning theories (Molenda and Russell, 2005). The design phase of ISD has been heavily influenced by the *behaviorist, cognitive,* and *constructivist* learning theories.

Figure 10-4. ADDIE Model and Learning Theories

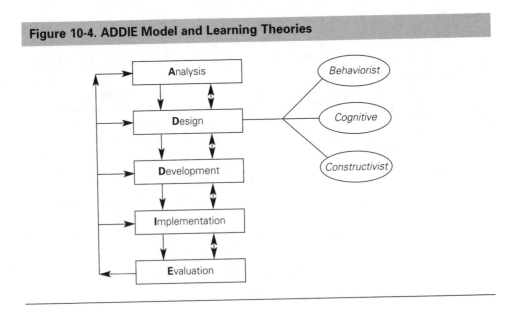

Behaviorist Approach

Behaviorists concentrate their efforts on what is observable learner behavior and reinforcement. Drawing on the research and theories of B.F. Skinner on stimulus-response learning, behaviorist training programs focus on observable behavior. Main tasks are broken down into smaller tasks, and each small task is treated as a separate learning objective. Input and practice, followed by reinforcement (positive or corrective), are the base components of the behaviorist approach.

Behaviorist learning theory gave rise to teaching machines and programmed instruction from which many practical and essential instructional design concepts are derived. Examples include

- Determining specifically stated descriptions of observable human performance (the objectives of the instruction)
- Using objective-based testing rather than topic-based testing (later called criterion-referenced testing)
- Using developmental testing of training material prototypes and approaches on members of the target learning populations for the purpose of improving the materials until learners can meet the preset criterion (a try-out and revision process)
- Chunking instruction and designing and writing based on learning objectives and content types such as facts, procedures, concepts, processes, and principles.

Current Uses of the Behaviorist Approach

A behaviorist approach is very useful in training intended to impart intellectual, psychomotor, and interpersonal knowledge and skills (that is, where the learner needs to gain fluency and automatic use of the knowledge and skills). A few examples will clarify the usefulness of this approach.

- Example 1: Teaching learners how to write user requirements for software development illustrates an instance when an intellectual skill should be practiced until learners can write user requirements within the context of their own work environments.
- Example 2: Teaching interpersonal skills related to conflict resolution requires repeated practice with feedback until learners gain enough confidence to use the skills in their own work environments.
- Example 3: Learning to drive a car is a psychomotor skill that must be practiced until certain sub-skills become automatic. Acquisition of automatic sub-skills enables learners to successfully drive without consciously focusing on each and every step in the procedure.

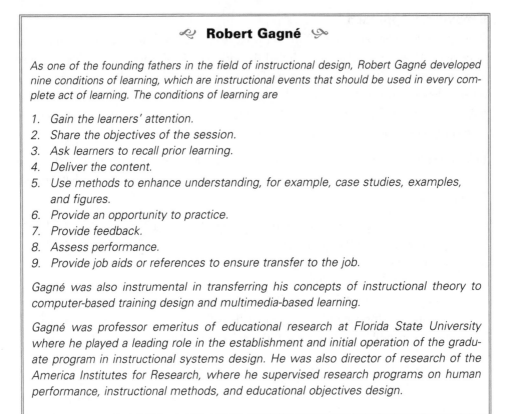

Another offshoot of the behaviorist approach is called programmed instruction. Programmed instruction is useful in e-learning courses. Within this context, substantial text and ideas are presented in manageable chunks, followed by an interactive question or an activity, and concluded with corrective or confirming feedback.

Benjamin Bloom's (1968) philosophy and concepts revolving around *Learning for Mastery* also have their roots in the behaviorist approach. The learning for mastery model is based on Bloom's premise that perhaps 95 percent of the learner population can learn what we have to teach them and that it is our responsibility as designers and educators or trainers to figure out the means to help those learners master the content we have to teach. In particular, learning for mastery makes use of performance or behaviorally stated learning objectives and criterion-referenced testing. It also emphasizes diagnostic testing and remediation strategies.

Learning for mastery has been very influential in public education and in military training.

Cognitive Learning Theory

Although behaviorist learning theory is focused almost exclusively on external events and processes, cognitive theories focus on what is happening to learners internally. Cognitive learning theories try to understand understanding (Clark, 1999).

The cognitive approach has contributed what we know about internal cognitive processes to the field of instructional design. Cognitive theory helps us provide conditions that make it more likely learners will acquire the thinking strategies necessary to improve their job performance. The cognitive view of how learning takes place is based on how information is processed, stored, and retrieved in the mind, rather than on how behavior changes (Foshay, Silber, and Stelnicki, 2003).

Cognitive approaches to training have given rise to more in-depth strategies and tactics for helping learners acquire cognitive skills. Gagné's nine events of instruction (listed below) are foundational for many cognitive training designs:

1. Gaining attention
2. Informing the learner of the objective
3. Stimulating recall of prerequisite learning
4. Presenting the stimulus material
5. Providing learning guidance
6. Eliciting the performance
7. Providing feedback about performance correctness
8. Assessing the performance
9. Enhancing retention and transfer.

The cognitive training procedure suggested by Foshay, Silber, and Stelnicki (2003) juxtaposes the five tasks learners have to accomplish with the elements trainers and designers must put into lessons. Table 10-1 shows lesson elements associated with each of the five learner tasks consistent with the cognitive approach.

Current Uses of Cognitive Theory

The cognitive approach is well suited to helping learners recall new information, comprehend how things work, and remember and use new procedures (Davis and Davis, 1998). It applies generally to objectives in the cognitive domain, particularly to tasks at the lower and middle levels of complexity.

Learning strategies and tactics from cognitive theory can be used to build on the behavioral approach to instructional design by expanding the instructional designer's repertoire of strategies and tactics for how people acquire and learn cognitive skills.

Table 10-1. Cognitive Training Model

Learners Must Do This to Learn	Trainers Put These Elements into Lessons to Help Learners
1. **Select the information to attend to.** Heighten their attention and focus it on the new knowledge being taught because that new knowledge is seen as important and as something that can be learned.	**Attention.** Gain and focus learners' attention on the new knowledge. **WIIFM.** Answer "What's in it for me?" for the learners. **YCDI.** Tell the learners "You can do it" regarding learning the new knowledge.
2. **Link the new information with existing knowledge.** Put the new knowledge in an existing framework by recalling existing or old knowledge related to the new knowledge and linking the new knowledge to the old.	**Recall.** Bring to the forefront the prerequisite existing (old) knowledge that forms the base on which the new knowledge is built. **Relate.** Show similarities or differences between the new knowledge and old knowledge, so that the new knowledge is tied to the old.
3. **Organize the information.** Organize new knowledge in a way that matches the organization of related existing knowledge to make it easier to learn, cut mental processing time, minimize confusion, and stress only relevant information.	**Structure of content.** Present the boundaries and structure of the new knowledge in a format that best represents the way the new knowledge itself is structured. **Objectives.** Specify both the desired behavior and the knowledge to be learned. **Chunking.** Organize and limit the amount of new knowledge presented to match human information processing capacity. **Text layout.** Organize text presentation to help learners organize new knowledge. **Illustrations.** Use well-designed illustrations to assist learners' organization and assimilation of new knowledge.
4. **Assimilate the new knowledge into existing knowledge.** Integrate the new knowledge into the old knowledge so they combine to produce a new unified, expanded, and reorganized set of knowledge.	**Present new knowledge.** Using a different approach for each type of knowledge, present the new knowledge in a way that makes it easiest to understand. **Present examples.** Demonstrate real-life examples of how the new knowledge works when it is applied.

5. **Strengthen the new knowledge in memory.** Strengthen the new knowledge so that it will be remembered and can be brought to bear in future job and learning situations.

Practice. Involve learners by having them do something with the new knowledge.

Feedback. Let learners know how well they've done in using the new knowledge, what problems they're having, and why.

Summary. Present the structure of content again, including the entire structure of knowledge.

Test. Have learners use the new knowledge again, this time to prove to themselves, you, and their employer that they have met the objectives of the training.

On-the-job application. Have learners use new knowledge in a structured way on the job to ensure they "use it, not lose it."

Constructivist Learning Theory

Constructivist pedagogy emerged in the 1980s. It revolves around the notion that "knowledge is constructed by the learners as they attempt to make sense of their experiences" (Driscoll, 2000). Constructivist theory sees learning as knowledge construction and is based on the idea that learning occurs when a learner actively constructs a knowledge representation in working memory. According to the knowledge construction view, the learner is a sense maker; the teacher is a cognitive guide who provides guidance and modeling on authentic learning tasks (Mayer, 1999).

The constructivist learning experience is more discovery oriented, rather than expository oriented. Constructivist learning experiences involve carefully crafted activities, multiple perspectives, and learner-driven knowledge creation. These techniques result in tasks similar to those learners would encounter in the real world, with the natural complexities that surround those tasks.

With constructivist strategies, the aim is to make the learning experience reflect real-world experiences, enabling learners to transfer what they learn more efficiently and effectively to their jobs.

Current Uses of Constructivist Learning Theory

Constructivist pedagogy is currently combined with the concept of performance-based training and has various names. Models that embrace performance-based training include problem-based learning (Nelson, 1999), goal-based scenarios (Schank, Berman, and MacPherson, 1999), and constructivist learning environments (Jonassen, 1999). In more general discussions, constructivist performance-based learning may be referred to as situated learning, authentic activities, or cognitive apprenticeship. Whatever name is used, the approach describes a learning experience that

- Has real-world relevance
- Requires learners to define tasks and subtasks to complete activities
- Enables learners to examine tasks and their deliverables from different perspectives
- Provides the opportunity to collaborate
- Allows for competing solutions and a variety of outcomes
- Aims to create polished products or job-related tools valuable in their own right (Reeves, Herrington, and Oliver, 2002).

An Eclectic Approach

Experienced instructional designers frequently take an eclectic approach when designing and developing training programs. One learning theory and its related strategies may dominate a particular course, but other theories and strategies may also be used within that same course. This diverse and flexible approach is usually more sensitive to the type and variety of content being taught, the learners, the context, and the results desired.

Figure 10-5 shows the connection among an instructional system design (in this case ADDIE), the three leading learning theories, learning strategies, and course design. The design provides the plan; the learning theories help instructional designers come up with plausible instructional strategies and tactics, which lead to course and lesson design.

Instructional designers and trainers can expand their approach to designing instruction by learning to pick and choose the strategies that work best for specific learning situations and goals. For example, in a course for information technology professionals called "Gathering User Requirements" the overall approach was constructivist. The first day of the course, however, was dedicated to writing and validating good user requirements. This portion of the training used a more behavioral approach of intensive practice and feedback relative to the writing and identification of good user requirements. The course then shifted to cognitive approaches throughout a two-and-a-half day simulation, including readings relevant to the simulation and just-in-time interactive lectures (which also included practice and feedback). Each morning learners received advanced organizers to clarify the mental schema for the day's learning experience. In addition, thought-provoking instructional games and JOLTS (for example, short experiences to help learners think outside of the box [Thiagarajan and Thiagarajan, 2000]) reinforced key processes and concepts.

Figure 10-5. ISD Models, Learning Theories, Strategies, and Lesson Design

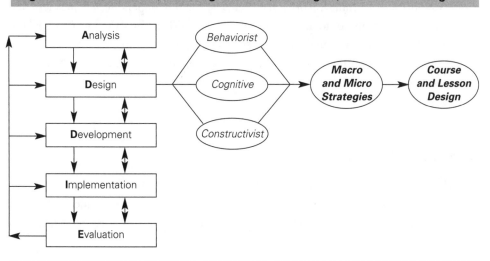

Crafting a design that used strategies and tactics from different learning theories ensured appropriate instruction while offering a variety of experiences that stimulated learners' full engagement in the training program.

Summary

Learning theories describe what's going on when people learn, which influences the ways that a learning designer approaches the design phase of ISD. Three learning theories are especially important in the context of learning design: behaviorism, cognitivism, and constructivism.

The behaviorist view focuses on observable behavior and suggests that learning occurs when a learner strengthens or weakens an association between a stimulus and a response. Thus, the theory influences learning design through the use of learning objectives, objective-based testing, and information chunking.

Cognitivism focuses on knowledge acquisition and is based on the idea that learning occurs when a learner places information in long-term memory. Learning designs that emphasize this theory consider how information is processed, stored, and retrieved in the mind, and frequently follow Gagné's nine events of instruction.

Finally, the constructivist view considers learning to be knowledge construction and is based on the idea that learning occurs when a learner actively constructs a knowledge representation in working memory. Thus, a constructivist learning design stresses activities that will enable learners to discover knowledge for themselves.

However, all three learning theories have their strengths, depending on business and learner needs, which argues for an eclectic approach to instructional design. This is where instructional design professionals select best practices from all three theories; apply the best strategies based on the desired results; and create learning experiences that effectively meet organizational, business, and individual needs.

∽

About the Author

Darryl L. Sink, EdD, is president of Darryl L. Sink & Associates (DSA). DSA has 26 years of experience designing and developing great learning experiences. His firm specializes in learning and performance consulting and custom training design and development.

His graduate work was at Indiana University, Bloomington, Indiana, where he specialized in instructional systems design and educational psychology.

He is the author of six comprehensive guides to instructional design and development that are used with DSA's workshops to provide fundamental instructional design training and processes. These processes have been adopted and are being used by many *Fortune 500* companies, public institutions, and nonprofit organizations.

He is a contributing author to the International Society of Performance Improvement's (ISPI) *Handbook of Human Performance Technology*. He is the recipient of ISPI's Professional Service Award and was three times awarded the Outstanding Instructional Product of the Year Award by ISPI.

References

Bloom, Benjamin. 1968. *Learning for mastery.* Los Angeles: The Center for the Study of Evaluation of Instructional Programs, University of California.

Clark, Richard E. 1999. The cognitive sciences and human performance technology. 2d ed. In *Handbook of human performance technology,* eds., H.D. Stolovitch and E.J. Keeps. Silver Spring, MD: ISPI.

Davis, James R., and Adelaide B. Davis. 1998. *Effective training strategies.* San Francisco: Berrett-Koehler.

Dick, Walter, Lou Carey, and James O. Carey. 2005. *The systematic design of instruction.* 6th ed. Boston: Allyn & Bacon.

Driscoll, Marcy P. 2000. *Psychology of learning for instruction.* 2d ed. Boston: Allyn & Bacon.

Foshay, Wellesley R., Kenneth H. Silber, and Michael Stelnicki. 2003. *Writing training materials that work.* San Francisco: Jossey-Bass/Pfeiffer.

Gagné, Robert M. 1997. Mastery learning and instructional design. *Performance Improvement Quarterly* 10(1): 8-19.

Gagné, Robert M., Walter W. Wager, Katharine C. Golas, and John M. Keller. 2005. *Principles of instructional design.* 5th ed. Belmont, CA: Thomson/Wadsworth.

Gustafson, Kent L., and Robert M. Branch. 1997. *Survey of instructional development models.* 3d ed. Syracuse, NY: ERIC Clearinghouse on Information and Technology.

Jonassen, David. 1999. Designing constructivist learning environments. In *Instructional-design theories and models: A new paradigm of instructional theory, Volume II,* ed., C.M. Reigeluth. Mahwah, NJ: Lawrence Erlbaum Associates.

Mayer, Richard E. 1999. Designing instruction for constructivist learning. In *Instructional-design theories and models: A new paradigm of instructional theory, Volume II,* ed., C.M. Reigeluth. Mahwah, NJ: Lawrence Erlbaum Associates.

Molenda, Michael, and Elizabeth Boling. 2007. Creating. In *Educational technology: A definition with commentary*, eds., A. Januszewski and M. Molenda. Mahwah, NJ: Lawrence Erlbaum Associates.

Molenda, Michael, and James D. Russell. 2005. Instruction as an intervention. In *Handbook of human performance technology*, eds., H.D. Stolovitch and E.J. Keeps. 3d ed. San Francisco: John Wiley & Sons.

Nelson, Laurie M. 1999. Collaborative problem solving. In *Instructional-design theories and models: A new paradigm of instructional theory, Volume II*, ed., C.M. Reigeluth. Mahwah, NJ: Lawrence Erlbaum Associates.

Reeves, Thomas C., Jan Herrington, and Ron Oliver. 2002. *Authentic activities and online learning*. Milperra, Australia: HERSDA.

Schank, Roger C., Tamara R. Berman, and Kimberli A. MacPherson. 1999. Learning by doing. In *Instructional-design theories and models: A new paradigm of instructional theory, Volume II*, ed., C.M. Reigeluth. Mahwah, NJ: Lawrence Erlbaum Associates.

Sink, Darryl L. 2002. ISD faster better easier. *Performance Improvement* 41(7): 16-22.

Thiagarajan, Sivasailam, and Raja Thiagarajan. 2000. *Interactive strategies for improving performance: 10 powerful tools*. Bloomington, IN: Workshops by Thiagi.

For Further Reading

Duffy, Thomas M., and David H. Jonassen, eds. 1992. *Constructivism and the technology of instruction: A conversation*. Hillsdale, NJ: Lawrence Erlbaum Associates.

Gagné, Robert M., and Karen L. Medsker. 1996. *The conditions of learning: Training applications*. Fort Worth, TX: Harcourt Brace.

Chapter 11

The Learner: What We Need to Know

Ann Herrmann-Nehdi

In This Chapter

- ➢ Understand how learners learn—learning styles and more
- ➢ Learn what's important about the brain in learning
- ➢ Apply learning styles and brain dominance to create effective learning

---

We have all experienced it—a frustrated learner who just doesn't seem to get it the way we or others seem to. Learning styles have emerged during the last 30 years as a path to diagnose and then design to meet the needs of our diverse learning populations. In addition, there continues to be a quest for greater return-on-investment (ROI). We have more learners and less time to get what they need to learn to them. It is time to redefine ROI as return-on-intelligence rather than just return-on-investment. For learners, this means getting as much out of their own brains as they can. For the organization, this means leveraging its learning power to build greater brain power, our most critical asset in the knowledge worker economy. To achieve return-on-intelligence, we must start by understanding and diagnosing the unique way people learn.

❧ **Ned Herrmann** ❧

Ned Herrmann was one of the first to study the human brain within the context of business—specifically, how individuals' thinking preferences affect the way they work, learn, and communicate. Herrmann developed the Herrmann Whole Brain Model, which concluded that the brain has four distinct types of thinking: rational, practical, feeling, and experimental.

However, each person tends to favor one type of thinking over the others. To gauge what type of thinking an individual favors and to what degree, Herrmann developed the Herrmann Brain Dominance Instrument in 1979. By gaining an understanding of their preferred thinking styles, individuals can be motivated to improve in the other styles.

In 1988, Herrmann published The Creative Brain, *which traced the historical and scientific background for his ideas. Later he expanded his ideas and showed how to apply them in* The Whole Brain Business Book *(1996).*

A recent Google search on the web found a range of references to inventories measuring learning styles from 13 primary models (Coffield, et al., 2004) to more than 80. Learning, personality, cognitive, and thinking styles are often intermixed and can be difficult to differentiate. How can workplace performance practitioners best use this information? What do you need to know? Why should you care? How can you best use it?

The best way to get started is to review the extensive ongoing research on the brain and our learning process. This chapter will highlight research on thinking and learning styles and how you can practically apply what we know about styles to workplace learning and performance challenges. Adopting and applying this research will improve results—return-on-intelligence—across the board for you, for your learners, and for your organization.

It's All in Our Heads

Anyone who has ever attempted to impart knowledge, teach, train, coach, or influence has experienced the different ways each individual takes in, processes, and reacts to information. There continues to be great debate over which of these three—taking in, processing, or reacting—is most important and critical to learning effectiveness. The reality is that all three are important, but they affect our learners and learning designs in different ways.

Thirty years of research has focused on what the brain has to do with how a learner learns and how you can practically apply that understanding to improve the effectiveness of the learning experience. Understanding what is happening in the heads of learners is what is critical in helping them apply what they have learned to achieve greater results. This work started at General Electric more than 25 years ago, where Ned Herrmann, my father, then head of management education at Crotonville, sought to understand why some programs were so effective and others were not. It was clear that some learners walked away with the intended outcomes, skills, and competencies, whereas others left with other unintended takeaways, like fond memories of the evening tour of New York. Why was it that the same training program could have such dramatically different results for attendees?

The brain became the obvious place to search for understanding. GE sponsored the research that started with electroencephalography (EEG) testing and later grew into a brain-based model for thinking and learning. It was interesting to grow up in a household where dad wired me up to an EEG to see how my brain and those of my friends worked as part of his initial research. The 30 years of ongoing research has proven that a brain-based approach to understanding learning provides us with a set of practical principles we can apply to learning challenges. In addition, there are many other models, such as Gardner's (1993a, b) work on multiple intelligences; Dunn and Dunn's (1999) work on visual, auditory, tactile, and kinesthetic processing; Kolb's (1984) learning style theory; or Gregorc's (1984) mind styles, that all are related to the findings that emerge from a neurological basis. Other models are psychological constructs, including models like the Myers-Briggs Type Inventory (MBTI) and a multitude of behavioral models (for example, DiSC, social styles). Each model provides a slightly different lens through which we look at the learner based on the different premise of the research. The model I will refer to in this chapter was selected in a comprehensive study as one of the most applicable and valid for a discussion of learning styles (Coffield et al., 2004). The core application tools and principles hold true for all learning style approaches. All converge on the following critical themes that this chapter will explore about learners:

- The brain is the source of all of our learning, memory, and performance; it is not fully understood; and it is underused.
- Our brains evolve throughout the course of our lives as we develop our unique learning styles that affect the way we take in, make meaning of, and retain information.
- As workplace performance professionals, our preferred learning styles will influence how we look at, design, and deliver learning. We are often unaware of the learning styles of our learners, designing to our preferences or the mentality of the content.
- All groups of learners represent the diversity of learning styles. Effective learning is whole brained—designing, delivering, and evaluating the learning to best meet the varying needs of diverse learners.

Brain Basics: What You Need to Know About Your Learners' Brains

The brain is our primary learning muscle, and we need to learn how to develop, practice, and maintain it. Michael Merzenich (1989), an expert on the brain's ability to change (known as plasticity), stated it this way: "The brain was constructed to change." It is the single body organ that is the central processor of all our learning activities. Our neurological system is involved in all aspects of the learning process. It is important to note that each and every brain is as unique and different as your thumbprint. We build that print throughout the course of our lives, creating and fine tuning our own unique learning processes and styles.

Just consider your own experience throughout your personal learning history. It is probable you did much better in some subjects than in others; you responded more to some teaching methods and teachers than to others, and you retained some material for a significant length of time, whereas other material was retained for a short time or not at all. There is no doubt that you had a favorite subject, teacher or trainer, or learning experience. Think back to your favorite subject. What was your energy like? Often the subject was not the easiest, but often the most interesting and even the most challenging. This sense of "turn on," or preference, is an essential element of what we need to know about our learners. When we can successfully engage the learner in a way that sparks some degree of turn on in his or her brain, we increase the engagement, sense of reward, and retention of the learning. Think back to your least favorite subject. What was that like? How much energy was required for you to stay engaged and focused? Did the style and delivery of the teacher or trainer have anything to do with your challenge as a learner? What would it have been like to do an advanced degree in that field of study? Painful? Probably. Doable? Perhaps. Is it an ideal condition for learning?

We have all had a disconnect with a teacher or delivery system. I recall a class on statistics that used M&M's as the data to be analyzed. This engaged learners who would have normally checked out of the content and disengaged the learners who were naturally inclined to learn statistics in a more traditional format. Learner preferences affect the effectiveness of the learning outcome, and the delivery system of the information for learning can either help or exacerbate the situation. In recent years, we have observed that e-delivery of content is effective for some and ineffective for others. When we miss the connection with the learner, we all lose. As Sir Winston Churchill stated in a December 26, 1941, speech to the U.S. Congress: "I am always ready to learn, but I do not always like being taught."

The Power of Mental Maps

Our preferences act as a foundation for the cognitive or mental maps we create as we learn and help define where we connect and disconnect. Those mental maps are built from our experiences in life. As we mentally explore a new situation, our brains will go to our experience base looking for patterns and the mental maps we already have. Sometimes our maps are helpful and sometimes they are not. For instance, I recently rented a car in Germany and was given an electronic keyless fob (remote entry clicker) and headed off to find the car. My current vehicle has a keyless fob as well, so this felt familiar enough. All I needed to do was place the fob into the vehicle with me and the car should recognize us and start. As I got into the vehicle, I spotted a start button on the dashboard. Once buckled in, I pressed the button and nothing happened. I went to my mental map and thought I would try pressing down on the brake first, as I had experienced that in other vehicles. I then tried the clutch. Still no start. I tried to check the glove compartment, which remained locked until the car was started. Finally, with some embarrassment, I reluctantly asked a passerby if he knew how to start the vehicle. With a friendly smirk he hopped into the car, took the electronic key fob and inserted it into a small hole in the dashboard, pressed the clutch, then the start button, and the car started with a friendly roar. My mental map was not a good fit, even though I thought it was. I was challenged by some subtle differences in a system I was sure I knew already. My knowledge actually stopped me from looking around for other options and noticing a small arrow on the key fob, placed obviously to indicate the direction you would insert the fob into the dashboard, which might have been a good clue to a new way to starting a car. Most learning requires that we challenge our mental maps and form new connections in the brain. This takes energy and motivation. When we understand how our mental maps are working, we are better prepared to adapt.

Our maps lead the brain to fill in gaps we might initially see and then quickly move on, but often with incomplete information. This is helpful when the map matches the situation and provides us with great efficiency so we do not have to sit and think about how we start our car every day. However, this is critical to understand because all learners are constantly filling in the blanks unconsciously, based on their prior experience. Look at Figure 11-1 and read what you see.

Figure 11-1. What Do You See?

What did you see? Ice cream is good? Groups around the globe who have completed this exercise are 100 percent sure that is the phrase provided. However, when you reveal the entire phrase you see: JGF GPFAM JS CQQD. (Take a piece of paper and cover up the lower portion of the letters and you will see how this works.) Thus all of our experiences will preprogram what we see and how we think about or feel about a given topic or model. Years ago in a program for headmasters of large private schools in the southeastern region of the United States, a headmaster stood up during a segment when a metaphor for the brain was being described and declared: "Excuse me, I do not *do* metaphors." It was clear that this person was shutting down his own mental process because of a previous experience. Think of the times you do that as a learner. What happens to you when someone presents a four-box (two by two) model? Do you become interested? Do you check out? How about a math problem? What if someone asks you to draw or dance? Do you roll your eyes into the back of your head when asked to do a role play? When we engage learners in a learning process, we are asking them to challenge their previous assumptions and make new neural connections in their brains. As you look at your learning designs, ask yourself these critical questions about your learners:

- What mental maps will my learners have around this topic?
- How do I build off of their existing experience to enhance their learning?
- How do I provide novelty and new insights that will help them from getting stuck in their predictive mindset?
- How can I build in ways for this learner to make new connections rather than try to rewire the old connections (often easier and more interesting for the learner)?

Mirror, Mirror, How Do I Learn?

The good news is that we know the brain has awesome capacity, with an exponential number of possible synaptic connections occurring among its 10 billion neurons. Our neurons are specialized and have an important impact on how we learn and what we learn. I will describe more on specialization later in this chapter, but a specific type of neuron has recently been described as having a significant effect on our learning. This research also explains the bewildering phenomenon we have all experienced: the contagious yawn. When we find ourselves yawning away after a colleague yawns, or delighted when we stick out our tongue at a baby who immediately responds in kind, what is at work are our mirror neurons. Why does this happen? Common regions of the brain process both the production *and the perception* of a given movement. Simply put, when we are observing someone doing something, mirror neurons in our brains will actually fire as if we were ourselves engaging in that activity. Eminent neuroscientist Vilayanur S. Ramachandran (2000) has suggested the discovery of mirror neurons may be as powerful a framework for our understanding of teaching and learning as the discovery of DNA was for our understanding of genetics (Sylwester, 2002). Athletes have long used this to their advantage in their training, using modeling, observation, and visualization to improve their skills, most likely without really knowing the technical reason why it worked so well. When observing or visualizing a situation, our brain will actually replicate that experience as if it is happening to us. Even sports fans watching a sport they do not actually play will have their mirror neurons activated. Those *who do* play a sport, like tennis for example, will have a much stronger activation of mirror neurons when they observe a great serve, further enhancing the learning. From a learning perspective, mirror neurons can play an important role when the activity is related to a specific goal. This means that we should use every opportunity to model and visualize as a way to prime the brain. Keep in mind that the more expert the learner is in a given domain, the stronger the mirror neuron activation will be.

Memories and How to Keep Them

There are many who believe that memory is essential to learning and that indeed without memory, learning is not possible. One challenge is that our system for taking in information has some limitations. When we look at memory processing, everything we take in goes through the memory sieve—our working memory. Our working memory systems are, by design, easily distracted, overwhelmed, and bogged down by too much input. Current research indicates that we can only keep a maximum of four (previously defined as seven, plus or minus two) bits of information in our working memory at any given time (Cowan, 2001). We all currently suffer from the plethora of numbers and passwords, web addresses, acronyms, and other tidbits of information we need to somehow retain. Chunking that information allows the learner to retain more, but context will often drive how we can easily chunk it. If you try to remember the letter sequence CIAJFKFBI, a system may pop out more quickly to a person in government because he or she might easily recall it as two federal organizations, the CIA and the FBI, with a former president JFK in between. Acronyms often provide a permanent chunking mechanism when the actual name is not as important to recall. For instance, many do not know what LASER stands for: light amplification by stimulated emission of radiation. There are three ways you can facilitate learning for better retention: be selective and thoughtful about how much and how you present your information, chunk data in ways that are easy to remember, and use tools like information mapping to better display what your learners are reading.

Overall, this translates into a need to be clear about what critical learning points you need to convey, focusing the learners' energy on acquiring those and making sure you are providing multiple ways for the learners to access them. Keep in mind that every time we think about something, write it down, develop a metaphor or analogy, visualize it, observe it in action or practice it, speak about it or gain insight, all of these methods provide us *new connections* that help us engage and move the learning into long-term memory. This is called *rehearsal*, and you want to make sure you are providing sufficient rehearsal for your critical learning points. Use variety because learners will gravitate more to some forms of rehearsal than others based on their preferences, level of knowledge, and style (see Figure 11-2).

Stress Can Affect Memory

Do you remember how you felt when you were preparing for a test in school? What we know about the brain shows that the effect of stress on our ability to process information and retain information is very tangible. We all have experienced the advantages of some degree of tension in creating selective, focused attention and motivation. There is also, however, a tipping point at which the tension turns to counterproductive anxiety. As Daniel Goleman (2006) states in *Social Intelligence*, "We do best at moderate to challenging levels of stress, while the mind frazzles under extreme pressure...the more apathy or angst we feel, the worse we do, whether on a term paper or an office memo." Although emotions can highjack our ability to process and think, emotions also hardwire memory. I recall quite vividly exactly where I was, the temperature in the air, and the time of day when I first heard that President Kennedy was assassinated. Many have

Figure 11-2. Memory Strategies the Whole Brain Way

Study Memorization Mnemonics Logical associations	Visualization Creating metaphors Creative mnemonics Visual association
A "capture plan" Writing it down, lists Categorization techniques Time management techniques	Emotional engagement and associations Link to music Use of rhythm Sharing with another person

Source: Herrmann International, © 1982-2007. All rights reserved. Used with permission.

reported the same high level of memory for the moment they heard about the events of September 11, 2001, or the death of a loved one. The implication for our profession is to take a hard look at our learning environments. The balance is critical. A positive environment leads to better brain function. Goleman further describes how physicians work with greater speed and accuracy when their mood is boosted, in addition to providing more suggestions to their patients (Goleman, 2006). A positive, stimulating environment is critical to effective learning. Too much anxiety will have a negative impact and actually shut down the learner. Watch your own emotional state and look for ways you can provide the balance between boredom and anxiety in your programs. When in doubt, solicit feedback from participants about the environment and how it can be changed to make it more balanced. Participants are often coming from a very stressful environment already.

Much of the learning process is happening outside of the actual time we spend on learning. We all know of the old adage, "let me sleep on it." Research conducted by Steffen Gais and Jan Born (2004) determined that memories are consolidated and memory performance improved after volunteers were tested after a deep sleep. Use time between learning sessions to strategically aid in the consolidation of memory, giving people an opportunity to consolidate and hopefully better retain the learning.

Learning with Style

Everything we have learned about the brain, our behavior, and our modes of learning requires that we assume differences in our learners. As the Talmud states: "We do not see things as they are, we see things as we are." Our knowledge of the brain and its inherent uniqueness shows that each individual is a unique learner with learning experiences, preferences, and avoidances that will be different from those of other learners. This means that learning designs must somehow factor in the uniqueness of the individual learner. An immediate implication for the education and training profession is that our assumptions about learning take this into account, that our unique learning similarities and differences become part of the learning design and experience and are made visible. As a result, learning is no longer one dimensional but rather includes the notion of multiple intelligences as Howard Gardner's (1993a, b) work has demonstrated, so that the subject matter is understood by all the participants, not just those who are in alignment with the design, delivery, and teaching/training style or mode.

Consider a learner whose unique learning style, a result of her mental preferences, led her to prefer a highly structured learning design, including step-by-step instructions and built-in practice segments. Attending a program with a trainer who focused exclusively on providing a flexible discovery and had a strong distaste for step-by-step approaches, the learner was soon overheated with frustration, trying to figure out where he or she was and began checking out from the course. Has this ever happened to you? Experience with thousands of learners in workshops and programs clearly demonstrates that when such differences are made visible and are recognized by the teacher or trainer and the designer and then a whole-brained approach is used, it is highly beneficial to the individual learner and also to the entire learning group.

The concept of Whole Brain teaching and learning is based on our distribution of specialized modes throughout the brain system. The metaphoric model that has been developed from the initial EEG research at GE is divided into four separate quadrants—much like most of the learning style models that exist today—each one being different and equal in importance. For the purposes of this chapter, I will refer to the Herrmann model.

In the Whole Brain model (see Figure 11-3), the two left quadrants (A and B) are specialized in left-mode thinking processes: logical, analytical, quantitative, and fact-based modes are in the upper left A quadrant; the more planned, organized, detailed, and sequential mode is processed in the lower left B quadrant. In contrast, the two right quadrants (C and D) make up right-mode specialization: synthesizing, integrating, holistic, and intuitive modes are in the upper right D quadrant; the interpersonal, emotional, kinesthetic, and feeling modes are associated with the lower right C quadrant. In addition, the upper two quadrants represent more cognitive, intellectual modes (A and D). The lower two quadrants (B and C) represent the more visceral, emotional modes.

If you think of each of these quadrants as four different people learning how to use a new computer, PDA, or mobile device, imagine how each might approach the process. Person A would relish the technical aspects of the device, would be very comfortable with the mechanics, and would approach the challenge quite logically. Person B, however, would be ready and organized, expecting a process to follow, and enjoying specific steps as she progressed: turn on the device, proceed through the set-up wizard, and so forth. Person C would be thinking about the fun he will have; how he will be able to enjoy this to connect with his friends; and will often spend time talking out loud throughout the whole process, often preferring to do it with someone else. Person D would be looking at all of the cool features and trying them out spontaneously, and would not be too worried about the set-up procedures or instructions—she will figure that out later. Anyone trying to teach these individuals may have all four at any given time and certainly may prefer teaching one or more over the others. Fortunately, we are not limited to a one-quadrant perspective but are "hardwired to be whole." All of us have some degree of the four characters available to us.

Figure 11-3. Whole Brain Thinking Model

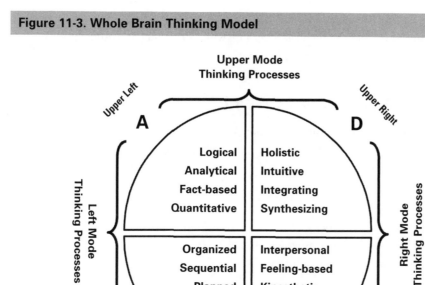

In fact, we all have connections that allow for direct interaction among these specialized areas, so we do have the bandwidth necessary to learn. Learning prompts interaction across this wiring. This also creates a sense of discomfort when we *don't know.* I invite participants to try writing their name with their nondominant hand. Try it! How does it feel? Responses often include uncomfortable, tiring, unpracticed, frustrating, and so forth. This is a terrific example of what is happening when we are engaging the brain in an area that is different and unusual. Does some discomfort mean we should not pursue this? Absolutely not. However, you want to maintain the balance between boredom and anxiety. This balance provides the energy required to make new neuronal connections. With motivation, preparation, time, and practice, the new connections will form and that feeling (which has actually been proven as a chemical reaction in the brain) of aha, insight, and accomplishment will eventually occur. The key message is not to "cave in" to the style of the individual learners but to plan around the challenges they present; learn the different languages they require; and design a whole-brained, multimodal experience. This will allow all learners to get what they need while stretching into other, less preferred but available modes their brain provides them.

What Does Age Have to Do With It?

Much has been written in recent years about generational style differences. As you design your learning, keep in mind the age groups you will be reaching. The following tips for each group may be helpful to consider:

Veterans (born 1922–1945)

- Give detailed directions
- Use clear language that is nonemotional
- Use organized and factual information.

Boomers (born 1945–1965)

- Let them know how to make a difference
- Focus on the future and challenges
- Present options
- Allow them to learn
- Try to build consensus.

Generation X (born 1965–1980)

- Share information on a regular basis
- Be straightforward, but use an informal style
- Allow for flexibility.

Millennials (born 1980–2000)

- Provide clear direction and share the whole story
- Discuss consequences
- Use humor
- Seek and provide them with regular feedback
- Use action words and challenge them at every opportunity.

Learning à la Mode

Most of us read at about 200–250 words per minute but think at speeds estimated of 350–500 words per minute. This is further complicated by the average speaking speed of

125 words per minute. This system design is set up to lose our learners' attention at any given moment. In addition, research has shown that your learner population will represent a diverse group of learners. Using the Herrmann Brain Dominance Instrument (HBDI), we have learned that the world, taken as a whole, represents an equal distribution across the four quadrants. We have also learned that most individuals are not singular in their preference. The data substantiate that everyone has access to all four modes. Only 7 percent of the global population under study strongly prefers one mode over the others. Less than 3 percent is whole brained in their preferences, preferring all four quadrants more or less equally. The balance, 90 percent, has dual or triple preferences across the model. We must plan for these differences. However, most learning design is reflective of either the mental tilt of the content itself, or the preferences of the designer, or both. How about your learning designs and programs? Where are your learners? Look over Figure 11-4 to identify which quadrants they fall into most frequently.

It is also useful to think about those students you think of as really smart. We all have different smarts—have you ever met someone who is socially dumb but quantitatively brilliant? Great at detail, but lousy at innovation? There are smarts all across the continuum as seen in Figure 11-5.

Figure 11-4. Preferred Learning Styles

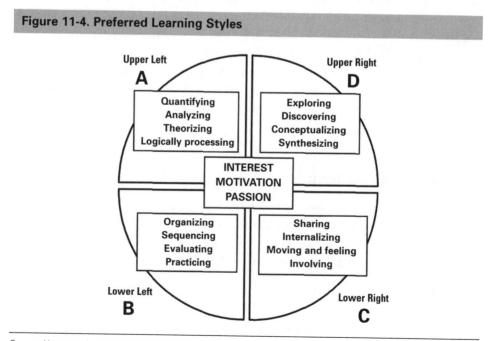

Figure 11-5. Smartness in the Four Brain Quadrants

Factual Intellectual Academic	Visual Street Artistic
Administrative Organizational Procedural	Communicative Social Emotional

Remember what it was like to be in a learning situation where you just didn't fit? It is pretty painful, and in today's world, learners do not have the patience or tolerance and will quickly check out. Stop and think about how you can be more effective in your design and delivery with those learners who do not fit your style. Start by looking at the programs you control and pick a learning program you think is really great. What styles does it appeal to most? Use the Learning by Design tool on the accompanying CD-ROM

 (Tool 11-1) to diagnose it and analyze which quadrants you tap into the most. Then look over Figure 11-6 to find ways you can further stretch the design to be more inclusive of multiple styles. Next, think of resources you have available to you, colleagues or other professionals who can bolster your ability to best reach those learners. What resources, people, tools, and activities can you use to make your learning more effective overall?

What About E-Learning?

An entire chapter could be devoted to the topic of what you need to know about the learner in e-deliverables and programs. Learners can easily check out of e-designs that do not engage the brain. The good news is that more and more e-deliverables today are part of some blended solution and provide multiple options for learners.

One key consideration is the potential challenges based on generational styles, habits, and comfort levels. Considering the age of the learner, veterans (born 1922-45) may be concerned about fraud, security issues, and overly technical applications; Boomers (born 1945-65) may prefer traditional modes of learning but are often open to technology-based

Figure 11-6. Instructional Strategies for Improved Learning Design

A	D
Lectures Facts Research findings Higher order reasoning Critical thinking Case studies, reference books, readings Use of experts Applied logic Metacognition Theories Technical approaches	Brainstorming Discovery learning Metaphors Active imagination Creativity Illustrations, pictures Simulations Mindmapping, synthesis Holistic exercises Storyboarding Visualization, mental pictures
B	**C**
Outlines Quizzes Practice Checklists, timelines Sequenced learning Policies, procedures Organization, summaries Who, what, why, when, where Exercises with steps Structured problem solving Clear examples, case studies, references	Cooperative and team learning Group discussions, chat Role playing, drama Body language Sharing personal experiences Listening and sharing ideas Writing, storytelling, and scenarios Auditory, musical, and rhythmic Physical, kinesthetic activities Interviews

Source: Herrmann International, © 1982-2007. All rights reserved. Used with permission.

approaches once they have developed a level of comfort with them; Generation X (born 1965-80) is accustomed to using a wide variety of media; and Millennials (born 1980-2000) prefer broad collaboration and expect e-deliverables.

As we look at the brain and e-learning, there is much we will learn in coming years. Four important elements will help make your e-learning more brain friendly:

- Human memory has two sources: pay attention to both visual and auditory inputs into memory—but do not overdo it.
- Only relevant, illustrative graphics really teach. Text and graphics need to be integrated and placed near each other to have full effect.

- Use job context in your e-lessons to provide "retrieval hooks." New knowledge needs to be retrieved from long-term memory back on the job and setting up that context will help set that up mentally.
- Learning is enhanced by challenge. Engaged learners' emotions are critical to retention and further engagement.

 On the CD-ROM, you have a practical e-learning checklist and locator map of e-learning activities (Tools 11-2 and 11-3) to aid in your design to make your e-learning programs more whole brained.

The Whole Is More than the Sum of the Parts

Our experience and data prove that different design and delivery approaches improve and facilitate the learning experience by tapping into each of these four specialized quadrants. As such, you need to provide options for learners. This must be done thoughtfully so you do not, by the same token, overwhelm learners by providing a deluge of modalities all streaming at them at once. Our preferences represent our default mode, but we often zig-zag around the model when we are learning, taking advantage of the array of processes we have available.

It is essential to consider the uniqueness of the learning group when designing programs, whether it is a classroom, coaching, e-learning, blended, or any kind of format. With the use of a diagnostic tool, it is possible to better design the learning program to meet that unique requirement. In most instances you will not have access to information on your learners, or at best you will have a guess, unless you are using an assessment tool. That means your most successful approach to your learning, design, and delivery is to create a Whole Brain experience for the learning group. A recent trip to Disney World reinforced that idea—the longest lines were for the experiences that were the most whole brained. Often the best websites appeal to different learning approaches in a very elegant way, not overwhelming the user. I believe good learning design is like a tapestry of these modalities that weaves through the learning, providing opportunities for learners to

- Understand how they learn
- Foresee and ramp up to what is coming (even if it is not in their preferred mode)
- Access what they need to continue the learning in a form they can learn from if the first pass did not work for them
- Have an opportunity to practice and reinforce what they have learned to strengthen the wiring and move it into long-term memory.

This tapestry approach creates a design that moves back and forth with techniques and activities from each of the four quadrants. Each critical learning point needs to be paraphrased in each mode at some point in the learning process. Considering how information is processed in different parts of the brain in your design and delivery helps ensure participants with different preferences and interests are able to learn effectively and consistently. Whether you are designing a learning point, module, workshop, or an entire course, look for ways to speak to the learners in all the styles they may bring to the table. This can also be applied to help nontrainers and learning professionals in the organization better reach their colleagues and associates when rolling out an initiative in response to an organizational challenge. Judy Strock, while at a large computer manufacturer, used this approach as part of a roll-out of a new performance management system that was delivered by call center managers. With some minimal investment, the managers were significantly more successful in getting the message across and encountered much less resistance to the proposed changes. Andrew Stagg at Bendigo Bank in Australia has used this approach to design its entire training curriculum with very positive results. So what can you do to more effectively apply what we know about the brain and our styles?

- Recognize the consequences of your preferences on how you think, learn, and teach.
- Understand that your learning community will always represent a very diverse thinking and learning group.
- Teach to the way the diverse, specialized brain likes and needs to learn, honoring the uniqueness of the learner's brain by learning to speak its multiple languages.
- Take the opportunity to use learning styles and brain-based methods to design and deliver learning.
- Remember that the learning environment and approach must not in any way dampen or diminish the motivation of the learner or his or her passion for the subject at hand.
- The proof exists that learning styles and brain-based theories of teaching and learning do improve the effectiveness of our learning under the right conditions. Learners should never feel like they are being trapped in one style or approach or put in a box.

What we know about the brain is that it can and will change. So for best results, use all styles regularly to ensure success!

About the Author

Ann Herrmann-Nehdi is CEO of Herrmann International, a 25-year-old global training and consulting company and publisher of the Herrmann Brain Dominance Instrument (HBDI), and has been featured in publications that include the *Harvard Business Review*. The company's Whole Brain Thinking model includes key applications: innovation, strategic thinking, problem solving, leadership, sales, teaching and learning, self-understanding, communication, and team/staff development. Clients being served around the globe include Cisco, IBM, Target, Novartis, PWC, MIT, and Wharton and Franklin Universities. She is active in the training industry, an ISA board member, and a featured writer and speaker for many training publications and training conferences, including ASTD. For more information, visit www.herrmanninternational.com.

References

Coffield, Frank, David Moseley, Elaine Hall, and Kathryn Ecclestone. 2004. *Learning styles and pedagogy in post-16 learning. A systematic and critical review.* London: Learning and Skills Research Centre, available at www.lsda.org.uk/files/PDF/1540.pdf.

Cowan, Nelson. 2001. Within fluid cognition: Fluid processing and fluid storage? *Behavioral and Brain Sciences* 24(1): 87-185.

Dunn, Rita, and Kenneth Dunn. 1999. *The complete guide to the learning styles inservice system.* Upper Saddle River, NJ: Prentice Hall.

Gais, Steffen, and Jan Born. 2004. Declarative memory consolidation: Mechanisms acting during human sleep. *Learning & memory* 11:679-685, available at http://www.learnmem.org/cgi/content/abstract/11/6/679.

Gardner, Howard. 1993a. *Multiple intelligences: New horizons.* New York: Basic Books.

Gardner, Howard. 1993b. *Multiple intelligences: The theory in practice.* New York: Basic Books.

Goleman, Daniel. 2006. *Social intelligence.* New York: Bantam.

Gregorc, Anthony F. 1984. *The mind styles model: Theory, principles, and applications.* Columbia, CT: Gregorc Associates.

Kolb, David A. 1984. *Experiential learning: Experience as the source of learning and development.* Upper Saddle River, NJ: Prentice Hall.

Merzenich, Michael. 1989. Holloway, Marguerite: "The mutable brain." *Scientific American* 289(3): 79.

Ramachandran, Vilayanur S. 2000. *The man with the phantom twin: Adventures in the neuroscience of the human brain.* New York: Dutton Adult.

Sylwester, Robert. 2002. Mirror neurons. *Connecting brain processes to school policies and practices,* available at www.brainconnection.com/content/181_1.

For Further Reading

Chapnick, Samantha, and Jimm Meloy. 2005. *Renaissance eLearning: Creating dramatic and unconventional learning experiences.* San Francisco: Pfeiffer.

Herrmann, Ned. 1996. *Whole brain business book.* San Francisco: McGraw Hill.

Herrmann, Ned. 1988. *Creative brain.* Lake Lure, NC: Brain Books.

Chapter 12

Instructional Design and Development

Karen Lawson

In This Chapter

- ➤ Learn to create learning objectives
- ➤ Learn to create a design matrix
- ➤ Understand how to create an instructional plan and clarify your methods

---

Instructional design and development is the structured process for creating the instructional means by which we help learners develop the knowledge, skills, and attitudes they need to succeed. Rooted in cognitive and behavioral psychology, the design and development of training programs is based on Benjamin Bloom's work in 1955 (Bloom and Krathwohl, 1956) in which he identified three learning domains: cognitive, affective, and psychomotor (behavioral). This taxonomy or classification of the processes of thinking and learning provides the framework for creating instructional strategies, materials, and activities used to improve individual workplace learning and performance.

Start with Learning Objectives

After the needs assessment has been completed and the data gathered, analyzed, and reported to the appropriate people, you are now ready to design the training program.

The first step in the design process is to write results-oriented learning objectives that align with business needs. Learning objectives or outcomes state what the learner will be able to do at the end of the training program or at the end of a phase of training. They describe the planned outcome of the training rather than the training process—results rather than procedure. Objectives serve as a type of contract. If participants know the program or session objectives from the beginning, they will know what they are expected to learn.

Why Set Objectives?

Objectives serve as the basis for the design and development of the program, that is, the instructional plan. They help the trainer focus clearly on the desired outcomes and determine what the participants need to know and do to meet those objectives. The concept of designing a training program is analogous to planning a trip: the objectives are the destination and the instructional plan is the itinerary. First decide where you want to go (objectives) and then decide how you are going to get there—how long the trip will take and what means of transportation you will use (methods and materials).

Objectives should be written from the participant's point of view, not the trainer's. The emphasis should not be on what you want to cover but what you want the participant to value, understand, or do with the subject, information, or skills after the training program is over.

Objectives are used also to measure success. Because they describe what the participant will be able to do at the end of the training, the objectives automatically become the standard against which success is measured.

Types of Objectives

Reflective of Bloom's taxonomy, objectives fall into three categories of learning: knowledge (cognitive), skill (behavioral), and attitude (affective).

Knowledge Development (Think). Knowledge development objectives have to address content or cognitive learning. They relate to critical thinking and the ability to demonstrate acquired knowledge, comprehend information, solve problems, analyze concepts, draw conclusions, make choices, and critique ideas.

Skill Development (Do). Objectives for skill development address behavior. These are much easier to identify and to determine if they have been met. They focus on a person being able to perform a task or procedure, use a tool, or demonstrate an action.

Attitude Development (Feel). Objectives that address attitude development address attitudes, values, or feelings. These objectives are appropriate when you want to change people's attitudes or increase their appreciation and awareness of or sensitivity to certain issues or ideas.

Components of an Objective

Writing objectives is not an easy task. The first challenge is to think of objectives from the participant's viewpoint, and the second challenge is to write them as performance outcomes. According to Robert Mager, world-renowned expert in instructional design, the easiest way to write an objective is to start by examining its three components: *performance*, *condition*, and *criteria* (Mager, 1984).

Performance. Ideally, the objective should describe behavior that can be observed, that is, what the participant will be able to *do* (not *know* or *understand*) as a result of the training. This is not always easy, particularly when dealing with attitude or affective objectives. When the objective is not observable, specify the consequences of the learned behavior that can be accepted as evidence of achievement. For example, for a diversity training program, an objective might be that the participants will "explore their feelings about workplace diversity issues."

The objective must use specific action words that are not subject to various interpretations. Words such as *understand, know,* and *learn,* for example, are not acceptable. You cannot observe those behaviors. For example, a performance component for a sales training objective might be that the participants will be able to "suggest other bank services to the customer." Tool 12-1 on the accompanying CD-ROM presents a chart of appropriate action verbs for each category of learning: knowledge, skill, and attitude.

Condition. The objective explains the circumstances under which the participant will be performing the activity. It also describes the equipment, supplies, and job aids that may or may not be used on the job. Furthermore, the objective describes the work setting and any information used to direct the action. For example, a statement such as "Using open-ended questions to identify customer needs, the participant will. . . " identifies the materials the participant will use to help him or her perform an action.

Criteria. Finally, the objective specifies the level or degree of proficiency that is necessary to perform the task or job successfully. It indicates the quality of the performance required

---

❧ **Robert F. Mager** ❧

Robert F. Mager made many significant contributions to the field of human perform-ance technology (HPT) and set the standard for measurable objectives. In his seminal 1962 book, Preparing Objectives for Programmed Instruction *(later retitled* Preparing Instructional Objectives*), he developed behavioral learning objectives with three key elements: what the worker must do (performance), the conditions under which the work must be done, and the standard, or criterion, that is considered acceptable performance.*

Another significant contribution Mager made was to develop criterion-referenced instruction (CRI). CRI is a framework around which training can be designed and deliv-ered, which includes identifying what needs to be learned, defining performance objectives and how to measure them, and developing learning based on the specified performance objectives.

Together with his colleague, Peter Pipe, Mager also developed a human performance equation that found performance (P) was a result of resources (r) plus consequences (c) plus skills and knowledge (s, k) plus the difficulty of the task (t), or $P = r + c + (s, k) + t$. Mager and Pipe also developed a human performance model that involves deter-mining the importance of the problem and the results of either solving or ignoring it. If the problem is deemed important, the next step is to determine if a skill deficiency is involved.

---

to achieve objectives. Thus, information in the criteria is used to evaluate performance. The objective may involve speed, accuracy with a margin of error, maximum of mistakes permitted, productivity level, or degree of excellence. Keep in mind that not all standards can be quantified. Following the sales example, the criteria might be to identify how many or which services the participant would tell the customer about. Putting it all together, the objective reads: "Using open-ended questions to identify the customer's needs (*condition*), the participant will suggest (*performance*) at least two additional products or services to every customer (*criterion*)."

In many cases, the trainer will need to rely on input from subject matter experts or super-visors to establish the criteria, especially if the objective relates to specific tasks that can be measured. This standard of performance is usually determined by the line manager and thus directly links the training to real-world projects and job expectations.

To gain a better understanding of the format and components of an objective, take a look at the following examples:

- "Using brochures and desk-top charts (condition), customer-service representatives will answer (performance) all customer questions about standard products and services (criteria)."
- "Employees will answer the telephone (performance) within three rings (criterion) using the standard identification message and greeting (condition)."
- "Following prescribed bank procedures (condition), employees will balance the teller windows (performance) each day within 20 minutes (criterion)."
- "Using PowerPoint software (condition), employees will create (performance) a 30-minute presentation that includes animation and sound (criteria)."
- "Managers will write (performance) a two-page, error-free request proposal (criteria) following the proposal format introduced in the business writing workshop (condition)."

At first, the practice of writing objectives may seem difficult, tedious, and time consuming. With practice, though, it will become easy. After you have determined your learning outcomes and written objectives, you are ready to design your training program.

Major Components of Design

As mentioned earlier, designing a training program is much like planning a trip. In both cases, you must ask yourself the whos, whats, whys, whens, and hows to build your case for going on the trip or planning your training session in the first place (see Table 12-1).

An instructional plan identifies what you are going to accomplish (*learning outcomes for the participants*), what will be said or presented (*content*), and how content will be

Table 12-1. Design Component Comparison

	Trip	Training Session
Who	Who is going?	Who should participate?
When	When are we going?	When will I conduct the training?
Where	Where are we going?	Where am I taking the learners (outcomes)?
Why	Why have we chosen this trip?	Why am I conducting this training?
What	What do we want to see and do?	What do I want the learners to know?
How	How will we get there?	How will I communicate the information or develop the learners' skills?

communicated (*methods and media*). The purpose of the initial design document is to organize one's thoughts and sequence the material and activities to create the optimum learning experience and meet learning outcomes.

After determining the objectives and before writing a detailed instructional plan, it is helpful to first design or lay out the course using a design matrix. This is truly the planning phase of the development process.

Creating a Design Matrix

A design matrix is used to visualize the course or session. It enables you to take a broad view of what you want to accomplish and visualize how to meet the learning outcomes. The design matrix provides a framework or skeleton for the course. (Tool 12-2 on the accompanying CD-ROM provides a blank design matrix for you to use.) You will then "put the meat on the bones" as you make decisions about methods and materials and prepare your instructional plan. The design matrix consists of four parts: duration, content or learning points, methods or activities, and materials or aids.

The design matrix is a rough sketch of the training session. Use it to identify and sequence content subtopics, estimate the amount of time devoted to each subtopic, consider the methods to communicate the content, and identify potential training materials and aids.

Determining Content

Content flows naturally from the learning outcomes or objectives. The important point to remember when developing or determining content is that you want to focus on what the participants need to know versus what's nice to know. This is particularly important when there are time constraints. Many trainers new to the profession with little or no experience in designing a training program often ask: "Where do I start?"

Researching the Topic

Unless you are a subject matter expert, start by researching the topic. Search the Internet and read articles to gather facts and other important information and, whenever possible, work with subject matter experts, especially for job-specific content. Approach the research process in much the same way you collected information for a research paper in school. In this case, however, be careful to collect information that is vital to the program, always keeping in mind your learning objectives and the need-to-know concept. In other words, don't go overboard collecting information. Read and distill the material. Make sure you cite sources of specific data and give credit for proprietary models. Include a full reference for every source cited, including the author's or editor's initials and last name, the title of the book (and article, if applicable), the city of publication, the name of the publisher, and the year of publication. Concentrate on recent sources—ones that have been published within the last three to five years.

Approaches to Organizing Training

After you have determined the major content and learning points for the training, determine the order in which you will present the content. This is the time to organize. You can use several methods, depending on the type of training and what you are trying to accomplish. Although there are no hard-and-fast rules for sequencing, the following guidelines may help you as you make decisions about the order of content and activities:

- Start with easy activities and move to more complex ones.
- Use less risky activities before those that some participants might find threatening.
- Vary your activities and methods in terms of length and format.
- Present easy concepts first.

Present the information in a way that will maximize the learning. You want the participants to retain the knowledge (*cognitive*), develop the skills (*behavioral*), or heighten their awareness (*affective*), and at the same time enjoy the learning experience.

Many of your designs will be variations of the behavior-modeling approach introduced in the 1970s by James Robinson and William Byham (Pescuric and Byham, 1996): content, positive role modeling, skill practice, feedback, and application on the job. There are, however, other ways to organize your session, depending on your intent. The following are other approaches to consider.

Sequential

Sequential designs present a step-by-step process leading to a conclusion. For example, in a sales-training seminar, the content might be presented in this order: (1) establishing rapport, (2) identifying customer needs, (3) matching product benefits to needs, (4) overcoming objections, and (5) closing the sale. With the approach, the subtopics follow the pattern of the process that serves as the training focus.

Job Order

This approach teaches tasks as they occur on the job. For example, a bank teller–training program might present subtopics for opening procedures in the following order: (1) getting cash drawer from vault, (2) verifying cash, (3) ordering cash, (4) logging on to the computer, and (5) preparing settlement sheet.

Priority

Skill or knowledge essential to the completion of a task is taught first as a prerequisite to the training that will follow. Returning to the teller-training example, trainees would need to have knowledge about how to log on to the computer before learning how to complete other transactions.

Topical

This approach addresses job knowledge in terms of topics rather than sequence of activity. Sales representatives, for example, would have to learn about the products before they could sell them; however, they would not have to learn about those products in any particular order.

Developing an Instructional Plan

The instructional plan is a detailed guide to delivering a training program. It serves several purposes:

- It forces you to organize material or content and present it in a logical manner.
- It identifies what materials are needed, learning points, and how content will be communicated.
- It helps you stay on track, make the points you want to make, and avoid spending too much time on a particular topic.
- In the long run, it saves time. After it is created, file it away until the next time you have to present this particular subject. Rather than reinventing the wheel, review the plan, assemble the necessary materials, and go.

Components of an Instructional Plan

An instructional plan consists of two parts: (1) the program overview and (2) the instructional guide.

Program Overview

The program overview details the components of the course or training session. It consists of the following:

1. **Title.** Make it brief but descriptive.
2. **Course Description.** Identify the overall goal of the course, along with a brief description of the content.
3. **Learning Outcomes.** List exactly what the participants should be able to do as a result of this program.

4. **Length.** Give the length of the course in terms of the number of sessions, number of hours in each session, frequency, time of day or day of week, if appropriate.

5. **Format or Methodology.** Describe the approach and methodology you will use, such as case studies, role plays, experiential learning activities, discussion, and so forth.

6. **Audience.** Identify who should attend (in terms of levels, job titles, or job duties) as well as group size.

7. **Participant Preparation.** If applicable, identify any pretraining assignments such as reading, completing assessment instruments, or meeting prerequisites.

8. **Instructional Materials and Aids**
   - *Document list:* Handouts, transparencies, textbooks, instruments, and so forth, along with the source
   - *Equipment list:* Computer, LCD projector, flipcharts, chalkboards, overhead projector, video equipment, whiteboards, and markers
   - *Media list:* Video titles (include name of producer and length of video), audio-tapes, or software.

9. **Reference List.** Identify sources used in putting the program together such as books and articles. This is particularly helpful if someone else delivering the program wants further information.

10. **Facility Check-Off List.** Create reminders or "to dos" such as table setup, water pitchers and glasses, refreshments, markers for flipchart, pointers, extension cords, and participant materials (folders, paper, pens, name tents).

Instructional Guide

Part 2, the instructional guide, is the real meat of the plan. It consists of the following four components: timeframes, content outline, training aids and materials, and trainer's notes. Let's take a look at each of these in detail.

Timeframes. Identify how much time each major content section takes. Indicate a time-frame for each by listing the number of minutes required (for example, 15 minutes) or express time as a digital clock (for example, 0:15).

Content Outline. This section outlines in detail the ideas, principles, concepts, or skills the participants are to learn. There are many possible formats; however, an outline is best as it helps you see relationships as well as the sequence of topics and subtopics. Although you do not have to worry about adhering religiously to the rules of outlining, it is important to observe some basic rules or guidelines:

- Main points and subpoints follow the order of general to specific.
- Subdivisions or subpoints must flow logically from each main point.

- Use the standard system of numerals, letters, and indentations as follows:
  I. Roman Numerals
     A. Capital Letters
        1. Arabic Numerals
           a. Small Letters
              (1) Arabic numerals in parentheses
                 (a) Small letters in parentheses
- If you have the heading *I*, you must have *II*. By the same token, if you have an *A*, you must have a *B*, and so forth. There cannot be just one point under a heading.

Training Aids and Materials. Training aids and materials include assessment instruments, videos or CD-ROMs, transparencies, slides, computer-generated visual aids, audiotapes, games, and evaluation tools. Include brief notations to cue you when to use a slide, an overhead projector, video, or handout. To make it easy for you (or someone else) to see at a glance what to do, you might use abbreviations or icons. Table 12-2 lists some ways to indicate your training aid without writing it out.

Trainer's Notes. In essence, your trainer's notes are your "stage directions" and methods. They tell you how you will communicate the content. They might include specific questions to ask the group or instructions for activities. Table 12-3 details some possible stage directions you might choose to use.

Table 12-2. Training Aid At-a-Glance

Training Aid	Abbreviation	Icon
Slide	SL	
Transparency	TR	
Workbook	WB	
Flipchart	FC	
Handout	HO	
Video/DVD	V/DVD	

Table 12-3. Sample "Stage Directions" for Conducting Your Activities

Distribute...	Write...
Conduct role play	Show video
Demonstrate...	Ask...
Discuss...	Instruct participants to...
Break into subgroups	Explain...

Instructional Methods

After you have determined the content and have some idea of the methods and materials you want to use, the next step is to come up with specific activities or structured experiences and specific training aids. Always keep your objectives and desired outcomes in mind as you design a training session.

Design Principles

The term *design* was used earlier to describe the process of planning or laying out the training session or program. Design also applies to the methods and materials chosen. Each technique or activity must be carefully thought out prior to developing the activity
 (see Tool 12-3 on the CD-ROM to help you determine when to use a specific instructional method). As you begin to develop your activities and materials, keep in mind the following three design principles:

- One design can accomplish two things at once. For example, an icebreaker can build group cohesiveness and assess group needs.
- The same design can often be used for different purposes.
- Published designs can often be modified to suit your own needs.

Instructional methods are the various means by which content or material is communicated. They include the use of assessment instruments; activities such as role plays, case studies, simulations, and other structured experiences; and training aids. Issues to consider when using some of the standard experiential methods are discussed below.

When selecting training methods, remember that there is no one best method; however, do try to use a combination of strategies. In selecting your methods of delivering instruction, consider the following:

- Subject matter
- Group's knowledge of the subject

- Training objectives
- Available time
- Group size
- Kind of participation desired
- Equipment available
- Type and size of room
- Cost
- Comfort zone of the trainer
- Comfort zone of the participants
- Participants' learning styles and perceptual modalities.

Table 12-4 lists the advantages and disadvantages of the various instructional methods.

Developing Materials

A critical issue in course development is the decision whether to use materials and activities already developed or to create your own. Many trainers, particularly those new to the field and often those faced with time and cost constraints, choose to use off-the-shelf training materials they integrate into their own designs.

Most trainers use a combination of developing their own, buying, customizing, and tailoring. For example, using published assessment instruments helps to maintain the integrity and professionalism of the program, providing a high degree of validity and reliability. Also, purchasing simulations is wise because of their complexity and their proven success. In general, customizing or tailoring published role plays and case studies to clients' specific situations is easier and less time consuming than writing your own.

Writing training materials is a time-consuming process. Not only do you have to create the participant materials, but you also have to create materials for yourself—or for another trainer, if applicable. Always keep your purpose in mind. Don't get carried away with including everything you know about a particular subject. It is also a good idea to have someone who is unfamiliar with the topic take a look at the materials to determine if they are understandable and user friendly.

Participant Materials

When creating participant materials, remember what you know about adult learners. First and foremost, keep in mind that you are dealing with a sophisticated audience with high expectations of the trainer, the course content, the methods used, and the materials they receive. The materials should be high quality, easy to read, and visually appealing. Also provide ample space on handouts and workbooks for participants to take notes. Workbook

Table 12-4. Instructional Methods

Method	Advantages	Disadvantages
Role Play Acting out real-life situations in a protected, low-risk environment	• Develops skills • Provides opportunity for participants to practice what they learn • Enables participants to gain insight into their own behavior	• Some participants are resistant. • Situations may be contrived. • Considerable planning is required.
Games An activity aligned to learning objectives and governed by rules entailing a competitive situation	• Promotes active learning • Provides immediate feedback • Boosts interest • Stimulates excitement • Increases learning • Improves retention	• It is time consuming. • It may lead to loss of facilitator control and is sometimes difficult to monitor. • It has some degree of risk.
Simulations Activity designed to reflect reality	• Promotes high level of motivation and participation • Provides immediate feedback • Approximates real-world environment	• It can be costly. • It is time consuming. • It requires significant planning and excellent facilitation skills. • It may require more than one facilitator.
Observation Watching others without directly participating; giving constructive feedback	• Generates interest and enthusiasm • Is less threatening than other methods • Promotes sharing of ideas and observations	• Focus could easily shift from learning factor to entertainment factor. • Demonstrators may not do adequate job. • A skilled facilitator is required.

(continued on next page)

Table 12-4. Instructional Methods (continued)

Method	Advantages	Disadvantages
Instruments Paper-and-pencil device used to gather information	• Helps to achieve participant buy-in and commitment because it is personalized • Helps focus on most appropriate material • Helps clarify theory, concepts, terminology	• Some participants might be fearful. • Participants might argue with data. • It is time consuming. • It requires a skilled facilitator. • In some cases, it leads to some participants feeling stereotyped or "pigeonholed."
Mental Imagery Exercises Visualize situations; mentally rehearse putting skills into action	• Enables everyone to participate • Stimulates thinking, imagination	• Some participants may be uncomfortable or impatient. • Monitoring participation is impossible.
Writing Tasks Worksheets in conjunction with materials; list and evaluate information	• Enables everyone to participate • Is particularly effective for shy participants	• Because it is an individual task, there is little or no interaction. • It is time consuming. • Some people are averse to writing.
Lecturettes Short, structured, one-way communication from trainer to participants	• Enables trainer to control what material is covered • Saves time	• Participants are put in a passive mode. • It may be boring to participants. • It uses one-way communication.
Small Group Discussions Small groups formed from larger group; composed of five to seven individuals; assigned to discuss a certain topic within certain time limit	• Increases participation • Creates risk-free environment • Stimulates thinking • Draws on knowledge and experience of all group members • Helps participants to assess their understanding of material	• One participant might dominate. • No guarantee that all will participate; some may choose to remain in a passive role. • It is easy for group to get "off track." • It is time consuming.

Method	Advantages	Disadvantages
Case Studies Written description of a problem or situation trainees might be faced with on the job; working in small groups, trainees read and discuss the case to determine the pertinent facts, identify problem, suggest alternative solutions, and agree on a final solution	• Allows participants to discover learning points by themselves • Enables participants to apply new knowledge to specific situations • Stimulates discussion and participation • Provides immediate feedback to recipients	• Situations may be contrived. • There is no opportunity to solve a real problem. • It can cause frustration because there is no one "right" answer. • It is time consuming.
Task Exercises or Activities Participants are divided into small groups of five to seven and work on a specific task or activity; often present results to the total group	• Stimulates thinking • Promotes group interaction	• It is time consuming. • It is difficult to keep groups on track.

Source: Lawson (2006). Used with permission.

materials should be presented in "chunks" so that the participants can quickly and easily digest the information. To make participant materials even more useful and meaningful, include specific work-related examples. Create memory aids (called mnemonic devices) such as rhymes, acronyms, or pegging (associating words with images) to help people remember lists or important points. Create models or flow charts to present processes and procedures. Participant materials also include other ancillary pieces and job aids that help reinforce the learning. These take-away pieces may include checklists; pocket-size reminder cards that list key points; computer screen savers; or CD-ROMs that could contain templates, forms, and checklists referenced or used in the session.

Trainer Materials

Trainer materials include the detailed instructional plan; master copies of the slides or computer screens and participant materials; background reading; and copies of the leader's guides for videos, games, and other activities. In some cases, you may want to include an actual script that would tell the person who delivers the training exactly what to say. This may be necessary if someone other than the designer or developer is going to conduct the training session. My personal philosophy and approach is that you prescribe what the trainer is to address or cover but the actual wording is left to the trainer. The amount of detail in the trainer's guide depends on several factors:

- Who is going to use it
- The experience level of the trainer(s)
- The budget
- Amount of detail required by the key decision maker.

Regardless of how elaborate the finished product needs to be, it should contain these basic components:

- Table of contents
- Introductory material providing background information
- Presentation guide that includes facilitation tips
- Instructional plan
- Master copies of handouts, participant workbook, and transparencies
- List of materials
- Resources.

Once the program has been designed and developed, complete with methods, participant materials, and trainer instructional guides, then it's show time! Just as the successful performance of a stage play depends on a carefully thought-out and well-written script, the delivery of an effective training program depends on the craft of instructional design and development. Training, however, is not an event—it is a process, one that involves thoughtful preparation, rigorous adherence to adult learning principles and practices, and a commitment to creating a rich learning experience that gives participants the knowledge and skills they need to meet the challenges of today's increasingly complex work environment.

∽⑤

About the Author

Karen Lawson, president of Lawson Consulting Group, is a consultant, executive coach, professional speaker, and author of 10 books. Specializing in management and organization development, she works with organizations that want to grow great leaders to outperform the competition. She conducts seminars on leadership, team development, communications, and quality service. Lawson is an adjunct professor in the International MBA program at Arcadia University in Philadelphia, Pennsylvania. She received her PhD in Adult and Organization Development from Temple University and is one of about 400 people worldwide to have earned the Certified Speaking Professional (CSP) designation awarded by the 4,000-member National Speakers Association.

References

Bloom, Benjamin S., and David R. Krathwohl. 1956. *Taxonomy of educational objectives: The classification of educational goals, by a committee of college and university examiners. Handbook I: Cognitive domain.* New York: Longmans.

Lawson, Karen. 2006. *The trainer's handbook.* 2d ed. San Francisco: Pfeiffer.

Mager, Robert F. 1984. *Preparing instructional objectives.* Rev. 2d ed. Belmont, CA: David S. Lake Publishers.

Pescuric, Alice, and William C. Byham. 1996, July. The new look of behavior modeling. *Training & Development* 50: 24-30.

For Further Reading

Anderson, Lorin W., and David R. Krathwohl, eds. 2001. *A taxonomy for learning, teaching, and assessing—A revision of Bloom's taxonomy of educational objectives.* New York: Longman.

Biech, Elaine. 2005. *Training for dummies.* Hoboken, NJ: John Wiley & Sons.

Mager, Robert. 1988. *Making instruction work.* Belmont, CA: David S. Lake Publishers.

Piskurich, George M. 2000. *Rapid instructional design: Learning ID fast and right.* San Francisco: Pfeiffer.

Piskurich, George M., Peter Beckschi, and Brandon Hall, eds. 2000. *The ASTD handbook of training design and delivery.* New York: McGraw-Hill.

Rothwell, William, and H.C. Kazanas. 2003. *Mastering the instructional design process.* 3d ed. San Francisco: Pfeiffer.

Best Practices in Online Course Development

Michael W. Allen

In This Chapter

➤ Set the right e-learning target to ensure success

➤ Take advantage of individualization

➤ Create meaningful, memorable, and motivational e-learning experiences

---

Although many instructional design principles are valid across all instructional media, online learning in the workplace presents new opportunities but also has limitations that need to be recognized. Additionally, developing online courses is a significant undertaking that demands not only excellence in design and a command of technology but also the support of many stakeholders with different perspectives and divergent responsibilities. This chapter reviews design principles that can lead e-learning development to success in the workplace and also reviews procedures that help break down bureaucratic barriers to win project support.

The opportunities new technologies provide aren't always obvious. It can take years, sometimes even generations, to understand what a new technology enables, just as it can take some time to recognize the dark side of otherwise beneficial technologies (like television, for example). Our vision can be blurred by traditional thinking, media, superstition, and fears. As long as we thought of robotics as mechanical humanoids, we weren't thinking of noise-canceling hearing aids, aviation auto-pilots, mobile music players, or laptop computers. As long as we thought of e-learning as an automated form of traditional classroom instruction, we weren't thinking of collaborative learning communities, supercharged explorations, simulations, or even personalized practice.

Conjure up a vision of a robot at the front of a classroom, and you might shudder. Rightly, you should. Many have worried the advent of online learning would allow impersonal, insensitive characteristics to dominate, if not eradicate, kindhearted nurturing of new skills and insights. And, unfortunately, although online learning has no visual semblance to a robot, it often exhibits inflexibility, insensitivity, and frustrating demands for conformity.

We've learned how to use computing technology for many purposes, especially after freeing our focus from replicating traditional instructor-led activities. Robots used in manufacturing plants have much of their unique value precisely because they differ from the physiology of humans. They are stronger, faster, and more precise. Computers similarly provide some unique instructional possibilities because of the very ways they differ from human teachers. They can precisely remember attributes, accomplishments, and difficulties of each learner. They are fair and unbiased, with limitless patience. They can reveal the results of each learner's choices and actions so that learners can explicitly see consequences and learn to evaluate alternative behaviors themselves. And computers can do much, much more in the process of developing skills and successful behavior patterns.

Setting the Right Target

It's important to be clear about the target. Learning in the workplace is all about success, and *success comes from doing the right thing at the right time*. Success does not come from just knowing what to do. The customer service representative, the doctor, the salesperson, and the truck driver all fail if they decline or neglect to do the right things, regardless of what they know. Some failures are disastrous, and although others may be minor infractions, they can add up to enormous costs and lost opportunities for organizations.

The target is success. It can be individual success. It can be individual *and* organizational success. But the target can't be organizational success without individual success, because organizational success is achieved by its constituents doing the right things at the right times.

Why is this assertion important? E-learning in the workplace is an expense not only because of the cost to provide instructional software (whether purchased or custom developed), the network, and computer hardware, but also because of employee time diverted from performing other services. Organizations cannot afford to provide e-learning if it just consumes employee time and fails to result in behavioral success. It's critically important to have the target of performance success clearly in mind because we design learning events differently if they are focused on performance outcomes than if they are focused on acquiring knowledge.

Best Practices

Best practices in online learning today are no longer focused on replicating instructor-led classroom experiences, although much effort has, unfortunately, been invested in attempts to do so. Rather, we now look to the unique capabilities of online systems to produce performance improvements while remaining mindful of their limitations. Computers don't recognize frowns, tears, grins, frustrations, and euphoric discoveries of learners, for example, but they can tell stories enhanced with music and special graphic effects. They can construct a learning problem that is at the optimal level of difficulty for a single learner and do it on the fly with nary a detectable pause as the learner moves from one problem to the next.

Computing and communications have essentially become one, creating opportunities for learners to communicate with each other and with instructors both synchronously and asynchronously, personally, publicly, and anonymously. Computers as instructors have infinite patience, total lack of bias, and the ability to flawlessly recall every learner's accomplishments and tendencies to err. With all this capability, a very wide range of instructional approaches can be supported, but not all will be successful.

Some of the attributes well-designed e-learning can have are listed together with their advantages in Table 13-1. These attributes are readily attained through skilled design and deployment and deliver valuable benefits.

Budget Versus Investment

Few would argue today that e-learning doesn't have big advantages in both reduced delivery cost and reduced learning time. However attainable, these are appropriate goals only if the effect is also sufficient to meet performance goals. Reducing training costs can actually increase mentoring and supervisory costs, product returns, and unmanageable customer complaints. In other words, damages from ineffective e-learning can easily increase overall costs. More than wiping out savings, poor e-learning can create unmanageable, enterprise-threatening expenses.

Table 13-1. Attributes and Benefits of E-Learning

Attribute	Benefit
Shorter learning time, often much shorter	• Less time away from productive work • Lower training costs
Adapts to learner needs (i.e., learning mastery is fixed but individual learning times may vary)	• Minimized time away from productive work (people return to work as quickly as individually able) • No waiting for those needing extra time • Extra attention for those needing more help
Actively involves learners; frequent activity	• In-depth learning experiences for each learner, not just for selected learners or those volunteering
Ensures learning	• No sliding by. Each learner must achieve and demonstrate competency.
Generates positive learner attitudes (When done well, learners often rate e-learning activities preferable over alternatives.)	• More enthusiastic participation • More receptivity • Greater likelihood learning will be applied to on-the-job performance
Provides consistent quality	• E-learning doesn't have bad hair days, headaches, or late nights out.
Allows instant, worldwide updates	• Through networked services, corrections, improvements, and new information can be made available to all learners instantly.
Is available 24/7/365	• Learning can start any day employees are hired or immediately upon assignment to new responsibilities. • Learning can be worked in and around higher priority activities. • Learner-managed schedules allow learners to work late into the night, in short sessions distributed throughout the day, or in long blocks of time. Whatever is best.
Is patient and treats all learners objectively and fairly	• Same options and same performance criteria for all learners • Blind to racial, cultural, gender differences • Offers no more or less learning support to any individual

Attribute	Benefit
Is highly amenable to systematic improvement	• Easily provides data necessary for evaluating each and every component
Saves money through low-cost delivery (no or minimized travel, fewer or even no instructors, automated administration, no classrooms, supplies, whiteboards, etc.)	• Even taking full account of development costs, e-learning has a big advantage of cost savings.
Allows options for more in-depth study or review whenever needed	• Support for learners with special interests or needs goes beyond the bounds of classes. • Material used for instruction can be accessed in well-designed applications for later use as reference material.

Training budgets are never unlimited and almost never commensurate with the potential business value an effective learning program can have. If a program can reduce costs or increase profits by a million dollars annually, would a $500,000, one-time development budget be too much? It would seem like a reasonable investment just from the financial perspective, but few organizations opt for it. Today's best practices are therefore a compromise between what we would see as ideal and what is deemed an acceptable expense by someone. To that end, e-learning best practices address economical ways to make every minute spent by learners a productive one, and this requires learner-centric design.

Learner-Centric Design

Although it's easy to focus on the content, making every learning minute count requires focusing instead on the successful behaviors each learner needs to acquire and the experiences each learner needs to acquire them. Designers produce quite different e-learning when they focus on developing behavioral skills and the desire to perform them than they do when they focus simply on a complete and orderly presentation of the content. Although designers have to fold appropriate content into learning experiences, learner-centric design focuses on individualization and making learning events meaningful, memorable, and motivational.

Individualization of Instruction

Research by pioneers in e-learning focused quite clearly on one of the primary strengths and unique capabilities of computers for assisting learning: individualization. By individualization we mean the optimal accommodation of differences that exist among learners, such as ability, readiness, and speed. There is actually a broad range of differences that affect what, how, and when we learn best, ranging from reading ability to need for social interactions, response to challenges, and need for control.

Online delivery of instruction provides a great range of pedagogical opportunities and ways of accommodating individual differences. Some take little special instructional design work at all. For example, e-learners can naturally work at their own speed without feeling pressured to keep up with or be delayed by others. Rapid readers and quick learners don't have to wait for other learners to catch up. Similarly, slower learners can take the time they need. Focus remains on learning rather than avoiding embarrassment or observing the progress of others.

Of course, books accommodate differences in speed too, but they have only a facile ability to assess learner progress and evoke remediation, all of which can be subverted easily by the learner. In contrast, online courses can assess learner abilities at the best times for each learner, if not continuously. They can evoke remediation both directly, by initiating appropriate learning events or alerting the instructor of the need, and indirectly, by providing learners easy access to additional materials, exercises, and aids.

Individualization can make learning experiences far more enjoyable and effective. It can avoid wasted time and increase engagement to the levels necessary to keep learners at task until performance goals have been achieved. But individualization comes at an expense. Although research on individualization has been of major interest in university labs since the first applications of technology to learning, it's rare to find corporate training departments undertaking the cost of developing alternate instruction to accommodate individual differences. Fortunately, there are many ways to individualize, and some are much less costly than developing multiple treatments of the same content. One technique is the bedrock of current design. For lack of a better name, I'll call it *challenge and rescue* and contrast it with the unfortunately commonplace content-centric design.

Content-Centric Design

Content-centric design is the antithesis of individualization. It's a logical but hapless design approach. Putting content front and center, as content-centric design does (see Figure 13-1), presupposes that learners will appreciate whatever is before them, regardless of its relevance to their needs or interests. Adding navigation helps make the content accessible and provides some often appreciated learner control, and a little interactivity may help overcome learning doldrums. These are common attempts to dress up content-centric designs and make them seem more interactive. But these elements don't magically turn content into powerful learning experiences. It's still pretty much a broadcast model where all learners receive the same content, ready or not.

Figure 13-1. Content-Centric Design

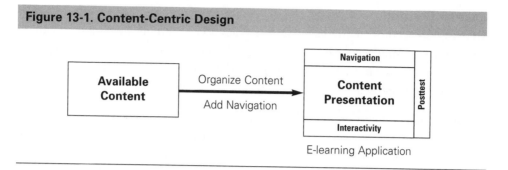

E-learning Application

Learner-Centric Design

Learner-centric designers focus initially on needed outcomes, or more specifically, on the behaviors successful learners will exhibit. Working backward, designers then determine what practice exercises would develop and demonstrate performance proficiency. If not all learners in the target population can be expected to succeed with these exercises that would immediately precede successful on-the-job performance, another set of exercises is devised as preparatory work for them. Once again, if not all learners could reasonably enter and succeed at this point, more precedent exercises are devised until a sufficient range of exercises is defined to match the variance anticipated in the target audience.

When looking at content from the perspective of learner-centric design, the question to ask of each element is, Will this piece of content help learners achieve proficiency? If so, it should be made ready in feedback messages and performance aids that learners can retrieve (see Figure 13-2). With typical budgetary and time constraints, e-learning projects are often further challenged with content overflow. Although there are always advocates for every scrap of content, content must be trimmed down and put in its place.

Figure 13-2. Learner-Centric Design

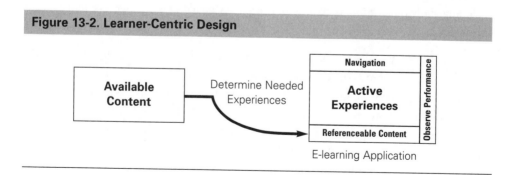

E-learning Application

Learner Control

Here's where learner control leads to an important layer of individualization. Learners like to browse through course materials to quickly get a sense of how much material is in front of them, what it looks like, where unusual elements lie, and so forth. A quick perusal helps them set a strategy and determine their options.

E-learning applications can, unfortunately, prohibit such perusal and confine learners to a sequence that may or may not have a revealed length, breakpoints, resources, review options, and so on. Cloaking content organization, length, and options prevents learners from determining how the learning application will fit their available time, their interest level, their goals, and preferred learning strategies. Whether or not their chosen strategy would be optimal is often a minor point, because feeling constrained and victimized, most learners set their sights on finding the earliest possible escape.

Although learner control can be a feature of both content-centric design (where it is greatly appreciated as an escape tool) and learner-centric design, it takes on particular power in challenge and rescue.

Challenge and Rescue

If no or little learning is needed, then simple access to information is sufficient. There's nothing wrong with page-turning applications if they're good at getting readers to the right page and the right page enables successful performance. Such solutions, however, shouldn't be confused with e-learning and are more appropriately classified as performance support aids. They can be enormously cost-effective, but when used where learning and skill development are needed, they are a mistake with costly consequences.

When significant learning is necessary to achieve performance, we're talking about learning *experiences* rather than merely presenting information. And here, the simplest and often most cost-effective approach that draws on many of e-learning's unique capabilities including individualization is to put performance challenges to learners and provide increasing or decreasing rescue options as their abilities require (see Figure 13-3).

Designers typically make a variety of rescue aids available to learners to adapt to varying individual needs. Aids include suggestions of what to try first, demonstrations, walk-throughs, and procedural guides or checklists. If the learner fails even with the use of explicit aids, a simpler challenge can be taken up to adapt to the lower level of learner readiness than was expected. If the learner succeeds without use of aids, a more advanced challenge is presented. Finally, if the learner succeeds with use of aids, the same or a similar level of challenge is presented so that the learner can demonstrate

Figure 13-3. Challenge and Rescue

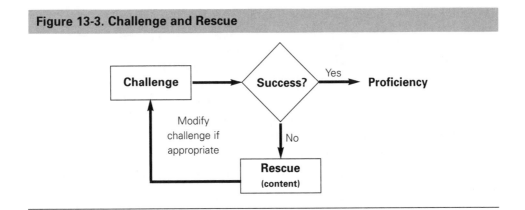

competency without use of aids, build confidence, and practice before going on to a higher level of challenge.

The challenge and rescue design provides a foundation that works well across a broad spectrum of learning needs. The design can become very sophisticated through fine tuning of rescue options made available or denied at certain points and through calibrating the levels and types of challenges that follow. Perhaps most notably, it is successful in simple, basic forms and manageable by somewhat inexperienced instructional designers. Finally, as we'll see below, it is also an excellent basis for achieving the three Ms—meaningful, memorable, and motivational learning experiences (Allen, 2003, 2007).

Meaningful Learning Experiences

Learning events that aren't meaningful to learners are a waste of time. Reading a book, attending a class, or participating in e-learning that doesn't make sense provides little benefit. Simply moving content to e-learning delivery doesn't somehow make it possible to learn things that don't make sense.

It's very easy for subject matter experts (SMEs) to make poor assumptions about what will make sense to learners and what will interest them. The paradox of expertise tells us, in fact, that the more expert one becomes in a subject, the less able one is to think like a novice and to communicate in terms understandable to novices. Experienced designers don't judge meaningfulness based on personal review, SME assumptions, or the assurances of the learners' supervisors. They verify content meaningfulness with representatives of the target audience before proceeding with detailed design and development.

Successful design techniques to ensure learning events are meaningful to each learner include:

- Using a context that relates to the learner's current situation or a situation and responsibility that learners expect to encounter
- Creating a compelling interest story that builds on a developed context and allows learners to select tasks of importance and relevance to them
- Basing each module or segment of instruction on learning skills that
  — Can earn learners' recognition
  — Look harder to do than they are (everybody likes to get in on the tips and secrets)
  — Are fun to do, yet valuable.
- Providing sideline resources that explain terms, concepts, or procedures learners should know but may have forgotten or missed
- Providing browsing capabilities.

Memorable Learning Experiences

Learning that isn't retained is also a waste of time. If the outcome we seek is improved performance, it's necessary for us to have persisting impact such that behavior occurring at any point after training will be as learned. Practice is one of the key ways we have of making new behavioral patterns last; yet many e-learning applications provide far too little. And if success is measured based on a posttest rather than long-term retention and performance, both designers and learners will probably succeed at achieving an inconsequential goal. Wherever possible, learners should understand that their learning success will be evaluated by observing their performance some weeks after the conclusion of a course of instruction. This framework actually causes them to mentally rehearse, create personal aids such as mnemonics, and otherwise work for retention rather than short-term recall.

It's much easier to remember things we've done than things we've been told or simply observed. You can ride with another driver to a location, for example, and easily not know how to get there on your own. You're much more likely to remember the route if you were driving. Similarly, when teaching software applications, everyone can click along with an instructor, but it can be very hard to remember what you clicked later when you're on your own. It's much better for learners to have to figure out where to click.

Best e-learning practices therefore include using interactive multimedia capabilities to have learners busy doing things frequently and practicing them often. Although the "doing" that we're talking about will be reflected by such input gestures as moving the mouse pointer, clicking buttons, typing, and talking into the microphone, the targeted activity is often mental. That is, we really want learners thinking and rehearsing mentally.

Instructional interactivity is an e-learning super power. Unfortunately, it's often confused with simple interactivity. Instructional interactivity is "interaction that actively stimulates the learner's mind to do those things that improve ability and readiness to perform effectively" (Allen, 2003). It's not pushing the enter key to go to the next page. Although that would be an interaction, an instructional interaction would be deciding, for example, what action to take when an employee displays disrespect in a public forum.

Context, Challenge, Activity, and Feedback

Instructional interactions have four components: context, challenge, activity, and feedback—CCAF, for short. Designing interactivity with this framework in mind leads to memorable learning events. The context can give the interaction authenticity by describing a situation the learner can expect to encounter. Imbuing the situation with dramatic tension, as any novel writer would eagerly do, can make the situation both more interesting and memorable. Building on the context, the challenge confronts the learner with a problem to solve. The challenge should stimulate the learner's mind to consider an alternate course of action, recall relevant information, and decide what to do.

The activity in an e-learning application is a gesture the computer can recognize and one that reflects the situation. Examples include a mouse click, pointer movement, voice command, or keyboard entry. Even the activity can assist in making the event memorable if it's visually interesting, amusing, or satisfying. Apple has dramatically demonstrated the power of pleasing activities in the interface of the new iPhone, for example. And finally, the feedback should be *intrinsic* in that it reveals the real-life consequences of the learner's action, rather than simply an *extrinsic* judgment of "Yes, that's correct" or "No, that wouldn't work." Intrinsic feedback relates back to the context and can create a memorable consequence—positive or negative alike—of an employee resigning, a customer committing to future purchases, or a truckload of products being sent to the wrong state.

One more best practice is especially worthy of note: spaced practice. Considerable research tells us that practice distributed over time with rest periods in between combats forgetting and makes learned behaviors more resistant to extinction (Thalheimer, 2006). Effective spacing can be as short as 15 minutes, but often much longer spacing, such as two or more days has more beneficial effects. If practicable, spacing should increase as learner skills develop and eventually equal the time that will actually occur between on-the-job performances of the behaviors being taught. Optimally spacing practice one task at a time can lengthen training programs considerably, but by interleaving practice of skills with the learning of additional skills as shown in Figure 13-4, spaced learning becomes not only a powerful, but also a practical solution.

Figure 13-4. Interleaving Spaced Practice

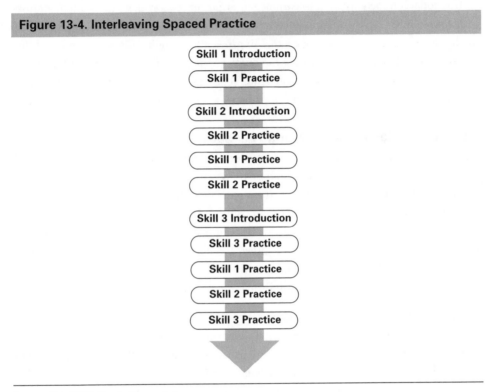

Source: Allen (2007). Used with permission.

Motivational Learning Experiences

Two important ways we can help learners most is to energize their motivation to learn and take advantage of whatever motivation they already have. In addition, because success comes only when new skills are applied, learners need motivation to change their behavioral patterns and perform in more effective ways. Motivation is clearly a topic of importance for e-learning developers. Let's briefly review best practices in heightening motivation to learn and to perform.

Motivation to Learn

Today's best practitioners work to engage learners so that they'll want to learn. If learners are spending their time developing abilities that have obvious benefit to them, for example, they are much more likely to attend to the learning experience and get something out of it. It's worth developing up-front learning activities that intrigue, excite, and captivate the learner's attention before launching into detailed skill development.

Listing objectives at the beginning of each module has been a traditional way of trying to help learners focus and of acquainting them with the beneficial outcomes to be expected. But lists of objectives rarely make interesting reading. Learners often report that they skipped over such lists. Instead of just listing objectives and expected outcomes, many designers now develop compelling stories, sometimes delivered through dramatic videos that reveal either the negative consequences of not having necessary performance skills or of the successes that have been realized through application of the skills being taught. Sometimes testimonials from previous learners are used to help boost initial motivation.

In concert with best practices in the psychotherapy of behavioral change (Prochaska et al., 1994), many designers are now going further to prepare learners for learning and change. They help learners contemplate whether making performance changes would be worth the effort, for example. When and if they come to the conclusion that making changes would be sufficiently beneficial, they then ask learners to devise a plan for making such changes—a plan that often includes learning. Sometimes, engaging informal learning (Cross, 2003) is helpful to avoid the backlash of what might be considered employer coercion and to facilitate social support for learners. With a plan in hand and help all around, learners can then make a critical step—they can make a commitment to their plan.

Boring e-learning, in contrast, quickly erodes whatever motivation learners have, making learning outcomes less probable. Unfortunately, so much e-learning is boring. Of course, it's much easier to create boring e-learning than that which engages and succeeds. Focusing on content, not individualizing, providing little learner control, and focusing on knowledge rather than action are just some of the many ways to make e-learning development easier. But the ease of development is little justification for boring e-learning and the expense that ensues.

Seven design techniques that fuel learning motivation, listed by CCAF component as discussed above, are listed below.

Context
1. Build anticipation of outcomes through authentic contexts.
2. Make the context appealing (use novelty, suspense, humor, fascinating graphics, sound, music, animation, and so forth).

Challenge

3. Put the learner at risk.
4. Select the right content for each learner.
   - If previously learned, repetition will be boring.
   - Adjust the challenge level to match the learner's readiness level.
   - Provide challenges that integrate previous learning and provide spaced practice.
   - Provide challenges that build confidence.

Activity

5. Have the learner perform multistep tasks.

Feedback

6. Provide intrinsic feedback.
7. Delay judgment.

Motivation to Perform

If motivation for change ends with acquiring new skills, the new skills aren't likely to be applied. For e-learning to be successful, learners need to follow through to complete the process of behavioral change and actually apply new skills and behavior patterns. Several techniques can be used to help maintain motivation into the postlearning performance stage.

Delayed, On-the-Job Evaluation

If learners know that their use of new skills is going to be observed and that this observation will be the basis for their performance evaluation (and maybe their salary, bonus, or other personal and meaningful consequences), they will study and prepare themselves very differently than if they feel the evaluation will be based primarily or even totally on posttest performance. It's important to delay the evaluation so that learners will practice their newly acquired skills and create new behavior patterns while the incentive of an upcoming evaluation is still in effect.

Of course, it's also important to alert learners to the evaluation program that will be used so that it will work as an incentive to prepare themselves.

Social Awareness

Publicizing the fact that people are participants in a program designed to create performance change can create the social support that will help learners reach the finish line. One of the best ways to do this is to nest the whole learning program in a change campaign, which uses events, communications, slogans, logos, and messaged items to keep everyone aware of the goal and progress.

Supervisor Training

Supervisors can help recent learners turn their new learning into successful behavior patterns. To provide needed mentoring, it's important for supervisors to have sufficient information about what their subordinates have been taught. In many cases, it's best for supervisors to experience the full training program themselves before taking on responsibility for guiding new learners. And, to be effective mentors, they often need training on the mentoring process itself.

Safety Nets

In many cases, learners can be expected to encounter situations not anticipated in training programs. Unless learners know what to do when their new skills seem inadequate, they are likely to fail to perform at desired levels. Best practices include providing learners knowledge of what to do when they feel unprepared or when they sense that their performance is inadequate.

Refresher Events

Don't forget that one of the most powerful influences we can wield is spaced practice. Even during periods subsequent to instruction in which learners are expected to perform, it can be very helpful to provide refresher learning events to counter forgetting and lowering performance quality.

Rapid Prototyping

Successful e-learning is engaging. It keeps learners focused and practicing authentic tasks that will be effective on the job. It has a powerful context, compelling challenges, intuitive activities, and effective feedback. It is intrinsically interesting and cognitively demanding. It uses interactivity and media well. It probably has a gripping storyline and much more. Design and development of successful e-learning is obviously a challenging, multifaceted, creative process.

Adding complication, there are typically many stakeholders. There is the executive who has made funds available and the executive whose profits and losses are most directly affected by success or failure. These are sometimes the same person, of course, but it's not uncommon for them to be separate individuals, which causes situational complexity. Then there are typically the supervisors of the trainees, the SMEs, and the training group. The IT department may well be involved, as may human resources and even the marketing department. With all these stakeholders, the creative problem-solving process has plenty of problems to address.

It's important to get the stakeholders in as much agreement with each other as possible. And knowing that there are often hidden agendas and a good probability that it won't be possible to get all stakeholders in full agreement, it's important to identify the key decision maker.

To achieve consensus and create a successful design that enjoys needed support, today's best practices use iterative design and development cycles rather than a linear process of analysis, design, and development (Allen, 2006).

Successive Approximation

Although there are many permutations of the iterative approach, they all build on the concept of *successive approximation*. It's the notion that no design—as complex as one that interfaces with humans; tries to engage, motivate, and enlighten them; and has many components to coordinate—is ever going to be perfect. Each design is only an approximation of a theoretical ideal.

There is necessarily an experimental attribute to the process in which needs are assessed, solutions are designed and prototyped, and results are evaluated. No one should expect a satisfactory outcome in one try. Evaluation of a series of design ideas can lead successively to a closer approximation of the ideal and eventually to a design that's acceptable. It's quite an efficient approach, especially in comparison to the process of preparing specification documents and storyboards, circulating documents for approval, and later finding people were expecting something quite different from what developed.

One such iterative approach is shown in Figure 13-5. The process proceeds from left to right, beginning with preparation by gathering information and concluding with the rollout of the gold release. The intervening design and development phases are both iterative and designed to produce successive products as they search for the best solutions. Typically, both design and development cycles iterate three or four times.

Design Iteration One

Sometimes called a savvy start, the initial design iteration is undertaken by as many of the stakeholders as you can get together. Ideally, but often not realistically, you'll have all of the following participants:

- Budget maker
- Person who owns the performance problem
- Person who supervises the performance
- SME
- Candidate learner

- Recent learner
- Project manager
- Instructional designer
- One or two prototypers.

The process begins by discussing the performance change that is needed (who needs to do what) and moves very quickly into brainstorming possible learning events. Although the intent is to generate functional prototypes for review as soon as possible, this first iteration is an effective way to validate background information collected earlier. One should be prepared for revelations and new directions. For example, it's not unusual for these sessions to determine that a different group or additional groups of learners should be targeted than originally thought.

Because of space limitations, I cannot discuss the importance of each person's participation. I will note, however, that having a recent learner involved is very helpful, especially in subsequent iterations when it's less likely that shifting to different targeted skills or learner groups will occur. Recent learners are often able to express what helped them learn, what caused their ahas, and what they found difficult or confusing. They are usually much more able to provide these insights than are SMEs who may think they can provide them, but think more as an expert than a novice and often steer design in the wrong direction.

Design Iterations Two and Three

Once the team has a prototype or two to look at, they are likely to have many new thoughts about what should be taught and how it should be taught. Giving prototypers the direction to build what was discussed in the first iteration, teams are often quite excited

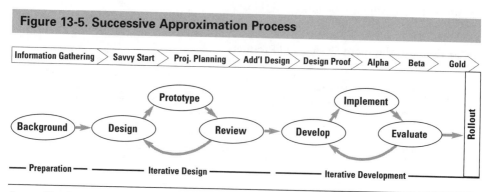

Figure 13-5. Successive Approximation Process

Source: Allen (2006). Used with permission.

about their ideas. As they see them come to life on the screen, however, it's almost certain that they will have new and better ideas—embellishments or completely new directions, but new ideas nonetheless—and they will appear to be much better.

At least one more iteration is usually necessary and sometimes a third is required to be sure the team has really identified the following core issues: Who should be trained? On what should they be trained? What will be satisfactory performance? How will it be measured? What is the appropriate look and feel of the e-learning interface? But getting these questions answered as efficiently as this process does and getting public agreement on a design that is visible on the screen (rather than expressed in easily misinterpreted design documents) are major accomplishments.

At this point, it's possible to generate a project plan and schedule additional, iterative design sessions that may be needed to cover all of the skills that need to be developed.

Iterative Development

The development iterations help ensure that the design is finalized and that development is true to the design. Each iteration and the product it produces are listed in Table 13-2 and described briefly below.

Development Iteration One: Construction Cycle

The construction cycle is the first major development effort. It produces the design proof—an intentionally incomplete release, in terms of content, that brings all the pieces of the design together for the first time. It's an important check to be sure expectations are being met and that the approach will work as a whole. Most important, the design proof is offered in the hope of rooting out problems as early as possible. Content and media development are limited so that if any change of direction occurs, minimal amounts of work will have been wasted.

Table 13-2. Development Cycles and Products

Cycle	Product
Construction	Design Proof
Production	Alpha Release
Validation	Beta Release and Gold Candidate
Correction	Gold Release

Source: Allen (2006). Used with permission.

Development Iteration Two: Production Cycle

Feedback from the design proof supplies all the information needed to finalize any models you're building and all structures you are using. Despite challenges, developing content is now a production-line issue. It may be possible to do many tasks concurrently. You should not have to fear that models and structures are going to change and require content rework. Once all the content is integrated, the alpha release produced by the cycle is intended to be a complete and fully functional release.

Development Iteration Three: Validation Cycle

During the validation cycle, the alpha release is tested and modified according to needs and problems identified. This work can range from adding practice exercises to deleting unnecessary instructions to replacing content and media. In general, however, work at this point is restricted to making corrections rather than making significant structural changes.

Development Iteration Four: Correction Cycle

In a perfect world, this cycle wouldn't ever be needed. Development iterations one, two, and three would have implemented the design perfectly and the design would be regarded as the very best possible compromise between what was affordable and what appeared to be ideal. But errors do creep in. To make sure that projects finish well and that bugs that surface late in the process can be addressed, experienced project managers always reserve funds and time for a fourth iteration in which to make corrections.

Summary

Success in the workplace comes from doing the right things at the right times. Therefore, for online learning to succeed, it must help learners develop and implement skills that result in valuable performance improvement. E-learning has the necessary capabilities but needs to be designed specifically for performance enhancement rather than just information distribution. It requires learner-centric designs that create meaningful, memorable, and motivational experiences.

Rapid prototyping in an iterative design-develop-evaluate process helps bring all key stakeholders to support a design solution, and further iterations in the development phase help assure everyone that the evolving solution will be what was expected. Today's best practices recognize the need for creative solutions that engage learners, help them develop and apply needed skills, and fit the resource constraints. Through advanced but practical design principles and development procedures, e-learning is not only able to reduce training expenses but also provide greater performance impact than ever before.

The sections on the three Ms draw heavily from *Michael Allen's Guide to e-Learning—Building Interactive, Fun, and Effective Learning Programs for Any Company* (Allen, 2003) and *Michael Allen's e-Learning Library: Designing Successful e-Learning—Forget What You Know About Instructional Design and Do Something Interesting* (Allen, 2007) and are used with permission.

The section on the iterative development process draws heavily from *Michael Allen's e-Learning Library: Creating Successful e-Learning—A Rapid System for Getting It Right First Time, Every Time,* (Allen, 2006) and is used with permission.

∽⟋

About the Author

Michael W. Allen has pioneered multimedia learning technologies, interactive instructional paradigms, and rapid-prototyping processes, bringing each forward into leading corporate enterprises. He led the design and development of Authorware Professional and was the founder and chairman of Authorware Inc., which merged to form Macromedia. He is the chairman and CEO of Allen Interactions, a company with East Coast, Midwest, and West Coast studios that build universally acclaimed custom e-learning, provide consulting on learning strategies, and train e-learning professionals in collaboration with ASTD. He holds a doctorate in educational psychology from Ohio State University and is an adjunct associate professor at the University of Minnesota Medical School, a popular conference speaker, and prolific writer on e-learning.

References

Allen, Michael W. 2003. *Michael Allen's guide to e-learning—Building interactive, fun, and effective learning programs for any company.* Hoboken, NJ: John Wiley & Sons.

Allen, Michael W. 2006. *Michael Allen's e-learning library: Creating successful e-learning—A rapid system for getting it right first time, every time.* San Francisco: Pfeiffer.

Allen, Michael W. 2007. *Michael Allen's e-learning library: Designing successful e-learning—Forget what you know about instructional design and do something interesting.* San Francisco: Pfeiffer.

Cross, Jay. 2003. *Informal learning: The other 80%.* Internet Time Group, available at http://internettime.com/Learning/The%20Other%2080%25.htm.

Prochaska, James O., John C. Norcross, and Carlos C. DiClemente, eds. 1994. *Changing for good: A revolutionary six-stage program for overcoming bad habits and moving your life positively forward.* New York: Quill.

Thalheimer, Will. 2006. *Spacing learning events over time: what the research says,* available at www.work-learning.com/catalog.

Chapter 14

Learning Transfer: The Next Frontier

Calhoun W. Wick, Andrew McK. Jefferson, and Roy V.H. Pollock

In This Chapter

- ➢ Learn why there is a lack of learning transfer
- ➢ Identify roadblocks for learners
- ➢ Get solutions for fixing the problem

"Houston, we have a problem." Three days into the flight of Apollo 13, Astronaut Jack Swigert radioed that famous understatement to Mission Control. They had a problem indeed—a ruptured oxygen tank scuttled the whole mission and threatened the lives of the crew. It was only through extraordinary teamwork to find creative solutions to never-before-solved problems that the mission was salvaged and the crew brought back safely.

Our recent research suggests that we have a problem in corporate training and development; one that threatens to scuttle our mission and undermine our contribution. The problem is learning transfer—or more precisely, the lack of learning transfer by many program participants. Like the challenges faced by Apollo 13, solving it is going to require teamwork, innovative solutions, and new approaches.

Dimensions of the Problem

In a recent series of seminars around the country, we asked more than 200 learning leaders in San Francisco, Chicago, Minneapolis, and New York to estimate from their experience the percentage of participants who transfer and apply what they were taught long enough and well enough to demonstrably improve their performance after a typical learning and development program. The distribution of responses is shown in Figure 14-1. Most estimates fall between 10 percent and 20 percent; the average was 16 percent and the median value was 15 percent.

We have a problem when most people responsible for planning and executing corporate learning programs estimate that more than 80 percent of participants fail to achieve the productivity gains that are learning's *raison d'être*. In our book, *The Six Disciplines of Breakthrough Learning*, we defined training and development that never gets transferred as "learning scrap"—analogous to manufacturing scrap in product production. The goal of Total Quality Management and Six Sigma is to reduce manufacturing scrap to an absolute minimum, because manufacturing scrap is expensive—it wastes time, money, raw materials, and opportunities. So does learning scrap.

Customers are unwilling to pay for defective products or services that do not meet their needs. Sooner or later (probably sooner), learning and development's customers are going to refuse to continue funding such an apparently inefficient process. That would be tragic;

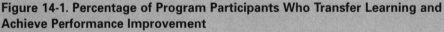

Figure 14-1. Percentage of Program Participants Who Transfer Learning and Achieve Performance Improvement

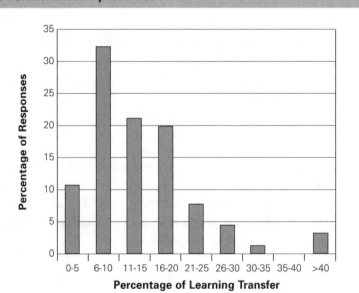

training and development can make a real difference for individuals, their teams, and our companies—provided it is used. The success of those individuals who take what they learn to heart, transfer it, and practice it until it becomes habit proves beyond a reasonable doubt the kind of positive impact training can produce. Those participants who do not achieve improvement, for whatever reason, represent significant lost opportunity and unrealized value. As a profession, we need to find much better ways to increase learning transfer to increase the value we create for our companies.

Where Is the Problem?

Borrowing a question originated by Robert Brinkerhoff of Advantage Performance Group, we asked the same learning leaders where they thought the process most often broke down—before, during, or after the formal instruction period. Figure 14-2 illustrates typical responses: although some failures occur before the program through lack of support, not enough experience, or poor selection, and some in the training itself, a great many of the learning transfer failures occur in the postcourse application environment.

The consensus in every group was that the most common point of failure was what happened—or rather failed to happen—after the training itself. Everyone acknowledged that some failures of learning transfer originate in the preprogram period and, to a lesser extent, some have their origin in the training itself (lack of relevance, insufficient

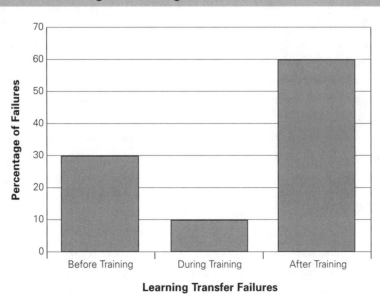

Figure 14-2. Percentage of Learning Transfer Failures

opportunity to practice, poor program design). But there was general agreement that the vast majority of failures to transfer occur during the postinstruction application period.

So what goes wrong that blocks transfer and application? Most people leave well-designed programs with new ideas and insights and enthusiasm for applying what they learned. What gets in the way?

We asked the learning leaders in our sample to identify the key impediments to transfer and application. The top five, in order of most frequently cited, were

- Conflicting priorities for participants
- No expectation of follow-through
- Lack of supervisor support
- No mechanism to assess application
- Lack of time for trainers to coach after program.

Clearly, there is linkage among these. If there is no supervisor support for learning transfer, and no expectation of follow-through, then other priorities will take precedence. Similarly, if there aren't the same clarity of expectations, means of assessing, and rewards for completing learning objectives as there are for other priorities, then learning transfer will get short shrift.

The catch-22 is that whether or not learning produces performance improvement and results depends on whether the organization—especially the participants' direct supervisors—believes that it will. If supervisors believe it will result in meaningful improvement, then it does. If they don't, then it doesn't. This self-fulfilling prophecy results because managers will invest the time to create learning intentionality beforehand, support attendance, and provide the accountability and coaching necessary to ensure transfer only if they expect real benefit for their direct reports and department. If the managers think the training is a waste of time, then they will telegraph that through their actions: there will be no expectation of follow-through; no coaching; and no encouragement or recognition for application of course principles. Learning transfer will fail. From management's point of view, the training failed. In fact, it was the performance management system that failed. No matter. It is the training budget that will suffer.

What's the Solution?

There was no one simple solution for getting Apollo 13 back safely. It took the cooperation of many people and many different steps. Likewise, there is no one magic bullet to solve the transfer of training issue. It will require new approaches and new cooperation between line management, learning leaders, and trainers to effect a cure. Three steps are essential: clarifying expectations, increasing support and accountability for training, and improving evaluation.

Clarify Expectations

Learning leaders in our survey selected "no expectation of follow-through" as the second greatest impediment to learning transfer. That is not surprising. The prevailing paradigm in the minds of both participants and instructors is that the program ends when the class is over. Our view is just the opposite: the real work begins when the class ends. The real work is applying the learning to the job and business needs.

Historically, what happened back on the job was outside of training's purview. That is why we consider it the "new frontier." Space was a new frontier in the last century; the post-learning follow-through period is training's new frontier in the 21st century. Its conquest is vital for companies to sustain leadership and competitiveness and the productivity of a changing workforce.

As a result of increased pressure for performance, global competition, and the accelerating pace of change in business, learning and development organizations are increasingly being held accountable for demonstrating on-the-job impact. Indeed, in our surveys of learning leaders, more than half reported increased pressure to demonstrate results. On-the-job productivity has become the new finish line for training and development. Providing a great learning experience is still necessary, but it is no longer sufficient.

Accelerating learning transfer, however, is going to require new approaches and a level of teamwork between line managers and learning professionals that, until now, has been the exception, rather than the rule. Teamwork needs to start by being much clearer about expectations, specifically:

- Better definition of the business impact expected from training
- Clearer articulation of the expectations for participants.

In our study of the most effective learning and development programs, we identified defining outcomes in business terms as the first, critical discipline for turning training into business results (Wick et al., 2006). Everything else—the design, the delivery, the learning transfer, and the overall success of the program—depends on reaching a clear and shared understanding with the business leaders around four questions:

1. What are the driving business needs?
2. If the program is a success, what will participants do better and differently to meet those needs?
3. Who will be able to observe and confirm the behavioral change?
4. How will we gather and evaluate the data?

In addition to defining the expectations for the program itself, we need to do a much better job of setting—or rather resetting—the expectations of the participants and their managers. People's prior experience has conditioned them to think that simply attending the program is all that is required: you go to a course, learn some cool stuff, put the notebook on the shelf, and go back to business as usual. That has to change; it is too inefficient and wasteful.

Resetting participants' expectations requires management support and a consistent message: just showing up is no longer enough. When you attend a program, you are expected to follow through on what you learned and put it to work in a way that improves your performance. Posttraining improvement will be measured, evaluated, and rewarded.

Finally, as learning professionals, we need to recalibrate our own expectations. We must recognize that we are in the business of delivering performance improvement, not training and development programs. Business leaders expect us to deliver terrific results, not just terrific end-of-course evaluations. We should expect no less of ourselves.

Increase Support and Accountability for Transfer

Communicating the expectation for improved performance is one thing. Making sure it happens is another. That is going to require a change in thinking, reallocation of some resources, implementation of new processes, and adoption of new tools. In other words, we cannot keep doing the same thing and expect a different result. Nor can we achieve significant improvement by fiddling with the instructional design; it is rarely the cause of transfer failure. We have to tackle the transfer problem directly.

The first task is to increase accountability for the transfer of training. We need to build mechanisms into the overall program design that require people to publicly commit to application goals, report periodically what they have done, involve others, and, ultimately, document what they accomplished with what they learned. Studies of expertise in a whole range of human endeavors have shown a direct correlation between excellence and the amount of practice (Ericsson, Prietula, and Cokely, 2007). We owe it to our instructors, our companies, and our participants to ensure that they practice their new skills long enough so they truly improve.

Various approaches can be used:

- Having teleconferences at specified intervals, ideally with participants' managers or senior leaders on the line
- Reconvening the group and having members or teams report their progress, lessons learned, and achievements
- Making learning objectives part of annual objectives; tracking and measuring them as part of the performance management system.

Our own efforts have focused on making the process scalable through the development and perfection of electronic follow-through management systems. An example of such a system is *Friday5s*, which automates, streamlines, manages, and supports learning transfer. Managing the postinstructional transfer period using a system like *Friday5s* differs in several key ways from the traditional "turn 'em loose and pray they'll use it" approach still practiced in far too many programs:

- *Learning goals are treated like business goals.* That is, they are collected, recorded in the system, and sent to the participants' managers, which helps address several of the main impediments to transfer.
- *People are reminded that they are expected to follow through.* Every two weeks or so, people are reminded of their goals and asked to report on what they have done, how much progress they have made, and their future plans.
- *Help is available.* Online help is available to suggest ideas for improving particular competencies, and there is a simple system to request input from managers and coaches.
- *The learning group is kept together.* Peer coaching and support are encouraged through online sharing of goals, progress, obstacles, and successes.
- *Results are documented.* The data are recorded in a shared database that allows learning leaders to analyze the kinds of goals, actions taken, progress made, manager involvement, and on-the-job achievements (see Figure 14-3).

Maximizing learning transfer requires not only postcourse accountability, but also ongoing support. As Donald and James Kirkpatrick point out in *Transferring Learning to Behavior* (2005), results are maximized when accountability and support are kept in balance.

Traditionally, however, learning and development organizations have invested more than 90 percent of their resources in planning and delivering the formal training and practically nothing in application support. Yet learning leaders in our seminars recognize that when learning transfer fails, the program fails; it does not deliver on its ultimate objective of improving business performance.

To optimize transfer and therefore results, learning organizations need to shift more of their resources to providing posttraining support for learning transfer. Support can take many different forms including

- *Ongoing facilitation.* Most learning organizations schedule their trainers so that as soon as one course ends, they immediately start teaching another. There is no time or expectation to follow up and support prior program participants. Some enlightened organizations have begun to recognize that reducing the number of programs to make time for ongoing support yields better results. In other words,

Figure 14-3. Sample Online Tool to Track Learning Transfer

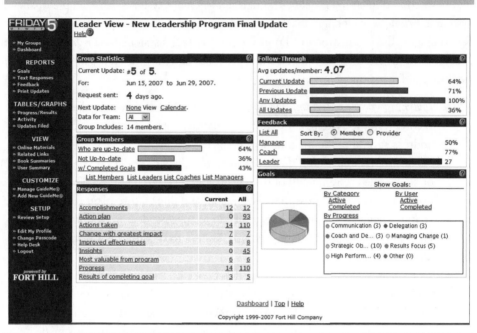

Source: Fort Hill Company, © 1999–2007. Used with permission.

teaching less but having more of it stick (get transferred) is a better strategy than continuing to "churn and burn."

- *Peer coaching.* Because peers, especially those who attended the same program, face the same kinds of challenges, their advice can be targeted and highly valued. Learning organizations can encourage and facilitate peer coaching in the postcourse period.

- *Manager involvement.* A participant's manager profoundly influences whether or not the learning gets applied. Learning organizations should ensure that managers have the information and skills they need to maximize the return on training investment. These include, for example, providing an executive summary of the program's business objectives and its content, a copy of their direct report's goals, and instruction or teleconferences on how to coach for maximum impact.

- *Relevant content.* Learning organizations should make implementation help available either in print or online. To be most effective, it should be action oriented, tightly coupled to the course content, and specific to the user's objectives.

■ *Follow-through support.* Automated follow-through management systems are available that include many of these features and also ensure greater accountability. The incremental cost of such systems is usually repaid many times over in greater learning transfer and performance improvement.

Improve Evaluation

Although it may seem counterintuitive, it turns out that better evaluation is key to improving learning transfer and the value that training and development delivers. That is because learning is a self-fulfilling prophecy: if managers and participants believe that the training is going to generate value, then they will take action to transfer and use it, and, in doing so, create greater value.

But for them to believe that the training will create value, they need compelling and credible evidence that it has done so for others. In this regard, the ubiquitous end-of-program evaluations fall short, as do typical approaches to return-on-investment (ROI). Scott Watson (2007) puts it well: "ROI has no soul."

For evaluation to help drive transfer and application, it needs to be compelling and memorable. It needs to provide relevant examples of success and underscore the importance of the extracurricular factors—especially managerial support, encouragement, and accountability—that drive performance.

In this regard, Brinkerhoff's *Success Case Method* (2003) seems particularly well suited. Its focus on gathering evidence "beyond a reasonable doubt," on acknowledging nontraining contributions, and on comparing successful and unsuccessful trainees provides compelling and credible evidence of the value that can be created, as well as how much potential value is being left "on the table" by failure to support transfer.

Whatever specific approach to evaluation is used, it needs to be discussed with and agreed to by the sponsors in *advance*. As van Adelsberg and Trolley (1999) point out, a training engagement should be approached as a business transaction that

■ Clarifies precisely what its customers expect from training
■ Negotiates a results contract
■ Guarantees customer satisfaction.

Measurement needs to be "baked into" the design from the beginning, and it must always provide data to improve as well as to prove training's value. In other words, it should actively attempt to identify weaknesses or points of failure in the entire process, as these provide the raw material for even greater success in the future.

Evaluation that focuses on real workplace outcomes is the essential "third leg" of the strategy to improve learning transfer. Assessment drives the PDCA process improvement cycle: *plan* a change, *do* it, *check* the results, and *act* accordingly to achieve continuous improvement and solve the learning transfer problem.

Summary

The Apollo 13 mission demonstrated that even when a problem is complex, urgent, and seemingly intractable, it can be solved through teamwork, innovative approaches, and focus. The learning transfer problem is urgent, complex, and hitherto intractable. Our experience suggests, though, that it is not insoluble. Many companies have made real progress in extracting more value from their learning and development programs by focusing on outcomes, increasing accountability for transfer, and improving the evaluation to provide power for further improvement.

About the Authors

Calhoun W. Wick is founder and chairman of the Fort Hill Company. He is nationally recognized for his work on improving the performance of managers and organizations. In 2006, he was named Thought Leader of the Year by the Association of Learning Providers (ISA).

Andrew McK. Jefferson, JD, is president and chief operating officer for Fort Hill. He is an accomplished executive with a passion for improving leadership and organizational performance. He has held leadership positions in both operational and legal capacity for technology companies.

Roy V.H. Pollock, DVM, PhD, is chief learning officer of Fort Hill. He has extensive experience in both line management and strategy development at SmithKline Beecham, Pfizer, and IDEXX. He is a fellow of the Kellogg Foundation National Leadership Program.

References

Brinkerhoff, Robert O. 2003. *The success case method: Find out quickly what's working and what's not.* San Francisco: Berrett-Koehler.

Ericsson, K. Anders, Michael J. Prietula, and Edward T. Cokely. 2007. The making of an expert. *Harvard Business Review* 85(07-08): 115-121.

Kirkpatrick, Donald L., and James D. Kirkpatrick. 2005. *Transferring learning to behavior: Using the four levels to improve performance.* San Francisco: Berrett-Koehler.

van Adelsberg, David, and Edward A. Trolley. 1999. *Running training like a business: Delivering unmistakable value.* San Francisco: Berrett-Koehler.

Watson, Scott. 2007. Ten reasons to get beyond ROI, available at http://www.getbeyondroi .com/news=topten.htm.

Wick, Calhoun W., Roy V.H. Pollock, Andrew McK. Jefferson, and Richard D. Flanagan. 2006. *The six disciplines of breakthrough learning: How to turn training and development into business results.* San Francisco: Pfeiffer.

For Further Reading

Broad, Mary L., and John W. Newstrom. 1992. *Transfer of training: Action-packed strategies to ensure high payoff from training investments.* Cambridge, MA: Perseus Books.

∽ **Chapter 15**

Off-the-Shelf Materials

George Piskurich

In This Chapter

➤ Learn what products are available

➤ Understand the pros and cons of off-the-shelf materials

➤ Get a buyer's checklist

There are about as many types of off-the-shelf training packages as there are vendors who sell them. Common wisdom is that most are second rate when compared with creating your own materials, but common wisdom is often mistaken. There are many wonderful training programs available directly from vendors. When used for the right needs and in the right training environment, they can save time and money and provide a great learning experience for the learner.

This chapter categorizes the various forms of off-the-shelf materials and describes the pros and cons of each type. (See Table 15-1 for an overview of this chapter at-a-glance.) This list, however, is not exhaustive because many of the products overlap into one another's categories; also, new products and enhancements are released regularly.

Table 15-1. A Comparison of Off-the-Shelf Products

Type	Pros	Cons
Complete Package	Comes with well-designed materials and an instructor who is certified in his or her field of expertise.	Can be cost-prohibitive.
Complete Package plus Train-the-Trainer	Comes with well-designed materials and a trainer who will teach your instructor the materials.	Can be cost-prohibitive, and expectations of what exactly constitutes "train-the-trainer" vary among vendors.
Lightly Customized Package	Vendor can customize for you, or you can customize yourself.	Can run into copyright infringements if you overstep your vendor agreement of what to customize.
As-Is Package	Cost-effective, good for self-instruction situations. Also good for very specific training that matches content.	Not customizable, may not get learner buy-in, may not be effective for learner, could be poorly designed or not the right fit for your needs.
License-to-Change Package	Is very customizable to blend segments into a course that the instructor is designing.	Can be cost-prohibitive, not very time efficient, can cause extra work for your instructor.
Technology-Based Asynchronous	Is cost-effective and strong on instructional design.	Instructor should carefully choose based on objectives, criteria, learning activities, and evaluation.
Technology-Based Synchronous	Is good for multisite simultaneous sessions.	May not be available in your geographic area or in your area of expertise.
Blended Package	Is cost-effective, time- and resource-efficient to develop.	May not be designed well enough to meet your needs.

The Complete Package

The best, most complete, and usually most expensive off-the-shelf programs are those that come with all the necessary, well-designed materials and are accompanied by a certified, experienced instructor. These are considered best because no matter how good your instructors may be, they will never be able to equal the program knowledge and, more important, the depth of specific delivery experience of facilitators who teach a program continually.

There are a few important aspects to consider when purchasing off-the-shelf programs with instructors. The first is cost. If you are looking for an inexpensive training solution, this may not be it. However, carefully consider all the costs inherent in developing your own materials, as well as the effectiveness of your instructors when teaching something they've never taught before, and may not have expertise in, before finalizing your decision. When you add together development time, facilitator preparation time, staff displacement from other important tasks, and other personnel constraints, you may find full-service packages are not so expensive after all.

A second consideration is how well trained and experienced the vendor's instructors are. Paying for expertise and experience and then getting an instructor who has not taught the class before is not fair value, and certainly not what you should expect. How will you know if the instructors are well qualified? Ask how the vendor internally certifies them! For example, companies I have worked for have had their new instructors attend an intensive session on course facilitation techniques. Afterward, the instructors did a "watch one, discuss, team-teach one" train-the-trainer session for each course they were certified by the company to teach, often with a master instructor sitting in on the rookie's first solo facilitation. This level of instructor expertise should be the minimum you expect when you purchase the instruction as well as the materials from a vendor.

The third aspect to consider is the company's reputation. Don't just rely on the sales pitch, on how big their ads are, or even on what you've heard—do your homework. Ask for a list of clients who have used the particular program you want to purchase, and even the particular instructor you'll be assigned, if possible. Then call a few of these at random. If they were satisfied with the materials and instruction, most will be glad to share their experiences and usually will be quite honest about the good and bad points of the program. If they don't want to talk about it, that may tell you something as well.

In the final analysis, if you have the financial resources, and a specific need that a vendor and its product can fulfill, why spend the time creating and facilitating your own materials? Let the pros in both the content and its facilitation take care of it for you.

Off-the-Shelf Materials with a Train-the-Trainer Session

One step below the complete package are off-the-shelf materials that come with a train-the-trainer session for your instructors. No matter how good the materials are and how detailed the instructor guide, having a facilitator who is experienced in both the content and the delivery come to your site to train your instructors is a great boon for them, and ultimately for your learners. A favorite basic form of train-the-trainer is when the client instructor has the chance to sit in on the class as it is being taught, and then is given time afterward with the master instructor to discuss the material and ask questions. Even better, after the client instructor is prepared and ready to teach, the master instructor sits in for the client's first facilitation to offer encouragement and words of wisdom. Unfortunately, this additional service is usually time and cost prohibitive.

A common train-the-trainer session is for the vendor's master trainer to do a run through of the program for the client instructor. It's not quite the actual class because there are usually no target learners involved, but it's more than just a question-and-answer (Q&A) session. This may occur at either your site or theirs. One disadvantage of this is that the client trainer may not get a real feel for the class and how it flows. However, cost constraints being what they are, you may insist that your trainers have a chance to review the course materials before their train-the-trainer session with the vendor's master trainer.

Even if the train-the-trainer session that the vendor provides is nothing more than a Q&A on a conference call, it is still better than no training at all. You'll want to pay in accordance with the vendor's training effort, so try to pick the vendors who plan to do the best job of preparing your trainers to use their off-the-shelf materials.

Lightly Customized Off-the-Shelf Materials

The third category of off-the-shelf programs comprises those that provide you with the course materials only, but allows you to slightly personalize them. This personalization may be as simple as your company logo on the front page of the learner guide or as complicated as your own situational activities and company-specific terminology.

There are two main ways that vendors allow for customization: first, by doing it for you, and, second, by giving you an incomplete computer file and allowing you to make the modifications yourself. Be aware, however, of your contractual parameters for editing. Modifying materials with reckless abandon may open the door to copyright infringement issues with your vendor. See the section below on License to Change Materials.

Many people have a "not invented here" bias, so even something as simple as adding a corporate logo can make your off-the-shelf programs more acceptable to your learners.

Better yet, if you have the vendor's permission and the ability, you might add things such as a message from your CEO, a company terminology list that is used throughout the training, situations that come from corporate history, and examples that are corporate or industry specific. Your learners are more likely to pay attention, and maybe even to learn, if you do.

"As Is" Off-the-Shelf Materials

Further down the line are the simple "as is" courses, which you buy and use. . . as is. When purchased for the right training need and used in the right environment, this type of off-the-shelf material can be effective and highly efficient because you do nothing but teach it or just provide access to it, as in the case of self-instructional materials. The number of these programs and the number of vendors that supply them have decreased dramatically in recent years due to the fact that their effectiveness has been found wanting. Many training managers who should have known better, and perhaps an even larger number of human resource managers who were a little light on training acumen, bought such courses by the hundreds as instructor-led training; as self-instruction in print, slide/tape, or video formats; as computer-based training (CBT); and delivered on the web in both synchronous and asynchronous configurations. They advertised these course libraries to their trainee populations, and then watched in consternation as the materials gathered dust, or as learners simply didn't complete or even sign up for them. There were a number of reasons for this failure, not the least of which was that much of the material was badly designed. However, the key issue was, and still is, that "as is" courses work best when they are targeted at a very specific training need that closely matches their content.

License-to-Change Materials

The fifth and final general category of off-the-shelf training materials comprises those that you buy a license to own and allows you to modify at will. This category is last, not because of lower cost, because this type of license can be very expensive, but because this type of material can fail to be time efficient. These programs are quite often more effective than the "as is" variety but may require a lot more design slicing and dicing to get them that way. This extra work is what you're trying to avoid by purchasing off-the-shelf materials to begin with.

This type of license shouldn't be confused with those that are basically a site license to teach a program. Microsoft would probably be very unhappy if you started to chop up, rearrange, and basically redo their software courses. No, this kind of license permits you to take the course apart and do whatever you need to it—from reestablishing objectives to cutting out entire units and replacing them with other materials more germane to your training requirements. Such extensive editing of off-the-shelf materials is often done in learning center deliveries of self-instructional packages, where only certain modules of a course might be relevant, whereas others require major adjustments or even complete deletion.

One of the best reasons for purchasing a full-use license is to blend pieces of the off-the-shelf program into a course that you're designing anyway, simply to save you development time. This might be a video slug that fits nicely into your content flow, or a computer-based simulation that you can repurpose and thus save yourself countless design hours. You might even wrap an entire new course around a module from an off-the-shelf program so that the final product fits your needs or reflects your organization better. The possibilities are endless, and the savings in development time, particularly in the technology world, can be huge. Unfortunately, few vendors are comfortable with this type of license, and it is often difficult to obtain one.

Technology-Based Asynchronous Off-the-Shelf Materials

The latest trend in off-the-shelf programs is a CBT or web-based technology (WBT) type of delivery. Even the old standard communications and supervisory skills courses have gone high tech with WBT deliveries and computer-based simulations.

For the most part, these materials are asynchronous in nature, which translates as self-instructional; and because there is no instructor, much of the previous discussion concerning the types of off-the-shelf materials is not as relevant. In the world of technology-based self-instructional materials, it is not the instructor or even the technical bells and whistles that are important—it's the instructional design that makes the program.

If you are considering any type of self-instructional off-the-shelf training materials, look for proper instructional design characteristics, such as:

- *Strong and plentiful learner-based objectives.* The objectives take the place of the instructor in guiding the learners to what is most important in the content. If there are few or no objectives that lead the learner through the activity, you probably want to look for another package, no matter how close the content itself is to what you need. You might consider augmenting the objectives with ones you create, but this will take time and be very cumbersome for the learner, particularly in a technology-based program.
- *Proper criterion-based evaluation activities.* With no instructor present, the only person capable of evaluating the learning is the learner. Good off-the-shelf self-instructional materials should have integrated evaluatory activities through-

out, as well as a final evaluation that makes it possible for the learner to evaluate objective mastery.

■ *Learner activities that are designed in, not just added on, and that help the learner master the content.* These learner activities are often referred to as interaction, although that term often means just pressing keys or moving a cursor around in a technology delivery. Look for true activities, such as the ones a good facilitator uses to help solidify learning the content or to introduce new concepts in ways that help the learners retain the information. The "choose an answer," or "drag and drop" activities so common in asynchronous technology-based programs are just the tip of the activities iceberg. The more well thought out and innovative activities a self-instructional off-the-shelf program has, the more likely your learner will be able to learn from it effectively. Of course, these activities come at a price, both monetary and in terms of learning time, but they are worth it if designed and integrated properly.

■ *A proper match among objectives, evaluations, content, and activities.* These aspects are not only basic requirements of a good self-instructional course, but they need to relate to each other as well. Do the objectives cover the content, or were they just added because you're supposed to have them? Do the evaluation processes truly reflect the key learning points, or do they evaluate minutiae? Do the activities really help the learners focus on the content? If there are performance objectives, do they allow learners to practice? Depending on the yeses and nos, some of which may need to be answered by your subject matter experts, you can decide if a self-instructional off-the-shelf program will really meet your training needs effectively.

Technology-Based Synchronous Off-the-Shelf Materials

Another type of technology-based delivery is synchronous web-based materials. *Synchronous web-based* means instruction using a computer network in which both the learners and the instructor are online simultaneously. There are not a lot of these around yet, but their numbers are growing quickly as vendors learn how to use synchronous learning software effectively, and companies begin to develop their own internal synchronous learning processes.

What's already been said for classroom-based off-the-shelf programs goes double for synchronous web deliveries. If a vendor offers it, and you can afford it, having experienced synchronous instructors facilitate the programs is your best alternative. Contrary to popular opinion (and some questionable promises) synchronous instruction is not the same as classroom instruction, and your own instructors will not be able to carry it off effectively without a lot of help, practice, and live experience. If the synchronous program vendor does not supply instructors, they should at least supply train-the-trainer sessions on both the learning materials and the software.

As for the programs themselves, look for plenty of activities that take advantage of the software's capabilities. These activities can range from simple polls and Q&A sessions to well-constructed group-based simulations and chat rooms that can carry over from one synchronous class to the next. As with face-to-face classroom programs, synchronous programs are only as good as the designer who designed them and the instructor who facilitates them, so be sure you get what you need, so your learners will get what they need.

Blended Off-the-Shelf Materials

Blended delivery of off-the-shelf products has become the new darling of the industry, and for good reason. It can be resource effective, time and cost efficient to develop, and it works. Today, most good off-the-shelf vendors sell blended programs. Usually they blend prework activities, such as self-instructional, technology-delivered materials, with a classroom session, in which the learners participate in activities and discussions that illuminate the content they mastered in the prework.

There are many problems inherent in such learning blends, however, not the least of which is that you as the savvy buyer need to analyze both the self-instructional and the instructor-led components in depth to make sure both are well designed and meet your needs. This takes time! Most of the other problems require a deeper consideration of this type of blended learning process itself, which is beyond the scope of this chapter.

There are many other types of blends as well, some of which you may discover in your research. They all have advantages and disadvantages, but if you "unblend" them and analyze each component, you'll find that the key questions are the same ones this chapter covers.

Hints for Analyzing Off-the-Shelf Programs

When looking at any off-the-shelf program, keep the following checklist in mind:

- Know your needs. Begin with a strong needs assessment or analysis to make sure you know what you're looking for.
- Write your own objectives. Before beginning your search, create your own set of objectives for the program so you can match that of the vendor.

- Decide on your delivery method and stick to it. Don't get stars in your eyes over a vendor's multilevel WBT program when your learners still can't turn on a computer without trouble.
- Ask for evaluation copies. Most reputable vendors will send you an evaluation copy for a specified period. If they won't, that should raise a flag for you.
- Don't go it alone. Pass around the evaluation copy to subject matter experts, supervisors, and even a few trainees to get their opinions.
- Look for good design aspects, objectives, activities, and criterion-based evaluations.
- Ask for references and call them.
- Check out the vendor's train-the-trainer processes.
- Describe exactly what you are planning to do with the program to the vendor to clarify your requirements and avoid misunderstandings.
- Keep your learners' needs and abilities foremost in your mind while deciding what to purchase.

Summary

In closing, remember that off-the-shelf training packages when selected and used properly can be a valuable training resource that saves money and time and provides learners with great learning experiences. This chapter has discussed several broad categories of off-the-shelf training packages and indicated some considerations to think about when making your selections. Foremost among these considerations are keeping your learner's needs, capabilities, and proclivities in mind and doing your research to ensure that the package you choose matches those learner characteristics.

About the Author

George Piskurich is an organizational learning and instructional design consultant specializing in e-learning design, performance improvement analysis and interventions, and telecommuting initiatives.

He has been a classroom instructor, instructional designer, and corporate training director for more than 20 years. He has developed classroom seminars, multimedia productions, and distance learning programs.

Piskurich has presented at more than 30 conferences and symposia, including the International Self-Directed Learning Symposium and the ISPI and ASTD international conferences.

He has authored books, journal articles, and book chapters on learning technology, self-directed learning, instructional design, and telecommuting, among other topics, and has edited books on instructional technology, human performance improvement, and e-learning.

For Further Reading

Biech, Elaine. 2005. *Training for dummies.* Hoboken, NJ: John Wiley & Sons.

Piskurich, George M. 2005. *Classroom facilitation: The art and the science.* Bellevue, KY: MicroPress.

Piskurich, George M. 2006. *Rapid instructional design: Learning ID fast and right.* San Francisco: John Wiley & Sons.

Steinmetz, Robert. 2000. Converting your curriculum: Choosing the right course. In *The ASTD handbook of training design and delivery,* eds., G. Piskurich, P. Beckschi, and B. Hall. New York: McGraw Hill.

Section IV

Face-to-Face Delivery— As Important as Ever

Face-to-Face Delivery— As Important As Ever

Luminary Perspective

William C. Byham

··· **In This Chapter** ···

➤ Recognize the importance of face-to-face delivery

➤ Understand the value of face-to-face delivery in blended learning

---

For years industry prognosticators have been predicting the imminent demise of traditional instructor-led training, opining that by the turn of the millennium a significant majority of organizations would turn to the Internet or local intranet as a means of delivering learning to their employees. For example, an article in the January/February 2000 issue of *The New Corporate University Review* cited an ASTD estimate that by 2001, 63 percent of organizations would offer courses over the Internet and 77 percent would provide training via their intranets. At about the same time, International Data Corporation predicted a 1,000 percent growth over a three-year period for the U.S. corporate e-learning market. And former U.S. Labor Secretary Robert Reich declared that "classroom training is a 19th century artifact—if not an artifact of medieval times."

E-learning proponents have often pointed to the host of powerful benefits e-learning offers: lower costs, consistency, scalability, 24/7 availability, transfer of the responsibility for development from the employer to the learner, less time away from the job for training, ability to further leverage investments in technology, and ability to deliver training just-in-time when learners need it.

In 2007, however, despite these purported advantages, face-to-face classroom delivery remains a strong and very viable training option. According to the 2006 *ASTD State of the Industry Report,* the percentage of learning hours delivered face to face by instructors hovered at about 53 percent. Although that represents a drop from 78 percent in 1999, it still remains a significant majority, and the percentage of technology-based training hours still falls below 40 percent (although it is up sharply from 14 percent in 1999).

The Human Touch

Clearly, face-to-face delivery is alive and well. All e-learning's virtues aside, there is one element unique to classroom training that no computer or software can ever match, one that ensures that face-to-face delivery as a training modality will remain vital: the human touch. Have you ever seen an e-learning program that could read its students' body language—sleepy eyes, slouched posture, or silent nods—and adjust accordingly? The classroom facilitator can not only do that but also can turn on a dime and adapt delivery to accommodate changes that are affecting the organization, such as shifts in strategic focus or expansion or contraction of the workforce.

Unlike preprogrammed e-learning products, the skilled facilitator can add to the depth and breadth of training by delving more deeply into content, if learners need it, and promoting more meaningful discussion around key learning points. E-learning typically offers limited, discrete answers and solutions, even in complex programs involving role plays and simulations. In parallel classroom situations, the facilitator can enrich learning by asking probing questions of all participants in the role play or by coaching them in a way that reveals details and nuances that an e-program can't.

One of the major benefits of e-learning is consistency—learners are guaranteed to get the same content, delivered in the same way, each time a learner takes a given course. Although consistency can be a potential problem with classroom delivery, it can be rendered a nonissue with a strong train-the-trainer curriculum, such as the one my company has developed. Each year we certify thousands of facilitators of all types, from those qualified to deliver specific classroom courses to master trainers. To date, we have directly trained and certified more than 50,000 trainers and facilitators. In addition, our clients who have master trainer eligibility have trained tens of thousands more. All were required to meet a set of stringent standards before being certified, and some have cycled through more than once to become certified to train other programs and courses.

Face-to-Face Delivery Defined

It might be helpful at this point to clarify what I mean by face-to-face delivery. I'm talking about training that takes place in large or small groups and that is conducted or monitored by a trained facilitator. Generally, this training occurs in a classroom setting, and the delivery is interactive, featuring behavior modeling, simulations, role plays, business games, and other activities—all orchestrated by a skilled facilitator who is most often certified to deliver a specific topic.

Face-to-face delivery should *not* mean lecture or traditional instruction where I talk and you listen. Although there might be times when the person delivering the training must lecture for brief periods, that person most often is there to impart key content, underscore it, effectively engage class members, guide them through the course, and help students practice what they've learned.

Why It Will Remain Important

Although the rate of business is increasing—both driven and enabled by advances in technology—compelling organizations to find newer, slicker, more expedient training modalities, face-to-face delivery hits that sweet spot innate to human beings: it's something most of us enjoy. From early infancy, humans are hardwired with a desire to learn from other humans: at first from parents, grandparents, siblings, and extended family members; later, from teachers, instructors, professors, and people met though life experiences. Every infant begins to learn at the sight of the first face and the sound of the first voice. Let's face it—we're social beings; we enjoy learning from others, and that desire stays with us through adulthood.

A skilled facilitator can tap into this desire like no e-learning program can, spotting subtleties in students' attitudes, learning preferences, personalities, and styles, then tailoring the learning to meet the need. The facilitator can customize delivery to an organization's culture or call on specific company examples or analogies that will resonate with specific audiences. Even when delivering somewhat static training, the facilitator can gauge an audience and match his or her pace to the time needed to cover the learning topics. Also, given the time required in the research-and-development cycle between e-learning versions, training content can quickly become out of date. The effective facilitator can make the adjustments for the classroom audience not only to hold its attention, but to keep the content current and relevant.

Aside from being the training modality that gives the facilitator latitude to adjust, adapt, and tailor his or her approach, face-to-face delivery is important for still another reason: the facilitator's skill. It's quite true that a good facilitator can make even a poor training program acceptable; similarly, a skilled facilitator can make an average program excellent. Contrast this with e-learning, where having even the best and newest PC will not make a poor e-learning course any better.

Blended Learning

Depending on an organization's culture, the acceptance of training modalities differs just as certainly as people's individual learning preferences. Some organizations foster independence as a value and, as such, rely heavily on distance learning or self-study. Others demand high-tech in all they do and eschew classroom delivery. In still others, the need for speed makes e-learning the primary choice for training. It might seem as if there is little opportunity for face-to-face delivery in these cultures, and sometimes that's true. However, an increasing number of organizations have turned to blended learning solutions; here, face-to-face delivery definitely plays a prominent role, especially in soft skills training, where the objective is not for learners to gain knowledge, but to build skills. To do that, learners need to be able to put what they've learned into context and have immediate opportunities for application and practice. In small learning lab settings post e-training, an effective facilitator can reinforce, follow up, and help participants more fully grasp and apply the skills they've learned online—via role play, group discussion, or other classroom-based methods. In these settings, face-to-face delivery has proven to be an excellent means of ensuring that technology-based learning achieves optimum results.

The fact that face-to-face delivery coexists so easily with and, in fact, complements high-tech training solutions in organizations that promote blended learning bodes well for the future of facilitator-led training. That definitely has been the case with many of the client organizations my company works with.

Alive and Well

Without question, the pulse of face-to-face delivery is strong and its prognosis excellent. Demand for trained facilitators remains high. Although they have the option of using e-learning versions of our courses, the majority of my company's clients still value—and even demand—facilitator-led training courses or blended learning solutions. Even clients that are primarily high-tech organizations emphasize the face-to-face delivery component.

Although electronic technology will surely be a big part of our learning profession's future, just as surely humans will remain at the heart of it. The following chapters in this section explore face-to-face delivery in depth, describing delivery techniques for large and small groups, interactive learning, coaching and mentoring, facilitation skills, and other key elements—all of which illustrate the vitality and importance of this time-tested training modality.

∽

About the Author

In 1970, William C. Byham, PhD, envisioned a business that would help companies make better hiring, promotion, and employee-management decisions. More than 37 years later, he is the cofounder, chairman, and CEO of Development Dimensions International (DDI), an internationally renowned human resource consulting and training company. Headquartered in Pittsburgh, Pennsylvania, DDI has more than 1,200 associates around the world.

During the last 37 years, he has forged important innovations in human resource technologies and systems that have had a significant effect on organizations worldwide. A best-selling author with his 22nd book, *70: The New 50,* he continues to write books and articles and deliver speeches on important management advancements and how they are affecting businesses. He is also a Distinguished Contribution to HRD Award recipient.

Chapter 16

The 10 Most Important Lessons I've Learned About Effective Classroom Presentation

Robert W. Pike

In This Chapter

➢ Discover the best ways to engage a group
of learners

➢ Encourage learners to discover learning
for themselves

➢ Learn how to teach from the heart and the head

Why would my top 10 tips on classroom training have any value for you? What gives me the right to share with you on this subject? These are questions you should ask whenever you read anything on the subject of training and performance improvement. Since 1969, I've given more than 100 presentations per year and worked in more than 40 countries. My *Creative Training Techniques Handbook* has more than 300,000 copies in print, making it the best-selling train-the-trainer book ever published. In addition, I've written more than 21 books in the field and produced a dozen training videos. These ideas have been built into more than 600 training programs designed for clients during my career—not counting the programs the consultants of the Bob Pike Group have designed using these principles. I've presented at ASTD's International Conference and Exposition each year since 1977 and for as long as I can remember I've been in the top five presenters based on both audience size and evaluations. More than 100,000 trainers on five continents have attended my two-day Train-the Trainer Boot Camp. These graduates will tell you that these ideas are simple—and, more important, they work. Don't let the simplicity fool you—read on—but don't simply read—put the ideas to work. Even as I write this, I am halfway through a two-day program in Japan for 25 corporate trainers. These ideas work around the world. So here we go.

Use the Dynamics of the Group

Today's adult learners are different from the adult learners of 30 years ago. The media that we are exposed to on a daily basis has made most of us more sophisticated and savvy. As a result, we no longer can overwhelm people with our effective presentation style.

Look at how the world of entertainment has changed. We can flip through the 68 channels of our local cable television system, then look at each other and say, "There's nothing on." We can wander up and down the aisles of a video store, past 5,000 titles, and after 15 minutes we still can't find anything to watch on a Friday night. Now, this is the adult learner you've got sitting in front of you. There is nothing you can do to match the kind of attention-getting entertainment that's available today. The most viable option I see is using the participant's own energy.

That means involving the participants, not talking to them. I don't know of anyone who's looking for a good talker. When was the last time any of us had 15 spare minutes and said, "I wish I had someone to listen to"? More often, we're looking for somebody who's willing to listen to us. Have you ever seen someone write on an evaluation form: I wish there was more lecture? I haven't. So the very first thing I suggest is that we teach more by covering less. There are many things we talk about during classroom presentations that could be better shared in other ways. Reference manuals are one example. Or if I'm teaching needs assessment, I don't need to lecture on The 10 Ways to Assess Needs. I'd be better off putting that in a handout and focusing on specific areas in which participants need some hands-on experience. Don't let anything come between you and your group's dynamics. Mobilize their energy.

Divide and Conquer

Most of us are familiar with the "terrible three" or the "dynamic duo" who come stalking into the classroom. Negative people can find one another. It's uncanny. Your response is to divide and conquer by breaking participants into smaller groups and moving them around. Take advantage of the ability to move resistant people away from each other so there's less support for the resistance. It may not enhance the learning of negative participants, but it will certainly enhance the learning of the other participants.

There are other ways to encourage positive group dynamics. All that is required is paying close attention to seating arrangements. In schoolroom, lecture-style, theater, and even U-shaped seating arrangements, the unfortunate message is: I'm going to talk, and you're going to listen. I frequently number people off, move them around the room, and cluster them in groups of five to seven. (If you've got fewer than five in a group, a dominant person can overpower the group and take control; with more than seven, shy people can get lost.) Again, you're taking advantage of group dynamics.

I've done this with groups as small as six (with two triads) and as big as 1,200. That may sound like a logistical nightmare, but it took about seven minutes. It was simply a matter of dividing the audience into parts and numbering them all at the same time.

People Will Not Argue with Their Own Data

This is one of Pike's laws of adult learning: The more involvement and the more participation, the more learning is going to occur. So let me suggest to you that there are three ways we can teach people—and why two of them generally don't work.

First, you can tell people things. For example, I could say, "I'd like you to get the most out of what I have to say, so I'd like to start by telling you all that you're lousy listeners. Having shared that, let me tell you that there are five power tricks for effective listening. I'll give them to you so you can get the most out of what I have to say." That is generally not what happens. Instead, people will say, "Wrong. I'm not a lousy listener. You're a lousy talker. If you had something interesting to say, I'd listen, but since you don't, I won't. It's your problem I'm not listening, not mine."

Second, you can use research and statistics. I could start the session by saying, "According to the latest behavioral studies, 95 percent of all people are lousy listeners." Your group's response: "Boy, you're right. What can I do to help them? I wish my boss was here; I wish my spouse was here; I wish my co-workers were here." In other words, they'll think the lousy listeners are everyone else.

Third, you can put people in situations where they can discover for themselves just how effective or ineffective they are. Remember: People do not argue with their own data. If I say it's true, you say "He's got to believe it; he's the one who's teaching." If you say it's true, it becomes a fact because you came up with it. You've got ownership of it.

Revisiting Is the Key

Notice that I said revisit, not review. Revisiting is when the participants look at content again—reviewing is when the instructor does it. Albert Mehrabian, who wrote the book *Silent Messages*, did a study that found that if people are exposed to an idea once, they'll remember 10 percent after 30 days. But if those same people are exposed to an idea six times with some interval between each exposure, they'll retain more than 90 percent after 30 days (1981).

Obviously, revisiting is essential. It doesn't matter what you've covered; what matters is what people can grab onto and recall when they need it. But you should be shot on the spot if you stop and tell a group, "Let's review what we've covered." Why? Because, in my experience, when you say, "Let's review," three quarters of the room will say, "It's time to check out for a few minutes because we've already covered this." What we need to do is review without calling it a review.

How? One thing I've done is ask people to keep an action or idea list during sessions. I'll stop every couple of hours and ask, "Would you quickly review your action or idea list and come up with the two most useful action ideas you've generated for yourself so far?" Or I'll say, "Would you take about five minutes and, as a group, share the action ideas you've come up with so far and create a master list? Now, take 30 seconds and pick the one idea you would take away with you. Then, take another 30 seconds to come up with two big takeaways for your group." Finally, I'll go from group to group and pick up a new idea from each one.

Notice what happened. You looked over your list. That's one revisit. You talked about it for 30 seconds—two revisits. You decided what you were going to share with the larger group—third revisit. And then we went around and polled ideas from the larger group—fourth revisit. But each review took a different angle. And many participants may have added an idea to their own thinking as they shared ideas in their small group. They also may have added ideas because of what was shared by the larger group. So revisiting, not review, is key!

Learning Is Directly Proportional to the Amount of Fun You Have

Learning is directly proportional to the amount of fun you have, but let your participants create it with all kinds of extensive debriefings. You may gain more participant energy in a series of quick activities. They can be as short as 30 to 45 seconds or up to three to five minutes. For example, instead of lecturing on the qualities of an effective supervisor, I could have small groups discuss the best supervisor they ever had and what made that supervisor effective. I could then draw from them those same qualities.

Notice I did not say "jokes." I said "fun." When participants are engaged in a way that honors the experience they bring to the classroom—they have fun and learn, too. When we honor their ability to think and share their thoughts and allow them to use the vast experience they bring to the classroom, they are energized, they have fun, and they learn!

Change the Pace

In his book *Use Both Sides of Your Brain,* Tony Buzan says that the average adult can listen with understanding for 90 minutes but listens with retention for only 20 minutes (1991). That means that you and I need a distinct change of pace every 20 minutes. Otherwise, here's what often happens: the minute the clock starts, our participants walk in with their 20-minute heads, and we start pouring from our 90-minute pitcher. They nod and smile and listen while we pour, and we think we're doing well. Finally, we cover all our material and feel great. They listened, nodded, smiled. They understood the whole time! But what do they walk out with? Twenty minutes worth of material.

Because participants can listen for only 20 minutes with retention, you need a distinct change of pace at least every 20 minutes. The techniques aren't hard. Move from a lecture to a small-group discussion. Move from something participants do as individuals to something they do as small groups. Number people off and move them around the room. It's like pouring gas into a funnel; you have to stop every once in a while and let it drain down. And that ties us right back to revisit. Give it a chance to sink in and then come back and hit it in another way.

Leave Participants Impressed with Themselves, Not Intimidated by the Instructor

The most successful training occurs when someone comes up to you and says, "You know, I didn't see you do anything I can't do." When that happens, you're a success. The last thing we want is participants saying, "Boy, if I could only be like that. But I can't—so now I can leave with an excuse for being less effective."

The purpose of training is to leave people thinking, "I'm great. I'm so excited about what I can now do that I couldn't do before, what I now know that I didn't know before, what

I now feel about myself." Those are really the three things we train for: knowledge, skills, and attitudes. I challenge anyone to show me a training text that says one of the objectives of training is to have the participants recognize the greatness of the instructor. But how many times does the ego of the trainer get in the way of training? If you use group dynamics and involvement, you'll be going a long way toward leaving people impressed with themselves.

An instructor who feels the constant need to lecture and who doesn't allow participation is saying, "I feel the need to control. I feel the need to be acknowledged as the expert. And I don't feel good enough about myself to let others feel better about themselves."

Allow Adults to Use Their Experience

Almost all of us have shared life experiences. We may never have been managers, but if I'm in a new-managers program, I have been managed. We may never have sold, but we've been sold to, so we have a lot of information about what we want in an effective sales presentation. We may never have handled a customer complaint, but we've sure been mishandled as customers. Think about the knowledge and experience participants have. Take advantage of it. Let them share it.

Help People Learn How to Learn

The old pedagogic model may have told us to memorize, but did it teach us how to learn? We're told to learn, but we aren't taught how to learn. For most of us, school was not about learning for living—it was about learning how to pass. Cramming for finals did not provide long-term memory to draw on later. Most of us could not pass a test today on what we should know because of the degrees we possess.

We need to use creative non-pedagogic techniques if we want to help adults learn how to learn. Our objective is not to drill information into people's heads. We need to realize, for example, that we think in pictures, that images are retained more readily than concepts. We can create pictures to help people retain concepts: a heart for love, a lion for confidence, and so forth. There are dozens of other ways to help people absorb knowledge that are in tune with the way we process information. An understanding of the concepts of adult learning is essential for anyone in human resource development. There are at least 36 alternatives to lecture. Mind mapping, creating windowpanes with both key words and icons to accelerate retention of processes, having participants create and periodically revisit their own personal action idea lists are all ideas we could explore. Space does not allow for that in this brief chapter—but other resources are available to help you dig deeper. Send me an email at BPike@BobPikeGroup.com with Five Free E-Lessons in the subject line, and I'll send you a link to five free e-lessons that can help you dig deeper into these topics.

Teach from a Prepared Life, Not Just a Prepared Lesson

It's not enough to know it in our heads; we need to know it in our hearts. Have we experienced what we're teaching? If not, we're missing a dimension of power.

In a college speech class I learned this poem:

> *The room was hushed, the speaker mute.*
> *He'd left his speech in his other suit* (McFarland, 1963).

Too many trainers are like that. DVD player doesn't work? No class today. LCD bulb burned out, and you can't use your Microsoft PowerPoint presentation? No class today. Someone asks a question, and you lose your place in your script? Better start over. Someone asks a question you can't answer? Stop letting people ask questions. It undermines your authority. I'm being facetious, of course. Yet we've all seen it—trainers who have not lived the content, but who try to act as though they have. They are largely ineffective—and most participants see through them.

Teach the things you know and have passion for, and you'll never be afraid to say, "I don't know, but I'll find out." I've been a full-time training and performance consultant since 1969. I am as passionate about what I do today as the day I first started. The years have added wisdom and experience that help me to be even more effective. I hope these 10 tips will increase your effectiveness as well.

About the Author

Robert Pike has developed and implemented training programs for business, industry, government, and the professions since 1969. He was senior vice president with Master Education Industries and vice president at Personal Dynamics. As founder and chairman of the Bob Pike Group and Creative Training Techniques Press, he leads sessions more than 150 days per year. A member of ASTD since 1972, Bob has been active in many capacities, including three national conference design committees, director of special interest groups, and former member of the ASTD Board of Directors.

Pike has presented at regional and national ASTD and Training conferences. In 1991 Pike was granted the professional designation of Certified Speaking Professional (CSP) by the National Speakers Association (NSA). In 1999 he was granted the professional designation of CPAE (Council of Peers Award of Excellence) Speakers Hall of Fame. He is a prolific writer, having edited and authored more than 10 books and 12 videos.

References

Buzan, Tony. 1991. *Use both sides of your brain: New mindmapping techniques.* 3rd ed. New York: Penguin.

McFarland, Kenneth. 1963. *Eloquence in public speaking: How to set your words on fire.* Upper Saddle River, NJ: Prentice Hall.

Mehrabian, Albert. 1981. *Silent messages: Implicit communication of emotions and attitudes.* Belmont, CA: Wadsworth.

For Further Reading

Biech, Elaine. 2005. *Training for dummies.* Hoboken, NJ: John Wiley & Sons.

Bowman, Sharon. 2003. *Preventing death by lecture.* Glenbrook, NV: Bowperson Publishing.

Ettington, Julius E. 2002. *The winning trainer: Winning ways to involve people in learning.* 4th ed. Woburn, MA: Butterworth-Heinemann.

Pike, Bob, and Lynn Solem. 2000. *50 creative training openers and energizers.* San Francisco: Jossey-Bass/Pfeiffer.

Pike, Robert W. 1994. *Creative training techniques handbook.* 3rd ed. Amherst, MA: HRD Press.

Piskurich, George. 2003. *Trainer basics.* Alexandria, VA: ASTD Press.

Scannell, Edward E., and John W. Newstrom. 1983-1998. *Games trainers play (McGraw-Hill training series).* New York: McGraw-Hill.

Silberman, Mel. 2004. *The best of active training: 25 one-day workshops.* San Francisco: Jossey-Bass/Pfeiffer.

Stolovitch, Harold D., and Erica J. Keeps. 2002. *Telling ain't training.* Alexandria, VA: ASTD Press.

Thiagarajan, Sivasailam. 2003. *Design your own games and activities.* San Francisco: Jossey-Bass/Pfeiffer.

Active Learning Strategies

Mel Silberman

In This Chapter

➢ Get eight strategies for successful active learning

➢ Engage your participants in your training sessions

I f you want to spark active learning in your training sessions, there are eight strategies that will bring you success. You don't need to heed all eight, but I have found that most of them are critical for any trainer, at any level, and in any subject matter. Table 17-1 summarizes the eight strategies and provides brief descriptions of them.

As I further acquaint you with each strategy, consider how it applies to your training situation. Understand that each training situation has its own unique context. For example, you might conduct some of your training in short, single sessions (from one to three hours in total length). In such brief periods, you might have time for only one short opening or closing activity. Therefore, limit yourself to a single technique and keep it quick. When your training involves a multisession format, there is time for more openers; closers; and nontraditional methods, such as team learning. In that case, make use of more techniques. Or you might be working with subject matter that is very technical in nature and

Table 17-1. Eight Strategies for Successful Active Learning

Strategy	Description
1. Engage your participants from the start.	Use activities at the beginning of an entire course or at the beginning of any single training session to develop a climate for active learning, promote peer interaction, and build immediate involvement in the learning topic.
2. Be a brain-friendly presenter.	Present information and concepts that maximize understanding and retention through techniques that stimulate participants' brains to be mentally alert and receptive to new data.
3. Encourage lively and focused discussions.	Structure discussion so that participants are motivated to participate and pursue the topic in depth.
4. Urge participants to ask questions.	Motivate participants to ask thoughtful questions and seek information that will answer them.
5. Let participants learn from each other.	Set up effective group learning and peer teaching activities that require peer collaboration.
6. Enhance learning by experiencing and doing.	Design and facilitate games, practice exercises, role plays, and other experiential activities to enhance the learning of information, skills, and values.
7. Blend in technology wisely.	Effectively integrate synchronous and asynchronous e-learning tools with classroom learning activity.
8. Make the end unforgettable.	Close a learning experience so that participants review what they have learned, reflect on its importance, consider future steps, and celebrate their accomplishments.

there is little, if any, need for extended discussion. In that case, ignore the strategies on lively and focused discussions. You might even be involved in a leadership development program that requires skill in managing real-world situations. In this instance, be sure to consider the advice on experiential learning. Although each strategy may be important to your specific situation, some will naturally have greater applicability.

Engage Your Participants from the Start

To learn something well, your participants need to listen, observe, ask questions, and discuss the material with others. Above all else, participants need to "do it." That includes figuring out things by themselves, coming up with examples, and doing tasks that depend on the knowledge they already have.

The success of active learning depends on your ability to form and sustain an environment in which participants take on the responsibility to be doers. Above all, they must be willing to use their brains—studying ideas, solving problems, and applying what they learn. You cannot depend on a grab bag of training tricks for success. There must be a climate right from the beginning that supports your creative methods. The longer you wait to create this climate, the longer your participants have to settle into being passive learners.

Engaging participants right from the start applies to both single session and multisession training events. If you want your participants to start learning actively, give them a taste of it right away. Get your participants to do something before you even start serious training. Think of it as the appetizer before the main course. Whet their appetites, and they will be hungry learners.

Be a Brain-Friendly Presenter

Your participants' brains are your best allies. Too often, trainers think that there is nothing going on in their participants' heads. Nothing could be further from the truth. Technically speaking, if nothing is happening in participants' brains, they are *dead.* Their brains are *alive* and working (even when they are asleep). The issue is what are their brains thinking about?

I appreciate the fear that participants are thinking about everything but what you want them to think about. Yes, participants, like all human beings, do a lot of "mind surfing." Your task is twofold: to interest their brains in what you are presenting and to help their brains to really go to work so that they learn and retain the presentation as well.

The brain does not function like an audio- or videotape recorder. Because of its storehouse of prior information, incoming information is continually being questioned. The brain asks questions such as

- Have I heard or seen this information before? What does it remind me of?
- Where does this information fit? What can I do with it?

The brain doesn't just receive information—it *processes* it. Our job, as trainers, is to facilitate that processing.

In many ways, the brain can be compared with a computer. Although a computer receives information, it needs software to interpret the data. Participants' brains need to engage their own software as well. Their brains need to link what they are being taught with what they already know and how they already think and learn. When participants are denied that opportunity, their learning is passive and their brains don't make these connections. Furthermore, a computer cannot retain information that it has processed without "saving it." Participants also need to be tested on the information, recap it, or perhaps explain it to someone else to store it in their memory banks. When learning is passive, the brain doesn't save what has been presented. It may stay in temporary memory for a short time but never makes it into permanent memory.

What occurs when trainers flood participants with their own thoughts (however insightful and well organized they are) or when they rely too often on "let me show you how" demonstrations and explanations? Pouring facts and concepts into participants' heads and masterfully performing skills can actually interfere with participant learning. The presentation may make an immediate impression on the brain, but it may lull participants into thinking that they will never forget what they heard and saw. However, participants cannot retain very much for any period of time unless they do the work to store information intelligently. That work can't be done solely by the trainer, regardless of how dynamic he or she is.

The bottom line is that just because you covered certain information with your participants does not mean that it was uncovered by them.

Encourage Lively and Focused Discussions

Lively, focused discussions are often the best moments in a training session. Participants are engaged and time flies. All too often, however, a trainer tries to stimulate discussion but is met with uncomfortable silence as participants wonder who will dare to speak up first. Sooner or later, some do. But, in your experience, how many? When I tell trainers that the average number of frequent participators in almost every training session is four, they are not surprised. The number comes close to their experience. When I tell them that they are not just any old four participants, but the same four participants, throughout the training program, they think a bit and usually agree that that's true in many of their classes as well. What is your experience? Do you hear from the same "usual suspects"?

The key to obtaining lively and focused discussion is to design into it some important elements, such as engaging participant interest before plunging into the discussion, stating effective questions, improving the quality by having participants prepare for the discussion, and using creative discussion formats.

Urge Participants to Ask Questions

The act of learning begins with a question. The brain starts the work of learning because it has a question about information it is obtaining from the senses (hearing, sight, touch, and taste) that feed it. If the brain could talk, it would say things like, "Where does this information fit?" "Does it confirm what I already know?" "Does it challenge what I already know?" If the brain isn't curious about incoming information, it takes the path of least resistance—it attends to something else.

When participants are asking questions, they are in a seeking mode rather than a passive mode. Their brains are activated to obtain answers rather than merely "logging in." If participants are asked to read some information or view presentation slides and they come to it with few or any questions, their brains treat the information superficially. If they are trying to find out something, their brains treat the information carefully.

Getting participants to ask questions is easier said than done. Many participants are so used to being told or shown things that they become consumers rather than seekers of knowledge. As a result, they may have few questions. Furthermore, many trainers are so accustomed to *asking* participants questions (for example, What's an example of that? How did you arrive at that answer?) that they forget to inquire of participants if they have any questions of their own. As a result, participants often receive little practice asking questions. Don't make that mistake.

Let Participants Learn from Each Other

Even if you put participants in small groups for brief periods of time, you probably would find it risky to leave them there for a long time. The risk may be worth it. Your participants can learn as much from each other as they can learn from you. After all, they "speak each other's language." They can also give each other more personal attention than you can give to each of them. Under the right conditions, learning that is collaborative is more active than learning that is trainer led.

In educational jargon, participants' learning from each other is referred to by such terms as *cooperative* or *collaborative learning, group learning, peer tutoring,* and *peer teaching.* I use the term *team learning* because it suggests that a team effort is needed for learning results to occur. Participants need to think *we* rather than *me.*

Team learning has many benefits. Participants develop a bond with their learning teammates that may motivate the team to sustain collaborative learning activity through complex, challenging assignments. Furthermore, participants in learning teams are willing to accept greater responsibility for their own development precisely because they have a sense of ownership and social support. Think how often you say to yourself the phrase "my class." Trainers naturally have a sense that they own their training session when they say things such as, "I hope my class goes well today," or "In my class, participants are very engaged." When team learning is happening, participants get the feeling that it's *their* class.

Enhance Learning by Experiencing and Doing

Jean Piaget, the renowned developmental psychologist, taught us that children learn concretely but become capable of abstract thought as they enter adolescence and adulthood. Unfortunately, many trainers have taken this change in mental capacity to mean that concrete learning experiences can now be curtailed.

Learning by experiencing and doing should continue throughout a person's life. For example, participants will understand project management concepts through actually managing a project. They can understand the dynamics of the stock market through managing an imaginary portfolio. They can understand the problems faced by visually impaired people through participating in simulated blindness. The need for concrete experience doesn't diminish, but, with the capacity for abstract thinking, participants can now go from the experience to much higher order understandings.

Experiential learning not only enhances the understanding of concepts but is also the gateway to skill development. Whenever you want participants to develop skills (for example, writing business memos, creating spreadsheets, operating a machine, interviewing job candidates), it's imperative to go beyond showing them how to do it. They must do it themselves, not just once but often, at first with your guidance and then on their own.

Blend in Technology Wisely

With widespread availability of computers, the development of new software, and the growth of the Internet, training does not have to be confined any longer to the classroom. Through the advent of computer-based training, participants can learn without an instructor and without the need to follow a single method and a single pace. Furthermore, the use of computers has the potential to engage participants in high-level, active learning. Because they can find information faster and use software that enables them to do many things with it, participants are freed up to engage in critical thinking, analysis, and application.

Of course, the use of technology in training can be handled wisely or unwisely. Some computer-based programs, for example, still turn participants into passive learners and low-level thinkers. Others seek to entertain but not to educate. Still others isolate participants from the support of peers.

Regardless of your circumstances, how you blend in technology will determine whether or not active learning, as I have been exploring it throughout this chapter, will be sustained.

Make the End Unforgettable

Many training programs run out of steam at the end. In some cases, participants are marking time until the close is near. In other cases, trainers are valiantly trying to cover what they haven't gotten to before time runs out. How unfortunate! What happens at the end needs to be "unforgettable." You want participants to remember what they've learned. You also want participants to think that what they learned has been special.

When you are preparing for the end, there are four areas to consider:

- How will participants review what you have taught them?
- How will participants assess what they have learned?
- How will participants consider what they will do about what they have learned?
- How will participants celebrate their accomplishments?

Final Advice

At the beginning of this chapter, I promised to share with you eight strategies to spark learning in your training sessions.

I hope you are inspired to apply these training strategies with your participants. I recognize, however, that inspiration doesn't ensure action. So, I would like to end with some final advice.

Focus on Outcomes, Not Content

All too often, training is designed around the information, concepts, or skills that appear to be central to the topic at hand. For example, if the topic is teamwork, a training design might cover subtopics, such as the team concept, goal setting, roles and responsibilities, managing conflict, problem solving, and decision making. As a result, separate modules might be developed for each topic. On paper, it seems that the design covers the topic of teamwork well, but what happens in the actual experience of the participants? Most will find that they "toured" the topic. They went from subtopic to subtopic, much like a sightseer goes from city to city or country to country, taking in the tour guide's patter but often forgetting where they were a few days ago. At best, participants walk away feeling "been there, done that."

Training that uses active learning strategies focuses on outcomes rather than content. The training is designed to achieve a result instead of covering a topic. Thus, training on teamwork will be concerned with outcomes:

■ Participants will assess how they contribute, as individuals, to their team's success and determine what they can do to make a stronger contribution.

■ Participants will experience a variety of team problem-solving approaches and decide how to apply them to their own team situation.

■ Participants will identify arenas of collaboration within their organization that are not currently happening and strategize how to take those initiatives.

My suggestion is to look at your current training sessions and ask yourself if they are focused on content or outcomes. If it's the former, start asking yourself this question: "What do I want participants to do with the training they are getting?" When you make this shift in focus, you will really appreciate the eight strategies explored in this chapter and start to use them consistently. For example, you will want to involve your participants from the beginning (with icebreakers) to the end (with closing activities) of the training program because they are the key to your success. What you tell and show your participants ultimately doesn't count. What they take away is paramount. It makes no difference how eloquent you are or how elegant your presentation slides appear. What's vital is how well they understand what you've taught and how motivated they are to apply it. When the training is focused on specific targets, the participants must take more active responsibility for the outcome. Having been trained using active learning, they are more likely to do so.

Assess Your Training Situation

Once you know where you're going, give hard thought to how you're getting there. As you consider the eight strategies in this chapter, assess how they may or may not contribute to the process of achieving success in your own situation.

In each instance, ask yourself these questions:

■ Who are the participants? Are they used to active learning? If they are accustomed to lecture and slides, I would advise you to go slowly. Keep activities short and highly structured. Use pairs rather than small groups. Ask one debrief question, not several. Use nonthreatening role-playing techniques. Keep the challenge level moderate.

- What is your comfort level? When you train actively, you don't have the same level of control that a traditional presenter enjoys. You give away a lot of control to the participants. If you don't feel confident that you can take such as risk, transfer control in small doses. Retain a presentation focus, experimenting with a few of the easier techniques to make it brain friendly. Hold off letting participants learn from and teach each other until you feel ready to take the plunge. When you do, be sure to follow up with an instructor-led summary and review.

- How much time do you have? If time is limited, don't waste it on social icebreakers, but do consider a learning icebreaker. If your training program is one or several days long or is distributed over several weeks, realize that you cannot sustain involvement being "front and center" most of the time. In this context, team learning activities are an important break in the process and help participants to "own" the success of the program. Add experiential activity to the mix.

- What can be done outside of the classroom? Consider whether questionnaires or inventories can be completed before class. Can a case study be presented prior to class? Can a reading that provides more detailed information be assigned after the session? Can an e-learning activity be used to supplement the training? Can a discussion use email, chat rooms, and the like?

Seize the Opportunity

Throughout this chapter, I have highlighted the theme that you can make a difference in your training if you take the eight steps to heart. You have the opportunity to rise above the usual norms prevalent in too many organizations today. Far too often, trainers tolerate practices that shut down, rather than open up, learning. By applying the strategies I have provided, there is a strong likelihood that your participants will become the active learners who are needed in a rapidly changing world.

Adapted from *Training the Active Training Way* by Mel Silberman (Pfeiffer, 2006). John Wiley & Sons, © 2006. Used with permission.

About the Author

Mel Silberman is president of Active Training in Princeton, New Jersey, a company that offers active-training seminars for educational, corporate, government, and human-service organizations worldwide. He is known internationally as a pioneer in training and performance improvement. As professor of adult and organizational development at

Temple University, he has won two awards for his distinguished teaching. He shares his original and practical ideas through numerous books, including *Active Training, The Best of Active Training, 101 Ways to Make Training Active,* and *The 60-Minute Active Training Series.*

Silberman's training skills, psychological insights, and engaging personality have made him a popular keynote speaker and workshop leader at conferences of ASTD, ISPI, and NASAGA. He served as the editor of *The ASTD Training and Performance Sourcebook* and *The ASTD Team and Organization Development Sourcebook,* annual collections of tools for trainers and consultants. He recently edited *The Handbook of Experiential Learning* (Pfeiffer, 2007).

Reference

Silberman, Mel. 2006. *Active training: Handbook of techniques, designs, case examples, and tips.* 3d ed. San Francisco: Pfeiffer.

For Further Reading

Barbazette, Jean. 2004. *Instant case studies: How to design, adapt, and use case studies in training.* San Francisco: Pfeiffer.

Jensen, Eric P. 2000. *Brain-based learning: The new science of teaching and training.* Rev. ed. San Diego: The Brain Store.

Silberman, Mel, ed. 2007. *The handbook of experiential learning.* San Francisco: Pfeiffer.

Silberman, Mel. 2006. *Training the active training way: 8 strategies to spark learning and change.* San Francisco: Pfeiffer.

Thiagarajan, Sivasailam. 2005. *Thiagi's interactive lectures.* Alexandria, VA: ASTD Press.

Instructional Facilitation

Sivasailam "Thiagi" Thiagarajan

In This Chapter

- ➢ Learn the difference between training and instructional facilitation
- ➢ Learn the functions of an instructional facilitator
- ➢ Understand the importance of flexibility in presentations

---

The dictionary defines *facilitation* as "the act of making easier." More specifically, Roger Schwarz (2007) in his book *The Skilled Facilitator*, provides this definition:

> Group facilitation is a process in which a person whose selection is acceptable to all members of the group, who is substantively neutral, and who has no substantive decision-making authority diagnoses and intervenes to help a group improve how it identifies and solves problems and makes decisions, to increase the group's effectiveness.

Using methods that range from simple brainstorming to elaborate computer-mediated problem-solving protocols, facilitators help groups to plan projects and strategies, collect and share information, interpret and analyze data, review and evaluate products, make and debate policies, deconstruct and reconstruct workflow procedures, handle crises, resolve conflicts, prioritize ideas, and make decisions.

Although many trainers call themselves facilitators, purists would argue that trainers cannot play the role of facilitators because they have pre-specified goals for the participants. There are also debates about whether facilitation is a subset of training or whether it is the other way around. I prefer to run away from these futile arguments and, for the sake of clarifying what I plan to explore in this chapter, offer the following definition:

> Instructional facilitation is a process in which a person assists a group of participants in selecting, modifying, or accepting a set of learning objectives and acquiring new skills, knowledge, and attitudes related to these objectives. The facilitator supports collective inquiry through the use of activities that encourage participants to interact with each other and with a variety of content resources.

Instructional Facilitation Compared with Training

Before discussing details of instructional facilitation, it will be a good idea to compare this approach with typical training in the corporate workplace. Table 18-1 attempts such a comparison. Here are two points from the table that need to be stressed:

- Both training and instructional facilitation aim at providing effective learning and improving workplace performance.
- Trainers focus on consistent presentation of content while facilitators focus on flexible use of activities that deliver the content.

Integrating Content and Activities

Pure facilitation (used for collaborative problem solving and decision making, for example) focuses on the process and helps participants generate any required content by themselves. Learning situations, however, frequently require the acquisition of new facts, procedures, and principles from the outside. Therefore, instructional facilitation requires integration of just-in-time, just-enough, and just-for-the-group content with collaborative activities. Different types of facilitated activities are available to leverage different content resources. These types are identified and briefly discussed in Table 18-2.

Competencies of Instructional Facilitators

What does an instructional facilitator do? Based on several years of field observations, I have identified a set of macro functions of a facilitator during a typical learning session.

Table 18-1. Comparison Between Training and Instructional Facilitation

	Training	Instructional Facilitation
Desired outcome	Effective learning and improved workplace performance.	Effective learning and improved workplace performance.
Role	Trainer is the presenter of content and manager of learning.	Facilitator supports collaborative learning by a group of participants.
Professional preparation	Train-the-trainer sessions emphasize consistent implementation of the training design and content.	Train-the-facilitator programs emphasize conducting activities that support the group to learn on its own.
Learners	All learners must have the prerequisite skills. Differences in learning styles are acknowledged, but the focus is on catering to linguistic and logical intelligences.	Current group of learners and their learning styles determine the choice of content and activities.
Overall design	Predetermined and consistently implemented.	Original design is viewed as a suggested safety net. Final design organically evolves during the session.
Goals and objectives	A standard set of precisely stated goals and objectives is specified for all participants.	Session begins with broad goals that are modified through the group's inputs.
Content	Content is the most important element. Based on task analyses, accurate and essential content is delivered through participant manuals, slides, and standardized trainer presentations.	Content is given lesser emphasis than the process. Content is obtained from different types of available resources, including participants' current expertise and experience.
Activities	Activities are given lesser emphasis than content. When there is a time crunch, trainers usually skip the activities or reduce the time spent on them.	Activities are considered to be the most important element. Activities require participants to gather, generate, process, and apply the content.
Interaction	Frequent interactions between the participant and the content are required.	Frequent interactions among participants are required.

(continued on next page)

Table 18-1. Comparison Between Training and Instructional Facilitation (continued)

	Training	Instructional Facilitation
Questions for participants	A standard set of objective questions, generated by the instructional designer, is interspersed throughout the training session.	Facilitator frequently makes up questions. Participants are encouraged to generate their own questions.
Questions from participants	Generally discouraged or postponed. Trainer responds with standard answers.	Encouraged and used to modify content and activities. Facilitator encourages collaborative inquiry to discover the answers.
Sequence	Trainers stick to single hierarchical sequence of content presentation based on task analysis.	Facilitators modify the sequence to suit the needs and preferences of participants.

Table 18-2. Types of Instructional Facilitation

Content Resource	Facilitated Activities
Participants' current expertise and experiences	Structured sharing activities facilitate mutual learning and teaching among participants. These activities involve special forms of brainstorming and dialogue and encourage the sharing of ideas, opinions, information, principles, and best practices with each other.
Subject matter experts' presentation of new principles and practices	Interactive lectures transform passive presentations into active experiences. The facilitator (or a subject matter expert) presents the content in suitable chunks and conducts interactive interludes that require participants to collaboratively recall, process, synthesize, and apply the content.
Printed materials (including books, manuals, articles, and handouts)	Textra games combine the effective organization of well-written documents with the motivational impact of interactive exercises. Participants read the content and complete an activity that uses peer support for the analysis and transfer of what they read.
Content on the Internet	Library-playground activities combine the effective organization of online information with the motivational impact of games. Participants study and review content on the Internet, play web-based games, and complete collaborative projects that require recall and transfer of the content.
Video or audio recording	Double exposure activities enhance the instructional value of mediated materials. In a sample double exposure activity, participants watch three-fourths of a video documentary and collaboratively prepare an outline for the remaining portion. Later they compare their outline with the original version and discuss the differences.
Interaction with low-fidelity simulations	Facilitated activities in this area include role plays, metaphorical exercises, and jolts that dramatically increase participants' level of awareness and force them to reexamine their assumptions and revise mindless automatic behaviors. As a part of the activity the facilitator conducts a debriefing discussion to ensure that participants reflect on their experience and share their insights.
Interaction with high-fidelity simulations	Facilitated activities in this area incorporate realistic physical and computerized simulators, authentic documentation, and real-world procedures. The facilitator supports participants' learning by providing just-in-time coaching during the activity and by conducting after-activity reviews.
Job-related experiences	Action learning involves a combination of action and reflection by a team to solve complex, strategic problems in a real-world organizational setting. The facilitator helps participants to effectively apply their current skills and knowledge and to create new skills, knowledge, and insights by continuously reflecting on and questioning the problem definition, the problem-solving processes, and the ensuing results.

Furthermore, my field observations have also identified various micro functions that the instructional facilitator performs according to the demands from the situation. Both the macro and micro functions are identified in the sidebar *Functions of an Instructional Facilitator.* Cutting across these macro and micro functions of an instructional facilitator is the important concept of flexibility that involves a combination of knowledge, skills, and attitudes.

Flexible Facilitation

In the early 1970s, my colleagues and I spent several years conducting some futile field research. We interviewed and observed several facilitators (selected for the high ratings they received from their peers and participants) and the participants they facilitated. Our goal was to discover the secrets of effective facilitation in terms of facilitator behaviors. Initial data from our observations and interviews were disappointing and confusing. We did not find consistent and common behaviors among the facilitators. Furthermore, the same facilitator appeared to use different behaviors with different groups, even when conducting the same activity. As we collected and classified more data and reflected on the patterns, we realized that the real secret of effective facilitators was buried within the apparent inconsistency. We reexamined the data and concluded that effective facilitators are flexible: they continuously modify their activities before and during implementation.

To understand the flexibility demonstrated by effective facilitators, we need to understand the attributes along which this flexibility is based. Following are six critical attributes of facilitated activities, each specified in the form of a behaviorally anchored rating scale.

Design: When Is the Activity Designed?
1. Most predetermined: Have a validated design for the activity.
2. Predetermined: Design the activity based on analyses and evaluation.
3. Neutral: Design consists of a recommended outline for the flow of the activity.
4. Improvised: Parts of the activity are designed while the facilitator is conducting it.
5. Most improvised: The entire activity is designed while the facilitator is delivering it.

Implementation: How Rigidly or Flexibly Should the Activity Be Implemented?
1. Tightest: Explain the rules in detail at the beginning and enforce them rigidly.
2. Tight: Announce the rules in the beginning and enforce them fairly strictly.
3. Neutral: Give an overview of the rules and enforce them flexibly.
4. Loose: Explain the rules only when needed and apply them loosely.
5. Loosest: Make up the rules as you go along and use them loosely.

Functions of an Instructional Facilitator

Macro

- Specifying and modifying goals and objectives
- Establishing ground rules
- Conducting learning activities
- Incorporating content presentations within learning activities
- Conducting practice and feedback activities
- Conducting performance-test activities

Micro

- Allocating roles
- Answering questions
- Arranging the room
- Asking questions
- Assigning partners
- Briefing
- Celebrating
- Challenging
- Checking for consensus
- Closing
- Coaching
- Co-facilitating
- Communicating nonverbally
- Confronting
- Contributing
- Converging
- Debriefing
- Diverging
- Encouraging
- Evaluating
- Focusing on commonality

- Focusing on diversity
- Focusing on the activity
- Focusing on the content
- Focusing on the group
- Focusing on the individual
- Forming teams
- Framing
- Gatekeeping
- Giving feedback
- Handling complaints
- Handling emotions
- Interpreting
- Interrupting
- Intervening
- Letting go
- Linking
- Listening
- Maintaining silence
- Mind mapping
- Mirroring
- Modeling
- Monitoring

- Motivating
- Negotiating
- Observing
- Opening
- Organizing
- Orienting
- Paraphrasing
- Preventing closure
- Questioning answers
- Receiving feedback
- Recording
- Redirecting questions
- Regrouping
- Resolving conflicts
- Rewarding
- Setting climate
- Stimulating
- Summarizing
- Sympathizing
- Taking charge
- Transitioning

Pace: How Rapidly or Leisurely Should the Activity Be Implemented?

1. Fastest: Constantly rush the participants and impose tight time limits.
2. Fast: Keep the activity moving at a fairly fast pace.
3. Neutral: Keep the activity moving at a comfortable pace.
4. Slow: Keep the activity moving at a fairly slow pace.
5. Slowest: Constantly slow down the activity.

Interaction: How Do Group Members Interact with Each Other?

1. Most cooperative: Maintain a high level of cooperation by focusing on external challenges.
2. Cooperative: De-emphasize scores and encourage the participants to help each other.
3. Neutral: Maintain a balance between cooperation and competition.
4. Competitive: Keep scores and encourage participants to outperform their opponents.
5. Most competitive: Encourage cutthroat competition by constantly pointing out that winning is the only important thing.

Focus: Which Is More Important, Process or Outcome?

1. Most process-focused: Keep the activity interesting and enjoyable.
2. Process-focused: Keep the activity enjoyable.
3. Neutral: Maintain a balance between enjoyable procedures and effective results.
4. Outcome-focused: De-emphasize the enjoyment of the activity and focus on getting the job done.
5. Most outcome-focused: Constantly emphasize the goals, results, and outcomes of the activity.

Tone: How Seriously Should We Take the Activity?

1. Most serious: Avoid activities. Present job relevant content through a no-nonsense lecture.
2. Serious: Use high-fidelity simulations and job-related contexts to conduct activities.
3. Neutral: Conduct playful activities and metaphorical simulations.
4. Playful: Conduct activities that involve some chance and fun elements.
5. Most playful: Conduct activities that have plenty of chance and fun elements. Use energizers and icebreakers that are unrelated to the content and objectives.

Mastering Flexibility in Facilitation

When a newcomer asks me, "Should I keep the facilitated activity moving at a fast pace or a slow one?" I usually answer, "Yes."

The appropriate position of an activity along the six attributes depends on several factors, including the number and type of participants and the structure and purpose of the activity.

The secret of effective facilitation is to make these attributes transparent so that if you ask a participant "Was the session slow or fast?" he or she responds, "I don't know. I wasn't paying attention to the pace of the activity."

This transparency is achieved by maintaining a balance between the two poles of each attribute. Balance resides in the context of the activity and the perception of participants. Thus, the balance between cooperation and competition may differ significantly between a group from California and a group from New York, or between a group of human resource people and a group of salespeople from the same organization.

Techniques for Making Adjustments

You may use a variety of techniques to change the position of the activity along each attribute. The sidebar *Sample Techniques for Adjusting Attributes* provides a couple of sample techniques for each attribute.

A Procedural Model for Flexible Facilitation

Learning the adjustment techniques presented in the sidebar does not guarantee you will become an effective facilitator. You also need to know when and how to use them effectively. Here's a six-step procedural model for using these techniques before, during, and after a facilitated activity.

Identify Your Preferences

Flexible facilitation does not mean that you should not have personal preferences, but you should be aware of these preferences and keep them under control. For example, I prefer an evolving design, a fairly loose structure, fast pace, cooperative interaction, results focus, and a playful tone. The best way to discover your biases is to recall your own facilitation experiences in which you felt very positive or very negative and to analyze the factors that contributed to the feelings. You may also talk to your colleagues and participants to get their opinions about your biases. Once you are aware of them, remind yourself that your preferences may not match those of your participants.

Identify Participant Preferences

Before planning a facilitated activity, collect information on the likely preferences of your participants along each of the six attributes. The best source of information is a representative sample from the group; the best strategy for collecting the information is to interview the participants using the behavioral scale presented earlier. To validate your information, talk to other facilitators, consultants, and trainers who are familiar with the group.

Revise the Activity to Suit Participant Preferences

Whether you are designing a new activity or using an existing one, integrate your understanding of the participants' preferences into the activity. Work through the steps and

Sample Techniques for Adjusting Attributes

Design

- *To increase the use of predetermined design,* use only field-tested and packaged materials. Become thoroughly familiar with the content, the sequence, and the timing.
- *To increase the use of evolving design,* avoid depending on packaged instructions. Treat the existing design as a set of flexible recommendations. Experiment with new activities and new twists to existing activities.

Implementation

- *To tighten the implementation,* begin with a detailed explanation of the rules of the activity. Stress the importance of adhering to these rules. Provide a printed copy of the rules to each participant. Frequently refer to these rules.
- *To loosen the implementation,* acknowledge that the participants will be initially confused. Reassure them it is not absolutely necessary to stick to the rules. Don't present all the rules in the beginning. Introduce the rules only if and when they are required.

Pace

- *To speed up the pace,* begin the activity promptly and get it rolling fast. Announce and implement time limits.
- *To slow down the pace,* announce and implement minimum time requirements. If a participant or a team finishes the task before this time is up, insist on review and revision. Introduce a quality-control rule that discourages participants from turning in sloppy ideas or products.

Interaction

- *To increase competition,* use a scoring system to reward effective performance. Periodically announce and compare the scores of different teams. Reward the winning team with a valuable prize.
- *To increase cooperation,* reduce the conflict among the participants and increase the conflict between the participants and external constraints (for example, time limits). Use multiple criteria for determining the winners: reward participants for speed, quality, efficiency, fluency, creativity, novelty, and other factors.

Focus

- *To increase the focus on the process,* make the procedure more salient. From time to time, stop the procedure and undertake a process check. Let the participants suggest changes for making the procedure more interesting.
- *To increase the focus on the outcome,* use a scoring system to reward efficient performance by participants. Stop the activity frequently and discuss the desired results. Have the participants commit themselves to getting the job done.

Tone

- *To increase the seriousness of the activity,* periodically relate it to serious events and decisions in the workplace. Repeatedly remind participants that learning requires serious study and repeated practice.
- *To increase the playfulness of the activity,* intersperse chance and fun elements at unpredictable intervals throughout the facilitated session. Repeatedly remind participants that having fun accelerates learning.

rules of the activity to decide where they are positioned along each attribute. For example, if there are several complex rules that are rigid, the activity will be perceived to be too tight by most participants—unless their preference is for a tight structure. When you identify attributes at one extreme or another, use appropriate techniques to make suitable adjustments. Whenever possible, work with a few members of your participant group to ensure that your design adjustments are appropriate.

Begin the Activity

With suitable adjustments, you should start the activity with confidence. Do not worry about making additional adjustments at this stage. Present a brief overview of the flow of the activity and get the group going.

Make Modifications on the Fly

As your participants work through the activity, continuously monitor their positions along various attributes. If the six attributes are at optimum levels, do not interfere. However, some attributes are likely to become salient from time to time. Wait a little while to see if participants make their own adjustments. If this does not happen, intervene with appropriate adjustments. Do this as unobtrusively as possible. Continue monitoring the group and adjusting the activity as required.

Debrief the Group

When the activity is completed, conduct a debriefing discussion to collect information on their perceptions of different attributes. This can be done in a few minutes by asking the participants questions such as, "When did you feel the activity was too tightly implemented?" or "When did you feel the pace was too fast?" Take notes on the participants' responses and use them to adjust the same activity with similar groups or other activities with the same group.

A major skill in facilitation involves the ability to reconcile the extreme dichotomies such as fast or slow or competitiveness or cooperation. This brings us to the primary dichotomy of training and instructional facilitation.

Not a Line but a Grid

In our initial discussion, I probably misled you into thinking that *training* and *instructional facilitation* are antonyms of each other. Actually, if we reflect on the fact that both aim to produce effective learning and improved performance in the workplace, we may see them in their true colors as complementary activities.

Training and instructional facilitation are not two ends of a continuum where you indicate your position by putting an X, preferably close to the center.

Training   Instructional
                                                                            facilitation

I would like to represent the relationship as a grid in which the two axes refer to training and instructional facilitation (see Table 18-3). Each axis is divided into three segments that represent low, medium, and high levels of effectiveness with respect to achieving improved performance. Our goal in the workplace should be to reach the upper right corner of the grid where highly effective training is blended with equally effective instructional facilitation.

Table 18-3. Relationship Between Training and Instructional Facilitation

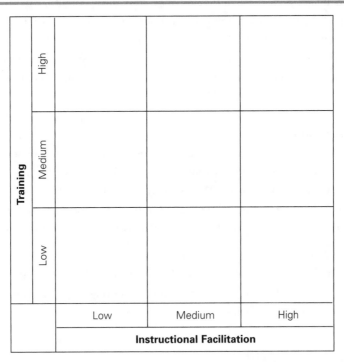

So don't worry about whether you must be a sage on the stage or a guide by the side. Try to become a sage by the side (or a guide on the stage) by blending the best practices from both training and instructional facilitation.

About the Author

Sivasailam "Thiagi" Thiagarajan, PhD, is currently resident mad scientist at the Thiagi Group where he plays games and helps others to play. Since March 21, 1999, he has been conducting a longitudinal research study that involves designing a new learning activity every day (including weekends and holidays). As a result of this obsession, he has published several books and articles related to facilitated learning strategies. A four-time president of North American Simulation Gaming Association (NASAGA) and two-time president of the International Society for Performance Improvement (ISPI), Thiagi has lived in three different countries and has worked and played in 25 others.

Reference

Schwarz, Roger. 2007. *The skilled facilitator: A comprehensive resource for consultants, facilitators, managers, trainers, and coaches.* Rev. ed. San Francisco: Jossey-Bass.

For Further Reading

Kaner, Sam, Lenny Lind, et al. 2007. *Facilitator's guide to participatory decision-making.* 2d ed. San Francisco: Jossey-Bass.

Schuman, Sandy. 2005. *The IAF handbook of group facilitation: Best practices from the leading organization in facilitation.* San Francisco: Jossey-Bass.

Thiagarajan, Sivasailam. 2003. *Design your own games and activities: Thiagi's templates for performance improvement.* San Francisco: Jossey-Bass/Pfeiffer.

Thiagarajan, Sivasailam. 2005. *Thiagi's interactive lectures: Power up your training with interactive games and exercises.* Alexandria, VA: ASTD Press.

 **Chapter 19**

Large Group Methods: A Shopper's Guide

Marvin Weisbord

In This Chapter

- ➤ Adapt methods to changing circumstances
- ➤ Empower your meeting participants
- ➤ Learn to work your plan for success

Well, here's your dilemma: There are now more brand name ways for getting numbers of people interacting than there are cereals in the supermarket. What are large groups good for? Practically anything you can imagine. They are used to bring people together across great distances, find common ground, reconcile conflicts, manage crises, facilitate mergers, redesign organizations, advise people in power, and implement complex strategies.

In their seminal 1997 book, Barbara Bunker and Billie Alban inventoried 12 large group methods. By 2007, Peggy Holman, Tom Devane and Stephen Cady had collected 61 methods and counting. With so many products on the shelves, how do you decide whether to grab Appreciative Inquiry, the Conference Model, Future Search, Open Space, Scenario Planning, Whole Scale Change, World Cafe, or to get a private label hybrid devised just for (or by) you?

This chapter is a guide both for those who purchase these methods and for consultants who offer them. You are forgiven if you have a hard time figuring out which aisle to shop. There's no way you can sample so many forms of interaction, not when your Palm Pilot already is full of meetings that have no names at all. Wise shoppers hire consultants. Maybe you are a consultant. I was. So I know that no consultant ever used 61 methods. What consultants provide are what they know how to do, and what they have passion for (two criteria that, alas, do not always go together like a horse and carriage).

In short, consultants have only a little more capability than do those soliciting their help; what the best ones have is deep experience, gained by reworking a few favorite methods repeatedly to unlock the mystery of their underlying principles. These methods enable them to take risks only when they believe they will succeed. If you're a diligent shopper, you'll figure out which principles matter most to you.

How do you sort nourishment from sugar coating? The books cited above will give you all the particulars, cases, and comparisons you can handle. My purpose in this chapter is to give you a wide-angle view on these matters that will help you choose wisely.

The Times Just Keep on Changing

> *"A large group event is always an unfolding mystery."*
> —Marie T. McCormick (2006)

Years ago I was a serious woodworker intent on cutting dovetails, mortises, and tenons by hand. These feats require sharp chisels—a dull chisel is not only useless, but also danger-ous. So I got a set of the finest Sheffield steel. The first step to using a chisel is to hone it so precisely that it will cut hard woods like a slicer through cheese. I invested in a pair of Japanese water stones that could put a razor edge on table knives.

For advice I turned to a symposium on chisels in *Fine Woodworking,* where a dozen experts advised me on achieving the perfect edge. One advocated rubbing the chisel back and forth in a straight line, another honing in an arc from side to side. A third swore by circular motions in one direction, then the other. I read the methods with increasing frus-tration. "This is no help at all!" I burst out to my wife. "Every expert says their method is best. But which one should *I* use?"

"The answer," said Dorothy, "is obvious. They *all* work!"

If you are shopping for the one best large group method, you could do worse than heed Dorothy's advice. They all work. Methods, however, don't care what you do with them. They remain blithely indifferent even to consultants who profess undying love.

Consequently, they also all fail. I can define failure precisely by telling you about its opposite, success. A meeting succeeds when people do things afterward that they couldn't or wouldn't do before. If that sounds too simple, try this: a successful method helps a system transform its capability for action.

You can succeed in large groups—say 50 to 2,000 people—in ways that people once considered impossible. You also can waste everybody's time. Simply getting platoons of people into a room, physical or virtual, all at once will get you nowhere unless you attend to such basics as the right people, worthy tasks, good leadership, adequate resources, and sufficient time. There is not one thing on that list that is peculiar to the 21st century. You could have made up the same story 100 years ago.

Why have large group "interventions" increasingly captured the imagination of so many people at this moment in time? I plead guilty to my role in this drama. More than 20 years ago I wrote a book tracing the evolution of my consulting practice from expert problem solving to getting everybody improving systems.

The methods I had learned in the 1960s seemed to work best on last year's problems. By the 1970s, we were embedded in systems of problems, what Russell Ackoff, the operations researcher turned management guru, called "messes." For years I had noticed myself panting along trying to keep up with an expanding repertoire of organizational fixes, using the Excalibur of systems analysis on one hand and the Holy Grail of participation on the other.

When I started consulting in 1969, nobody had cell phones, pagers, fax machines, personal computers, PowerPoints, CDs, DVDs, PDAs, Googles, or Wikipedias. The now obsolete Sony Walkman would not be invented for 10 years. My "personal digital assistant" was a little black book in which I wrote dates in pencil because they were sure to change. Blackberries were something you put on pancakes. To research a topic, I went to the library, looked up sources in a card catalog, and made notes on 5 × 8 index cards. I wrote whole books on a typewriter. I backed up with a carbon copy, something you may never have seen. It's a wonder anybody accomplished anything. But they did. My father, born in 1903 just before the Wright brothers' first flight, had by 1969 lived long enough to see a man walk on the moon. What will you live to see?

That life is speeding up is not a new observation. In the 1960s a mentor of mine, Eric Trist, and his collaborator Fred Emery, wrote a ground-breaking paper describing how outside events affected organizations in ways that they could neither control nor ignore. In *The Causal Texture of Organizational Environments*, Emery and Trist (1964) were the first to identify external conditions—more uncertainty, greater interdependence among systems—that called for new systemic responses. What none of us fully appreciated in those years was that the *velocity* of environmental change was accelerating at warp speed. The pace was outstripping our methods.

When I started consulting, business schools taught that big companies reorganized every seven years. Those that were centralized, decentralized. Those that were decentralized, centralized. If they were in aerospace, they had a matrix, and people kept fiddling with it but never quite got it right. For consulting firms this was a windfall. You diagnosed the problem for a year, then recommended to the client the structure they did not have. The seven-year cycle got to be five years in the early 1970s, then three years, and by the 1980s, reorganizations were as predictable as the seasons: mergers, acquisitions, downsizings, globalizings, right sizings. The organizational charts had hardly come out of the copy machine before they had to be changed.

When I left full-time consulting in 1992, the cycle was more like seven weeks. Nobody could study anything for a month, let alone a year. By the time you wrote the consulting report, the scenario had changed. Companies and communities also were diversifying, making every encounter a dynamic social challenge. During the next 15 years, I found myself helping people make plans in many of the world's cultures. The meetings I ran grew more diverse with multiple ethnic groups speaking a Babel of languages, bound together only by the task at hand—improving economic conditions, extending health care, marketing new technologies, or reducing the risk of natural disasters. But what became of the stable old cultures that needed prodding to unfreeze, move, and refreeze at some elusive higher level of functioning? Those were the ones for which *my* tool kit was designed.

The Learning Curve

> *"Problem-solving and invention are greatly simplified*
> *when you're asking the right question."*
>
> —Peter Homer, inventor of a superior
> space glove for astronauts (Hitt, 2007)

In 1987, I wrote *Productive Workplaces*, tracing my consulting ancestry back 100 years to Frederick Taylor, "the father of scientific management." I saw my practice on a learning curve, starting in the 19th century with experts solving problems and dictating the one correct solution (see Figure 19-1). Taylor in 1893 appointed himself the world's first "consulting engineer." He institutionalized his expertise to the point where, just as fish do not know they swim in water, we take for granted our sea of fragmented work systems—in stores, restaurants, offices, and even our homes, from whence we try to connect via crazy-making automated phone loops to what is called oxymoronically "the service economy."

Figure 19-1. The Learning Curve

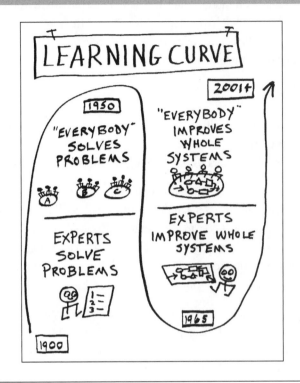

Experts Solve Problems

My interest in Taylor was more than academic. In 1981, I had followed in his footsteps at the Bethlehem Steel Corporation. That's the firm where Taylor from 1898 to 1901 installed innovative work systems under a contract you might envy: if anyone resisted his methods he could have them fired. Despite this (or maybe because of it) he had great success improving output, quality, and working conditions. His systems integrated cost accounting, training, personnel records, inventory control, goal setting, feedback, and wage incentives.

Eighty years later, my consulting firm was hired to help untangle the mess created by the mindless repetition of Taylorism. We found 400 industrial engineers timing jobs and setting rates and 3,400 wage incentive plans. Workers averaged 130 percent of base pay and the company was losing $80 million a month. Bethlehem came through the crisis, in part with "whole system in the room" activities that, with draconian downsizing, kept it going for 20 more years. In the end, this iconic company fell victim to global economic forces that no one could control. It went bankrupt in 2003.

Ah, there is a moral to this story. Taylor's success centered on breaking jobs into little pieces. Our success hinged on integrating what had been split apart. Yet Taylor had many values you would applaud. What happened to his values is the plot line that intrigues me. In his magnum opus, *The Principles of Scientific Management* (1911), arguably the first human resources textbook, Taylor advocated

- Science, not rule of thumb
- Harmony, not discord
- Cooperation, not individualism
- Maximum output, not restricted output
- Development of all workers to their "greatest efficiency and prosperity."

He asserted that "whenever these principles are correctly applied, results must follow that are truly astounding," a claim with a familiar ring if your toolkit has in it Appreciative Inquiry; Open Space Technology; or, for that matter, Future Search. Taylor insisted that techniques were a minor part of his system. Rather, his was "a complete mental revolution" in the relations among working people. Testing and slotting people into the jobs they did best and paying big bonuses for superior output were just the tip of a systemic iceberg.

Many people came to see Taylor as the boogeyman who dehumanized work. His intention was exactly the reverse. Having grown up in an egalitarian Quaker family, he believed his expert methods would so motivate workers that he could cut out authoritarian supervision and do away with labor-management conflict. He lived long enough to see greedy executives and consultants reduce his high-minded systems to time and motion study. He died in 1915 frustrated that so many people had divorced his values and married his techniques.

Everybody Solves Problems

The 1950s brought new insights into group dynamics, leading to the second point on my learning curve: the naming of group dynamics by Kurt Lewin and Ronald Lippitt in 1938, the codification of group processes in the 1940s, and the refinement of group problem solving in the heady years after World War II, which made possible new ways of cooperating and innovating. Participative management became the mantra of the 1960s. Pooling their experience, people could solve hosts of problems in parallel, a development that in the 1970s would inundate the work world with quality circles.

Dazzled by T-groups (human relations training) in the 1960s, many of us believed that experienced-based workshops in decision making, conflict management, group and interpersonal skills, collaboration, and self-awareness would lead to a workplace revolution. We devised cultural change strategies in the 1960s and 1970s that consisted of training hundreds and sometimes thousands of people in groups. We theorized that when everyone got greater personal and group skills, they would transform their organizations.

This turned out to be an iffy proposition. We considered it risky business, for example, to have people from different levels learn together. Too much self-exposure across the hierarchy could derail your career. Yet it's hard to gain influence on the whole in peer groups. In companies "flavor of the month" fixes came and went like songbirds with the seasons. Alas, people improved themselves more than their organizations. We were always getting people ready to do something that they never actually did.

In my favorite musical, *Guys and Dolls*, Miss Adelaide develops a psychosomatic head cold induced by her unreliable fiancé: "You can feed it all day with the Vitamin A and the bromo fizz," she laments, "but the medicine never gets anywhere near where the trouble is." What people could not get in 1970s training groups was influence over an organization's policies, procedures, systems, and structure—the heart and soul of systemic change.

Experts Improve Whole Systems

About this time, organizational experts began to catch on to biologist Ludwig von Bertalanffy's (1950) paradigm-shifting concept, general systems theory. It's a hard read, but I will give you a one-sentence summary that could change your life:

Everything is hooked up to everything else!

This concept made possible the third station on my learning curve. Into organizations heavy with problem-solving task forces and tiger teams came a new expert capable of thinking through every aspect of the mess. It became somewhat easy, for example, for my consulting company circa 1980 to interview dozens of people in a solar energy startup and diagram systemic issues—the connections among the design and engineering of solar cells, the disappointment with leadership, the problems of development, the failures in the marketplace, and the demotivated employees.

We self-styled systems experts offered a solution: more research and development, less marketing pressure, and more patience in corporate headquarters could do wonders at all levels. The sad fact that our clients could not implement our wisdom emerged in participative meetings involving "everybody" except executives from the parent company. We simply validated the hopelessness. Within a year, the startup was gone without a trace (Weisbord, 2004).

Nonetheless, whole systems expertise brought new dimensions to the art of change. Leaders began noticing the interactions among economics, technology, and people. They could see the order in apparent chaos, the links between the laws of nature and organizational life, an understanding that flowered with Margaret Wheatley's (2006) *Leadership and the New Science.*

Inevitably expert analysis and participation would meet, fall in love, and move in together. This evolution started even before "systems thinking" became a buzzword. Shortly after World War II, ex-British Army officers led by psychiatrist Wilfred Bion and psychologist Eric Trist started the Tavistock Institute of Human Relations in London, intending to devise ways to rebuild a war-ravaged British economy using social science knowledge. In South Yorkshire, they found coal miners performing in leaderless work teams, bringing coal to the surface around the clock, with less waste, higher output, and fewer accidents than other mines. More remarkably, union workers and managers had planned the innovative system together in response to a new roof control technology. The miners had turned Taylorism upside down!

In *Organizational Choice* (1963) Trist and colleagues described the empirical and theoretical roots of "sociotechnical systems" design from their study of coal mines. You started with a system's core mission, its so-called primary task. If people internalized the social, technical, and economic assumptions behind the task, they could invent flexible, dynamic, and self-renewing organizations. Emery, Trist's collaborator, soon dubbed a key aspect of their framework the "second design principle." Instead of Taylor's "one person, one task" dictated by engineers, self-managing multiskilled teams controlled and coordinated their own work.

What happened later, however, makes me less sanguine about the future of large group methods. In the 1960s and 1970s, what British coal miners had devised spontaneously became the province of expert systems improvers. Their methods became an infinite charting of variances and a detailed social remapping of jobs, high-level Taylorism with a patina of labor-management participation by a design team. I found an awesome paradox in getting multitudes of people in a company to embrace the hard-won conclusions of a representative 12-person team.

But that is not the last word. Just as Taylor's systems were boiled down to time and motion study, so did sociotechnical systems become a self-regulating team package installed like software. In the late 1980s, I was invited to a manufacturing meeting in a venerable paper company suffering the aftereffects of such an exercise. The managers were angry, and they got sympathy from me but not help. Having sacrificed participative values on the altar of canned techniques, they were not about to do it once more with feeling. This company too, like so many I worked with in those years, is no more. (So much for our fantasies of building for the ages!)

Everybody Improves Whole Systems

To ameliorate alienation and get better designs, some of us in the 1980s began redesigning systems in a series of large conferences of 60 people and more. This lengthy process nonetheless involved many more people, cutting implementation time from years to only months. It was a principled effort to involve people across levels and functions at the same time. Sometimes customers and suppliers came in. *Collaborating for Change: The Conference Model* (Axelrod and Axelrod, 2000) describes a notable example.

Maybe now you can see where I'm going. A series of projects I reported in my 1987 book led me inexorably toward a scary, and liberating, conclusion. If we truly wanted to realize values for workplaces in which productivity rested on a bedrock of dignity, meaning, and community, we ought to figure out how to get *everybody improving whole systems*. Processes that involved everybody in improving the whole seemed to me the design spec for a diverse world of nonstop change. Such methods would make it possible for everybody to use the brains they were born with, bring their experience to bear, appreciate the whole and their part in it, and be capable of taking responsibility. How to do that became for me the right question.

I had noticed that in successful cases there was an attractive goal, a leader with an itch to scratch, and some energized people with expertise and commitment. I observed a few practices that seemed to make my elusive goal attainable: get the "whole system" in the room, focus on the future rather than the problem list, and set things up so that people could do the work themselves. Pushing further into this dimension of group dynamics, I learned that mine was not the only way to do such work. In *Discovering Common Ground* (Weisbord, 1992) I brought together many cases that I thought pointed toward unifying principles for successful large group methods.

The future search model Sandra Janoff and I (2007) have experimented with since 1987 is one outgrowth of that inquiry. We built on procedures I had borrowed from my mentors, notably Eric Trist and Ronald Lippitt, as well as Fred Emery, going back to the 1970s. Over time, Janoff and I concluded that nobody could facilitate his or her way to success in meetings in which key people were missing. We learned to define "whole system in the room" as people with authority, resources, expertise, information, and need. (A colleague noted the acronym "AREIN" years later. In such ways do life and art become one!) For us this was a conceptual leap that rationalized bringing in customers, suppliers, bureaucrats, community leaders, and even family members.

When diverse groups meet to pursue a given goal, they effectively redefine a system's boundaries. They turn "systems thinking" into an experiential rather than a conceptual activity. They enable everybody to use for a few hours, days, or months, what they already have on behalf of goals larger than themselves. People who *are* each other's environment share what they know. Instead of talking about "them," whoever they are, people dialogue with "them." Everybody comes to understand the whole in a way that no one person had done days or hours before. Thus, they empower themselves. Although these are structural interventions, paradoxically, many people voluntarily change their behavior (Weisbord and Janoff, 2007).

Unless "everyone" is present, it's very easy for people to slough off responsibility to those who aren't there. This last point is not trivial. In a contentious meeting of stakeholders in the air traffic system, for example, a participant looked around the room after a few anxious hours and said, "Well, we're all here. If *we* don't fix this system, no one else will do it" (Weisbord and Janoff, 2000).

So, now you have a key criterion for assessing any large group method, including those not yet invented. To what extent will method X help you prepare everybody to act responsibly on behalf of the whole? Anything less, and you run the risk of prescribing more of the medicine that makes people cynical. Even that's not enough. You still need to find all the mundane stuff that preceded cyberspace—leadership, resources, and a worthy task that people cannot do alone.

Just Do It

> *"It ain't bragging if you can do it."*
>
> —Dizzy Dean, legendary baseball player (1931)

That somebody did miracles with Appreciative Open Strategic Holistic Future Conversations (I made that one up, but just wait) tells you nothing about what *you* could do with this imaginary hybrid. If somebody claimed they got a miracle putting all that together, he or she probably did. For evidence, check the cases in the 2006 edition of Bunker's and Alban's large group methods book. They will knock your socks off. I was involved in one of them, and while I read the others with awe, I can't imagine replicating any of them. Indeed, I'm not sure I could pull off my own high wire act again.

Knowing that something "worked" once before leaves me with no more certainty than believing that because a train arrived on time yesterday the same will be true today. The best way to apply any method is with wonder, high tolerance for anxiety, patience, and an open mind. Still, you need not fly blind. Get the basic principles, whatever you believe them to be, firmly fixed in your psyche. That's your insurance policy. Find a good match among leader, goal, timeframe, and procedure. After that, leave it up to the cosmos—and to the people in the room.

Some Dos and Don'ts That Correlate with Success

In our 2007 book, Janoff and I described 10 principles that we have applied worldwide to meetings of all sizes. A few points are worth iterating:

- Get the whole system in the room. That's the shortest road to getting out all the key information, making informed decisions, and building commitment.
- Explore the "whole elephant" before acting, meaning have people educate each other on what they know, what they believe, and what they want.
- Encourage self-managing and responsibility. With a little prompting, groups of up to eight people can manage themselves with no facilitation. You can put on huge meetings with building blocks of eight.
- Seek common ground rather than rehash old issues. We like to treat past problems and conflicts as information, not action items, until people have a vision they all share.
- Self-managing groups function best with a goal accepted by all. For people to "self-organize" they need a shared task. A well-balanced top will spin a long time on its own only after somebody spins it.
- Allow enough time. People who do this work have learned that faster and cheaper does not always correlate with shorter.
- Choose good meeting rooms. These are not easy to find for large groups. The usual settings are hotel ballrooms and high school gyms. Eventually people will build more big conference spaces that include windows and skylights and acoustics that favor dialogue over dance bands.
- Prepare yourself by accepting that anxiety usually precedes productivity.

Events vs. Processes

Some people worry over whether a particular meeting represents just an "event," rather than something larger, grander, nobler, and more far-reaching, that is to say, a "process." Only processes, it is said, result in cultural change that will be self-sustaining and self-organizing, making organizational learning a way of life. (Whew, I managed to put five bromides of the change business into one sentence!)

Having pursued that phantasm to the far side of the galaxy and come back empty-handed, I would rather put the energy that goes into debating processes versus events into real work. The real work is planning and running the best meeting you are capable of running, every single time, with as many of the right people as you can squeeze in. Do such events periodically with intention, and, voila, you have a process.

That is something anybody can do if he or she has the authority and chooses to do it. What happens after each meeting will depend on who is willing to take responsibility and what resources he or she has. No matter how much you preplan, such matters are unknowable until people do new things purposefully that they didn't used to do.

Technology, Again

In the four decades that I have been on this quest, I have learned to work comfortably with groups of up to a few hundred without resorting to electronics beyond the cordless microphone. I consider myself a technological illiterate in this age of multitasking, even though I have lived long enough to see Chloe and Isabel, my granddaughters, sitting on the same couch text messaging each other while watching TV and doing their homework.

The integration of the Internet, television, the telephone, art, music, literature, science, and so much else has made possible astounding feats. You can work with hundreds or even thousands of people if you have the time, resources, and technology. In every meeting we now have more resources a mouse click away than most people who ever lived could mobilize in a lifetime. People are now experimenting with simultaneous online meetings around the globe, some participants in the same room, others sitting alone. There seems no end to the permutations, combinations, and applications. Consider, for example, the BBC's involving 17,000 people in a drive to make their company the most creative in the world using every known form of interaction (Cheung-Judge and Powley, 2006).

And yet, and yet…nobody I know claims that interacting at a distance makes a wholly satisfying substitute for meetings in the flesh. The most successful large group methods, now and later, I believe, will involve both forms. I also am too much of a historian to imagine that today's eye-popping large group methods are the end of history. Every method has its limits, as we all are destined to learn.

Our ancestors gave us priceless gifts, but none has prepared us for a world that lies beyond the Internet, virtual teams, and BlackBerries that are not edible. More to the point, we live in a global economy that is consuming resources at a rate far beyond our ability to replace them. Indeed, sustainable organizations have no future in an unsustainable world of our own making. That is a topic that ought to be on every meeting agenda.

The future of our organizations, communities, nations, and planet does not rest on any particular method. It lies with what we do every day. With large group methods, we have evolved the capability to screw up on a grand scale. We can choose to continue to run meetings with key people missing in timeframes so short that more meetings are unavoidable, closeted in dungeon rooms that deplete body, mind, and spirit. We can perpetuate the practice of having experts talk at people followed by questions but never dialogue. We can treat anxiety and chaos as problems to be solved rather than the context for productive work.

We also can involve everybody in improving the whole. For most of us the only way we ever will change the world is one meeting at a time. You can make a difference every day, if you decide to do it; but sharpen your chisels. Otherwise, you just won't cut it.

About the Author

Marvin Weisbord co-directs Future Search Network, an international nonprofit service agency, providing communities, nonprofits, and NGOs with whole system planning workshops for whatever they can afford. He was a business executive in the 1960s. For 20 years he was a partner in the consulting firm Block, Petrella, Weisbord and a member of NTL Institute. He is on the resource faculty of the Organization and Systems Renewal Program at Seattle University, an emeritus member of the European Institute for Transnational Studies, an elected fellow of the World Academy of Productivity Science, and an honorary lifetime member of the Organization Development Network, which gave him a Lifetime Achievement Award in 2004 and voted *Productive Workplaces* one of the most influential books of the last 40 years. In addition to books listed in the references, he is author of *Organizational Diagnosis* (Perseus Books, 1978), still widely used as a college text and consulting guide.

References

Axelrod, Emily M., and Richard H. Axelrod. 2000. *Collaborating for change: The conference model.* San Francisco: Berrett-Koehler.

Bunker, Barbara Benedict, and Billie T. Alban. 1997. *Large group interventions: Engaging the whole system for rapid change.* San Francisco: Jossey-Bass.

Bunker, Barbara Benedict, and Billie T. Alban. 2006. *The handbook of large group methods: Creating systemic change in organizations and communities.* San Francisco: Jossey-Bass.

Cheung-Judge, Mee-Yan, and Edward H. Powley. 2006. Innovation at the BBC: Engaging an entire organization. In *The handbook of large group methods: Creating systemic change in organizations and communities*, eds., B. Bunker and B. Alban. San Francisco: Jossey-Bass.

Dean, Dizzy, available at www.quotationsbook.com/author/1931.

Emery, Fred E., and Eric L. Trist. 1964. The causal texture of organizational environments. *Human Relations*, 18(1): 21-32.

Hitt, Jack. 2007, July 1. The amateur future of space travel. *The New York Times Magazine*, 66.

Holman, Peggy, Tom Devane, and Stephen Cady. 2007. *The change handbook: The definitive resource on today's best methods for engaging whole systems.* San Francisco: Berrett-Koehler.

Lewin, Kurt, and Ronald Lippitt. 1938. An experimental approach to the study of autocracy and democracy: A preliminary approach. *Sociometry* 1: 292-300.

McCormick, Marie T. 2006. "Speakup! Bringing youth, educators, and parents together for critical conversations. In *The handbook of large group methods: Creating systemic change in organizations and communities*, eds., B. Bunker and B. Alban. San Francisco: Jossey-Bass.

Taylor, Frederick W. 1911. *The principles of scientific management.* New York: Norton, 1967.

Trist, Eric L., G.W. Higgin, H. Murray, and A.B. Pollock. 1963. *Organizational choice.* London: Tavistock Publications.

von Bertalanffy, Ludwig. 1950. Theory of open systems in physics and biology. *Science* 111: 23-29.

Weisbord, Marvin R. 1987. *Productive workplaces: Organizing and managing for dignity, meaning, and community.* Rev. ed. San Francisco: Jossey-Bass/Wiley.

Weisbord, Marvin R. 2004. *Productive workplaces revisited: Dignity, meaning, and community in the 21st century.* San Francisco: Jossey-Bass/Wiley.

Weisbord, Marvin R., ed. 1992. *Discovering common ground.* San Francisco: Berrett-Koehler.

Weisbord, Marvin, and Sandra Janoff. 2000. *Future search: An action guide to finding common ground in organizations and communities.* 2d ed. San Francisco: Berrett-Koehler.

Weisbord, Marvin, and Sandra Janoff. 2007. *Don't just do something, stand there! Ten principles for leading meetings that matter.* San Francisco: Berrett-Koehler.

Wheatley, Margaret J. 2006. *Leadership and the new science: Discovering order in a chaotic world.* 3d ed. San Francisco: Berrett-Koehler.

The 25 Competencies of a Master Trainer

Jean Barbazette

In This Chapter

- ➤ Learn the best practices of master trainers
- ➤ Apply effective behaviors to get better training results

How do you recognize a master trainer or facilitator? A master trainer or facilitator makes the entire learning process look deceptively easy. They exhibit an advanced level of competence when completing a variety of tasks both inside and outside the physical or virtual classroom. The 25 competencies presented in this chapter are built from knowledge and skills. Following each competency is a list of behaviors exhibited by master trainers. Beginning and intermediate trainers usually exhibit the first two to three behaviors listed for each competency, whereas master trainers use all or most behaviors.

This chapter's aims are twofold: a snapshot of desired skills for the beginning trainer and review for the advanced trainer. For beginners, it is necessary to develop skills, and it's essential to know which skills are most useful to trainers. By understanding the attributes that are exhibited by master trainers or facilitators, a beginner can identify his or her own skill gaps. Then, by selecting two or three areas for improvement, the beginner can look for opportunities to grow and develop his or her level of competence by using the additional behaviors suggested after each competency. For the advanced trainer, these competencies present a refresher—of the behaviors listed, which ones are absent from your practice? Which ones have you mastered?

 Refer to the Master Trainer Self-Assessment in Tool 20-1 on the accompanying CD-ROM to assess your own skill set.

Prepare for Instruction

Preparation is critical to successful training. It helps to ensure that the trainer understands the learners' needs, that the learners are ready for the training, and that the training environment is optimized for learning. To prepare for instruction, the master trainer completes the following prior to the day of training:

- Create and distribute appropriate prework assignments
- Set up the classroom for optimum learning
- Check classroom equipment for proper running condition
- Partner with supervisors of participants to prepare learners for results
- Revise participant training materials based on the needs of this group
- Customize the lesson plan to the needs of this group
- State course outcomes as benefits to the participants.

Set the Learning Environment

Master trainers know that a poor learning environment can seriously detract from the learning. To set a learning environment that's conducive to learning, master trainers complete these tasks at the beginning of a training session:

- Conduct introductions that place the learners at ease
- Establish ground rules and announce the schedule for the course
- Ask for information from the learners about their objectives, experience, and motivation for the course topic
- Design a course graphic to provide a visual overview of the course
- Select appropriate music or other audiovisuals to play while participants assemble
- Show electronic slides that will preview the training session concepts
- Identify risk factors of activities relevant to the specific target population
- Conduct a session starter that involves everyone, is low risk, and is related to the course content
- Help participants tie course objectives to a business need.

> ### ✐ **Leonard Nadler** ✐
>
> *Leonard Nadler was an integral figure in the birth and rise of human resource development (HRD). In 1965, Nadler started the oldest HRD program in the United States at George Washington University. Five years later, Nadler published his revolutionary book* Developing Human Resources, *in which he was the first to truly define and identify the field of HRD. Nadler is also recognized for coining the term* human resource development. *He was integral in laying the framework for HRD and identified the three important roles of a human resource developer: learning specialist, administrator, and consultant.*

Use Adult Learning Principles

Much research indicates that adults have different learning needs than do children. To capitalize on that research and enhance the learning experience for adults, master trainers use these adult learning principles during training:

- Provide a practical and useful learning experience
- Acknowledge participants' prior knowledge and skills
- Use many training methods to appeal to different learning styles.

Use Lectures Effectively

Typically lectures are viewed as one of the least effective methods for enabling learning. However, lectures are sometimes necessary. To make the best use of lectures, successful trainers

- Set up the lecture by telling the objective and giving an overview of the content
- Provide clear and accurate examples
- Supplement verbal comments with written handout materials and visuals
- Make a summary
- Answer questions accurately
- Involve learners in brief activities at least every 15 minutes
- Maintain eye contact and use appropriate gestures
- Avoid distracting words, such as "ah," "um," and "ya know"
- Vary speaking rate, pitch, and volume
- Have learners develop or use the concepts from the lecture
- Have learners finish the lecture or make a summary or application of the ideas presented.

Conduct Discussions

Discussions are a good way to get learners engaged with the training material. When conducting discussions, accomplished trainers often

- Set up the discussion by stating the objective and giving an overview of the agenda
- Ask general questions to begin the discussion
- Ask direct questions to gain fuller participation
- Ask participants to clarify the concepts
- Make a summary
- Ask redirected and reverse questions to gain fuller participation
- Ask a variety of open and closed questions to appropriately direct the discussion
- Challenge generalizations and irrelevant digressions and probe for deeper meaning
- Draw out quiet or reluctant participants without embarrassing them
- Ask participants to clarify the concepts and make a summary.

Facilitate Exercises

Exercises are another excellent way to get learners engaged with the material. Advanced trainers use the following behaviors when facilitating exercises:

- Set up the learning activity by telling the objective and giving an overview of the activity
- Group participants and assign roles appropriate to the activity
- Observe the participants and assist groups as needed
- Conduct a debrief to get learning points
- Make a summary of key points
- Conduct a debrief of the activity by asking participants to share and interpret their reactions to the activity through appropriate questions
- Ask participants to identify learning points that usually emerge from the activity
- Handle unexpected learning appropriately
- Ask participants to identify how they will use or apply the concepts learned from the activity.

Conduct Demonstrations

Demonstrations are a way to help visual learners understand the learning material better and provide an additional way for nonvisual learners to grasp the information. When conducting a demonstration, master trainers

- Set up the demonstration by telling the objective and giving an overview of the process or procedure to be demonstrated
- Show the process or procedure while explaining what learners see and hear
- Supervise participant return demonstrations, give feedback, and make corrections
- Supervise practice sessions to complete learning
- Evaluate learning through tests
- Evaluate learning through appropriate skill performance tests
- Ask appropriate questions
- Ask learners questions so learners develop concepts and make a summary.

Conduct Role Plays

Role plays are activities in which participants act out new roles, attitudes, and behaviors to practice skills and apply what they've learned. Successful trainers use the following behaviors when conducting role plays:

- Set up the role play by sharing the objective, selecting a volunteer, and preparing the volunteer for his or her role
- Make a summary of skills demonstrated
- Structure the role play to be completed simultaneously in groups of three
- Instruct observers and provide a checklist for completion during the observation
- Ask participants to play the scene without overdirecting
- Ask participants to share and interpret their reactions to the role plays
- Ask participants questions to develop the concept or focus on the skills being developed
- Ask participants questions to summarize and apply what was learned to the job.

Provide Feedback

Feedback is important to correct learners when they have misunderstood something and to provide reinforcement when they get it right. However, feedback needs to be appropriate and given in the correct way. Master trainers

- Describe specifically what the learner does and says that is incorrect
- Offer an appropriate model
- Avoid commenting on attitude or values, or making a judgment
- Focus on limited issues and avoid describing behavior as "always" or "never"
- Focus on behavior the learner can do something about
- Give well-timed information

- Use paraphrasing to ensure learner understanding and clear communication
- Help learners gain insights and verbalize the rationale for changed behavior.

Use Audiovisuals

Audiovisuals are a way to capture learners' attention. When using audiovisuals, successful master trainers

- Show or customize visual images that support the learning objective
- Select a variety of media to enhance different learning styles
- Use color appropriately
- Do not read to the learner from the visuals
- Operate equipment with ease and troubleshoot minor mechanical problems.

Administer Tests and Evaluate Skills

Tests and skill evaluations can be used to gauge the learners' comprehension of the content, which in turn enables trainers to adapt to the needs of the learners. Master trainers should

- Select appropriate content and test items
- Administer the test fairly
- Answer participant questions without providing unwarranted assistance
- Correct tests promptly
- Provide feedback to learners to improve performance.

Handle Problem Learners

Training sessions are frequently disturbed by problem learners. To avoid disruptions to other learners and to get the training back on track, master trainers

- Use disciplinary strategies to correct problem learner behavior
- Ignore minor problem learner behaviors and talk to disruptive participants privately
- Use interactive training methods to redirect the focus of a problem learner
- Ask disruptive participants to leave the classroom
- Identify whether or not a problem is caused by the content or process of instruction

- Anticipate problem learners by using prevention strategies, such as setting ground rules
- Use high-risk disciplinary strategies to correct problem learner behavior as a last resort
- Assess the effectiveness of problem learner strategies.

Use Technology to Deliver Training

Myriad technological options are now available to trainers. It is important, however, that they be used judiciously. When using technology to deliver training, master trainers use these behaviors:

- Operate software and hardware that are a part of the course
- Provide written directions for others to operate technical tools
- Seek support for technical assistance
- Place learners at ease when introducing new technology through learning activities
- Interact appropriately with technical support personnel
- Complete system and sound checks prior to conducting a course.

Promote Learning Transfer

However valuable and entertaining training may be, if it does not transfer to the job through improved skills, knowledge, and attitudes, it is simply a waste of money and time. To promote the transfer of learning from the classroom to the workplace, master trainers

- Use adult learning methods to facilitate content that addresses the participant's real issues
- Provide appropriate practice and feedback to learners
- Set objectives with the participant's manager that are based on needs defined with the manager
- Customize content to meet the participant's needs
- Provide follow-up information to assist coaching and support by the participant's manager
- Assist the manager in evaluating the transfer of learning and bottom-line results of training.

Conduct Online Learning

Master trainers use the web to deliver training with increasing frequency. They generally

- Use lecture appropriately in a virtual classroom
- Help learners become familiar with a few tools in the technology by pointing them out
- Facilitate threaded discussions
- Use appropriate visual support
- Use a variety of training methods appropriately in a virtual classroom
- Help learners become familiar with tools in the technology that promote participation
- Compensate for a lack of face-to-face contact appropriately
- Depart from the prepared script to promote learning.

Recommend Course Changes

By delivering training and getting immediate feedback from learners, trainers are in an ideal position to identify areas to improve in courses. When recommending course changes, master trainers

- Identify appropriate changes to make a course more effective
- Identify when a course does not match the job and is out of date
- Tactfully make appropriate recommendations for course changes.

Plan Meetings

When planning team or training meetings, master trainers use an agenda or meeting content description and exhibit these behaviors prior to the meeting or training:

- Solicit agenda items from participants
- Tie agenda items to a business need
- Contact participants from prior meetings to obtain updated information and completed assignments
- Circulate the agenda prior to the meeting.

Set a Productive Climate for Discussions

Trainers frequently find themselves facilitating discussions. To set a productive climate and begin a discussion, master trainers or facilitators

- Set a productive climate through room setup
- Collaboratively set ground rules
- Place new group members at ease through an appropriate introduction that acknowledges expertise
- Begin a meeting with an appropriate introduction of a new topic or an update on a continuing matter
- Ask appropriate general questions to initiate the discussion.

Orient Meetings Toward Outcomes

To get a group to focus on defining and reaching outcomes, master trainers or facilitators use these behaviors:

- Chart suggestions and ideas from the group
- Ask questions to bring clarity or develop a topic
- Use brainstorming and other idea development techniques to keep the group thinking divergently
- Organize information from the group into a plan
- Get the group to summarize and reach a decision by consensus where appropriate
- Use time efficiently to help groups summarize
- Keep the group on track and bar irrelevant diversions
- Help the group through storming and norming phases of group development to get to the performing and productive phases.

Enable Group Communication

Good communication is important in most areas, but it is especially true when facilitating meetings. To help a group communicate effectively, master trainers or facilitators exhibit the following behaviors:

- Initiate, propose, and make suggestions that bring clarity to the communication
- Use paraphrasing and ask questions to clarify meaning
- Accurately record group member ideas
- Encourage divergent thinking and use a variety of idea generation techniques
- Organize information
- Encourage diverse opinions and facts from reluctant participants
- Keep the conversation civil, even with disagreement
- Acknowledge all points of view.

Encourage Creative Problem Solving

One way for groups to address issues is to engage in creative problem solving. One technique to encourage members of the group to come up with innovative solutions is brainstorming. To encourage creative problem solving, such as brainstorming, master trainers or facilitators

- Conduct brainstorming sessions
- Help participants identify problems
- Use a variety of creative techniques to get participants to identify solutions
- Keep the problem solving divergent until enough ideas are generated
- Assist participants in reaching a decision.

Encourage Participation

Full participation from all group members is important to capture people's ideas, experience, and knowledge and to surface additional issues. To support and encourage participation, master trainers or facilitators use these behaviors:

- Ask appropriate questions
- Initiate, propose, and make suggestions
- Divide the group into subgroups to increase participation
- Encourage diverse opinions and facts from reluctant participants
- Organize a sequence of speakers
- Chart group ideas
- Draw out quiet participants in a nondefensive manner.

Foster Self-Discovery

Establishing a sense of ownership of a solution or change is critical to its successful implementation. One way to establish a sense of ownership is through self-discovery of alternatives and solutions. To foster such self-discovery, master trainers or facilitators

- Use questioning appropriately
- Use brainstorming and other creative problem-solving methods
- Assign specific tasks to subgroups to foster self-discovery
- Use inventories and questionnaires as a means of fostering self-discovery of alternatives
- Use convergent techniques to get participants to decide upon a solution.

Enable Decision Making

To help a group make decisions, master trainers or facilitators often

- Help the group summarize areas of agreement
- Use questions to clarify points of difference
- Use a variety of techniques to be sure all points of view are explained
- Ask questions to help build a consensus when appropriate
- Ask the group to provide a rationale for its decision.

Select Team Leaders

To select a team leader, master trainers or facilitators use these behaviors:

- Solicit group input for leadership criteria
- Ask questions to help the group evaluate team leader candidates
- Collaboratively get groups to choose a team leader.

Other Behaviors of Master Trainers

In addition to exhibiting these 25 competencies with ease, master trainers or facilitators usually mentor less-experienced trainers to help them develop advanced levels of competence. Mentoring can be formal or informal. Mentors are often called upon to offer peer instruction or advice to those who are interested in development.

Master trainers are visible at trainer association conferences and give back to their profession by conducting workshops and sessions to benefit their peers. They often conduct or participate in research and serve on task forces to better the profession. You'll find master trainers in leadership positions in professional organizations and in their own organizations. Master trainers are generous with their time and often conduct pro-bono training sessions for community organizations.

Adapted from *The Trainer's Journey to Competence* (Barbazette, 2005). John Wiley & Sons, © 2005. Used with permission.

About the Author

Jean Barbazette, MA, is president of The Training Clinic, a training consulting firm she founded in 1977. Her company specializes in train-the-trainer programs, new employee orientation, and quality enhancement of training and instruction for major national and international clients. Her degree from Stanford University is a master's in education. She's the author of the bestselling book *Successful New Employee Orientation* (Pfeiffer, 2007) and *The Trainer's Support Handbook* (McGraw-Hill, 2001). She has authored three training packages: Customer Service: Back to the Basics, Telephone Techniques, and Dealing with Difficult Customers. She is a past contributor to McGraw Hill Sourcebooks, Pfeiffer Annuals, and ASTD publications. She received The President's Award from Orange County ASTD in 1998 for 20 years of continuous and outstanding service to the chapter. OCASTD awarded her the 1999 Distinguished Service Award.

Reference

Barbazette, Jean. 2005. *The trainer's journey to competence: Tools, assessments, and models.* San Francisco: Pfeiffer.

For Further Reading

Barbazette, Jean. 2006. *Training needs assessment.* San Francisco: Pfeiffer.
Barbazette, Jean. 2006. *The art of great training delivery.* San Francisco: Pfeiffer.
Barbazette, Jean. 2007. *Managing the training function.* San Francisco: Pfeiffer.
Biech, Elaine. 2005. *Training for dummies.* Hoboken, NJ: John Wiley & Sons.
Carliner, Saul. 2003. *Training design basics.* Alexandria, VA: ASTD Press.
Lawson, Karen. 1998. *The trainer's handbook.* San Francisco: Jossey-Bass/Pfeiffer.
Piskurich, George. 1999. *The ASTD handbook of training and delivery.* New York: McGraw-Hill.
Piskurich, George. 2003. *Trainer basics.* Alexandria, VA: ASTD Press.
Rosania, Robert J. 2003. *Presentation basics.* Alexandria, VA: ASTD Press.
Stolovitch, Harold D., and Erica J. Keeps. 2002. *Telling ain't training.* Alexandria, VA: ASTD Press.

Chapter 21

Coaching: A Customized Learning Approach

Madeline Finnerty

--------------------------------------- **In This Chapter** ---------------------------------------

➤ Understand the difference between coaching and training

➤ Learn approaches to coaching

➤ Get resources for coaches

Coaching has become increasingly important as a strategy for workplace performance improvement. Over the past 25 years, rapid organizational change has created a need for customized solutions that effectively target the development needs of each employee or client. Coaching differs from training, as this chapter points out, and requires a particular set of skills. As the demand for acquiring and hiring those skills has grown, coaching resources have proliferated.

Coaching has evolved to include several different approaches, all based on different assumptions about how people are motivated to change behavior, the role of the coach, and the nature of the relationship between the coach and the employee or client. This chapter outlines the behavioral, ontological, and appreciative inquiry based approaches. Additionally, this chapter addresses specific coaching applications such as executive coaching, mentoring, and dealing with difficult coaching situations.

Coaching: An Approach

Coaching has become an important approach in the repertoire of workplace performance improvement strategies. From an organizational perspective, a rapidly changing business environment created by a global marketplace and technological innovation has resulted in the need for a workforce that can deal with complexity, ambiguity, and continuous change (see Figure 21-1). From the individual's perspective, the expectation to be actively

Figure 21-1. Factors Driving the Growth of Coaching

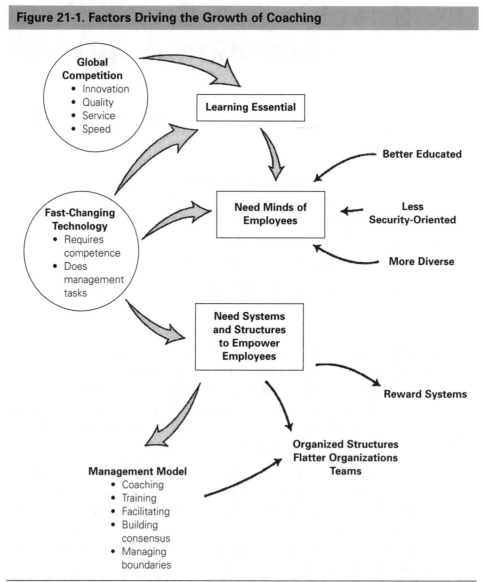

Source: Finnerty International, © 2007. Used with permission.

engaged in meaningful work has replaced the assembly line days where workers were hired for their hands. The role of management is no longer command and control. As Flaherty (1999) points out, "Command and control organizations cannot bring about the conditions and competencies necessary to successfully meet the challenges holistically."

Managers today need to be able to influence performance quickly and effectively. The learning needs of employees are changing as rapidly as the business environment. In addition, the development needs of employees often vary significantly in scope, level, and focus. Just as industries are realizing the need for mass customization of products for clients with diverse needs and preferences, organizations are increasingly turning to a mass customization approach to workplace learning. That approach is coaching.

At a minimum, coaching enables one manager and one employee to resolve a specific performance problem through analysis, discussion, and feedback. In its more complex forms, coaching may facilitate redefining a client's dreams and reality in a way that causes dramatic change. Coaching may also be used to enable a team of individuals to work together more effectively. In each case, the coaching engagement is uniquely structured by the coach and the client. The approach and the outcomes depend upon the situation or focus of the coaching session, the participants (coach and employee or client), the particular coaching method, and the skill of the coach. In successful coaching applications, the learning resolves a problem, positively affects an issue, imparts learning, and advances the goals of the manager, the employee, and the organization. In the individuality of each coaching relationship, coaching is both a learning approach and a metaphor for the customization in today's workplace.

What Is Coaching?

There are as many definitions for coaching as there are practitioners and scholars who work in this field. Some examples of how coaching is defined include

- "The face-to-face process [intended] to redirect a subordinate's behavior to stop doing what he shouldn't be doing or to start doing what he should be doing" (Fournies, 1987).
- A process by which one individual, the coach, creates enabling relationships with others that make it easier for them to learn. The coach helps other people set and achieve performance goals at levels higher than those at which they are currently performing (Mink, Owen, and Mink, 1993).
- A service-oriented practice that is squarely focused on the goals, desires, and intentions of the client (Haneberg, 2006).

- A healthy, positive, and enabling process that develops the capacity of people to solve today's business problems. Transformational coaching is the art of assisting people in enhancing their effectiveness in a way so they feel helped (Crane, 2001).
- A professional partnership between a qualified coach and an individual or team that supports achieving extraordinary results, based on goals set by the individual or team. Through the process of coaching, individuals focus on the skills and actions needed to successfully produce their personally relevant results (ICF, 2007).

The commonalities include that coaching is a goal-directed process, not an event, and that it involves a relationship between the coach and a single individual or a team. At one time, there would have been agreement that coaching is a face-to-face process as well. An initial face-to-face meeting is probably still the norm. However, with new communication technologies, people today are more accustomed to working together online. Whether or not they are using an enabling technology such as video conferencing, many coaching relationships today are managed via telephone or Internet connections.

Differences among the definitions of coaching include the extents to which the coach is directive or enabling, the outcomes are individually or organizationally prescribed, and the learning is specific to a problem or generally applicable to overall performance. These variations are related to different coaching methodologies and their underlying assumptions. A subsequent section, Approaches to Coaching, will explain this in further detail.

Evolution of Coaching

Coaching is a somewhat new approach to employee development and performance improvement. Although supervisors have always been responsible for the work of their employees, management literature has only differentiated coaching as a specific learning approach (versus a management skill) since around 1980. Senior leaders may have always relied upon trusted friends, and more formally on boards of directors, for counsel, but it is only recently that training and development professionals have represented themselves as coaches, that businesses have existed for the purpose of training workplace coaches, and that companies have created mentoring programs for the specific purpose of enhancing the performance of their junior managers.

The evolution of coaching has paralleled a number of other developments in the business landscape. Initial approaches to coaching followed a behaviorist approach and were intended primarily to resolve performance problems. As the workplace changed and management practices evolved from command and control toward more participatory practices, coaching became more focused on employee learning and longer-term development in addition to the performance goals of the organization. The coach also became a collaborator in learning with the employee.

Recognition that employees bring all of themselves into the workplace has legitimized coaching discussions of a more holistic nature. Goleman's (1995) work on emotional intelligence is one example of research on workplace skills that delves into more personal territory. Coaching practices have evolved to reflect this emergent understanding of workplace management. "Coaching as it is being practiced today is a new field," according to Orem, Binkert, and Clancy (2007). "Its rapid growth is an indication that it is tapping into a fundamental need to make people's lives and work more meaningful, balanced, and holistic."

Seeking alternative ways to address complex workplace issues that are far more difficult to resolve than well-bounded problems has led to the development of new technologies, such as appreciative inquiry. This in turn has influenced the ways in which we approach coaching. Orem, Binkert, and Clancy (2007) conducted research using the application of appreciative inquiry methodology to the coaching process. They have developed a new template for workplace learning that does not begin with a problem or area for improvement focus. Their process breaks new ground for what is possible in structuring the coaching relationship.

Coaching versus Training

Coaching and training serve different purposes. Training builds skill and imparts knowledge. Although the instructional methodology may be self-paced or instructor led, face-to-face in a classroom, web-based, workbook, or some combination of technologies, the intent is to instruct in some aspect of the learner's work. Generally, there is also an assumption that the learner does not yet know how to do the task or does not have the knowledge required for the assignment. Although training may be customized to fit the learning needs of the learner, the focus remains on communicating the predetermined content of the curriculum. The instruction serves to prepare the learner for a specific task or ground the learner in the knowledge necessary for a particular role or career path.

Coaching may also build skill and impart knowledge. However, coaching is an approach that is customized to the needs of the person being coached, even when the setting is a team. A coaching solution is tailored to the needs of the client, the organization, and the situation. The purpose, for example, may be to motivate an employee to work, to help a client develop alternative and more productive choices, to resolve a problem by understanding and expanding an associate's perspective, or to identify and build upon a manager's strengths. The coach will attempt to find, draw out, and develop the client's unique abilities to resolve a situation or create a desired outcome.

In addition, coaching is dependent on a relationship. The relationship between coach and employee or client attributes adult responsibilities to the client as co-contributor and decision maker in the learning process. Coaching can often stimulate introspection at a deep level and extend beyond the contract to accomplish business results. The process can legitimize looking at emotions or lack thereof that are integral to getting things done. Although the intent of workplace coaching is both to help an individual grow and develop and to help the organization achieve its goals, the individual's learning, and the coach's learning, are not predictable but evolutionary. Development can occur at an intensely personal level.

Approaches to Coaching

Every process used to coach employees and build teams is based on underlying assumptions about human behavior. Coaches choose particular methods with the expectation of a successful outcome. They may select a strategy based on skills training, learning from previous coach-employee or coach-athlete relationships, or simply from identifying what works through trial and error. As our understanding about organizations, management, employees, and the nature of work has changed, so has our understanding of coaching. Three significantly different approaches to coaching are behavioral, ontological, and appreciative coaching. Together, they represent an evolution in our understanding of human behavior and the dynamics of performance improvement.

Behavioral Coaching

The behavioral model of coaching is best articulated by Fournies who presented this approach first in workshops and then in print. It is based on a Skinnerian orientation toward performance. The underlying assumption of behavioral coaching is that human beings respond to stimuli, sustain behaviors that are pleasurable, and cease behaviors that produce pain. People's actions represent a continuous process of selecting between alternatives that bring rewards or punishment. The role of the coach is to create a clear understanding for the employee of what performance is expected and also what rewards will come from satisfactory achievement and what penalties will come with failure to achieve.

For example, a coach may get agreement from an employee that the expectation for satisfactory performance is to produce 20 widgets per hour. In return for doing so, the employee will be given compensation at a particular rate. Failure to achieve this goal within 90 days will result in termination. The employee is expected to opt for meeting the production quota to be paid and avoid the consequence of being fired. Where behavior doesn't meet expectations, the behavioral coaching process is an appropriate solution. As Fournies (1987) explains, "If you want people to select better alternatives, let them understand the consequences of the alternative they are selecting and give them more alternatives to select from."

Fournies describes two parts to the behavioral coaching process. The first is the coaching analysis, the process of determining whether the problem is one that can be fixed through coaching. If the problem is related to lack of training or ability, coaching may not be the best option. If positive consequences accompany nonperformance, for example, someone else will do the employee's work, or negative consequences result when the task is well done, for instance, the employee will have extra work, then the system needs to be redesigned. Coaching, particularly behavioral coaching with clear outcomes for noncompliance, may change the behavior temporarily, but in the long term, the problem is not at the individual level. The key question is whether or not the employee could do the task if he or she wanted to.

Once the coaching analysis is complete, the face-to-face coaching process begins. In this discussion, the coach's first objective is to get agreement that a problem exists. Those who are unwilling to see their behavior as problematic are probably not coachable. The employee and the coach then mutually discuss alternative solutions and agree to actions that will be taken to solve the problem. Here the coach is able to draw on experience to contribute alternatives that the employee may not have considered. Finally there is agreement to follow up to measure results. Coaches are also encouraged to recognize achievement when it occurs. The boundary of the coaching engagement is limited by the behavior that needs to be improved. As Fournies says, "When you employ someone, you are not buying people, or their minds, or their values; you are only renting their behavior. As a manager, your job is not to change people, but to manage and change their behavior in your restricted environment" (Fournies, 1987).

At this basic level, the process may seem simplistic. Today's coach may provide directions as to how to achieve a goal and feedback to assist the employee in correcting performance in the direction of improvement. The process may include mutually negotiated goals and a more holistic relationship between the coach and the employee. According to the Behavioral Coaching Institute's Graduate School website (2007), "Coaching is all about achieving behavioral change and change is a psychological process. A successful, professional, ethical coach has to understand, be confident and competent in the psychological aspects of coaching and a master in the use of a range of behavioral change coaching techniques and validated psychological-based tools that bring about genuine, lasting, measurable results." Fournies would disagree, suggesting that psychology is not a prerequisite knowledge for motivating people to behave according to an organization's purpose. Either way, the behaviorist approach is evident in the assumption that feedback on performance and defined consequences are principal tools for coaching an employee toward performance improvement.

Ontological Coaching

Although the roots of ontological coaching began in the 1980s in the work of Julio Olalla, Fernando Flores, and Rafael Echeverria, Flaherty's *Coaching: Evoking Excellence in Others* is frequently cited as a definitive description of this approach (1999). The underlying assumption of ontological coaching is that, "It isn't events, communication, or stimuli that lead to behavior, it is the interpretation an individual gives to the phenomenon that leads to the actions taken." The first job of a coach is to understand the client's structure of interpretation, the worldview that is bounding the person's possibilities for action. Then, in partnership, the coach and client alter this structure so that the actions that follow bring about the intended outcome.

Like behavioral coaching, there is an outcome that precipitates the coaching, a problem, an issue, a limitation to be overcome. However, rather than expanding the list of alternative responses that the client has in the situation, ontological coaching seeks to alter the way of being that the client experiences in relation to the situation. The expectation is that the new, altered way of being will make possible behaviors that result in learning, growth, and resolution of the situation. When using this approach, Flaherty (1999) notes, "It's sometimes easy for a coach to slip into a more familiar role of being a teacher or a therapist or a manager and many times when we are under pressure we will return to one of these roles." However, the task is to have the client observe something in such a way that competence improves.

Flaherty (1999) describes five principles upon which ontological coaching is structured. First of all, the relationship between the client and the coach is the context for all that happens in the coaching engagement. This relationship depends on mutual trust, respect, and freedom of expression. Second, he states that coaching must be pragmatic, and for it to be so, coaches must be willing to innovate, correct, and reassess as they proceed. Achieving the wrong goal is not success. Because of the fluidity of the process, a third and parallel expectation is that coaching is a learning experience for both the coach and the client. That clients are always and already in the middle of their lives is the fourth principle. This means that coaches have to adapt their work to fit with the interpretations and habits that individuals bring to the relationship. Each and every client is different in this regard, which is why "Techniques don't work" is Flaherty's fifth principle. Coaches must be ever mindful of their process and not become prisoner to what has worked before. This also means that clients will quickly recognize when technique is primary and will not feel that the coaching is genuine.

The steps that Flaherty (1999) proposes for an ontological coaching process include establishing a relationship, recognizing an opening for coaching, and observing or assessing the situation to determine and understand the client's structure of interpretation. Once this part of the work is finished, the coach enrolls the client in the work. Enrollment includes mutual commitment of the client and the coach, established outcomes for the relationship, and identification of any hindrances to the coaching process. With these steps in place, the coaching conversations begin. These conversations ultimately enable the client to see things differently and determine new ways of being. Because ontological coaching is focused on deeper discovery, this approach to coaching is more fluid and requires more mindfulness on the part of the coach. Flaherty allows much latitude as to the form of the coaching activity. He believes that any work grounded in these principles, based on the assumption that actions are driven by interpretations of phenomena, and focused on a goal of long-term excellence, can be called ontological coaching.

Appreciative Coaching

Appreciative coaching is a third coaching process. It is grounded in newer assumptions about change management that propose, "If people manage their strengths and past accomplishments wisely, they can achieve far greater benefits than if they toil away at incremental improvements to their weaknesses" (Orem, Binkert, and Clancy, 2007). Whereas both behavioral coaching and ontological coaching are based on the principle of a problem-solving approach, appreciative coaching is a process of discovery centered around a topic. It is an inherently positive approach.

This coaching methodology was developed by Orem, Binkert, and Clancy using the principles of appreciative inquiry. As with appreciative inquiry, they found incredible power in asking the right questions. "The appreciative approach assumes that the questions people ask affect the way they think about their past, present and potential future" (Orem, Binkert, and Clancy, 2007). In this process, the authors sought to discover questions that "create a joyfully focused state of mind" and "engage people in thinking about their own best selves."

Five principles make up the core philosophy for appreciative inquiry and appreciative coaching: the constructionist principle, the positive principle, the simultaneity principle, the poetic principle, and the anticipatory principle (Orem, Binkert, and Clancy, 2007).

Collectively these principles form a belief that people create their reality through language and metaphors, and that an important part of that reality is the stories they tell about their past, present, and future. Through a process of positively focused inquiry, the coach can be a catalyst for retelling stories, reinterpreting reality, and creating a dream for a different future. This act of telling a new story in and of itself begins the process of change.

To accomplish this coaching process, the coach follows a cycle with four distinct parts: discovery, dream, design, and destiny. Through a series of questions, discussions, and reflections, the coach guides the client to discover what gives meaning in his or her life; to imagine possibilities for a preferred future; to focus the dream in mindful choices and actions; and, finally, to recognize the dream as reality in the present. Essential to appreciative coaching is the underlying assumption of social constructionism that people are "active, independent, and spontaneous beings who, consciously or not, form images of the future toward which they then grow" (Orem, Binkert, and Clancy, 2007).

Skills for Coaching

To be a successful coach, one needs several basic skills. Communication is absolutely essential. To accurately assess a coaching situation, the coach needs to be an expert at listening and observing. Communication is also integral to building a relationship between the coach and the client. Asking questions is an important skill. For appreciative coaching it is imperative, because asking the right questions is the foundation of this coaching methodology. Being able to analyze data allows a coach to assess the information gathered from listening to the client and observing what is happening. Within this assessment lie the keys to new possibilities for action. Delivering feedback is another communication skill that enables coaches to achieve success with their clients. Finally, the coach's negotiation skills assist the employee in forming a plan of action for resolving a problem or perhaps for determining the goals of the coaching contract.

Being a good coach also requires self-understanding and self-management. Coaches often have to challenge their assumptions about control, caretaking, and learning. Being a coach demands letting go of the reins and letting the individual or team play the game, run the race, succeed, or fail. Managers often act as parents to their child, trying to prevent the child from making mistakes. In *Stewardship*, Peter Block (1993) explores the shift from patriarchy to partnership. He writes, "Dependency rests on the belief that there are people in power who know what is best for others, including ourselves. We think the task of these leaders is to create an environment where we can live a life of safety and predictability." Letting go of the need to be the leader who provides this safety and predictability for others is essential for coaches. Caring, but not caretaking, is key to empowering others to take risk, try new things, learn, and grow.

Difficult Situations

Coaching will not solve all performance problems. Executive coach Marshall Goldsmith (2006) suggests five situations where coaching will likely be a waste of time:

- The person you're coaching is not willing to make a sincere effort to change.
- The person has been written off by the company.
- The person lacks the intelligence or functional skills to do the job.
- The person has the wrong strategy, mission, or direction.
- The person lacks ethics or integrity.

Managers may also be faced with employees whose performance appears to be the result of problems that they suspect, but are not trained to diagnose, such as mental illness or alcoholism. Coaching may be successful in changing a problem behavior, such as excessive absenteeism, but should only address the observed deficient behavior and the desired performance. Implying a suspected cause could place the coach in jeopardy for damaging the person's reputation. If an employee discloses personal problems of a serious nature, then the coach should seek assistance from the human resources department.

Many companies have employee assistance programs that can provide a solution. Some performance problems involve temporary situations that the employee can master over time such as a divorce or financial crisis. Others are more serious long-term problems. Mink, Owen, and Mink (1993) offer more ideas for coaching people who have failed, including the healing process, forgiveness, letting go, and self-renewal. Good coaching is able to inspire employees to satisfactory or exceptional performance. However, in rare cases, the counseling a person needs far exceeds the ability of a coach.

Executive Coaching

The rapid pace of change in today's world necessitates continuous learning at all levels of the organization. However, senior managers often have difficulty finding objective feedback about their performance and sound counsel. Recognizing the benefits for an entire organization of personal growth at the executive level, many corporations today provide executive coaches for their top managers. Many *Fortune* 500 companies now provide coaches for their leaders.

Coaches who work at this level need a broad understanding of business principles as well as a firm grounding in personal and organization development. The type of strategies that may be included in a developmental plan or goal set for an executive can create significant impact on the organization. The questions that the coach chooses to ask and the feedback support that the coach provides must reflect an understanding of the implications of these goals. Personal confidence is also a requisite for executive coaching. Being intimidated by the client will diminish a coach's effectiveness. The coach must be willing to challenge a person in a senior and powerful position, provide honest feedback, and manage any negative repercussions during the coaching engagement.

Mentoring

Mentoring is a specialized form of coaching (Finnerty, 1996). Typically, mentoring involves a relationship between a more senior or experienced manager and a new or less experienced employee. In Homer's tale, *The Odyssey,* Mentor was a friend of Odysseus whom he entrusted with the education of his son, Telemachus. The mentor then is a trusted friend given to assist with the education of his or her charge. This differs from the relationship one has with a supervisor who has direct responsibility for the performance and learning of an employee. Because mentors are more senior, they may also have the ability to influence other senior level managers in support of the career path of their protégés.

Some organizations establish formal mentor programs to assist new or high-potential employees with their careers. For example, newly hired college interns might be assigned a senior manager as their mentor. Historically, other organizations have established mentor programs to assist disadvantaged populations such as women and minorities. This type of program provides the employee with a coach other than his or her supervisor. Mentors provide valuable information and feedback employees might otherwise not have. Often employees gain knowledge from mentors of organization culture and unwritten organization norms.

If an organization does not have a formal mentor program, mentoring is still possible. Given the advantages of having one's own coach, employees may chose to seek their own mentors. In fact, some young managers elect to have multiple mentors to advise them given the complexity of today's business environment. Whether the mentor relationship is initiated by the mentor or the mentee, it is typically a power-neutral relationship that is intended to last for a longer term than a coaching contract. The success of mentor relationships often depends on the quality of the personal dynamics that evolve in the partnership. Discussing the choice of a mentor with one's supervisor can help ensure a positive outcome.

Resources for Coaching

As coaching has become a major element in the workplace learning tool kit, there has been a corresponding growth in resources to develop and supply these skills to individuals and organizations. Many books have been written on the subject from guidelines for those interested in learning how to coach or making an argument for coaching to be part of an organization's development strategy, to specific methodologies for coaching and detailed processes for implementing these approaches. Long-standing resources for training and development such as ASTD, the American Management Association, and the Society for Human Resource Management have recognized coaching as an important component of workplace performance and have added services to support coaches.

In 1991, Julio Olalla founded the Newfield Network; in 1992, Thomas Leonard founded Coach University. Today several other institutions have emerged to offer coaching curricula and, in some cases, corresponding certification. The International Coach Federation is the most well known of various membership organizations for those professionals who represent themselves principally as coaches. These organizations are also a source of information about coaching for those who seek to hire coaches for themselves or their organizations. They offer suggestions for criteria to be used in selecting a coach, as well as references to assist in locating coaching professionals. As the coaching field evolves, Internet searches will continue to produce a wealth of information on the topic and the market for resources will continue to grow.

Summary

Coaching is an increasingly important strategy for workplace performance improvement. Different approaches to coaching are based on different theories about how people are motivated, the role of the coach, and the nature of the coaching relationship. Common themes among these approaches are that coaching involves a goal-directed process, rather than an event, and it involves a relationship between the coach and a single individual or team.

The three approaches to coaching outlined in this chapter are behavioral, ontological, and appreciative coaching. Behavioral coaching focuses on clearly defining desired performance and the consequences of achievement as well as failure and enabling the coachee to achieve high performance. Ontological coaching focuses on understanding and altering the individual's worldview so that the actions that follow bring about the intended outcome. Finally, appreciative coaching approaches the relationship by asking questions that stimulate the individual to imagine and achieve new possibilities.

Regardless of the approach used, coaches must be authentic; that is, they must avoid adherence to process at the expense of the relationship. Other important skills of a coach are the ability to listen well, provide feedback, analyze data, and negotiate. Coaches must also be aware of their own tendencies to steer the relationship and allow the individual being coached to drive performance.

⤳

About the Author

Madeline Finnerty is president of Finnerty International, a consulting practice specializing in the design and facilitation of strategic planning, organization change, and team-building processes. Her domestic and international clients have included financial services, transportation, manufacturing and service companies, public school systems, social service agencies, churches, libraries, and large consulting firms. Finnerty has more than 15 years' experience as an independent consultant and more than 20 years in line and staff management positions within multiple *Fortune* 500 telecommunications companies. She has extensive national leadership experience serving ASTD. She is also active in the Rotary Club of Ashland.

References

Behavioral Coaching Institute. 2007. Graduate School of Master Coaches: Deliver results, available at www.behavioral-coaching-institute.com/Courses.html.

Block, Peter. 1993. *Stewardship: Choosing service over self-interest.* San Francisco: Berrett-Koehler.

Crane, Thomas G. 2001. *The heart of coaching: Using transformational coaching to create a high-performance culture.* San Diego: FTA Press.

Finnerty, Madeline. 1996. Coaching for growth and development. In *The ASTD training and development handbook: A guide to human resource development,* ed., R. Craig. New York: McGraw-Hill.

Flaherty, James. 1999. *Coaching: Evoking excellence in others.* Burlington, MA: Butterworth-Heinemann.

Fournies, Ferdinand F. 1987. *Coaching for improved work performance.* New York: Liberty Hall Press.

Goldsmith, Marshall. 2006, March 1. *Behavioral coaching: How not to waste time.* Blog entry, http://www.marshallgoldsmithlibrary.com. (Blog now discontinued.)

Goleman, Daniel. 1995. *Emotional intelligence: Why it can matter more than IQ.* New York: Bantam.

Haneberg, Lisa. 2006. *Coaching basics.* Alexandria, VA: ASTD Press.

ICF (International Coach Federation). 2007. *Frequently asked questions about coaching,* available at www.coachfederation.org/ICF/For+Coaching+Clients/What+is+a+Coach/FAQs/.

Mink, Oscar G., Keith Q. Owen, and Barbara P. Mink. 1993. *Developing high-performance people: The art of coaching.* Reading, MA: Addison-Wesley.

Orem, Sara L., Jacqueline Binkert, and Ann L. Clancy. 2007. *Appreciative coaching: A positive process for change.* San Francisco: Jossey-Bass.

✌ Section V

Delivering Technology-
Enabled Learning

What Is the Meaning of the *e* in e-Learning?

Luminary Perspective

Elliott Masie

In This Chapter

➢ Learn the history of e-learning

➢ Learn new meanings for the *e* in e-learning

The small letter *e* at the start of the term of *e-learning* has a rich history, a varied set of meanings, and a quite fascinating future.

Almost every week, someone asks me what the *e* in e-learning represents. The simple answer is "electronic"—as in using the tools of the electronic age—from personal computers (PCs) to the Internet—for learning. But that is just the start of a more interesting response. Let's embrace the *e* and explore how it has changed learning and is in the midst of dramatic change itself.

First, a bit of history. The term *e-learning* started to be used by me and other analysts in the training and learning field in 1997. But that was the not the beginning. For decades, the idea of using technology, computers, and machines as part of the learning and training process has fascinated both geeks and teachers.

Admiral Grace Hopper, the godmother of mainframe computing who led the Navy's information technology innovation, predicted that the bulky first computing machines, loaded with electronic tubes, would someday "be used to teach our sailors."

First, there were standalone teaching devices, using what was called programmed instruction, that taught a specific set of skills or procedures. I had the privilege of using an early teaching machine that taught Morse code to telegraph operators.

As mainframe computers integrated into the world of business, computer languages were used to create learning, training, and information transfer programs. Tens of thousands of programmers learned the languages of COBOL, JCL, and other mainframe applications by taking structured e-learning, which was then called computer-based training (CBT).

These early e-learning efforts combined the concept of behavioral reinforcement for learning that was pioneered by B.F. Skinner with the explosive ability to use computers to deliver content based on the user's successful (or failed) responses to questions.

Video became an aspect of e-learning with the rise of video disks. This now allowed instruction that included images, sound, and motion rather than just text. As the standalone PC and then the network was born, e-learning took a massive step forward—first spreading from just technical folks to a wider mass of desktop users. And networked PCs allowed for the delivery of more video and sound—adding to an enriched e-learning experience, although we weren't yet using the *e* phrase.

In 1997, the *e* was popping out everywhere. The popularization of the Internet and the browser led to e-mail, e-business, and e-commerce. I was at a strategy meeting with IBM senior executives when we suggested that they use the phrase *e-learning* to reflect the combination of e-business and CBT. At that time, many believed (and wrote about) a multibillion dollar business that would grow up around the ability of every person to buy the learning they needed right from their computer. Conferences ranging from my original *TechLearn* to *e-Learning* to *On-Line Learning* all generated great excitement about what e-learning would do to the world of business and training.

In the past 10 years, e-learning has continued to change—as technology has matured—embracing synchronous and asynchronous training and spanning K–12 and a rapidly exploding marketplace for online higher education degrees. We have seen the rise of learning management systems and learning content management systems take e-learning across the entire organization and manage and track its deployment and outcomes. And change continues with the rise of search (for example, Google), collaborative environments (for example, wikis and blogs), and web services innovations (for example, Web 2.0 and software as a service).

So, what does that *e* in e-learning stand for? Here are a few meanings that the *e* has for me:

Electronic. E-learning is about the use of electronics to create, deliver, track, enhance, and manage learning. Our electronics will continue to get faster, smaller, more flexible, and more integrated. Each leap forward of electronics creates new opportunities for e-learning. As your mobile phone evolves, for example, e-learning can become more portable and context specific. You will be able to access a lesson or information from your mobile device, and it may automatically know where you are, based on the integrated GPS chip, and give you location-specific e-learning (for example, tourism information about a town or the customer service record of the office that you are about to visit).

Enterprise. Leveraged well, e-learning is a powerful tool for the enterprise. Just as we are weaving together all of our employees around the globe—along with our suppliers and customers—we can use that same enterprise network to create and deliver e-learning globally. The goal of great e-learning is to provide a link between expertise (whoever may have it in the enterprise) and the learner who needs that knowledge.

Empowerment. As the tools for fingertip knowledge become more pervasive, our workforce is growing an expectation that they can get at knowledge from their keyboards at any time. The employee of a retail store in the middle of Kansas wants to be empowered to find the learning and knowledge he or she needs, without having to ask a manager for permission to learn. The empowered employee will have a wide range of e-learning tools, resources, and systems in his or her workplace.

Enforcement. Legal and compliance offices have fallen in love with e-learning. One major retail chain added e-learning to a recent settlement of a class action lawsuit. The organization agreed to provide 30 minutes of training to every employee about a workplace safety issue. The good news is that e-learning is providing a simple way for organizations to deliver and track compliance-oriented learning offerings. The bad news is that e-learning is viewed as a simple way to deliver compliance—often resulting in hours of mandatory and unmotivating training that can damage the brand of e-learning in the eyes of employees and their managers.

Everywhere. Learning is something that can't be limited to the classroom. E-learning provides a process for allowing learners to learn anytime and anywhere. As e-learning grows in acceptance and deployment, learning can become more democratic and global in distribution.

Expensive? I am adding expensive to this list to destroy a myth that e-learning is cheap or even free. Sure, you can create very rapid, simple e-learning that does not cost much to develop. But the real costs of learning are usually the wage hour costs and the remediation or transfer costs as employees attempt to actually use the new skills or procedures in their work settings. E-learning can be less expensive than some forms of classroom training—but it is not cheap or free!

Evolving. The use of e-learning is evolving dramatically, even as this book goes to press. Here is a short list of evolutions that our Learning CONSORTIUM has been tracking about e-learning:

- Content is becoming less structured and programmed. Although some courses are still following a show-test-remediate model, a large amount of e-learning is becoming less formal.
- Performance support grows. More and more e-learning is following the model of performance support—learning at the moment of need: pop-ups, sidekicks, and frequently asked questions.
- Content is more collaborative. E-learning content is coming from the "wisdom of the crowd" rather than a single subject matter expert.
- 3D and virtual learning is on the horizon. Experiments in the use of avatars, virtual worlds, and persistent gaming environments for e-learning are intriguing to many of us in the learning field.
- Blending continues. Although e-learning is widely deployed, a large amount of it is actually consumed in a blended learning format—either through designed blending (for example, classroom with e-learning) or informally by the learner himself or herself (for example, e-learning followed by peer coaching).

Evaporating? How many of us still say e-commerce when we go to Amazon to buy a book? It has been a while since I said that I was sending an email to someone—I just talk about sending a note or answering my mail. Well, the *e* in e-learning may also start to evaporate. Personally, I won't mourn its passing! Remember, it has only been used for 10 years of a multidecade history. As our technology and methods evolve, we will assume that electronics, computers, and networks will be useful and used to support learning, knowledge, and performance.

Experimental. In conclusion, let's think of the *e* in e-learning as standing for our experiments in connecting technology and learning and performance. Let those experiments continue, focusing on how we combine what we know (and will discover) about how people learn with an ever-changing set of technologies. As experimenters, let's focus on the "affordances" of e-learning: what can it do for learners and learning professionals that we could not do without it? The experiment of e-learning is exciting and the future of *learning*, no matter what we call it next, is bright! Let's learn about learning together.

About the Author

Elliott Masie is an internationally recognized futurist, analyst, researcher, and organizer on the critical topics of learning, technology, business, and workplace productivity. He is the founder of the Learning CONSORTIUM, a coalition of more than 252 *Fortune* 500 companies cooperating on the evolution of learning strategies. He is the editor of *Learning TRENDS* by Elliott Masie, an Internet newsletter read by more than 50,000 business executives worldwide, and is a regular columnist in professional publications. He is the author of a dozen books, including the recent *Learning Rants, Raves & Reflections* and the free digital book *My Most Memorable Teacher (or Trainer)*. He is the convener of Learning 2008 and Learning Systems 2008. He heads The MASIE Center, a Saratoga Springs, New York, think tank focused on how organizations can support learning and knowledge within the workforce. He is also a Distinguished Contribution to WLP Award recipient.

Learning Technology Primer

Bryan Chapman

In This Chapter

- ➢ Use technology to achieve learning goals
- ➢ Target learning technologies to specific learning needs
- ➢ Understand the types of learning technologies that are available

---

Technology has had a major effect on the way we learn today, whether the learning takes place formally through structured courses provided by an employer or informally by browsing the web. Learning technology can provide 24/7/365 access to training materials, compress learning times by 50 to 60 percent versus classroom instruction, provide personalized instruction at the learner's own pace, and deliver instruction with optimal consistency. Many organizations have also learned—by experience—how to find reasonable balance in applying technology for the right content at the right time. The *ASTD 2006 State of the Industry Report* indicates that technology-delivered learning accounts for 36.3 percent of all training content delivered across member organizations of the ASTD benchmarking forum. Figure 22-1 suggests a trend toward increasing the mix of technology-delivered learning with a corresponding decrease in classroom-based learning.

Figure 22-1. Comparison of Average Percentage of Learning Hours Provided via Instructor-Led Real Time vs. Technology-Based

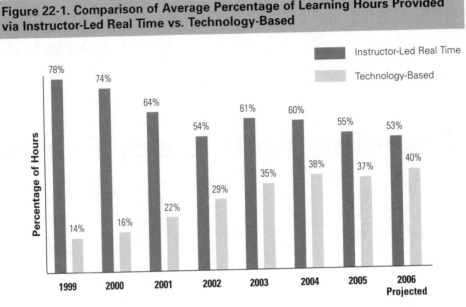

Source: *ASTD 2006 State of the Industry Report.*

Consider how the dynamic of shifting learning delivery formats affects the skill sets required by training professionals. In the early days of technology-delivered learning, at a time when only a small percentage of training was delivered via computer-based training (CBT), there was often a clear delineation between those who designed instruction and those who coded, assembled, and authored courses using technology. Today, there is greater demand for training developers who can both design and create learning content using authoring tools such as Adobe Flash, Dreamweaver, Authorware, ToolBook, Articulate, and other rapid-development tools. In a random sampling of 100 job postings for instructional designers on Monster.com, HotJobs.com, and CareerBuilder.com, 68 percent of the postings specifically listed the ability to use authoring tools as a requirement for the job (see Figure 22-2). The postings came from a wide array of organizations, large and small, public and private.

As technology becomes a greater part of how training and learning take place, it is incumbent on all of us to become learning-technology literate and develop a vision for how and when to apply it for specific purposes and objectives. One barrier to understanding the technology is the sheer volume of learning technologies available. In fact, there are more than 500 companies that provide learning technology solutions today. This primer is designed to help you quickly classify systems according to their primary purpose and to

Figure 22-2. Percentage of Instructional Design Job Postings Requiring Authoring Tool Experience

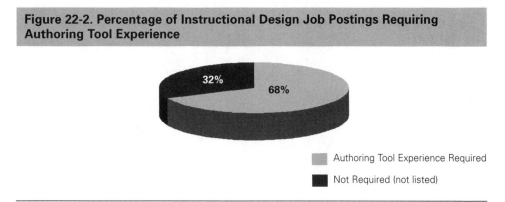

□ Authoring Tool Experience Required

■ Not Required (not listed)

Source: Chapman, et al. (2007a). Brandon Hall Research, © 2007. Used with permission.

understand their role in an organization's learning infrastructure by providing a taxonomy as a guide to sort out systems by role.

Learning Technology Components and Taxonomy

Most corporate learning systems contain at least some of the core components shown in Figure 22-3, forming the main category headings for the learning technology taxonomy. In many organizations, especially large ones, you are likely to find multiple instances of some components. For example, different lines of business may use different virtual classroom or live meeting software.

In addition to the major groupings, further classifications will help you better align technology with critical business and instructional scenarios (see Figure 22-4). The question, "What is the best authoring tool?" is a difficult one to answer without knowing what is to be taught. For example, are you teaching how to use a business-critical software application? Or, is the goal to increase leadership capabilities in mid-level managers? Or perhaps you are creating courseware to teach troubleshooting skills in a manufacturing setting? In each of these scenarios, the scope and range of recommended authoring tools would vary based on desired outcome. The following simplified taxonomy will help you further focus on learning technologies targeting specific needs.

Authoring

By definition, an authoring tool is nothing more than "a software application that allows individuals to create their own e-learning content, without needing programming skills"

Figure 22-3. Major Learning Technology Components of a Full Learning Infrastructure

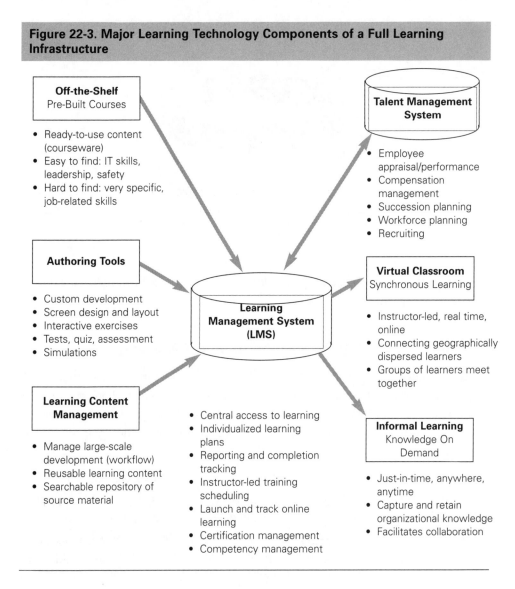

Off-the-Shelf
Pre-Built Courses

- Ready-to-use content (courseware)
- Easy to find: IT skills, leadership, safety
- Hard to find: very specific, job-related skills

Authoring Tools

- Custom development
- Screen design and layout
- Interactive exercises
- Tests, quiz, assessment
- Simulations

Learning Content Management

- Manage large-scale development (workflow)
- Reusable learning content
- Searchable repository of source material

Learning Management System (LMS)

- Central access to learning
- Individualized learning plans
- Reporting and completion tracking
- Instructor-led training scheduling
- Launch and track online learning
- Certification management
- Competency management

Talent Management System

- Employee appraisal/performance
- Compensation management
- Succession planning
- Workforce planning
- Recruiting

Virtual Classroom
Synchronous Learning

- Instructor-led, real time, online
- Connecting geographically dispersed learners
- Groups of learners meet together

Informal Learning
Knowledge On Demand

- Just-in-time, anywhere, anytime
- Capture and retain organizational knowledge
- Facilitates collaboration

(Clarey, 2007). Writers use Microsoft Word to write. Engineers use AutoCad to design devices. Business analysts use Visio to organize business processes into flowcharts. Similarly, instructional developers use authoring tools to create learning events and activities, delivered and tracked online for the purpose of learning. However, not all authoring tools are designed for the same purpose, and there are more than 150 authoring tools available on the market. Some can be used to create both websites and online learning,

Figure 22-4. Simple Taxonomy of Key Learning Technologies

- **Authoring**
  - General Purpose, Course Authoring
  - Rapid Development
  - Simulation
    - Software Simulation Tools
    - Soft Skills Simulation Tools
    - Technical Skills Simulation Tools
  - Instructional Games
  - Assessment
- **Learning Content Management System (LCMS)**
- **Learning Management System (LMS)**
  - Locally Installed
  - Hosted Solutions or SaaS
  - Open Source
- **Live, Synchronous Learning**
- **Informal Learning**
  - Wikis
  - Blogs
  - Collaboration Systems
- **Off-the-Shelf Courses**
  - IT and Computer Skills
  - Soft Skills, Professional Development
  - Safety and Regulatory Training
  - Vertical Market Focus
- **Talent or Performance Management Systems**

others are used to create time-based animations, some convert Microsoft PowerPoint presentations (used in a classroom setting) to online courses, and still others allow you to use templates to create highly interactive simulations that allow learners to run a mock business and see the results of decisions made over an elapsed number of years. Studies have indicated that most companies use multiple authoring tools (Nantel et al., 2007), selecting the right tool for the job.

General Purpose, Course Authoring

The practice of using authoring tools has been around since early CBT times. Authoring tools have evolved to embrace delivery over the Internet. Leading software application provider Adobe dominates the general purpose authoring category when it comes to brand recognition and popularity of use (see Table 22-1).

Table 22-1. Authoring Tools Most Frequently Used by Professional Learning Developers

Authoring Tool	Vendor	Percentage of Companies That Use This Authoring Tool
Flash	Adobe	92
Dreamweaver	Adobe	6
Authorware	Adobe	34
Director	Adobe	27
Lectora Publisher	Trivantis	21
Captivate	Adobe	18
ToolBook	SumTotal	18

Source: Chapman, et al. (2007a). Brandon Hall Research, © 2007. Used with permission.

Rapid Development Tools

Even though authoring tools are targeted to the nonprogrammer, many authoring tools have a steep learning curve. They allow for considerable flexibility in creating high degrees of interactivity. Studies indicate that it takes 220 person-hours of development to create a single hour of finished e-learning courseware (Chapman et al., 2006). Vendors have been working to shorten development times, make authoring easier for nontechnical content contributors, and make learning development more cost effective. Some rapid development tools allow novice developers, instructors, and subject matter experts to work in familiar tools, such as Microsoft PowerPoint, to create learning content. PowerPoint files are then converted into online courses, complete with narration and additional interactivity. Rapid development tools that have gained popularity and widespread adoption are listed in Table 22-2.

A survey of rapid development tool users suggests a dramatic savings in development time: 33 person-hours for each finished hour of courseware created—a significant reduction from the 220:1 ratio—when creating traditional e-learning (Chapman, 2008). Rapid development, however, is not well suited for all types of learning content. Respondents indicated that they achieve the best results by using rapid development tools and mixing them with the rich interactivity of other applications, such as Flash exercises or simulations.

Table 22-2. Rapid Development Tools: PowerPoint to E-Learning

Product	Company
Articulate Presenter	Articulate
Acrobat Connect Professional	Adobe
Impatica for PowerPoint	Impatica
Camtasia Studio	TechSmith
Rapid E-Learning Studio	Rapid Intake
MindFlash	MindFlash

Simulation Tools

From the very beginning of technology-based learning, simulations and games have been an important instructional tool to support experiential learning and to reinforce higher-level, cognitive learning methodologies. Early simulations and games were often custom programmed or assembled through sophisticated use of standard authoring tools. Of course, simulations have been around for many years in a variety of forms, from large-scale flight simulators to role-playing simulations in the classroom to computer-delivered simulations and, most recently, to high-fidelity simulations that can be delivered through cyberspace.

In a recent study, organizations indicated that they would like to use more simulations as part of a blended curriculum, but they think that the barriers to entry (such as high development costs and difficulty of creating simulations on their own) are simply too prohibitive (Chapman et al., 2007b). The study also found that the average development time to create one finished hour of simulation is 750 hours of development time (with a range up to 1,300:1), compared with an average of 220:1 for standard e-learning courses. This explains why simulations are currently underused in online learning courses.

This has, however, also resulted in an explosion of a whole new line of instructional design and development tools that focus on developing simulations as well as teaching software applications, teaching soft skills, and creating simulations that teach technical skills, such as troubleshooting.

Software simulation tools. Software simulation tools allow novice developers to record screen interactions while walking through a procedure. The tool remembers each mouse click and keystroke for the purpose of later creating interactive simulations, for example, registering the coordinates and creating a click area for each mouse click. Simulation authors need only clean up the recording and add feedback and remediation to complete the simulation. This is considerably quicker than using standard authoring tools to capture screens, manually add touch areas and text input fields, create prompts and instructions for the learners, wire each click or correct key entry into a branching pattern, and so forth. Software simulation tools have significantly reduced development time, while preserving a high degree of fidelity and interactivity in the learning event.

Table 22-3 lists some of the leading tools that can be used to create software simulations.

Soft skills simulation tools. Soft skills simulation tools are usually based on a template for quickly creating specific types of interactions, such as developing a dialogue, choosing on-screen characters, and creating a role-play simulation with graded responses and comparison with expert paths through the simulation (how they may have handled the situation). The difficulty for makers of simulation tools is that they must try to provide as much flexibility to vary the simulation for different purposes while keeping focused on delivering high-fidelity, workplace-relevant scenarios created in a very short amount of time. Here are some examples of subtypes of simulations:

- Role play (for example, conversation with on-screen characters)
- Business skills (for example, making decisions to play out a business scenario, such as running a mock business)
- Business modeling or analytical (for example, setting variable conditions and observing the outcome based on business rules, learning how to interpret data)
- Story problem or scenario based (for example, set up story problem, have learners make decisions to solve the problem)
- Sales process simulator (for example, simulating mock sales scenarios).

Figure 22-5 is an example of a sophisticated simulation in which the learner makes decisions about how society may potentially reverse the effects of global warming. The simulation, from Forio, is capable of simulating elapsed time because the learner may run the scenario over months or years (compressed to an hour or less online).

There are several tools emerging that will help novice developers create their own simulations. Table 22-4 lists a few that are gaining traction.

Table 22-3. Leading Software Simulation Tools

Product	Company
Captivate	Adobe
OnDemand	Global Knowledge
FireFly	KnowledgePlanet
STT Trainer	Kaplan IT Learning
Assima	Assima
SoftSim	OutStart
RapidBuilder	XStreamSoftware

Figure 22-5. Global Warming Simulation Developed Using Forio

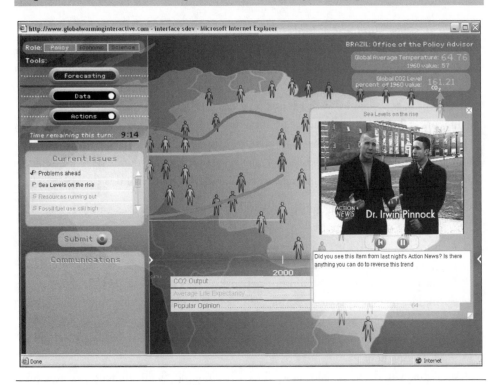

Source: Hillinger (2007). Used with permission.

Table 22-4. Examples of Commercially Available Soft Skills Simulation Development Tools

Product	Company
Redwood Development Platform	Redwood e-Learning Systems
Forio Simulation Development Software	Forio
KDSimStudio	Knowledge Dynamics
Experience Builder	ExperienceBuilders LLC
RealCall	SIVOX
StarTrainer	Knowlagent
Simulated Role Play	SIMmersion LLC
SimWriter	NexLearn

Technical skills simulation tools. The technical skills simulation category covers a broad range of skill areas. Think of systems in this category as being capable of modeling physical systems, such as some machinery or an electronic measurement system. This category also covers "task simulators" designed to teach and measure a learner's ability to follow steps in a procedure with various levels of guidance. A good example of how this might work is flight simulators in the aviation industry. Many airlines have figured out how to pass performance data from sessions in a flight simulator back to a central learning management system, which also keeps performance records for classroom-based learning and e-learning courses. Here are some subtypes of simulation that fit in this category:

- Troubleshooting or diagnostic (for example, making decisions and observing the outcome of each action)
- Procedural walk-through (for example, learner performs steps in a procedure)
- Simulating physical systems (for example, simulating pieces of equipment, other objects, or setting up a computer network)
- Simulating concepts (for example, simulating a schematic diagram, or simulating how weather patterns work using a diagram)
- Emergency response simulations (for example, performing actions as a result of an emergency)
- Virtual worlds or spatial relationships (for example, flight simulators; simulating an office environment, cockpit, or factory).

There is a whole new class of emerging technologies that are designed to streamline the development of technical skills simulations (see Table 22-5).

Instructional Games

Games play a unique role in deploying an enterprise-wide learning strategy by providing support in achieving specific instructional outcomes. Although not primarily designed to do an entire training or teaching job alone (Kirk and Belovics, 2004), games provide a level of motivation in learning areas, such as classification (matching games), reinforcing factual information (question and answer games), and rote learning (memorization games). In addition, as the new gaming generation enters the workforce, lecture-based training will likely be less effective (Kirk and Belovics, 2004).

Both simulation and gaming development tools are unique in that the instructional design guidance is not obvious through the interface. Rather, the guidance comes from the intelligence and flexibility of the simulation or game designed to achieve a specific learning outcome. The primary instructional benefits of using focused, learning-activity-based tools is the depth of interaction and rich feedback available for learners, achievable through relatively rapid development processes and minimizing the authoring savvy required on the part of instructional developers (see Table 22-6).

Assessment Tools

Although many authoring tools provide the ability to create and deliver online tests, quizzes, and exams, there are tools designed specifically for the purpose of developing robust, stand-alone tests or testing strategies. Many organizations are rethinking their testing models, patterning them more closely with the way universities administer tests; namely, instruction takes place in the classroom, but tests are often administered in a

Table 22-5. Technical Skills Simulation Development Tools

Product	Company
Humentum	Humentum
Multigen Creator	Multigen-Paradigm
KD-Calc	Knowledge Dynamics
NGRAIN Producer	NGRAIN
Visual Purple	Visual Purple

Table 22-6. Popular Development Tools for Instructional Games

Product	Company
Raptivity	Harbinger Group
GameShow Pro (Web)	Learningware
Composica Enterprise	Composica
Games2Train	Games2Train
Game Development Environment	Galaxy Scientific

testing center, staffed and equipped to deliver and record test results. In an online model, the same technique can be used to deliver nontracked instruction separately from tests and exams. Table 22-7 presents some authoring tools that specialize in creating assessments.

Learning Content Management System (LCMS)

Since 2000, a new classification of instructional development tools has evolved and is beginning to gain traction as a commercially viable option for developing online learning through creating reusable learning objects. Many of the most popular traditional

Table 22-7. Authoring Tools that Focus on Online Assessment

Product	Company
QuestionMark Perception	QuestionMark
TestCraft	Ingenious Group LLC
ExamBuilder	ExamBuilder
Pedagogue Testing	Pedagogue Solutions
Respondus	Respondus
Exam Engine	Platte Canyon Multimedia

authoring tools are available as desktop applications, meaning that they typically can be used by only one instructional developer at a time to create interaction. By contrast, this new classification of tools is groupware based on a publishing model for online learning development and uses multiple-concurrent content contributors where each works on learning content and interactive exercises that are part of a larger course or curriculum. To illustrate the point, consider the following question. Could the publishers of the *Los Angeles Times* use Microsoft Word to lay out and organize each daily newspaper? The answer is yes. How efficiently, however, could it be produced? The answer is not very efficiently.

Such groupware or publishing systems are called learning content management systems (LCMSs). By definition, an LCMS is a multideveloper environment where developers can create, store, reuse, manage, and deliver learning content from a central object repository (Chapman et al., 2007a). Although many LCMS solutions have built-in authoring capabilities, most are also designed to assemble individual learning activities that may have been created using a variety of traditional authoring tools and storing the learning events as "learning objects." A learning object is a reusable learning activity that can be metadata tagged for easy retrieval; standards conformant so that it can communicate with other learning technologies; and combined or clustered with other learning objects to create new, derivative learning structures such as lessons, units, or entire courses.

Table 22-8 lists some of the most frequently used commercial LCMS solutions to date.

Table 22-8. Most Frequently Used LCMS Solutions

Product	Company
Evolution LCMS	Outstart
Total LCMS	SumTotal
ForceTen	Eedo
Saba LCMS	Saba
Learn.com	Learn.com
Generation 21	Generation 21
TopClass	WBT Systems

Source: Chapman et al. (2007b). Brandon Hall Research, © 2007. Used with permission.

Learning Management System (LMS)

Of all the components in the learning infrastructure, the learning management system is considered one of the most critical. By definition, an LMS is "software that automates the administration of training events" (Clarey, 2007). The LMS provides a common interface and functionality to all types of users including learners, instructors, managers, training administrators, content developers, managers, and supervisors. In many organizations, the learner interface serves as the company's central learning portal, with catalogs of courses delivered self-paced, online; registration and enrollment for classroom events; and virtual classroom for live, distance learning. Here are some of the main features provided by LMS solutions:

- Secure access and login
- Ability to launch and track e-learning
- Ability to launch and track off-the-shelf courses
- Learner surveys or smilesheet evaluations
- Basic test and exam creation and delivery
- Classroom management (scheduling, enrollment, notification, and wait listing)
- Reports for test scores, class rosters, learning gains, and test item analysis data
- Advanced classroom management (scheduling instructors, rooms, and equipment)
- Regulatory and compliance tracking
- Collaborative learning
- Certification management
- Multilingual support
- Skill-gap analysis
- Back office integration
- Advanced learning analytics
- Talent management capabilities, such as employee appraisals and compensation management.

Although there are approximately 140 LMS solutions that are commercially available, through acquisition and consolidations, there are fewer LMS vendors gaining significant market share and brand recognition. One way to further subdivide, according to the taxonomy, is key to how the LMS solution is provided to customers. Some install the LMS on their own local servers (behind their firewall), and others have the system externally hosted to minimize the amount of internal support required to maintain the system. Still others gradually ease into using an LMS by leasing time on the system, rather than buying it outright. This model is called software as a service (SaaS). Finally, some use open source solutions to forgo licensing costs and customize for their own internal use. Again, this becomes a useful differentiator for narrowing down the list of LMSs you might consider for use inside your own organization.

Locally Installed Solutions

Approximately 62 percent of companies install their LMSs on their own internal servers (Chapman et al., 2007a). Although most vendors will install according to your preference, the truth is that some vendors specialize and are well equipped to provide quality services around hosted or SaaS offerings. Table 22-9 lists learning management systems that excel in this area.

Hosted or SaaS Solutions

Some LMS vendors specialize in providing a full set of services around the learning management system, whether you license the full solution and have it hosted by the vendor or one of its partners (hosted), or you lease individual user licenses without purchasing the LMS (SaaS). Table 22-10 lists LMS solution providers that have built their businesses around providing this type of offering.

Open Source Solutions

By definition, open source learning management systems are free to the general public, with some minor restrictions on how they can be used. Code developers work as a

Table 22-9. Locally Installed Solutions

Product	Company
TotalLMS	SumTotal
Saba Enterprise Learning Suite	Saba
Plateau Learning Management System	Plateau
Meridian KSI	Meridian
Training Partner	GeoMetrix
Blackboard	Blackboard
SAP LS	SAP
PeopleSoft ELM	Oracle

Table 22-10. Hosted and SaaS Solutions

Product	Company
GeoMaestro	GeoLearning
KnowledgePlanet OnDemand Learning Suite	KnowledgePlanet
LearnCenter	Learn.com
Cornerstone OnDemand Enterprise Suite	Cornerstone OnDemand
Intellinex LMS	ACS Learning
TrainingEdge	Outstart

community to design, develop, maintain code, and add new features and upgrades. Some examples of open source LMS solutions include

- Moodle (www.moodle.org)
- Sakai (www.sakaiproject.org)
- Claroline (www.claroline.net)
- LRN (www.dotlrn.org).

Live, Synchronous Learning

Virtual meetings have become mainstream at most organizations, but did you know that many of the most popular virtual meeting software applications initially targeted training and learning events? Live, synchronous learning tools are software applications that allow multiple attendees to connect in real time from remote geographic locations throughout the Internet for the purpose of learning (Wexler et al., 2007). The advantages of using virtual classrooms include low-cost development of learning content (similar to developing training for the classroom); live sessions that allow for interpersonal communication between instructor and learners and learner to learner; sessions that can be easily recorded for later playback; and sessions that can be set up quickly and easily, regardless of the location of the learner (as long as he or she has a computer and an Internet connection). The disadvantages include the fact that learning is generally not self-paced or available at any time; the challenges of different time zones; and the need for an instructor to deliver the training, as opposed to asynchronous, online courseware.

Table 22-11 lists some of the leading systems in this space.

Table 22-11. Leading Live, Synchronous Learning Systems

Product	Company
Webex Training Center	Webex
Adobe Acrobat Connect	Adobe
Microsoft LiveMeeting	Microsoft
Saba Centra Live	Saba
Elluminate Live	Elluminate
Interwise Connect	Interwise
Horizon Wimba	Horizon Wimba

Informal Learning

The model used most frequently for training today is the same model that has been patterned around the way we learned in school. Using this model, information is basically dispensed and learners are tested for recall of facts and concepts. The problem with this model is that it doesn't match how businesses operate. We need information on demand to do our jobs well. At times, information is overabundant and comes in many forms, as opposed to formal, structured, training events. How we access and use information will ultimately determine our effectiveness in the workplace.

Information evolves, and new information is created rapidly as people are retiring from the workforce and taking valuable knowledge with them. To remain competitive, an organization needs to transition from one that dispenses information in the form of training courses to one where employees have greater stewardship for their own learning. That information should also be easily accessed on demand. Rather than test employees in the traditional sense, the real assessment comes when staff uses resources to perform more effectively.

The best way to meet this need is to create a learning environment composed of both structured and unstructured learning (informal learning) that draws on several delivery formats, including classroom-based learning, self-paced e-learning, virtual classrooms, knowledge management repositories, and simulations.

There are many tools and technologies to create support for informal learning (short of converting the content into structured learning), including using knowledge bases or newer Web 2.0 technologies such as wikis, blogs, collaborative discussion groups, online communities, and, most important, utilities that facilitate the exchange of expertise. Web 2.0 technologies are often low cost or free and easy to deploy.

Wikis

By definition, a wiki is a website created by a group, rather than an individual. One of the most popular web destinations on the web is Wikipedia, an online encyclopedia with thousands of volunteer writers and editors and nearly two million articles. The core technology used to create Wikipedia is open source, as are many other wiki technologies. Many organizations are using wikis to create informal knowledge bases containing learning entered by a wide array of content contributors. Content can be edited by anyone with the right security access and a computer with Internet access. Here are some wiki technologies (most are open source) for your consideration:

- www.socialtext.com
- www.wikibooks.org
- www.twiki.org
- www.zwiki.org
- www.snipsnap.org
- www.pbwiki.com
- www.mediawiki.org.

Blogs

Blogs have exploded all over the Internet as a primary method of peer-to-peer communication. Training organizations are also taking the opportunity to leverage this Web 2.0 or social networking technology. In fact, many learning technology vendors, such as LMS vendors, are adding wiki and blog utilities to their core platforms. Like wikis, blog technology is frequently available for little to no cost, so it is an ideal technology to use for informal learning purposes. Here are some leading blog technologies:

- www.blogger.com
- www.wordpress.com
- www.textpattern.com
- www.bblog.com
- www.b2evolution.net
- www.movabletype.com.

Collaboration Systems

Perhaps one of the most important innovations in learning technology and in support of informal learning are systems designed to capture and share expert knowledge through frequently asked questions, discussion groups, knowledge bases, or direct contact with experts. Some of the applications in this space are listed in Table 22-12.

Off-the-Shelf Courses

One of the quickest ways to put learning online is to identify and license off-the-shelf courses that meet your specific learning outcomes. There are more than 200 companies that provide ready-built courses. Some of these companies also allow you to adapt their courses for your own use. It is important to ensure that the courses will be interoperable with your LMS. Ideally, both the LMS and library of courses use the same standards, such as SCORM 1.2 or SCORM 2004. However, I recommend that you simply check with your LMS vendor to make sure they've tested the desired library of courses for interoperability in areas such as bookmarking, tracking scores, and setting completion status.

IT and Computer Skills Courses

Here are some of the most well-known companies that provide IT and computer skills online courseware:

- SkillSoft
- ElementK
- MindLeaders
- LearnKey.

Table 22-12. Collaboration, Knowledge Capture, and Sharing Systems

Product	Company
Participate	Outstart
SupportPoint EPSS	SupportPoint
eRoom Collaboration	Documentum
TotalCollaboration	SumTotal
Saba Collaboration	Saba

Soft Skills and Professional Development Courses

These companies provide courses in areas such as interpersonal skills, leadership development, coaching, and management:

- SkillSoft
- Richardson
- PrimeLearning
- MindLeaders
- Harvard Business School Publishing
- DDI
- Ninth House.

Safety and Regulatory Courses

One of the key business drivers for using online learning is the need to meet mandatory training requirements in areas such as meeting OSHA safety training requirements (industrial and manufacturing) or HIPAA training (health care). Here are some examples of companies that specialize in providing safety and regulatory courseware:

- Syntrio
- Coastal Training Technologies
- Eduneering
- Brightline Compliance
- QuickCompliance.

Vertical Market Courseware

Beyond the general types of training that apply across many companies, there are specific training requirements within vertical market sectors. There are many companies that employ subject matter experts for the purpose of creating market-specific courses in areas such as finance or health care. Some vendors that provide focused training are featured in Table 22-13.

Talent and Performance Management Systems

A recent trend in establishing a learning platform is the idea that learning can have a broader effect when coupled with areas typically handled by human resources, such as recruiting talent, compensation based on performance, succession planning, and workforce planning. One area where there is significant overlap is competency management, or, in other words, defining competencies by job role and monitoring performance in each competency area.

Table 22-13. Off-the-Shelf, Vertical Market Focus

Company	Vertical
ESI International	Project Management
Omega Performance	Banking and Finance
HealthStream	Health Care
MEDSN	Health Care
ITC Learning	Industrial Plant
MC Strategies	Health Care
Kaplan Financial	Finance
Auralog	Language
Berlitz	Language
GlobalEnglish	Language
CCIM Institute	Real Estate
GeneEd	Biotechnologies

Although competency management is considered standard functionality in most LMS solutions, there is usually little carryover to how this information can be used during annual employee appraisals or for determining compensation based on performance.

Some organizations are working toward full convergence between their learning platforms and human resource back office tools to automate the exchange of data in a meaningful way so that learning and career development become completely seamless.

Making the leap to a fully integrated talent management or learning platform can dramatically drive up the cost of your learning platform. In short, making the decision to go this route needs to be done with clear strategic vision and a budget to match. Beyond cost, another important consideration is that the technology isn't the hardest part of this convergence (Albrecht et al., 2007). The hardest part is developing a common strategy that will meet the objectives of both human resources and training (see Figure 22-6).

Figure 22-6. Convergence of Learning and Talent Management

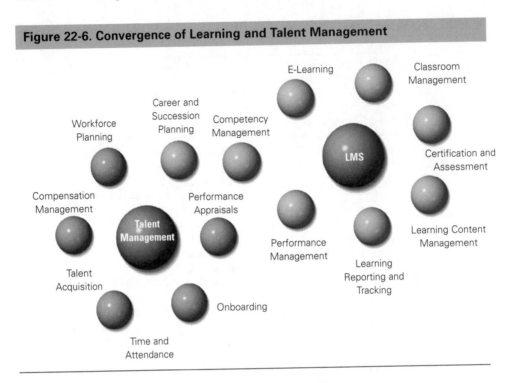

LMS vendors are building out much of this functionality and providing it through their LMS platforms. Here are some of the leading LMS providers, blazing a trail in the area of talent management:

- Saba
- SumTotal
- Cornerstone OnDemand
- Plateau
- GeoLearning
- TEDS
- KnowlegePlanet
- Learn.com.

Conclusion

The learning technology space is evolving quickly, sometimes faster than our ability to plan how we can leverage the technology to keep pace with what our learners need. With numerous learning technology components available, it is becoming increasingly important to keep up with what's happening in each category area. A simple taxonomy will help quickly classify and short-list technologies that will align with your most critical business and instructional goals.

About the Author

Bryan Chapman is chief learning strategist at Chapman Alliance, a provider of research-centric consulting solutions that assist organizations to define, operate, and optimize their strategic learning initiatives. As a veteran in the industry, he has more than 20 years' experience and has worked with such organizations as American Express, Avon, Honda, IBM, Kodak, Microsoft, Sharp Electronics, Shell, Sprint, UNICEF, the U.S. Food and Drug Administration, and the U.S. State Department to help them optimize learning efficiency through the use of innovative learning techniques and technologies.

Chapman was formerly the director of research and strategy for independent research and consulting firm Brandon Hall Research, where he served as the primary author and researcher on high-profile projects such as the LMS Knowledgebase, LCMS Comparative Analysis Report, and Comparison of Simulation Products and Services.

References

Albrecht, Mark, Janet Clarey, and Brandon Hall Research. 2007. *Talent management: A complete guide to strategies, systems, and issues.* Sunnyvale, CA: Brandon Hall Research.

ASTD. 2006. *ASTD 2006 state of the industry report.* Alexandria, VA: ASTD Press.

Chapman, Bryan, and Brandon Hall Research. 2006. *PowerPoint to e-learning development tools: Comparative analysis of 20 leading systems.* Sunnyvale, CA: Brandon Hall Research.

Chapman, Bryan, and Brandon Hall Research. 2007a. *LMS Knowledgebase 2007: In-depth profiles of 60+ learning management systems.* Sunnyvale, CA: Brandon Hall Research.

Chapman, Bryan, and Brandon Hall Research. 2007b. *Online simulations 2007: A knowledgebase of 100+ simulation development tools and services.* Sunnyvale, CA: Brandon Hall Research.

Chapman, Bryan. 2008. Tools for the design and development of online instruction. In *The handbook of research for educational communications and technology*, eds., J.M. Spector, M.D. Merrill, J. van Merriënboer, and M.P. Driscoll. 3rd ed. New York: Taylor & Francis.

Clarey, Janet. 2007. *E-learning 101: An introduction to e-learning, learning tools, and technologies.* Sunnyvale, CA: Brandon Hall Research.

Hillinger, Michael. 2007. Global warming interactive, available at http://www.globalwarminginteractive.com.

Kirk, James J., and Robert Belovics. 2004, April. An intro to online learning games. *Learning Circuits*, available at www.learningcircuits.org.

Nantel, Richard, Sharon Vipond, and Brandon Hall Research. 2007. *Authoring tool knowledgebase 2007: A buyer's guide to 105+ of the best e-learning content development applications.* Sunnyvale, CA: Brandon Hall Research.

Wexler, Steve, Brent Schlenker, Paula Canero, Bryan Chapman, Karen Hyder, Karl Kapp, Ann Kwinn, and Tony O'Driscoll. 2007. *Synchronous learning systems (SLS): Benchmarks, best practices, and real-time analysis about real-time learning.* Santa Rosa, CA: eLearning Guild.

For Further Reading

Brandon Hall Research. 2006. *How to buy e-learning systems, tools, and services.* Sunnyvale, CA: Brandon Hall Research.

Chapman, Bryan. 2007. *Creating a learning culture: Jumpstart toolkit.* Whitepaper. Salt Lake City, UT: Chapman Alliance.

Chapter 23

Authoring Techniques and Rapid E-Learning

Thomas A. Toth

In This Chapter

- ➤ Learn the three tools you need to build e-learning programs rapidly

- ➤ Recognize the value of saving your prototypes

- ➤ Learn the secret of rapid e-learning development

E-learning. Distance learning. Web-based training. Online learning. It's had a variety of names over the years, but at the end of the day, it's just people learning through the medium of technology. Whether it's through an iPod, from a web browser, or off of a network server, online learning offers people a new way to learn. Although online learning is an excellent way to deliver training, addressing the needs of a variety of learners sitting at desktops or working virtually around the world, developing it in a timely fashion is challenging. Trainers want to use this technology, but are often challenged about how to implement it.

Building online learning requires a proficiency in online technology: HTML, XHTML, PHP, ASP, Flash, Photoshop, and web video editing just for starters! Trainers who have dedicated their professional careers to the art of instructional design and facilitation are now being asked to learn web programming languages and graphic design. Some are comfortable with the challenge. Others prefer to bring on specialized technology gurus who can do some of the work for them. Some embrace this change and are learning and expanding their skill sets. This chapter will be most helpful to those who take the challenge to build new and innovative ways to learn.

Gone are the days of the six-month development timeline. As the technology gets easier to learn and implement, users who dabble on the weekend programming an HTML "ego site," blog, or MySpace page don't accept vendors that dramatically expand deliverable timetables. Yes, programming takes a long time, but web users are more educated about the technologies and won't accept unreasonable delays. Some people believe that putting together a good online learning project should take about as long as it takes to put together a good PowerPoint presentation. Although this is unreasonable, the belief is out there and is perpetuated by software vendors who advertise about how "easy" it is to create online learning if you buy their software or attend one of their classes.

As an online learning developer, how can you rapidly create online learning projects, using the proper web technologies and learning strategies? You need to have a toolbox—one full of templates, libraries of sample script, and graphic resources you can use to get what you need built, and built fast. (See the sidebar for some tools and processes for getting started.)

Image Libraries

In most cases, your online learning project will be made up of two things—text and images. Users read the text and learn, or text appears on the page as an accent to a running voice over. Users are familiar with textual elements and expect them to appear in any online learning course.

Images and graphics have three distinct roles in online learning—instructional, functional, and cosmetic.

Instructional graphics explain a series of learning points, illustrate a difficult concept, or help a learner understand the content through animation. These should be the most common types of images you add to your online learning program because they address a specific learning point and then expand upon it.

Functional graphics are essential to the interface and navigational aspects of an online learning course. Buttons, lines, and other elements that the user interacts with as part of the interface are considered functional graphics—buttons can light up or pulsate,

Tools and Processes for Getting Started

The definition of rapid e-learning differs among experts, but generally it's considered to be e-learning that can be developed quickly and inexpensively. Rapid e-learning uses tools and processes that decrease development time dramatically. Traditional courseware development timelines are measured in terms of months whereas rapid e-learning timelines are measured in terms of days and weeks. This makes it an attractive solution for many companies.

Tools to Develop Rapid E-Learning

As the popularity of rapid e-learning grows, the number of development tools increases. Tools on the market include

- Macromedia Breeze
- Articulate
- Lersus
- SNAP!
- Studio
- Content Point
- Webex
- mindflash.

These tools leverage common business tools, such as Microsoft PowerPoint, and automate applications to accelerate and simplify the development process, which means that editing and updating content can be done quickly and painlessly. Some of these tools offer the benefits of easily adding an audio track to the courseware by using a standard computer microphone; providing assessment and tracking tools; publishing to Flash, thus presenting the courseware to the learner in a user-friendly medium that is available on 98 percent of browsers; and using XML tags, enabling the content to be indexed and fully searchable.

Processes

In addition to using tools to help shorten the duration of development time, some advocates of rapid e-learning also propose a change to the design process. Some companies using rapid e-learning have subject matter experts (SMEs) develop the content and work directly with rapid e-learning tools to design the courseware. This process can work very well for content management. Updating sales staff on new features and developments, or critical information transfers that must be done quickly, are two examples where using both the rapid e-learning design process and tools are beneficial. However, in situations where the integrity of the instructional design is critical, there may be a considerable trade-off in using the SME to design the learning solution—unless the SME is trained in courseware design.

There are three possible solutions to this problem. With the traditional approach, you may have the SME work directly with the instructional designer. Using this approach, no time is saved in the design phase, and only the development time benefits by using rapid e-learning tools. The second option is to have the SME initially develop the content slides but have an instructional designer modify the content based on instructional design requirements. The final option is to have instructional designers carefully create templates that will guide the SME through the design phase.

(continued on next page)

Tools and Processes for Getting Started (continued)

Still, some traditional courseware designers may argue that having the SME develop the content, even in conjunction with an instructional designer, will compromise the courseware. Unfortunately, the alternative is that courseware may not be developed at all.

Another concern for traditional courseware designers is the lack of a programmer component to the solution. By having the person who knows the content develop the content quickly and easily, the time for development decreases dramatically, as does the time for quality assurance. Ask any programmer what the actual content of a course was and you will generally receive a blank look. The argument: If the designer is actually developing the courseware, there will generally be fewer errors because there are fewer people involved. While it is true that programmers are generally not required for rapid e-learning, this will give them more time to concentrate on high-end solutions that require their skills.

Source: Archibald (2005).

---

links can blink, and the navigation bar can be moved around the screen. All these elements are part of the functionality of the online learning project, but they can also be animated to provide additional interactivity to the learner.

Cosmetic graphics are background elements that can add to the look and feel of the online learning project. The interface itself, with its many graphical enhancements that users don't interact with, is considered to be a cosmetic graphic. Background animations, "mouse chasers" (animation tied to mouse movement), and between screen transitions are considered to be cosmetic graphics.

Motion graphics, or animations, can fall into any of these three categories. You can have an instructional motion graphic that explains a key learning point with voice over and animation. You can create buttons that jump around and interfaces that blink and glow. All of these elements are implemented by using motion graphics, but they can be hard to create unless you are very comfortable with Flash or other animation software.

As a developer, you need to have an arsenal of all three types of graphics at your disposal. Although you will be custom building most instructional graphics from scratch based on the needs of the learning module, having the graphic staples is critical to the rapid development of your online learning project. There are four media collections you should consider owning or purchasing: a collection of photo-realistic images, a collection of buttons and icons, a collection of background images, and a collection of motion graphics and animations.

Photo-Realistic Images

A collection of photo-realistic images should include images of office equipment, office people, and buildings. Transportation and industry-specific images (like banking or construction) are also helpful. These images should be high-quality photographs that you can edit with graphic design software and use throughout your online program. These images can form the basis for your instructional motion graphics or be standalone pictures that add to the screen. Just be sure to purchase photo images, not clip art.

Clip art is inexpensive. Don't be tempted to buy 20 CDs of it, because it has fallen out of favor. Programs with photos are viewed as more professional than programs with clip art.

Don't know where to go for images? Try www.gettyimages.com for the high-end, expensive shots, and www.istockphoto.com for more reasonable selections. Although istockphoto.com doesn't sell images by the CD, you can get a good collection going for a small investment.

Buttons and Icons

You can find collections of buttons and icons online, and they are a must for quickly building online learning. You can usually find them in sets at fairly inexpensive prices. Have them available and use them as a starting point for your interfaces and prototypes. Your objective is to get the visual and textual aspects of your online program completed in the least amount of time—find a set you like and tweak it for your use.

Background Images

When looking for background images, don't look for "tiles" or "textures." Most of these are cheesy and unprofessional (unless you can figure out a way of incorporating the look of "dragon skin" into your online learning!). What you are looking for are the large image files that contain the color smears, light effects, and other lined effects that you can drop into your solid color areas to add some additional professionalism to your images and interfaces.

Motion Graphics and Animations

Although you should not use repetitious, animated GIFs as a part of your online learning projects, a good animation can add tremendous value to your learner. But you don't have to build these from scratch. For Flash animations, try www.flashkit.com and download several you think can be used as is or modified for your use. I once created an entire snowball fight learning game from the structure and code downloaded from Flashkit.

Other people have done it before you, and if you don't have the time to develop something from scratch, this is an excellent alternative. Spend some time on this site and you will find amazing things you can download for free.

Once you have selected your collections, buy an external hard drive and save all your images and motion graphics to a single location. Create a good file folder system to help keep you organized. Use a software tool like Adobe Bridge or Aperture to scan your image library and quickly identify the image that will work best and drop it right into your program. Getting this library together and then not being able to easily find what you are looking for defeats the whole purpose.

Now that you have your images archived and organized, you can start thinking about building a rapid prototype, the second tool in your online learning toolbox.

Rapid Prototyping

After the learning objectives are created, the content built, the scripts written, the interactions designed, and the animation or video planned, this pile of information lands on your desk. As the developer, you are required to turn this stack of notes and paperwork into a fully functional online learning program.

You must take the time to review the outlines and have an opportunity to meet with the design team to ask questions and receive clarification before any programming starts. You may be inclined to jump right in, but meeting with the designer before programming begins ensures that you have a good feel for the content and expected deliverables. Begin with the end in mind—don't start programming or you will extend the timelines for development, especially if you have to keep going back to the designer to get answers to questions. Schedule a long meeting, get your questions answered, and then begin the rapid prototype process.

The rapid prototype process is used to clarify the general look and feel of the interface. What are the basic colors of the project? Is there a company template or color scheme that must be followed? Is there a theme? Are there menus and buttons? What do they look like? The graphical structure where the content will be placed is the interface, and the rapid prototype is developed using graphic design software (like Photoshop or Fireworks). Creating a rapid prototype ensures that the tiny snafus that occur during the development of the interface get corrected before the project moves into full development.

In its simplest form, the rapid prototype is a preview of the online learning program so that it can be evaluated based on its visual appeal. It is the user interface and perhaps a few learning screens or an animation that can be adjusted to meet the designer's expectations. The four or five pages of graphics and sample interactions can be changed or modified to fit the needs of the designer.

If everyone on the design team has the opportunity to evaluate the prototype before the majority of the content has been inserted into it, drastic, time-consuming interface over-hauls can be avoided. Imagine if the designer wanted to change the colors of the program from red to green, or he or she didn't like the position of the company logo on the screen? What if the fonts were hard to read or the positioning of the feedback area was not easy to find? It is much easier for you to change a few pages of code and graphics than to return to an entire program of hundreds of pages. Edits to the graphical design of the prototype are easy. Performing these changes at a later date can add days or weeks to the development cycle.

If this is the first online learning program you've developed, this rapid prototyping stage may take a few days. However, if you've developed online learning in the past, you may already have previous work that you can reuse.

In a perfect world, your initial prototype design will be perfect, the designers will love it, and you can move forward. That usually isn't the case. In some instances, you are required to make simple tweaks and edits to positioning. However, you may also have to throw everything out and start from scratch. As you are tweaking and building, *don't delete any-thing*. Everything you build now, even if the client or design team hates it, can be used to build rapid prototypes for other clients or other programs. Get in the habit of using "Save As" for your graphic and program files, because you can always go back and reuse this work at a later time. Get into the habit of saving your files separately. For example, you build an interface and save it as interface001.psd. The design team comes back and asks for a tweak to the colors, and a rebuild of the program navigation elements. Open inter-face001.psd and "Save As" interface002.psd. Even though the first navigation prototype didn't work for this project, you now have a perfectly good interface and navigation that you can reuse for any new projects.

The more interfaces you develop, the more you will have in your library of prototypes. The more sample prototypes you have, the easier and faster it will be for you to develop new ones. Save these interfaces onto the same hard drive you are using for your generic stock images. Extract the buttons and other navigation elements from these interfaces and save them as their own elements so that they can be quickly reused in other programs.

If you are building a series of online courses for a single company or client, don't rein-vent the wheel for every learning project. The more programs you build, the less time it should take you to develop your rapid prototype. You should consider branding your online learning projects—each program's interface should look similar, act similarly, and be comfortable for your learners to jump into. Once you have a prototype that the designer likes, keep using it for all subsequent online learning courses. Naturally, you will need to change titles and module section names, but everything else should stay the same. Following this method can take your prototyping timetable from several days to several hours.

Once the rapid prototype has been approved, the coding begins. This is where you can take advantage of the final tool in your toolbox: script libraries.

Script Libraries

Creating interfaces, code, and interactions from scratch each time you develop an online learning product is a waste of time. There are some elements common to every online learning project you create. Write a list of those items and then save the lines of code you create to make these elements work.

Your list could look like the following:

- Page counter
- Back and next buttons
- Directions for the learner
- Multiple-choice interactions
- Drag-and-drop interactions
- Data tracking
- LMS-specific code
- Flyout menu elements
- Web form processing
- User authentication.

Depending on your choice of programming language, these bits of code could be in HTML, JavaScript, PHP, ASP, or ActionScript. It doesn't matter which language you use, but once you figure out the code to make something work, save it and reuse it. Continually go back to these bits and use them as a basis for all your future coding.

Dreamweaver or Flash come with a library of commonly used commands called Snippets. Breadcrumb code trails, navigation elements, JavaScript, ActionScript functions, and other goodies are easily located on the Snippets tabbed menus. Using these programs and the Snippets included with the software can rapidly accelerate your development time. Also, companies like WebAssist (www.webassist.com) sell readymade Snippets for use in Dreamweaver and other web development software packages.

Something else to consider when working to rapidly develop online learning code is to become familiar with the online resources available to you. Simply Google the technology you are using, and you will be amazed to find hundreds of sites offering free code: www.javascript.com, www.phpfreaks.com, www.asp101.com, www.csszengarden.com, and www.htmlgoodies.com all contain free code samples for you to use and reuse. Although these sites are not online-learning centric, they contain information about the core technologies you need to make your online learning work.

Don't Reinvent the Wheel

The secret to rapid development is to reuse, recycle, and reinvent. Software and technology are available to quickly program code and design graphics, but taking the time to figure out what your common online learning elements are and then figuring out how to quickly copy those into new projects is the key. It is also important to determine if the project is appropriate for rapid e-learning. The sidebar describes the best uses for rapid e-learning.

Best Uses of Rapid E-Learning

It's important to keep in mind that the tools and technology used in e-learning need to be appropriate to the instructional objectives of the courseware. As the instructional objectives become more complex, typically the complexity and the cost of development also increase.

Rapid e-learning is most useful for low- to mid-range levels of e-learning complexity in which knowledge and comprehension is key. It's typically considered less effective to use rapid e-learning for high-end solutions in which evaluation and synthesis are critical. However, many rapid e-learning tools have the capacity to embed more engaging and rich media for projects that may need a blended solution. This easy interoperability increases the versatility of the product. By blending rapid e-learning with other forms of training, it may be considered part of a valid e-learning solution in a wide range of situations.

In traditional courseware development, long design and development cycles that lead to higher costs have usually precluded content that has a short shelf life, content that needs to be developed quickly, or content that isn't substantial enough to merit the time and cost of traditional e-learning. Institutions with limited budgets have also foregone e-learning as a means of workplace development. But by developing content quickly and cheaply with very little risk, rapid e-learning processes and tools allow e-learning to be an effective alternative in situations where previously it wasn't considered feasible. As it continues to grow in popularity, rapid e-learning processes and tools will continue to evolve, making it an even more attractive option for many e-learning solutions.

Source: Archibald (2005).

Don't be concerned about reusing images or prototypes for other clients or projects. Remember, the client or the designer rejected the prototype you want to reuse. They didn't like something about it and asked for another sample. That doesn't mean that the original was a bad design, it just meant that this client or designer didn't prefer it. Tastes are different, and everyone has a different opinion. Try using the same interface with another client or designer and see if you get a different reaction. I've submitted things to clients that I've loved and things I've hated. The client or the designer needs to be happy, and if you provide something that they adore, it doesn't matter if three other clients or designers have seen it before and hated it.

Don't be too concerned with reusing your code. It is the true secret to rapid development. Review your functionality list, and you will see a list of the common online learning interactions and programming activities; copy and paste that code to make the new program work as well as the original program. The functionality is the same across all online learning programs. Capitalize on your expertise and your experience, as well as the experience of others.

Can you create an online learning program as quickly as someone making a PowerPoint presentation? Certainly not. The instructional design, scripting, and interaction design can take a very long time depending on the size of the program, the amount of content, and the intensity of the interactions. However, you can make your life easier and produce a fantastic online learning project by adding these three tools to your toolbox: an image library, rapid prototypes, and reused code.

About the Author

Thomas A. Toth, based in the Denver, Colorado, area, is a Macromedia-certified developer with a decade of training, management, and design experience in the computer and technical education industries. He has designed and programmed several dozen online and computer-based training courses using Macromedia and Adobe products and has personally created and maintained more than four dozen websites for corporate clients. He is the president of dWeb Studios, a web and e-learning design and development firm in Parker, Colorado.

He has his bachelor's degree in human communication and his master's degree in education with a focus on educational technology and belongs to several professional organizations such as ASTD, the American Marketing Association, the eLearning Guild, Toastmasters, and the HTML Writers Guild. He is also a published author, a performing magician, a trained chef, and a musician.

Reference

Archibald, Dianne. 2005, January. Rapid e-learning: A growing trend. *Learning Circuits*, available at http://www.learningcircuits.org/2005/jan2005/archibald.htm.

For Further Reading

Allen, Michael. 2002. *Michael Allen's guide to e-learning.* Hoboken, NJ: John Wiley & Sons.

Horton, William. 2000. *Designing web-based training: How to teach anyone anything anywhere anytime.* Hoboken, NJ: Wiley & Sons.

Horton, William, and Katherine Horton. 2003. *E-learning tools and technologies: A consumer's guide for trainers, teachers, educators, and instructional designers.* Hoboken, NJ: Wiley & Sons.

Toth, Thomas. 2003. *Technology for trainers.* Alexandria, VA: ASTD.

Chapter 24

What Is a Simulation? The New Structure of Actions-Systems-Results

Clark Aldrich

In This Chapter

> ➤ Learn what simulations are
>
> ➤ Understand four genres of simulations
>
> ➤ Learn a new way to organize simulation content

When I am in front of a group of training professionals, I usually ask them to define the word *simulation*. I give them a minute to think about it, and then poll the room. Frequent responses include "a model of reality," "a place to learn by doing," or most commonly, "a safe place to practice skills." Everyone agrees to the definition, including me.

I then ask, "What has been your actual experience with simulations?" It is harder now to get replies. One person might mention a sales role play she did a few years ago. Someone else might mention a computer game that he or his kids play. Another might mention a military or airline flight simulator. Or someone might mention a business school company simulator. Soon, the group that was so united around the concept of simulations is talking about totally different things.

This might be the single biggest challenge of simulations (or *sims* for short) today. Everyone likes them in theory, but most groups have different expectations and experiences with them and don't ever realize their bias. This not only hinders implementations, but also comparisons of best practice, and even research. Articles that say simulation-based learning programs improve retention by x percent, make me think, what kind of simulation? What kind of content? What kind of audience?

For a training professional, however, the different types of simulations—or genres—once understood, make creating and using simulations much easier and more predictable.

In this chapter, I first define simulation. Then I discuss four common genres of simulation: branching stories, interactive spreadsheets, virtual labs, and minigames. Next, I compare development prices for each. Then, I discuss the whole philosophy of sims, including how they are structured and even how they might change the way we capture and share experiences, and, finally, what to expect when they are deployed.

A Scary Definition

I first want to put forth my own broad definition of simulations. But be warned, it is a scary definition:

> Educational simulations are a broad genre of sims that focus on increasing participants' mastery level in the real world. Educational simulations use *simulation elements* to model and present an abstracted reality, including
>
> - Real-life or target *actions*, reflected in the interface
> - How the actions then affect relevant *systems*, including any units, maps, and work processes
> - How those systems produce feedback and *results*.
>
> The simulation elements are then mixed with *game elements* to make it engaging and *pedagogical elements* (including coaching) to make it effective.
>
> Simulations are also organized into tasks and *levels* to create incrementally challenging practice environments and can be engaged by one or more participants and often surrounded by a community.

Genre 1: Branching Stories

A branching story is an educational simulation genre in which learners make a series of multiple-choice decisions to progress through and affect an event.

Specifically, learners start with a briefing; they advance to a first multiple-choice decision point, or branch; then, based on the decision or action they make, they see a scene that provides some feedback, advances the story, and then sets up another decision. Learners

---

✍ **Roger Schank** ✎

Roger Schank is one of the most respected and influential members of the e-learning community. An outspoken critic of conventional educational models and traditional curricula, Schank favors learner-based and performance-based learning solutions, particularly through e-learning and multimedia. Throughout his career, Schank has advocated the use of story-centered curricula, often referred to as SCC, which is based on the idea that a good learning program should tell a good story.

Schank based his educational models on the idea that traditional curricula used for decades in various levels and types of schools—from kindergarten right up through corporate training universities—use outdated concepts and teaching methods that disregard how people really learn. Common educational tools such as reading assignments and lectures often do not make the content stick and do not promote a love of learning. According to Schank, the only way to learn is through experience, practice, and memorable storytelling. His learning-by-doing approach in the classroom, whether virtual or otherwise, allows people to grasp concepts, apply them, practice the application, and then learn from mistakes in a safe environment.

In 1989, Schank founded the prominent Institute for the Learning Sciences at Northwestern University in collaboration with Andersen Consulting. In 1994, he started Cognitive Arts Corporation, which designs and builds multimedia simulations for corporate and online university training. Then in 2002, he founded Socratic Arts, which creates e-learning for schools and businesses. He was also named chief learning officer at Donald Trump's Trump University in 2005. Schank is the author of more than 20 books on learning, artificial intelligence, education, reading, e-learning, and storytelling, among other topics.

---

continue making decisions, traversing some of the available branches, until they either win or lose by reaching either a successful or unsuccessful final state. Learners then get some type of after-action review.

Again, the branching story's basic input is typically a multiple-choice interface. Also typically, actions are invoked by the player's character saying different statements to direct other people.

The simplicity of the interface is branching stories' greatest strength and weakness. Their ease of use, ease of deployment, and dynamic visual content make them highly appropriate for entry-level salespeople, call center representatives, freshmen, customer-facing retail positions, and entry-level managers. Any high-turnover position should be trained, although not exclusively, using branching stories. However, some critics call them all trigger and no complex systems. Many high-potential or highly creative individuals eschew their simple, all-or-nothing interface. Companies like WILL Interactive have advanced the genre to handle more moral and complex situations, making a few, unlike most other examples of the genre, also appropriate for higher-level employees.

Branching stories can be presented in text, full motion video, pictures, and sound, and can take on an almost cinematic quality. Branching stories are often designed to be used multiple times so learners can practice or try different alternatives to get different results. When this is the case, the program might use bread crumbs, or indicators such as active links that change color when traversed, to show what decisions the player made last time.

There are no technology barriers to creating content in branches. Papers and Microsoft PowerPoint presentations can be designed to take the user where he or she wants to go, although more powerful tools for creating branching stories include

- Adobe Captivate 2
- NexLearn SimWriter
- Trivantis' Lectora
- SuddenlySmart's SmartBuilder
- Hot Potatoes
- Hard coding in Flash, HTML, Dreamweaver.

Creating branching stories is, in fact, a first crack at dismantling the monopoly of linear content.

Genre 2: Interactive Spreadsheets

The second popular genre of educational simulation is the interactive spreadsheet. This is an educational simulation genre in which learners typically try to affect three or four critical metrics indirectly and over time by allocating finite resources along competing categories over a series of turns or intervals.

Learners get feedback on their decisions through graphs and charts after each interval. The entire sim might continue for between three and 20 intervals.

For example, the head of a nonprofit organization might try to optimize the variables of "funding" and "impact to community" by allocating his or her time during the course of each week among fundraising, creating new services, doing menial tasks, doing paperwork, and evaluating existing services.

Interactive spreadsheets are often deployed in a multiplayer or team-based environment, with significant competition among learners and often with a coach or facilitator to help everyone along. Used as such, interactive spreadsheets are often the cornerstones of multi-day programs to build shared knowledge and understanding.

Interactive spreadsheets typically focus on business school issues such as policy, supply chain management, product life cycle, accounting, and general cross-functional business acumen. Despite the genre name, spreadsheets like Microsoft Excel are not a platform for deploying these models, although they may be used in the design document.

The subtlety, unpredictability, and variability make them appropriate for training business school learners and high-potential supervisors through the direct reports to the chief executive officer. They require, and are a pure introduction to, dynamic systems.

Genre 3: The Virtual Lab

The third genre is virtual labs, in which learners are given realistic, online versions of objects or applications, and given challenges to solve. For example, automotive dealers might be given a smoking car. They have to find the right tools, such as a diagnostic computer terminal, pop the hood by pressing the right buttons, attach the cable to the right spot in the engine, and start the computer by pressing the right sequence of buttons.

What is really interesting about the virtual lab model is that now the interface becomes part of the content. What you do, where you do it, how hard you do it, and how long you press the "turn the wrench" button all matter a lot; it is not just a matter of clicking A, B, or C. There is kinesthetic learning going on as well. Here we are focusing on the actions of the participant in a realistic setting that transfers nicely to real life.

Genre 4: Minigames

The final popular genre of simulations is called minigames. Minigames, also called casual games or microgames, are easy to access, most often Adobe Flash based, and represent between five and 20 minutes of learner engagement. Minigames are both fun, in terms of quick gameplay, often-bouncy music, and appealing graphics, and educational. And with their somewhat low development cost, they are actually attainable for many organizations.

Minigames are perfect when there are a few skills or activities that need repetition and practice to be able to apply well, or there is some counterintuitive system in place, or some new sets of results are desired. The scenarios in the sidebars illustrate some successful applications of minigames in the workplace.

Minigames: Cisco Systems

"My audience consists of people who are preparing for a Cisco certification," explained Jerry Bush, program manager, Cisco Systems. "We have tried pure games in the past and had a bit of success. For example, I have used multiplayer quiz games to review key points before certification tests, which participants seemed to really like; so we wanted to go to the next step."

Jerry first surveyed the audience. "One skill that was giving a large number of people some problems was the binary number system. So we decided to create a Cisco binary game."

"I am an instructional designer, so I mapped out some ideas. I then hired a game developer, who added a lot of great ideas. He built it more Tetris like and added music and sound effects. We came out with the binary game about a year ago. The first year we had 30,000 to 40,000 people using it. As our second year began, it went viral and has now had about 200,000 downloads. I also sent out a survey to about 300 people asking, "Did this game help you pass the Cisco certification? Fifty percent said yes, 25 percent said they thought it will (they hadn't taken the test yet), and 25 percent gave it a more mixed review."

Jerry then took the Cisco binary game into traditional classes. (Cisco Network Academies helps prepare high school and college students to take the certification exam.) Although he has not done formal surveys yet, anecdotally, the program seems to have helped students better learn binary numbers on their own time and more enjoyably.

Next? Cisco just released the Subnet Game to help participants understand the concepts of subdividing networks for traffic and security. Its theme is Area 51, and involves battling malicious hackers.

Minigames also work well when much of the raw information is already "out there," whether on corporate websites or in newsletters, but the rate-limiting step is the uptake and "caring." The point isn't to shovel more raw data into the learners' heads, but to build interest and ownership.

As a result, some minigames straddle the line between being simple and simplistic. Many training people will bristle at the over-abstractions of some minigames, but both corporate communications and salespeople will feel right at home.

Costs for Simulations

The next question is, of course, what are the costs? Table 24-1 lists some examples of retail costs for access by corporations, but your mileage may vary.

A New Theory of Content: Actions-Systems-Results

Let's now look more at the big sim picture. To a lot of people, the whole sim movement appears to be the dumbing down of content while increasing cost, all to pander to computer-game-addled slackers.

Table 24-1. Simulation Costs

	Branching Story		Interactive Spreadsheets		Minigames		Virtual Lab	
	Perpetual Site License (Custom)	Per User (Off-the-Shelf)	Perpetual Site License (Custom)	Per User (Off-the-Shelf)	Perpetual Site License (Custom)	Per User (Off-the-Shelf)	Perpetual Site License (Custom)	Per User (Off-the-Shelf)
Short	10 minutes: $30K	$30	Less than 1 hour: $30K[a]	$30[b]	5 minutes: $10K	n/a	30 minutes: $30K	$10
Medium	10–30 minutes: $100K	$100	1–4 hours: $100K[a]	$100[b]	10 minutes: $15K	n/a	1 hour: $75K	$30
Long	30 minutes–2 hours: $500K	$500	4–8 hours: $500K[a]	$500[b]	30 minutes: 40K	n/a	4 hours: $150K	$100

[a] plus cost of facilitation
[b] including cost of facilitation

Minigames: Miller Brewing Company

Miller Brewing Company is testing a game called *Tips on Tap* for bartenders. The core gameplay is around the activities of being a great bartender, including serving up the perfect draught beer, carding customers, and serving them quickly for the goal of getting great tips.

Tips on Tap includes embedded minigames, including *Score Your Pour*, which teaches people how to pour beer using proper angle and height to achieve the perfect "head."

Score Your Pour provides a continuous practice environment for participants to precisely move the glass using the mouse, which measures distance and angle of the glass to the tap to create the proper head. Points are subtracted if participants hit the tap (bacteria buildup), or spill the beer (waste).

After each play, the participant gets feedback, tips, and motivational thoughts.

This level of kinesthetic knowledge is impossible using traditional linear methods of instruction, but it is also quite expensive, less convenient, and even often less instructional using real product. Jon Aleckson of Web Courseworks, the lead for the project, noted, "In the end, the minigame, *Score Your Pour*, is a reusable, updatable learning object that Miller Brewing Company can use in live classroom training, webinars, and as a part of a larger immersive learning simulation."

In some early cases, that is probably true. But ultimately, something else is happening. A new science is being defined—a new way of representing the world—that will be as transformational as Isaac Newton's *Philosophiae Naturalis Principia Mathematica*.

As mentioned in the scary definition, educational simulations are a broad genre of sims that focus on increasing participants' mastery level in the real world.

Educational simulations use *simulation elements* to model and present an abstracted reality. This includes three parts that have traditionally been only minimally captured in classrooms and books: actions, results, and the invisible system that connects them.

Actions

Actions are what a person does in real life and in a simulation at the most tactical, or basic, level, be it "pat person on the back" in one type of simulation or "buy small company" in another.

In a simulation, actions are accomplished by basic inputs. These can include pressing buttons, moving sliders, entering numbers, clicking on a text window or icon, or moving a joystick. Although multiple-choice inputs in branching stories are somewhat interesting, real-world actions are better represented by 10 or 15 options, each with two analogue components: magnitude and timing.

Minigames: Canadian Standards Association

The Canadian Standards Association (CSA) wanted a way to let users practice establishing emergency procedures learned in class through an interactive experience.

They looked at the way other people have approached the problem, such as using three-dimensional environments and accurate simulations of how fire burns. "The games industry has solved a lot of hard problems, but making products that look like games that came from Electronic Arts might not be the right approach," said Kenton White, CTO of CSA's implementation partner, DISTIL. For example, "In CSA's market of standards and certification, replayability is not a necessary feature. If in a single play through, a student encounters all of the required content and has responded appropriately, there is no benefit to having them play it again." The Canadian Standards Association also realized that what they wanted to teach didn't need to have high graphical fidelity or gameplay sophistication.

They focused on creating a product in which the learning objective was raising the awareness of the participant to think broadly about a disaster site and learn that missing something could have fatal consequences. And they wanted to do it in a way that was memorable, and where the player would take ownership for any failure.

"So we modeled the interface off of causal games, such as Bejewled, and hidden pictures games," said Kenton White. The result was a minigame called *Response Ready. Response Ready* gave people the ability to identify potential hazards and, for each, determine emergency response procedures.

In the minigame, participants are given a broad panorama of a city scene. Their goal is to identify places on that map that are of high risk. They assign to these areas both a probability of problem and severity of problem if it does occur, which in turn unlocks procedures specific to that risk.

Kenton White explained, "So if I go to the gas station part of the map, I have to identify things that could give you spills, such as gas pumps, tanker trucks, and propane tanks. Then, after I identify risks and put in place procedures, life happens. A tanker truck comes in, and there is a spill. I now see how well my rules handle the situation."

In some cases, there may even be two different spill procedures, and a real-time challenge is to match the right procedure to the right spill.

Response Ready does not set participants up to fail the first time, but many do. A common problem is the amphitheater, which people think is just background art. But it represents a place where there needs to be evacuation processes, just as much as the office buildings.

As is typical of creating any new type of experience, many participants are initially unsure of it. Some game-literate people at first are disappointed because they have different expectations about what a game is. Meanwhile, some people who are not game literate briefly experience an initial frustration with the game interface. Both issues are self-resolved quickly. But the content replaces an hour of classroom time with about 15 minutes of self-paced time, in a way that, most important, better enhances public safety. These are the types of criteria, more than pure fun or replayability, that justify minigames.

For example, in driving a car, it is not enough to "turn right," but to turn the steering wheel the right amount and at the right time. Likewise, in managing a project, it is not enough to increase the budget, but to increase the budget the right amount and at the right time. In eating well, it is not enough to eat protein. One has to eat the right amount and at the right time.

Actions are effective in contexts and combinations. The collection of actions is ultimately as logical and fluid as collections of words in a sentence, or notes of music in a concerto, and needs as much practice to master.

Here's a leadership example (see Figure 24-1). Although they go by many different names, the broad categories of leader actions are

- Focus on current goal (positively or negatively)
- Focus on current active person or parties (positively or negatively)
- Switch goals (positively or negatively)
- Switch (or bring in) new people or groups (positively or negatively)
- Do nothing.

As I hope this example shows, the presentation and availability of actions through basic inputs can greatly influence the look and functionality of the simulation display. Meanwhile, the granularity and scope of the simulation also determines the granularity of the actions. For a country president, an action might be "to send an assertive letter to another country's leader." But if the simulation is about the staff writer, an action might be "to start off the letter recalling a shared positive experience."

The educational challenge of actions is building a new awareness of learners' real-world options. Almost always, it means at least some of the time not allowing learners to do things the way they have in the past to break bad habits.

Meanwhile, giving learners so many options, dozens at any given time, is unnerving at first (and good level design will slowly increase the number of options) but is necessary to personalize the experience and enable learners to own the outcome.

The challenge of actions is also the challenge of applying what one learned in the world. Most traditional courses leave the task of applying the material learned for the learners to figure out after the class, which means that most do not do it. By forcing the practice of the application of the material to the front of the program, it paves the way for the materials' productive use after the program.

Figure 24-1. Explanation of How Interface Was Built to Map to Leadership Actions

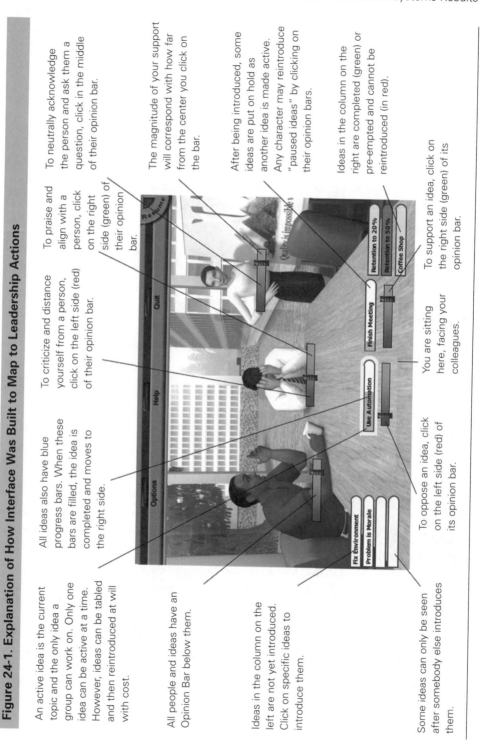

An active idea is the current topic and the only idea a group can work on. Only one idea can be active at a time. However, ideas can be tabled and then reintroduced at will with cost.

All people and ideas have an Opinion Bar below them.

Ideas in the column on the left are not yet introduced. Click on specific ideas to introduce them.

Some ideas can only be seen after somebody else introduces them.

All ideas also have blue progress bars. When these bars are filled, the idea is completed and moves to the right side.

To criticize and distance yourself from a person, click on the left side (red) of their opinion bar.

To oppose an idea, click on the left side (red) of its opinion bar.

To neutrally acknowledge the person and ask them a question, click in the middle of their opinion bar.

To praise and align with a person, click on the right side (green) of their opinion bar.

The magnitude of your support will correspond with how far from the center you click on the bar.

After being introduced, some ideas are put on hold as another idea is made active. Any character may reintroduce "paused ideas" by clicking on their opinion bars.

Ideas in the column on the right are completed (green) or pre-empted and cannot be reintroduced (in red).

To support an idea, click on the right side (green) of its opinion bar.

You are sitting here, facing your colleagues.

Results

After actions, the next content and design issue is that of results (sometimes called the mission). This is what a participant or team is trying to accomplish in the experience.

A mission can be as simple as arriving at a certain location at a certain time with a certain item, or can be as complex as combinations of

- Managing a process
- Defeating a competitor
- Developing a functioning ecosystem or re-engineering a set of processes
- Discovering or implementing a new process
- Creating an outcome that is measured against a balanced scorecard.

Each level has its own results, and typically gets more complex as one progresses through levels.

Systems

Most people naturally think about actions and results. This is even truer of real life than it is of sim design.

But it is almost always a system, and almost always a hidden system, that connects actions and results. And it is a lack of understanding of the invisible system that leads to failure of many hardworking and well-meaning individuals. This is a huge concept, critical to sim design.

Here's an example. We all play variations on this type of scenario: What if someone from 200 years ago watched us live today? What if an ancestor watched us, say, wash dishes? The steps we took, from scraping off the remaining food, to loading up the dishwasher, to putting some form of soap in a small box, to running the disposal, to pressing some buttons and turning a knob, to walking away for an hour, would seem like we were performing mystical incantations. More specifically, some steps would make sense, some would seem random, and some steps would actually appear to be the opposite of what we should be doing.

Here are some other examples of successful uses of systems that would seem bizarre to anyone who did not understand the invisible systems connecting actions and results:

- A couple falls in love with a house on the market. But when the salesperson enters the room, they act uninterested.

- A project manager, with a deadline fast approaching, fires two programmers.
- A health-conscious actress, a week before a big scene, injects a neurotoxin into her face.
- An environmentalist forester cuts down a third of the trees in a grove.
- A dieter eats a large breakfast.
- A doctor deliberately exposes a patient to a small quantity of a fatal virus.

By not understanding the invisible system, some people are always surprised by unintended consequences; they naively optimize just one part of a complicated system and have no positive impact on the entire system, and possibly a negative impact. Meanwhile, other people perform concise actions and get remarkable results. These are the people who understand and can use the invisible systems. "Going to where the puck will be, not to where it is now" requires a working knowledge of the system.

Our world is filled with systems, as complex as the universe or simpler than a light switch. And complicated systems are made up of simpler systems, equations, variables, relationships, processes, units, and actions.

There are six different techniques for building out systems in sims, all compatible with each other, overlapping, scalable, and recursive:

- *Pure mathematical system.* Some systems are purely mathematical, where, for example, primary variables are affected by aggregations of secondary variables, as defined by equations and relationships. This is the primary model for the sim genre of interactive spreadsheets.
- *Units on maps as system.* Some systems are best captured by the activities of units on maps. Games, such as Roller Coaster Tycoon, perhaps best model this.
- *State-based system.* Some systems are best modeled through the abstracted "state-based systems," such as maps of museums or subway stops.
- *Artificial intelligence (AI) as system.* Directing or competing against AI characters can represent compelling and repeatable engageable systems.
- *Work process as system.* One type of system is a work process. Just knowing who gets what business form can spell the difference between success and failure for an activity.
- *Community as system.* Perhaps the least predictable system is a real community, such as one organized by a social networking model.

Using various levels of abstraction and techniques, a good simulation models the invisible system that connects actions and results. Modeling simulations will become a critical skill, not just for sim designers, but for the creators of any intellectual property.

Mix Well with Game and Pedagogical Elements

The simulation elements (actions, systems, and results) then must be mixed with various levels of *game elements* to make the content engaging, and *pedagogical elements* to maximize the learning and time spent.

Game elements are techniques that motivate people to want to engage, not just have to engage. Game elements include fantasy, whimsy, competition, beauty, and a great story. It is a game element that positions the participant in the role of a hero, or gives him or her a high score to pursue.

Game elements can do a lot of good in a serious game or educational simulation. Game elements drive engagement, and such elements, great graphics, for instance, can make a boring simulation much more tolerable. A good sense of humor can build goodwill, which is often then transferred to the content itself. A game show format can lower tension, making it potentially more accurate than assessing with a traditional test.

But game elements are also very controversial. Game elements surround and dilute the learning. They take up developer time and they take up end-learner time, ultimately taking resources away from the primary content.

They are also subjective. What is fun for one person, such as gambling or treasure hunts, can be tedious for someone else. Different cultures, ages, genders, experiences, and needs all create complex demographics.

Game elements can also sometimes subvert the learning. A developer can make things happen faster or more dramatically, or abstract tedious steps, which increases the fun but at the expense of accuracy.

Fun elements can often also be leveraged by a learner to "game" the sim. And certain game elements, like competition, can focus users on getting a high score rather than learning the material.

Having too few game elements results in a boring, dry experience, and having too many game elements creates something that is silly and distracting. As a rule, the more one cares about content, the more one is intolerant of game elements. If the orphanage is burning and you need to learn how to put out the fire, the last thing you want is to play Wheel of Fortune to get the information.

Pedagogical Elements

Pedagogical (also called didactic) techniques and elements surround an experience, ensuring that a participant's time is spent productively. Pedagogical elements in real-life range from speedometers and caller identification to mentors, supervisors, or guides.

In sims, pedagogical elements can include in-game tips and directions, graphs, highlights, forced moments of reflection, bread crumbs, a coach or facilitator, background material, and after-action reviews.

In educational experiences, pedagogical elements help the learners

- Know what to do
- Use the interface
- Avoid developing superstitious behavior, such as believing they are influencing something by a particular action when they are really not
- See relationships faster
- Work through frustration-resolution pairs
- Try different approaches
- Apply lessons to the real world.

Pedagogical elements have to balance the challenge of giving neither too much nor too little help. Pedagogical elements take the place of the wise instructor (or the form of a virtual mentor, supervisor, or guide), watching, commenting, pointing out key relationships, and knowing when not to say anything.

In addition to game elements and pedagogical elements, simulations are finally organized into tasks and levels to create incrementally challenging practice environments, and can be engaged by one or more participants.

Deploying Sims

Once you have created or bought a sim, you will discover that deploying sims is significantly different than deploying other types of formal learning programs. To fully appreciate this, we should step back and reexamine learning itself, not classroom or book learning.

It all comes down to this. In any transformation (from getting a big promotion to moving to a better house), things get worse before they get better, even when the transformation is sought after and desired. New clarity only follows frustration. New power comes from not being able to do things the way you have in the past. Likewise, a moment of learning is marked first by a participant being frustrated at not being able to do something that one wants to do, and then resolving that frustration.

Compare your own experiences. When learning to ride a bike, or swim, or drive, or speak a foreign language, the process was most likely uneven and filled with lows and highs, frustrations and resolutions.

There are first moments when any learner wants to give up. Then there are aha moments where everything starts clicking together. The exaltation is then followed by another, more interesting frustration, and the cycle continues and one's capabilities increase.

In real learning, the frustration-resolution sensation is the sensation of new mental muscle forming. Likewise in real learning, learners have difficulty summing up what was learned, to themselves and to others. Words just trivialize the learning. But what was learned sticks with us. Hence learners remember riding a bike forever, while forgetting what year the Magna Carta was signed five seconds before they need to write it on the test.

Sims, and educational simulations in particular, only minimally smooth out the peaks and valleys of real learning. Instead, they compress them and make them more predictable.

That said, when learners hit the valleys of frustration, this can present problems of expectations for the simulation coach or sponsor. There is a "threshold to quit" for different end learners, that if the experience dips below the threshold, the learner will opt out of the course with a negative bias.

Factors that raise the threshold to quit (making it more likely a learner quits) include

- The learner is "evaluating" or "surveying" the material.
- The program has little support.
- The expectation of the sim experience has been poorly set up.

Factors that lower the threshold (making it less likely a learner quits) include

- A live coach or facilitator assists with the learning.
- The learners understand that they really need the content.
- The program has a lot of credibility or good "buzz."
- The learners are being graded in an academic setting or ordered to take it in a corporate or military setting.

Do They Work?

Do sims work better than traditional methodologies? The bad news is that there will never be a silver bullet argument that sims do or do not work better. This is for many reasons, including that we still don't know how to measure traditional learning and that developing big skills, such as leadership, project management, stewardship, and security, completely falls off the map in any evaluation scheme.

But there is also good news. I have been involved in many studies of one simulation, SimuLearn's Virtual Leader, by handing off the simulation to credible third-party evaluators, letting them evaluate, and then reading over the results. In military, academic, and corporate settings, the independent evaluators have gone public in academic dissertations and speeches—all outside of SimuLearn's influence—with their results. Independent third parties evaluated the effectiveness of this simulation approach. Following is a typical case study, one from a corporate *Fortune* 100 environment.

Corporate Case Study: *Fortune* 100 Company: An Extra Day Every Week of Work

Background

A *Fortune* 100 company needed groups to relate better across departments, achieve desired meeting outcomes, better use time, and build healthy relationships. To create "influential leaders," the division heads brought in this action-system-results model of leadership.

Process

A 360 preassessment was conducted around the participants. The managers themselves, their peers, their subordinates, and their supervisors were given an extensive questionnaire about the managers' performances.

The managers were introduced to VLeader and were required to spend eight two-hour lab sessions practicing on the simulator, broken up over four weeks. The labs were available twice a week, allowing flexibility for the managers, and were staffed with a facilitator to answer questions and provide background. Halfway through the lab sessions, the facilitator spent one-on-one time with each participant, reviewing the results of their original 360 assessment and putting it in context of their behavior in the simulator.

The participants "graduated" five weeks after they began the program. Then, six months after the program began (five months after the last contact), the managers again were assessed on business performance changes (something the organization rigorously tested) and given a second 360 evaluation.

Results

The participants who went through the actions-systems-results model of leadership improved their teams' relative performance rankings (a nonsubjective metric on volume of successful client jobs completed), on average, 22.0 percent (see Figure 24-2).

Just as relevant was the way that these managers got these accelerated results. Six months after the program, the increases in positive behaviors and the cessation of

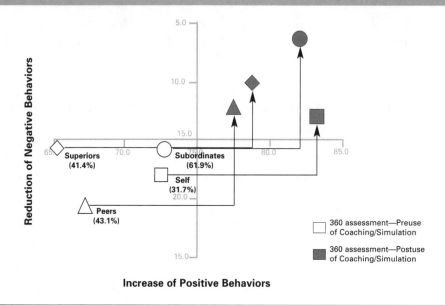

Figure 24-2. Pre- and Postuse Measurements from Coaching Simulation

negative behavior among peers, subordinates, and superiors were unprecedented in GEMA-Lead360's 15-year history (see Table 24-2).

The action-system-results model of leadership supported the increase of positive behaviors, but even more, reduced the occurrences of negative behavior. The learners themselves, curiously, were least aware of their new capability, suggesting the value of external measurement rather than self-assessment.

Summary

The corporate managers that completed the program significantly improved their value to their organization, including their professional value, while strengthening their relationship with their peers, supervisors, and subordinates.

Conclusion

Simulations take on many forms and will continue to do so. Genres will be created and refined. Even more relevant, this action-system-results approach to content has revolutionary implications to everyone who is in the business of capturing or propagating intellectual property, including formal learning programs, publishing, and even strategic

Table 24-2. Positive and Negative Changes After Completing Simulation

Positive Behaviors—Service Beyond Self				
		Pre	**Post**	**Difference Scores**	**Percentage Increase**
Contribution	Self	69.2	81.1	11.9	17.2%
	Superiors	61.3	72.5	11.2	18.3%
	Peers	63.9	75.5	11.6	18.2%
	Subordinates	69.4	77.6	8.2	11.8%
Cooperation	Self	75.8	86.3	10.5	13.9%
	Superiors	65.2	86.2	21.0	32.2%
	Peers	68.3	77.0	8.7	12.7%
	Subordinates	71.8	82.8	11.0	15.3%
Connection	Self	72.6	82.4	9.8	13.5%
	Superiors	69.2	77.6	8.4	12.1%
	Peers	69.7	80.0	10.3	14.8%
	Subordinates	76.8	85.8	9.0	11.7%
Average Increase					**16.0%**
Negative Behaviors—Self Beyond Service				
		Pre	**Post**	**Difference Scores**	**Percentage Decrease**
Superiority	Self	15.8	9.4	−6.4	−40.5%
	Superiors	12.8	7.8	−5.0	−39.1%
	Peers	21.6	10.4	−11.2	−51.9%
	Subordinates	13.2	4.6	−8.6	−65.2%
Domination	Self	16.1	13.6	−2.5	−15.5%
	Superiors	15.4	10.0	−5.4	−35.1%
	Peers	20.1	10.4	−9.7	−48.3%
	Subordinates	17.3	6.6	−10.7	−61.8%
Withdrawal	Self	22.1	15.9	−6.2	−28.1%
	Superiors	18.7	12.5	−6.2	−33.2%
	Peers	19.6	15.5	−4.1	−20.9%
	Subordinates	16.7	7.6	−9.1	−54.5%
Average Decrease					**−41.2%**

planning. As computer games and other forms of interactive content and Flash and other types of interactive authoring tools become more prevalent, we may be entering into a next generation of literacy. Here, we will finally be able to be farmers, not just hunters and gatherers, for many of our most valued and critical skills, including project management, stewardship, security, and innovation. This will be done by looking rigorously at new actions, results, and the often-invisible system that connects them.

About the Author

Clark Aldrich is the author of two award-winning books, *Simulations and the Future of Learning* and *Learning by Doing,* creator of the online glossary *Clark Aldrich's Style Guide for Serious Games and Simulations* (available at http://clarkaldrich.blogspot.com), and founder of and former director of research for Gartner's e-learning coverage.

His work has been featured in hundreds of sources, including the *New York Times,* the *Wall Street Journal,* NPR, CNET, Business 2.0, *BusinessWeek,* CNNfn, *U.S. News and World Report;* and, among other distinctions, he has been called an industry guru by *Fortune* magazine.

He graduated from Brown University with a degree in cognitive science and worked on special projects for Xerox's executive team.

For Further Reading

Aldrich, Clark. 2004. *Simulations and the future of learning: An innovative (and perhaps revolutionary) approach to e-learning.* San Francisco: John Wiley & Sons.

Aldrich, Clark. 2005. *Learning by doing: A comprehensive guide to simulations, computer games, and pedagogy in e-learning and other educational experiences.* San Francisco: John Wiley & Sons.

Crawford, Chris. 2003. *Chris Crawford on game design.* Indianapolis, IN: New Riders.

Salen, Katie, and Eric Zimmerman. 2003. *Rules of play: Game design fundamentals.* Cambridge, MA: MIT Press.

Koster, Raph. 2004. *A theory of fun for game design.* Scottsdale, AZ: Paraglyph Press.

Chapter 25

Performance Support: Anytime, Anyplace, Including the Classroom

Allison Rossett

In This Chapter

➤ Harness fingertip knowledge and information to improve performance

➤ Recognize when to use on-demand resources and when to avoid them

---

On July 18, 2007, Elliott Masie and M. David Merrill presented at the Learning Strategies Conference sponsored by the U.S. Navy's Human Performance Center. Masie touted the value of fingertip knowledge, where critical content is delivered in context, not in the classroom. Merrill agreed with much that Masie said, but differed about knowledge and information, "It is not fingertip *knowledge*," he noted, "It is fingertip *information*." The job of learning professionals, according to Merrill, is to turn information into knowledge.

Does it matter? Are they the same?

They are not the same. Information, according to many sources, is there to reduce uncertainty. Available in many forms, such as documentation, posters, and performance support tools, people reach outside themselves for information to get things done. The *Oxford*

English Dictionary says knowledge is (1) facts, information, and skills acquired by a person through experience or education; (2) the theoretical or practical understanding of a subject: (3) what is known in a particular field or in total, facts and information; or (4) awareness or familiarity gained by experience of a fact or situation.

Although information resides in a context, knowledge has found its way into the individual, into memory, typically achieved through practice, feedback, and repetition over time. That is education and training.

Knowledge and information are both valuable. Both involve investment. And both profit from fingertip availability.

To get to those fingertips requires delivery into the workflow, where lessons, advice, and smarts exist in close proximity to where they are used. Fingertip information and knowledge are available as needed, in the car, on the plane, in a hospital room, in a foxhole, or even in a living room or at a kitchen table. This chapter is about learning *and* information products and services available every time and every place, but not in the place where we are most accustomed to them, in the classroom.

Background

In the first edition of the *Handbook of Job Aids,* Rossett and Gautier-Downes (1991) expanded the definition of a most basic form of information: job aids. To traditional job aids that supported *information* (the Yellow Pages, for example) and *procedures* (documentation that reminded one how to change the message on an answering machine), Rossett and Gautier-Downes added job aids that *coached and advised on decisions.* Is this the right graduate school for me? How do I work with an employee who is often tardy? Checklist heuristics help people reflect hard and well before deciding what to do.

Although information, procedures, and guidance remain distinct, what we see today is that performance support often *brings these purposes together in one computer-based program that is delivered where and when it is needed.* For example, a performance support program for a salesperson who is attempting to tailor a proposal for a customer might include a database of possible products and features, a template and heuristics for proposal writing, interactive checklists that query about the client, and access to a database that "knows" this client and then generates recommendations congruent with the client's priorities and installed technology base.

People don't want to go to school to learn how to change the message on their answering machines or make comparisons between their product and that of a competitor. Most prefer information and advice on demand.

But what of the spirited interactions and ambiguous challenges at the heart of customer service? Yes, knowledge is involved and commitment, too. Developing customer service fluency requires access to scenarios, worked examples, practice, and feedback. Think of the knowledge to be derived through access to structured assets, experts, coaches, and communities—online and in person—and all delivered in the midst of work.

When to Move Learning and Reference into the Work?

Even Albert Einstein favored on-demand assets. A famous story tells of Einstein admitting to not knowing his own phone number. He didn't see any reason to know it, because he called it rarely and could look it up when necessary.

When do we move learning and information into the workplace?

When Information Is Difficult

Performance support and on-demand knowledge make good sense for individuals who confront *lengthy, difficult, and information-intensive challenges,* such as those presented by Sarbanes Oxley and HIPAA. How does an employer secure data in a computer system so that certain employees may access the data but others may not? What factors must a manager keep in mind when putting an employee on notice, or when terminating an employee, or when helping an employee deal with the loss of a loved one?

When Information Is Copious

Getting work done in the information age depends on *ready access to large amounts of information about people, places, things, and policies.* On-demand resources are essential when there are voluminous answers to questions about who, what, when, where, and how. Training catalogs provide a good example. Not even the most motivated student can be expected to know the entire list of options. Technology steps in here, allowing employees and supervisors to search the database for the right offering, right time, and right place. More often now, the system communicates with employees to point them to offerings that will fulfill requirements or meet needs.

When Information Is Ever Changing

The need to shift knowledge and information closer to work is also driven by the *short shelf life of knowledge, procedures, and approaches.* The contemporary salesperson, for example, must stay abreast of changing products, features, and compatibilities. Answers that are right on Monday afternoon, after training, could be wrong on Tuesday. In fact, they might be wrong by close of business on Monday. On-demand resources keep people up to date.

When the Consequences of Error Are Intolerable

Sometimes *the consequences of an error are intolerable.* When that is the case, on-demand information and knowledge make good sense. Imagine what could happen when a doctor prescribes a medication that causes a patient to suffer a grave reaction because the physician had forgotten the interaction between the new drug and medication the patient was already taking. Or think how awful it could be when a soldier attempts to communicate with a man on the street in Afghanistan but is unable to discern whether the information is credible.

When Information Is Cross-Referenced in the Workplace

Vickers (2007) described a study conducted by the Institute for Corporate Productivity. He wrote:

> Higher-performing organizations are much more likely than their lower-performing counterparts to have clear, well-thought-out strategies that are matched up well with performance measures. This sounds a bit like Management 101, but it actually reveals two critical and related organizational characteristics that managers often lose sight of amid the hubbub of new business ideas: *consistency and clarity.*

Learning and reference materials, including policies and rubrics, can be provided within the workflow. A manager can conduct a more sensitive performance appraisal when he or she can examine exactly what is expected of him or her, for these particular challenges. A novice sales professional could boost his or her confidence and skill by referring to podcasts delivered in the car on the way to negotiate a sale.

When Temporary Employees Require Information

Organizations are *less willing to invest in training* when employees might be short-timers. For example, a woman I know publishes a small, commercial directory of goods and services. Her salesforce is active for only a few months each year, turns over frequently, and handles a very simple product line with a rate card that changes rarely. She relies on support in the workflow because she wants her salespeople in the field, not in training.

When More Knowledge Is Needed and Less Training Is Desired

Another reason to bring information and education close to work is *that executives favor investing in more knowledge and less training.* Organizations favor an investment in reusable assets that remain with the organization. Lou Iorizzo, executive director of the U.S. Army Training Support Center, made his general's goal clear: less time in classrooms for soldiers. At the same time, the Army wants performance and results. Iorizzo described how they now turn to what he called guided experiential learning, an array of rich resources and interactions delivered into the field, as part of a blended solution that retains roots in the classroom.

When Integrated Learning Strategies Are Desired

Learning and reference on the job are not distinct from training in the classroom, of course. They belong together in *a blend, an integrated strategy* for delivering on promises about learning and performance. Blending, according to Rossett and Frazee (2006) involves a planned combination of approaches, such as coaching by a supervisor, participation in an online class, a breakfast meeting with colleagues, competency statements, reference to documentation, e-coaching by a supervisor, and participation in an online community. Blending happens in classrooms and on the job, in a concerted fashion. In some cases, blended learning has been shown to achieve the same results as instructor-led training in 40 to 60 percent less time (Zenger and Uehlein, 2001).

Should We Avoid On-Demand Resources?

There are circumstances in which a workforce learning professional might want to avoid performance support, such as when credibility would be damaged, speed matters, high performance is expected, or when morale might be adversely affected.

When Professional Credibility Would Be Damaged

Imagine that you find yourself in an elevator with the manager of manufacturing. She says, "We put a new supervisory development program in place two months ago, and I'd like you to evaluate it. Could you do that?" You must know enough about the topic to ask good questions and add some value, on the spot. Later, you would take time to refer to references and even take a face-to-face class or e-learning modules.

When Speed Matters

Does your organization value throughput? Does a life hang in the balance without speedy actions? Would valuable equipment be harmed if employees fumbled for references? If you answered yes to any of these questions, on-demand resources might not be the best option.

Are novel or unpredictable challenges involved? Such situations demand intangible abilities to handle surprises, stresses, and the unforeseen. School districts expect good judgment from employees when they are confronted by parents upset about their child's test results; the Navy also expects good judgment from pilots when they are subjected to combat situations. Brecke (1982) explored the topic of training to instill judgment in pilots. He provided a useful definition of judgment as the "right stuff" evoked in situations that include uncertainty, lack of complete information, stress, task difficulty, cognitive complexity, and time constraints. There are many reasons to worry that reference to fingertip assets will not clinch victory in the skies.

When High Performance Is Expected

When smooth, fluid, and elegant performance is on the line, it is best to avoid on-demand resources. Think about a great public speaker. World-class athletes, too, do not typically use performance support on the field of play. Successful performance depends on habitual, automatic, flexible, and seamless performance. The design of the public speaker or athlete's job does not allow reference to an online module, an e-coach or knowledge base, or performance support.

When Employee Morale Is Compromised

When employees are not motivated, on-demand resources are of no use. If organizations provide on-demand assets, they only gain value when they are used. Wallflower reference and learning materials are useless.

What Might Performance Support Look Like?

Two dimensions are critical for learning and reference on the job. The first dimension is the degree of *integration* into the task or context. Is the support inside or outside of the task? Is it support you get when you use an ATM or that a phone coach provides when you are filling out a travel reimbursement request? Or is it a website that provides information to help the family assess its readiness for a natural disaster? ATM and phone coaching are integrated into the task. Disaster preparedness support, for example, stands apart; it nudges you to think about this, worry about that, and plan for every eventuality.

The second dimension is *tailoring*. Is the support standard for all or actively tailored to your situation? Does it know you and act differently as a result of that knowledge of disease state, location, medication, or inclinations? Is it a mass mailing from your city government about fire danger in California or a notice sending you to a website because the system recognizes that your home is on a canyon and you must do special kinds of cleanup to mitigate fire danger? Is it dad's counsel about selecting a used car that is right for your commute and financial realities, or is it a brochure that tells everybody what to keep in mind when considering auto options?

Finding Your Way on the Streets and in the Organization

Imagine that you have an important appointment across town, at a place you have never been. Training makes no sense at all here. Instead, consider reference and support available on demand, as depicted in Table 25-1.

Table 25-1. Integration and Tailoring for Getting Directions to a Destination

Consult the city map you have pinned to your wall before you leave.	The map is a job aid but is not integrated into the task and is not tailored to you. It doesn't know where you are going or offer guidance on the best way to get there. It will not adapt to your twists and turns or local detours.
Listen to advice from your brother-in-law who describes the route and what to watch for as you go from here to there.	Very generous coaching provided by your brother-in-law but wouldn't support while engaged with the task by much better? This support is tailored to you, but not sufficiently integrated.
Go to MapQuest and enter your address and the destination address. Print the results.	Here we see the blending of computer-based performance support and job aids. The online tool is used prior to undertaking the challenge. It is preparation for it.
Refer to the printed results as you drive.	Here we have a conventional print job aid that is integrated into the task, albeit precariously. As you negotiate the highways and byways, a trusty piece of paper points the way. Note, there is no adaptation to detours or distractions.
As you head out the door, ask your brother for directions. He generously provides them.	This may get you there if you have a good memory and your brother is reliable. But integrated into the task? Definitely not. And when you get distracted and turn left instead of right, his directions will not adjust to your errant ways.
Hop in the car. Dig through the glove box. Pull out a map. Read the map while you drive.	This dangerous support is integrated into the task. It is there as the need to decide right or left. While integrated into the task, *you* have to tailor it to you, and at some risk.
Hop in the car and fire up the global positioning system (GPS). Key in the destination address. A sultry voice tells you how to get there, no matter where you start or how you diverge.	The GPS support is identified with the task. While there is a display with directions, the directions are little more than comfort because a voice is anticipating what you will need to do and then prompting you to do it. Most interesting is how *active* the system is, how it adjusts to your location and actions. When you refuse or skip guidance, new advice is calculated for you, tailored to your current location. GPS is both tailored and integrated.

Getting from one location to another is one kind of challenge. But what of something more complex, something more typical of knowledge work? Let's imagine that we are eager to help supervisors run more effective meetings. We'll presume that an analysis served as the basis for the approaches and emphases presented in Table 25-2 (Rossett, 1998).

Should We Always Maximize Integration and Tailoring?

The previous examples make integration and tailoring look great. And they are. There are, however, things to say in favor of less integration and not so much tailoring. Let's look at integration first.

Table 25-2. Integration and Tailoring to Improve Meetings

Review a checklist of criteria for running an effective meeting; reflect on the two most recent meetings you have run in light of criteria.	These guidelines are not tailored for you, nor are they integrated into the meetings that you are offering.
Visit with a colleague known for running good meetings. Bring along feedback from participants in your meetings and your checklist.	This is a great idea, and it is tailored to you, based on two sources of feedback about your meeting patterns in light of criteria. Although closer to the challenge than the training you took in February, it is not fully integrated, of course.
Use a performance support tool to generate ways to improve your meetings. The tool solicits feedback from participants in your meetings, asks you for your reactions, and checks on follow-up actions items.	This nifty tool is tailored, with several sources feeding into individualized recommendations. It is not, however, integrated into the task. The online tool is used prior to undertaking the challenge.
The tool then generates recommendations to be used when running a meeting.	The recommendation is meant to help while you are running a meeting. It reminds, nudges, and points to what to do to improve individual efforts. This aspect is integrated into the task.
Take an e-learning module (approximately 10 minutes in length) about preparing a meeting agenda.	This is not tailored, but it is integrated into work because it delivers critical skills just as the supervisor is working to put a meeting agenda together. Because it is an effective module, it asks the supervisor to judge agendas, correct them, improve them, and then enables the supervisor to receive feedback on his or her efforts.

✍ **Gloria Gery** ✍

Gloria Gery is considered a pioneer in the field of e-learning and performance support systems due in large part to her groundbreaking work in defining the field of electronic performance support systems. An electronic performance support system, commonly referred to as an EPSS, is a computer application that runs simultaneously with another application, or is a component of a software package, used to guide workers through a task in the target application. Examples of EPSSs are tutorials or hypertext links. EPSSs deliver just-in-time information with minimum staff support. EPSSs are unique in that they have a performance-centered design, which aims to train workers to be more productive with less effort.

As early as 1976, Gery was beginning to experiment with and implement various forms of e-learning tools while she worked at Aetna Life & Casualty. Based on her previous training experience, she noted that much of the task-oriented training given prior to performing a task did not help much when a worker was faced with the intricacies of executing the actual task. This served as her inspiration to write Electronic Performance Support Systems *(1991), which "serve[d] as a rallying call to examine whether a new alternative of providing direct support of work processing by technology would be a more powerful alternative to traditional training." This book is now considered a classic in the training and development field because it sparked the EPSS movement.*

Gery also developed the three levels of performance support: external support, extrinsic support, and intrinsic support. External support is the most basic type of help or support system. It is usually developed after the fact to help with a deficiency in the system. Some examples are job aids and help desk documentation. Extrinsic support is a help system that does not require a user to stop work to get support but does require the user to decide how to use certain features, such as an online database or help center. Intrinsic support is an intelligent help system that has the ability to adapt to a user's needs based on patterns. Examples are Microsoft Word help resources and certain toolbars.

The opposite of integration is not disintegration. In this case, it is having a plan, being ready, and taking a reflective stance. It is information and advice consulted in advance of performance. How can we use delivered knowledge to prepare, to mitigate, and to make better decisions about what to do in the future? Hurricane Katrina raised motivation to turn to such tools. Consider the many websites that provide lists to help prepare for hurricanes, earthquakes, floods, and fires. All are examples of the value of thinking ahead in a systematic fashion.

In a 2003 study, Jupiter Research found that only 8 percent of respondents pointed to personalization as a reason for increased visits to web content. Think about that. This number contrasts with 54 percent of consumers who cited faster-loading pages and 52 percent cited better navigation as greater incentives to visit.

Personalization sounds good, but is it as good as it costs? A single, standard message costs far less to produce and maintain. With the cost of personalization estimated at four or more times basic costs, Jupiter Research and respondents favored attention to usability over a tailored experience.

Regulatory content is also an issue. The pharmaceutical industry must receive regulatory approvals for what is said about medications. One way of controlling the content, of making certain that there is no gap between intended message and received message, is to craft, codify, and distribute *standard, approved* content.

Planners and Sidekicks

Fingertip knowledge and information can appear in many forms, from notes on slips of paper to e-coaching, archived virtual classroom sessions, live virtual classroom sessions, documentation, checklists, ehelp.com, 2-D and 3-D e-learning modules, performance support tools, and online communities. Rossett and Schafer (2007), acknowledging contributions from Cavanaugh (2004), Gery (1991), and Raybould (2000), suggested two overarching forms for these on-demand resources: planners and sidekicks.

Planners are in our lives *just before or after* the challenge. They help us decide if avian influenza virus should alter trip plans or to reflect on how we could have improved the presentation offered at the sales meeting.

Sidekicks are at our side *during* the task. For example, the quick food cook reads the job aid as he or she creates the new food product. The writer pecks away and smiles at how Wikipedia sported a red line under it last year, but no longer, since Office Suite 2007 emerged. Sidekicks vary in how close they are to the task. They might be next to the task, as is the case with the cook and quarterback, or integrated into it, as in the spelling checker.

How might this model extend to *knowledge and learning* in the workflow? What of bringing lessons out of the classroom and closer to work? In brief, programs that are devoted to knowledge must be short, targeted, and connected to the work. If they do not add obvious value, as perceived by employees, they will be ignored in favor of nuggets of information. Table 25-3 illustrates the model for sales and makes an extension to knowledge on the job.

Table 25-3. Knowledge and Information in the Workflow

	Standard	Tailored
Sidekicks: They are with us in the work, as we act.	***Information:*** Here the customer and salesperson look together at a PC to examine a table that compares a recommended product with its competitors. ***Knowledge:*** No time for the reflection, practice, and feedback involved in learning in the workflow, not here, not with the customer.	***Information:*** When the customer picks a product configuration, the salesperson identifies the customer and the system details what it will take to achieve compatibility with this customer's current installed base. ***Knowledge:*** No time to build skills in the midst of the interaction. That must happen before and after engagement with the customer. It is best, though, if those lessons happen in close proximity to when they are needed.
Planners: They are there when we get ready to act and afterward, when we reflect on our efforts.	***Information:*** This is a print or automated program that reminds a salesperson what to keep in mind when selling at higher levels in the organization. Afterward, the salesperson can reflect on the interaction in light of criteria. ***Knowledge:*** The salesperson accesses an e-learning module that reviews how to sell at higher levels in the organization. The program offers relevant work examples and presents opportunities for practice and success—because confidence is at issue here. Feedback is generic, as users compare their efforts on the practices with model answers. ***Knowledge:*** The salesperson searches in the knowledge base for a related sales proposal, reviews one, identifies strengths and weaknesses, and then reads about how the proposal fared, including how the sales expert would have improved, if he or she was able to do it over again.	***Information:*** This is an automated program that seeks data about a potential customer, qualifies the customer, and then informs the salesperson about appropriate products and loan size, based on data about this customer, his or her needs, and installed base. The rationale is provided to the salesperson to aid in making the case and countering objections. ***Information:*** This is an opportunity to participate in a blog, led by one of the leading sales reps in the organization. ***Knowledge:*** The salesperson takes an e-coach along on a ride-along. The coach provides the salesperson with feedback as soon as the interaction has been completed. Ideally, the coach also looks at the salesperson's plans and approach and works with him or her to generate more targeted and effective approaches prior to meeting with the client. ***Knowledge:*** The salesperson accesses short, scheduled virtual classroom sessions about changes in the product and service line. Attendees ask questions, tackle customer questions, and receive feedback from experts.

Knowledge and Information Where and When It Matters

This chapter is not an ode to technology or blends or performance support. Instead, my intention was to focus on the possibilities that emerge when the walls of the classroom are permeable and the voices of experts and instructors are projected. When that happens, through e-learning modules, blogs, virtual classes, documentation, performance support, and e-coaching, attention and resources are where they need to be—within the work, with the worker, and at the workplace. It makes sense to move from knowledge and information in the classroom to all of it everywhere, because that is where life, work, and satisfaction are to be found.

Adapted with permission from *Job Aids and Performance Support: Moving from Knowledge in the Classroom to Knowledge Everywhere* by Allison Rossett and Lisa Schafer (2007), published by Pfeiffer, an imprint of John Wiley & Sons, www.pfeiffer.com.

About the Author

Allison Rossett, long-time professor of educational technology at San Diego State University, is in the HRD Hall of Fame, served as a member of the ASTD Board of Directors, was honored by selection as an ISPI Member-for-Life, and is a member of the eLearning Guild's advisory board. She is also a recipient of the ASTD Distinguished Contribution to WLP Award. Rossett's 2007 book, co-authored with Lisa Schafer, is *Job Aids and Performance Support: Moving from Knowledge in the Classroom to Knowledge Everywhere.* She has authored six books, including *First Things Fast* and *The ASTD E-Learning Handbook.*

References

Brecke, Fritz H. 1982. Instructional design for aircrew judgment training. *Aviation, Space, and Environmental Medicine* 53(10): 951-957.

Cavanaugh, Thomas B. 2004. The new spectrum of support: Reclassifying human performance technology. *Performance Improvement* 43(4): 28-32.

Oxford English Dictionary. 1989. 2nd ed. New York: Oxford University Press.

Gery, Gloria. 1991. *Electronic performance support systems.* Tolland, MA: Gery Associates.

Jupiter Research. 2003. Jupiter Research reports that web site "personalization" does not always provide positive results, available at www.jupitermedia.com/corporate/releases/03.10.14-newjupresearch.html.

Raybould, Barry. 2000. Building performance-centered web-based systems, information systems, and knowledge management systems in the 21st century. *Performance Improvement Quarterly* 39(6): 69-79.

Rossett, Allison. 1998. *First things fast: A handbook for performance analysis.* San Francisco: Jossey-Bass/Pfeiffer.

Rossett, Allison, and Jeannette Gautier-Downes. 1991. *A handbook of job aids.* San Francisco: Pfeiffer.

Rossett, Allison, and Lisa Schafer. 2007. *Job aids and performance support: Moving from knowledge in the classroom to knowledge everywhere.* San Francisco: Pfeiffer/Wiley, available at www.colletandschafer.com/perfsupp.

Rossett, Allison, and Rebecca Frazee. 2006. *Blended learning opportunities.* Online White Paper, American Management Association, available at www.amanet.org/blended.

Vickers, Mark. 2007, July 20. The essentials of high performance organizations. Leader's edge 2(8), available at http://www.amanet.org/LeadersEdge/editorial.cfm?Ed=575& BNKNAVID=61&nws/D=104&display=1.

Zenger, Jack, and Curtis Uehlein. 2001. Why blended will win. *T+D* 55(8): 54-60.

For Further Reading

Kirkpatrick, Donald J. 1998. Evaluating training programs: Evidence vs. proof. In *Evaluating training programs: The four levels*, ed., D.J. Kirkpatrick. San Francisco: Berrett-Koehler.

Kirkpatrick, Donald J. 1959. Techniques for evaluating training programs. *Journal of the American Society of Training Directors* 13(3-9): 21-26.

Wexler, Steve, Brent Schlenker, Paula Cancro, Bryan Chapman, Karen Hyder, Karl Kapp, Ann Kwinn, and Tony O'Driscoll. 2007. *Synchronous learning systems: Benchmarks, best practices, and real-time analysis about real-time learning.* eLearning Guild Research, available at www.elearningguild.com/pbuild/linkbuilder.cfm?selection=doc.1455.

Distance Learning and Web-Based Training

Jennifer Hofmann

with Jane Bozarth

In This Chapter

> ➢ Learn about the newest generation of distance learning delivery tools

> ➢ Get examples of ways to use new technologies in learning

> ➢ Compare technologies, such as blogs, wikis, discussion forums, and communities

---

It might surprise you to know that distance learning is not a new concept—formal distance learning in the United States can be historically traced as far back as the first half of the 19th century. The introduction of every new communication medium seemed to be fast followed by a desire to use it to distribute education in a nontraditional manner. As early as 1913, Thomas Edison was forecasting the demise of traditional educational models, asserting that "It is possible to teach every branch of human knowledge with the motion picture" and "Books will soon be obsolete in the public schools."

Although technology innovators, like Edison, have always been certain that their latest contributions to the media field would be the way to get education to everyone, everywhere,

---

Evolution of Modern Educational Technologies

Generation 1: 1840—First correspondence study via mail (shorthand)

Generation 2: 1900s—Audio recordings

Generation 3: 1910s—Motion picture cinema

Generation 4: 1920s—Radio stations

Generation 5: 1930s—Television

Generation 6: 1960s—Satellite

Generation 7: 1980s—Fiber optic, audiovisual technology, CD-ROM

Generation 8: 1990s—World Wide Web, email

Generation 9: 2000s—E-learning, virtual learning, mobile learning, blogs, wikis, discussion forums, and online communities

---

and anytime, technology alone wasn't the answer. Educators soon realized that using the media for instructional purposes required special instructional design considerations that were different from mainstream applications of the media.

The focus of this chapter will be the newest generation of delivery tools, focusing especially on asynchronous e-learning, synchronous virtual learning, and mobile learning. Informal e-learning tools, specifically blogs and wikis, will be explored to identify ways of incorporating them into a blended learning environment. All of these are being promoted as effective educational tools—but a tool is only as good as its wielder. These are all extensive topics, and all by themselves deserving of book-length explorations. This short overview is intended to provide some ideas as to how you might incorporate distance learning into your blend, and what tools might effectively create the level of personal interaction desired.

Asynchronous E-Learning

According to the glossary at *Learning Circuits* (2008), asynchronous learning is "learning in which interaction between instructors and students occurs intermittently with a time delay. Examples are self-paced courses taken via the Internet or CD-ROM, Q&A mentoring, online discussion groups, and email."

Asynchronous e-learning is certainly the most familiar form of Internet-delivered distance learning. It became somewhat commonplace in the 1980s when content become more easily accessible via diskette, CD-ROM, or internal networks. It was adopted by organizations rather quickly because of the apparent advantages—content could be quickly disseminated to large audiences, who could then participate at a time of their own choosing. Content could be revisited easily, or the entire course could be retaken without incurring additional cost. Being with a trainer at a particular time was not a requirement, so the cost of travel, classrooms, and related items were eliminated.

There were many roadblocks that kept asynchronous e-learning from meeting the expectations. Early asynchronous content was characterized by text-heavy "page-turners" that dumped everything a classroom trainer might say into an electronic format. Courseware might take hours (or even days) to complete, and it was not always easy to stop and then pick up where you left off. Early developers often did not consider the social aspect of learning, so they did not prepare learners for this new experience. Consumers of early asynchronous e-learning were often left feeling overwhelmed, isolated, and frustrated. The result was libraries full of (often) expensive content that was not being used.

As the industry developed, several factors have allowed asynchronous e-learning to be viewed by both learners and organizations as a more viable and accessible delivery mode. From a technological perspective, the learning industry has been able to take advantage of less expensive and easier-to-use software and hardware. The World Wide Web has grown with accessible bandwidth, and authoring technologies (products like Adobe Flash and Articulate Presenter, for example) have been created that allow nontechnical instructional designers to create compelling content.

Today, the category of asynchronous e-learning includes myriad solutions, from collaborative discussion boards to self-contained tutorials on the web. All types of topics are taught, from engineering (for example, the University of Illinois at Urbana-Champaign) to front-line leadership (for example, AchieveGlobal) to technical training (for example, Sun Developer Network). Simulations and game playing are continuing to develop. Asynchronous learning has been implemented everywhere, and it is trying to teach just about everything—but is it working?

Kruse and Keil (2000) in their book *Technology-Based Training* have identified two major drawbacks to this type of learning compared with traditional classroom learning. The first is the "lack of human contact, which greatly impacts learning." The second drawback is the use (or the lack of) multimedia components. Adding audio and video can make learning programs much more engaging and interactive and, when done well, can begin to appeal to multiple learning styles at the same time. Kruse and Keil make a strong point by saying that "both [of these drawbacks] will be overcome in the next five to ten years as high bandwidth network connections become as common as telephones."

Technology has not, of course, been the only problem. A lack of systematic instructional design was a huge culprit in early failures. It seems strange that organizations were willing to discard their understanding of what makes a good learning solution simply because the delivery method had changed. In my experience, two factors seemed to drive this:

- There was a misguided perception that the use of technology eliminated the need for a designer, much in the same way a dishwashing machine eliminated the need to wash dishes by hand.
- Organizations had already invested so much time and money in purchasing and installing e-learning technologies that it seemed the best use of resources was to get as much content out to the users as quickly as possible.

A common result was training that did not meet the mark and fell far short of the quality standards expected in the traditional setting. Many made the assumption that technology was not the appropriate delivery medium for the content. Although that may have indeed been the case, most of the issues were due to the lack of solid instructional design and assessment techniques.

As the technology continued to evolve, so did instructional design techniques. Organizations understood that the technology had to be adapted to content, and not content adapted to technology. Today, we have excellent examples of asynchronous e-learning content that has been successfully deployed at organizations, from topics ranging from the mundane to the high risk. Especially relevant is the *Advanced Live Emergency Response Training* (ALERT) system, developed by the Mass Transit Railway for first responders in Hong Kong. This training, using simulations and asynchronous role plays, increased the confidence level of emergency responders by 120 percent and received an Excellence in Practice citation by ASTD in 2006.

Synchronous Virtual Learning

If you've been working in the training field for the last decade or so, you've heard of the virtual classroom, synchronous learning, live online learning, e-meetings, and webinars. All of these terms mean basically the same thing: content delivered live over the Internet to geographically dispersed participants.

The first major public introduction of online synchronous technology to the training community may have been in early 1998 in Atlanta at the "Training" show, an annual conference for thousands of training professionals and vendors. It was the height of the dot-com craze, and early live online learning mirrored the same trends. People were throwing money at technology, thinking it was the answer they needed to solve any training issue. Organizations were willing to spend tens or hundreds of thousands of dollars on these new technologies—but these same organizations didn't allocate money and time to develop new best practices, new training designs, or new facilitation techniques. And the idea of managing the transition from the traditional classroom to the virtual classroom was largely ignored.

The dot-com bubble soon burst, of course. In the ensuing economic downturn, some learning technologies had more staying power than others; organizations began to realize that merely having the technologies was not enough. Managers wanted to see some kind of measurable return on their investment in learning technologies. So organizations began an urgent search for best practices and case studies.

Then came the terrible events of September 11, 2001. For a short time, the fear of travel heightened the prospects for live online learning. Its advocates geared up for what promised to be a busy and profitable future. However, changing workforce priorities and an American economy that continued to struggle meant that once again adoption and use of synchronous technologies was underwhelming at best.

The corporate propensity for throwing money at technology has abated, thank goodness. The focus has returned to teaching and learning. In corporate circles, instructional technology now needs to work.

Helping trainers and participants accept live online learning as legitimate is fundamental to the success of any live online learning initiative. Because live online learning is somewhat new, training professionals have been creating programs without the benefit of successful models, without best practices, and without full knowledge of how to use the technology to its best advantage. Best practices are developing but haven't been widely shared. So a promising tool has gone misused and underused despite its bright prospects.

Many practitioners are nevertheless convinced that live online learning works. The live online learning environment can be good for all types of courses and all types of skills—technical, business, soft skills. But you must know your tools inside out and design an entire experience. If you want the same quality from your synchronous deliverables that you expect from your face-to-face programs, you must invest the same time and effort, the same instructional design resources, and the same needs analyses. You must pay attention to all the components—support materials, visuals, communications, interactions and collaborations, scripts, and more—to make this delivery format a success.

We are only beginning to realize the promise of live online learning. It is still not well understood at many companies; thus, a great need persists for more information about how it works.

Live online learning has great potential for delivering training to audiences who may otherwise not have the opportunity to participate in a learning event. The implications are immense for improving communication among organizations, bridging cultural divides, and providing educational opportunities to global destinations that might be expensive or time consuming to travel to in person. The Brandon Hall Research report, *Live E-Learning 2004: Virtual Classrooms, Synchronous Tools, and Web Conferencing Systems,* explains that "Live e-learning systems provide an excellent way for an organization to have its experts teach a geographically dispersed group of participants. In addition, live e-learning systems enable real-time collaboration between participants, often allowing them to break out into smaller 'rooms' to discuss and share ideas" (Brandon Hall Research, 2004).

So, why isn't the live online learning approach used more? Learning professionals new to live online learning don't realize that "live and online" can mean more than a 60-minute lecture. Too many creators of live online learning give participants little or no opportunity for interaction with the course content and too few chances to collaborate with other participants. When participants encounter programs that bore them, when session leaders don't prepare, when technical goofs slow a program, participants may get the impression that virtual classrooms are not as effective as traditional classrooms. Trainers may not know how to assess participants' performance in a live online session to prove that it was a success. Indeed, trainers may not realize that assessment is as important online as it is in a traditional setting. The reason that these issues have merit is because synchronous learning has an identity crisis. Participants and training professionals alike don't think synchronous learning actually qualifies as real learning. "If this content was really important," participants think, "they would send me to a *real* class."

Not so long ago, participants had the same reaction to asynchronous e-learning when it was first introduced. Self-directed, asynchronous learning on the Internet left participants alone at their desktop without any live instructional assistance. They were often frustrated and felt lost in cyberspace. Unsatisfactory experiences with self-paced e-learning have probably contributed to a negative perception of the live virtual classroom as well—even though in a live online classroom a facilitator is on hand to help participants learn. In fact, it's a shame that live online learning technologies came out only after self-paced e-learning technologies became popular because it probably would have made for an easier transition. People who use live online learning find that indeed you can teach effectively with it—but first its advocates must convince trainers and participants that live online learning is *real* learning. Although implementation has been slow, the idea of virtual classrooms in corporate training had staying power. Practitioners seem to have an instinctive belief that live online learning is a promising delivery system whose time is near.

Today, it's obvious to most professionals that live online learning does indeed have a bright future. In fact, live online learning is an easier transition for participants who are accustomed to the traditional classroom. The online learning environment resembles the old-fashioned classroom by allowing participants to interact with facilitators and other participants. That makes live online learning more intuitive for participants than previous forms of e-learning. Using a virtual classroom means you can pull workers off the job for two hours, train them, and get them back to work with a limited interruption to productivity. In the old days, if a course took a half day or less, sending workers to the course almost always meant they would be away from their jobs for a full day. A lost day of productivity may not justify the training. Therefore, partial-day courses often didn't come to pass because content had to wait until it could be combined with other material—allowing for a full day of training (or it may never have been taught at all). With the rise of live online learning, however, trainers found they could deliver half-day courses, two-hour courses, even one-hour courses without pulling workers off the job for a full day. In fact, a live online course as short as 30 minutes can be effective. Participants can work until class time, set aside what they are doing, take the class, and be back on the job as soon as the class ends. After that 30 minutes, participants can often immediately apply the content they have learned.

Mobile Learning

One of the latest trends in distance learning is mobile learning. According to the Learning Citizen, mobile learning is "the use of mobile or wireless devices for learning on the move." Mobile learning provides curricula where and when you need it, using delivery technologies that enable you to carry learning with you. After all, even the best e-learning tutorial on agricultural pest identification does you no good when you are in the middle of a field and the tutorial is on a computer back at the farm.

The technologies involved can include many types of devices, including MP3 players, pocket PCs, mobile phones, and personal digital assistants (PDAs). There are certainly many other miniature devices being developed that will fall into this category, not to mention the combination of technologies to create new learning devices. The incredibly successful June 2007 launch of the Apple iPhone is an example of the convergence of these technologies—consumers are becoming less willing to carry around multiple devices. As this convergence continues, the types and amount of instruction that will be delivered via mobile learning will surely exponentially explode.

Sometimes, content is accessed from the local hard drive; other times it is accessed from the Internet—the idea is that mobile learning is ultimately convenient. Learning can occur when you need it (just in time) and, in theory, from wherever you happen to be. Do you need to know how to fix a pressure gauge on an agricultural vehicle when you are 20 miles from the office? Use your PDA to help guide you through the steps. Learning a new language? Listen to a "podcast" on your MP3 player with headphones while on the train to work. If you have an MP3 player with video capability, you can observe a process, like the cleaning of a machine designed to shred cheese and listen to the instructions as delivered by the narrator. If you need to review a step, it is easy to rewind and watch again. Museums and National Parks (like the Minute Man National Historical Park in Massachusetts) are allowing visitors to use their mobile phones to access an audio-tour of their sites. Mobile learning is already all around us.

Educational institutions and businesses alike are seeing great advantages to using mobile learning. It is inexpensive to create, often depending on audio-only or text-only technologies. Because the use of graphics are minimal or nonexistent, bandwidth requirements are not high. And, for delivery technologies like audio-only podcasts, you don't need to have a multimedia production background to create content.

The ease of use, low cost, and accessibility of mobile learning can lead practitioners into the trap of creating too much content with not enough thought about design. Those of us who recall early web-based training remember page-turners filled with useful content but lacking a systematic instructional design plan. Eventually, we learned that listening, reading, or watching four hours of content did not constitute learning. Content needed to be chunked by learning objective, learning needed to be assessed, learning styles needed to be considered, and learning needed to be active. Today's mobile learning producers need to learn from those lessons and find ways to incorporate those best practices into mobile learning design. When this is accomplished, mobile learning will become a ubiquitous delivery technology, providing access to content when it's needed and where it's needed.

Blogs, Wikis, Discussion Forums, and Online Communities—and More

Inexpensive and easy to set up and manage, wikis and, especially, blogs have most often been viewed as vehicles for first-person online diaries or even rants. But there are many possibilities for the use of blogs and wikis, and other networking technologies as instructional tools: they offer free or low-cost means for encouraging interaction and collaboration and can help to engender a sense of community and reduce the "distance" between learners and between learner and instructor. And they are simple for instructors to create, update, and manage, and can easily exist outside the grip of the organization's IT department.

Blogs and wikis are similar; with the major difference lying with the amount of control users are given. Simply, a blog allows one person (or others as designated) to post a thought or item, such as an image, link, or video clip, and optionally allows others to comment on that item. A wiki is more dynamic: everyone with access can start discussions, change, add, or delete content and even pages. Used as defined here, both blogs and wikis are simple means of creating class discussion sites, a place for intersession assignments (such as Insync Training's "A-Ha" blog, to which learners are expected to post within a day following a synchronous class session) and areas for student reflection or journals and updates from instructors.

But they can be so much more. The Mecklenburg County, North Carolina, Public Library uses a free blog as a mechanism for hosting its wonderful "23 Things" online course. A nine-week program of structured assignments designed to help learners develop experience and confidence in using new technologies (such as posting a picture to Flickr, creating a customized search tool, and creating a blog) 23 Things is, essentially, just a list of items on a single blog page with links to corresponding information, tutorials, and sometimes the technologies themselves. The program was originally created for the library staff who, upon completion of all 23 Things, were eligible for prizes, such as flash drives and iPods.

Similarly, instructor James Hall has found innovative, meaningful use for blogging for instructional purposes in his work teaching native Japanese speakers to become teachers of English. His blog serves as a place for presenting issues in teaching English as a Second Language (ESL) and also serves as a repository for links to the *students'* blogs, on which the Japanese students post reflections, in English, on their learning and evaluation of their skills. It is the perfect marriage of technology, reflective practice, and real-world application of training.

Wiki technology also allows for hosting course sites, as with M.C. Morgan's site for his "Teaching Writing with Technology Course," and allows for collaborative work on entire projects, such as the book currently being written by dozens of contributors in dozens of locations in an effort sponsored by the B.C. Campus initiative (British Columbia, Canada). Other organizations use wikis in knowledge management pursuits, such as creating collaborative libraries of best practices and other knowledge management pursuits.

In considering the instructional uses of these technologies, give some thought to what we do in the traditional classroom to encourage collaboration, interaction, and community. Discussions, role plays, debates, written assignments, and projects come to mind, as do casual hallway, break, and lunch conversations. Blogs and wikis provide the perfect means for replicating many of these same activities, as do additional technologies such as discussion forums and online communities. Discussion forums allow for threaded discussions, that is, several conversations can be going on simultaneously, and the software keeps them organized in sequence and by topic. These forums offer great opportunities for activities like online role plays and debates.

Finally, free online communities such as Yahoo! Groups and Google Groups offer, for free, fully functional websites with many features. The group sites come with a home page, and sometimes subpages, with storage space for documents and other files—like Microsoft PowerPoint shows—easy linking to outside resources, a discussion or message board, storage for photos and images, simple database or spreadsheet tools, a shareable calendar, and polling features. They are excellent for hosting a site for a community of practice, as with the 4,000+ member Tr-Dev Yahoo! community. It's also a simple matter to use one of these groups to support a multiweek online (or blended) course: the course syllabus, handouts, and lessons can be stored in the files section; learners can be directed to external links where appropriate; quizzing can be done via the polling feature; and discussions can be facilitated throughout via the group message board. And for those concerned about security: depending on the particular product you use, all of the technologies discussed here allow for measures like password protection.

So far we've looked at asynchronous technologies, that is, those that can be accessed by learners at any time. Discussions take place across a span of time rather than in "real" time, which is especially useful to learners working in different time zones or on different shifts. For those wanting some real-time interaction, instant messaging, or chat, tools allow for quick in-the-moment conversations, and those with licenses for a virtual classroom or web meeting product can arrange for scheduled get-togethers as well as impromptu meetings. Again, activities common to the traditional classroom are easy enough to repurpose for use here.

Technologies like blogs, wikis, discussion forums, and online communities, along with synchronous tools like chat and virtual classrooms, offer many possibilities for instructional applications (for a summary, see Table 26-1). They are (usually) free or very inexpensive; easy for the instructor to set up and manage; and, used creatively, go a long way toward bridging distance, real or imagined, in the online world. And remember, while these technologies may be new to many of us, they are already old hat to the next generation workforce. We haven't even yet talked about what newer, youth-used social networking technologies like Facebook, MySpace, and Second Life might bring to training in the coming years. But maybe we could ask Ashley, Jordan, and Madison about that, because they're already big contributors to the blog for Mr. Hall's third-grade class.

Table 26-1. Technologies Overview

	Blog	Wiki	Discussion Forum	Community
Example products	• Blogger • Wordpress • Bravenet • Blogeasy	• Pbwiki • Seedwiki • Wikispaces • Wikia	• Voyforums • Forums.com • Forumsforfree	• Yahoo! Groups • MSN Groups • Google Groups
Overview	• Page on which one person starts a post, others can comment	• Site on which everyone can post, edit, change	• Site offering threaded discussions tracked by topic	• Entire password-protected site with preprogrammed functionality for storage, links, message board, polling, shared calendar, and database
Typical features	• Posts are time stamped • Audio and video posts can be uploaded	• Wiki owners receive e-mail notification any time a change is made	• Discussions are threaded and searchable • Some allow attachments	• Message board • Chat • Files • Links • Photos • Polls (quiz) • Shared calendar
Security	• Can be password protected for posting and/or viewing • Posts can require moderator approval	• Can be password protected for posting and/or viewing	• Can be password protected • Posts can require moderator approval	• Can be password protected for posting and/or viewing beyond the main page • Posts can require moderator approval

(continued on next page)

Table 26-1. Technologies Overview (continued)

	Blog	Wiki	Discussion Forum	Community
Cost	• Externally hosted: Free • Internally installed: Varies	• Externally hosted: Free • Internally installed: Varies • Free hosting may be limited to number of pages or server space	• Externally hosted: Free • Internally installed: Varies	• Free
Examples of use	• Hosting course • Journaling • Discussion • Reflective activities • Writing assignments	• Group project • Class site • Sharing best practices	• Intersession discussion • Team assignments • Role plays • Debates • Knowledge sharing	• Community of practice • Repository for materials • Hosting online course
Sites	• "23 Things": http://plcmcl2-things.blogspot.com/ • Teaching English in Japan: http://englishiwate.blogspot.com/ • Mr. Hall's Third Grade Class: www.lakesideusd.org/hall/ • Blogging in Corporate America: www.nycupa.org/past_events/blogging-in-corporate-america.pdf	• http://biro.bemidjistate.edu/cgi/twwtwiki.pl • Library best practices wiki: www.libsuccess.org/index.php?title=Main_Page	• ASTD discussion boards: http://community.astd.org/eve/ubb.x	• http://finance.groups.yahoo.com/group/trdev • http://groups.yahoo.com/group/bozarthzone/ • Hosting entire catalog of courses/replicating learning management system (LMS): http://groups.yahoo.com/group/bozarthzone2

Summary

Where is distance learning headed? It's difficult to imagine. Five years ago blogs were just coming into their own, and few had heard of a wiki before the advent of Wikipedia in 2001. In another five years we may be talking about virtual avatars, and virtual machines to allow practice for high-risk procedures will be more commonplace. New learners will be expecting quality content using the latest technologies, and we need to be ready to provide it.

The section on synchronous virtual learning was adapted with permission from *How to Design for the Live Online Classroom: Creating Great Interactive and Collaborative Training Using Web Conferencing*, Hofmann (2005).

The section on blogs, wikis, discussion forums, and online communities was contributed by Jane Bozarth, author of *E-Learning Solutions on a Shoestring* and *Better Than Bullet Points: Creating Engaging E-Learning with PowerPoint*.

About the Author

Jennifer Hofmann is a synchronous learning expert and the president of InSync Training (http://www.insynctraining.com), a consulting firm that specializes in the design and delivery of synchronous e-learning. In the e-learning field since 1997, she has experience using all of the major web-based synchronous delivery platforms.

Hofmann is a recognized thought leader in the field of synchronous learning. Publications include *How to Design for the Live Online Classroom, The Synchronous Trainer's Survival Guide*, and *Live and Online!*

References

AchieveGlobal, available at www.achieveglobal.com/Solutions/Leader_eLearning.

Brandon Hall Research. 2004. *Live e-learning 2004: Virtual classrooms, synchronous tools, and web conferencing systems.* Sunnyvale, CA: Brandon Hall Research.

Hofmann, Jennifer. 2005. *How to design for the live online classroom: Creating great interactive and collaborative training using web conferencing.* Sunnyvale, CA: Brandon Hall Research, available at http://www.brandon-hall.com/publications/lol/lol.shtml.

Kruse, Kevin, and Jason Keil. 2000. *Technology-based training.* San Francisco: Jossey-Bass/ Pfeiffer.

Learning Circuits. 2008. Learning Circuits glossary, available at http://www.learningcircuits.org /glossary.

The Learning Citizen, available at http://www.learningcitizen.net.

Sun Developer Network, available at http://java.sun.com/developer/onlineTraining.

The University of Illinois at Urbana-Champaign, available at www.uiuc.edu.

For Further Reading

Bozarth, Jane. 2005. *E-learning solutions on a shoestring.* San Francisco: John Wiley & Sons/Pfeiffer.

Bozarth, Jane. 2008. *Better than bullet points: Creating engaging e-learning with PowerPoint.* San Francisco: John Wiley & Sons/Pfeiffer.

Clark, Ruth, and Richard Mayer. 2003. *E-learning and the science of instruction.* San Francisco: Jossey-Bass/Pfeiffer.

Hofmann, Jennifer. 2003. *The synchronous trainer's survival guide.* San Francisco: Jossey-Bass/Pfeiffer.

Rosenberg, Marc. 2006. *Beyond e-learning.* San Francisco: John Wiley & Sons.

Shank, Patty. 2007. *The online learning idea book.* San Francisco: John Wiley & Sons.

Learning Meets Web 2.0: Collaborative Learning

Marc J. Rosenberg

In This Chapter

➢ Understand the demands and pressures of modern-day work and their effects on learning

➢ Use collaborative tools and techniques to share knowledge and improve learning and performance

➢ Create a collaborative learning environment

In an age of constant change and transformation, when information is relevant one day and useless the next, how can we learn all that we need to learn? On whom should we rely to teach us? And what are the best tools and techniques to make this happen? As workplace learning and performance professionals, we are called upon to address these questions all the time. The answers are profound, game changing, and full of promise.

We are all learners, and, increasingly, we are all e-learners. We know that learning is a 24/7/365 activity. More and more, employees and customers aren't just saying "bring the training to me," but they are also saying "let me define what learning is for me." This means that to meet the learning and performance demands of 21st century workers, we need to let them take more control of what they learn, where they learn, and from whom they learn.

Training's place in the learning strategy of any organization is more certain than ever. However, the role of training is changing, and new approaches to facilitating learning and performance must find room in our repertoire.

This chapter focuses on new forms of collaborative learning. Taking advantage of new Web 2.0 technologies, we can now significantly enhance learning directly in the workplace and, in doing so, more fully involve the greater organization in the creation, distribution, and use of new knowledge. The opportunities for a new and expanded focus on workplace learning and performance—learning 2.0—are here. What will we make of them?

The Accelerating World of Learning

According to InternetWorldStats.com, there are approximately 1.26 billion Internet users worldwide (237 million in North America), slightly more than 19 percent (71 percent in North America) of the population (2007). The adoption of the web has been faster than any other technology, with the possible exception of the cell phone. And it has been no less so in learning and performance. Although there have been various iterations of computer-based training around for more than 30 years, there has not been much to show for it until the mass adoption of the Internet. The ubiquitous browser and the advent of common and inexpensive networking protocols eliminated many of the technical and distribution headaches that limited online learning for so long. Starting in the mid- to late-1990s, the shift to technology-based learning has been explosive, despite the disruption caused by the collapse of the Internet bubble in the early 2000s. The increased use of online courseware, either acquired from vendors or home grown, built with ever-easier authoring tools and the adoption of sophisticated supporting technologies, such as learning management systems, have been hallmarks of the field for the past decade.

Despite the growth of online training, or perhaps because of it, we now realize that learning is not the sole province of "the course," in a training center or online. And as important as online training is, we are beginning to recognize that formal instruction, be it instructor-led, technology-based, or a blend of the two, cannot address all learning and performance problems in an organization.

Why is this? Most corporate and government (except the military) employees only spend about two weeks in any form of formal training, three if they're lucky. The rest of the time, they are working. Yet learning doesn't stop at the classroom door or on the last screen of an online course. We have a strong need, even a biological need, to learn, but we surely don't always have the time to go to class.

Formal training cannot possibly keep up with the pace of information change. Not only is it becoming increasingly difficult, if not impossible, to create courses fast enough, but if formal courses were the only way to deliver new knowledge and skills, everyone would be in class for so much time there would hardly be time to get any work done. Speed of knowledge deployment has become as much of a critical challenge as speed of knowledge creation.

The demands of modern-day work also play a part. Time is an increasingly precious commodity. Although the web has enabled the delivery of online courseware 24/7, the job continues to take up more and more of the day, leaving less time to devote even a couple of hours to training. Allocating time for learning, therefore, is becoming more difficult.

The growing mobile workforce also plays havoc with traditional notions of training. Mobility has been called "one of the most dramatic megatrends in modern history," according to Sam Smith at RazzberrySync (Gronstedt, 2007). In the past, the largest segment of mobile workers was the telecommuter who worked from home on occasion. Now, the mobile worker's *only* workplace may be the home, and actual work locations may change on a weekly or daily basis, as people move from customer to customer, client to client, and even city to city. It is simply becoming too difficult to predict where or when workers will need access to knowledge. "Anytime" and "anyplace" are now front and center in a list of requirements for learning.

Individual needs are driving demand for more personalized learning. Just as new techniques of e-commerce focus on the unique customer (a customer of one), new techniques for learning focus on the unique learner (a learner of one). Even the most sophisticated online course will likely not be customizable enough to meet the needs of a much more sophisticated and specialized workforce who, above all, does not want to waste time.

One might argue that these new realities in the way learning is delivered were met by the onset of online training. It is certainly true that online training is a valuable tool that enables formal courseware to reach people in ways that are more convenient for them and more efficient for the business. Traditional e-learning has been a great addition to training's repertoire, but the fundamental changes in the workplace outlined above have pushed it about as far as it can go by itself. The need for learning that is even more individualized, is available wherever and whenever, is highly reliable and up to date, and does not waste a moment of time is driving workers and organizations to demand something more and to redefine e-learning as we have known it. Workers are seeking more informal ways to get the know-how they need to do their jobs. And, in a growing number of situations, they are increasingly turning to new, yet familiar and important, sources of knowledge: each other.

The Emergence of Web 2.0

"I get by with a little help from my friends."

—The Beatles

In 2005, the most popular search term on the web was Paris Hilton. In 2006, it was MySpace (Bingham, 2007). Although one might surmise that the big news here is that Paris's 15 minutes of fame might be over, for the learning and performance profession, the bigger news is Web 2.0.

The early web, Web 1.0, emerged in the late 1990s and was primarily one way and informational in nature. Massive amounts of good information (and some not so good) became readily available. Today, almost 80 percent of American adults are online (*New York Times*, 2007), and we have become very comfortable with the Internet as a primary information source. Between 1998 and 2003, new features were added to the web (sort of a Web 1.5) that enabled secure transactions to take place. E-commerce was one of the first opportunities for people to have an interactive experience with the web (for example, Amazon.com or eBay), and comfort levels with online transactions increased significantly. Learning management systems allowed sophisticated transactions (for example, registration, tracking, or billing) in the training arena.

Now we see the emergence of Web 2.0, not just a technology, but a significant change in direction, characterized by dynamic person-to-person and group-to-group interactions (for example, Linkedin or Facebook). These interactions are driving the transformation of e-learning into much more of an instantaneous collaborative experience.

Collaborative Learning

What is collaborative learning? There are really two ways to look at it. The first is more formal. We build collaborative experiences into formal courseware in the form of group work, case studies, and other active learning approaches. There is no doubt that such techniques enhance the learning experience, but the collaborative learning discussed here doesn't happen in the context of a course or a classroom (although courses certainly can be part of an overall learning strategy), but rather in the context of the workplace. And, it happens informally, driven by the individual's or group's immediate need to connect to others to answer a question, assess a situation, solve a problem, or develop a solution.

Information flows within organizations are often very chaotic. Knowledge seekers are constantly trying to get answers to myriad questions, get information or advice to help them in performing their jobs, or seek expert feedback on a new idea. "Who can help me do x?" "Does anybody know y?" "Where can I find z?" We ask our colleagues and search the web for answers. And we often spend hours of inefficient time doing it. David DeLong (2004) cites research that points to as much as 40 percent of corporate users cannot find the information they need to do their jobs on their own company's intranet and suggests that the cost of intellectual rework, substandard performance, and inability to find knowledge resources (or at least find them easily and efficiently) can amount to $5,000 per worker per year (or more).

Compounding the problem is that too many times, knowledge seekers, in their continued search for help, find neither the expert nor the nonexpert, but the *false* expert. False experts are individuals who may believe they have the right information but in fact are unknowingly misinformed. Or it is a person that the knowledge seeker believes to have the information, but the knowledge seeker has been misinformed. In such situations, inaccurate or incomplete information is conveyed, and, because one or both parties believe the expertise to be authentic, actions are taken based on the provided information—actions that may be inappropriate and could result in negative consequences.

Conversely, knowledge providers are constantly bombarded by knowledge seekers. It's no wonder people with expertise are often loath to identify themselves as such; the phone would never stop ringing. Yet the ability to quickly and reliably connect with expertise and to get questions answered correctly the first time is critical for true organizational learning. So the goal of collaboration in the workplace is to enhance connectivity between people and between groups so that knowledge can be shared and thus improve individual and organizational learning and performance.

Tools and Techniques for Collaborative Workplace Learning

Web 2.0 technologies have opened the floodgates of opportunity for collaboration online. They can do the same for learning. We can look at a few of these tools to better understand how they work and, from this examination, draw some new conclusions about the direction e-learning, and learning in general, is heading.

Communities of Practice

Communities of practice (CoPs) can serve as organizing structures and platforms for the entire workplace-based collaborative learning effort. CoPs are trusting groups of professionals united by a common concern or purpose, dedicated to supporting each other in increasing their knowledge, creating new insights, and enhancing performance in a particular domain. These are people who need to work with, learn from, and help each other achieve business goals (Hessan and Vogt, 1999). Much more than chat rooms or discussion threads, CoPs do not sit on the periphery; they are more fully integrating into actual work. Although we have been part of *vertical* CoPs for decades (just look at any organizational chart), where most information flows up or down, the biggest value to be gained from communities is when they are *horizontal*, where the information flows from side to side. It is in horizontal communities that people can find a professional identity and collaborate with others who have similar interests and needs. All Java programmers, all salespeople, all administrative assistants, all vice presidents, all accountants, and, of course, all trainers or all e-learning professionals, across the hall or across the globe, can participate in a horizontal CoP that focuses on their unique work.

Community building and management technologies continue to add power to the ability of the CoP to function effectively. Communications technologies, from email and instant messaging, to synchronous application sharing and meeting technologies, such as Webex, Microsoft LiveMeeting, Adobe Acrobat Connect (formerly Adobe Breeze), GoToMeeting, and others, are incorporated into communities to enable members to keep in touch easily. Document and content management systems allow members to contribute knowledge assets to a community knowledgebase, and affinity and alert tools allow members to keep tabs on who is doing what inside the community. Finally, portal technologies allow CoP members to have a single, unified access to the community that's easy to enter, leave, monitor, and return to on a regular basis.

The rap against communities is that no one uses them, especially on a regular basis. However, this problem is just as much of a cultural and sponsorship issue as it is a technology issue. So besides having good community tools, there are several key requirements for community effectiveness. Communities flourish when members think their time in the CoP is spent wisely and valued by their peers and managers. So, above all, communities must provide content that is deemed critical and important to members now, not at some point in the future, and they must provide easy access to that content. There should be incentives that encourage community participation, including recognizing membership as an achievement, without any risk or punishment (perceived or otherwise) for the time spent in CoP activities. Although it is true that communities often begin as grassroots initiatives, long-term effectiveness is almost impossible without good leadership and facilitation, the "secret sauce" of community success. Having people who step up to motivate participants, organize community activities, promote membership, resolve disputes (remove barriers), and generally provide stewardship for the CoP without dominating it, are essential. Finally, communities thrive in a culture of knowledge sharing. Organizations that horde, rather than share information, may not create an environment for CoP success. However, effective communities, those that are embraced by users and by their organizations, can be the seed corn for building a true organizational learning culture.

Companies often form horizontal communities of practice around specific job functions and subject matter expertise. This is especially valuable when the supply of subject matter experts (SMEs) is limited and the demand for their expertise is huge. Getting together in a virtual community allows everyone, wherever they are, to get the benefits of organizational expertise. Communities are also formed around projects. More short lived than those formed around content domains, these communities allow project team members to collaborate and keep track of who's doing what. Sales teams might form communities around a specific customer or market segment so that everyone has access to the latest competitive intelligence. When the salesforce resists coming to class because they need to spend more time with their customers, a community of practice may be the answer to keeping them informed, helping them learn, and still allowing them to focus on their jobs.

CoPs can create logical and long-term extensions of training. Participants in a formal training program can form their own community to keep in touch down the road, or community formation may happen as part of the instructional design, so that it is already functioning when class is over. This is especially valuable following orientation types of programs, where people come together for a brief time, meet each other, and then return to their own regions or countries. As work becomes more virtual, having a community of peers can be invaluable for sharing knowledge or just maintaining ties with the larger organization.

What other types of resources and tools can be integrated into CoPs to support collaboration? There are many ways to support communities and collaborative learning environments. Seven of the most promising and prominent of these approaches include presence awareness, social networking, next-generation knowledgebases, podcasts, wikis, blogs, and alerts and subscriptions.

Presence awareness. Presence awareness, an emerging technology designed to enhance collaboration, lets people see the real-time online availability of others within their community. When people make themselves available, and others "see" them, opportunities for instant contact become apparent. Learning is facilitated because answers to questions are more instantaneous, available at the moment of need, as opposed to waiting for an email or telephone reply. Presence awareness is not a stand-alone capability. Common in today's instant messaging software, it is showing up in a variety of knowledge management, CoP, and other collaboration tools, where it helps facilitate real-time conversations.

Social networking. Social networking lies at the very core of collaborative learning. John Seely Brown, former chief scientist at Xerox, first popularized the idea that learning and information sharing are social activities. People learn much more from each other than they do from more explicit information in books, magazines, websites, or videos. Adding social networking to CoPs ensures that conversations become more informal and personal, just like they are among friends and colleagues in the workplace. Tools that allow people to build online networks of other professionals within and outside of their own organizations are proliferating. Websites like Facebook and MySpace show how collaboration can work (collaboration is no flash in the pan; according to ComScore.com, together, these sites had approximately 166 million visitors in the last year). Today's teenagers are experts at it. Watch them multitask, holding multiple online conversations and interacting with several communities across a variety of interests (school, hobbies, careers) simultaneously.

Online social networks can be extensions of personal networks in the workplace (expanding the people you know), or can focus on personal interest areas outside of work. They can be general in nature or very domain specific (for example, gardeners, sports fans, automobile buffs, instructional designers, e-learning specialists). Social networks can also support specific learning activities, including simulations and games. Networks of gamers have grown up around popular online games, and these communities have become the primary source for learning about strategy, new features, and industry news.

When people can easily find others with common experience and expertise, shared knowledge can be significantly increased. The ability to instantly reach out to "people like me" is a powerful force in collaborative learning. In addition to discovering people with common interests and needs in a community, organizations can build online profiles of employees that are linked to human resource databases or the corporate contact directory. People identify their skills and projects and allow the network to find others like them. As a side benefit, the business gains a much more robust and valuable employee resource.

Talking about shared problems and common goals and helping one another improve performance are important first steps in building a collaborative learning environment on the web. Network building can bring experts together, foster innovation, and reduce redundant work. The next step is to allow these interactions to be enhanced with the ability to create and share a wide array of knowledge assets.

Next-generation knowledgebases. Next-generation knowledgebases are emerging that contain all the attributes of good content or document management systems (such as version control, shelf-life management, search and browse, metatagging, and entitlements) but go further to personalize the experience and create links not just among documents, but among users. New tools in this area allow connections to be made with others who may be doing the same work. Taking a cue from Amazon.com's "people who looked at this product also looked at...," these systems are now developing ways to link people who are accessing similar content from the system, allowing them to make connections with others who may be working on the same type of project, thereby reducing redundancy and concentrating the effort. As an example, one such product, Qexchange (www .qinnovation.com), provides the user with three views of "affinity" information: people who use the same content as you, people who contribute a lot of the content you use, and people who use a lot of the content you contribute. The benefit for workplace learning is clear. When people can search not only for a wide array of explicit content but make links with others who value that content, redundant work can be eliminated and the collective smarts of the organization can be better marshaled.

Social networking, presence awareness, and next-generation knowledgebases form the building blocks of solid communities of practice. Today, thousands of CoPs operate in every industry and in every size organization. On the business side, one of the earliest and best documented case studies was the Eureka! project at Xerox, where copier repair technicians found that the best source of information on how to repair increasingly complex machines was not the manual or the training, but each other (Barth, 2000; PARC Research, 2002; Roberts-Witt, 2002). On the military side, when front-line commanders on the ground in Iraq found that they couldn't get answers to their questions fast enough, they formed their own online community, CompanyCommand (www.companycommand.army.mil). In the workplace learning and performance community, ASTD serves the broader profession (including e-learning), and the eLearning Guild serves the niche e-learning market exclusively.

Podcasts. Podcasts (audio) and vodcasts (video) represent a new take on old technology. What was once sent out on audiocassettes, videotapes, and CD-ROMs/DVDs is now downloaded directly off the web, a key difference. Along with easier-to-use production tools, the ability to distribute a wide variety of audiovisual material over the Internet has made the podcast and all its cousins extremely popular and far less costly than past approaches. Another contribution of the podcast is that it has transformed our perceptions of what a knowledgebase is. After years of thinking about them as simply repositories for text-based documents (Microsoft Word, PowerPoint, or Excel), we now see a knowledgebase as containing a more complete array of resources that transcend text, simple graphics, and numbers. Of course, as with any form of information, care must be taken in developing podcasts that are reasonably short, but to the point and precisely targeted to intended users (nothing is worse than listening to an audio presentation on something that is not relevant to you). As instructional designers expand their skills into information design, this is a natural.

As mobile devices proliferate and grow in sophistication, so have podcasts. The ability to learn on the go, from experts who otherwise would have a more limited reach, and to get updates to the content every day if desired (just sync with your computer), makes this technology a no-brainer in knowledge dissemination and learning.

Wikis. Wikis are generating a great deal of excitement in learning circles. A wiki (Hawaiian for *quick*) is a software tool that supports collaborative knowledge creation. Wikis allow groups of people to contribute and edit content in a knowledgebase that has been defined and structured by the group, practically in real time, without the need for any programming knowledge. The most popular wiki by far is Wikipedia, the online encyclopedia, where almost anyone can contribute, edit, and manage information (sure sounds like a community).

The interesting idea that drives Wikipedia and other wikis is that they are based on both group-think and individual expert models. Knowledge contributions by a wide variety of participants can help to ensure that, as the group authors and edits content over time, all perspectives and points of view are heard. In addition, individual experts can evaluate and edit the content to ensure accuracy and completeness. This group collaboration, in addition to being a learning activity on its own, can serve as a collective intelligence around a particular knowledge domain. In this way, wikis are organic, self-organizing, self-correcting, and more accurate than people realize. As an example, according to the journal *Nature* (Giles, 2006), despite common belief, Wikipedia is only slightly less accurate than *Encyclopedia Britannica,* although on any given day the accuracy of any particular article may be called into question (and likely addressed by other Wikipedians).

The concern of most business and government organizations is that no knowledge domain should be open for everyone to contribute to or edit. They all don't have the subject matter expertise or the security clearance to do so. This is a legitimate concern, but what is often missed about wikis is that authorship and editing can be managed so that a qualification or certification process can control access to the content. Just because Wikipedia allows everyone to participate does not mean that all wikis have to function that way. In fact, most do not. Once past this misnomer, people begin to see the opportunities for quick, collaborative knowledge creation that wikis present.

Wikis present a great opportunity for communities of people to create knowledgebases in very short order. Project teams, subject matter experts, market managers, and other groups of workers, often spread out geographically, can quickly use wiki technology to create and maintain repositories of information. These resources can then be made available to the broader organization. Wikis can also become part of course design as primary resources (perhaps replacing the traditional print participant guide in whole or in part).

More collaborative assignments might have participants create a wiki during class and then add to it once they are back in the field. It's an excellent adjunct to an emerging CoP.

Blogs. Blogs, short for "weblogs," are, for the most part, online diaries or web journals that allow authors (bloggers) to easily and quickly "speak" with large numbers of readers who then collaborate with the author by adding comments, links, and other insights and materials that might be useful to the conversation. In 2006, 14 million blogs were launched, and there are an estimated 70 million blogs worldwide, albeit most of them tiny (*The McLaughlin Group*, 2007). Blogs are extremely easy to create and maintain; like wikis, no authoring or HTML expertise is required, just the desire to communicate. Blogging tools make it easy to immediately start writing and inviting others to comment and share what they know. Unlike a wiki, however, a blog is usually authored by a single individual, and its format is almost always chronological.

People who think about blogs often think of them in the public domain—political blogs or entertainment blogs. But CEOs are now writing in the "blogosphere," sometimes to communicate with customers and the marketplace in general, but also to communicate with employees. Bill Marriott (Marriott Hotels, blogs.marriott.com) blogs, as does Bob Lutz (vice president, General Motors, fastlane.gmblogs.com). Today it is possible to find blogs on almost every content area in business: project management, leadership, information technology (IT), marketing and sales, customer care, and product development, to name a few. Even the workplace learning and performance industry has dedicated blogs (for example, www.internettime.com and www.astd.org/content/publications/blogs). Because of their chronological nature, blogs can be useful sources of expertise and commentary that is usually more up to date than a general website, magazine article, or textbook.

Blogs can be powerful learning tools. They can maximize how new ideas are disseminated and discussed by a larger audience. Although it is important to ensure that those doing the blogging know what they are talking about, there is no need to restrict blogs to just a few "anointed" subject matter experts. Project managers can use a blog to keep teams, or even entire organizations, informed about a project's status. Product managers can keep sales and marketing staffs updated on new product features and functionalities, or document activities around a new product launch. IT organizations can use blogs to offer end-user advice and respond quickly and in one central place to technical problems that arise in the workplace. Community leaders can use a blog to communicate with members and generate interest and participation in knowledge creation. Much better than email updates, blogs form a permanent, organized record of activities and progress that can be archived and referenced. Instructors can use blogs to chronicle course activities, perhaps over multiple offerings. Insights from one class would not be lost to the next.

Alerts and subscriptions. Alerts and subscriptions add an important element of personalization to a CoP. By allowing authors of content, leaders of CoPs, subject matter experts, bloggers, and others who are responsible for organizational knowledge to alert people who might be interested in new information as it becomes available and notifying them not just that the new content is out, but exactly where to find it, knowledge sharing is significantly enhanced. Similarly, by allowing users of content, the consumers of knowledge, to subscribe to areas of interest and request notification when something new becomes available, information clutter is significantly reduced. Through alert and subscription personalization, each person's view into his or her CoP and associated knowledgebases becomes unique and more targeted to his or her needs, fulfilling one of the major requirements for community success and learning: delivering content that's valuable to the user.

Subscriptions go even further through the advent of RSS feeds (really simple syndication). When content is updated frequently, such as with current events, financial information, even the weather, an RSS feed provided by an organization that is publishing that information, or collecting it from third parties (an aggregator), sends the information to subscribers regularly. Today RSS feeds operate on a common standard that is compatible with most web browsers and portals (Google, AOL, Yahoo, and others that are referred to in RSS terminology as _readers_). From the user's perspective, all that needs to be done is subscribe and sit back as updated information is sent on an ongoing and regular basis. To experience RSS, subscribe to any of the feeds from the popular news sites like CNN, _USA Today,_ or _The New York Times._

One of the major issues in organizations is information overload. Too much knowledge being pushed out to everyone in the organization can backfire. People spend valuable time simply filtering incoming messages to determine what's important and what's not, what's urgent and what can wait, and what's mandated reading and what's optional. It seems that every organization in the business has _urgent_ content that _everyone_ must access _immediately._ Companies have tried to triage this problem at the source, developing guidelines and protocols for information dissemination, with some success. Subscriptions and alerts allow knowledge producers and knowledge consumers to manage this problem locally. Giving people some control as to what information they want to receive, within a broader set of organizational guidelines, appears to help manage the overload and enhance information productivity. Less is sometimes more.

With the right information targeted at the right people; with easy-to-use knowledge creation and dissemination tools like blogs, wikis, and podcasts; with next-generation knowledgebases that link both content and people; with social networking and presence awareness tools that keep people in touch with others like them; and with CoPs that bring all of these features together, the stage is set for effective collaborative learning. Just one more crucial component to add to the mix: the right environment.

Creating a Collaborative Learning 2.0 Environment

As we have seen, Web 2.0 tools and techniques, especially those that enhance workplace collaboration, offer great opportunities to enhance workplace learning and performance. From Web 2.0 we can create new forms of collaborative learning—learning 2.0. These new approaches do not diminish what has been accomplished through more traditional forms of training, they add to it.

The challenge for workplace learning and performance professionals in adopting learning 2.0 is threefold. First, we must recognize that not all learning takes place in the classroom and not all learning and performance problems are addressable by formal training. Second, once we get past the "training is all we do" barrier, we must focus considerably more resources on more informal learning in the workplace. And third, when we look at workplace learning and performance, we must devote more of our attention on building learning models that are far less dominated by training paradigms and far more collaborative in nature.

Assuming the first two challenges are met, what are some ways to address the third? There are several important environmental issues to consider. A good place to start is by *thinking holistically*. All the approaches used to support collaboration have value, but their value increases exponentially when they are combined. We learned this when we blended classroom and online training; it is no less so here. CoPs should be married with next-generation knowlegebases. Community members should have the opportunity to personalize access to information through alerts and subscriptions. One-way, top-down knowledge distribution might be augmented by more participatory approaches using wikis and blogs.

Combining these tools into more effective collaborative learning strategies will be for naught if they don't support the organizational strategy. Therefore, it is essential that any collaborative learning venture has a clear *strategy and value proposition* that is driven by organizational goals and objectives. The days of using learning metrics, such as pre- and posttest scores or learner satisfaction surveys as sole measures of effectiveness are over, replaced by a *measurement plan* that defines success criteria from the business's or client's perspective, not the trainer's. What benefits will collaborative learning bring and how will we know when we get there? This is one of the first questions that should be answered, not one of the last.

Leadership will also play a pivotal role in the success of any collaborative learning venture. Implementing collaborative learning in the workplace can be initially disruptive and stressful. Having leaders at the executive level and at the front line who are supportive of the change will pay off handsomely. Before any pilot project begins, be sure the leadership is truly on board, not just with words but with a commitment to serve as a role model in addition to providing the resources necessary to get the job done.

Finally, know the *culture* of the organization. When great learning initiatives, especially ones that are new and different, come up against a lousy organizational culture, the culture wins every time. If people are resistant to knowledge sharing, if collaboration is almost always forced, if change is a dangerous word in the organization, then it would be prudent to focus on improving the learning culture first before beginning a new and unique learning program.

Redefining E-Learning

The reality of learning 2.0 and workplace-based collaborative learning requires a redefinition of e-learning. From a learning psychology perspective, learning 2.0 takes on more of a constructivist approach, where learners, guided by appropriate models and supported by well-designed resources, increasingly define their own paths through content and organize knowledge in ways that have unique meaning for them. Contrast this with more traditional cognitive approaches where programs are specifically designed for instructional effectiveness, in lessons, modules, and other structures, offering far less individual flexibility.

From a use model perspective, learning 2.0 takes on more of a resource or reference approach, where individual learners seek out answers to questions, procedures, or other information at the moment of need. Contrast this with scheduled training programs that try as best they can to approximate the needs of an entire population of learners. For learning 2.0, the metaphor changes from the classroom to the library.

Finally, from a workplace learning and performance professional's perspective, learning 2.0 requires several new skills and areas of expertise in addition to traditional instructional design. Specialties like information design, knowledge architecture design, library science, user interface design, community facilitation, collaboration strategy, content analysis, and change management are becoming increasingly important. For learning 2.0, the work challenge moves beyond just building, maintaining, and delivering finite course products (that have a beginning and an end) to building, maintaining, and delivering workplace-based information and collaboration services on an ongoing basis as well.

Learning 2.0 represents more than significant changes in technology, it is a profound change in the workplace learning and performance field. To some this is disconcerting; it's too much of a shift. But more and more of us see this as a golden opportunity to move into the mainstream of our organizations and get more involved in the day-to-day life of the business. It means, to paraphrase an ancient proverb, going out on a limb. But isn't that where the fruit is?

About the Author

Marc J. Rosenberg is a management consultant in training, organizational learning, e-learning, knowledge management, and performance improvement. He is the author of the best-selling books *E-Learning: Strategies for Delivering Knowledge in the Digital Age* and *Beyond E-Learning: Approaches and Technologies to Enhance Organizational Knowledge, Learning, and Performance* (Pfeiffer). He is a past president of the International Society for Performance Improvement (ISPI) and holds a PhD in instructional design, plus degrees in communications and marketing. He is a recognized thought leader in the field. He has spoken at the White House, has been the keynote speaker at numerous professional and business conferences, has authored more than 40 articles and book chapters, and is a frequently quoted expert in major business and trade publications.

References

Barth, Steve. 2000. Eureka! Xerox has found it, available at choo.fis.utoronto.ca/mgt/KM .xeroxCase.html.

Bingham, Tony. 2007. Learning gets personal. Keynote address presented at ASTD TechKnowledge conference, Las Vegas, NV.

Delong, David W. 2004. *Lost knowledge: Confronting the threat of an aging workforce.* New York: Oxford University Press.

Giles, Jim. 2006. Internet encyclopedias go head to head. News@Nature.com, available at www .nature.com/news/2005/051212/full/438900a.html.

Gronstedt, Anders. 2007, January. The changing face of workplace learning. *T+D*, 21-24.

Hessan, Diane, and Eric Vogt. November 1999. Presentation at the Workforce Performance TechLearn conference, Orlando, FL.

Internet World Stats. 2007, November 30. Available at http://www.internetworldstats.com.

PARC Research. 2002. Eureka, available at www.parc.xerox.com/research/projects /commknowledge/eureka.html.

Roberts-Witt, Sarah L. 2002. A "Eureka!" moment at Xerox, available at www.pcmag.com
/article2/0,4149,28792,00.asp.

The McLaughlin Group. 2007, August 31.

New York Times. 2007, August 14. Harris Poll conducted in July 2007.

For Further Reading

Brown, John S. New learning environments for the 21st century, available at www.johnseelybrown
.com/newlearning.pdf.

Cross, Jay. 2007. *Informal learning: Rediscovering the natural pathways that inspire innovation and
performance.* San Francisco: Pfeiffer.

Goldsmith, Marshall, Howard J. Morgan, and Alexander J. Ogg, eds. 2004. *Leading organizational
learning: Harnessing the power of knowledge.* San Francisco: Jossey-Bass.

Richardson, Will. 2006. *Blogs, wikis, podcasts, and other powerful web tools for classrooms.*
Thousand Oaks, CA: Corwin.

Rosenberg, Marc J. 2006. *Beyond e-learning: Approaches and technologies to enhance organizational knowledge, learning, and performance.* San Francisco: Pfeiffer.

Rossett, Allison, and Lisa Schafer. 2007. *Job aids and performance support: Moving from knowledge
in the classroom to knowledge everywhere.* San Francisco: Pfeiffer.

Saint-Onge, Hubert, and Debra Wallace. 2003. *Leveraging communities of practice for strategic
advantage.* Burlington, MA: Butterworth-Heinemann.

Surowiecki, James. 2004. *The wisdom of crowds.* Boston: Little Brown.

Wenger, Etienne, Richard McDermott, and William M. Snyder. 2002. *Cultivating communities of
practice.* Boston: Harvard Business School Press.

Section VI

Measuring and Evaluating Impact

Evaluating Training Programs

Luminary Perspective

Donald L. Kirkpatrick

In This Chapter

➢ Learn how the four evaluation levels came to be

➢ Understand the four levels of evaluation

In today's competitive environment, there's no question that we need to evaluate and prove the value of our training programs. That, of course, is easier said than done. Fortunately, the four-level evaluation model simplifies what can be a complex process.

History of the Four Levels of Evaluation

Although it may seem like the four-level evaluation model has been around forever, this now-standard method of evaluation wasn't introduced until 1959. Many years ago I was teaching a human relations for supervisors course at the Management Institute of the University of Wisconsin in Madison. I had earned a BBA and an MBA in the School of Business. I decided to work toward a PhD, so I decided to use an evaluation of the human relations for supervisors program as my dissertation topic.

In selecting the contents of the dissertation, I decided to measure four things:

- Reaction: A measure of the satisfaction of the participants who attended the program
- Learning: The extent to which participants increased their knowledge, learned or improved present skills, or changed their attitudes
- Behavior: The extent to which participants applied what they learned when they returned to their jobs
- Results: The improvement of morale, the increase in sales or production, the reduction in turnover, the increase in customer satisfaction, the return-on-investment (ROI), and any other benefits that came from attending the program.

Five years later, I received a call from Robert L. Craig, the editor of the *Journal of the American Society of Training Directors* (now *T+D* magazine), who asked me to write an article on evaluation based on my dissertation. I told him I would write four articles for successive months. He agreed, so I wrote an article on each of the four items I had evaluated.

Then a funny thing happened. Trainers began to call my concepts the "Kirkpatrick model." They began to call the four items "the four levels." I began to get requests to conduct in-house programs and speak at national conferences and ASTD chapters about "Kirkpatrick's Four Levels." I remember one comment from a trainer who said, "Don, you have broken down that elusive concept, 'evaluation,' into four simple and practical terms that we can all understand." Trainers began to write articles such as "How to Evaluate at Level 2" or "How to Measure Level 3," assuming that every reader would know what that meant.

It wasn't until 1993, 34 years later, that I wrote the first edition of *Evaluating Training Programs: The Four Levels* after a friend suggested that it should be a book. And now, the book is in its third edition and has been translated into Chinese, Polish, Spanish, and Turkish (Kirkpatrick and Kirkpatrick, 2006).

There are several reasons for evaluating programs: to determine if they should be continued or dropped, to learn how they can be improved, to justify the training budget, to ensure learning compliance, to maximize the value of training, and to align training with strategy. Let's examine the four levels and find out why each is important.

Level 1 Evaluation: Reaction

Evaluating reaction, often called a level 1 evaluation, typically consists of a reaction sheet. The purpose is to measure how the attendees feel about the program. Unfortunately, some people put little faith in this evaluation level and negatively refer to it as *smile sheets*. In fact, some recent literature suggests that these smile sheets do more harm than good. Instead of perpetuating that notion, let's review the definition of *reaction*, which measures customer satisfaction.

Customer satisfaction is essential. If customers report bad things on a reaction sheet, they likely will say bad things when they return to their job. The result: Higher management may judge the training based on what they hear. Therefore, reactions are important to evaluate, not only to benefit the instructor, but to know that customers have gone back to their jobs with a positive attitude toward the program and the trainers who presented it.

Additionally, if you don't measure customer reaction and satisfaction, you are subtly telling them that their feedback isn't wanted or needed. The answer is simple: use reaction sheets for *all* programs.

Guidelines for evaluating reaction include

1. Determine what aspects of the program you want to evaluate.
2. Design a form that will quantify reactions.
3. Encourage written comments.
4. Get 100 percent immediate response for an instructor-led program or as close to 100 percent you can get if evaluating an e-learning program.
5. Develop acceptable standards against which to measure actual ratings.
6. Make trainer decisions based on actual ratings against the standard.

Level 2 Evaluation: Learning

After evaluating reaction, you can move on to evaluate level 2, learning. Learning consists of what knowledge was learned, what skills were developed or improved, and what attitudes were changed.

Why do we measure learning? Simply put, if the training course does not meet one or more of the learning objectives, you cannot expect any change in behavior. Moreover, if we were to measure behavior change (level 3) and not learning, and if we found no change in behavior, the likely conclusion would be that no learning took place. This conclusion could be very wrong.

Evaluating learning is important for two reasons. First, it measures the effectiveness of the instructor in increasing knowledge and changing attitudes. If little or no learning has taken place, little or no change in behavior can be expected.

Just as important is the specific information that pretest and posttest evaluation of learning provides. By analyzing the change in answers to individual items, instructors can see where they have succeeded and where they have failed. If the program is going to be repeated, instructors can plan other techniques or aids to increase the chances that learning will take place. Moreover, if follow-up sessions can be held with the same group, the things that have not been learned can become the objectives of these sessions.

Here are some guidelines for evaluating learning:

1. Measure knowledge, skills, and attitudes before and after.
2. Use a paper-and-pencil test for measuring knowledge and attitudes.
3. Use a performance test for measuring new or improved skills.
4. Get 100 percent response if possible.
5. Use a control group (did not receive the training) and an experimental group (received the training) if practical.

Level 3 Evaluation: Behavior

What happens when trainees leave the classroom and return to their jobs? How much transfer of knowledge, skills, and attitudes occurs? That is what level 3 attempts to evaluate: behavior. In other words, what change in job behavior occurred because people attended a training program?

This level is more complicated than the first two levels. First, trainees cannot change their behavior until they have an opportunity to do so. For example, if you decide to use some of the principles and techniques described here, you must wait until you have a training program to evaluate. Likewise, if the training program is designed to teach a person how to conduct an effective performance appraisal interview, the trainee cannot apply the learning until an interview is held.

Second, it is impossible to predict when a change in behavior will occur. Even if a trainee has an opportunity to apply the learning, he or she may not do so immediately. In fact, behavior changes may occur at any time after the first opportunity, or they may never occur.

Third, the trainee may apply the learning to the job and come to one of the following conclusions:

- The participant liked what happened and will use the new behavior.
- The participant didn't like what happened and will continue the old behavior.
- The participant liked what happened, but the boss or time restraints prevent him or her from changing.

We all hope that the rewards for changing behavior will cause the trainee to come to the first of these conclusions. It is important, therefore, to provide help, encouragement, and rewards when the trainee returns to the job from the training class. One type of reward is intrinsic. This term refers to the inward feelings of satisfaction, pride, achievement, and happiness that can occur when the new behavior is used. Extrinsic rewards also are important. These rewards come from the outside. They include praise, increased freedom and empowerment, merit pay increases, and other forms of recognition that come as the result of the change in behavior.

Guidelines for evaluating behavior include

1. Measure on a before-and-after basis if possible.
2. If not possible, measure on an after basis and ask the participant to compare it with his or her before behavior.
3. Allow time for new behaviors to be used. This may vary from one day to three to six months.
4. Get 100 percent response or a sampling. The sampling depends on the resources available.
5. Repeat at appropriate times. For example, if the first measurement was done after three months, the second might be done after six months. During that period, some new behaviors might have occurred or some behaviors that were tried were no longer used and the participant went back to the old ways.
6. Use a control group if practical.

One good way to measure change in behavior is to use a patterned interview with a select group that includes the participants and possibly their supervisors, peers, and even subordinates. In the interview, ask to what extent the participant has changed his or her behavior because of attending the program. Possible answers are

- To a large extent
- To some extent
- Not at all.

If the participant says, "Not at all," ask him or her, "Why not?" with the possible answers being

- The training did not apply to my job.
- I intended to change but had higher priorities.
- My boss prevented or discouraged me from changing.
- I have had no opportunity to use it yet.

Be sure when asking these questions that you do not put the participant on the spot by putting pressure for a positive answer. Emphasize that you want the truth so that the program can be evaluated and improved.

Level 4 Evaluation: Results

Finally we get to what it's all about: results. It is important to go through all three evaluation levels before trying to evaluate results—and ROI in particular. Results are the last thing to evaluate, but the first thing to consider when planning a training program. When planning a program, the questions to ask, in order, are

- What results do we hope to achieve through a training program?
- What behaviors are needed to accomplish those results?
- What knowledge, skills, and attitudes are necessary to initiate these behaviors?
- How can I present a training program that is practical, interactive, and enjoyable?

Some guidelines for evaluating results include

1. Measure on a before-and-after basis.
2. Allow time for possible results to take place.
3. Repeat at appropriate times.
4. Use a control group if practical.
5. Consider costs versus benefits.
6. Look for "evidence" because absolute "proof" is not possible.

Evaluating results is usually easier than evaluating changes in behavior because specific data are often readily available. For example, when measuring the reduction in turnover, figures are easy to get. Likewise, increase in sales, increase or retention of customers, change in profits, amount of scrap, and time to complete a job are usually available.

Soft skills such as leadership, communication, managing change, and decision making are more difficult to measure and cannot be measured in dollars or in ROI. Some specific measures are available that can relate to these programs if the organization has an annual attitude survey, but converting the comparisons to money is not viable unless they can be converted to such measurable items as turnover.

Note that a "chain of evidence" can be created by evaluating all four of the levels in sequence. Each bit of evidence can help build the overall case that the program was effective. So, when evaluating, do all four levels and don't yield to the temptation of jumping from learning to results or ROI.

Summary

What began as a dissertation topic in the 1950s has become an integral part of training programs around the world. Four simple and practical words have formed the basis for this phenomenon: reaction, learning, behavior, and results.

These four levels can be used not only to evaluate the effectiveness of a learning program but can also be useful in getting the desired changes to take place. Although learning is the desired goal of any training program, the most critical aspect is that the learning creates the desired change in behavior that must take place for positive results to be achieved.

✧

About the Author

Donald L. Kirkpatrick holds BBA, MBA, and PhD degrees from the University of Wisconsin in Madison. He served as human resources manager of Bendix Products Aerospace Division and is a former national volunteer president of ASTD, where he received the Gordon Bliss Award and the Lifetime Achievement in Workplace Learning and Performance Award. He is a member of the HRD Hall of Fame. In 2007, he received the Lifetime Achievement Award from the Asia HRDCongress. He is the author of seven management inventories and seven management books, including *Evaluating Training Programs: The Four Levels*, which has become the basis for training evaluation worldwide. As a consultant, he presents programs to many U.S. organizations, as well as organizations in Argentina, Australia, Brazil, Greece, India, Korea, Malaysia, the Netherlands, Saudi Arabia, Singapore, and Spain.

Reference

Kirkpatrick, Donald L., and James D. Kirkpatrick. 2006. *Evaluating training programs: The four levels*. 3d ed. San Francisco: Berrett-Koehler.

For Further Reading

Kirkpatrick, Donald L., and James D. Kirkpatrick. 2005. *Transferring learning to behavior*. San Francisco: Berrett-Koehler.

Kirkpatrick, Donald L., and James D. Kirkpatrick. 2007. *Implementing the four levels*. San Francisco: Berrett-Koehler.

Level 1:
Reaction Evaluation

Nancy Kristiansen

In This Chapter

➤ Use a level 1 evaluation strategy to make
   training more effective

➤ Learn the elements of a successful level 1 evaluation

Why do level 1 evaluations and their associated forms—the so-called "smile sheet"—get such a bad rap? Is it because they have become no more than a formality and are barely tolerated at training events? Have we watered them down just to avoid offending anyone so that they no longer serve any purpose? What makes trainers the most resistant opponents? Do we see level 1 evaluations as behavior modifiers or score cards rather than as data collection tools that can help us improve the training process? If so, we may have missed the whole opportunity, in many cases the *only* opportunity, to ensure participants' learning needs are met. The key to an effective level 1 evaluation is good design that doesn't lower the bar or underestimate participants' ability to give us valuable feedback and, thus, enhance the overall strategy that we use. A well-designed level 1 approach incorporated into a closed loop training design will transform the smile sheet into an effective data collection tool that provides invaluable information to trainers, instructional designers, facilitators, training coordinators, and managers. That will lead to good decision making for our classrooms and computer-based training (CBT) programs.

Benefits and Advantages

Depending on the organization, the benefits and advantages of developing and using a well-designed level 1 evaluation strategy can be many:

- Manage multiple facilities, resources, providers, and contractors
- Improve decision making
- Prepare for levels 2, 3, and 4 cross-functional strategies
- Meet regulatory compliance requirements
- Reinforce a culture of learning
- Involve participants as contributors to the betterment of the training process
- Model a closed loop process of continuous improvement for others in the organization
- Inquire directly whether or not what was learned met participants' expectations and objectives
- Avoid knee-jerk reactions and decisions made out of context.

Some organizations evaluate every program at level 1, and results are calculated, monitored, and used for decision making. Large organizations, especially those that employ or contract a group of instructors, find level 1 evaluations useful for managing the quality of training delivery when multiple sessions of the same course are scheduled at various locations. Managers can use the data to identify recurring issues or trends, such as poor facilities or inadequate instruction, and draw on the information for problem solving and decision making. For example, if the same training course was being delivered by 15 instructors at three different locations across several months, without having to physically observe each session, a manager reviewing trends in the data would be able to identify low performance among instructors or catering services that weren't up to par. It is important that the data themselves should not spark the decision making but should trigger inquiry into the causes of low ratings. Perhaps there is a reason for the low ratings, which did not indicate a trend. Or conversely, perhaps there is a problem that, through root cause analysis, could be identified and solved.

Another advantage of using a level 1 evaluation is avoiding emotional reactions when only a few participants have complaints. Reactionary decision making based on feedback from a single source may be ill-informed or insincere and also costly at this stage of the training process.

Yet another advantage of these evaluations is having employees of all ranks of the organization collaborate to ensure training courses and programs are meeting the learning needs of its members. Training departments can easily become silos when communication is one-sided and decisions are made without direct input and feedback from others.

Undisciplined assessments are nothing more than the "blame game": they need this training, they need that instruction, and they don't know their jobs. Level 1 evaluations can serve cross-functional efforts, at least as a starting point. As training evaluation strategies rise to levels 3 and 4, the ability to work with other teams and departments becomes increasingly necessary and the experience gained from practicing level 1 evaluations can pave the way.

Many organizations must meet some sort of regulatory compliance program, such as ISO 9000, or quality system regulation (QSR). These programs typically require that at least a minimum effort is made to ensure the effectiveness of its training programs; a level 1 effort to capture the reactions of participants is often sufficient to meet such requirements. On a more critical level, the requirement will most likely be linked to a concern that people are qualified for their jobs. Measuring training effectiveness is a logical outgrowth of implementing training programs to ensure people are qualified. In other words, to answer the question, "How do you ensure people are qualified for their jobs?" you could answer, "We assess the new hire's skill sets against the job description to determine if there are any gaps." The statement, "We provide training to all employees," will inevitably lead to the next question, "How do you know the training was effective?"

Level 1 evaluations also reinforce a culture of disciplined learning through reflection. Most organizations are so focused on the present and immediate future, it is difficult to reverse the focus and take time to reflect on the past. In adult learning, whether at the individual or organizational level, learning is often a function of taking time for reflection. Without it, the potential for learning is weakened and many valuable lessons can be lost to the moment and trampled by the next big crisis. Busy training participants generally aren't encouraged to take time to reflect on their experiences because it seems useless. When participants complete a well-designed level 1 evaluation form, they can pause, consider, and reflect on their recent experience. This practice, while seemingly little more than a routine administrative task, can actually instill the habit of reflecting on learning experiences, which holds everyone, including the learner, accountable to the process. When seen in this context, the actual ratings and answers the participant provides become secondary. The humble smile sheet, warts and all, when used to actively engage participants in reflecting on the learning process, can prove its value.

Unfortunately, even seasoned trainers are reluctant to distribute evaluations at the end of a class, and level 1 evaluations continue to get a bad rap. Why is this? If the questions on the evaluation form are too few and too simple, participants may oversimplify their replies by responding negatively to the whole training event, just because, for instance, the facilities were uncomfortable or the food was not appetizing. This leads us to the following premise: well-designed level 1 evaluation forms that ask specific questions that cover the entire training process can provide useful information for developing a habit of reflection and for real improvement. When the forms are too vague or general, it's the instructor who takes one for the team.

A Closed Loop Process

Training evaluation is typically not considered during the initial assessment and design stages of the training process, so level 1 evaluation is generally the only method used. It may be that this deliver-first-ask-questions-later approach has done the most damage to the level 1 evaluation. If we were to include the evaluation strategy in our initial assessment and design stages of the training process, two important things would happen. First, participants' reactions might just yield valuable information that links their experience to their expectations and objectives. Second, we might discover opportunities to deploy a comprehensive evaluation strategy that either combines level 1 with levels 2, 3, and 4 feedback or frees us from deploying level 1 methods because we determined ahead of time that the effectiveness of our efforts and the quality of our programs can be ascertained without them. The point is that training effectiveness findings at any level are only as informative as our assessment and design strategies allow them to be. Reaction feedback is hindered the most when we treat the data collection process as a reactive strategy. Certainly the data are intended to reflect participants' reaction to their learning or training experience, but the methodology should be well planned and designed from the start. Well-planned and -designed level 1 evaluation strategies can provide valuable information that, in a spirit of continuous improvement, closes the loop on the training design process.

The Deming Cycle

Integrating a continuous improvement or total quality management (TQM) model into a process approach to training affords the opportunity to develop effective strategies that evolve as changes occur, ensuring that programs remain fresh and relevant. The well-known plan-do-check-act cycle, pictured in Figure 28-1, first introduced by Walter A. Shewhart in the 1930s and later popularized by W. Edwards Deming and the TQM movement in the 1950s (Deming, 2000), has been wholeheartedly adopted by organizations and professionals who care about quality—of services, goods, or programs—worldwide.

The Deming Cycle provides a roadmap for just about any process improvement strategy, including the training cycle, as we see in Figure 28-2.

Figure 28-1. The Deming Cycle

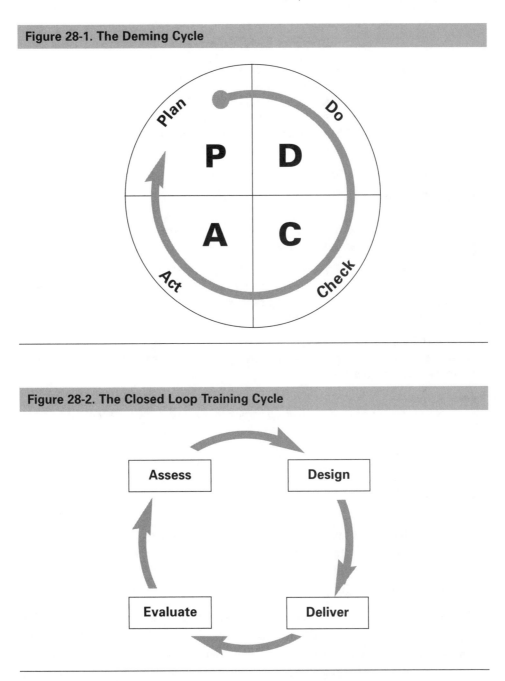

Figure 28-2. The Closed Loop Training Cycle

✍ **Donald L. Kirkpatrick** ✍

Donald L. Kirkpatrick is considered the father of training evaluation. Renowned for developing the four levels of evaluation, he first presented his ideas on the topic in the article "How to Start an Objective Evaluation of Your Training Program," which appeared in the May-June 1956 issue of the Journal of the American Society of Training Directors *(later* T+D*). These ideas were then compiled into his seminal book,* Evaluating Training Programs: The Four Levels *(1994).*

Kirkpatrick's four levels of evaluation are as follows:

Level 1: Reaction
Level 1 evaluation focuses on the reaction of participants to the training program. Although this is the lowest level of measurement, it remains an important dimension to assess in terms of participant satisfaction.

Level 2: Learning
This level determines whether the participants actually learned what they were supposed to learn as a result of the training session. It measures the participant's acquisition of cognitive knowledge or behavioral skills.

Level 3: Behavior
Level 3 focuses on the degree to which training participants are able to transfer learning to their workplace behaviors.

Level 4: Results
The last level moves beyond the training participant to assess the impact of training on organizational performance.

The Training Cycle

Following the training cycle, or closed loop process approach, our level 1 evaluation tools and strategies should be designed to capture reactions from participants that reflect our assessment and course design and delivery efforts. That said, level 1 evaluations should be subjected to the same careful attention to instructional design principles as other aspects of the course or program will be.

Following Donald Kirkpatrick's four levels of evaluating training programs, level 1 is geared toward ascertaining participants' *reaction* to training. If we ask participants for feedback about their whole experience with the training, rather than just an overall reaction to aspects of it, they become part of the whole cycle of the training process: the assessment, design, and delivery stages, as well as the evaluation and assessment/reassessment stages of the cycle. In this holistic approach, continuous improvement and quality are inevitable as the learners become collaborators whose input can contribute to continuous improvement within the training cycle. What a great example to model for other groups within the organization seeking to implement similar processes. The marriage of the concepts and tools from Shewhart, Deming, and Kirkpatrick form a powerful strategy that can grow and mature with the organization as it seeks to continually improve in all areas.

Focus on the Assessment Stage

The assessment stage of the training cycle typically involves research into all of the aspects of a sound training design. The research may be conducted by a training team consisting of one individual, several members, or an entire department that is scattered among different facilities. We begin by considering who is involved in the design and delivery process and include information that will help everyone involved. Although collaboration among team members is a vital part of course development, individual roles and responsibilities can be broken down as follows:

- Instructional designers are usually responsible for researching the needs, content, and appropriate methods of instruction.
- Subject matter experts provide content and performance information.
- Training coordinators negotiate schedules, make facility and instructor arrangements, and notify participants.
- Trainers or instructors deliver instruction.
- Training managers oversee projects and teams, manage budgets, and report on program results.

Whether one person or a team is responsible for the whole process, the assessment consists of an inquiry into many aspects of the training design:

- What do the learners need to know?
- What are the learning needs and objectives?
- What content will be included?
- What will the participants be expected to know or do as a result of the training?
- What methods of instruction will be used?
- What activities should be included to support course objectives?
- Who should deliver this course?
- Where should the training be conducted?
- What is the best seating arrangement?
- How should the training be scheduled?
- How long should the session last?

- What kind of incentives, if any, should be provided?
- How will we know the training was effective?
- Will the training taste like a bitter pill and will that be reflected in the ratings?

By considering who will benefit from results of a level 1 evaluation and the type and nature of the assessment questions, we can develop a comprehensive strategy that will provide valuable decision-making information to everyone concerned, upfront and proactively. A well-designed evaluation strategy can capture data about the whole assessment, design, and delivery process and how well the answers to these questions addressed the design of the instruction, the instructor selection and performance, logistics, and relevance and applicability of the training. Through direct questioning of participants for specific feedback about their whole experience, rather than just an overall reaction, they become collaborators in the design and delivery process.

The Level 1 Evaluation Strategy

The evaluation strategy should consist of two tools: a form for capturing participants' reaction to their training or learning experience as data and a tool for analyzing and presenting the data captured from the forms.

For both tools, the design principles involved are derived from several sources. From a designer's standpoint, knowledge management concepts, as well as standard technical writing practices and popular structured writing methods, inform the overall design of the evaluation form and analysis tools.

Level 1 Evaluation Form Design

A well-designed form takes advantage of a whole $8\,1/2''$ x $11''$ sheet of paper when you think of this paper not so much as a document but as a container (see Tool 28-1 on the CD-ROM that accompanies this book). Although many documents benefit from white space, this document is most efficient when it is thought of as a divided container that maximizes the utility of a small space. The form will be organized and structured around three main sections to capture and organize participants' reactions to different aspects of their training experience.

Evaluation Categories

First, the form should include basic course information, such as the title of the course, the instructor's name, and the date of the instruction. Second, the main part of the form is the evaluation section, where most of the data collection is focused (See Table 28-1).

This section is divided into categories that mirror questions asked and resulting decisions from the assessment, design, and planning processes. When considering what categories to include, it is most important to consider who will complete the form and design it from *their* point of view.

Third, provide a comments section. It is helpful to include some white space for each of the evaluation categories. Participants are more likely to provide honest information when they are not required to provide their names.

Each category on the form should contain carefully crafted statements so participants can reflect and respond. The evaluation will capture their reactions as ratings for every aspect of the training design and delivery process: the needs assessment, the clarity and appropriateness of the objectives, the duration and scheduling of the training, the facilities and support, the methods of instruction, and the instructor's performance.

Develop three to five statements for each category using language that will elicit thoughtful responses. Many of the statements you include, such as those addressing objectives, level of difficulty, and methods of instruction, directly address the initial needs assessment and will provide valuable information for that important aspect of the design-redesign process.

Table 28-1. Sample Evaluation Categories

Category	What to Evaluate
Training Design	Objectives Topics Pace Level of Difficulty
Instructor	Overall Performance Knowledge Time Management Responsiveness
Exercises	Helpful Meaningful
Application	Relevance (personal or professional)
Logistics	Facilities Seating Lighting Food

Make statements very specific and focused to help participants form an opinion as they read and reflect on them. This will help the reader to rate his or her level of agreement with the statement. Save questions that require detailed responses for the comments section. Table 28-2 provides some examples of statements that reflect the assessment and design stages of the training cycle to include in the evaluation section of the form.

A comments section is an important feature on the evaluation form even if it is often left blank. But rather than just leaving a block of white space labeled comments, help the participants by providing questions that relate directly to the evaluation section categories they just rated. A few questions allow participants to provide specific supporting opinions,

Table 28-2. Sample Evaluation Statements That Reflect Assessment and Design

Training Design Statements
• The training objectives were clearly communicated and met my satisfaction. • The pace of the training was appropriate for the topics covered. • The level of difficulty of the content was appropriate for me.
Statements About the Instructor
• The instructor performed well overall. • The instructor is knowledgeable about the subject matter. • The instructor practiced effective time management. • The instructor answered my questions adequately.
Statements About the Exercises
• I found the exercises valuable in helping my understanding of the concepts discussed and how to apply them. • There was an adequate amount of time to practice the new skills. • The exercises were helpful in learning the concepts covered.
Relevance Statements
• I will apply what I learned in my work. • I will apply what I learned in my personal life. • I will recommend this training to others in my department or organization.
Statements About the Logistics
• The seating arrangement was appropriate for the content and duration of the training. • Visual media and lighting were conducive to participation and learning. • Breaks, beverages, and snacks were ample for the session as it was scheduled. • The length of the session was appropriate for the topic presented. • I was able to see and hear the entire presentation.

suggestions, or concerns. In their answers, participants can provide descriptive data that might be useful when low ratings indicate research or improvement is needed, or to offer praise for something they liked about the session or event. Their input may be superfluous to the data; however, should low ratings occur for some aspect of the program, comments can be the first stop in researching problems, root causes, and even suggestions for improvement. You don't need a question for each statement, just one for each category, as in Table 28-3.

Computer-Based Training

As distance education increasingly becomes the norm and choices abound, the market for CBT has resulted in myriad new and exciting training products and services. And as human resource and training professionals can attest to, the mountains of flyers, demo CD-ROMs, and persistent telemarketers are downright staggering. A well-chosen CBT product or program can be a highly appropriate method for bringing much needed instruction to those who need it—when and where they need it.

Choosing the most effective program, however, can be confusing and overwhelming. Unfortunately, many seemingly great products are actually very content- or media-centered, showcasing the vast knowledge of the subject matter experts or the creative talents of the programmer. Video, animation, graphics, and clever little "click on" devices can be as misleading as any Hollywood movie set—great façade, but nothing inside. On the other end of the spectrum, highly technical material may be too complex and beyond

Table 28-3. Sample Evaluation Questions for Comments Section

Question	Category to Support
What topics would you have like to have spent more or less time on?	Design
What might you suggest the instructor do to improve his or her effectiveness?	Instructor
What was most useful about the exercises?	Exercises
What changes would you recommend to improve the course to make it more effective?	Application
What are your suggestions concerning improvement of the facilities and accommodations in the future?	Logistics

the needs of the users. Application of sound educational principles and learning theory can anchor us in reality when we are tempted by technological illusion or overly impressed with content density.

A well-designed CBT program reflects unrelenting insistence that objectives, content, and methods be learner centered. In assessing the appropriateness and evaluating the quality of computer-based programs, assessors should

- Develop awareness of the CBT development process.
- Conduct thorough informal assessments of the target audience.
- Be methodical, using a form that incorporates into its design the considerations of the target audience.
- Remain focused on the needs of the learners—even when the graphics and sound effects are exciting and entertaining.
- Compare similar programs. You may find that the less expensive program. actually meets the needs of your learners better than the glitzier model.
- Maintain records of assessments for future reference.

CBT presents us with many important reasons for conducting level 1 evaluations. The statements or questions are slightly different on a CBT evaluation form (see the example provided in Tool 28-2 on the CD-ROM) but will reflect the same closed loop process: assess, design, deliver, evaluate, assess/reassess. Sections on the CBT evaluation form should focus on design principles and include several specific ratings for structure, objectives, content, instructional methods, technical quality, and overall impression. Whether you are purchasing a CBT or developing one, consider user testing and evaluating the program using a structured form before releasing it to your organization. This will help to focus reactions and feedback, important because it is very easy to lose sight of training objectives when you get distracted by the bells and whistles, especially if they don't work the way they should. And although some CBT programs are very expensive and can serve your organization's needs for flexible schedules and remote locations, sometimes behind the bells and whistles there is little substance or even technical glitches.

What to Do with the Data

Whether for classroom or CBT, when we think of the process as data collection, a form serves as a vessel for capturing the data, but it is not very useful for analyzing data. In comes the spreadsheet. Spreadsheets are useful tools in this process because once they have been designed and all of the calculations are formulated, they can be used on an ongoing basis to bring your data collection activities easily into the analysis and presentation steps of level 1 evaluation. The spreadsheet design should mirror the evaluation form itself, including rows for training sessions held and columns for each of the categories on the evaluation form. For each session, ratings from each form are added together and the

 categorical ratings averaged, automatically. (Tools 28-3 and 28-4 on the CD-ROM are Microsoft Excel spreadsheets designed to capture and average data, and Tool 28-5 provides an explanation of how to use them.)

The resulting spreadsheet data should produce a chart that also mirrors the evaluation form, with averaged ratings for each of the evaluation categories: design, instructor, application, exercises, and logistics. Compare Figures 28-3 and 28-4. As you can see, Figure 28-3 is too general to provide any meaningful information for decision making. In Figure 28-4, the combination bars on the chart are divided by different shades, indicating specific results based on the averaged ratings for each category. Which chart is more informative?

Analyzing the Data

Figure 28-4 with its combination bar chart, data labels, and text boxes is more informative for a few reasons. The data bars are divided shaded sections that show the averaged ratings for each category from the level 1 evaluation form. Notice that Figure 28-4 also includes a legend, along with actual values in the shaded bars. In addition, there are notes that tell the story behind low ratings. This is an extremely effective strategy when presenting data to others. Do the analysis and research work upfront and provide as much information as possible to eliminate the possibility of getting stuck in lengthy explanations or off track from the reason for meeting. Figure 28-3 only presents general questions, whereas Figure 28-4 presents answers.

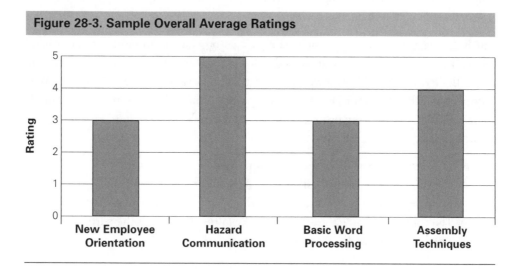

Figure 28-3. Sample Overall Average Ratings

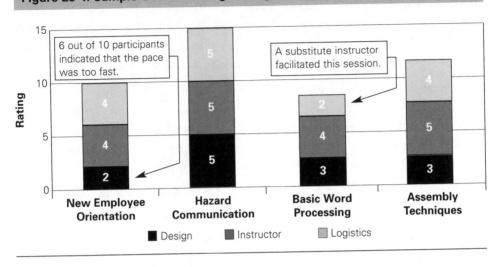

Figure 28-4. Sample Overall Average Categorical Ratings

If the spreadsheet is designed well, it can easily be used to enter the data from the forms for all training events on an ongoing basis. This enables all sorts of data analysis where elements of the training—relevance, for example—can be analyzed independently of the other categories. In Figure 28-5, the training manager was able to share with her team that the assessment stage decision-making process behind determining what training should be provided to the organization was yielding reactions no lower than a 3.5 out of 5. She was able to account for the low rating (3.5) and reported the changes that were implemented after determining the root cause—which she ascertained from the comments section on the evaluation forms.

Analyzing data can be as simple or as complex as you make it. In most cases, our needs are informal and should not be subjected to formal statistical techniques. It may be helpful to think of the individuals involved in the training design and delivery process. What information will help them? Develop your reporting around their needs and focus on the training design and delivery process. Combination bar charts can be used to analyze and provide a variety of information:

- Key design aspects of a course that is presented frequently
- Consistency of ongoing sessions of a course or group of courses
- Periodic reports presented at quarterly management review meetings
- The courses and programs that are really hitting home with the participants
- Immediate feedback about a new training course.

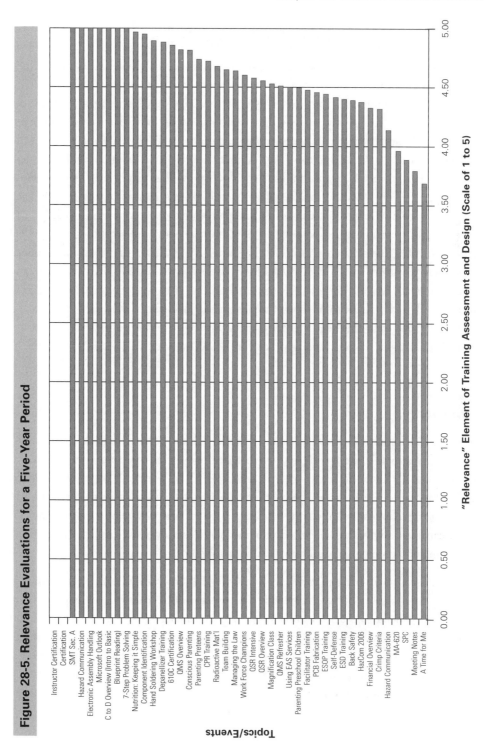

Figure 28-5. Relevance Evaluations for a Five-Year Period

One of the main aims of collecting data is avoiding extreme or emotional reactions without sufficient information. Use the data collected to avoid knee-jerk reactions and *over-reactions* resulting in unnecessary or premature decisions to spend excess money on a CBT, cancel a course, or dismiss an instructor. In other words, use data to create a window that allows you to see your processes in action. The knowledge captured from the data can be used to develop effective decision-making abilities that go beyond event level reactions and treat situations according to their context. The data alone are not the answer; data are only an indicator and should not be used without understanding the context (Kim, 2002). Data should trigger questions that can be used to develop a clearer picture of a situation that may have simply been a random event, or may have deeper, underlying issues that will result in a pattern of repeated occurrences. By asking the right questions, it is possible to develop a deeper understanding of the real issues and then develop an appropriate response. Was this a one-time occurrence? Or is there a pattern in the data? Does there seem to be a trend? If there is a trend, what seems to be the underlying structure of the situation (Senge, 2006)? What questions should you ask to improve the design and delivery of the course? By asking questions that get to the heart of the matter, you can use the information to inform your re-assessment of the training process to close the loop in a spirit of continuous improvement.

Summary

Data alone do not provide answers. Involve everyone in the design and delivery process—managers, instructors, designers, and subject matter experts—by sharing the data and talking about it. One of the most powerful outcomes of this work is the ability to align and sustain the focus of team members who are looking at the data you have presented in easy-to-interpret, meaningful charts. The resulting dialogue can help to foster advanced understanding and problem-solving capability. When improvements are made, continue the closed loop training cycle and review the data again.

Never underestimate what participants know about their learning needs. The simplest and sometimes most important training needs assessment begins with a simple question: What do you need to learn to improve your performance? When a training solution evolves from the answer to this question, an appropriate evaluation of their training might consist of one question directed to the learners, as well: "Did you learn what you needed to learn from this training experience?" Simplistic? Yes. Appropriate? Absolutely. In fact, when really effective assessments are performed, level 1 evaluations may be all that are needed.

Finally, be proactive. Include questions about what evaluation method will be used during the assessment stage of the training cycle and maybe you and your team will be able to advance the level of evaluation that is performed and become increasingly less reactive in your approach to measuring the effectiveness of training.

About the Author

Nancy Kristiansen draws from more than 30 years in the electronics industry to serve as a training and organization development consultant, independently and through a partnership with Blackfox Institute. Having earned her master's degree from Suffolk University, she has branched into new territories, including becoming an adjunct faculty member for Saint Joseph's College of Maine in its highly innovative MBA quality leadership program. Her own continued development rests in her conviction that training and development is a helping profession and that teaching is a learning process. Her practice is founded on a belief that effectiveness in any endeavor is achieved through balanced management of discipline and creativity.

References

Deming, W. Edward. 2000. *Out of the crisis.* London: MIT Press.

Kim, Daniel. 2002. *Foresight as the central ethic of leadership.* Indianapolis, IN: The Greenleaf Center for Servant-Leadership.

Senge, Peter M. 2006. *The fifth discipline: The art and practice of the learning organization.* Rev. ed. New York: Doubleday.

For Further Reading

Carey, Lou, and Walter Dick. 1996. *The systematic design of instruction.* New York: Harper Collins College Publishers.

Kemp, Jerrold E., Gary R. Morrison, and Steven M. Ross. 1998. *Designing effective instruction.* Upper Saddle River, NJ, and Columbus, OH: Merrill.

Kirkpatrick, Donald L. 1998. *Evaluating training programs: The four levels.* 2d ed. San Francisco: Berrett-Koehler.

Kristiansen, Nancy. 2004, February. Making smile sheets count. *Infoline* 0402, eds., M. Morrow and T. Estep. Alexandria, VA: ASTD.

Ross, Rick, Bryan Smith, and Charlotte Roberts. 1994. The wheel of learning. In *The fifth discipline fieldbook,* eds., P.M. Senge, A. Kleiner, C. Roberts, R.B. Ross, and B.J. Smith. New York: Currency/Doubleday.

Tufte, Edward R. 1997. *Visual explanations, images and quantities, evidence and narrative.* Cheshire, CT: Graphics Press.

Tufte, Edward R. 2001. *The visual display of quantitative information.* Cheshire, CT: Graphics Press.

Risher, Howard, and Fay Charles. 1995. *The performance imperative: Strategies for enhancing workforce effectiveness.* San Francisco: Jossey-Bass.

Chapter 29

Level 2: Learning— Five Essential Steps for Creating Your Tests and Two Cautionary Tales

William Coscarelli and Sharon Shrock

In This Chapter

- ➢ Learn the value of well-designed level 2 assessments
- ➢ Understand the distinctions between norm-referenced tests and criterion-referenced tests
- ➢ Learn the five essential steps of creating effective, valid tests

---

Any organization can vastly improve its level 2 assessments with little additional investment. Testing properly costs little more than testing improperly and yields significant results for the individual and the organization. Testing is important in that it provides feedback to the learner about his or her competence, it helps the organization determine whether a person can do the job, it informs the training function of the effectiveness of instruction, and it provides the foundation for level 3 and 4 assessments.

Organizations that think sophisticated testing is too expensive should at least consider that resources they currently spend on testing may very well be wasted and that in most instances testing correctly is no more expensive than testing incorrectly. This chapter describes five fundamental steps that should be considered in creating any level 2 assessment and then concludes with two cautionary tales on the process and outcomes of testing well.

Five Essential Steps for Creating Your Tests

As you contemplate creating level 2 assessments, the first distinction you need to understand is the difference between norm-referenced tests (NRTs) and criterion-referenced tests (CRTs). NRTs are designed to sort test takers in relation to one another. They are useful for selecting and ranking people. NRTs can be very useful when we have a large number of people to choose from for a limited number of positions or ranks. The SAT, ACT, and other such tests are NRTs that work well for their purposes. Creating a valid NRT requires a different set of techniques and assumptions than are commonly found in the corporate world. The danger of NRTs in corporate training situations is that, without reference to specific competencies, what test takers can actually do is unverifiable.

CRTs, by contrast, define the performance of the test taker against a given standard, for example, "initiates the landing gear at the proper time and altitude." In the world of training we hope for the kind of outcome where all who are trained succeed. Thus, we want to create a test that allows us to measure this positive outcome. The technology for creating a CRT is different from that for creating an NRT and understanding and implementing the full process is especially important in high-stakes situations where health, safety, or legal consequences must be managed. However, even if the full model for CRT development isn't or can't be implemented, a basic understanding of the CRT development process should be essential knowledge for any trainer or performance technologist. Figure 29-1 illustrates this full process.

The first step in the process is the analysis of the job content. All valid CRTs (and successful legal defenses) begin with this step. With a certain understanding of the job skills, instructional objectives are usually created for training, and the subject matter experts (SMEs) who created the job analysis sign off on their validity. With the formal documentation of the job-task analysis complete, the developer can then create any cognitive or performance items that would be used to assess test-taker skills. The items are then reviewed by the SMEs for their validity. An initial pilot of the test follows and is followed by the statistical analysis needed to create a reliable test and parallel forms or item banks. A passing score for determining mastery is then set, and the reliability of the test can be established. Finally, the score can be reported, although it is critical to note that with CRTs you should only report a master/nonmaster distinction. CRTs do not allow for rank ordering of test takers. Of course, throughout the process there should be continuous

Figure 29-1. The Criterion-Referenced Test Development Process

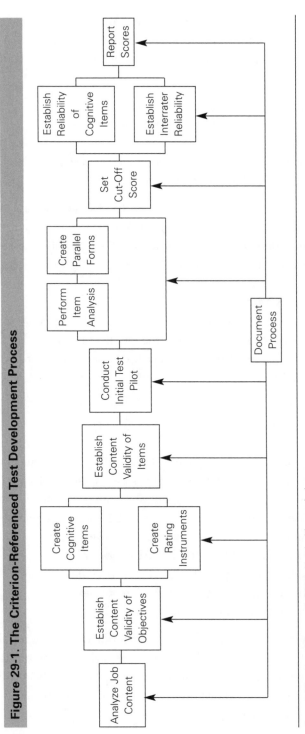

Source: Shrock and Coscarelli (2007). Used with permission.

513

documentation for both professional review and legal defense. We realize that not all situations require use of the full model, but it has been our experience that quality CRT development addresses at least five steps from the model that will provide the best outcome for the effort:

1. Analysis—Determine what to test
2. Validity—Determine if the test measures what it purports to measure
3. Construction—Write the test items
4. Standard setting—Establish a legally defensible cut-off or mastery score
5. Reliability—Show that the test provides consistent results.

 Each of these steps will be summarized in the following pages. The focus in each step is on the techniques that are important, powerful, and doable in most organizations. For further help in developing test items, refer to the test-writing checklist provided on the accompanying CD-ROM (Tool 29-1).

Analysis—Determine What to Test

The validity of your test depends entirely on your ability to determine what you are going to assess. Your goal here is to create a test that looks like the job that the test takers do, not a test that looks like most of the tests that we have taken in school. There are two strategies for implementing this advice:

- Use more performance tests
- Test at the top of the skills hierarchy.

Performance tests. A performance test relies on a rater who uses the proper rating tool to observe and record the performance of the test taker or to assess the quality of a product that was produced during an assessment. The test administrator uses a rating scale to assist in the observation and scoring of the performance or product. Performance tests are often a better choice than cognitive (or so-called knowledge) tests, even though most of us have more experience with taking tests of the latter kind. The primary issue in deciding between the two is determining which type of test is a better reflection of what test takers must do on the job. However, as technology has evolved, more and more jobs blur the distinction between cognitive and performance test designs.

Successful performance tests usually require careful preparation by the rater to ensure all logistics—such as proper location, materials, and so forth—are managed before the assessment. Using multiple raters, training them well, and verifying their reliability are three issues to consider if you are working with high-stakes tests in which safety or significant costs are associated with performance.

Top of the skills hierarchy. Most of us are familiar with the use of hierarchies to describe or visually represent the components of a job. The most powerful—and most efficient—way to create a test that matches the job is to base the test on the higher super-ordinate skills.

The point here is that level 2 assessments are most efficiently created to measure the highest strata of these hierarchies, not the lower levels. The highest levels reflect the nature of the job to be accomplished by those who pass the test; therefore, measuring them improves job relatedness. Furthermore, the higher levels of a hierarchy subsume the lower levels, so if we measure at the higher levels, we automatically determine competence in the subordinate skills. For example, if we want to measure the competence of loan officers, we are well advised to give test takers loan applications in response to which test takers must make "loan" or "no loan" decisions. Instead, too many test writers compose items that require recall of the rules for making such decisions. In fact, the single most common error in test design is the tendency for untrained test developers to write questions at the bottom of the hierarchy. Without training, many test developers write tests that look like the majority of tests they have taken through their school years. And these tests tend toward low-level memorization questions rather than items that assess higher-level skills such as application or analysis.

Validity—Determine if the Test Measures What It Purports to Measure

Validity means that the test measures what it claims to measure. While a number of types of validity exist, content validity is the most important. Content validity is established through the use of SMEs who review the items and formally certify that the test measures what it is supposed to measure. It is the most important form of validity from both training and legal perspectives.

Establishing content validity is the most cost-effective way to address the validity issue for most organizations giving CRTs. Establishing content validity is a straightforward matching process. Content experts are identified, and their credentials for serving as experts are documented. Then these experts are given the competency statements (or objectives) upon which the test was based and the test items or rating scales. For each item or point, the experts judge whether the desired competency is or is not being measured. The test is revised until the experts agree that it has content validity. Content validity helps ensure and document the job relatedness of the test, a critical hurdle if litigation over test results is pursued.

Construction—Write the Test Items

A common tendency in organizations is that when a test needs to be created, the developer, with no real training in test design and development, skips the first two steps:

analysis and validity. The developer's first reaction is to write items or performance scales. Skipping the first steps and beginning with item writing is akin to constructing a building without a blueprint. Our advice at this point is to create checklists to support performance tests and to write multiple-choice items above the recall level for cognitive tests.

Checklists. Performance tests require instruments to assess the skill or product being observed. Descriptive or numerical scales (scales that only have words, such as superior, excellent, average, and poor; or numbers, for example 1 to 7) are unreliable and should be avoided. The checklist that breaks down the process or product into a series of binary choices, for example, "present" or "absent," is the most reliable rating tool available.

Multiple-choice items above the memory level. For the traditional paper-and-pencil or computer-displayed test, the single most useful technique is to create items using the multiple-choice format. Multiple-choice items reduce the chances of guessing the correct answer; they can be written to assess higher-level thinking skills, such as comprehension, application, and analysis; and are easily and reliably scored both for score reporting and for statistical analysis of item quality.

The most common hurdle for the new test designer is to write tests that do more than simply measure the ability to memorize information. The easiest way to determine if you are writing items at the higher cognitive levels—which is where most jobs operate—is to create items that use previously unencountered examples of situations, concepts, or principles. Learning to write such novel items turns out to be a difficult task for new test developers. Usually there is a need for practice and feedback in a workshop setting that clarifies the job-objective-test item link. However, once the item writers master this skill, the time spent proves well worthwhile as the final test will be one that operates at the job level, not at the memorization level. (When management starts doubting the value of training because workers pass the test but can't do the job it was designed to test, the most likely cause is that the test was written at the memory level. Management calls for level 3 and 4 evaluations of training are often really symptoms of bad level 2 test design.)

Standard Setting—Create a Professionally and Legally Defensible Cut Score

CRTs are developed to determine who has mastered the material or performance and who has not. CRTs do not allow subtle distinctions between test-taker scores as is the case with NRTs. The only distinction CRTs allow among test takers is pass or not pass. You can't decide that a score of 80 is significantly different than a score of 85 if both scores fall into the same classification, for example, "master." (This quality often creates concern among managers who are looking for ways to rank order people.) The tendency of organizations to set passing levels based on tradition ("passing is always 85 percent here") is neither professionally nor legally defensible.

There are three common approaches to standard setting: informed judgment, conjecture, and contrasting groups. Of these three the most commonly used method is probably the Angoff technique, which is one of the conjectural approaches. The Angoff technique uses two to three SMEs to review the items and estimate the probability that a minimally competent test taker would pass the item. (Note that minimally competent doesn't mean incompetent. For example, the minimal competence level of professional pilots is very high.) Each judge's estimate is expressed as a decimal (from 0–1.0), and the estimates are summed to determine a raw cut score for mastery. Judges can then average and negotiate the final cut score for the test. Over time, the Angoff technique has proven to be efficient, effective, and legally defensible. It isn't an immediately intuitive process, but with practice, most SMEs seem to grasp the principles.

Reliability—Show That the Test Provides Consistent Results

Reliability means consistency; it means that you will get similar scores given similar situations. Reliability is a fundamental property of all well-developed tests; no test can be valid if it is not reliable. It is important to understand that with CRTs reliability means consistency of a master/nonmaster decision. Traditional NRT methods such as Cronbach alpha or Kuder-Richardson should be avoided because they do not meet CRT assumptions. Our advice here is to skip the formal calculation of reliability for cognitive tests and calculate a percentage of agreement among raters to determine the interrater reliability of performance tests.

Skip the reliability calculation. Any traditionally schooled test and measurement professional might cringe at this advice, but there are some strong arguments for skipping this step. First, human performance changes over time due to any number of factors such as practice or lack of practice in the performance. Attempting to establish a test-retest estimate of reliability is usually not warranted in most corporate settings. Second, because most CRTs are designed to assess distinct skill sets and are usually associated with mastery learning systems, most test takers will do well, which creates a skewed distribution of performance with most test takers scoring on the high end of the scale. These two conditions will result in low estimates of reliability if you use any of the traditional measures of reliability because the items don't interrelate and the spread in scores is not very great—which, for statistical reasons, negatively affects the quality of the reliability estimate.

Calculate a percentage of agreement. Many test administrators incorrectly assume that a good rating scale is all that is required to rate behavior or products of test takers reliably. However, the reliability of performance tests is a function of both the quality of the rating scale and the accuracy of the observers using the scale. It is important that all observers rate similar behavior and product attributes the same way. Therefore, the type of reliability most important for performance tests is interrater reliability.

It is important that any rating scale have clear and concise definitions for each of the rating points on the scale. Precision in creating the scale descriptors increases the consistency of rater judgment and thus scale reliability. If you are designing a test that would be considered high stakes, it is imperative that the observers be trained in using the scale and that the consistency of their judgments be determined. The easiest way to do this is to calculate a simple percentage of agreement between or among the raters. If the agreement is below 90 percent, however, other, more sophisticated statistical analyses are probably warranted as well as a reexamination of the checklist and rater training.

Two Cautionary Tales

When we first began our work in CRT, we thought of the work as an expansion of the "final" box in an instructional design model where data are gathered on learner performance and added into the formative evaluation process for consideration of revisions. What came as a surprise to us, however, was what happens when you take CRT seriously, develop tests that aren't subject to belittlement, and provide accurate results on test-taker behavior. We found that creating such a precise measurement of performance can create newfound opportunities for performance improvement as well as organizational resistance to testing as a process. The two tales that follow capture two issues we feel are important for test designers to understand as they interact with the organization as a whole.

You Can't Do Level 3 and 4 Evaluations If You Haven't Done Level 2

Here is Kirkpatrick's (1994) first piece of advice on the levels:

> Some trainers are anxious to get to level 3 or 4 right away because they think the first two aren't as important. Don't do it. Suppose, for example, that you evaluate at level 3 and discover that little or no change in behavior has occurred. What conclusions can you draw? The first conclusion is probably that the training program was no good, and we had better discontinue it or at least modify it. This

conclusion may be entirely wrong…the reason for no change in job behavior may be that the climate prevents it. Supervisors may have gone back to the job with the necessary knowledge, skills, and attitudes, but the boss wouldn't allow change to take place. Therefore, it is important to evaluate at level 2 so you can determine whether the reason for no change in behavior was lack of learning or negative job climate.

Kirkpatrick's point was driven home for us in a very telling episode. We were working with a global business that depended on call centers for managing a large part of the customer interactions. New hires were placed in a well-designed course to teach the essential skills of the position, but as they moved to the floor their performance degraded. As management became disgruntled they began to ask level 3 and 4 questions, as they are prone to do when things don't go well. Two managers lost their jobs over the performance of the call centers before the third arrived. The third manager arrived with the title of director of human performance. She began with a thorough look at the instructional system. She found the level 1 evaluations indicated learner satisfaction with the training and then moved on to the level 2 evaluations. She determined that tests that had been created were reliable and valid measures of what was expected for the job. She now knew the problem had to be elsewhere. Where previous managers had jumped to level 3 and level 4 questions, leading to frustrations and firings, she asserted to senior management that the problem couldn't be in training. Knowing that training wasn't an issue, and she could only know this because of valid level 2 tests, she began to consider other hypotheses. She left her office and began to systematically wander around the call center. Shortly thereafter she found the problem. The call center, it turns out, was operating with six different keyboards for the computers with the function keys inconsistent across different keyboards. The students left training competent with one keyboard system, only to be sent to the job where there was an 80 percent chance they would be working with a tool they hadn't been trained on—and to make matters worse, leaning over the cubicle to ask a colleague how to perform a specific operation was likely to lead to a wrong answer. Standardized keyboards solved the issue.

This case exactly mirrors the outcomes Kirkpatrick warned about. You can't be accurate in your level 3 or level 4 evaluations of training if you don't know what was learned, and only a valid criterion-referenced test will tell you that. Very often level 3 and level 4 evaluations are requested when management becomes dissatisfied with the performance of trained employees. Well-designed training and assessment will probably mean fewer level 3 and 4 requests from management, but those that come will prove most fruitful to the organization.

Serious Level 2 Assessment Is Really an Organization Development Initiative

We encountered one very large corporation with numerous regional offices that invested in the creation of a sophisticated appraisal instrument for measuring soft skills attainment among recent hires for the purpose of making a hire-fire decision. The appraisal was based on a high-fidelity role-playing scenario and came at the end of 10 weeks of corporate-based and office-based training. During the first evaluation of 12 new hires, three failed. The three, as it turned out, all came from one office. Because the test was valid it became apparent that the performance problem wasn't with the training or new-hire motivation. Clearly, the data suggested that the regional manager had not supported new employees as required. This revelation was entirely attributable to the use of an appropriately created and validated organization-wide level 2 test. However, this knowledge created the discomfort of having to deal with the manager's incompetence. The discomfort was evidenced in a series of phone calls from the one manager with the failing employees to other managers. The manager appealed to fears of a loss of control and loss of a job and fanned the flames of rebellion even before a single vice president became aware of the issue. With a sense of fear in the air, senior management chose to convert a sophisticated hire-fire program into a sophisticated coaching exercise.

The lesson here is that creating a test without understanding and managing the related aspects of the system is likely to result in failure. Criterion-referenced test designers who are engaging in high-stakes tests should consider that their role is as much about the human performance perspective of managing a systemic intervention as it is about test development.

Conclusion

The advice in this chapter is designed to help those who want to develop defensible CRTs that will yield useful information while expending minimal resources. The good news is that most organizations can improve their testing quality dramatically and take action to capture the benefits of performance assessment. Good assessment throws light in every direction, informing workers, training and performance staff, and management at every level. It is very costly to stay in the dark. If you are doing so, at least consider that an invalid test is not worth anything to anybody, at any time, for any purpose. So you might as well light the candle and do level 2 evaluation right!

About the Authors

William Coscarelli is a professor in the Instructional Design specialization at Southern Illinois University Carbondale and the former co-director of the Hewlett-Packard World Wide Test Development Center. He has been elected president of the International Society for Performance Improvement and the Association for Educational Communications and Technology's Division for Instructional Development. He is the founding editor of *Performance Improvement Quarterly,* author of the *Decision-Making Styles Inventory,* and co-author of the *Guided Design Guidebook* and *Criterion-Referenced Test Development.*

Sharon Shrock is professor of Instructional Design and Technology at Southern Illinois University Carbondale where she coordinates graduate programs in instructional design and technology. She is the former co-director of the Hewlett-Packard World Wide Test Development Center. She is a past president of the Association for Educational Communications and Technology's Division of Instructional Development and has served on the editorial boards of most of the major academic journals in the instructional design field. She is the senior author of *Criterion-Referenced Test Development.*

References

Kirkpatrick, Donald. 1994. *Evaluating training programs: The four levels.* San Francisco: Berrett-Koehler.

Shrock, Sharon A., and William C. Coscarelli. 2007. *Criterion-referenced test development.* 3rd ed. San Francisco: Pfeiffer.

For Further Reading

Browning, Anne H., Alan C. Bugbee Jr., and Meredith A. Mullins, eds. 2006. *Certification: A NOCA handbook.* [CD ROM]. Washington, D.C.: National Organization for Competency Assurance.

Cizek, Gregory J., and Michael B. Bunch. 2007. *Standard setting: A guide to establishing and evaluating performance standards on tests.* Thousand Oaks, CA: Sage Publications.

Downing, Steven M., and Thomas M. Haladyna, eds. 2006. *Handbook of test development.* Mahwah, NJ: Lawrence Earlbaum.

Eyres, Patricia. 1997. *The legal handbook for trainers, speakers, and consultants.* New York: McGraw-Hill.

Chapter 30

Level 3 Evaluation

Robert O. Brinkerhoff

and Timothy P. Mooney

In This Chapter

- ➤ Learn how level 3 evaluations can help improve learning effectiveness
- ➤ Understand different level 3 evaluation methods
- ➤ Get answers to two common questions about level 3 evaluations

---

When we think about evaluating training, an old but timely aphorism concerning weather comes to mind. Everybody talks about it, but that is about as far as it goes. This is especially true for evaluation beyond levels 1 and 2.

The purpose of this chapter is to take a candid look at level 3 evaluation, and explore what's working when human resource development (HRD) professionals undertake it, what are the challenges, and what's not working. We also take the view that level 3 evaluation is the most important and productive of all of the levels of evaluation and, we hope, explain our rationale in a way that will compel more practitioners to conduct useful level 3 efforts.

What Is Level 3 Evaluation?

The term *level 3 evaluation* comes from the seminal work by Donald Kirkpatrick in 1959 and is part of his four-level training evaluation taxonomy. Level 3 refers to gathering information on how (and how well) the skills, knowledge, and attitudes that were acquired in a training program are being used in workplace performance. In a word, level 3 is principally about *application.*

Most HRD professionals today are familiar with this term and the concept of level 3 evaluation. Many have also attempted to conduct evaluation studies using level 3 principles. Many of these same HRD professionals have also experienced some difficulties in the process and are less than satisfied with the information they obtain and the response this information elicits from senior or line management.

There are several reasons that practitioners give in response to the question as to why level 3 evaluation should be conducted:

- We want to see *if* trainees are actually using what they learned in a learning event.
- We want to see *how often* trainees are using what they learned.
- We want to see *exactly how* trainees are using what they learned.
- We want to see if training makes a *difference* in how people do their jobs.
- We do it because we know we *should* be doing it. (It is an HRD "good housekeeping" practice.)
- We want to prove that training makes a difference and *adds value* to the organization.
- We conduct level 3 evaluations because level 4 evaluations are too difficult.
- We do it to *justify the training* budget and satisfy skeptics that our training is making a difference.
- We do it because we are being pressured to show results.

To some extent, any of these reasons are probably good reasons to do something. But we believe there are even better and clearer reasons for level 3 evaluation, and we'll explain what these are. We also will make the case that being very clear about why to do level 3 evaluation is an absolute prerequisite for doing it well, because a lack of clarity about the reasons for doing it makes it far more difficult than necessary and undermines the credibility of the results.

The Logic of Training and Level 3 Evaluation

To truly understand level 3 evaluation—why, when, how, and so forth—one needs to understand the logic of training. Most kinds of training conducted in organizations currently are based on the belief that some employees need certain skills to perform their jobs correctly, and thus training is conducted to give them those skills. Trainees are then supposed to return to their jobs and correctly use the training-acquired skills to perform in their jobs. Eventually, so goes this rationale, the company will benefit from the application of these skills in increased revenues, higher-quality products, increased output, decreased scrap rates, and so forth. The benefit to the organization derives not from what was learned but from what actually gets used—that is, value doesn't come from exposure to the training or the acquisition of new capability. Instead value comes from the performance changes that the training eventually leads to.

There are other reasons that training is conducted, such as to avoid legal exposure, or to meet regulatory requirements to provide certain training, or simply to offer training because it is perceived as a staff benefit and may help recruitment and retention of personnel. These sorts of training do not necessarily require application of skills to produce value, and thus they are not the focus of our discussion.

So for most training, impact and value are achieved only when the training gets used to improve or sustain job performance. And this is what provides the basic reason for the existence of level 3 evaluation: Training is not done for the sake of learning alone but for the sake of providing value to the organization through improved job performance. We represent this logic in Figure 30-1.

Figure 30-1. The Logic of Training

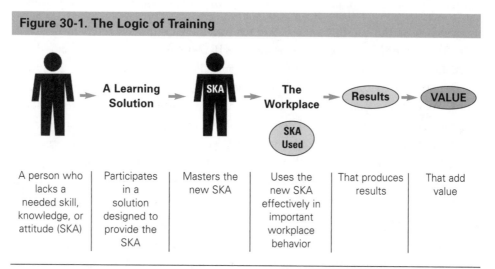

Source: Robert O. Brinkerhoff and Advantage Performance Group, © 2007. Used with permission.

As the figure shows, training logic operates such that a person who lacks a certain skill or knowledge participates in a training session intended to provide him or her with certain skill or knowledge—a capability. If the learning solution (a workshop, an online module, a job rotation, and so forth) is efficacious, then when the participants have completed it, they exit with that new capability in their behavioral repertoire. Then, they use that new capability in some aspect of their job performance. That skill application then results in an improved result in their job, which in turn contributes to some worthy organizational goal.

For example, imagine a training program that teaches service technicians to use a new time-saving troubleshooting procedure. Value to the organization will occur when service technicians correctly use the new procedure, which will in turn translate into greater productivity and quality (more repairs completed, more repairs completed correctly, and more problems fixed the first time), which should lead to lower costs and greater profits. In this example, the logic of training projects a behavior change (using the new procedure) that results from learning how and when to use the new procedure (the learning). Then, so goes the logic, a savings in time will occur, resulting finally in some benefits to the organization (for example, more productivity, more profit). Level 3 evaluation as applied in this example would focus on whether and why anyone was using this new capability, who was using the new procedure, how and when they were using it, and whether they were using it correctly. Eventually, of course, level 4 evaluation would pursue the question of how much these productivity and quality improvements were adding up across uses and how much value to the organization was being achieved as a result.

Let's go back to the question we posed in the beginning of this chapter: Why do you do level 3 evaluation? The most common reason HRD professionals cite for doing level 3 evaluation is to *prove* or document for the organization that the training they are providing does in fact make a difference (that is, that it changes behavior back on the job that is worthwhile to the organization). And this helps them justify their budgets, reputations, and the value of the learning and development (L&D) department to the organization. Thinking about this for a moment or two really leads to an unfortunate commentary on the state of our HRD profession, that we are undertaking evaluation primarily as a defensive strategy, and we have to justify our existence in this way. We label this motive as defensive, because we are doing it out of a need to defend our turf or our value.

We have seen, however, a number of progressive and enlightened HRD professionals use evaluation for purposes that are more strategic, more proactive, and more constructive. They are doing evaluation for the same reasons that they are doing training in the first place—to create value for the organization. Specifically, they are using level 3 (and level 4) strategically to change how well their organizations use training to drive organizational outcomes. In other words, they are not doing evaluation to *prove* the value of training. They are doing evaluation to *improve* the value of training.

How Level 3 Evaluation Can Yield Value

Level 3 evaluation can help improve the value of training in two primary ways:

- Uncovering what skills, knowledge, and tools from the training that trainees are using, who is using it, where and when they are using it, and how they are using it—so you can improve the learning solution itself and make it more relevant and effective.
- Identifying the performance system factors that facilitate or hinder using the skills and knowledge acquired in training—so you can work on strategies for ensuring that more of the new skills or knowledge get used by more people, more effectively, in more situations that are critical to their performance and will drive important organizational results.

In other words, the first use is to improve the training itself, whereas the second use is to improve the organizational conditions that affect the application of the training. Each of these purposes is worthwhile, and they are both interdependent. They are interdependent because good training itself does not ensure application—it only makes it more likely.

As the logic of training shows, the value of training is achieved only when training is actually applied on the job. And on-the-job application is driven in part by capability (whether you are able to do something), and in part—an even greater part—by the context in which you work. Consider this example:

Imagine that some people have just participated in some training, and imagine further that the training was good—it was relevant to their jobs, they really mastered new capabilities, and the capabilities, if used, could lead to improved value for the organization. Now, imagine that one of the people has just returned from this training and encounters the boss, and the following exchange occurs:

Manager: I see you're back from training. Did you enjoy the training?

Employee: Yeah, it was great! I really got a lot out of it and picked up some new ways to do my job.

Manager: Good, I'm glad you liked it. But, let me give you my thoughts now that you're back from this training. There are two ways we can look at things. There is the theoretical way they teach you in the training and the real-world way we do things here.

Employee: Hmmm, I see.

Manager: And...where are you now?

Employee: I'm here?

Manager: Right. And so how do you think you should do your job?

Employee: The way we do things here?

Manager: Right again! I thought you would understand. I'm glad we're on the same page. Now, feel free to try some of the things you may have learned in the training, but just make sure it doesn't slow you down or upset things from the way we like to do them here. OK?

Employee: Umm, OK! I get it.

Although this example may be extreme, it does illustrate the point that how well (or even if) an employee uses training back on the job is likely to be more influenced by the work environment (for example, a boss's support, day-to-day work pressures, conflicting performance incentives) than by what happens in the learning event—no matter how stellar the design, materials, and facilitator. All HRD professionals have seen plenty of examples of where factors back on the job got in the way of an employee using the new skills or knowledge that he or she recently acquired in a training program.

It Takes Two to Tango

Now, imagine the reverse of this scenario. Employees may return from training *not* having learned a new capability adequately, or having learned an irrelevant skill or knowledge. If these employees encounter a manager the opposite from our previous illustration, a manager who wants and expects the new capability to be used, it is still not going to lead to improved performance, because the employees did not learn the right information well enough in the first place. The result again? No value.

Our point is that the L&D organization cannot be held solely accountable for whether training gets applied on the job even when it does an outstanding job of imparting new capability. Nor can we expect a supportive performance environment alone to drive new or better performance—and the results that are derived from it—if employees lack the essential capability to perform better. Level 3 evaluation is an important tool for helping the L&D department help the entire organization. Learning new skills is often a necessary

---

❧ **Rensis Likert** ❧

Rensis Likert was a social scientist who spent much of his time researching human behavior within organizations. Likert is best known for developing the Likert scale, a linear scale used in data collection to rate statements and attitudes. An example of a Likert scale involves asking a participant to rate a statement on a scale of one to five: 1 = strongly disagree, 2 = disagree, 3 = neutral, 4 = agree, 5 = strongly agree.

Likert also developed the linking-pin model, which concerns the manager's role. The linking-pin theory suggests that a manager is a member of multiple groups, serving as a subordinate to upper management and as a superior to direct reports. The manager acts as the link between these two groups. For a manager to be effective in this position, he or she must be invested in the objectives, projects, and successes of each group.

In The Human Organization: Its Management and Value *(1967), Likert developed a theory of business management that identified four types of organizational systems:*

- *System 1: Exploitive-authoritative*
- *System 2: Benevolent-authoritative*
- *System 3: Consultative*
- *System 4: Participative-group.*

Likert argued that System 4, participative management, provided the best working climate. Participative management ensures that subordinates feel trust and support from management and are comfortable going to management with problems.

---

condition for improving performance and eventually improving organizational performance. But it is never a sufficient condition. We need both good new capability and a supportive performance environment to see worthwhile performance improvements that can and will lead to worthwhile organizational results. Level 3 evaluation, constructively applied, can help achieve both of these conditions.

Using Level 3 to Help Improve Learning Effectiveness

It is clear that the L&D organization should not solely be held accountable for whether training produces business impact, because so much of this impact is eventually driven by those outside of L&D—supervisors, managers, senior leaders, human resource systems owners, and all the others who create and control the performance culture and environment. But even though getting results is a whole-organization responsibility, L&D plays a very critical role in the equation. There are specific conditions that L&D can control that will drive positive behavior change and lead to performance improvement and measurable results. The responsibilities that L&D owns are all those that are subsumed by the concepts and practices of effective instructional design and adult learning, such as:

Identifying the right behavioral goals before the training. The behavioral goals are more than the learning objectives from the training program. Behavioral goals should bridge the chasm between training and the workplace and identify where, when, how, and with whom those new skills should be applied on the job. The more context-specific the behavioral goals are, the more likely the learning will be applied back on the job.

Including the right concepts and content. The content of the training program should be based on the behavioral goals. The content includes the concepts or principles that need to be understood, the skills that need to be learned, the models that will help the learner understand the concepts, and the tools and processes that will help him or her effectively perform the desired behaviors.

Including effective learning methodologies for conveying the information. The goals and content of the training program in conjunction with adult learning principles should drive the learning methodology for any program. Quality learning solutions avoid lecture and overuse of Microsoft PowerPoint slides. Instead, discovery learning, simulations, and structured role plays should be the foundation for the learning design.

Including the right examples in training content. Learning content should accurately and realistically reflect the actual job circumstances that employees will encounter. Although learning can certainly be achieved with novel content, it must also be sure to help people bridge the gap to their own context and realities.

Including skill practice with feedback. Skill mastery and durability of skills depends in a large part on practice. Good trainers know this and are sure to include practice exercises, in a "safe" setting, in their learning designs. And practice also requires feedback, so skills can be refined.

Including action planning. Helping learners plan their applications and helping them forecast obstacles also help to increase the likelihood of application.

These are just some of the more important learning design and delivery factors that drive the depth and durability of learning. These are covered more completely elsewhere in this handbook and in other publications and programs. They are pertinent to level 3 evaluation, for if we find during a follow-up inquiry that training skills are not being applied, it may mean that one or more of these factors is out of synch and or not aligned. Employees may not be applying their skills, for example, because their job environment factors may have changed since the training was designed and delivered, and the examples and practice sessions included are no longer relevant or realistic.

Thus, negative level 3 results (people are *not* using their training) may have root causes that lie in the design and delivery of the training program itself. This possibility should always be explored, and, if there are root causes that explain a lack of application, then the L&D function should take immediate action to make corrections.

But we must add the point that a level 3 evaluation is a "last resort" methodology and a poor, suboptimal, and late way to uncover training design and delivery failures. Good evaluation of the design itself, good adherence to the right instructional design processes, and good level 2 evaluation (measurement of learning mastery) should uncover these failures well before a level 3 evaluation is pertinent or implemented. It is somewhat akin to attaching motion sensors to a barn door long after one knows the horse has escaped.

We also recognize, however, that L&D practitioners may encounter situations where they are engaged in the process after design and delivery has taken place, and there is no alternative but to explore the relevance and quality of the learning by finding out what is actually happening on the job. It is also true that things change quickly in organizations, and so what was a great learning design at the time of delivery can be quickly overwhelmed by a change in market and workplace conditions. In this respect, a level 3 evaluation is a lot like a needs assessment and, in fact, is a great way for an L&D function to stay in touch with a dynamic workplace and the needs it is presenting.

Using Level 3 Evaluation to Improve the Performance Environment

Using level 3 evaluation to focus on improving the performance environment produces the greatest leverage and value. Why? Consider this fact: Most often, training programs across a broad sample produce reliable results. Some people use their learning in ways that get great results for their organizations. Some others do not use their learning at all. The large bulk of the remaining others may try some parts of it, notice little if any changes or results, and eventually go back to the ways they were doing things before. Never have we seen a program where absolutely everyone used their learning and got good results. Likewise, almost never have we seen a training program where absolutely everyone failed to use their learning at all.

And very often as well, the people who do use their training in improved workplace behavior help produce valuable results. Thus, the typical training program leaves money on the table. It does not produce anywhere near all of the value it could, because not enough people use the training. Given this, the challenge for getting more value from training is not about doing training better; it is about getting better results from the training that we're doing (assuming, of course, that it is good and important training in the first place).

This leads us directly to the really high-value focus for level 3 evaluation, which is to find out not just how and whether people are using their training, but why they are or are not using it. Level 3 inquiry can and should, we believe, look closely at the factors that are enabling employee application of learning and the factors that are impeding employees from using it. With this knowledge in hand, HRD practitioners are then empowered to provide useful feedback to the organization that can really leverage greater results. If, for example, perceived job priorities are keeping employees from taking the time to try out new learning, feedback about this can be given to their supervisors. Armed with this knowledge, supervisors can help their employees reprioritize their responsibilities and refocus their energies on applying new learning more strategically, thus dramatically increasing the effect of the training.

Level 3 Evaluation Strategy

The strategy for level 3 evaluation is to first discover to what extent training is being used or not being used. Assuming that there is some application, the second thrust is then to dig into the reasons that training is being used or not used. Sometimes, although not often, these reasons will lead one back to deficiencies in the training design or delivery. In these cases, feedback to the L&D function is provided, enabling leaders there to make the changes needed to resolve the problems. More often, though, the reasons that training is being used (or not used) will lie in performance factors under the control of managers and others outside of the L&D function. In these instances, the strategy directs us to provide feedback to the roles in the organization that can effect needed changes, such as supervisors, line managers, senior leaders, and human resources and other (for example, IT) system owners. These people have their hands on the levers that can drive changes in the performance environment, thus enabling dramatic increases in the numbers of people trying out new learning, and leading to more leveraged and strategic application of learning. Figure 30-2 illustrates the evaluation strategy.

Level 3 Evaluation Methods

There are many possible ways to peel the level 3 apple. The principal aim is always to uncover the extent to which training is being applied, and how well it is being applied, and

Figure 30-2. Evaluation Strategy

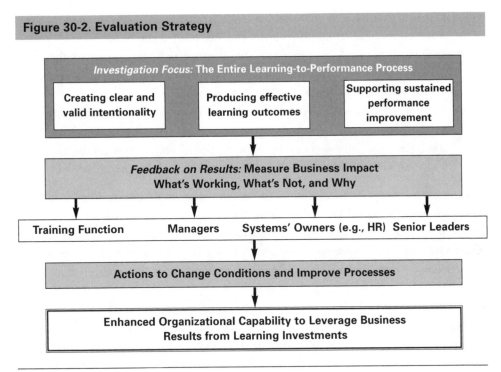

Source: Robert O. Brinkerhoff and Advantage Performance Group, © 2007. Used with permission.

why or why not, as we have seen. There are several ways to do this, some more simple and effective than others. We'll provide a summary listing of the most common methods, briefly noting the pros and cons of each. Then, we'll close the chapter with a brief description of the Success Case Method, a hybrid approach that takes the best of each method and is being used increasingly by organizations to conduct both level 3 and level 4 and even return-on-investment studies—all at the same time.

The focus of level 3 evaluation is, as we have said, the application of learning, or behavior. Studies of human behavior are notoriously problematic, as data collection methods are threatened and influenced by many sources of unreliability and bias. For example, if you were to ask your teenage son, as he is heading out the door, if he finished his homework, he'll likely respond "yes," irrespective of the reality of the state of completion. Consider for a moment these sources of bias in this little example:

- Your teenage son wants to go out, and he knows if he says "no" you will make him stay home. So to be able to go out, he says, "yes."
- Your teenager has a different definition of "finished" than you do. By "finished" you mean that he has done a thorough and complete job. By "finished" he

means that he has gone through the motions and has at least attempted the work. So truthfully from his perspective he is finished and he says, "yes."

- Your teenager doesn't see the value of homework, or he disagrees with this particular assignment. By "finished" he means that he is done trying and doesn't care to spend more time. So he says, "yes."

- Your teenager doesn't even really listen to your question. He simply says "yes" to anything you ask him because he's in a hurry to get out the door. You could have asked him if he had taken out the trash, robbed a bank, or noticed the nice new wallpaper in the living room. The answer would have been the same "yes."

In every case, the answer to your question was the same "yes," but it meant a different thing each time it was said. Any self-report methodology, such as a survey or interview, suffers from the same threats to accuracy—bias due to differing standards, misinterpretation, self-serving motivations, posturing. Because of this, research practitioners and evaluators have tried to develop more reliable and accurate methods other than self-report:

Direct observation. Sitting with the employee and watching the job performance directly, taking note of who does what, when, and so forth. This method is more accurate and less susceptible to misinterpretation bias, but is also expensive and impractical. It is also threatened by the bias of the person being observed knowing he or she is being watched. Thus, very often what you are observing is "best behavior," not routine, daily performance. In this way, direct observation is closer to a level 2 test (can they do it?) rather than a level 3 measure (are they doing it?).

Covert observation. This is similar to observation described above, but the observer is hidden and undetected. This is highly accurate, although also highly impractical, and perhaps unethical or even illegal. In any case, it is not a very promising level 3 method.

Analysis of records and other unobtrusive metrics. This is a highly accurate method and very bias resistant, because it gathers data about the effects of behavior rather than the behavior itself. So, for example, if we want to know if salespeople are using a new method for planning their sales strategy, we could collect samples of their sales plans and analyze them. Analysis of work records, work samples, and other "tracks" left by behavior is a very powerful level 3 method, although it may not always be practical or applicable. Another problem is that many records of behaviors tend to be recording less consequential aspects of behavior, and thus may not get to the heart of whether new learning is really being applied well or in the most strategic ways.

Surveys. This is the most common method for level 3. But although it is highly practical and somewhat easy, a survey also leaves a lot to be desired. First, people are pretty much "surveyed out" and are resistant to taking the time to complete yet one more. So response rates are low, thus leading to bias (you may tend to hear from extreme groups versus typical performers). The length of the survey also presents a problem to the researcher. To get all the information the researcher needs to address all the relevant issues, the survey is usually fairly long—25 to 30 questions is not unusual. The longer the survey is, the less likely the typical employee or manager is to take the time to complete it. If the survey is streamlined (forgoing some important questions to make it easier for managers to complete), it frequently leaves the researcher with many unanswered questions. Also, because surveys have to be reduced to numbers, they tend to ask forced-choice questions that may not get at qualitative nuances of learning application. As we have already explained, surveys are also subject to bias of people telling you what they think you want to hear, or what they know should be the "right" answer: "Of course I am using my training. I am supposed to, after all." People may also not trust your motives in asking. If they think the level 3 survey results will influence a performance appraisal, and thus a raise or promotion, or sanctions from their bosses, don't expect accurate results.

The Success Case Evaluation Method or SCM (Brinkerhoff, 2003, 2006). SCM is increasingly being adopted as an effective "hybrid" method for getting accurate, credible, and compelling level 3 (and level 4) results. The SCM combines survey and interview methods together in an effort to be as efficient, reliable, and valid as possible. A very brief survey is used first to ask participants to self-report the extent to which they believe they are using, or not applying, training they received. Because the survey is brief—just a few questions—and is done with an iron-clad assurance of confidentiality, response rates tend to be high. It is not unusual to get a response rate of more than 80 percent. Then, using a rigorous sampling process, a small number of respondents from the "high" and "low" application groups are interviewed in-depth. The interview documents actual application behaviors (level 3) and results achieved for the business (level 4). It also seeks out and explains the factors that are helping, or hindering application, so that these can be reported to parties outside the L&D function, where, it is hoped, they will be acted on to enable increasingly higher application rates.

To eliminate the inherent biases in self-report survey data, the interviewers are highly trained to seek authentication of the information. They don't accept the information at face value but ask probing questions that uncover specific instances and examples to avoid misinterpretation and control for biases. Companies using the SCM report that they are leveraging level 3 evaluation results to increase training effectiveness, sometimes at very dramatic rates. They also find that they are able to make a compelling business case for investing in training and ways to gain senior management commitment, because the SCM data tie actual application, results, and performance system information together into an actionable improvement plan.

Two Commonly Asked—and Commonly Misanswered—Level 3 Questions

In closing, it is worthwhile for us to reflect on two questions that we are often asked by our evaluation clients. These are important questions, and, too often, we have heard and seen misguided advice given in response.

How Soon After Training Should You Follow Up with Trainees?

It is a mistake to use a standard timeframe, such as after three months, six months, nine months, and so forth. The right way to determine the correct lag time prior to level 3 inquiry is to ask: How soon after the training is it reasonable to expect that people should have been able to apply their learning? In some cases, this may be a matter of days, such as with call-center employees learning a technique for routing calls more effectively. In other cases, such as purchasing executives learning a new method for conducting negotiations with suppliers, it may be necessary to wait a full quarter, depending on the cycle time for applying the skills. But always it is wise to remember this guideline: most training, if it is not applied in the first two to three weeks after training, will probably never be used.

What Courses or Programs Should Be Evaluated at Level 3?

Again, it is a mistake to have a set formula, such as 40 percent of our courses will be evaluated at level 3. The correct process is to ask, for each learning intervention: How important is it to our organization for this training to work? If the organization is gambling its future success on people acquiring and applying new skills, for example, to execute a vital new strategy, then it would be unwise not to conduct a level 3 evaluation, perhaps even several cycles of level 3. The less important it is that people use their skills, then the less the need for level 3. Of course, in these cases of low importance, one should wonder why the training is being conducted in the first place. The reality is that no training is likely to be applied by 100 percent of the trainees. So, one must ask: What is the consequence to our business if this training is not applied well, or is applied only by small numbers of people? If the business vitally needs broad and effective application, then by all means, level 3 is needed, as it can drive application quantity and quality upward.

Summary

The goal of level 3 evaluation—as with all training evaluation—should be to improve the value of training, not to prove after the fact that the training is valuable and worthwhile. Level 3 evaluation is a useful tool for helping the organization understand the extent to which trainees have changed their behavior on the job to improve their performance. It should also identify what factors facilitated or hindered this change in behavior. This type of information will help the L&D organization work more effectively with line management to ensure that the future sessions of the studied course and all other training implementations yield the greatest possible return for the organization. In this regard, level 3 can be a great forward-looking process for helping the L&D organization gain commitment from senior managers and line management on the whole-organization effort required to turn training into behavior change and business results.

About the Authors

Robert O. Brinkerhoff is an internationally recognized expert on training effectiveness and evaluation and is author of 14 books and many articles. A popular speaker, he provides keynote addresses and hundreds of sessions at professional association conferences and institutes. His latest books are *High Impact Learning* (Perseus, 2001), *The Success Case Method* (Berrett-Koehler, 2003), and *Telling Training's Story* (Berrett-Koehler, 2006).

Timothy P. Mooney is a vice president for the Advantage Performance Group, a wholly owned subsidiary of BTS Group AB. He is a seasoned performance consulting expert who specializes in assessment and organizational change. He works directly with clients on consulting projects, and is the practice leader for *The Advantage Way*. He is a frequent speaker and writer on achieving measurable business impact from training. Prior to joining Advantage in 2000, he served in a senior management capacity for DDI, working closely with leading global organizations.

References

Brinkerhoff, Robert O. 2003. *The success case method.* San Francisco: Berrett-Koehler.
Brinkerhoff, Robert O. 2006. *Telling training's story.* San Francisco: Berrett-Koehler.

For Further Reading

Drasgow, Fritz, and Neil Schmitt. 2002. *Measuring and analyzing behavior in organizations: Advances in measurement and data analysis.* San Francisco: Jossey-Bass.

Kirkpatrick, Donald, and James Kirkpatrick. 2006. *Evaluating training programs: The four levels* 3rd ed. San Francisco: Berrett-Koehler.

Kirkpatrick, Donald, and James Kirkpatrick. 2006. *Transferring learning to behavior: Using the four levels to improve performance.* San Francisco: Berrett-Koehler.

Phillips, Jack, and Ron Stone. 2002. *How to measure training results: A guide to tracking the six key indicators.* New York: McGraw-Hill.

Chapter 31

Level 4: Results

Donald V. McCain

In This Chapter

- ➤ Learn what a level 4 evaluation is
- ➤ Know when to conduct a level 4 evaluation
- ➤ Get guidelines for conducting a level 4 evaluation

A topic of interest to trainers and clients alike is what impact or results did a training initiative have on the organization. After all, clients support the training effort by supplying their time, sending their employees, providing dollars, sustaining evaluation efforts, and supporting environmental change to enable new knowledge, skills, and attitudes (KSAs). The training organization spends significant resources to design, develop, and implement learning experiences. Its credibility is at stake as it seeks to have the new KSAs transfer to the job and demonstrate tangible, bottom-line results. So, it is in the best interest of both the client and the training organization to provide a level 4 analysis.

This chapter defines the level 4 evaluation and discusses when to conduct level 4 analyses. The evaluation plan for level 4 provides a structure to discuss the business analysis and the evaluation process. Although several guidelines are presented, this chapter presents five specific steps for conducting a level 4 analysis. Because separating the variables to determine the results of training only is critical, ways to address this issue are presented, followed by an example to bring clarity to the process.

A Working Definition of Level 4 Evaluation

Level 4 evaluation is the process of determining what final business results occurred as a result of the training. It is the process of determining how much the training contributed to the shift in the business metric, identified in the initial business analysis and recorded on the evaluation plan. The effect is the actual shift in the business metric. Were there fewer grievances or defects? Was turnover reduced? Did sales increase? Did costs decline? Did we get the product to market faster? To provide answers to questions like these, the evaluator must monitor results to measure the outcome. After all, the change in the business metric is the reason for the training in the first place.

Identifying the business metric came from the initial conversations with the client. In those conversations, the following took place:

- You discussed and completed the initial evaluation plan.
- You identified the business metric. This measures the results of the training.
- You identified the tracking mechanism. In most cases, the metric is already being tracked by the organization.
- The client provided access to the data and to the people knowledgeable about the operations supporting the business metric. The evaluator must have access to the field.
- You determined the dollar value of the business metric.

The challenge is to identify the change in the business metric that is attributable to training. For example, if the training is designed to increase unit sales, the impact is the change in unit sales that are attributable to the training program. Not all increases are due to the training program. Impact or results are only the increase in sales due to the participants' involvement in the training program and the transfer of their KSAs to the job.

When to Conduct a Level 4 Evaluation

The evaluation plan provides a structure to guide your thinking about evaluation. The extent to which you will evaluate any given course depends on several factors. You will conduct a more extensive evaluation under the following conditions:

- The course is expected to be part of a core curriculum and have a long life.
- The training is linked to client's objectives and is important to meet organizational or corporate goals.
- The course supports a strategic initiative for the training organization.

- The greater the total cost, the more extensive the evaluation.
- The training has high visibility with senior management.
- There is a large target audience.
- Data are readily available.
- There is a defined business metric that has a dollar value associated with it.
- Change in performance is measurable.
- Participants are required to attend.
- Senior management requests the training.
- The redesign or development effort to improve the course is not significant.

Level 4 and the Evaluation Plan

The evaluation plan makes this level of evaluation easier. The evaluation plan in Figure 31-1 is developed with input from and support of the client early in the design process. Notice that the four levels contain subparts, allowing more discrimination in data collection for decision making. The first area to complete is the business metric section, provided by the client. Then, for each level, you complete the matrix.

Figure 31-1. The Evaluation Plan

Business Metric(s):
(from business analysis) ——————— ——————— ———————

Level	What	Why	How	Sources	When	Where	Who
1 Reaction							
2 Learning Application							
3 On-the-Job Environment							
4 Impact ROI							

Source: Performance Advantage Group, © 2004. Used with permission.

The following discussion details each area of the evaluation plan. The columns "what" and "why" identify what you want to know and why you want to know it. The why relates to the decisions to be made. For example, the what and why could include questions similar to those in Table 31-1.

Once you determine what and why, the remainder of the evaluation plan indicates a process to gather the required information. The "how" refers to the methods used to collect the information. Some of the methods are better for one level than for another (for a resource to help you evaluate data collection methods, see Tool 31-1 on the accompanying CD-ROM). "Sources" are where you get the information. "When" refers to the timing of the collection of the information for your evaluation. "Where" is the physical location where the information resides. "Who" is the person or people responsible for providing the information. Table 31-2 provides a sample completed matrix with some ideas. You will need to align the information with your course and organization.

Evaluation for level 4 results is conducted after the training and in the field. The timing is a function of the skill difficulty and the environment. First, the more complex the skills, the longer it would take for a participant to get proficient, that is, a longer learning curve requires more reinforcement. Second, you must wait long enough for the environment to take its effect. It is not unusual for participants to go back and start using their new KSAs only to run into barriers. So there must be time to identify barriers. Third, there must be enough time for the business metric to shift. Generally, level 4 evaluation is conducted nine to 12 months following the training event.

Table 31-1. Sample Answers from an Evaluation Plan

What?	Why?
Did the business metric change?	Effectiveness of the training, meeting client's needs, value to the client, course continuance, course redesign or development
How much did the business metric change?	Value for the client, content for a communication plan, degree of effect, continued funding, allocation of resources
What part of the business metric change is attributable to the training?	Separate variables to see training's contribution to the impact, value for the costs, program continuance
Were there other benefits?	Added value for client relationship and communication, residual benefits

Table 31-2. Level 4 Evaluation Plan

Level	How	Sources	When	Where	Who
4	• Monitor performance records • Track business metric • Monitor performance contract • Monitor learning contract • Monitor action plans • Use interviews and focus groups • Use questionnaires • Make estimates • Use control groups • Analyze extant data • Use program cost worksheet • Conduct primary and secondary research • Use trend lines and regression analysis	• Extant data • Performance reviews • Performance and learning contracts • Action plans • Participants, peers, and managers of participants • External research • Internal or external experts • Professional organizations • External studies • Government • Vendors	Three to nine months after the training	On the job	• Evaluator • Participants • Managers of participants • Clients • Internal and external experts • Peers • Vendors • Course designers and developers

Instruments: Advantages and Disadvantages

The how refers to the method and instrument used to do the research. In selecting the method or instrument, you should also consider

- The time it takes to develop the instrument, and collect and analyze the information for decisions
- The skills on staff to develop data collection and assessment instruments
- The culture's support for a more or less intrusive methodology
- The knowledge and skills of the participants
- The use of the instrument
- The way feedback will be presented and to whom.

Guidelines for Level 4 Evaluation

Here are a few guidelines to follow in conducting a level 4 evaluation:

- Conduct levels 1, 2, and 3 evaluations first.
- Verify that there are learning objectives written for level 4.
- Allow enough time for the environment to take effect and for achieving business results.
- Demonstrate the causal link between the business metric from the business analysis or needs assessment and the training.
- If you can, measure both before and after the training. The before measurement gives you the baseline performance data, whereas the after measurement provides the change in the business metric.
- Continue to track the movement of the business metric.
- Conduct no more analysis than is needed to make your decisions.
- Separate the variables, that is, determine the effects of training vis-à-vis other factors that are changing the business metric.
- If possible, use control groups to help separate the variables.
- Put the business metric (which is the benefit) in monetary terms.
- Use appropriate statistical analysis.
- Select appropriate programs for level 4 evaluation. You will actually conduct very few level 4 analyses. Table 31-3 provides some factors to consider when determining which programs are best for a level 4 analysis.

Steps in Conducting a Level 4 Analysis

There are five steps to analyzing the results of a training program. These steps are discussed below.

Step 1: Conduct Business or Needs Analysis

The actual results or impact analysis process begins with analyzing the business needs, identifying the business metric, determining the value of that metric, and setting learning objectives. Barksdale and Lund (2001) in their book *Rapid Evaluation* provide several examples of business metrics. Some of these are listed in Table 31-4, as well as other measures.

Step 2: Develop an Evaluation Plan

The evaluation plan, Figure 31-1, was completed with input from the client. For level 4 evaluation, Table 31-2, you need to complete the evaluation plan for all four levels. Be as complete as possible.

Table 31-3. Training Program Criteria for Level 4 Analysis

Criterion	What You Need to Consider
Long Life	How long will this training course be offered? The longer the time, the stronger the case for level 4 evaluation.
Very Important	How important is this program in meeting the organization's goals? Is the course part of a strategic initiative? If so, you may want to consider level 4 evaluation.
Link to Program Objectives	Do the program's learning objectives state what is to be implemented and the change in the business metric? You want alignment among business metrics, statement of objectives, and the measurement.
High Cost	The higher the cost of program design, development, and implementation, the greater the need for level 4 evaluation.
Highly Visible	How visible is the program to senior management? The greater the visibility, the greater the likelihood that it is a good candidate for level 4 evaluation.
Large Target Audience	The larger the size of the target audience, the stronger the case for level 4 evaluation.
Data Readily Available	Is the business metric currently being tracked? Would it be a simple matter to collect the data for level 4 evaluation? If the data are not readily available or very difficult or expensive to obtain, you may not want to conduct a level 4 evaluation.
Mandatory Participation	Everyone in the organization being required to attend supports the need for level 4 evaluation.
Executive Request	If an executive is requesting the information, you will need to respond.
Levels 1, 2, and 3 Evaluation Already Conducted	Have previous levels (1, 2, and 3) of evaluation been carried out? If not, you will need to conduct a comprehensive evaluation of the training course.
Direct Cause and Effect	How direct is the connection or link between the training program and the business metric? The more direct the linkage, the stronger the case for level 4 evaluation.
Easy Conversion to Monetary Value	If it would be straightforward to convert the business metric to a monetary value, this fact builds a case for level 4 evaluation.

Table 31-4. Measures to Determine Effectiveness

Type of Measure	Potential Measure	Type of Measure	Potential Measure
Operations	• Revenue per employee • Time to delivery • Warranty claims • Cycle time • Returns • Unit costs • Scrap • Rejects • Number of accidents • Errors • Error rates • Defect-free products or parts	Customer	• Customer acquisition • Customer profitability • Customer retention • Customer satisfaction
		Employees	• Problem resolution • Safety incident rate • Delivery time • Employee satisfaction • Yield per employee • Overtime • Efficiency • Productivity
Productivity	• Number of calls answered • Response time to inquiry • Throughput time	Innovation and Creativity	• Product launch success • Product development • Suggestions for improvement
Management	• Employee retention • Employee satisfaction • Budget goals met • Safety goals met • Employee profitability • Employee law suits • Absenteeism • Tardiness • Turnover	Marketing and Sales	• Revenue per employee • Market share • Improved delivery • Cross-sell ratio • Percentage revenue from new product
Financial	• Operating income growth • Sales per employee • Revenue generated • Expenses as a percentage of sales • Expense ratio • Budget variance • Financial penalties • Inventory turnover		

Step 3: Design and Develop Instruments and Methodologies

In this step, you actually design and develop the instruments and methods for data collection. In some cases, the instruments are already a part of the program design, as action plans or performance contracts. In other cases, you must develop the instruments, for instance, surveys, interview and focus group protocols, and so forth.

For example, you may elect to develop a *survey* or a *questionnaire*. At level 4 you may want to include a reliability or confidence level to represent the degree of confidence the responders have in their estimates. This is discussed in detail in Step 5 below. The respondents indicate their degree of confidence by assigning a percentage to it in their estimate. A 100 percent confidence level indicates that they are positive in their estimate. Jack Phillips popularized this thinking in many of his workshops and books. See For Further Reading at the end of this chapter for some of his books.

You can elect to collect data through *interviews* and *focus groups*. Again, you may want to include a discussion of other factors affecting the results and use the estimate and confidence methods as discussed. Other methods include follow-up on action plans, performance contracts, observations, and performance tracking. Performance tracking allows you to determine a baseline of performance before the training. The performance is continually tracked until you conduct your level 4 evaluation. At that time, the difference between the pretraining baseline and current performance is the effect of training. A variation of this is the *trend-line* approach. Using previous information (at least six months before the training event if possible) you draw a baseline of the data and extend it into the future (beyond the point of the training event). Following the training, the actual performance data are plotted and compared with the original extended line. The difference between the two lines is the result of training. Again, you will want to separate the variables. This is discussed further in Step 5 below.

For the initial baseline trend line, you plot the data and then statistically determine the line of best fit. This line is then extended into the future. The trend-line method assumes that the forces driving the initial trend line will stay in place and have the same intensity of effect on performance. In essence, the future (extended trend line) is subject to the same forces as the initial baseline. This is a huge assumption.

You may elect to use a *control group* to conduct your level 4 evaluation. In the control group design, one group receives the training (experimental) and the other group (control) does not. You then compare their performance following training. Ideally, control groups need to

- Be demographically similar
- Have similar environmental influences or working conditions

■ Be isolated from each other (no communication)
■ Have participants of the groups randomly selected.

Step 4: Collect the Data

Now is the time to implement the data collection part of the evaluation plan. You have made decisions regarding instruments and methods, identified and developed the instruments, identified the sources of information and the timing, and identified the people responsible.

Step 5: Analyze and Interpret the Data

Based on the method selected above, analyze the data and identify nontraining variables affecting the change. Separation of variables is one of the most difficult tasks of evaluation. Some methods include using control groups, making estimates, and using trend lines. Again, Phillips has done extensive work in this area. The concepts are included in the *Handbook of Training Evaluation and Measurement Methods* (1997).

Control Groups

Using the control group design, one group receives the training (experimental) and the other group (control) does not. Compare performance following the training; the benefit is the difference between those receiving the training (experimental) and those not receiving the training (control), that is, Benefit = (Train – Nontrain). The result is then standardized in terms of percentage of job performance improvement. Calculate this by dividing the net benefit by the average nontraining or pretraining performance:

$$\text{Standard Training Impact} = \frac{\text{Net Benefit}}{\text{Average Nontraining Performance}}$$

An example will help clarify the use of control groups. Suppose there are two groups, Group A and Group B. Group B receives the training. The results are below in Table 31-5.

$$\text{Standard Training Impact} = \frac{500 \text{ (Posttraining: 900 Group B} - 400 \text{ Group A)}}{400 \text{ (Group A posttraining)}}$$

$$= 125 \text{ percent increase}$$

Table 31-5. Sample Control Group Results

Group	Production Pretraining	Intervention	Production Posttraining
Group A	400 units	—	400 units
Group B	400 units	Training	900 units

Because production of Group A remained the same, we can assume that no other factors other than training influenced the results.

In some instances, production may go up in both groups during the training. This is because something influenced the groups other than training (see Table 31-6).

$$\text{Standard Training Impact} = \frac{300\ (\text{Posttraining: 900 Group B} - 600\ \text{Group A})}{600\ (\text{Group A posttraining})}$$

$$= 50\ \text{percent increase due to training}$$

In this case, something influenced the control group (Group A) that caused the production to increase by 200 units. This reduces the effect of training, that is, something else influenced the production. At this time, you do not know what it is.

Table 31-6. Sample Control Group Results with Other Unknown Factor Affecting Results

Group	Production Pretraining	Intervention	Production Posttraining
Group A	400 units	—	600 units
Group B	400 units	Training	900 units

Estimates

For some reason, many HRD professionals do not put much faith in people's estimates. Yet, it is a fairly common practice. Estimates are based on individuals' experience and expertise and therefore are "informed" estimates. The key is to have the people closest to the data and who have the greatest relevant perspective make the estimates. These individuals are usually the participants, their managers, or internal experts.

This method, popularized and applied to training by Phillips, can be used in conjunction with surveys, interviews, or focus groups. You will want to ask the following questions:

- What percentage of the improvement is due to applying the training?
- How reliable is this figure? What degree of confidence do you have in your estimate? The respondents are to provide a percentage, with 100 percent being fully confident. You can improve the reliability for this method by adding this factor to your research.
- What is the basis for your estimate?
- What other factors contributed to the improvement? This helps with the separation of variables.

For example, in a focus group, you may state that, based on the data, defects declined from 100 per quarter to 60 per quarter—a decrease of 40 per quarter or 160 defects per year. You would then

- Ask the respondents for other major factors, other than training, that could influence the decrease in defects. The process is separation of variables. Include another category for minor factors affecting the results.
- Have respondents indicate what percentage of the improvement was related to each major factor. This should add up to 100 percent.
- Last, have them indicate how confident they are of their estimate. Again, this is a percentage. You could provide a table for them to complete (see Table 31-7).

In this case, the respondent thinks that training was 40 percent responsible for the decrease in turnover. In addition, the respondent has a lot of confidence in his or her thinking, 85 percent. This table also tells us that there was another factor that had a significant effect on the decrease in defects. In this case, there was an initiative that resulted in providing incentives for reducing defects. According to the respondent, the incentives had a greater effect on the decrease in defects.

Table 31-7. Confidence Levels for Decrease in Defects

Factors	Percent Decrease by Factor	Reliability or Confidence
Training	40	85
Career Path and Coaching	58	90
Other	2	98
Total	**100**	

Trend Lines

Phillips applied this statistical technique to training evaluation. To track performance you may use the trend-line approach. This is where you plot the data over time (time series). You plot the performance data on the X axis and the timeline on the Y axis (see Figure 31-2).

The first line to plot is the business metric using extant data, reflecting the movement of the business metric up to the point of the training (line A to A1). As noted before, it is good to have at least six months of prior data. You will use historical data for this. Then,

Figure 31-2. Example of Trend-Line Analysis

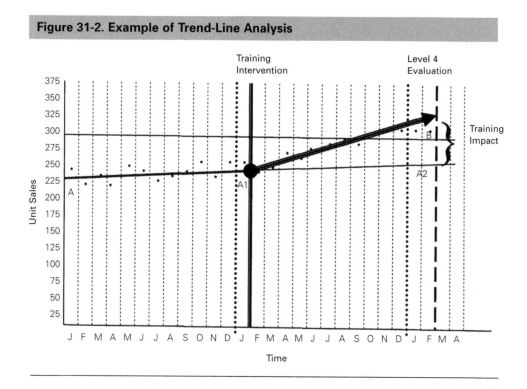

statistically determine the line of best fit and extend that line into the future to the point when you conduct your level 4 evaluation (line A1 to A2). This line represents the continuation of the business metric if there was no training intervention. Line A1/A2 is just the extension of line A and A1.

Following the training intervention, continue to track and plot the business metric.

At the time of the level 4 evaluation, you will statistically determine the line of best fit for the data points from the time of the training intervention to the time of the evaluation, line A1 to B. The difference between the data points at A2 and B represents the difference due to training.

As stated before, you must separate other factors (separation of variables) that could have affected the results. To do this, you combine two methods, including using estimates. For example, on completing the trend-line analysis, you have a change in the business metric. You would then use the estimate approach to separate the variables.

An example using the reduction in defects will reinforce the concepts. Assume that each defect represents a total cost of $2,250. This cost was established with the client.

Table 31-8. Estimated Effect of Different Variables on the Costs of Defects

Factor	A Percent of Estimated Contribution of Factor to the Decrease in Defects	B Percent of Confidence in Estimate	C Dollar Impact (Cost x A x B)	D Impact per Quarter (C x 40 reduced defects)	E Annualized Dollar Impact (D x 4 quarters)
Training	40	85	$2,250 × 40% × 85% = $765/defect/quarter	$30,600	$122,400
Quality Incentives	58	90	$2,250 × 58% × 90% = $1,174.50/defect/quarter	$46,980	$187,920
Other	2	98	$2,250 × 2% × 98% = $44.10/defect/quarter	$1,764	$7,056
Total	100	—	—	—	—

Using the previous information, you can now establish the annual savings accruing to the organization by reducing the number of defects by 40 per quarter. To summarize the situation:

- An organization is experiencing 100 defects per quarter.
- The human resource development (HRD) department conducted a training program to reduce defects.
- The number of defects dropped to 60 per quarter, representing a savings of 40 defects per quarter (benefit).
- The cost of each defect is $2,250 per defect (provided by the client in conjunction with HRD).
- The other factor affecting turnover was the implementation of a quality incentive program.

As you can see from Table 31-8, the quality incentive program contributed more toward the reduction in defects than did the training. Does this mean that the training did not achieve a positive return-on-investment (ROI)? Does it mean that the organization should put more resources into incentives? At this point, you don't know the answer because you don't have the cost information to determine ROI.

Now that training's effect has been determined, the ROI can be calculated by comparing total training costs to the dollar value of the net benefit. The benefit is the shift in the business metric due to training.

✍

About the Author

Donald V. McCain is founder and principal of Performance Advantage Group, an organization dedicated to helping companies gain competitive advantage through developing their human resources. He also consults in HRD processes, including design and development, competency identification and development, certification, evaluation, presentation and facilitation, and managing and marketing the HRD function.

McCain has a bachelor's degree in business administration, a master's degree of divinity, a master's degree in business administration with a concentration in human resources and marketing, and a doctorate in education in HRD from Vanderbilt University, Nashville, Tennessee. He is a member of the Society for Human Resource Management and the Academy of Human Resource Development. In addition, McCain is a former visiting professor at the School of Business at Tennessee State University and is also on faculty at the University of Phoenix and the University of Fredericton.

McCain is the author and co-author of several ASTD Press books, including *Evaluation Basics, Facilitation Basics, Facilitation Training,* and *Needs Assessment Basics* and has published several articles and evaluation instruments.

References

Barksdale, Susan, and Teri Lund. 2001. *Rapid evaluation.* Alexandria, VA: ASTD Press.

Phillips, Jack. 1997. *Handbook of training evaluation and measurement methods.* 3d ed. Houston: Gulf Publishing Company.

For Further Reading

Brinkerhoff, Robert O. 1987. *Achieving results from training.* San Francisco: Jossey-Bass.

Kirkpatrick, Donald. 1994. *Evaluating training programs: The four levels.* San Francisco: Berrett-Koehler.

McCain, Donald V. 2005. *Evaluation basics.* Alexandria, VA: ASTD Press.

Phillips, Jack, Patricia P. Phillips, and Toni K. Hodges. 2004. *Make training evaluation work.* Alexandria, VA: ASTD Press.

Robinson, Dana Gaines, and James Robinson. 1989. *Training for impact.* San Francisco: Jossey-Bass.

Swanson, Richard A., and Elwood F. Holton. 1999. *Results? How to assess performance, learning, and perceptions in organizations.* San Francisco: Berrett-Koehler.

Return-on-Investment

Jack J. Phillips

In This Chapter

- ➤ Understand what the ROI methodology is all about
- ➤ Learn to isolate the effects of and evaluate a program
- ➤ Gain benefits from using the ROI methodology

"**S**how me the money." There's nothing new about that statement, especially in business. Organizations of all types value their investments. What's new is the method that organizations can use to get there. Although showing the money may be the ultimate report of value, organization leaders recognize that value lies in the eye of the beholder; therefore, the method used to show the money must also show the value as perceived by all stakeholders. Just as important, organizations need a methodology that provides data to help improve investment decisions. This chapter presents an approach that does both; it evaluates the value that organizations get from investing in learning and development programs, and it develops data to improve those programs.

Value Redefined: The Value Shift

"Show me the money" represents the newest value statement. In the past, a learning program's success was measured by activity: number of people involved, money spent, days to complete. Little consideration was given to the benefits derived from these activities. Today the value definition has shifted: value is defined by results versus activity. More frequently, value is defined as monetary benefits compared with costs, which is return-on-investment (ROI).

Although this ROI methodology to "show the money" had its beginnings in the 1970s, it has expanded in recent years to become the most comprehensive, documented, and used approach to demonstrating the value of learning and development.

Many people are concerned that there is too much focus on economic value. But it is economics, or money, that allows organizations and individuals to contribute to the greater good. Monetary resources are limited and can be put to best use—or underused or overused. Organizations and individuals have choices about where they invest in learning and development. To ensure that monetary resources are put to best use, they must be allocated to programs that yield the greatest return.

The Show Me Generation

Figure 32-1 illustrates the requirements of the new show me generation. Show me implies that stakeholders want to see actual data (that is, numbers and measures) to account for program value. But financial results alone do not provide evidence that programs add value. Often, a connection between programs and value is assumed, but that assumption soon must give way to the need to show an actual connection. Hence, "show me the real money" was an attempt at establishing credibility. This phase, although critical, still left stakeholders with an unanswered question: "Do the monetary benefits linked to the program outweigh the costs?" This question is the mantra for the new show me generation: "Show me the real money and make me believe it." But this new generation of program sponsors also recognizes that value is more than just a single number. Value is what makes the entire organization system tick—hence the need to report value based on people's various definitions.

Value must be balanced with quantitative and qualitative data, as well as financial and nonfinancial perspectives. The data sometimes reflect tactical issues such as activity, as well as strategic issues, such as ROI. Value must be derived using different timeframes and not necessarily represent a single point in time. It must reflect the value systems that are important to the stakeholders. The data that indicate value must be collected from credible sources, using cost-effective methods; and value must be action oriented, compelling individuals to make adjustments and changes.

Figure 32-1. The "Show Me" Evolution

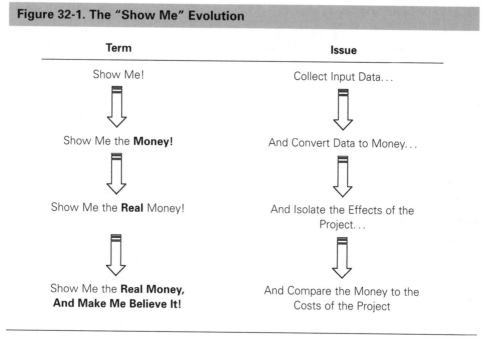

Term	Issue
Show Me!	Collect Input Data...
Show Me the **Money!**	And Convert Data to Money...
Show Me the **Real** Money!	And Isolate the Effects of the Project...
Show Me the **Real Money, And Make Me Believe It!**	And Compare the Money to the Costs of the Project

The processes used to calculate value must be consistent from one performance improvement project to another. Standards must be in place so that results can be compared. These standards must support conservative outcomes, leaving assumptions to decision makers. The ROI methodology presented in this chapter meets all these criteria. It captures six types of data that reflect the issues contained in the new definition of value: reaction and planned action, learning and confidence, application and implementation, impact and consequences, ROI, and intangible benefits.

Types of Data

The richness of the ROI methodology is inherent in the types of data monitored during the implementation of a particular performance improvement project or solution. These data are categorized by levels. Table 32-1 shows the levels of data and describes their measurement focus.

Level 0 represents the input to a program and details the numbers of people and hours, the focus, and the cost. These data represent the activity around a program versus the

Table 32-1. Types and Levels of Data

Level	Measurement Focus	Typical Measures
0. Inputs and Indicators	Inputs into the program, including indicators representing the scope of the project	Types of programs Number of projects Number of people Hours of involvement Cost of projects
1. Reaction and Planned Action	Reaction to the project, including the perceived value of the program	Relevance Importance Usefulness Appropriateness Fairness Motivational
2. Learning and Confidence	Learning how to use the program, content, materials, system, including the confidence to use what was learned	Skills Knowledge Capacity Competencies Confidences Contacts
3. Application and Implementation	Use of program content, materials, and system in the work environment, including progress with implementation	Extent of use Task completion Frequency of use Actions completed Success with use Barriers to use Enablers to use
4. Impact and Consequences	The consequences of the use of the program content, materials, and system expressed as business impact measures	Productivity Revenue Quality Time Efficiency Customer satisfaction Employee engagement
5. ROI	Comparison of monetary benefits from project to program costs	Benefit-cost ratio (BCR) ROI (%) Payback period

contribution of the program. Level 0 data represent the scope of the effort, the degree of commitment, and the support for a particular program. For some, this equates to value. However, commitment, as defined by expenditures, is not evidence that the organization is reaping value.

Reaction and planned action (level 1) mark the beginning of the program's value stream. Reaction data capture the degree to which the participants involved in the program, including the stakeholders, react favorably or unfavorably. The key is to capture the measures that reflect the content of the program, focusing on issues such as usefulness, relevance, importance, and appropriateness. Data at this level provide the first sign that program success may be achievable. These data also present learning and development leaders with information they need to make adjustments to help ensure positive results.

The next level is learning and confidence (level 2). For every program there is a learning component. For some—such as programs to implement new technology, systems, competencies, and processes—this component is substantial. For others, such as a new policy or new procedure, learning may be a small part of the process but is still necessary to ensure successful execution. In either case, measurement of learning is essential to success. Measures at this level focus on skills, knowledge, capacity, competencies, confidence, and networking contacts.

Application and implementation (level 3) measure the extent to which the program is properly applied and implemented. Effective implementation is a must if bottom-line value is the goal. This is one of the most important data categories, and most breakdowns occur at this level. Research has consistently shown that in almost half of all learning and development programs, participants are not performing at desired levels following solution implementation. Evaluation at this level involves collecting data about measures such as the extent of new knowledge or information used, task completion, frequency of use of new skills, success with use, and actions completed—as well as barriers and enablers to successful application or on-the-job performance. Data captured at this level provide a clear picture of how well the organizational system supports the successful transfer of desired knowledge, skills, and attitude changes.

Level 4, impact and consequences, is important for understanding the business consequences of the program. Here, data are collected that attract the attention of the sponsor and other executives. This level shows the output, productivity, revenue, quality, time, cost, efficiencies, and level of customer satisfaction connected with the project. For some, this level reflects the ultimate reason the learning program exists: to show the effect within the organization on various groups and systems. Without this level of data, they assert, there is no success. When this level of measurement is achieved, it is necessary to isolate the effects of the program on the specific measures. Without this extra step, alignment with the business cannot occur.

The ROI (level 5) is calculated next. This shows the monetary benefits of the impact measures compared with the cost of the program. This value is typically stated in terms of either a benefit-cost ratio, the ROI as a percentage, or the payback period. This level of measurement requires two important steps: first, the impact data (level 4) must be converted to monetary value; second, the cost of the program must be captured.

Along with the five levels of results and the initial level of activity (level 0), there is a sixth type of data—not a sixth level—developed through this methodology. This consists of the intangible benefits—those benefits that are not converted to money but nonetheless constitute important measures of success.

The Initial Analysis

Our research suggests that the top reason for the failure of learning and development programs is the lack of alignment with the business. The first opportunity to obtain business alignment is in the initial analysis. Several steps are taken to make sure that the program is absolutely necessary. As shown in Figure 32-2, this is the beginning of the complete, sequential model representing the ROI methodology. The first step in this analysis examines the potential payoff of solving a problem or taking advantage of a performance improvement opportunity. Is this a problem worth solving, or is the project worthy of implementation? For some situations, the answer is obvious: yes, the project is worthy because of its critical nature, its relevance to the issue at hand, or its effectiveness in tackling a major problem affecting the organization. A serious customer service problem, for example, is one worth pursuing.

The next step is to ensure that the program is connected to one or more business measures. The measures that must improve as a reflection of the overall success of the program are defined. Sometimes the measures are obvious; at other times they are not.

Next, the job performance needs are examined with the question, "What performance must change on the job to influence the business measures previously defined?" This step aligns the program with the business and may involve a series of analytical tools and questions to solve the problem, analyze the cause of the problem, and ensure that the program is connected with business improvement in some way.

After job performance needs have been determined, the learning needs are examined by asking, "What specific skills, knowledge, or perceptions must change or improve so that job performance can change?" Every solution involves a learning component of some sort,

Figure 32-2. Sequential Model Representing the ROI Methodology

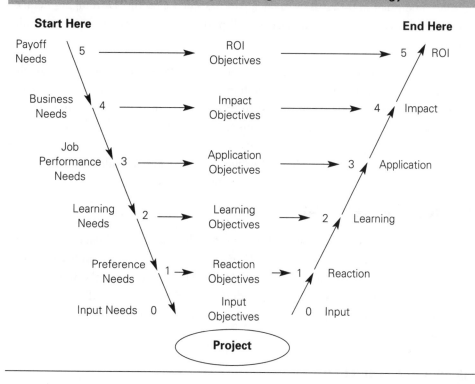

and this step defines what the participants or users must know to make the program successful. The needed knowledge may be as simple as understanding a policy, or be as complicated as learning new competencies.

The final step is identifying the design of the program. How best can the information be presented to ensure that needed knowledge will be acquired and job performance will change to solve the business problem? This level of analysis involves issues surrounding the scope, timing, structure, method, and budget for program implementation and delivery.

Collectively, these levels clearly define the issues that led to initiation of the project. When these preliminary steps are completed, the project can be positioned to achieve its intended results.

Understanding the need for a learning program is critical to positioning it for success. Positioning a program requires developing clear, specific objectives that are communicated to all stakeholders. Objectives should be developed for each level of need and should define success, answering the question, "How will we know the defined need has been met and the performance gap has been closed?" Developing detailed objectives with clear measures of success will position the program to achieve its ultimate objective.

Before a program is launched, forecasting the outcomes is important to ensure that adjustments can be made or alternative solutions can be investigated. This forecast can be simple, relying on the individuals closest to the situation, or it can be a more detailed analysis of the situation and expected outcome. Recently, forecasting has become a critical tool for program sponsors who may need evidence that the performance improvement project will be successful before they are willing to plunge into a funding stream for it.

The ROI Process Model

The next challenge for many program leaders is to collect a variety of data along a chain of impact that shows the project's value. Figure 32-3 displays the sequential steps that lead to data categorized by the five levels of results. This figure shows the ROI methodology as a step-by-step process beginning with the objectives and concluding with reporting of data. The model assumes that proper analysis is conducted to define need before the steps are taken.

Planning the Evaluation

The first phase of the methodology is evaluation planning. This phase involves several procedures, including understanding the purpose of the evaluation, planning data collection and analysis, and outlining the details of the project.

Evaluations are conducted for a variety of reasons:

- To improve the quality of projects and outcomes
- To determine whether a project has accomplished its objectives
- To identify strengths and weaknesses in the process
- To enable the benefit-cost analysis
- To assist in developing marketing projects or programs in the future
- To determine whether the project was the appropriate solution
- To establish priorities for project funding.

The purpose of the evaluation should be considered prior to developing the evaluation plan because the purpose will often determine the scope of the evaluation, the types of instruments used, and the type of data collected. As with any project, understanding the purpose of the evaluation will give it focus and will also help gain support from others.

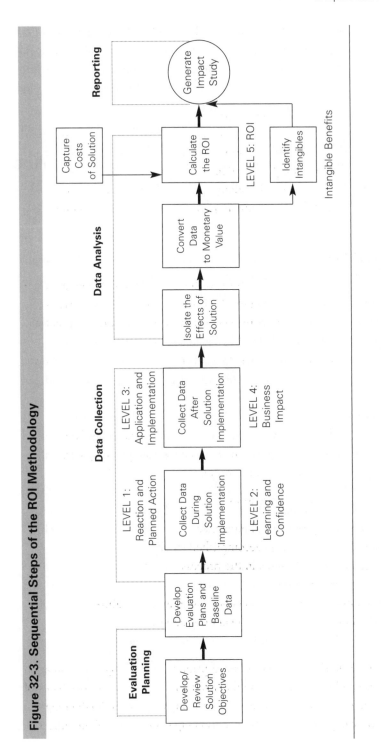

Figure 32-3. Sequential Steps of the ROI Methodology

Three simple planning documents are developed next: the data collection plan, the ROI analysis plan (see Figure 32-4 for a sample plan), and the project plan. Collectively, the three planning documents provide the direction necessary for the ROI study. These documents should be completed during evaluation planning and before the evaluation project is implemented—ideally, before the program is designed or developed. Appropriate up-front attention will save time later, when data are actually collected. The remainder of the performance improvement project becomes a methodical, sys-

 tematic process of implementing the plan. On the accompanying CD-ROM are a sample data collection plan, a sample ROI analysis plan, and a sample ROI project plan (Tools 32-1, 32-2, and 32-3).

Collecting Data

Data collection is central to the ROI methodology. Both hard data (representing output, quality, cost, and time) and soft data (including job satisfaction and customer satisfaction) are collected. Data are collected using a variety of methods, including

- **Surveys** are taken to determine the degree to which participants are satisfied with the program, have learned skills and knowledge, and have used various aspects of the program. Survey responses are often developed on a sliding scale and usually represent perception data. Surveys are useful for levels 1, 2, and 3 data.
- **Questionnaires** are usually more detailed than surveys and can be used to uncover a wide variety of data. Participants provide responses to open-ended and forced-response questions. Questionnaires can be used to capture levels 1, 2, 3, and 4 data.
- **Tests** are conducted to measure changes in knowledge and skills (level 2). Tests come in a wide variety of formal (criterion-referenced tests, performance tests and simulations, and skill practices) and informal (facilitation assessment, self-assessment, and team assessment) formats.
- On-the-job **observation** captures actual skill application and use. Observations are particularly useful in customer service training and are more effective when the observer is either invisible or transparent. Observations are appropriate for level 3 data.
- **Interviews** are conducted with participants to determine the extent to which learning has been used on the job. Interviews allow for probing to uncover specific applications and are usually appropriate with level 3 data but can be used with levels 1 and 2 data.

Figure 32-4. Sample ROI Analysis Plan

Program: _____ Interactive Sales Training _____ Responsibility: _____ P. Phillips _____ Date: _____

Data Items	Methods of Isolating the Effects of the Program	Methods of Converting Data	Cost Categories	Intangible Benefits	Communication Targets	Other Influences and Issues
• Weekly sales per associate	• Control group analysis • Participant estimate	• Direct conversion using profit contribution	• Facilitation fees • Program materials • Meals and refreshments • Facilities • Participant salaries and benefits • Cost of coordination • Evaluation	• Customer satisfaction • Employee satisfaction	• Program participants • Electronics depart-ment managers at targeted stores • Store managers at targeted stores • Senior store executives (district, region, headquarters) • Training staff: instructors, coordinators, designers, and managers	• Must have job coverage during training • No communication with control group • Seasonal fluctuations should be avoided

- **Focus groups** are conducted to determine the degree to which a group of participants has applied the training to job situations. Focus groups are usually appropriate with level 3 data.
- **Action plans and program assignments** are developed by participants during the training program and are implemented on the job after the program is completed. Follow-ups provide evidence of training program success. Levels 3 and 4 data can be collected with action plans.
- **Performance contracts** are developed by the participant, the participant's supervisor, and the facilitator who all agree on job performance outcomes from training. Performance contracts are appropriate for both levels 3 and 4 data.
- **Business performance monitoring** is useful where various performance records and operational data are examined for improvement. This method is particularly useful for level 4 data.

The important challenge in data collection is to select the method or methods appropriate for the setting and the specific program, within the time and budget constraints of the organization. Data collection methods are covered in more detail in other books, such as *Show Me the Money: How to Determine ROI in People, Projects, and Programs* (Phillips and Phillips, 2007).

Isolating the Effects of the Program

An often overlooked issue in evaluation is the process of isolating the effects of the program. In this step, specific strategies are explored that determine the amount of the business effect that is directly related to the program. This step is essential because many systemic factors will influence performance data. The specific strategies of this step pinpoint the amount of improvement directly related to the program, resulting in increased accuracy and credibility of ROI calculations. The following techniques have been used by organizations to tackle this important issue:

- A **control group** arrangement is used to isolate the effects of training. With this strategy, one group receives training, while another similar group does not receive training. The difference in the performance of the two groups is attributed to the training program. When properly set up and implemented, the control group arrangement is the most effective way to isolate the effects of training.
- **Trend lines** are used to project the values of specific output variables if training had not been undertaken. The projection is compared with the actual data after training, and the difference represents the estimate of the effect of training. Under certain conditions, this strategy can accurately isolate the training effect.

- When mathematical relationships between input and output variables are known, a **forecasting model** is used to isolate the effects of training. With this approach, the output variable is predicted using the forecasting model with the assumption that no training is conducted. The actual performance of the variable after the training is then compared with the forecasted value, which results in an estimate of the training effect.

- **Participants estimate** the amount of improvement related to training. With this approach, participants are provided with the total amount of improvement, on a preprogram and postprogram basis, and are asked to indicate the percent of the improvement that is actually related to the training program.

- **Supervisors of participants** estimate the effect of training on the output variables. With this approach, supervisors of participants are presented with the total amount of improvement and are asked to indicate the percent related to training.

- **Senior management** estimates the effect of training. In these cases, managers provide an estimate or "adjustment" to reflect the portion of the improvement related to the training program. Although perhaps inaccurate, there are some advantages of having senior management involved in this process.

- **Experts** provide estimates of the effect of training on the performance variable. Because the estimates are based on previous experience, the experts must be familiar with the type of training and the specific situation.

- When feasible, **other influencing factors** are identified and the effect estimated or calculated, leaving the remaining, unexplained improvement attributed to training. In this case, the influence of all the other factors is developed, and training remains the one variable not accounted for in the analysis. The unexplained portion of the output is then attributed to training.

- In some situations, **customers** provide input on the extent to which training has influenced their decision to use a product or service. Although this strategy has limited applications, it can be quite useful in customer service and sales training.

Collectively, these techniques provide a proven, comprehensive set of tools to handle the important and critical issue of isolating the effects of projects.

Converting Data to Monetary Values

To calculate the ROI, business impact data are converted to monetary values and compared with program costs. This requires that a value be placed on each unit of data connected with the program. Many techniques are available to convert data to monetary values. The specific technique selected depends on the type of data and the situation. The techniques include

- **Output data** are converted to profit contribution or cost savings. In this strategy, output increases are converted to monetary value based on their unit contribution to profit or the unit of cost reduction. Standard values for these items are readily available in most organizations.

- The **cost of quality** is calculated, and quality improvements are directly converted to cost savings. Standard values for these items are available in many organizations.

- For programs where employee time is saved, the **participants' wages and employee benefits** are used to develop the value for time. Because a variety of programs focus on improving the time required to complete programs, the value of time becomes an important and necessary issue. This is a standard formula in most organizations.

- **Historical costs,** developed from cost statements, are used when they are available for a specific variable. In this case, organizational cost data establish the specific monetary cost savings of an improvement.

- When available, **internal and external experts** may be used to estimate a value for an improvement. In this situation, the credibility of the estimate hinges on the expertise and reputation of the individual.

- **External databases** are sometimes available to estimate the value or cost of data items. Research, government, and industry databases can provide important information for these values. The difficulty lies in finding a specific database related to the situation.

- **Participants** estimate the value of the data item. For this approach to be effective, participants must be capable of providing a value for the improvement.

- **Supervisors and managers** provide estimates when they are both willing and capable of assigning values to the improvement. This approach is especially useful when participants are not fully capable of providing this input or in situations where supervisors need to confirm or adjust the participant's estimate. This approach is particularly helpful to establish values for performance measures that are very important to senior management.

- **Soft measures are linked mathematically to other measures** that are easier to measure and value. This approach is particularly helpful when establishing values for measures that are very difficult to convert to monetary values, such as data often considered intangible, like customer satisfaction, employee satisfaction, grievances, and employee complaints.

- **Staff estimates** may be used to determine a value of an output data item. In these cases, it is essential for the estimates to be provided on an unbiased basis.

This step in the ROI model is important and absolutely necessary in determining the monetary benefits of a program or solution implementation. The process is challenging, particularly with soft data but can be methodically accomplished using one or more of these strategies.

Tabulating Program Costs

An important part of the ROI equation is the calculation of program costs. Tabulating the costs involves monitoring or developing all the related costs of the program targeted for the ROI calculation. Among the cost components to be included are

- Initial analysis costs (usually prorated)
- Cost to design and develop the program
- Cost of all program materials
- Costs for the learning and development team (for example, facilitator, coordinator)
- Cost of the facilities
- Travel, lodging, and meal costs for the participants and team members
- Participants' salaries (including employee benefits) for the time involved in the program
- Administrative and overhead costs, allocated in some convenient way
- Evaluation costs.

The conservative approach is to include all these costs so that the total is fully loaded.

Calculating the ROI

The ROI is calculated using the program benefits and costs. The benefit-cost ratio (BCR) is calculated as the program benefits divided by the program costs. In formula form,

$$\text{BCR} = \frac{\text{Program benefits}}{\text{Program costs}}$$

The ROI is based on the net benefits divided by program costs. The net benefits are calculated as the program benefits minus the project costs. In formula form, the ROI becomes

$$\text{ROI } (\%) = \frac{\text{Net program benefits}}{\text{Program costs}} \times 100$$

This is the same basic formula used in evaluating other investments, in which the ROI is traditionally reported as earnings divided by investment.

Identifying Intangible Benefits

In addition to tangible, monetary benefits, intangible, nonmonetary benefits also accrue to most performance improvement projects. Intangible benefits include items such as

- Increased job satisfaction
- Increased organizational commitment
- Improved teamwork
- Improved customer service
- Fewer complaints
- Reduced conflict.

During data analysis, every attempt is made to convert all data to monetary values. All hard data—such as output, quality, and time—are converted to monetary values. The conversion of soft data is attempted for each data item. However, if the process used for conversion is too subjective or inaccurate and the resulting values lose credibility in the process, then the data are listed as an intangible benefit with the appropriate explanation. For some programs, intangible, nonmonetary benefits are extremely valuable and often carry as much influence as the hard data items.

Reporting Results

The final step in the ROI process model is reporting results, a critical step that often lacks the attention and planning required for success. The reporting step involves developing appropriate information in impact studies and other brief reports. At the heart of this step are the different techniques used to communicate to a wide variety of target audiences. In most ROI studies, several audiences are interested in and need the information. Careful planning to match the communication method with the audience is essential to ensure that the message is understood and that appropriate actions follow.

Operating Standards and Philosophy

To ensure consistency and replication of impact studies, operating standards must be developed and applied as the process model is used to develop ROI studies. The results of the study must stand alone and must not vary with the individual who is conducting the study. The operating standards detail how each step and issue of the process will be handled. Following are the 12 guiding principles that form the basis for the operating standards:

- When conducting a higher-level evaluation, collect data at lower levels.
- When planning a higher-level evaluation, the previous level of evaluation is not required to be comprehensive.

- When collecting and analyzing data, use only the most credible sources.
- When analyzing data, select the most conservative alternative for calculations.
- Use at least one method to isolate the effects of a project.
- If no improvement data are available for a population or from a specific source, assume that little or no improvement has occurred.
- Adjust estimates of improvement for potential errors of estimation.
- Avoid use of extreme data items and unsupported claims when calculating ROI.
- Use only the first year of annual benefits in ROI analysis of short-term solutions.
- Fully load all costs of a solution, project, or program when analyzing ROI.
- Intangible measures are defined as measures that are purposely not converted to monetary values.
- Communicate the results of ROI methodology to all key stakeholders.

The guiding principles serve not only to consistently address each step but also to provide a much needed conservative approach to the analysis. A conservative approach may lower the actual ROI calculation, but it will also build credibility with the target audience.

Implementing and Sustaining the Process

To date, there are more than 4,000 users of this methodology. Its success rests with the efforts to implement and sustain it. A variety of environmental issues and events will influence the successful implementation of the ROI evaluation process. These issues must be addressed early with specific topics or actions, including

- A policy statement concerning a results-based program approved for learning and development
- Procedures and guidelines for different elements and techniques of the evaluation process
- Formal effort to develop staff skills with the ROI process
- Strategies to improve management commitment to and support for the ROI process
- Mechanisms to provide technical support for instrument design, data analysis, and evaluation strategy
- Specific techniques to place more attention on results.

The ROI process can fail or succeed based on the success of these implementation issues.

In addition to implementing and sustaining ROI use, the process must undergo periodic review. An annual review is recommended to determine the extent to which the process is adding value. This final element involves checking satisfaction with the process and determining how well it is understood and applied. Essentially, this review follows an assessment with the five levels of data, including the ROI on the ROI.

Benefits of This Approach

The evaluation methodology presented here has been used consistently and routinely by thousands of organizations in the past decade. It has been more prominent in some fields and industries than in others. Much has been learned about the success of this methodology and what it can bring to the organizations using it.

Aligning with Business

The ROI methodology ensures business alignment by defining desired business results as an up-front planning process at the time the program is validated as the appropriate solution. Second, by requiring specific, clearly defined objectives, the program focuses and drives business measures over the course of solution design, delivery, and implementation. Third, in the follow-up data, when the business measures may have changed or improved, a method is used to isolate the effects of the program on those data, consequently proving the connection to that business measure (that is, showing the amount of improvement directly connected to the program and ensuring there is business alignment).

Validating the Value Proposition

In reality, most learning and development programs are undertaken to deliver value. As described in this chapter, the definition of value may on occasion be unclear, or may not be what a program's various sponsors, organizers, and stakeholders desire. Consequently, there are often value shifts. Once the values are finally determined, the value proposition is detailed. The ROI methodology will forecast the value in advance, and, if the value has been delivered, it verifies the value proposition agreed to by the appropriate parties.

Improving Processes

ROI is a process improvement tool by design and by practice. It collects data to evaluate how things are—or are not—working. When things are not where they should be—as when projects are not proceeding as effectively as expected—data are available to the various stakeholders to indicate what must be changed to make the project more effective. When things are working well, data are available to show what else could be done to improve the program. This continuous feedback cycle is critical to systemic process improvement and is inherent in the ROI approach.

Enhancing the Image, Building Respect

The learning and development function is often criticized for being unable to deliver what is expected. For this, its image and credibility suffers. The ROI methodology is one way to help build the respect that the function or profession needs. Many learning and development executives have relied upon ROI data to show how programs add value and achieve desired results. This methodology connects a project to the bottom line and shows the value that it delivers to stakeholders. Consequently, its use can help professionals enhance the image and perceived value of the performance improvement function within the organization.

Improving Support

Securing support for learning and development programs is critical, particularly at the middle-manager level. Many programs enjoy the support of the top-level managers who allocated the resources to make learning and development programs viable. Unfortunately, some middle-level managers may not support certain projects because they do not see the value the projects deliver in terms they can appreciate and understand. Having a methodology that shows how a project or program is connected to the manager's business goals and objectives can change this support level. When middle managers understand that a learning and development program is helping them meet specific performance indicators or departmental goals, they will usually support the process, or will at least resist it less. In this way, the ROI methodology might actually improve manager support.

Justifying or Enhancing Budgets

Some organizations have used the ROI methodology to support proposed budgets. Because the methodology shows the monetary value expected or achieved with specific programs, the data can often be leveraged into budget requests. When a learning and development program is under budget review, the amount budgeted is often in direct proportion to the perceived value that the function adds. If little or no credible data support the contribution, the budgets are often trimmed—or at least not enhanced. Bringing accountability to this level is one of the best ways to secure future funding.

Building a Partnership with Key Executives

Almost every function attempts to partner with operating executives and key managers in the organization. Unfortunately, some managers may not want to be partners. They may not want to waste time and effort on a relationship that does not help them succeed. They want to partner only with groups and individuals who can add value and help them in meaningful ways. Showing the results from performance improvement programs will enhance the likelihood of building these partnerships, with the results providing the initial impetus for making the partnerships work.

Earning a "Seat at the Table"

Many functions are attempting to earn a seat at the table; however, that must be defined. Typically, "earning a seat at the table" means being at the strategy- or decision-making table and in high-level discussions at the top of the organization. Using the ROI methodology to show the actual contribution of the performance improvement function may be the single most important action that professionals can take to earn a coveted seat at the table. Most executives want to include those who are genuinely helping the business and will seek input that is valuable and constructive.

Final Thoughts

This chapter presents the overall approach to the use of the methodology to evaluate learning and development. This ROI methodology is the most used system in the world to show the value of learning and development; it is now used in 50 countries. This chapter presents the different elements and steps in the methodology, the standards, and the different concepts necessary to understand how ROI works and brings the process into

 focus as a critical strategic tool. To fully understand the methodology, please review the case study on the CD-ROM (Tool 32-4). For more tools, templates, and information on the methodology, please visit www.roiinstitute.net.

About the Author

As a world-renowned expert on accountability, measurement, and evaluation, Jack J. Phillips provides consulting services for *Fortune* 500 companies and major global organizations. The author or editor of more than 50 books, Phillips conducts workshops and makes conference presentations throughout the world.

His expertise in measurement and evaluation is based on more than 27 years of corporate experience in the aerospace, textile, metals, construction materials, and banking industries. This background led Phillips to develop the ROI methodology—a revolutionary process that provides bottom-line figures and accountability for all types of learning, performance improvement, human resource, technology, and public policy programs.

Phillips is chairman of the ROI Institute.

References

Phillips, Jack J., and Patricia P. Phillips. 2007. *Show me the money: How to determine ROI in people, projects, and programs.* San Francisco: Berrett-Koehler.

Phillips, Jack J., and Patricia P. Phillips. 2005. *ROI at work: Best practice case studies from the real world.* Alexandria, VA: ASTD Press.

Chapter 33

Bottom Line Measures in the ASTD WLP Scorecard

Ray J. Rivera

In This Chapter

➢ Learn to demonstrate the business value of learning

➢ Understand why improvements in workplace measurement are needed

➢ Get an overview of the WLP Scorecard

As more organizations answer the call to run learning as a business, measuring workplace learning and performance (WLP) activities has become a crucial part of transforming the learning function into a value-producing business function. Measurement is an integral part of managing any business function, from the development and implementation strategy to establishing the targets that drive performance. Traditionally, business functions have been managed using performance measurement systems built up from financial statements, profit plans, and budgets. However, because learning is situated in other activities and results in the accumulation of intangible assets invisible to most financial statements, the learning function is unable to be managed using standard performance measurement methods.

The WLP Scorecard is a comprehensive online benchmarking, decision support, and performance measurement tool capable of tracking a wide range of learning investments and performance activities, and reporting business results in business language. The WLP Scorecard was developed by researchers at ASTD in collaboration with learning executives and measurement experts. It provides learning managers with a standard set of metrics and reporting methods within an automated online environment. WLP Scorecard users are able to measure across the learning and performance value chain and map the learning function to a scorecard framework. Through a set of meaningful indexes, users are able to visualize the learning function's strengths and weaknesses and make comparisons with peers. WLP Scorecard users are also able to determine where to focus their learning and performance improvement efforts and how changes in learning investment affect both learning and business functions.

Workplace Performance Measurement and Management: Transforming the Learning Function into a Business Function

Many learning managers struggle to quantify the work they perform and to fend off proposed reductions or elimination of learning budgets during economic downturns. Although senior management values learning and talent development, they also need evidence that investing in learning is appropriate; targets the right people and competencies; and drives productivity, innovation, and differentiation.

So how do learning managers overcome these barriers to demonstrate value? All business functions rely on measurement as a means of finding gaps and targeting improvements. Measurement enables management to identify, develop, and implement strategies based on hard and soft targets to drive performance. For most learning functions, measurement currently focuses on levels 1 through 4 evaluation, the amount and quality of throughput (that is, number of learners trained, number of courses delivered, and completion percentages), and learning function efficiency.

Learning managers facing pressure to manage learning as a business need to demonstrate the learning function's contributions to achieving organizational objectives. To manage the learning function as a business function, learning managers must

- Plan a course that leads to value creation
- Determine which learning investments contribute most to value creation
- Set up the decision-making mechanisms that achieve business results
- Create a measurement strategy that allows the precise management of learning function resources (Vanthournout et al., 2006).

The WLP profession currently monitors learning at various levels, yet possesses limited ability to transform measurement into a blueprint for managing learning, discovering the mechanisms that transform learning into value, and creating control systems for optimizing human performance technology.

Why All Business Functions Need a Measurement Strategy

Measurement governs both the development and implementation of business strategy and creates soft and hard targets that drive individual and group performance. For many decades, business functions have been managed using performance measurement systems, at the core of which are financial statements, profit plans, and budgets. These documents have traditionally provided the means necessary for communicating strategy, allocating resources, and driving performance.

Financial statements served as the basis of performance measurement in the 20th century, when organizations were made up of primarily tangible assets. Yet financial statements are becoming less effective in managing organizations in the 21st century, whose most valuable assets are knowledge assets, and whose value and efficacy are increased through learning.

Why Learning Cannot Be Managed Using Standard Performance Measurement

Intangible assets represent the unique capabilities and competencies controlled by an organization, and learning is the means by which organizations increase and accumulate intangible assets. The issue is that most intangible assets never appear on financial statements unless some transaction has occurred—thus making it a poor basis for measurement and probably the worst basis for managing.

Management of intangible assets requires special measurement treatment to feed back timely information into business processes to achieve desired performance. Traditional hard financial measurements are too blunt and coarse to fulfill all the management needs of intangible-heavy organizations.

Why Current WLP Profession Measurement Methods Are Inadequate

Benchmarking and program evaluation, despite being the bulwark of workplace performance measurement, are often criticized for being lagging indicators. They tell us what we want to know after we need to know it and are often disconnected from business strategy. Because most benchmarking and evaluation uses learning-centered metrics instead of business-centered metrics, the information rendered allows limited ability to manage the resources used in providing effective workplace learning.

The balanced scorecard (Kaplan and Norton, 1992) has emerged as the most prominent strategic management and performance measurement system used by organizations today. The balanced scorecard derives its name, and achieves its thrust, by balancing traditional performance measures with more forward-looking indicators in four key dimensions: financial, integration/operational excellence, learning and growth, and customers.

In the past decade, numerous scorecard-based methods have arisen to help measure and manage learning activity over a broader scope. Scorecard-based measurement strategies connect learning to business strategy and treat learning as a business value driver. Despite this benefit, results from most scorecard-based methods that include learning as a measurement dimension are typically neither prescriptive nor diagnostic. Users of these scorecards often find that learning requires separate analytical treatment, and scorecard methods that do not capture the economic value of learning are often regarded as no more useful than benchmarks.

Despite great sophistication in the areas of program evaluation and even capital budgeting, the WLP profession has failed to create a balance sheet that captures and communicates the value proposition of the learning function. Although the profession has made great strides in terms of measurement—creating tools with the look and feel of balance sheets, cash flow analyses, and budget variance reports—these reports don't really tell us what is going on in the learning function.

The few organizations that do have such measurement systems are tracking only a fraction of the learning opportunities and activities that occur, usually formal learning. Furthermore, these organizations often base their data collection and reporting on learning-centric models, that is, models that evaluate learning strictly in terms of learning outcomes, such as a test score, rather than on common business metrics (see Figure 33-1).

Just as all business functions have inputs, processes, outputs, and measures and controls, so does the learning function. Learning in today's organizations is not a single, monolithic event, but a dynamic set of events with a beginning, middle, and end, like most other business functions. Therefore, one learning activity does not support all learning objectives. One metric does not capture the impact value of an organization's learning and performance activities. And one evaluation method does not measure all the important parts of an organization's learning.

Figure 33-1. WLP Scorecard Reports Overview

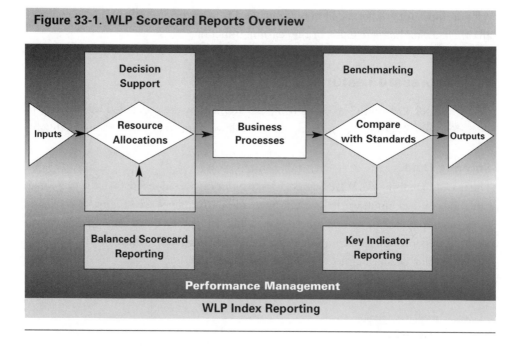

The WLP Scorecard Overview: What Is the WLP Scorecard?

The WLP Scorecard is an online benchmarking, decision-support, and performance measurement and management tool, used by learning and nonlearning executives. This tool connects learning investments and activities to business outcomes, reports results in business terms, and allows users to see how changes in learning investments move the dials of both learning and business functions.

Using a standard set of workplace learning, performance, and business metrics, the WLP Scorecard provides a complete performance measurement system. By reporting both common business metrics *and* learning-centric metrics—rather than learning-centric metrics alone—the WLP Scorecard provides a common language for learning professionals, learning executives, and nonlearning executives. By enabling cost-effectiveness comparisons, WLP Scorecard users can identify not only what learning functions spend, but they can also discover what levels and types of expenditures on learning and performance activities are most effective.

The WLP Scorecard helps illuminate the link between learning investments and individual, group, and organizational performance. Users can explore causal chains and relationships and predict the effects of changes in single or multiple indicators on overall efficiency and effectiveness of the learning function.

WLP Scorecard Features

 Tool 33-1 on the accompanying CD-ROM provides a detailed user's guide for the ASTD WLP Scorecard, but the following sections provide some highlights.

Entering Data

The first step in using the WLP Scorecard is to enter organizational data in the three main categories of data input: workplace, learning, and performance (see Figure 33-2). These three categories include several subcategories. Taken together, these data input categories and subcategories reflect a comprehensive set of learning and performance inputs across the WLP value chain (Sugrue, O'Driscoll, and Blair, 2005).

The three main categories of data input are organized as follows:

- Workplace
  — Workforce
  — Compensation
  — Talent management
  — Performance management
  — Employee engagement
  — Innovation.
- Learning
  — Investment
  — Learning function staff/talent
  — Learning function processes
  — Output (formal learning)
  — Output (work-based learning)
  — Infrastructure
  — Outsourcing
  — Integration
  — Usage (formal learning)
  — Usage (work-based learning).
- Performance
  — Capability
  — Productivity
  — Business outcomes
  — Perceptions.

Figure 33-2. WLP Scorecard Data Entry (Input) Screen

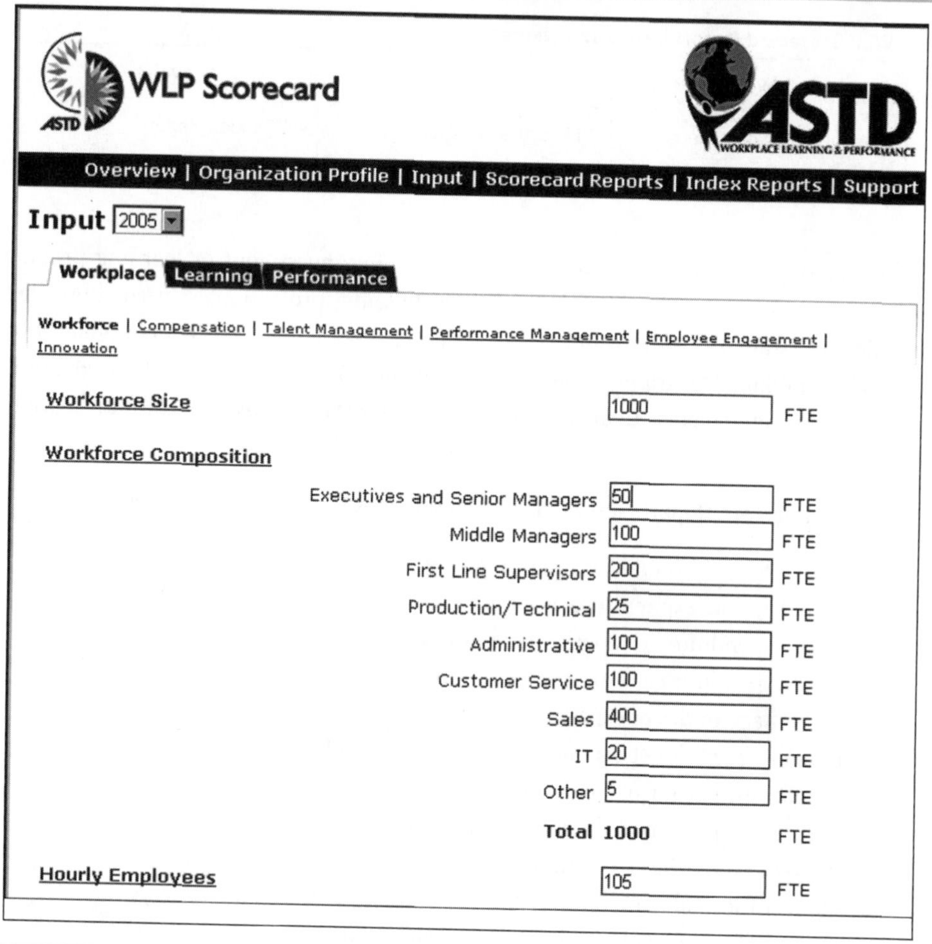

Exploring the WLP Scorecard Reports

The WLP Scorecard reports enable users and organizations to transform the learning function from an expense function into a powerful business function able to communicate the direct and indirect relationships between learning and business value. Table 33-1 displays the levels and names of each WLP Scorecard report.

Level 1 reports: Benchmarking using key learning indicators. The first level of WLP Scorecard reporting contains most of the key learning indicators found in ASTD's annual *State of the Industry Report.* Taken together, these indicators are useful for benchmarking the effectiveness and efficiency of learning investments, the production and delivery of learning content, and usage.

Table 33-1. WLP Scorecard Reports Overview

WLP Scorecard Report Levels and Names		
Level 1	**Level 2**	**Level 3**
Free Key Indicators Report	WLP Scorecard Reports	WLP Index Reports

Benchmarking is typically performed after a learning investment or learning program has been completed and is useful in allowing learning professionals to compare their learning investments with best practices and industry leaders. Nearly every organization, when determining its learning budget, refers to benchmarking data (sometimes over several years) for guidance as to an acceptable range for the various areas of their learning investments.

The Key Indicators Report (see Figure 33-3) provides the following metrics:

- Direct formal expenditure per employee
- Direct formal expenditure as a percentage of payroll
- Total expenditure as a percentage of revenue
- Total expenditure as a percentage of income/profit
- Percentage of direct expenditure on external services
- Percentage of direct expenditure on tuition reimbursement
- Direct cost per formal learning hour available
- Direct cost per formal learning hour used
- Ratio of employees to learning staff
- Hours of formal content available per learning staff member
- Hours of formal content usage per learning staff member
- Formal learning content reuse ratio
- Formal learning hours available by content area
- Formal hours available by delivery medium
- Formal learning hours used by delivery medium
- Formal learning usage per employee
- Percentage of formal learning delivered online.

Tool 33-2 on the accompanying CD-ROM displays the WLP Scorecard worksheets, which are a full list of all WLP Scorecard input fields and descriptions. This quick reference document facilitates the planning and data gathering processes to begin using the WLP Scorecard.

Figure 33-3. The Key Indicators Report Financial Dimension

WLP Scorecard®

ASTD WORKPLACE LEARNING & PERFORMANCE

Overview | Organization Profile | Input | Scorecard Reports | Index Reports | Support

Scorecard Reports - Year: 2006 - OPEN

Financial | Operations | Customer | Innovation | Customize | BMF

Financial Indicators	Your Organization		All Organizations				
	Value	Rank	Mean	Median	Min	Max	n
Expenditure (total) per employee							
Expenditure (total direct) per employee							
Expenditure (direct formal) per employee	$1,104.77	38	$705.43	$433.89	$0	$7,172.57	194
Expenditure (direct work-based) per employee							
Expenditure (direct formal) as percentage of payroll (excluding benefits/taxes)	2.26%	40	1.96%	1.18%	0%	27.08%	174
Expenditure (total) as percentage of total compensation							
Expenditure (total) as percentage of payroll							
Expenditure (total) as percentage of revenue	0.43%	74	0.97%	0.37%	0%	18.18%	164
Expenditure (total) as percentage of income/profit	2.79%	63	9.1%	2.79%	0.01%	97.44%	125

Level 2 reports: Decision support using a balanced scorecard framework. Level 2 reports, also called the Scorecard Reports, contain rankings of standard sets of learning and performance indicators within a balanced scorecard framework (see Figure 33-4). In a Scorecard Report, a standard set of learning indicators is classified according to four performance dimensions—financial, operations, customer, and innovation—allowing users to compare their organizations' learning and performance indicators with those of other organizations.

- **Financial** indicators cover the financial aspects of the learning function, such as expenditures and cost ratios.

- **Operations** indicators treat the major operational aspects of the learning function: staffing, processes, and production and output indicators.
- **Customer** indicators monitor the learning function's internal customer behavior and satisfaction in such areas as usage and learner and manager satisfaction.
- **Innovation** indicators monitor and compare innovative aspects of the learning function, such as integration, work-based learning, and performance improvement.

The Scorecard Report can be customized by selecting the indicators of greatest interest and comparing the selected learning function values with those of organizations similar in size, in different geographic regions, or across different industries.

Figure 33-4. The Key Indicators Report Customer Dimension

WLP Scorecard®

ASTD
WORKPLACE LEARNING & PERFORMANCE

Overview | Organization Profile | Input | Scorecard Reports | Index Reports | Support

Scorecard Reports - Year: 2006 - OPEN

Financial | Operations | **Customer** | Innovation | Customize | BMF

Customer Indicators	Your Organization		All Organizations				
	Value	Rank	Mean	Median	Min	Max	n
Formal learning usage per employee	54.4	43	35.23	19.8	0	396.98	197
Work-based learning usage per employee	178.76	3	158.75	178.76	0	256	5
Knowledge repository usage per employee	37.76	1	3.57	0	0	37.76	11
Knowledge sharing usage per employee	81	6	119.72	100.5	0	480.21	10
Challenging work assignment usage	2	7	17	5	0	90	11
Discretionary learning per employee	20	6	59.18	20	0	400	11
C-level satisfaction with learning function	6.3	14	6.97	7	1	9	19
Business unit leader satisfaction with learning function	7.3	11	7.22	7.75	1	9	18
Overall employee satisfaction	7.3	8	7.04	7	4	9	25
Employee satisfaction with learning opportunities	7.2	9	6.75	7	2	9	25
Learner satisfaction with formal learning	7.5	15	7.81	8	3	9	21

Why use a balanced scorecard framework for decision support? Benchmarking provides limited opportunity for managing the learning function in the short term, or executing on an existing learning strategy. As illustrated in Figure 33-1, for a performance measurement system to be truly useful as a management tool, it must feed back information about the performance of the learning function to the point where resource allocation decisions are made, and before value-producing business processes are committed. In this sense, a balanced scorecard approach provides proper decision support, and illuminates the power that learning has in many organizations.

A balanced scorecard framework clarifies and communicates the role of learning within a larger context. Because the balanced scorecard framework requires users to articulate cause-and-effect relationships between activities and performance, this process often forces users to revisit learning function assumptions that had been taken for granted. This framework helps to translate an organization's mission and strategy into clear, actionable measurements and performance goals organized into four equally weighted perspectives: financial, operations, customer, and innovation.

Finally, the balanced scorecard framework was one of the first management systems able to account for significant accumulations of intangible assets, intellectual capital, and other learning assets that would never appear on financial statements. Although the balanced scorecard framework does not solve the problem of determining the financial value of these enormous stores of assets, it prevents them from becoming lost in the management shuffle.

Level 3 reports: Managing performance strategically using the WLP Index Reports. The WLP Index Reports, the highest level of reporting, allow users to measure and manage the learning function strategically, over a longer-term view than with the Scorecard Reports. WLP Index Reports map a standard set of learning function predictors to four WLP Indexes—alignment, efficiency, effectiveness, and sustainability—and enable users to visualize the areas of the learning function that contribute most to its strength and fitness (see Figure 33-5).

The WLP Index Report displays five main tabs:

- **WLP Index tab** combines the four index dimensions to display an overall index for each dimension and an overall WLP Index rollup score.
- The **four index tabs** measure the alignment, efficiency, effectiveness, and sustainability of the learning function compared with all organizations in the database and display a diagnostic report for each dimension.

Table 33-2 describes each of these elements in the WLP Index Reports and what they measure.

Figure 33-5. The WLP Index Report Screen

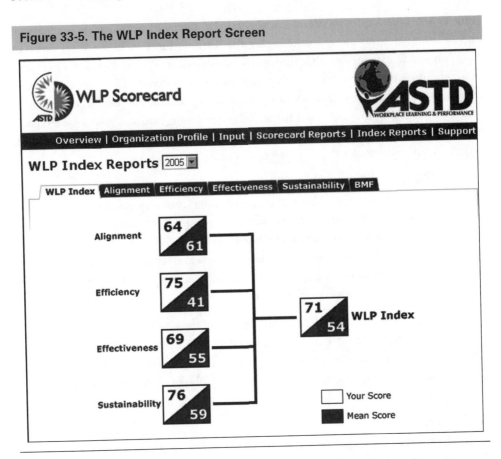

Together, the first five tabs display values enable comparison of the learning function to the entire workplace learning and performance industry. The WLP Index scores for alignment, efficiency, effectiveness, and sustainability—and the overall WLP Index score—appear in a square graphic, with the score for your learning function in the upper left section of the square, and the average score for all organizations in the database in the lower right.

In each of the diagnostic reports, the WLP Scorecard identifies indicators that are likely to exert the greatest effect on your WLP Index score and consequently may be priorities to strengthen the alignment, effectiveness, efficiency, or sustainability of the learning function (see Figure 33-6). For example, a red-shaded bulb in the WLP IndicatorWatch column denotes an indicator that is substantially and negatively affecting the WLP Index score. A red- and yellow-shaded bulb denotes an indicator that is moderately and negatively affecting the WLP Index score. A yellow- and green-shaded bulb in the WLP IndicatorWatch column denotes an indicator that strengthens the Index Score.

Table 33-2. WLP Index Diagnostic Reports and Descriptions

	Report Name	Description
Overall Report	**WLP Index Report**	Displays scores based on alignment, efficiency, effectiveness, and sustainability index scores as well as an overall WLP Index Score, which represents the overall quality of the learning function. Users can compare their organization's WLP Index Scores with the average WLP Index Scores for all organizations in the database.
Diagnostic Reports	**Alignment Index**	Measures the extent to which the learning function is aligned with organizational goals and the defined strategic aspects of the organization.
	Efficiency Index	Measures the extent to which the learning function executes and uses resources prudently and judiciously.
	Effectiveness Index	Measures organizational productivity, human capital, financial performance, employee retention, and satisfaction.
	Sustainability Index	Measures the extent to which the learning function can both maintain its current level of success, and scale to meet future strategic needs.

Users may also perform powerful sensitivity analyses by modifying Index Scores on any or all of the index indicators. Entering a new or revised value in the "Change Your Score" column changes the Index Score in the "New" square graphic. This feature enables users to experiment with scores on any or all indicators to determine the overall effect of a different set of indicator values on an Index score.

For all Index scores, the scale on which scores are reported is a continuous integer scale ranging from 0 to 100, where 0 represents the lowest score, and 100 the highest score.

Why Measure Alignment, Efficiency, Effectiveness, and Sustainability?

In the past 20 years, ASTD research has studied hundreds of learning functions—including ASTD BEST award winners—and has found that top-performing learning functions share certain common characteristics, including

- Overall higher levels of investment in the learning function
- Deliberate alignment of learning with business strategy
- Explicit strategies for measuring effectiveness and efficiency
- Maximized efficiency throughout the learning function

Figure 33-6. The Alignment Diagnostic Report

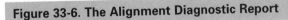

WLP Scorecard

Overview | Organization Profile | Input | Scorecard Reports | Index Reports | Support

WLP Index Reports - Year: 2005 ▾

WLP Index | **Alignment** | Efficiency | Effectiveness | Sustainability | BMF

Current   **New**

Alignment   63 / 66   ☐ Your Score   Alignment   63 / 66
                              ■ Mean Score

Indicator	Your Value	WLP Elite Value	WLP IndicatorWatch	Change Your Score
Individual and Organization Goal Linkage	7	8		
Individual Performance Goals	70%	100%		
Individual Learning Plans	45%	100%		
Alignment of Individual Performance Goals and Learning Plans	4.5	8		
Job Competency Documentation	90%	20%		
Individual Competency Profiles	85%	15%		

- Demonstrated effectiveness using both qualitative and quantitative methods
- Broad range of both formal and work-based learning opportunities
- Executive-level involvement
- A habit of combining innovative nonlearning solutions with learning to facilitate value-producing performance improvement.

ASTD's findings are corroborated by a landmark study of high-performing learning organizations by Accenture (2004). This study found that the most successful learning functions possessed these similar characteristics:

- Articulated alignment of learning strategy with business needs
- Competency development focused on critical job families

- Leadership development treated as high priority
- Integration of learning into other processes and the daily worklife of the employee
- Establishment of a measurement system in focusing on effectiveness, efficiency, and organizational effect.

Running Learning Like a Business

Just as the traditional balanced scorecard is a management tool that is used to map an organization's strategic objectives into performance metrics, the WLP Scorecard is an online benchmarking, decision support, and performance measurement tool that connects learning investments to business results. The WLP Scorecard helps decision makers understand business drivers and how the organization currently stacks up based on a variety of metrics and indicators for work-based learning, human capital, and business outcomes.

The WLP Scorecard reports are beyond descriptive; they are predictive, diagnostic, and prescriptive—meaning they tell you much more than where you have been. WLP Scorecard reports give you a sense of where the learning function is going, what it is going to take to get to where you really want to go, and what needs to be done to get there.

Ultimately the WLP Scorecard provides workplace learning professionals, learning executives, and upper management with a common language to communicate with each other about the diversity of learning function activities and the means by which learning is measured.

By reporting the learning function accomplishments based on these four dimensions, WLP Scorecard users can make use of the same powerful business tools frequently used by nonlearning counterparts. The benefits of each measurement dimension include

- Effectiveness dimension—allows users to connect learning budgets to an overall profit plan and to create a learning function value plan.
- Efficiency dimension—provides measures that help ensure the learning function has the necessary operating platform to fulfill overall performance and strategy goals.
- Sustainability dimension—supplies the learning professional with the means to ensure the learning function remains connected to organizational strategy.
- Alignment dimension—allows learning professionals to manage budget and performance variances, while ensuring alignment at all levels.

About the Author

Ray J. Rivera is the director of the WLP Scorecard at ASTD. He has a master's degree in instructional design and technology from the University of Iowa and is completing his PhD at Stanford University. His dissertation research focuses on using intangible asset valuation methods to determine and measure the effects of learning on performance. He is co-author of ASTD's 2005 and 2006 *State of the Industry Report,* along with numerous other articles and reports covering areas such as business impact measurement, the strategic value of learning, learning function globalization, and challenges of a maturing workforce.

References

Accenture. 2004. *The rise of the high-performance learning organization: Results from the Accenture learning 2004 survey of learning executives,* available at www.accenture.com/NR /rdonlyres/27C2CE28-8274-433F-8EC0-350DCF2502A9/0/HPLO_fullreport_final.pdf.

Kaplan, Robert S., and David P. Norton. 1992. The balanced scorecard: Measures that drive performance. *Harvard Business Review* 70(1): 71-80.

Sugrue, Brenda, Tony O'Driscoll, and Daniel Blair. 2005, January. What in the world is WLP? *T+D,* 51-52.

Vanthournout, Donald, Kurt Olson, John Ceisel, Andrew White, Tad Waddington, Thomas Barfield, Samir Desai, and Craig Mindrum. 2006. *Return on learning: Training for high performance at Accenture.* Chicago, IL: Agate Publishing.

For Further Reading

Beatty, Richard W., Mark A. Huselid, and Craig Eric Scheier. 2003. Scoring on the business scorecard. *Organizational Dynamics* 32(2): 107-121.

Fitz-enz, Jack. 2000. *The ROI of human capital: Measuring the economic value of employee performance.* New York: American Management Association.

Holton, Elwood F., and Sharon S. Naquin. 2004. New metrics for employee development. *Performance Improvement Quarterly* 17(1): 56-80.

Huselid, Mark A., Brian E. Becker, and Richard W. Beatty. 2005. *The workforce scorecard: Managing human capital to execute strategy.* Boston: Harvard Business School Press.

Lazear, Edward P. 1998. *Personnel economics for managers.* New York: John Wiley & Sons.

Rivera, Ray J., and Andrew Paradise. 2006. *2006 State of the Industry Report.* Alexandria, VA: ASTD Press.

Section VII

Organizational Level Applications

Organizational Level Applications

Luminary Perspective

John Coné

In This Chapter

- ➤ Understand what the people you serve expect from you

- ➤ Learn three new roles for workplace learning and performance professionals: the synthesist, the experimenter, and the enviroguide

- ➤ Discover who your friends are in the organization

If you are going to leverage major change in your organization, you have to be standing on solid ground. Are you? Everything we do happens in a rich and complex context, and the more we know about it, the better our chances of success. The next section of this book looks at some really huge leverage points. Among them are things like organizational culture, knowledge management, organization development, and consulting. I've learned a lot from the authors and hope to learn more. And because I don't think I can add to or improve on what they have to teach us, I wanted instead to share a few practical lessons I've learned over the years as I did my best to put their ideas into practice. Here are five suggestions for getting clarity about where you stand before you even start to make a change.

Know the Deal

It is critically important to understand the often unspoken agreement you have with the people you serve. It's true that at a fundamental level the relationship between organizations and the learning professionals who serve them is pretty straightforward. We are expected to enable the people in that organization to have the knowledge and skills needed to meet the organization's goals. It is worth noting that business leaders are becoming much more sophisticated regarding the role of learning and performance in achieving business success, and they are much more sophisticated consumers of the services we can provide. They know that more is not always better and less not always worse. And our most basic contract with each individual in the organization is to help him or her succeed, although those individuals, too, are more sophisticated consumers. These expectations form the basis of a contract, implied or explicit, between us and the organizations we serve.

But beyond that, every organization has a deal with its learning function, a set of expectations about what we will deliver. Every organization is somewhere on a continuum of needs, and the deal is based on where the organization is. Although it is seldom this simple in real life, it's easiest to talk about that continuum in order of increasing complexity.

Talent Delivery (Employee Orientation and Job Skills Development)
At the most basic level the biggest organizational need is new talent. People need to be trained on how to do all of the things the organization requires. Often, the emphasis is on creating common practices, common processes, and even common language. That becomes the primary expectation of the learning function.

Capture and Replication of Success Models
As an organization evolves, it invents or discovers the most effective ways to get things done. The most important learning need is focused on replicating those models of success and the deal with the learning function is primarily meeting that expectation. Our job becomes figuring out how that highly successful division or department or group does it so well and then teaching that to everyone else.

Tactical Business Issues
If the learning function has done its job well, the organization begins to call on it to aid in the pursuit of key goals. The learning is integrated into critical processes and into action

plans. Tactical business issues are big but are typically of shorter terms and are often things the organization has done before. Opening a new plant, implementing a new pay-roll system or sales process are examples. In this setting, we find ourselves more likely to be working as part of a larger team or task group, and it can be more difficult to address the need with traditional training alone.

Strategic Initiatives

It often seems that all learning professionals aspire to a fourth type of "deal" with the organizations they serve, that of supporting broadly based strategic initiatives. Strategic initiatives are larger in scope, longer in duration, and often are things the organization has never done before. Globalization, total quality management (TQM), and leadership development are examples. These can be the most complex, highest payoff interventions with lots of variables that can affect the outcome.

Organizations may expect one or any combination of the above. And because the needs are so basic and natural for the organization, the deal is implied, not stated. But precisely because the needs are so fundamental, it is critical to know what your deal is, and whether in the estimation of the organization, you are fulfilling it. Trying to be one thing when the organization is expecting another is a formula for failure.

And don't forget the ante. Every organization has a very basic set of expectations by which you prove your competence, your right even to be in the game. It may be managing class-rooms, registering and tracking students, or managing tuition assistance. These are the nuts ands bolts that you have to get right to be considered worthy of any deal at all.

Know Yourself

For the first 10 years of my work experience, I saw myself as having four primary roles. First, I was the *analyst,* who identified the needs of the organization, the conditions pres-ent that affected the ability to change, the size and type of gaps, and so forth. Second, I was the *coach,* who convinced and supported the organization and leaders through decid-ing to change and through the process of change. Third, I was the *strategist,* who looked at the big opportunities, the broad pathways to learning, and constructed the means for learning to be an integral part of the organization. And fourth, I was the *futurist,* who looked at where the organization was heading, and where the field of learning was going to bring the future of one to bear on the future needs of the other.

As time went on, it became clear that there were other roles worthy of note that con-nected the big four to each other. Between being the analyst who sees the gap and the coach who encourages bridging that gap, I also had to be a problem solver. I had to help the organization define the issue and select from alternatives. As learning strategies were developed, I found myself somewhere between strategist and coach, marketing and promoting support for those strategies.

Because the future is never precisely clear, I had to develop processes by which the leaders of the organization and I explored potential strategies together based on shared predictions of the future state we wanted. And once those future strategies were agreed upon, I had to apply the knowledge of the analyst to become the architect of new structures, systems, and processes that would be robust enough to meet future as well as current needs. But even roles like promoter and architect still allowed me, if I chose, to act purely as a servant. I could be a strategic business partner who never led the business. There had to be more.

Over the last several years, I have become convinced that the changes in the organizational, human, and learning environment, but most significantly in the new obligation of the learning function, require another way of looking at our roles. And they are new enough (at least to me) that I had to make up words to describe them. They may not be the best words, and smarter folks may replace them but for me they help to explain how we can be true servant leaders.

The first such role is that of the *synthesist*. The synthesist sees the patterns of ongoing learning moments (in addition to discrete programs or events). By seeing the big picture, the synthesist can recognize broad patterns of need, of essential fundamental issues. He or she sees basic connections to existing business issues and business measures and patterns of remediation options. The synthesist may be the only person in a position to see that a whole group of seemingly unrelated performance problems are due to a lack of project management skills in the organization. The learning and performance vantage point may be the only one from which it becomes clear that the organization learned best through action learning or responds most quickly to online performance support tools.

Because learning is now so fast, so distributed, and so individualized, we have a new responsibility to be the source of reflection on how learning happens. We must concern ourselves with metacognition. We must be the experts on how the organization learns best, and we must leverage that expertise to influence the organization. We must call attention to fundamental issues, call out the needs, and insist that the gaps be filled. We must do more than offer choices of remediation; we must recommend among options.

It is our duty to know more than anyone else in the organization about how learning works and how it should work. And it is our obligation to do everything in our power to lead the organization into that mode of learning.

The second new role is that of *experimenter.* I chose the word because these days many of the most important solutions we manage are truly experiments. With thousands of moving parts and interacting variables affecting the organization, our job becomes one of applying our experience and expertise to maximize the likelihood of success. As an experimenter, we must practice development forensics: the capture, use, modification, and re-use of deliberately or spontaneously generated capability from around the organization. We must establish momentary alliances with consultants, companies, universities, and individuals. The experimenter is not afraid of management fads but sees them as windows of opportunity. Instead of trying to resolve a dispute among division training groups over which supervisory program is best before launching a new initiative, the experimenter may devise a way to try all three versions.

Our expertise positions us uniquely to help the organizations we serve maximize the leverage that can be gained from the inevitable and pervasive experimentation.

If and when we know that an experiment has worked, our obligation is to promulgate both the results and the method that led to it.

Of equal importance is insisting that the organization move past those experiments that have the least leverage or that have outlived their utility. The notion of learning as experiment requires us to reconsider how we design the learning tools we create. Simply stated, you build things differently when you think of them as transient and disposable. Another factor that influences how learning is designed is understanding that, in the experimental world, we cannot control or often even predict who will use the tools we create.

The third role worth considering is that of *enviroguide.* For decades, learning professionals have honed the skills needed to identify the areas of development that are most likely to positively affect individual and organizational performance, select from all of the available information and tools in those areas those that will have the greatest leverage and are most likely to be learned and used, and determine optimum ways to organize learning, check progress, test use, and measure results. We honed those skills in an environment where we were likely the only ones in the organization who knew of the many developmental options available. Now that has changed—radically. Today, anyone can almost instantly access thousands upon thousands of potential sources of information and development. And that is precisely the problem.

An enviroguide may build self-assessment tools that help people focus their learning, create a portal with search criteria that locates learning programs consistent with company culture, or add staff who act as advisors to key groups on how best to learn.

As enviroguides, we must help those we serve to better understand where they want to go and help them to get there as quickly and safely as possible. In a world of too many options, we must help select those with the greatest potential. That means constantly exploring the changing landscape of learning and development, finding or building pathways that get to the changes the organization needs, and coaching and guiding those who want to be more deliberate in their development. It requires us to think about outcomes and vectors of change rather than programs and schedules and to think of assessment as trip planning, not just evaluation as trip reporting.

Whatever you decide is your role, it fundamentally affects how you will carry out your deal. If you accept this different view of your role as a learning professional, being a synthesist suggests that your job is not about organizing and integrating everything in advance, it is about seeing the organizing principles and ideas that already naturally exist and helping the organization to take full advantage of them. If you are an experimenter, you will spend less time trying to bundle knowledge and capability into courses and curricula and more time unbundling it into learning objects. And if you decide your role is being an enviroguide, you will be less concerned about collecting, coding, and warehousing knowledge and capability, and more interested in creating access to it wherever it naturally resides.

To truly lead, our obligation is to be on the leading edge of awareness of the many possibilities open to those we serve. Our greater commitment must be to strongly advocate the directions and resources we know will produce the best results. The difference between a vast repertoire of developmental resources and a confounding chaos of alternatives, between thousands of individuals controlling their learning and performance improvement anarchy, will be our willingness and ability to demand that learning—the right learning—takes place.

Where, when, and how we take a stand will rarely be dramatic. It will seldom be in the boardroom or the executive offices. Most often it will be a series of small decisions and choices to insist rather than concede.

Know the Language

I can't begin to count the number of times I've come across a training group that is agonizing over what to call itself. At least twice in my career I've participated in such a renaming exercise. Once, we decided that "The Organizational Effectiveness Group" was the title that would best describe the wide-ranging work that we did. In another case it was either the "Performance Improvement Group" or maybe "Team." Either way, it wasn't just the acronym that was unfortunate. After spending seemingly endless cycles selecting the right moniker, we spent even more time trying to explain to our customers who we were. (The conversation usually ended with them saying something like, "Oh, you mean you're the training guys.") We in the training (performance improvement/OD/HR/and so forth) world have a penchant for trying to teach everyone else to use the specialized language of our profession. We're not alone in that. Bits of the language of information technology have crept into most places. So have parts of sales speak and marketing language and engineering talk. But we in the development world are often not satisfied with that kind of entrée. We want our clients to speak with us about adult learning theory, enabling objectives, and intervention design. In reality, the language of pretty much any organization is about money, competition, and problems. Whether the organization is public or private, nonprofit, governmental, social, or religious, every organization has a budget. Making money may not always be the point of the organization; but managing money is always a necessity. When we speak the language of finance we are likely speaking a language already understood by our customers.

Which statement do you think would get a more enthusiastic response?

1. We're going to improve sales call planning.
2. We're going to increase sales quota attainment.

1. Our solution will introduce the new material handling program.
2. Our solution will reduce scrap by 20 percent.

1. As a result, we will greatly improve call center customer management skills.
2. As a result, we will reduce receivables cycle time.

When you can discuss your work in terms of revenues, expenses, earnings, margins, market share, and quotas, you are speaking a powerful language that needs no translation.

And every organization competes in a marketplace. We may be competing for buyers, members, users, or supporters. Every marketplace has a language, and everyone in it speaks that language. So should we.

The language of problems is unique to the organization we serve and the circumstances of the time. It is the language of the top management of the organization as they struggle to succeed and grow. It could be to "improve customer satisfaction," "increase membership," or "decrease operating expenses." It may be all about innovation, consolidation, or acquisition. Whatever the issues, the key is to learn and speak the language of the organization, and not spend too much time trying to teach everyone else the language of learning.

Know Your Limits

Don't overreach. People in our profession share a desire to make a difference, to make things better. We want to help as much as we can. And we are honored and excited to be asked to serve at increasingly complex and strategic levels. Our natural instinct is to say yes, and that's a really good approach as long as it is followed by a realistic assessment of what we can actually do.

We must objectively consider the talents and skills we bring to the organization. We may possess immense talent and experience in the design and delivery of workshops, be somewhat less gifted when it comes to job analysis, and really in the dark about job redesign. Our skill set may include process improvement, but not TQM. Being aware of our limitations doesn't have to stop us from accepting the challenge. But it should significantly influence how we get the job done. This is especially important the first time you get asked to take on a more expansive role. I have noticed (in myself and others) a tendency to resist outsourcing. But sometimes the best thing we can do is admit our own limitations and bring in an expert. When we do, we must also consider what value we add to the relationship between the outside expert and our customer. Often we can add significant value by managing the relationship or maintaining links between the outsourced project and the larger organizational context. But sometimes the best thing we can do is to just step out of the way. If we accept that our role is increasingly one of directing people to the resources they need, stepping aside gets easier.

It is also important to have a realistic view of how many things you can do at once. It's pretty common to hear training professionals talk about having too much on their plate. Getting involved beyond your capacity to deliver can hurt the organization and your reputation. And determining how many things you can do simultaneously is not just a function of your capacity. It has even more to do with the absorption rate of the organization. It is critical to consider how many solutions your customers can handle at the same time.

And finally, consider being "narrow and tall." Often we operate on the premise that any intervention must be universal in scope. (For instance, a sales skills program must reach all sales people globally, or a process improvement solution must be launched in all affected departments.) Especially in large organizations, one or two massive interventions can use up all of our bandwidth. In the worst cases, we find our efforts to be a mile wide and an inch deep. Both we and the organization we serve may find it possible to manage several interventions at the same time if each is initially a more narrowly targeted effort. And each may have much greater impact.

Know Who Your Friends Are

The majority of learning professionals I have encountered report into the HR function, and for many it is an uneasy relationship. In some cases this results from a belief that the learning function has a vastly different agenda from the rest of HR. In other cases the learning professionals don't want to share what they consider to be the less than stellar reputation of HR. I have never seen this conflict produce positive outcomes. But when the relationship is positive, those folks in HR are the best friends we can ever have. The basis of that friendship is a sobering realization: most of what we do in learning and development is a subset of a larger HR agenda. (This is true whether we report to HR or not.) They are concerned with optimizing the use of all human assets in the organization. They must be concerned with finding those assets in the first place and managing the larger processes that reward them and move them through the organization. When training is not enough to solve a performance problem, they are the ones who get the call. And just as we have seen the portfolio of the learning function expand, so has that of HR. We can argue the case that when we get involved in business process improvement, cycle time reduction, development of new management reporting systems, that we have gone outside the traditional HR charter, but even those arguments are pretty weak. More significantly, they are unnecessary.

Working together with our HR friends, we can take a much broader look at things like competencies, skills-based compensation, mentoring, and much more. There will probably always be skirmishes over turf; but in most organizations there is much more work to do than can be done by all of the available resources—yours and theirs.

In some places, organization development (OD) is another separate function. In such cases, tension usually exists with them as well. And although there are often real issues to be worked through to become friends with OD, another insight has helped me here. In organizations where OD does not exist as a separate function, OD work is still going on. And in organizations where training does not exist separately, it is still happening. We are all perfectly capable of working in the broader HR world, and our customers expect us to get things done regardless of charter. When a specialist shows up, it means that we are likely to get even better at serving the organization. Rather than worry about turf, we can focus on getting more done and on learning from the experts.

There are lots of other potential friends out there in the organization. Everyone wants the CEO (or equivalent) to be a friend of learning, and that sure beats indifference or hostility. But there are a few other friends worth making if you can. I learned about most of these the hard way. First, have a friend in finance. If it can be the CFO, that's great. You need a friend who can help you quantify the cost and benefit of what you do, and who can partner with you as you develop and manage the business of learning.

You need a best friend in IT. Nowadays most of what we do has a technology component. The days are long past when training can sneak by on a rogue server and buy applications that don't integrate with the larger IT system. Your friend in IT can help get what you do onto the master plan for the organization and avoid the black hole of technology reviews.

You need a lawyer. Your friend in legal can help you create a process that doesn't add six months of legal reviews to your critical projects but helps you to manage the risks inherent any time you are communicating to employees on behalf of the organization.

And last, make friends with centipedes. These are the people in the organization who can vote with lots of feet. If you are planning to roll out an intervention aimed at first-line managers, wouldn't it be great if your friend was the person that manages 40 percent of the first-line managers in the organization?

The time to make friends is not when some new project demands it. In fact, all five of the suggestions listed here are aimed at laying the groundwork for everything we do. It may be that the lessons I've learned won't be a perfect fit for you. As I look back, I see that the chances are good that you're a lot smarter than I was and have already avoided most of the mistakes I made. Still, it's worth asking the questions:

- Do you know the deal?
- Are you clear about your role?
- Do you know your capabilities and limitations?
- Do you manage your business using the language of the organization?
- Do you have all the right partnerships in place?

I don't know about you, but for me five positive answers would make me feel much more ready to learn what comes next.

❧

About the Author

John Coné consults on issues of organizational learning and to CLOs and others working to create great learning functions. He was one of the founders of Motorola University and was vice president of HR and CLO for Sequent, where he launched Sequent University and created the company's first comprehensive quality strategy. He was creator and vice president of Dell Learning and served briefly as interim CEO of ASTD.

He has been featured in *Fast Company, T+D, HR,* and *Selling Power* magazines, *Corporate University Review,* and was named by *Training* magazine as a visionary in organizational learning. His work has been profiled in four books on organizational learning, and the organizations he has led have received numerous awards.

He has served as chairman of the ASTD Board of Directors, the board of ASTD's certification institute, the editorial board of *Strategic HR Review,* and the board of SumTotal Systems. He is also a Gordon Bliss Award recipient

Learning in Organizations

Chris Argyris

H uman beings as a species are not really programmed to thrive in organizations. In fact, it would be accurate to say that we are skillfully incompetent and skillfully unaware of the counterproductive consequences of the behaviors we exhibit in our interactions with co-workers, managers, and leaders. If that were not enough, behavioral systems we have created reinforce counterproductive behavior. Is it any wonder that organizational learning often suffers from the consequences of our own natural tendencies?

To my point, human beings seem to gravitate naturally toward any excuse that relieves them of responsibility (that is, the spinning of truth, whether that means covering up, withholding information, or blaming others). This tendency is especially predominant when discussing organizational learning. Learning often suffers in organizations where:

- Leaders proclaim their focus is on learning, yet they support policies and values that inhibit learning.
- Organizational culture rewards the spinning of truth and cover-ups instead of an honest dialogue on the effectiveness of learning. These organizations are often very hierarchical and have unclear goals.
- Goals and self-confidence are high without a corresponding reality feedback loop.

Why Counterproductive Behavior Continues

So how do individuals become skillful at these counterproductive behaviors? How are organizations built to support and reinforce them? I suggest two answers. The first is the mindset human beings have when they create and attempt to correct these types of problems. The second is the theory of effective action that human beings have stored in their heads that informs their action.

Defensive Reasoning Mindset

Reasoning is defensive when its purpose is to protect individuals, groups, or organizations from being embarrassed or threatened. People with this mindset do not test the validity of their diagnoses and actions in the service of discovering some semblance of truth upon which they can design corrective actions and evaluate the effectiveness of their implementation. Their primary reason for testing is to protect the actors. Self-referential logic is a key reasoning process. The logic used to create the claims is the same as the logic used to test the claims—for example, "Trust me, I know this individual (or group or organization)," or "He will never agree." (See the case study in the sidebar.)

Another underlying feature of defensive reasoning is that it is mostly kept private. Transparency is poor, and asking for transparency is dangerous. Self-referential logic combined with a lack of transparency and bolstered with the belief that all is done in the name of concern and caring is a recipe for disaster.

Theories of Action

All human beings hold what might be labeled "microtheories of action" that specify what effective action is and how it can be produced. The theories of action people espouse vary widely, whereas the theory-in-use does not vary. Research has shown that

Case Study

One of the most common problems identified in the literature is leaders that espouse learning, but who act in ways that inhibit it.

Former secretary of state Dean Rusk organized a conference of senior State Department officials to explore ways of reducing the dysfunctionalities described by many as "foggy bottom." In one session, an assistant secretary of defense described how former defense secretary Robert McNamara's program on planning and budgeting could help make the State Department more effective. Immediately after his thoughtful presentation, secretary Rusk asked me to respond. I predicted that the State Department officials would resist. Secretary Rusk said that he found both presentations to be of value and asked others to give their reviews. Silence. Rusk then asked one of the United States' most senior ambassadors to respond, especially about the concerns that I mentioned. The ambassador thought for a moment and then he said, in effect, "Mr. Secretary, if you and the president ask us to implement these new programs, we will do so." After the session ended, the ambassador came to me and said, in effect, that he agreed with me, and he would say so to the secretary at a meeting later. I asked him why he did not state his thoughts during the meeting. He replied that doing so would be counterproductive and inappropriate.

The next day secretary Rusk told me that he was surprised the ambassador did not speak out during the meeting. After all, he selected him to attend because he thought the ambassador would be candid and honest. I asked the secretary if he said as much to the ambassador. The secretary responded, no, it would have been inappropriate.

Both men covered up their feelings and views on very important issues. Secretary Rusk, at that time pleading with the Foreign Service officers to be candid and honest, was not honest with the ambassador, whom he had personally selected to attend the meeting because he believed he would speak candidly. The ambassador, who knew that he was flown in to attend the meeting because the secretary counted on him to help lead a lively and candid discussion, also covered up his views during the meeting. Neither the ambassador nor the secretary was honest with the group.

For a cover-up to be effective, it must be covered up by another cover-up. The actor must behave as if he is not covering up. At the least, this is accomplished by spinning at best, by designed lying at worst. Both of these men disliked spinning, and both were against designed lying. They lived with this personal inconsistency by believing their actions were necessary to show concern and caring—to minimize upsetting the other, to minimize being held responsible for making the other defensive, and to set the stage for a successful implementation.

---

they are the same regardless of a person's gender, race, education, wealth, or organizational setting (for example, private or public, large or small; Argyris, 1982, 1985, 1990, 1993, 2000, 2004; Argyris, Putnam, and Smith, 1985; Argyris and Schön, 1996). The governing values of the theory-in-use instruct the leader to be in unilateral control, to seek to win and not lose, to suppress negative feelings, and to deny personal responsibility under conditions of embarrassment or threat. The dominant action strategies are to advocate one's position in ways that do not encourage inquiry into them and to deny that this is the case because one's unilateral actions are in the service of effectiveness. The consequences are self-reinforcing error and self-reinforcing and self-sealing process.

Human beings use this master program to create organizational defensive routines. They sanction and reward self-protective actions. Thus, they reinforce the unilateral, top-down model used by individuals who then reinforce the organizational defensive routines. These consequences create an underground world that competes with the above-ground world in organizations. Defensive reasoning mindsets and unilateral theories-in-use make it unlikely that the underground world will be dealt with.

Learning and Change: Professional Efforts

I believe it is fair to say that the early founders of organization development strove to develop theories and practices that were inconsistent with defensive reasoning. Beginning with the personnel growth movement, the argument was that the requirements for rigorous testing were "too rational" and "too scientific" (Argyris, 1967, 1968, 1972). The underlying reasoning used by these practitioners was that their orientation was "humanistic." A humanistic orientation did not require independent testing of claims. Indeed, independent testing was probably impossible.

The difficulty with this position is that it is impossible to test either the claims made or the effectiveness of the actions produced. It is impossible to answer the question of whether or not we are unrealizingly kidding ourselves and others because the logic is self-referential and self-sealing. The theory underlying this position when practiced leads to important inner contradictions. For example, contrary to its claim that the humanistic approach encourages learning and competence, it may do neither.

John, an active senior consultant, holds that an approach that emphasizes rigorous testing inhibits the expression and understanding of emotions. We jointly designed an experiment to test his claim. I became the client. I claimed that John's position would inhibit learning. I also acknowledged that I could be wrong and blind to the fact that I was wrong, which is why I "hired" him as my consultant. The experiment we designed called for John to help me see that my approach inhibited learning and emotions. We held our dialogue over the Internet. It lasted for about six months (Argyris, 2005).

The dialogue began with John's premise that there are two basic mindsets in consulting: one scientific and analytical, the other subjective and humanistic. The former places feelings in the background; the latter gives feelings a prominent foreground position. He characterized my approach as objective and his as subjective.

Each of us held a different position. I was objective and scientific; he was subjective and humanistic. He stated, "This in no way makes your position wrong."

If I accepted his reasoning—in effect, that each of us was correct—how would I ever learn that I may be unknowingly kidding myself and others? How could he ever help to generate such learning for me?

The following are some illustrative quotes taken from email composed by John (John has read and approved these comments as representative of his position):

- "It must be obvious by now, if the claims I am making are correct, your request (of how do I test the validity of my claim) is impossible to fulfill. There should not be a way to describe objectively a subjective mindset."
- "I believe that objectivity is likely to ruin the effect of emotional understanding. Making and sharing analytical observations will interfere with the conditions required to achieve the outcome that the client and the consultant want."
- "My hypothesis is that people would trust you more, like you more, and feel better about their relationships with you when you adapt what I have been describing as an empathetic or subjective mindset, as opposed to a distant or objective one."
- "I am arguing that we cannot obtain objective answers regarding emotional experiences, and that I cannot provide objective reasons why these answers are impossible."
- "Since I experience my own subjective feelings directly, a test (of their validity) is unnecessary."
- "My reasoning is that if you feel something, then for you, ipso facto, it is true."

As I read these claims I expressed questions about how John may help me to discover any potential blindness that I have. For example:

- "I agree that there are consultants who believe their position is correct (as illustrated by John). I do not agree when they claim that analysis of emotion necessarily ruins the experiences of these emotions. I could be wrong."
- "How can I learn from John about my errors if he tells me that objective understanding of his claims is impossible and that he cannot provide reasons that his 'impossibility' claim is valid?"
- "If I were to accept John's position as correct, would it not require that I accept the reasoning processes he uses to produce effective action? Would this not lead to my becoming dependent upon him?"
- "If I were to accept John's advice that thinking about my position 'too much' is counterproductive, what criteria would I use to judge when I am thinking 'too much' or 'too little' (if there is such a state as too little)?"

This dialogue continued throughout the experiment. I finally concluded that I could not learn about my possible blindness and how to correct it. John responded in a way that surprised me. He said, in effect, that he did not understand that the purpose of our experiment was to help me to see and correct my blindness. I referred to our early emails, in which this reason was stated as my purpose for "hiring" him. He said that there was a misunderstanding.

I do not agree. I interpret the claim of "misunderstanding" as a self-protective defense. I expressed feelings to John of betrayal. John responded to those feelings by repeating his claims that he never intended to enter into such an agreement with me.

From my perspective, John distanced himself from having any responsibility in dealing with my feelings by claiming there was an obvious misunderstanding. The irony is that his defense of "misunderstanding" was based on rational-objective reasoning. As his client, I felt that he reasoned in ways that made it possible for him to be blind to his part in the causal responsibility for the failure in our relationship.

Change and Human Nature: Is Participation Possible?

Another fundamental assumption of the humanistic approach is that genuine participation could lead to effective problem solving. Consultants often tell their clients that they represent hundreds of years of experience that could help the clients find new and practical solutions to their problems consistent with the humanistic approach, but the consultants do not test the validity of this claim.

For example, Tom is a senior organization development (OD) consultant in a very large corporation (Argyris, 2000). He was enthusiastic about a request by senior line management that the OD problems and business problems be integrated. Tom and some line managers designed such a change program.

The enthusiasm and commitment of the line managers deteriorated. Over time Tom became upset. He felt that the line managers were going back on their commitment. Tom decided to confront the line managers, who agreed that they were no longer enthusiastic because they felt the integration of human and business issues was not succeeding. They admitted that they did not know how to accomplish the goal. Moreover, they told Tom that they concluded that he did not know how to accomplish the objective, either. Tom admitted that it was true; however, he expressed confidence that with genuine participation, these problems could be overcome. The line managers disagreed. As one put it, it meant having confidence in participative processes of the blind leading the blind.

In my opinion, this case illustrates two fundamental problems. Tom activated his defensive reasoning mindset when he was having trouble. He acted in ways that he recommended against in his leadership skills workshop.

The second problem was that Tom had no theory of genuine integration. There was little basis for activating a productive reasoning mindset. Yet the line managers were using productive reasoning in dealing with the business and technical problems.

During the past five years, I have used this case in workshops that are attended by OD and other human resource (HR) professionals. The attendees are asked to read the case ahead of time. I then ask them to act as consultants to advise Tom on how to prevent this problem from recurring. The following excerpts were taken from taped transcriptions of these responses (Argyris, 2000):

- "I think the key (for Tom) is not to respond, but to be responsive."
- "Yes, I agree. Tom should try to develop, in some kind of a conversation, a real sense of what the survival issues are for the client."
- "Yes, and help the client to feel that all is not lost."
- "These are some ways that working to this end can really build some shared views of what might be possible."
- "And try to frame that in terms that are pretty understandable for folks (which is difficult to do) to connect directly to business performance."

Consider their responses:

- The advice is phrased in terms of end results: be responsive, develop a real sense of the survival issue, encourage the client not to feel lost, and craft the conversation in understandable language.
- The contributions do not specify what Tom might say to produce these end results. For example, what is the difference between responding versus being responsive? What is the nature of "some kind of conversation" or building "shared views" of what is possible? And what is "understandable language"?
- The causal theory in each bit of advice is not made explicit, which makes it difficult to test its validity. The speakers appear to believe that their advice is valid; they do not strive to test its validity. The features are similar to those produced in the previous two cases.
- The HR professionals were unable to produce the positive consequences they espoused in dealing with Tom. For example, I asked them to produce the conversations they would use with the "resisting" line managers. The conversations

---

❧ **W. Warner Burke** ❧

W. Warner Burke is a leading figure in the organization development and change fields. Burke is known for his emphasis on organization development as a change process designed to bring about a specific end result. Burke believes that organization development should involve such steps as organizational reflection, system improvement, planning, and self-analysis. Using a combination of theory and research to bolster his case, Burke stresses that organization development should be a deliberate, radical change instead of the gradual process typically exercised in organizations.

Burke is a professor of psychology and education at Teachers College, Columbia University. He has served as executive director of the OD Network. Burke is a one of the top 50 executive coaches and has consulted with a variety of organizations in diverse industries. Burke is the author of more than 130 articles and book chapters in organizational psychology, organization change, and leadership. He has authored, co-authored, and edited 14 books. In 1993 Burke was awarded the Lippitt Memorial Award (the Organization Development Professional Practice Area Award for Excellence) from ASTD.

---

were consistent with an easing-in process. Easing-in means asking the line managers questions, which, if answered correctly, would lead them to become aware of the ineffectiveness of their actions.

There were two negative consequences of the easing-in strategy. First, the line managers did not believe their actions were ineffective. They believed it was Tom who was ineffective, and that is why they refused to attend further sessions with him.

The second consequence was that the HR professionals sought data from the line managers about their pain and disappointments on their job. The line managers responded that their major pain was dealing with Tom. The following conversation illustrates the issues:

HR: First, I would start by asking the "resisting line managers" what is really on your mind at the moment. What keeps you awake?

Line manager (LM): I'll tell you. I want to make sure I get those business processes done because that is how I am being evaluated. I am a loyal manager—by that I mean a manager who produces the numbers, especially those I agree to.

A different HR: I would not talk that way.

Faculty member (FM): Fine, what would you say?

HR: I would ask what other things are on his mind.

LM: I am bewildered. You asked me what was on my mind. I told you. Did you hear me?

HR: I think I am trying to understand why these ideas are on your mind. I want to understand what is on your mind now.

LM: I am doubly bewildered. I thought I made it clear. I am striving to be a productive manager. So, I am going to produce according to the targets that I helped to set.

HR: What kind of targets are we talking about?

LM: You know. Produce X and Y with Z quality and do so consistently.

HR: What I am trying to understand is, given the targets, what is the disappointment at this point?

LM: The idea of disappointment is in your head, not mine. I am quite happy to do what I am doing. I am not feeling disappointed. In fact, if you would let me get on with my work, I would be quite happy.

I halted the role-play and asked the group members to reflect. I said, "One of you began the session with the advice, 'be responsive.' How responsive were you when you crafted this advice to Tom?"

HR: Not very.

FM: Would you please illustrate?

HR: Maybe Tom was not totally listening to the line managers. I would be ready to roll up my sleeves and ask, "How can I really help these guys? How can we really enter some meaningful dialogue to address their problems?"

HR: And do so in a way to find out what's wrong. There has to be something wrong, or else there is not much leverage.

HR: I start with a different premise. I do not go to "sell" to anyone. I require that they come to me. It's not manipulative. It's just the way it is.

The discussion here again becomes abstract. What does it mean, concretely, to "roll up one's sleeves," and "enter into meaningful dialogue?" The discussion also illustrates two assumptions often held by HR professionals: first, that to have progress, the client must feel some pain; and second, that HR experts should not "sell," but await initiatives from the line. In both cases, it is fair to ask why. The HR professionals seemed bewildered that I would question their two fundamental assumptions.

As the discussion continued, more of the participants began to make explicit their own sense of limitations:

HR: I am sitting here thinking, OK. Let us admit that we do not know. Maybe we should say so and ask them to work with us to figure it out.

HR: Yes, if we can admit that what we are doing isn't working, we would then all be aligned. We have no idea what the right "what" is, but let's figure it out together.

The Role of the HR Professional

When the HR professionals realized that they did not know as much as they should if they were to be helpful, they recommended shared dialogue and participation to figure out possible answers. But how can the blind responsibly hope to lead the blind? Imagine if other types of professionals—say, accountants—were to admit that they did not know how to produce a balance sheet and then asked their clients to participate jointly to prepare one.

To summarize, the HR professionals used defensive reasoning to craft their interventions. Their advice was abstract; it lacked explicit specification of how to produce the consequences they advised. Therefore, it was difficult to produce robust tests of the validity of their claims, and they provided themselves little opportunity to test where they may be unknowingly causing the very consequences they advised against (for example, making others defensive, acting inauthentically, and bypassing their own defensive reasoning and actions).

Finally, the HR professionals had no theory that could be validated and implemented for integrating the technical features of organizations with the leadership, learning, change, and commitment they espoused.

Interestingly, socialist planners in the former Soviet Union made similar errors. Participation by the workers was a key feature of their society. Many workers had doubts that were similar to the idea of the blind leading the blind. The socialists insisted that the workers participate and created the Red Guards to monitor their actions (Argyris, 2004).

Research: Part of the Problem or the Solution?

When we examine scholarly research on issues like openness, trust, honesty, and concern, we find that such research produces generalizations that if these behaviors are used correctly, they will necessarily lead to cover-up spinning, denial of the cover-up spinning, undiscussability, and cover up of the undiscussability.

❧ **Richard Beckhard** ❧

Richard Beckard was one of the founders of the field of organization development and is responsible for creating its standard definition: "an effort planned, organization-wide, and managed from the top, to increase organization effectiveness and health through planned interventions in the organization's 'processes,' using behavioral-science knowledge." This definition was published in his seminal work, Organization Development: Strategies and Models *(1969).*

Beckhard also worked in the field of change management. He helped develop the Formula for Change (also known as Gleicher's formula) with David Gleicher. The formula is used to determine how successful a change is likely to be, indicating that dissatisfaction (D) times vision (V) *times first steps (F)* is greater than resistance to change (R) or $D \times V \times F > R$.

The cause of these consequences is the rules in good currency about conducting rigorous research and generalizations whose validity is testable (disconfirmable; Argyris, 1980, 2004).

For example, some highly regarded studies on communication and trust concluded that if you are communicating to a large audience that you believe is smart, present more than one alternative if you seek to generate trust (Argyris, 2004). If you believe the audience is not so smart, present only one recommendation. Let us assume a practitioner seeks to use these findings. Does he or she tell the "smart" audience that they are getting several alternatives because that is the way to establish trust with them? If a member of the "dumb" group asked why the other group got several alternatives, would the practitioner tell the truth? I suggest that a politically correct lie is activated all in the name of trust (Argyris, 2004).

Studies of frustration and regression concluded that mild frustration increases creativity (Argyris, 2004). Beyond the threshold of mildness, the frustration leads to regression. Let us assume that a manager wishes to encourage creativity in her group meetings. Would she tell them ahead of time of her intention to frustrate them mildly? How does she determine when the threshold has been reached? How would she deal with any feelings on the part of the group members about being manipulated? Would they tell her?

In both examples, the research leads to advice to spin, cover up, cover up the cover-up, and to do all this to avoid upsetting others and getting defensive reactions.

Interventions for Effective Change

The first step toward effective action is to make valid sense of the problem at hand. The second step is to hold theories-in-use that act as master programs informing actors of the actions required if they are to achieve their intended consequences (that is, to act effectively). According to the research, most human beings in organizations (and across cultures, sexes, educational backgrounds, income brackets, and age groups) hold one theory-in-use, which is labeled Model I (see Figure 34-1).

Model I Versus Model II Theory

Model I theory-in-use is grounded in basic values. They are to maintain unilateral control; win, do not lose; do not express emotions; and act rationally. As illustrated, this model leads to skilled incompetence that produces such consequences as escalating errors, self-sealing processes, and self-fueling processes. Human beings and organizations have a theory-in-use that is counterproductive to their intended consequence, and a key reason they are unaware of this dilemma is the defensive reasoning mindset that accompanies Model I.

To begin to resolve the problem, it is necessary to help individuals become skillful at Model II (see Figure 34-2). Model II governing values, which are not the opposite of those in Model I, produce valid information, create conditions for free and informed choices, and promote acceptance of personal responsibility for one's actions. Model II action strategies include advocacy, evaluation, and attribution in ways that combine inquiry and public testing. The consequences of Model II include the reduction of self-fulfilling, self-sealing, and error-escalating processes and effective problem solving.

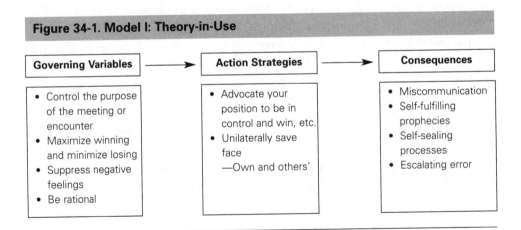

Figure 34-1. Model I: Theory-in-Use

Governing Variables	Action Strategies	Consequences
• Control the purpose of the meeting or encounter • Maximize winning and minimize losing • Suppress negative feelings • Be rational	• Advocate your position to be in control and win, etc. • Unilaterally save face —Own and others'	• Miscommunication • Self-fulfilling prophecies • Self-sealing processes • Escalating error

Figure 34-2. Model II: Theory-in-Use

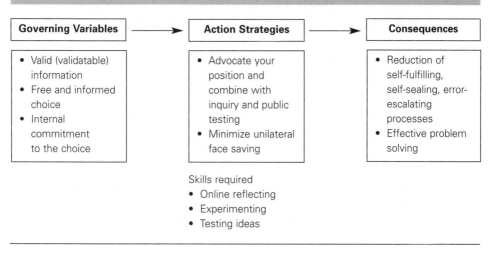

Governing Variables	Action Strategies	Consequences
• Valid (validatable) information • Free and informed choice • Internal commitment to the choice	• Advocate your position and combine with inquiry and public testing • Minimize unilateral face saving	• Reduction of self-fulfilling, self-sealing, error-escalating processes • Effective problem solving

Skills required
• Online reflecting
• Experimenting
• Testing ideas

The intent of the intervention is to help individuals become aware of the degree to which they use Model I and their defensive reasoning mindset. The interventions are also designed to help the participants become skillful at Model II and productive reasoning.

Single- Versus Double-Loop Learning

Moving from Model I to Model II requires not only changes in actions, but changes in the governing values and action strategies as well. This, in turn, requires double-loop learning to create organizations that have fewer defensive routines.

The reason that many leadership and change programs are often limited is that the designs focus on single-loop learning because the changes being proposed are consistent with Model I, and leaders are skillfully unaware of other possibilities. Finally, much of the academic research being produced also remains within Model I, even though researchers document its counterproductive consequences and defensive reasoning mindset. What is somewhat more bewildering is that the same researchers who document these patterns appear to cut off their own research on how to make progress away from the status quo, so that the new conditions required for double-loop learning can flourish (Argyris, 2004).

Key Features of Successful Change Programs

It is impossible within the scope of this chapter to present a detailed description of the interventions used in various organizations that are based upon the theory of action. Such descriptions are available elsewhere (Argyris, 1982, 1985, 1990, 1993, 2000, 2004; Argyris, Putnam, and Smith, 1985; Argyris and Schön, 1996). The following overviews the more fundamental ideas used to develop interventions and implement the designs.

The major focus is to obtain data from which it is possible to infer the theories-in-use of each participant, as well as the degree to which they use a defensive reasoning mindset. Thus, the data obtained should describe the actions and conversations that the participants use when they are actually dealing with the problems (that is, it should be in the form of tape recordings or actual observations of dialogue). Instruments such as questionnaires are adequate to infer espoused theories of action, but not theories-in-use.

The advantage of generating directly observable data is that it increases the likelihood that one can make valid inferences about the reasoning processes used to plan actions and implement a design. Another advantage is that by making the reasoning processes transparent, it is difficult for individuals to deny their personal causal responsibility in producing their actions. For example, they cannot claim that they did not interpret the researcher's inquiries differently, because the researcher's and subjects' inferences generated from the same directly observable data (for example, a conversation).

A final advantage is that subjects realize that if they attempt to deny their causal responsibility (that is, to blame any misunderstandings on the researchers), researchers are able to activate an inquiry into the validity of the inference processes used by the subjects and themselves.

Instruments used should be able to capture private data as well as crafted conversations. Any discrepancies between the two become an important basis for examining possible defensive reasoning and organizational defensive routine.

For example, subjects are asked to complete a somewhat simple case study that describes an important issue they are facing. They are asked to recall the conversations between themselves and others, as well as any thoughts and feelings they had that they did not express. Typically, for the kinds of problems that can be embarrassing or threatening, we find significant differences between the private thoughts and the public dialogue. We also find that the subjects cover up the differences and act as if they are not covering up (see Table 34-1).

If the spinning and undiscussables become public, it becomes legitimate to examine the discrepancies. Typically, the subjects respond that they have to hide the discrepancies in

Table 34-1. Private Thoughts Versus Public Conversation

Private Thoughts	Public Conversation
I am going to get attacked, straight out of the box.	I'm so happy to meet you and to get to know you. I think we will have a great working relationship and can learn a lot from each other.
What a bunch of garbage. I don't want to get drawn into this discussion.	I'd like you to know that I believe in open, direct communication.
Did he say *our* plan? He must have meant *his* plan. Doesn't he know I disagree with his decision?	No problem. It seems like we are at a crucial point.
Winning the Nobel Prize will not help the company. Perhaps it is time to expand development and downsize research.	I am sure you all realize that we work in a for-profit industry and must be realistically oriented.

the name of caring and concern and to avoid getting mired in organizational defensive routines. This response, in turn, often activates their stance that they are victims and helpless to change the situation.

As was shown in the sample cases, the claim that they are victims of the culture has some validity. But in making public their unilateral theories-in-use and their defensive reasoning mindset, they realize that they have built-in modes of reasoning and designs for action for which they are causally responsible. They would reason and act as they do in other situations, such as those involving family or close friends, or in learning settings.

Often this situation reveals a double bind. If they make their private thoughts and feelings public, they are likely to make others defensive. If they maintain their privacy, they create relationships that inhibit learning. This is why we recommend starting at the top of an organization.

Designing for change means that human beings have to become skillful at a new theory-in-use (ironically, one that many espouse). The governing values of this theory are creating informed choice, enabling learning as a key objective, and acknowledging personal causal responsibility. Productive reasoning is the mindset used, and its purpose is to test the validity of any claims made. The test should be independent of the reasoning used to create the claims. Self-referential logic is not used because of its self-sealing weak tests (Argyris, 2000, 2004). The key to making these require-ments part of the theory-in-use is practice so that the participants develop the requisite skills—within the seminars, but more important, in everyday life.

If Tom (in the earlier case) had been skillful at productive reasoning, he would have recognized what the line managers reported; namely, that his theory of effective inter-vention was equivalent to the blind leading the blind. If the OD and change profession-als had been skillful in productive reasoning, they would have recognized that they adhered to a theory of organizational change that was ineffective and, when used, made them skillfully unaware.

An important advantage of the theory-in-use that requires productive reasoning is that this direction is where information science is going. Information technology professionals tell us that truth (even with a small *t*) is a good idea. "Garbage in, garbage out"—IT is also grounded on the idea of rigorous testing of claims.

To summarize, whatever interventions are designed for organizations with the intent of encouraging learning around whatever substantive issues whose diagnosis and correction may be embarrassing or threatening (double-loop learning), they require at least the following properties:

- Collect data from which theory-in-use inferences can be made about the degree of defensive reasoning mindset and the degree of unilateral, win–lose suppression-of-feelings theories of action.
- Make public the degree of nontransparency, especially when issues are crucial, yet activate cover-up and cover up of the cover-up.
- Specify the organizational defensive routines. Specify the degree to which individuals enter organizations skilled with defensive reasoning mindsets and unilateral, top-down theories of action.
- Realize that ethical choices are required if people go with the status quo, or if they seek changes in organizations that are nontrivial.
- Realize that double loops in theories-in-use and defensive mindsets cannot be genuinely produced without individuals becoming skilled at producing these features, especially when the issues are difficult, embarrassing, or threatening.
- Practice is necessary to develop skills. The development of these skills is most likely to be effective when it is connected to actual "substantive" problems.

The good news is that the theories of managerial disciplines are increasingly being informed by the powerful developments of information science. The use of information science generates an ethical and moral flow. If IT supports truth as a good idea, it means it cannot produce its potentialities if human beings agree that truth is only a good idea if it is not upsetting, embarrassing, or threatening, or if they support practices under circumstances of massaging the truth, spinning it, covering up these defensive strategies, and denying that it is being done.

Closing Comments

I suggest that the examples in this chapter illustrate that behavioral systems exist in organizations with a way of reasoning and a theory of action that are counterproductive to the learning required to deal effectively with problems that are difficult, embarrassing, or threatening. This behavioral system may be characterized as an underground organization. It resists transparency and open inquiry because it violates the theories and practices acceptable in the above-ground organization.

I believe it is likely that above-ground organizations will try to deal with the underground organization by surfacing features that are counterproductive to learning. Unfortunately, this situation will tend to occur only when there is a tragedy.

Once the underground features have surfaced, the strategies tend to be to create new controls, produce new measures, and design new structures that specify responsibility. These strategies are helpful, but limited. It is time, I suggest, that when we try to understand the tragedies that occur as a result of these behavioral systems, we include a thorough analysis of the underground organization.

About the Author

Chris Argyris is the James Conant Professor of Education and Organizational Behavior Emeritus at Harvard University. He has consulted to numerous private and governmental organizations. He has received awards including 13 honorary degrees, as well as lifetime contributions awards from the Academy of Management, the American Psychological Association, and the American Society of Training & Development. His most recent books are *Reasons and Rationalizations: The Limits to Organizational Knowledge* (2004), *Flawed Advice* (2000), and *On Organizational Learning* (1999). He is a director-emeritus of Monitor Group.

References

Argyris, Chris. 1967. On the future of laboratory education. *Journal of Applied Behavioral Science* 3(2): 153-183.

Argyris, Chris. 1968. Conditions for competence acquisition and therapy. *Journal of Applied Behavioral Science* 4(2): 147-177.

Argyris, Chris. 1972. Do personal growth laboratories represent an alternative culture. *Journal of Applied Behavioral Science* 8(1): 7-28.

Argyris, Chris. 1980. *Inner contradictions of rigorous research.* San Diego: Academic Press.

Argyris, Chris. 1982. *Reasoning, learning, and action.* San Francisco: Jossey-Bass.

Argyris, Chris. 1985. *Strategy, change, defensive routines.* New York: Putnam.

Argyris, Chris. 1990. *Overcoming organizational defenses.* Needham, MA: Allyn Bacon.

Argyris, Chris. 1993. *Knowledge for action.* San Francisco: Jossey-Bass.

Argyris, Chris. 2000. *Flawed advice.* Oxford, England: Oxford University Press.

Argyris, Chris. 2004. *Reasons and rationalizations: The limits to organizational knowledge.* Oxford, England: Oxford University Press.

Argyris, Chris. 2005. On the demise of organizational development. In *Reinventing organizational development,* eds., D.L. Bradford and W. Burke. San Francisco: Pfeiffer.

Argyris, Chris, and Donald Schön. 1996. *Organizational learning II.* Reading, MA: Addison Wesley.

Argyris, Chris, Robert Putnam, and Diana Smith. 1985. *Action science.* San Francisco: Jossey-Bass.

For Further Reading

Argyris, Chris. 1991. Teaching smart people how to learn. *Harvard Business Review* 69(3): 99-109.

Argyris, Chris. 1996. Good communication that blocks learning. *Harvard Business Review* 72(4): 77-85.

Argyris, Chris. 2002. Double-loop learning, teaching, and research. *Academy of Management Learning and Education* 1(2): 206-219.

Edmonson, Amy C., and Diana Smith. 2006. Too hot to handle. Working paper, Harvard Business School.

Organizational Culture

Lisa Haneberg

In This Chapter

- ➤ Understand the importance of culture in an organization's success

- ➤ Learn ways to create and change cultures

- ➤ Align learning programs with culture for improved outcomes

---

Improving an organization's success through aligning its culture became a popular focus of work in the 1980s. During this time, many behavioral science researchers acknowledged the power and importance of organizational culture. In the last 25 years, organizational culture has become a frequent topic of discussion among a broad audience of leaders, including managers and organization development, human resources, and training professionals. Culture is now a regular topic during strategic planning sessions and throughout change management initiatives. The concept of corporate culture is important for all learning professionals to understand and use to construct their training plans and to align their development offerings for optimal effect and success.

What Is an Organization's Culture?

Many definitions of organizational culture can be found in behavioral sciences literature. A frequently cited definition comes from organization development pioneer Edgar Schein. In his book, *Organization Culture and Leadership,* Schein described culture as being deeper than behaviors and artifacts (1985):

> I will argue that the term "culture" should be reserved for the deeper level of basic assumptions and beliefs that are shared by members of an organization, that operate unconsciously, and that define in a basic "taken for granted" fashion an organization's view of itself and its environment.

Schein emphasized assumptions and beliefs while others see culture as a product of values. In *Culture's Consequences,* Geert Hofstede (1980) wrote, "I treat culture as 'the collective programming of the mind which distinguishes the members of one human group from another.' ... Culture, in this sense, includes systems of values; and values are among the building blocks of culture. Culture is to a human collectively what personality is to an individual." Beliefs and values are linked. What about understanding?

In "Organizations as Culture-Bearing Milieux," Meryl Reis Louis wrote that, "any social group, to the extent that it is a distinctive unit, will have some degree of culture differing from that of other groups, a somewhat different set of common understandings around which action is organized, and these differences will find expression in a language whose nuances are peculiar to that group" (1983). These three descriptions of organizational culture find root in collectively held individual thinking processes.

In their piece titled "The Role of Symbolic Management," Caren Siehl and Joanne Martin argued that "culture consists of three components: context, forms, and strategies" (1984). This description suggests a more systemic description of culture with both internal and external components. In *Riding the Waves of Culture,* Fons Trompenaars (1993) offers another systemic model and described three levels of culture: (1) the explicit layer made up of artifacts and products and other observable signs; (2) the middle layer of norms and values; and (3) the implicit layer, which comprises basic assumptions and beliefs. In *Corporate Culture and Performance,* John Kotter and James Heskett (1992) acknowledge internal and external components of culture, too. They see organizational culture as having "two levels, which differ in their visibility and resistance to change." The invisible level is made up of shared values that tend to persist over time and are harder to change. The visible level of culture includes group behaviors and actions, which are easier to change.

Is it important, or even possible, to sort out these definitions and decide which is most accurate? Schein, for example, argued that artifacts and products "reflect the organization's culture, but none of them is the essence of culture." The differences and interconnectedness of assumptions, beliefs, understandings, and values could be studied further to determine what is more elemental to culture, but would that be time well spent? What is more important, that a definition be right or that it be helpful? Although we cannot determine the right definition, each of these descriptions adds value to our approach to strengthening organizational culture. Based on the work of these and other researchers, we could make the following conclusions about organizational culture:

■ Each company has a unique culture built and changed over time.

■ Beliefs, assumptions, values, and understandings and the actions and norms they produce are important components of culture.

■ We recognize culture by observing actions and artifacts (explicit factors).

■ While some call it a subculture and others a climate within the larger culture, there may be cultural differences within subgroups of an organization.

■ Observable behaviors and actions are easier to change than are beliefs and values.

■ The observable elements of culture affect the invisible elements and vice versa. Change in one cultural element will affect other elements.

Although not apparent in these definitions, it is also important to consider how cultures external to the organization affect the organization's culture. For example, a silicon chip manufacturing plant in Portland, Oregon, employs workers from much different cultures than do plants in New Mexico or South Carolina. A strong internal culture will be enriched by the employees' diverse individual backgrounds.

Employees sense their organization's culture soon after they join the company. They might have a hard time describing the culture, but they know it when they feel and see it. There may be similarities in particular industries or regions (start-ups are fast paced, high-tech companies feel creative, Seattle-based companies are more relaxed), but each company will have unique cultural attributes.

How Are Organizational Cultures Formed and Changed?

Organizational culture is socially constructed—it is created and changed through conversations. Each conversation reinforces, builds upon, or challenges the current cultural norms and beliefs. The concept of social construction of organizational culture is vital for learning professionals and offers them a wonderful opportunity and poses two concerns.

The opportunity: Change the conversations, change the culture for the better. The concerns: (1) If you don't change the conversations, the culture will not change, and (2) conversations *not* for the change will make progress doubly hard to achieve.

One type of conversation involves the voices of the marketplace and customers. In *Corporate Cultures* (1982), Terrence Deal and Allan Kennedy suggest that each company's business situation creates its culture:

> Each company faces a different reality in the marketplace depending on its products, competitors, customers, technologies, government influences, and so on. To succeed in its marketplace, each company must carry out certain kinds of activities very well. In some markets that means selling; in others, invention; in still others, management of costs. In short, the environment in which a company operates determines what it must do to be a success. This business environment is the single greatest influence in shaping a corporate culture.

As market-related conversations change, so too will the company's. For example, if customers expect the option of online ordering, these conversations—in the form of demands and compliments and complaints—will reinforce this service as a basic requirement. In time, the organizational culture will reflect the movement to online order processing (or the aversion to it).

Edgar Schein believed that managers and leaders—through their daily conversations—create and change culture. Here is another quote from *Organization Culture and Leadership:* "Organizational cultures are created by leaders, and one of the most decisive functions of leadership may well be the creation, the management, and—if and when that may become necessary—the destruction of culture" (1985).

It is through conversations—talk, observed actions, listening, writing—that leaders manage, reinforce, and create culture. Leadership is a social act, and a leader's greatest tool for shaping culture is the conversation.

Improving the Organization's Culture

A culture can enable or hinder success. Learning professionals can affect the alignment of the culture with the company's mission and strategies. How? Culture is socially constructed, and managers and leaders have a significant effect on culture. Management development, then, ought to help build the skills needed to create great conversations and align conversations to best support organization goals. Training programs should also define, clarify, and reinforce the conversations that build the desired culture.

The organizational culture is particularly important when implementing companywide change. Many companies are struggling to keep up—they layer new initiatives onto the work processes before previous initiatives have taken hold. A culture can either enable or be a barrier to change. If the culture is nimble and constantly realigned, change will be more fluid and effective. Most large-scale changes need to be supported by complementary changes in the organization's culture. Change plans, then, should address current and desired cultural elements. Learning professionals can play a key role in facilitating change by aligning development programs to reinforce the desired culture through conversations.

Table 35-1 presents a set of questions you can use to assess and improve the alignment of development programs to better support the desired culture.

Table 35-1. Aligning Development Programs with the Desired Culture

Questions to assess current and desired cultural elements	Questions to identify alignment improvements
What are the desired cultural elements for this organization? How are each presented, explained, and reinforced in your development programs and activities?	In what ways should you change your development programs to better present, explain, and reinforce the desired culture?
In what ways do your development programs help build the managers' skills for facilitating great business conversations and using conversations as enablers to change?	What can you do to better build the organization's capabilities for using transformative conversations?
How well does the overall look and feel—the experience—of your development programs model desired cultural elements?	What improvements could you make to your training programs to better model the desired organization culture?
How current are your development programs—do they reflect the coming changes and help prepare the organization for new ways of working?	What can you do to stay abreast of major change initiatives and help prepare employees for these changes?
How many development conversations are there in your organization?	How can you create a culture of learning that goes beyond traditional classroom training?

✍ Chris Argyris ✎

Chris Argyris is a leader in the field of organizational learning. His early research concerned the effects of organizations on individuals. He found that traditional organizational structures caused individuals discomfort, damaged creativity, and reduced productivity. Instead of being free to work, employees have to expend energy navigating communication channels, levels of power, and performance goals. Because the needs of the organization are put before the needs of the individual, neither ends up being met.

Argyris and co-author Donald Schön wrote Theory in Practice: Increasing Professional Effectiveness *(1974). In this book, they developed the classic theory of action, which focused on the difference between what people say and believe they will do and what they actually do. The former became known as espoused theory and the latter theory-in-use. Argyris felt that people were most effective when their espoused theory and their theory-in-use were similar.*

From the theory of action, Argyris and Schön developed the concepts of single- and double-loop learning. Single-loop learning involves finding a problem and correcting it without altering the organizational model. Double-loop learning seeks to correct a problem by looking for the values or practices that might be causing the problem in the first place.

Argyris and Schön also identified two models of behavior. Model I behavior is evident in many people. People who exhibit this kind of behavior tend to work in ways that cannot be judged by others. This is seen as defensive behavior. People who exhibit model II behavior illustrate how they have achieved results and look for the input of others; this model of behavior facilitates double-loop learning. Both models of individual behavior can then apply to the organization as a whole if many employees exhibit the same type of behavior. Argyris found that model I behavior could actually inhibit organizational growth because employees act only in their own interest, while model II behavior promotes productivity and organizational learning.

Building a Learning Culture

Many companies say they want to build a learning culture. What does this mean? Generally, what they are saying is that they want people to be good learners, receptive to change, and willing to take on new tasks. A learning culture goes deeper than this, although these behaviors are certainly important. A learning culture is one where employees value continuous self-development and make learning a priority in the face of competing demands. A learning culture exists when a collective understanding of the importance of personal and team growth is backed up by a resolve to inject learning into everyday work practices.

Many development professionals dream of working for an organization that is sponge-like in its interest in continuous learning and growth. Trainers become trainers because they want to help people, and they know this is best done when people value development. There's nothing worse than having to cram training down people's throats all day, every day.

Development professionals can help their organizations build cultures of learning. Here are several important indicators of a learning culture:

- People are curious and adventurous. They value mental exploration. To what degree does the work environment encourage people to be curious and adventurous at work?
- People are allowed and encouraged to experiment. People believe is it safe to venture out and explore (within limits). Can people try new ways and approaches?
- The work environment is stimulating—sensual. The sights, sounds, smells, and textures are interesting and engaging.
- People at all levels seek and embrace learning in a variety of forms. This is the most telling clue. What level of participation is there in development programs?
- There is a healthy view of failure and mistakes. People are held accountable, but productive recovery is also rewarded, and mistakes are viewed as learning experiences.
- The workplace is intrinsically rewarding. When people are self-motivated, they seek more learning and development.
- The company is proactive about succession. It develops and promotes its people.
- The company has a focus on innovation—in all functions and at all levels.
- The company embraces omnimodal learning and communication—in-person, over the web, virtual, formal, informal, one-on-one, group, as part of regular meetings, separate courses, on site, off site, and so forth.

How does your work environment stack up? Development professionals can help build these conditions by offering valued and engaging learning opportunities in a variety of ways. Being a learning role model is important too. Development professionals need to practice what they preach and find ways to fit learning into their busy

schedules. Use the worksheet in Tool 35-1 on the accompanying CD-ROM to determine effective and aligned actions that will help build a learning culture.

Organizational culture is like the rudder of a large ship. To turn the ship, the rudder must move in the right direction. A company's culture can help it explore new horizons when it is aligned and properly managed. Like an inoperable rudder, if the culture does not move, or moves in the wrong direction, it is hard to make progress. Development professionals can build stronger training plans and programs by aligning their work to model and reinforce desired cultural elements.

About the Author

Lisa Haneberg (www.lisahaneberg.com) is an expert in the areas of management, leadership, organization development, human resources, and training, with more than 25 years' experience helping companies optimize results. She is the author of six books: *Organization Development Basics, Coaching Basics, 10 Steps to Be a Successful Manager, Focus Like a Laser Beam: 10 Ways to Do What Matters Most, High Impact Middle Management: Solutions for Today's Busy Managers,* and *Two Weeks to a Breakthrough.* Lisa authors a popular management development blog called Management Craft (www.managementcraft.com).

References

Deal, Terrence, and Allan Kennedy. 1982. *Corporate cultures.* Reading, MA: Addison-Wesley.

Hofstede, Geert. 1980. *Culture's consequences.* Newbury Park, CA: Sage.

Kotter, John, and James Heskett. 1992. *Corporate culture and performance.* New York: The Free Press.

Reis Louis, Meryl. 1983. Organizations as culture-bearing milieux. In *Organizational symbolism,* eds., L.R. Pondy, P.J. Frost, G. Morgan, and T.C. Dandrige. Greenwich, CT: JAI Press.

Schein, Edgar H. 1985. *Organization culture and leadership.* San Francisco: Jossey-Bass.

Siehl, Caren, and Joanne Martin. 1984. The role of symbolic management: How can managers effectively transmit organizational culture? In *Leaders and managers: International perspectives on managerial behavior and leadership,* eds., J.G. Hunt, D. Hosking, C.A. Schriesheim, and R. Stewart. New York: Pergamon Press.

Trompenaars, Fons. 1993. *Riding the waves of culture.* London: The Economist Books.

Chapter 36

Leading Complex Change

Patricia A. McLagan

In This Chapter

➢ Understand how the differences among transactional, transitional, and transformational change affect change initiatives

➢ Learn the four major responsibilities of change leaders

➢ Learn how to select appropriate change models and methods for effective change

---

Change guidance for organizations is a somewhat new discipline. It emerged as a recognized field of study in the 1980s, as a follow-up to the new emphasis on strategic planning. In most employee and management surveys, the concern for managing change trumps strategic planning as a key concern. Fortunately, models and tools exist to help address these concerns. What follows is my amalgamation of actions based on research, literature reviews, and my own decades of experience with changes of many kinds. I have organized them into phases. However, successful changes require both left brain (following steps) and right brain (sensing opportunities, learning and redirecting, knowing when to be assertive and when to stand back) thinking. Remember, part of any change process happens in the belly of the whale (Jonah), on the turbulent seas (Odysseus), or in the dark forest (Red Riding Hood) where road signs don't exist.

The change leader today has four major responsibilities when guiding a planned change. First, we must test the change and ensure it will add value. The second responsibility is to triage the change—identify whether it is simple or complex—and decide how much energy (resource) is needed for success. Third, the change needs an appropriate design and plan. The fourth responsibility is implementation. This requires commitment to the change plan while also being open to new options.

Test the Value of the Change

How many changes get started for the wrong reasons? Think about how often some organizations change their structures, their performance appraisal forms, their leadership, or their processes of all kinds. Recall the many fads and new initiatives accompanying leadership changes where new is something for its own sake: a transition or style shift, a departure from the old, even a critique of the old. Millions in time, money, and resources are wasted to support goals that could be achieved in other ways or may have already been in progress.

The change leader's first task is to query the value of the change, to estimate the costs, benefits, and risks. The change leader must help articulate the business case for change. His or her role is also to

- Help decision makers articulate the "why" of the change
- Articulate the value of what exists
- Assess whether what already exists is a better horse to ride to the finish than its replacement
- Speak up for appropriate actions that are under way but not yet completed.

Many ill-conceived changes only destabilize the organization. At times, this is good. It wakes people up, shakes the 80 percent of behavior that is automatic to life. But then what? Are there other, less costly ways to reenergize the organization than to restructure or introduce a radically new approach? Change leaders must speak out at this point, for the role requires it. Yet most change leaders stay still, accepting any change as fait accompli marching orders.

Triage

If we have determined that a proposed change is good for the organization, then the next step is to triage—decide how much energy will be required to ensure success. A key question to ask here is, "How much risk does the change present to the organization and its stakeholders?" One way to find out is to determine what kind of change we are talking about:

■ Is the change a simple one (a *transactional* change) that asks people to continue to do what they are doing, but in a faster, better, cheaper way?

■ Is it a change that is more complex, but others have done it and their best practices (benchmarks) can guide your success (*transitional*)?

■ Is this a change that will alter the course of things in your industry and put you at the front of a new paradigm (*transformational*)?

If the change is transactional, and people's roles are not in jeopardy or big systems and processes around people won't change, then a simple response is adequate. What's required may include communicating the "why" effectively, making single interventions like training, introducing a better machine or technology, or issuing a new policy. However, many changes today go beyond the transactional and thus require more complex responses: They are transitional or transformational.

Transitional changes involve multiple shifts and role changes where others have paved the way to success. Introducing a quality management process, a new enterprise-wide technology, or a more participative performance management process are examples. In these cases, the change has multiple facets: new approaches, new roles, new relationships and hierarchies, and radical skill shifts. But, for transitional change, even though the changes present multiple big challenges, there are precedents and benchmarks; other organizations have implemented them, and there are success formulas to follow. Because people's roles and the context for their work must change, however, the likelihood of failure is greater than for transactional changes. Thus the changes require more sophisticated change guidance methods and thought processes.

Transformational change is the most complex. It is like a transitional change in its scope, but there are no or minimal precedents or guidelines to follow. Benchmarks and history don't provide guidance. Consider the redirection of a company into bio-energy in the mid-2000s. This kind of change involves breakthrough strategies, a new vision of the future, major role shifts, significant new responses to customer or environmental needs, and attempts to introduce dramatically different product or service paradigms.

Clayton Anderson, in *The Innovator's Dilemma,* says that successful organizations are wired to prevent transformational shifts because their key internal and external structures and forces are wedded to how things are today (2003). Customers, suppliers, investors, and employees hold them to the past and resist implementing risky new ventures. The classic case is Bill Gates' and Paul Allen's launch of personal computer software before any of the big guys (including IBM) could reorganize around the emerging market. They went to their garage and started one of the major communication paradigm changes in history. On their own, they didn't have to face an entire value chain of suppliers, organization factors, and customers designed around mainframe and minicomputers. Gates and company started from scratch with little to lose and launched a transformational change that still rocks the planet.

Design and Planning

Designing and planning organizational change take different forms depending on whether you are dealing with transactional, transitional, or transformational change.

Planning and Executing Transactional Changes

Transactional changes are the simplest to plan and execute. Examples are changing to new collaboration software, installing a new machine, launching a new advertising plan, and implementing a product upgrade or a new product within an existing line. These changes involve three planning considerations:

- Plan how the technical aspects of the change will be implemented
- Identify what people need to know or learn
- Develop the communications, training, practice opportunities, or incentives that will prepare people to successfully act.

If it will help accelerate adopting something new, get opinion leaders or the affected people themselves involved in identifying their own needs and desired change support. Many other chapters in this handbook can help address transactional changes.

Planning and Executing Transitional and Transformational Changes

Transitional and transformational changes require more resources and more complex plans and actions than transactional changes. Why? Because these more complex changes involve major role shifts and realignments of systems, processes, and culture. Many failures occur because organizations treat these more complex changes as transactions, thinking that a communication from the president or a training program will suffice, as it does for a transactional change. Leaders of more complex changes want the water on the stove to boil (a major change), but they only turn up the dial to low or medium low. A cardinal change rule from physics is that the energy applied must match the energy required.

Transitional and transformational changes require a great deal of planning energy. The task is to develop a change map while getting support from and involving people who can make or break success (see Figure 36-1).

Figure 36-1. Change Map

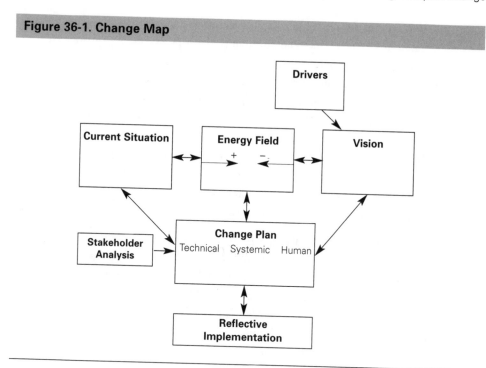

A change map answers these key questions:

- *Driver.* Why is the change required? What external or internal forces are driving it?
- *Vision.* What is the best, most desired result of the change? What will be happening in the desired future? What is the "to-be" situation?
- *Current state.* What is happening now? How do things work now? What is the "as-is" situation?
- *Energy field.* What are the current and expected forces for and against the change?
- *Stakeholder analysis.* Who are the key stakeholders—the people and groups whose support will be critical for success in the short and long term?
- *Change plan.* What is the action plan for bringing the change about? Group these into three categories and then place them on a time line:
  - *Technical* actions that directly relate to the change (for example, purchase new equipment, test it, redesign work to include new techniques, and train people in the new technical skills and requirements)

> — *Systemic* changes that must happen to support the change (for example, create new performance measurements and reports, redesign work spaces, and implement a new planning process)
>
> — *Human* interventions during the change to help stakeholders understand and support the changes (for example, involve equipment operators in planning the change, have team discussions of issues and benefits, and celebrate completed steps in the change process).

- ■ *Reflective implementation.* Change processes are dynamic. Plans are only guides. Effective change leaders make process interventions and modify change plans as they go. They continually ask, "What is working? What isn't working? What do we need to do differently to ensure success?"

Answering these questions is, by itself, a powerful change accelerator, especially when people from key stakeholder groups are involved. Many organizations create a change leader team, representing key stakeholders, to help define and then implement the changes. Change leaders can be middle management heads of affected units, or they can be opinion leaders from all levels selected by members of affected groups. The important thing is that successful transitional and transformational changes engage stakeholders in the planning as well as in the action stages.

Anyone in or around an organization can be a change leader. However, any time an organization asks individuals to be part of a change leadership team, it is important to provide the training and tools for guiding complex change. It makes no sense to put people on change committees without preparing them for their role. This is a key consideration during the planning phase.

Implement

Implementing a transactional change is a somewhat simple process compared with the other two options. It requires communication, training, and incentives. But transactional changes don't require complicated and costly attempts to get stakeholder ownership and support, and they don't cause major ripple effects across the organization. Transitional and transformational changes, however, require more careful attention to stakeholder buy-in and broader organization changes.

What can change leaders do to successfully implement transitional and transformational change? We haven't yet discovered all the possibilities, but, in addition to following and revising the change plan, actions include providing optimism and long-term view,

---

✍ **Kurt Lewin** ✍

Kurt Lewin is recognized as the father of social psychology. He was one of the first researchers to study group dynamics and organization development and was influential in the study of group dynamics and experiential learning.

Lewin may be best known for his three-step change model, which he developed in 1947 and which maintained its fundamental integrity through several iterations for nearly 50 years. The three steps in the model are unfreezing, changing, and refreezing. Unfreezing refers to the work that is required to move people out of their safe and comfortable status quo. To do this requires an understanding of forces that drive change as well as those that stand in the way of change. Lewin's force-field analysis identifies and measures the strengths of these forces. Driving forces are listed and given a value from one to four, and restraining forces are listed and given a value of negative one to negative four. This analysis helps the decision maker to assess the forces acting on a proposed change.

Changing is the process of doing all that is required to effect change. An important idea that Lewin put forth in this context is that change takes time and may involve several iterations of moving forward and sliding back before it begins to stick. Finally, refreezing involves institutionalizing the change and getting comfortable with the new status quo.

Lewin was also famous for his field theory, which emphasized how individuals' relationship with their environment affected their work. Lewin found that human behavior (b) was a result of an individual's activity (p) and the environment (e) in which the person works or b = (p, e). This was one of the first attempts at creating what is now known as a human performance equation.

---

working from change dynamics models, using situation-appropriate change methods, being reflective practitioners, and helping make change everybody's business.

Approach Complex Change with Optimism, Commitment, and Long-Term View

Any planned change is initially a wish, not a reality. Until it becomes real, one of the most powerful forces for change is the belief, confidence, and commitment of the people who are driving it. Complex changes inevitably involve barriers, challenges, resistance, inadequate resources, and pressures from the status quo. But change leaders must keep the long-term view, be optimistic, keep the torch glowing, and remain calm and centered as the organization (including change leaders themselves) moves through the dark forest and turbulent waters that precede transformation. A key goal is to get as many people committed to the dream as possible, making it clear that commitment is most valuable when results are uncertain.

Draw on Change Dynamics Models

Change seldom proceeds in logical steps, even though we may plan that way. There may be fits and starts, periods of rapid progress followed by plateaus and setbacks, times when resistance hardens, and phases of learning and redirection. The change leader must be equipped with mental models and ways of thinking that help make sense of and bring new insights to the seemingly irrational paths that changes take. The change leader who can filter changes through a variety of mental models is inevitably more centered and able to react with wisdom and with options that more reactive thinkers may miss. Among the many useful change models and frameworks are

- *The grief cycle.* Elizabeth Kubler-Ross depicted the process we go through when we experience a major loss: denial, anger, bargaining, insecurity or depression, acceptance, and adaptation (1997). This is the cycle that many people experience when they face a change that challenges their roles, capabilities, and position. A change leader must see these as healthy reactions rather than as resistance that must be put down. People need time, empathy, and appropriate support to experience and then to move through the cycle.

- *Complexity and chaos theory (the new science).* This presents an organic rather than a mechanistic view of change. The emphasis is on influential events, feedback, interdependencies, and the influential role of all parts of a system. Thinking from a New Science perspective, change leaders look for small changes that can trigger major changes. They feel free to work with groups who are most ready to change, even though they may not be the logical starting point, because change leaders know that change at any level can spawn changes at other levels. They know that the natural tendency of any organism is to solve its own problems. Knowing this, they may decide to back off and let groups figure things out themselves, or they may increase the amount of feedback related to the change. They don't try to control all aspects of the change, because they know this is impossible and futile and may create additional problems.

- *Time span thinking.* Change leaders think of the short, medium, and long term simultaneously, knowing that too much emphasis on one over the other will deplete energy. There must be enough short-term successes to fuel energy and optimism. There must be enough attention on the long term to keep the end state in view and support judgments that must occur along the way. And mid-range plans need to continually provide benchmarks and resource planning criteria.

■ *Quality and acceptance criteria.* Years ago, Norman Maier (1982) suggested a simple decision model for determining whom to involve in decision making and planning: "Involve people who have information that is necessary to make a quality decision or plan; and involve people whose acceptance of the decision will make or break its success." This is an excellent guideline for plans and decisions at all phases of a change process.

■ *Organization design models.* For organizations to work, several elements must align: structure, strategy, work and job designs, systems and processes, people, rewards, culture. One vital role of a change leader is to help ensure that these elements incorporate and support the change. Changes often create major disconnections among critical design elements (for example, the shift to a team-based approach won't work if rewards or the culture itself doesn't support teamwork). If design discrepancies are not addressed, both the change and the organization will suffer.

■ *Diffusion of innovation curve.* People vary in their speed of adopting change. Some are more apt to propose changes and get them into the change agenda. Others are early adopters: adventurous, committed to the end goal, able to accept uncertainty, on board early. Others get involved at various stages of planning and implementation. Still others hold out until major parts of the change are implemented and working. Personality characteristics, legitimate concerns, and fears all affect where people fall on the innovation curve. The change leader needs to expect these individual differences, use the energy of the early adopters, and find ways to respectfully help others get on board faster. The next section suggests techniques that can help shorten the curve.

Use Situation-Appropriate Change Approaches

Years ago, a fundamental goal in managing change was to prevent and subdue resistance and to expect people to quickly comply with change demands. Managing change was the equivalent of controlling resistance. Today, we have a more sophisticated understanding of the role of resistance in helping to test and refine changes, to increase adrenaline for learning, and even to provide some of the emotional energy that ultimately helps drive change. Also, early deliberate change efforts assumed a compliant workforce content to operate under command-and-control conditions.

Today's change leaders go beyond tell-and-sell tactics. They draw on a variety of approaches to help accelerate people's constructive engagement with important changes. Approaches range from leaders mandating changes to workers deciding what must be done. They include the following methods:

- *Directives.* Even though participative techniques are in style today, there are many times when it makes sense for management to make and impose decisions. Leadership teams may face a crisis or use their executive authority and strategic responsibility to steer the organization in a different direction. This approach is grounded in insights and theories about uses of power.

- *Rewards and other consequences.* Behaviorist theories hold that people pursue rewards and incentives and avoid punishing consequences. So, connecting consequences to change-supporting behavior can be a powerful change approach. This approach is grounded in behaviorist theories and insights.

- *Persuasion.* Persuasion involves understanding what affected people will see as the natural benefits of a change and then selling these benefits to them. This approach draws from studies of values, beliefs, and attitudes.

- *Education.* Education and training help people learn about the changes—why they are happening and what knowledge and skills are involved. Education and training are usually biased in favor of the change and what will make it work. This change approach has an obvious grounding in education and training theories and practice.

- *Role redesign.* When people's roles change, new expectations and behavior change often come with it. Think about how behavior changes when individuals become formal leaders—supervisors, project leaders—after being individual contributors. This approach draws on insights and theories related to organization structure and work design.

- *Opinion leader involvement.* Every organization and group has people who are opinion leaders. Regardless of their formal titles, they operate as communication facilitators and network nodes. Their support is vital for success, and they can be very powerful roadblocks. Engaging them in a formal way can be a key change accelerator. The theoretical base for this approach is sociology.

- *Collaboration.* This change approach involves meaningful interaction—in planning and implementation—among formal leaders, technical experts, or people who must implement. Collaboration differs from the grassroots technique below because it includes a variety of relevant perspectives beyond those of the people affected.

- *Open information.* Here, there, everywhere is full disclosure...everyone has access to change-related information, whether it is supportive, contrary to, or neutral related to the change path. The assumption is that reasonable people, given full information, will appreciate the complexity of the conditions surrounding the change and will know enough to appreciate and participate in decisions and plans. A somewhat new information science underlies this approach.

■ *Grassroots.* In this approach, people who must support and implement changes make decisions about what to do or how to do it. It is the most bottom-up approach. Sometimes people will launch this change approach without it being part of the organization's formal change strategy. The wise change leader will incorporate grassroots actions into the change process even when they spontaneously arise—perhaps sensing them before they become major movements. Find the best insights about the dynamics of grassroots change actions in studies of mass movements and action and even revolutions.

These nine change approaches fall along a continuum ranging from top-down to bottom-up (see Figure 36-2). The top-down end of the continuum puts *pressure* on people to change. This creates quick response and compliance and can help redirect energy, but obviously can also create resentment and backlash. The bottom-up end of the continuum creates *space* for people to go through their grief cycle and become owners of the change. Space techniques take time and are more chaotic, though, and require participants to have skills in areas like decision making and collaboration. Running across the entire continuum is *empathy.* Empathy involves listening and seeing situations through others' eyes.

Figure 36-2. Change Strategies Continuum

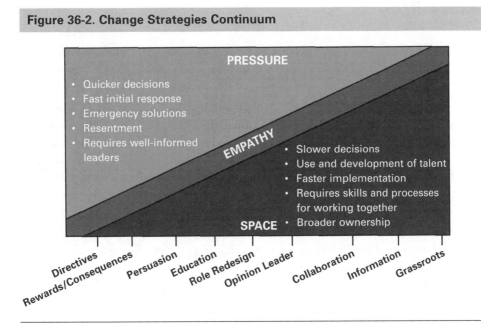

✒ **Edward E. Lawler III** ✒

Edward E. Lawler III is an influential scholar in the fields of improving organizational performance, change management, and human resources development. In addition to being a well-respected scholar and professor, Lawler is a perennially popular consultant, author, and speaker on a diverse range of topics such as motivation, organizational change, high-performance organizations, strategic human resources management, reward systems and pay, organization design, corporate boards, and organizational effectiveness.

In 1979 Lawler founded the Center for Effective Organizations (CEO) at the University of Southern California's Marshall School of Business. The CEO conducts research on organizational design and effectiveness, and its academic theories and research inform and influence corporate practices worldwide. The CEO has a corporate sponsorship network of more than 60 major Fortune 500 corporations.

Lawler's research method, with its blend of theory and practice, appeals to both the mass market as well as scholarly journals. Some of his more popular works include Motivation in Work Organizations *(Jossey-Bass, 1994), in which he theorized that an effective organization must motivate and encourage employees to perform well;* From the Ground Up *(Jossey-Bass, 1996), in which he completely rethought the old ways of organizational structure and formed six principles for organizing and managing a company based on a new logic intended to rebuild the organization from the ground up; and* Tomorrow's Organization *(Jossey-Bass, 1998), which offers solutions and guidelines for creating organizations that can compete successfully in the 21st century, including progressive ideas about customer product structures, design issues in networked organizations, and the structuring of global organizations.*

It is a very important change technique throughout the change process and may be the only effective action when people are in various early stages of the grief cycle, especially anger or insecurity.

Many successful complex change processes follow a common pattern. They start with a decision (*directives*) about what will change, presented in a way that connects with stakeholders (*persuasion*). Then come more participative approaches regarding how the change will be implemented (*opinion leader involvement, grassroots planning, information, collaboration*). These are followed by middle-range techniques (*role redesign, education*). By this point, people have had a chance to understand and contribute to the changes and to go through their own change process: more top-down methods (*directives* and *rewards and other consequences*) come into play. This is the time to sustain the changes and also to deal with any resistance that persists because some people may not be able to adapt and contribute to the new ways.

The point here is that change leaders can facilitate and draw on any and all of these approaches. Each has advantages and disadvantages, each is appropriate at various times in a change process, and each must be effectively integrated if forces beyond the control of the change leader bring it to the fore.

Here are some general guidelines for selecting from the change options:

- For changes relating to crises or survival and for changes that have been identified through thoughtful strategic planning processes, pressure techniques can introduce the change. But these must be immediately followed by space techniques that involve people in deciding how to refine the plans and implement them.

- When facing early stage resistance, use empathy and space methods to help reduce the disruptive forces and to give people time to work through their own emotions and reactions.

- When resistance patterns repeat, use collaboration and opinion leader approaches to help bring implementers into closer contact with change-related expertise. This may also help identify any shortcomings in the change itself and new actions for dealing with them.

- Use middle-range techniques (education, social influence, and structure) after the early introductions of the change to reinforce the nonreversibility of the change and to build commitment and skills, while also keeping open to new insights.

- Change peoples' roles after the new change requirements for deliverables, tasks, and technology are clear. Because this clarity may not occur until the organization is well into the change, an interim solution is to overlay temporary task and project groups on the old structure. Waiting to make permanent role changes helps avoid excessively destabilizing the organization and ensures the best work designs for sustainable change. However, new roles do spawn new behaviors. The change leader has to weigh costs and benefits of using this approach earlier versus later in the process.

- If change isn't happening after people have had time to work through their grief cycle, get information and education, participate in the change process, then shift toward the higher-pressure end of the continuum. At this point confront lingering resistance as a performance problem (move to the pressure end), but only do this if it is clear that you are dealing with personal resistance and not a fundamental deficiency of the change itself.

- Whenever possible, work at the space end of the continuum. Excessive and ill-timed use of pressure tactics increase resistance and don't ensure lasting commitment. Space methods are more likely to generate deep levels of commitment. Pressure methods generally create compliance—which you'll have to continually enforce after the change.

- When resistance is virulent, first make sure the resistance is not due to major faults in the change plan itself. Then, use empathy and space both to help people work through their personal change fears and also to mine their ideas. However, if resistance continues, take decisive and clear action—giving the resister a choice of taking time off, getting on board, or leaving.

- When resistance is passive, use space techniques to help people get actively involved. It's easy for people to hide and be passive when change approaches are at the pressure end of the continuum.

Be a Reflective Practitioner

Change leadership is as much about being as it is about doing. Who the change leader is as a person is a powerful driver (or inhibitor) of the process. Personal qualities include emotional maturity, a learning orientation, and the ability to stand outside the process and apply a variety of relevant thinking frameworks (see the change dynamics models presented earlier in this chapter).

The effective change leader is what Donald Schon (1983) calls a "reflective practitioner." He describes the reflective practitioner as someone who "appears to be an artist...responding in simple, spontaneous ways to complexity, spinning out long lines of invention and inference, holding several ways of looking at a problem without disrupting the flow of inquiry, and shifting paradigms when stuck."

Obviously, to be a reflective practitioner, the change leader must approach the role as a professional: learning about change issues and approaches, taking time to reflect on what is going on, and helping others think from a change perspective. This means that guiding change cannot be just another task. It must be a passion, a commitment, and a special practice with unique skills and thought processes. Reflective change practice may be the most important success factor of all, for it ensures that the change process remains alive and vibrant throughout all of its stages.

Make Change Everybody's Business

Most people's education prepared them for more stable times. "I can't wait for this change to be over so we can get back to business as usual," they say. Stability is the assumed norm. However, especially in these knowledge-work times, all three forms of change—transactional, transitional, and transformational—are continually under way. This requires everyone to be a change agent—to understand change dynamics and models, to be reflective practitioners. Today this happens mainly by osmosis. But in the future, everyone's ability to recognize and deal with his or her own resistance, for example, will be a real personal and organizational advantage. Passing on change leader skills is an important emerging challenge for all of us.

Moving Forward

Today's organizations face many change drivers, both from within and without. Increasingly, training, restructuring, and other unilateral methods to increase efficiencies are not robust enough by themselves to deliver the transitional and transformational changes that are required. Many linear and mechanistic models and maps exist to guide more complex change processes. However, unless they are implemented in a dynamic, responsive, flexible, and sensitive way, linear approaches often fail.

It is up to the change leaders—people who study models and practices for guiding the often nonrational paths of change—to help ensure that the changes we desire are good ones and are implemented successfully by maintaining optimism, working from change dynamics models, using situation-appropriate change methods, being reflective practitioners, and helping to make change everyone's business.

❦

About the Author

Patricia A. McLagan's first change program was for NASA in 1975. Since then, she has worked on major change projects and taught leadership courses on change for public, private, government, and nonprofit organizations throughout the world, including extensive work in South Africa. She is a passionate student, teacher, consultant, leader, and writer in the change field. Her 2002 book, *Change Is Everybody's Business*, has sold more than 135,000 copies and been translated into eight languages.

References

Anderson, Clayton. 2003. *The innovator's dilemma: The revolutionary book that will change the way you do business.* Boston: Harvard Business School Press.

Kubler-Ross, Elizabeth. 1997. *On death and dying.* New York: Scribner.

Maier, Norman R.F. 1982. *Psychology in industrial organizations.* 5th ed. New York: Houghton Mifflin.

Schon, Donald A. 1983. *The reflective practitioner: How professionals think in action.* New York: Basic Books.

For Further Reading

Campbell, Joseph P. 1972. *The hero with a thousand faces.* Princeton, NJ: Princeton University Press.

Christensen, Clayton. 1997. *The innovator's dilemma.* Boston: Harvard Business School Press.

Conner, Daryl. 2004. *Leading at the edge of chaos: How to create the nimble organization.* New York: John Wiley & Sons.

Kotter, John. 1996. *Leading change.* Boston: Harvard Business School Press.

Galbraith, Jay. 2001. *Designing dynamic organizations: A hands on guide for leaders at all levels.* New York: AMACOM.

McLagan, Patricia A. 2002. *Change is everybody's business.* San Francisco: Berrett-Koehler.

Pinkola-Estes, Clarissa. 1992. *Women who run with wolves.* New York: Ballantine Books.

Chapter 37

The Learning Organization Today: An Interview with Peter Senge

Elaine Biech, interviewer

How do you define a learning organization and how has your definition changed over the years—or has it?

I think the people and organizations throughout the Society for Organizational Learning (SoL) network still define a learning organization as "an organization that is continually expanding its capacity to create its future." The underlying ideas—systems thinking, mental models, personal mastery, shared vision, and dialogue—predate *The Fifth Discipline* by more than 10 years, and the term *learning organization* eventually arose as a convenient umbrella term to designate the kind of organization that commits itself to such disciplines to develop its learning capabilities.

The basic meaning hasn't changed over the years. There are two ways we think about learning. We *learn about* a lot of things, which is acquiring information. But we *learn how* to do something, which is a more fundamental and pragmatic notion of learning. Organizations need to continually learn how—because it is key to their survival and ability to innovate, generative learning. Because information is so widely available today, learning *about* is much easier, but by itself does little.

What is the key differentiating factor between learning organizations and other organizations? Does an instrument exist that measures the degree or extent that an organization has reached a certain level of being a learning organization?

Learning organization was always meant to describe an ideal. In one sense, all organizations that continue as the world around them changes are learning. But some are much better at it than others. I prefer to avoid labeling—saying this organization or that is a learning organization—because I really don't think that sort of labeling helps very much.

I don't have a tool to measure a learning organization, nor would I be interested in one. I think it would be superficial to try to measure. I know that some people do have tools but I try to avoid that. It would be like asking the question, "What makes a good person?" There is no tool to measure that because it is not possible to measure the various attributes that one could use to decide whether a person was "good." We are always in the process of becoming a better people as we mature. And, in the abstract sense, measuring a learning organization would be about assessing its people. We are always in a state of incompleteness. Assessing an organization sets the organization in a fixed state and has the potential to undermine its ability to continually expand its capacity to create its future.

I don't think we can characterize an ideal and embody it in an assessment tool. What does help, as a person, is having some idea of what is possible in my development as a person and having principles and methods to guide me in the journey. The same is true for organizations.

What is the role of the workplace learning and performance (WLP) function in a learning organization?

I'm not sure what you mean by the workplace learning and performance function, but if you are referring to something like a training department in human resources (HR), this is where many organizations must reconsider how to learn, grow, and adapt to future requirements.

It is the line manager who must be the most responsible for employees' growth and development—not an HR department. It is the line manager who must be committed to learning as an organization. A line manager in a learning-oriented organization is responsible for producing results and enhancing the capacity of people to produce results in the future. The HR function can be an important complement in this work, but it is the learning environment in the day-to day work that truly matters in growing people. Unfortunately that attitude is not present in many managers.

Specifically, it is the capability of working teams that determines what an organization can achieve. Very early in *The Fifth Discipline*, I asserted that the "working team" is the fundamental learning unit in any organization. Learning that affects performance is never just a matter of adding up individual skills or learning. For example, one could not just gather a group of excellent basketball players or a group of exceptional performing artists and expect to get good results. A team of any kind must grow and develop together.

Unfortunately when we place learning in the hands of an HR department, it takes on the guise of a class. Classes take learners out of their natural environment, which is why activities such as mentoring and coaching have received more attention recently. Those are more natural than a classroom setting.

Training departments or HR must partner with line managers. As partners they must examine the business strategy and the goals required to grow the business. They can help line managers in growing their people, but they are no substitute for managerial commitment, nor should they take on the accountability for workforce learning, lest they "shift the burden" away from managers.

What support do learning and performance professionals require to ensure their organization is doing all it can to expand its capacity to create its future? How do you recommend they obtain that support?

Most of the support is tied to budgets and financial constraints. When times are good there are usually few problems, but when cost-cutting measures are required, support is in jeopardy. For example, I have watched some otherwise good organizations in recent years cut their internal consulting drastically, even though many managers found it a useful process. This is a classic problem of misused metrics and myopic cost management. It is inherently difficult to measure the results of internal consulting. Internal consulting is available to help working teams. If the consulting was successful, the team gets the credit; if it was not successful, people say, "See, consulting doesn't work!" Rather than creating an internal market where managers can pay for this help if they find it useful, many companies set it up as part of HR and then, when a new cost-cutting HR head arrives, it is cut.

Similarly, the impact of training is also hard to measure. So, people rely on metrics that are easier to count, such as "butts in seats." This really doesn't help much—because it still avoids the fundamental question of real value to the business and leaves the training department a likely target when cost cutting arrives.

The best way to obtain the support required is to understand the systematic needs of the business and build a rich network of business partnerships. In this way, learning and performance professionals must become coaches and mentors to line managers, helping them develop their own skills to solve their own problems and to build strong teams. They must understand that it is all about teams and that they must focus on results. In the end, results are difficult to measure, but so too are the effects of most investments. Good organizations get good at assessing what sorts of investments are working in what ways through a mix of qualitative and quantitative means. But this only happens when enough managers are genuinely engaged in growing people and looking for better and better ways to help this.

Systems thinking is of course one of the five disciplines. What is the link between systems thinking and learning in an organization?

An organization's problems are easy to articulate but often difficult to resolve. Part of the reason is that the solution rarely addresses the underlying systemic cause. Most people do not know how to identify or solve the root cause of the problem. It may be difficult to see the interrelationship of causes that have existed for 10 or 20 years, whereas the problems of today are very visible. This results in superficial Band Aids put in place that may appear to resolve problems temporarily but do not touch forces that maintain the status quo.

This is similar to the dysfunctions of a family. Everyone knows they exist, but no one does anything about them. The same is true for an organization. Interrelated patterns are deeply embedded in the way an organization operates. These patterns and ways of acting become habitual, and people get stuck saying things like, "That's the way it works around here," or "It's the stupid system." The problem may be justified by believing that no one can do anything about it.

It takes organizational learning and team learning at many levels to identify and resolve the underlying systemic cause.

What is the relationship between learning and culture and how do they affect each other?

The culture is influenced by what is being learned. Most often a culture learns from what's not working. People discuss what's difficult, what they understand, and what they don't understand. In a learning organization, people learn from what's not working, and they have high aspirations when they fail. The key is not to just get it right, but to discover what works and what doesn't. We don't get things right the first time. When we learn to walk, we fall down a lot. When this happens in an organization, the organization is learning, and the culture changes. A learning culture is one that is continually regrouping.

Children begin life with a natural desire to learn. They love to learn, think of learning as fun, and are not concerned about looking foolish. Unfortunately schools often change that playful attitude, and children soon learn that school is about getting the right answer and that mistakes are bad. By the time children leave school, they have been conditioned to appear self-assured and certain that they have their acts together. Unfortunately, once we cannot embrace uncertainty, we are not able to continue to learn.

If learning is truly a part of an organization's culture, there is an attitude that we are never "there" because there is always more to learn. Learning is a sign of an organization that is expanding its capacity to create its future. One of W. Edwards Deming's favorite quotes was, "Learning is not compulsory; neither is survival." He believed that management must undergo a transformation and that the first step was transformation of the individual. This transformation comes from understanding what he called "the system of profound knowledge," which started with "understanding a system." But such a transformation is only possibly through continual learning.

One could say that learning and culture depend upon one another; when learning is low, cultures tend to become rigid, and adaptation becomes difficult or impossible.

How about organizations? What's on the horizon for organizations, and what do they need to learn to do better?

Organizations will need to learn how to better deal with the external forces that are fundamentally reshaping their environment. We are facing a huge shift over the next couple of decades. The last 25 years of embedding the basics of organizational learning have just been a warm-up act, because the wheels are about to come off the train of globalization. We are violating the basic laws of nature. Nature produces no waste. We in the United States produce one ton of waste per person, per day. Carbon dioxide in the atmosphere is now 30 percent higher than at any time in the past half million years, and emissions entering the atmosphere worldwide are three or four times what is being removed; climate instability is affecting people, especially poor people, around the world. Available water is arguably the most acute problem in the world, with a growing percentage of us having no access to drinkable water, while those of us in the rich northern countries spend twice as much for bottled water as we do for gasoline.

The global systems for food and water, energy and transportation, and material waste and toxicity are out of balance throughout the world and getting worse. For example, it takes 200-300 gallons of water to make one gallon of Coca-Cola. The food we buy in the United States travels an average of 2,000 miles to us—many of the products travel much farther. Yet more people live on less than $1 per day today than were alive 100 years ago.

What can we do? Many people see these problems and are offering significant ideas for the types of innovations needed—such as William McDonough, a world-renowned architect and designer, who believes we can accomplish great and profitable things within a new conceptual framework—one that values our legacy, honors diversity, and feeds ecosystems and societies. For example, McDonough says that, in nature, "waste equals food," and we must think about everything we design from the standpoint of how it, as Dr. Seetha Coleman-Kamula says, moves on to its "next higher life." McDonough is the winner of three U.S. presidential awards: the Presidential Award for Sustainable Development (1996), the National Design Award (2004), and the Presidential Green Chemistry Challenge Award (2003). *Time* magazine recognized him as a "Hero for the Planet" in 1999, stating that "his utopianism is grounded in a unified philosophy that—in demonstrable and practical ways—is changing the design of the world" (Rosenblatt, 1999).

His book, *Cradle to Cradle: Remaking the Way We Make Things,* written with his colleague, German chemist Michael Braungart, calls for the transformation of human industry through ecological design (McDonough and Braungart, 2002). Through historical sketches of the roots of the industrial revolution; commentary on science, nature, and society; descriptions of key design principles; and compelling examples of innovative products and business strategies already reshaping the marketplace, they make the case that an industrial system that no longer is based (in Paul Hawken's words) on "take, make and waste" can become a creator of goods and services that generate ecological, social, and economic value (Hawken, 1994).

Organizations will face a great deal of pressure to transform, to become dramatically less wasteful. Some of the pressure will come from more than one million nongovernmental organizations throughout the world. The transition will be turbulent, but this is what all organizations will need to learn to do better.

One of the five disciplines of the learning organization is personal mastery. How do you define your personal mastery— what lifelong learning are you committed to?

Personal mastery is the discipline of continually clarifying and deepening our personal vision, of focusing our energies, of developing patience, and of seeing reality objectively. It is an essential cornerstone of the learning organization.

An old idea, but a common one, is that we are not born a human being, but that we spend a life becoming a human being. So how do I prioritize my life? First, I am fortunate that my personal vision is embodied in the work I do. It has always been integrated in that manner. I have had the good fortune to always work within networks of friends who share the same commitments.

Developing our personal mastery also depends on regular practices—be they yoga, meditation, or contemplative prayer. The key is that your practices must be integrated into your life. For example, because of the nature of our work, I focus on conversations. Following any conversation, and especially difficult ones, I think about how well I listened. For example, do I listen from my perspective, or do I listen from inside their experience? The opportunities to integrate the development of personal mastery into your life are limitless. At the end of a meeting or event, whether difficult or easy, one can ask, "What did I learn? What did I want to create and what happened, and what I can do better?"

What are you reading to stay current or even ahead of the curve?

I am reading books about natural systems and the universe: food, water, energy. Right now I am reading Paul Hawken's new book *Blessed Unrest* (2007). Hawken writes about the historic growth of civil society organizations as a response to the deterioration of ecosystems, loss of habitat, and of biodiversity around the world—losses that are not only continuing but are in fact accelerating. Hawken is a fierce critic of multinational corporations, which have become so successful at exploiting the earth's natural resources that we are approaching the physical limits and seeing large arrays of toxic waste products being released into the environment where they take centuries and millennia to be broken down. Although I agree with Hawken's sense of urgency, I also think these corporations can be part of the solutions, especially as they learn to work with civil society organizations, which are a particular area of our focus. In general, I am always interested in what is emerging from leading philosophers of the sustainability movement. For those interested in this, I recommend another of his books, *The Ecology of Commerce* (1994) as well as the writings of Joanna Macy, Brian Swimme, and Thomas Berry. These sorts of writers are especially good at helping us understand the underlying shifts in thinking and being that will be needed in the future.

About the Author

Peter Senge is a senior lecturer at the Massachusetts Institute of Technology and founding chair of the Society for Organizational Learning (SoL) Council. He is the author of *The Fifth Discipline: The Art and Practice of the Learning Organization;* co-author of three related fieldbooks; and, most recently, *Presence: An Exploration of Profound Change in People, Society, and Organizations.* Senge lectures throughout the world about decentralizing the role of leadership in organizations to enhance the capacity of all people to work toward healthier human systems. He is also a recipient of the Distinguished Contribution to WLP Award.

References

Hawken, Paul. 1994. *The ecology of commerce.* New York: HarperCollins.

Hawken, Paul. 2007. *Blessed unrest.* New York: Viking.

McDonough, William, and Michael Braungart. 2002. *Cradle to cradle: Remaking the way we make things.* New York: North Point Press.

Rosenblatt, Roger. 1999, February 15. The man who wants buildings to love kids. *Time,* available at http://www.time.com/time/reports/environment/heroes/heroesgallery/0,2967,mcdonough ,00.html.

For Further Reading

Senge, Peter M. 1990. *The fifth discipline: The art & practice of the learning organization.* New York: Doubleday Currency.

Senge, Peter M., Charlotte Roberts, Richard B. Ross, Bryan J. Smith, and Art Kleiner. 1994. *The fifth discipline field book: Strategies and tools for building a learning organization.* New York: Doubleday Currency.

Managing Knowledge in Organizations

Ralph E. Grubb

In This Chapter

➢ Learn what knowledge management is and why it is important

➢ Understand the factors necessary for knowledge sharing

➢ The role of the learning and performance professional in knowledge management

---

In today's global economy, with its emphasis on speed to market and developing innovative products and services, business leaders are compelled to ask: What do we need to know, who knows it, and what do we not know that we should know? Knowledge management is not just the latest management fad, but rather the confluence of three major forces from the last half century. These include the developmental efforts to extend the lessons from the intellectual capital movement, the applications of information technology (IT), and the best practices from total quality management (TQM).

This chapter outlines several major factors that are necessary for a collaborative synergy of knowledge sharing to occur in organizations. Among the most important are creating a corporate culture that reinforces a knowledge-sharing environment, providing an infrastructure and tools to facilitate this interactivity, and transitioning to a performance management organization. Workplace learning and performance professionals will have a special responsibility in this transition so that there's less reliance on classroom training and more emphasis on supporting the performance of knowledgeable workers on the job.

What Is Knowledge Management and How Did It Evolve?

Almost everyone has an intuitive understanding of the term *knowledge management* (KM). In earlier days, people went to the nearest bookshelf or library to locate the information they needed, or perhaps made a well-placed phone call to someone in the know. In the Internet age, a particularly popular choice now involves "Googling" a topic and receiving results that number in the tens of thousands, or perhaps even more, within subsecond response time. So, within the context of multiple sources available in the information age, let's begin with a simple, yet powerful characterization of KM: the ability to store, organize, and retrieve information. Add to this mix a corporate culture of sharing job experience with the right infrastructure, and we have most of the basic ingredients of knowledge management. We'll build on these ideas as our discussion develops. The lack of a widely accepted definition of KM shouldn't dissuade practioners in this field; after all, epistemologists have been debating the nature and definition of knowledge for millennia. Whatever the definition, the field of KM views *knowledge* as residing on top of a three-tier hierarchy in which the term *data* provides the base. Raw data, in turn, are transformed into *information* through such means as organization or reduction, much the way an arithmetic mean can represent raw data. In this parlance, when experience and understanding are added to information, much the way best practices can help establish run control limits on a process, only then can one be said to have knowledge about that process.

In an organizational context, the goal of the KM process is to use a firm's intellectual assets and capabilities to derive *value* for the enterprise. More specific benefits include issues such as fostering innovation, increasing productivity, reducing time to market, improving employee retention, increasing revenues, improving quality, reducing costs, and working toward continuous improvement and organizational growth. Indeed, the very fate and survival of an organization depends, in large part, on the efficiency and the effectiveness of its knowledge management process.

KM is not a new idea in business circles. Organizational experts such as Daniel Bell, Peter Drucker, and Peter Senge have, for many years, used the term *knowledge worker* to describe modern-day employees who use their minds more than their hands. Building on this, the concept of *intellectual capital*—the sum total of all the knowledge assets that a company uses to earn profits—has emerged. Advocates for this position have even suggested that the intellectual capital assets of an organization be placed alongside the company's financial balance sheet to create a more thorough picture of the firm's overall health and viability.

In its 1985 intellectual capital report, Skandia identified 112 metrics by which intellectual capital can be measured, including such variables as the number of PCs per employee, the number of days employees visited their customers, annual turnover, average age of patents, and so forth. A large patent portfolio, for example, is not only important for producing innovative products, but also permits one to cross-license patents with others, thus enabling access to a treasure trove of knowledge worldwide. IBM has been the world's leader in new patents for the last 13 years. Not only is this the heart of their future technology, but it also happens to result in approximately $1 billion per year in revenue from licensing fees. Although some of Skandia's historical metrics have diminished in importance as desktop computers have become commodities, the concept is still an important one today.

Formal Versus Tacit Knowledge

Let's now discuss the distinction between kinds of knowledge. Michael Polyani (1967) has proposed a useful dichotomy: *formal knowledge* and *tacit knowledge.* Formal knowledge, on the one hand, is information that can be documented in some manner and made available to various audiences in the form of publications, patents, reports, and so forth. On the other hand, tacit knowledge resides within the personal realm of the individual and is unknown to the general public. Let's consider a simple example. A consumer purchases a pair of bookcases and, as is often the case, those dreaded words *some assembly required* are printed on the cartons. After struggling for an hour with the printed instructions (formal knowledge), the first bookcase is successfully assembled. The purchaser now tackles the second and notes that this time the task only takes 30 minutes. What has happened? The tacit or private knowledge the consumer has acquired by following the instructions, use of trial and error, and hands-on experience has made the assembly of the second bookcase far easier and more efficient than the first. Unhappily, there's no market force at work to document or quantify this particular consumer's learning curve for use by subsequent customers. I call this a *lost learning curve.*

What effect might this phenomenon of lost learning curves have on business and industry? Imagine for a moment that just 25 percent of the 146 million workers in the U.S. labor force have "some assembly required" on their jobs each day. This means that 37 million workers are walking out the door each evening with tacit knowledge that seldom if ever gets captured. Furthermore, much of this knowledge may never be captured because of business environments that reinforce competition among employees, departments, and work groups rather than collaboration and that have few hardware and software solutions that foster and enable collaboration. Additionally, such routine business forces as downsizing, retirement, and employee turnover result in billions of dollars in lost knowledge, none of which ever appears on a profit-and-loss statement. Contrast the KM potential in this hypothetical case with the meager productivity increase of 0.5 percent reported for the U.S. business sector for the first quarter of 2007, and you'll see the opportunity for huge organization and individual productivity gains.

Roles and Responsibilities in KM

Far from being the exclusive domain of management, KM, both as a process and a firm resource, has the potential to affect every member of the organization—management, technical professionals, and administrative support personnel alike. Management has the responsibility to foster a corporate culture of collaboration and provide an infrastructure to facilitate this interchange (see below). In the area of training and performance support, a 2004 ASTD competency study made clear that KM is one of the key areas of expertise that workplace learning and performance (WLP) professionals need to do their jobs more effectively, because they have a responsibility to be catalysts in bringing KM to the performance improvement domain of the organization (Bernthal et al., 2004). These activities range from adopting smarter and more comprehensive approaches to conducting a needs analysis to using performance support aids and systems to support job performance. In the past, the training department's motto was "the right person in the right course at the right place at the right time." That statement is now giving way to "the right knowledge at the right time." The importance of place drops away in an Internet world where the perception of proximity depends more on the level of interactivity than one of physical distance.

Factors that Contribute to KM Success in Organizations

Research suggests that certain factors are critically important for the successful implementation of KM in organizations. A particularly elegant and well-constructed study by Choi (2003) provides insight into what these variables are and how much they contribute to the total effectiveness of programs. Choi sampled 225 firms with a questionnaire that contained 39 KM-related attribute statements. Executives and managers were the primary respondents because they were the ones who were most likely to be familiar with operations. A statistical factor analysis routine was used to extract five major factors from the data that were perceived as important to KM. These factors, and the amount of variance accounted for, were a supportive corporate culture (44 percent), top management leadership and commitment (7 percent), IT capability (5 percent), performance measurement (4 percent), and KM education (3 percent).

Perception of importance is one thing, but how do these factors contribute to the success of KM in firms that already have operational programs? Because there were 59 organizations in the Choi study that had already implemented KM, a dependent variable or statement of success was regressed onto each of the five success factors. The IT factor was the only one of the five to be statistically significant ($p < 0.01$) and positively associated with KM success and effectiveness. In sum, the study suggests that four of the five factors cited above are necessary conditions for KM programs in organizations, but IT is seen as the enabling factor to help realize the objectives of the initiative.

Conversely, what factors are associated with programs whose KM expectations were not realized? A study of 423 organizations in Europe and the United States conducted by KPMG (2000) found that 36 percent of the respondents said that the KM benefits had failed to meet expectations. The most often cited reasons for this included lack of user uptake owing to insufficient communication (20 percent), failure to integrate KM into everyday working practices (19 percent), lack of time to learn how to use the system or a sense that the system was too complicated (18 percent), a lack of training (15 percent), and a sense that there was little personal benefit in it for the user (13 percent).

The Importance of IT and the Sharing of Tacit Knowledge

Sharing valuable personal knowledge and experience with other coworkers is key to realizing the value propositions inherent in the KM movement. One major approach involves developing communities of practice (CoPs). The term describes a dispersed group of people who possess a common interest and who collaborate over a period of time to share ideas and solutions to further their own work. The word *dispersed* as used here is synonymous with distance; therefore, IT becomes a crucial enabling mechanism. Not surprisingly, this movement of building social capital exploded with the growth of the Internet and intranets. These CoPs can range from a simple ad hoc engagement team working remotely with a client over an extended period of time, sharing ideas and work products in a central repository (also known as groupware) to a prestigious group of researchers scattered internationally and focused on a common problem or developmental tool.

Tools of Collaboration

The groupware concept catapulted the software Lotus Notes to fame and became the early tool of choice to enable team members to collaborate on projects in real time. When Ray Ozzie, the inventor of Notes, left the Lotus Corporation to found Groove Networks, now Microsoft Office Groove 2007, a more interesting virtual office desktop and graphic user interface emerged. The new desktop computer display device consisted of multiple windows or task panes that permitted team members to share computer files in real time with other team members, conduct meetings, post instant messages, sketch diagrams in a whiteboard section of the display, and perform other miscellaneous tasks. This real-time collaboration of CoP members represented a quantum improvement over LISTSERVs and other collaborative networking arrangements, which were largely designed for an interested community of people to send email messages to a list of subscribers organized around a common interest. Well-known topics include distance learning (DEOS-L), a statistical application (SPSSX-L), and a statistical methodology (structural equation modeling via SEMNET). In most LISTSERV instances, a nonprofit organization, such as a university, provides the hosting service necessary for the network and also makes available a searchable repository of all the past communiqués of its members.

IBM provides an exemplar of how tacit knowledge can be integrated into the very workflow of its employees and is described in the cover story of *Training* in April 2007 (Weinstein, 2007). In this application, employees can access all types of information concerning their jobs through an avatar-rich desktop computer display. As a necessary building block for this project, an extensive effort was undertaken to develop a taxonomy for the organization's knowledge assets, job types, and levels, so that knowledge can be organized, stored, and retrieved in a systematic way. This information system component alone requires considerable expertise and is frequently subcontracted to or developed in collaboration with outside information specialists.

Another component of the IBM system is called Expert Tracker, an online tool that permits users to find experts in the company and communicate with them directly online concerning job and project issues. As one might imagine, certain logistical constraints need to be put in place to protect the valuable time and privacy of the experts in the database. This peer-to-peer learning and performance support, all from one portal, is viewed as the wave of the future in KM. However, there are numerous low-tech projects and intermediate steps that organizations can take to move along on the KM journey. Said differently, you don't have to be an IBM to create a dynamic KM learning community.

Other Ideas for KM Collaboration and Dissemination

Most firms already make extensive use of project teams and job rotations to boost the exposure of their employees to other knowledge workers. A second way to extend that reach is to set up a wiki—a web application where collaborative authors contribute to an online job knowledge encyclopedia. Benchmarking studies are yet another low-tech approach that enables managers and decision makers to capture best practices in other organizations that have similar processes to their own, and then incorporate these practices wherever feasible and practical to their own workplace.

At first blush, many people don't think of benchmarking as a part of KM, except for the fact that each best practice is a collection of information and processes that have been honed through experience. Although many examples of best practices come from outside the company, many excellent ideas come from inside the organization itself. Organizations that have formal supply chains, or better still, value chains in which the ends of the supply chain are extended both into the vendor processes and into client relations, have documented internal best practices around each step of the process. This process of eliminating defects in each step of the process and improving quality and productivity is known in some circles as *lean manufacturing*. If the supply chain or value chain process is documented and controlled by IT processes, then the KM process becomes an integral part of the business process. The concept is the same, regardless of whether the business process produces a product or a service.

Knowledge as Process and as Object

The idea of knowledge as a process is fairly easy to grasp and seems to be a widely accepted concept. After all, we acquire most of what we know through repetitive experiences and practice. Documenting these thought processes and making them public throughout the organization is a major goal for KM practitioners. An excellent example from the field of project management is the *Project Management Body of Knowledge* (PMBOK). This book serves as the reference standard for anyone working in project management and provides a common vocabulary and standard set of procedures for successful execution of a project. Mastery of the material is necessary for certification as a professional project manager. The Project Management Institute, the society responsible for PMBOK, has divided the practice of project management into 44 processes. Each process has inputs, tools and techniques, and outputs (see Figure 38-1).

Using each of these processes coupled with the knowledge and experience from fields such as TQM, communications, cost, risk, human resources, and procurement management provides a repeatable process for successfully managing projects. But what about knowledge as an object? How do we get to that level? Perhaps the best way to understand this concept is to go back to what many believe is its modern-day origin. In the 1960s, Christopher Alexander, an architect on the faculty of Harvard's School of Architecture, was lamenting the fact that there seemed to be little or no carryover from one design project to the next. It was as though the architect was starting each project with a clean sheet of paper. Not only did this process seem inefficient; it also meant that the designer could easily overlook critical regulations and requirements that often accompany important technical spaces in buildings, such as computer centers, wiring closets, elevator banks, heating and ventilating facilities, and so forth. To overcome this, Alexander started

Figure 38-1. Project Management Processes: Perform Quality Control

Inputs	Tools and Techniques	Outputs
.1 Quality management plan .2 Quality metrics .3 Quality checklists .4 Organizational process assets .5 Work performance information .6 Approved change requests .7 Deliverables	.1 Cause and effect diagram .2 Control charts .3 Flowcharting .4 Histogram .5 Pareto chart .6 Run chart .7 Scatter diagram .8 Statistical sampling .9 Inspection .10 Defect repair review	.1 Quality control measurements .2 Validated defect repair .3 Quality baseline (updates) .4 Recommended corrective actions .5 Recommended preventive actions .6 Requested changes .7 Recommended defect repair .8 Organization process assets (updates) .9 Validated deliverables .10 Project management plan (updates)

Source: *A Guide to the Project Management Body of Knowledge (PMBOK Guide)*. 3rd ed. Project Management Institute, © 2004. Copyright and all rights reserved. Used with permission.

collecting best practices for each type of space in a building and its surroundings, even including designated parking areas. For example, if a space was to be used as an interview room, such best practices were written on one side of a card, with the other side containing the purpose of the space. This amounted to a series of written if-then statements—for example, if the space was to be used as an interview room, then the door is wider than that of an office, contains preferably a round table (not a desk) that is never more than 40″ across, the floor is carpeted, and so forth. Alexander called this design vocabulary and grammar an *environmental pattern language* (Alexander, 1968).

Alexander then encoded each of these spaces with icons on small objects, similar to pieces from the game of checkers. The next step came when Alexander sat down with the client and, using a board representing a footprint of the future office, asked the client to verbalize his office requirements. Alexander would then arrange and rearrange the design objects on the board as the interview proceeded until the client agreed that the resultant pattern fairly represented his requirements. Alexander would then give the board to an assistant to draw up the architectural plans. In the context of today's technology, he probably would have turned the production task over to a computer, or better still, accomplished the entire requirements and design process in real time at a computer screen by dragging and dropping these icons from his design library into an AutoCAD drawing.

No sooner had Alexander published his design process and language than the computer programming community came to the conclusion that this approach was exactly what was needed for their endeavors. After all, computer programmers were creating millions of lines of code, and trivial errors in smaller repeatable blocks of coding were causing havoc in lost time and rework because of the scope of the debugging process. Hence, the new metaphor for building large computer programs in the manner of snapping together Lego blocks became known as *object-oriented programming*—named partly to honor its source of inspiration, Christopher Alexander.

Using Learning Objects in the Instructional Design Field

The instructional design field has followed suit with the use of learning objects and other reusable virtual coded computer training segments that will accept new content and parameters in programs as the need arises. The previous discussion concerning project management and PMBOK is open to the same knowledge object developmental possibilities. This would mean that project managers could code their own best practices into each of the 44 PMBOK processes and lay out a project plan at a meta-language level, similar to the way Alexander worked with his architectural clients. This is hardly farfetched as evidenced in a recent project I conducted. The goal was to fix performance problems in a client's software development shop where projects were frequently over budget and late. This kind of problem is hardly newsworthy, since national studies show that approximately 80 percent of all projects are over budget and late. More startling, the same studies show that 90 percent of that 80 percent number is over budget by 200 percent or more.

I concluded that it was feasible neither to place the entire development shop's personnel in a program leading to project management certification (the typical time may be approximately three years or more) nor to create a course that would pull most if not all the developers off the line for a week or more. Instead, a KM-performance support approach was taken in which templates were developed for those project management processes that were deemed by executives to be pinch points in the process. These templates, 21 in all, were developed in Microsoft Word so that developers could type into formatted blocks that contained expert coaching questions designed to elicit well formed responses from the users. Not only had the templates captured the knowledge of local best practices through direct and experienced coaching questions, but a local computer server provided a repository for these documents. Best-of-breed documents were identified so that others in the organization could see *what good looks like*. Supervisors reported that the quality of project management documents that they received improved significantly, thus saving valuable project time normally used for multiple reviews and rewrites.

The Project Management Connection to Instructional Systems Design and Quality Improvement—A Powerful Synergy

Can instructional systems design (ISD) benefit from the experiences and the best practices found with the previously cited project management templates? Furthermore, what about the lessons learned within the quality movement? The first transition is an easy one, because, at one level, the traditional ISD model—otherwise known as ADDIE for analysis, design, development, implement, and evaluate—is in fact a project management model. In addition, it captures and codifies a number of best practices from everyday experiences. For example, the classic ISD model that was created in the 1970s for the Training and Doctrine Command of the U.S. military can be traced back to the best training practices that evolved from the various Job Corps projects in the 1960s (see Figure 38-2).

The answer to the second question, the importance of the TQM movement in shaping and influencing the classic ISD model, is similar because they all share the same parent-child relationship. The modern quality movement can be directly traced back to the 1950s with Deming's plan, do, check, act cycle; the continuous cycle was repeated again and again with a monitoring function until a defect free product or service emerged.

Additional Low-Tech Ways to Retain Brainpower

IT has played a critical role in KM in this discussion, but there are other low-tech (also read low-budget) ways to approach some of the critical issues in KM. For example, Fisher (2006) reports that several years ago the Tennessee Valley Authority (TVA) recognized that an aging workforce would be retiring and huge amounts of know-how would be walking out the door. This also happens to be a national problem because Morton, Foster, and

Figure 38-2. The Evolution from Quality Management to Project Management to ISD

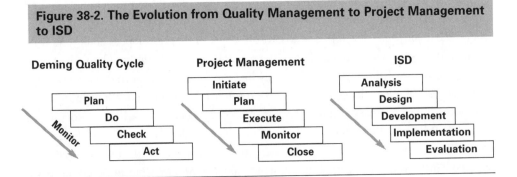

Sadler (2005) estimate that 40 percent of the U.S. workforce will be eligible to retire by the end of this decade. What's to be done to capture and retain these potentially lost learning curves?

TVA decided to do something about this. First, the organization surveyed all of its 13,000 employees, asking who would be planning to retire within the next several years. Management scored each of the responses according to the number of years to retirement (attrition score) and then applied a second scoring scheme based on how essential each person's knowledge was to the power plant's operations (critical knowledge skill score). Managers then multiplied the attrition score by the critical knowledge score to get a high priority target list of scarce job knowledge and skills that had to be captured in one way or another. The solutions ranged from simple troubleshooting charts, to contact lists for help, to assigning young engineers to shadow experts and formalize the tacit knowledge acquired from many years on the job. This latter approach also proved especially helpful in recruiting, because new engineers had an immediate opportunity to work with senior engineers rather than on routine entry-level tasks.

Other organizations have reported success by merely having their employees list the top five most difficult tasks they perform and where they go to get assistance, if necessary. Another variant is a list of the top five tasks that occupy most of their time—the 80/20 rule—with many brainstorming sessions conducted to develop ideas as to how to shorten the process.

Summary

In today's global economy, with its emphasis on speed to market and developing innovative products and services, business leaders are compelled to ask: What do we need to know, who knows it, and what do we not know that we should know? KM is not just the latest management fad, but rather the confluence of three major forces from the last half century. These include the developmental efforts to extend the lessons from the intellectual capital movement, the applications of information technology, and the best practices from TQM. In sum, this places a unique responsibility on management at every level in organizations to leverage each knowledge worker's assets and find common cause to collaborate in ways typically not seen before. The KM enterprise is unique, however, and differs from other business innovations because it is an initiative without an endpoint and will only grow larger and more complex with each passing day.

This chapter has outlined several major factors that are necessary for this collaborative synergy to occur. Among the most important are creating a corporate culture that reinforces a knowledge-sharing environment, providing an infrastructure and tools to facilitate this interactivity, and transitioning to a performance management organization. Workplace learning and performance professionals will have a special responsibility in this transition to rely less on classroom training and more on supporting the performance of knowledgeable workers on the job.

About the Author

Ralph E. Grubb is an industrial-organization development psychologist and president of Performance Improvement Associates in Yorktown Heights, New York. He founded the consulting firm after a distinguished career at IBM. In recent years he has been a consultant to many of the top *Fortune* 100 firms on subjects ranging from distance learning to performance improvement. He has served on the board of trustees for both the Graduate School of Education and Human Development at the University of Rochester and the Regents College, the University of the State of New York, Albany. He has authored more than two dozen publications on the topics of instructional technology and performance improvement.

References

Alexander, Christopher. 1968. The environmental pattern language. *Ekistics* XXV(150): 336-337.

Bernthal, Paul R., Karen Colteryahn, Patty Davis, Jennifer Naughton, William J. Rothwell, and Rich Wellins. 2004. *ASTD 2004 competency study: Mapping the future*. Alexandria, VA: ASTD Press.

Choi, Yong S. 2003, March. Reality of knowledge management success. *Journal of the Academy of Business and Economics*, 113-123.

Fisher, Anne. 2006, July 24. How to plug your company's brain drain. *Fortune*, available at http://money.cnn.com/magazines/fortune/fortune_archive/2006/07/24/8381688/.

KPMG. 2000. *Knowledge management research report 2000*. Annapolis, MD: KPMG Consulting.

Morton, Lynn, Lorrie Foster, and Jeri Sadler. 2005. *Managing the maturing workforce: Implications and best practices*. New York: The Conference Board.

Polyani, Michael. 1967. *The tacit dimension*. London: Routledge & Kegan Paul.

Project Management Institute. 2004. *A guide to the project management body of knowledge*. 3rd ed. Newtown Square, PA: PMI.

Weinstein, Michael. 2007, April. Virtually integrated. *Training*, 10-14.

For Further Reading

Davenport, Thomas H., and Laurence Prusak. 2000. *Working knowledge: How organizations manage what they know.* Boston: Harvard Business School Press.

Grubb, Ralph E. *Redeeming lost learning curves.* Unpublished manuscript.

Lambe, Patrick. 2007. *Organising knowledge: Taxonomies, knowledge, and organisational effectiveness.* Oxford, England: Chandos Publishing.

Consulting on the Inside

Beverly Scott

In This Chapter

- ➤ Understand the advantages and challenges of internal consultants
- ➤ Learn the roles, competencies, and requirements for consulting
- ➤ Discover some career options for internal consultants

"I was reminded during my time inside that when you are in the system you are part of the system—for better and for worse. Being inside inhibits your detachment. I think the main difference between internal and external consultants is that the internal consultant is more focused on task and the external on process. Neither is 'better' than the other: In order to have strategic change, you must have both."

—Amanda Trosten-Bloom, Corporation for Positive Change
(Scott and Hascall, 2002, 2006)

The term *consultant* often raises images of highly paid business consultants from large firms brought in by senior management to address problems that the organization cannot solve. External consultants from large or small firms bring the advantages of outsider status and expertise drawn from a wider base of experience—the basis for their perceived value to executives. It is also easier to understand their role as a temporary advisor who helps and influences management to address specific issues and then leaves the organization. However, the setting and environment of the consultant as an employee consulting on the inside creates different requirements, advantages, and challenges. (See Table 39-1 for a comparison of internal and external consulting roles and Table 39-2 to determine when to choose an internal versus an external consultant.) This chapter explores the advantages and challenges of the internal consultant, the roles, unique competencies, and other success requirements as well as the career options for internal consultants.

Advantages of Internal Consultants

The internal consultant offers unique benefits as an insider with deep knowledge of sensitive issues, cultural norms, and organizational history. External consultants are often engaged for their unique and specialized skills and knowledge, but the internal has the benefit of an intimate, detailed, hands-on knowledge of the business, strategy, and culture of the organization. Internal practitioners develop detailed understanding of the power and politics, the webs of relationships in the organization, and the details of what has been done in the past to a degree that few externals are able to learn. Internals can use inside jargon and language. Their deep, sometimes personal relationships with clients and colleagues, with whom they work closely with over a period of years, build trust and credibility. Consequently, internals have an enhanced ability to assess and use the right approach with a shorter ramp-up time on new projects.

A second advantage is that internal consultants participate in the life of the organization. They are aware of daily business challenges, customer issues, management decisions, and actions. In contrast, the external consultant often enters the system for a short time to implement a specific solution, but the internal consultant remains in the organization long after the project is completed. As a result, internal practitioners can follow the progress, identify challenges, or barriers facing the solution, and can immediately follow up with members of the organization to support the effort or ensure actions are carried out or adjusted as necessary. In addition, knowledge of the inside of the organization allows internals to more quickly recognize potential linkages to allied initiatives in other parts of the organization, involve other functional staff, or expand an initiative to include other issues. Thus, change efforts benefit from this insider knowledge of the internal consultant who remains an active part of the organization.

Table 39-1. Comparison of Internal and External Consulting Roles

Similarities	Differences	
	Internals	**Externals**
Knowledge of human systems, organization, and individual behavior	Accepted as members of the "group," congruent with culture	See culture and organization with outsider perspective
Understanding the process of change	Have credibility as an insider	Have credibility as an outsider
Desire to be successful and recognized for the value they bring to the client	Know organization and business intimately	Bring broader experience from other organizations
Commitment to learning	Can build long-term relationships; establish rapport more easily	Can confront, give feedback, take risks with senior management more easily
Passion about their work	Coordination and integration of project into ongoing activities	Focused involvement on a project that ends
Ability to influence and lead	Opportunities to influence, gain access, sit at the table as an insider	Once invited in as outsider, broader experience offers credibility, power, and influence
Skills to analyze needs and design interventions	Leverage and utilize informal and formal organization structure	Can avoid or ignore the organization structure, move around organization to achieve results
Credibility or "authority"	Lead from position and character (trust)	Lead from competence (expertise) and personality
	Know the cultural norms that should not be violated	Can acceptably challenge or violate the informal rules of the culture

(continued on next page)

Table 39-1. Comparison of Internal and External Consulting Roles (continued)

Similarities	Differences	
	Internals	**Externals**
	Know the history, traditions, and where the "bones are buried"	Seen as objective and not part of the problem
	Can take an advocacy role	Bring more objectivity, neutrality
	May be expected to be broad generalists	Often seen as specialists with narrow expertise
	As "one client" consultants, have a lot more "skin in the game"	If it doesn't work out here, can always move on to other clients

Source: Scott and Hascall (2002, 2006). John Wiley & Sons, © 2006. Used with permission.

Table 39-2. When to Use Internal or External Consultants

When to Use External Consultants	When to Use Internal Consultants
To support development of strategy or facilitate corporate-wide initiatives or key priorities	To support implementation of strategic priority, or initiative as an operational focus
Internal expertise does not reside within the organization	Organization possesses the needed internal expertise
Deep expertise is needed	Broad generalist knowledge is needed
An outside, neutral perspective is important	Knowledge of the organization and business is critical
New, risky alternatives require validation from an outside expert	Speaking the jargon or the language of the organization and the culture is important
Internal does not have status, power, or authority to influence senior management or the culture	A sensitive insider who knows the issues is needed
CEO, president, or senior leaders need coach, guide, or objective sounding board	Need to sustain a long-term initiative where internal ownership is important
Initiative justifies the expense	Cost is a factor
Project has defined boundaries or limits	Follow-up and quick access is needed

Source: Scott and Hascall (2002, 2006). John Wiley & Sons, © 2006. Used with permission.

A third advantage is that internal practitioners are a ready resource to senior leaders, internal change partners, and employees. As internals collaborate across the organization, they build commitment for the change initiative and can give immediate coaching or provide advice on an impromptu basis. Immediate action may head off a potential problem, defuse a budding conflict, encourage a project leader, or provide needed support in developing new behaviors.

Issues and Challenges

Internal consultants' intimate knowledge of the organization and the business makes them valuable business partners. Yet, it challenges their role of neutrality and objectivity, and they may be seen as too familiar and not capable of bringing the objective outsider world view. As internal consultants, they must stand at the edge, operate at the margins, and maintain distance. This delicate balance of knowing organizational knowledge and keeping a marginal position at the boundary of the organization defines the paradoxes that confront the internal consultant. Belonging to the organization and finding acceptance helps internal consultants be congruent with their clients; yet they must be cautious and avoid collusion by failing to tell senior managers the truth.

Internal consultants are often placed on a middle tier of the organizational reporting hierarchy through the human resource function because many organizations lack knowledge of the value of a strong and skilled internal consulting function. Internals then find their status and reporting relationships a barrier to establishing their own competence and credibility. Sometimes their mid-level positioning hinders establishing a consultant-client relationship with a senior executive who sees the consultant as a subordinate. Many internal consultants face pressure from senior-level clients to break confidences, take unrealistic projects, or make inappropriate changes. These challenges and paradoxes create conflict and stress for the internal consultant who joins the organization unprepared for these challenges (Foss et al., 2005; Scott, 2000).

Opportunities

Despite the challenges, internal consultants have a unique opportunity to exploit their position inside the organization and have a long-term, significant influence on the organization. Internal consultants' holistic knowledge of the organization enables them to take a systems view and ensure that linkages and processes successfully support the change targets. When they partner with external consultants, they can be a multiplier by disseminating and reinforcing the expertise and cutting-edge concepts, integrating them into the culture of the organization through their day-to-day work. Using their inside knowledge of the business and the organization, they can serve as catalysts for needed change, ensure organizational alignment with the business strategy, prepare employees with skills to cope with forthcoming changes from the tumultuous business environment, and provide candid perspectives as confidential sounding boards for senior executives.

Traditional Internal Consulting Roles

The internal consultant, similar to the external consultant, uses expertise, influence, and personal skills to facilitate a client-requested change without the formal authority to implement recommended actions. The change usually solves a problem, improves performance, increases organizational effectiveness, or helps people and organizations learn. The role the internal consultant plays in the change initiative reflects four considerations: the characteristics of the consultant, the characteristics of the client, the client-consultant relationship, and the organizational situation (see Table 39-3).

Discussions about consulting roles often reflect the tension between process consulting and technical or expert consulting (Marguilles, 1978). Technical consultation, or "expert" consulting as Block (1981) calls it, relies on the knowledge and expertise of the consultant to solve the client's problem. The expert approach uses data collection and analysis to determine solutions that are recommended to the client. This is the traditional model of

Table 39-3. Four Considerations in Choosing a Role

Characteristics of the consultant

- What are my interpersonal strengths?
- What is my consulting competency?
- What is my technical expertise?
- How is my expertise relevant to the client?

Characteristics of the client

- What support is there for the initiative at different levels in the organization?
- Is the client willing to be involved and participate in the projects?
- What is the client's readiness for change?

The client-consultant relationship

- Does the consultant understand the client's definition of success?
- Is there a commitment to help the client learn skills and insights?
- Have expectations been explored and clarified?

The organizational situation

- Are the organizational vision and strategy clear and understood?
- What are the key strategic needs of the organization?
- What are the effects of the current market and competition on the organization?
- What is the focus of attention?
- What resources are available to support the project?
- Are other strategic initiatives being driven in the organization and how might they affect the current initiative?
- What are the cultural norms and mindset that will influence the project?
- What organizational needs are not being met?
- Is the expertise of the consultant relevant to the organization's needs?

Source: Scott (2000).

business consulting. Process consulting relies more on the intuitive awareness of the consultant who attends to and observes the emotional, nonverbal, perceptual, and spatial aspects of human behavior. Process consultants help the client understand what is happening, identify solutions, and transfer skills to the client to manage the ongoing process. Their focus is on the energy of the client system and a heightened awareness of the dynamics in the group or organization.

It takes both process and expertise. Internal consultants are expected to bring more than their presence, process, and observation skills. They also bring technical competence and expertise. Drawing on the four considerations, consultants may balance the process or technical roles or may emphasize one over the other. The sidebar lists some of the roles an internal might choose, such as traditional organization development (OD) roles, classic business consulting roles, or new consulting roles. These descriptions were developed by the author in collaboration with Joseph Lipsey for the OD Network website (Lipsey and Scott, 2008).

Competencies

We have discussed the advantages and the roles of an internal consulting function. However, the competencies required for the internal to deliver the desired results are perhaps even more critical. Competency has been defined as the skills, knowledge, and attitudes (KSAs) or the sum of everything needed to be successful. Many basic competencies needed for external and internal consultants are similar: professional theories, techniques and methods, self-knowledge, and performance skills. However, internal consultants report that success as an internal does require *consulting* competencies that are different from external consultants. Table 39-4 shows the categories of internal consulting competencies and some of the descriptive behaviors developed from the results of interviews with internal consultants. In some cases the descriptive phrase might seem to be the same as for external practitioners. Internal practitioners, however, demonstrate the competencies differently because the context of the internal practitioner is different. Foss et al. (2005) report that other competencies may be needed but suggest that these are a starting point for discussion and future research.

Keys to Success

The most critical key to success as an internal practitioner is gaining the trust and credibility of both leadership and employees. Trust and credibility are part competency and part personal integrity. The credibility of the internal consultant, more than any other

Traditional OD Roles

- Change agent: The classic OD consultant role who serves as a catalyst for change as an "outsider" to the prevailing culture and external to the particular subsystem initiating the change effort (French and Bell, 1999).
- Process consultant: Emphasizes the consultant's observation and insights, often at a larger system level, which helps sharpen the client's understanding of the problem (Schein, 1988).
- Collaborative: Similar to both the change agent and the process consultant with the key assumption that the client's issues can be addressed only by joining the consultant's specialized knowledge with the client's deep understanding of the organization. The client must be actively involved in the data gathering, analysis, goal setting, and action plans, as well as share responsibility for success or failure (Block, 1981).

Classic Consulting Roles

- Doctor: The consultant's role is to make a diagnosis and recommend the expertise to solve the problem. The client depends on the consultant to offer a prescription.
- Expert: The client determines what the problem is and what kind of assistance is needed and whom to go to for help. Then the consultant is asked to deliver the solution.
- Pair of hands: The consultant serves as an extra "pair of hands," applying specialized knowledge to achieve goals defined by the client (Block, 1981).

New Consulting Roles

Some new roles for consultants are emerging as the competitive environment has intensified and organizational complexity has increased. These include performance consultant, change leader, and trusted advisor.

- Performance consultant: The demand for increasing organizational and employee performance has contributed to a role that transcends the traditional "skills trainer." This role combines the "whole system" focus of OD with the skill development characteristics of training. The performance consultant partners with the client to identify and address the performance needs within the organization and provide specialized services that change or improve performance outcomes.
- Change leader: As organizations continue to cope with a rapidly changing business environment, efforts at organization-wide change require facilitators as well as leaders to guide the implementation and support of their change initiatives. Many internal consultants are asked to both guide the process and be the driving force of a change initiative. This demand is based on the bottom-line business needs for expertise in change leadership and organizational alignment. The change leader becomes both an advocate and project leader for a change initiative. This results in the consultant being lifted from a neutral process role and becoming strongly identified with the project's success.

(continued on next page)

- Trusted advisor: The rapid pace of change and the complexity of the environment place organizational leaders in unforeseen and unknowable challenges and dilemmas, such as competitive global markets, rapidly changing technology, and new strategic directions for their organizations. In the midst of this turmoil, they must simultaneously focus internally on maintaining cultural alignment and meeting the ever-higher expectations of employees. Executives are often in lonely and isolated positions. The consultant who can serve as a sounding board—imparting insight into the "human organization" within the context of business demands—can be very valuable to top executives. The trusted advisor serves as a confidant and provides authentic communication and reaction based on an awareness and understanding of the human organization, critical performance issues, and the pressures of the business.

staff function, is influenced by the integrity, self-awareness, and self-management of the individual practitioner. This strong foundation of relationships relies on developing authentic partnerships with clients and making careful judgments regarding the client's resistance, readiness to take the risk of change, need for support, ability to lead the organization through transition, and openness to tough feedback. To achieve the successful outcomes internal consultants envision with their clients, they must, because they live inside, also build strong relationships with their bosses, other levels of management, and their peers and colleagues in HR or other staff functions. Building strong relationships requires that internal consultants educate and prepare others to understand and appreciate the role of consultant, take the initiative to understand the others' perspectives, be strong and clear, and use self-awareness and self-management. A misperception of shared confidences or misunderstanding of behavior or agreements can quickly destroy many years of effort by the internal practitioner (Foss et al., 2005).

More than the external who often specializes in a limited area of practice, the internal consultant must be a generalist, familiar and competent with a broad range of approaches and solutions. The internal practitioner has to master a wide range of potential initiatives to assist in a wide range of organizational situations. This also represents a potential pitfall. Internals cannot be successful trying to do everything but must be selective in offering their services to maximize the benefits of their efforts. With conscious choice and alignment with organizational strategy and priorities, the internal consultant will add more value and better meet the needs of the organization (Foss et al., 2005).

Table 39-4. Competencies Critical to the Internal Consultant

Competency	Behavioral Description
Collaborates with others	Ensures that interpersonal relationships with clients, peers, and others in the organization are collaborative, healthy, and team based. Seeks balanced, win-win partnerships. Emphasizes follow-up and good customer service. Is humble, caring and compassionate, and capable of celebrating client's success.
Establishes credibility	Establishes credibility and respect by doing good work, delivering value, and achieving results. Holds high ethical standards, maintains integrity through professionalism, ethics, and contracting. Provides realistic picture to client of what is achievable in the time available through clear expectations for the roles of client and consultant partners, the degree of difficulty of change, and the approach used.
Takes initiative	Is assertive in taking a stand, delivering tough messages, and pushing for decision and outcomes. Demonstrates entrepreneurial spirit. Acts to achieve results tied to the organization's goals. Understands, respects, and effectively uses power in the organization to assist clients in achieving their goals.
Maintains detachment	Is able to remain detached from the organization to maintain independence, objectivity, and neutrality. Is able not only to be sufficiently congruent with the client organization to find acceptance, but also able to keep an external mindset to provide more balanced perspective. Avoids getting trapped into taking sides or carrying messages.
Markets the value of OD	Helps clients and the organization understand the practice of OD and the value the practice delivers to them and the organization. Works toward clarity of roles with other staff assistance units (e.g., HR consultants, quality improvement staff, finance, or information technology consultants). Offers clear statement of organization development products and services as distinct from products and services offered by others in the organizations. Also clarifies products and services as distinct from external consultants. At times manages contracts with external consultants.
Demonstrates organizational savvy	Understands and knows how to succeed in the organization. Builds relationships with senior leadership and develops an extensive network of contacts at all levels. Leverages insider knowledge to address organizational issues. Uses appropriate judgment, recognizing cross-functional interdependencies, political issues, and the importance of cultural fit. Recognizes the importance of systems thinking.

(continued on next page)

Table 39-4. Competencies Critical to the Internal Consultant (continued)

Competency	Behavioral Description
Acts resourcefully	Is able to use imagination, creativity, and forward thinking. Is resourceful, flexible, and innovative in utilizing methods and resources. Is not wedded to a specific approach. Takes advantage of windows of opportunity; most often functions with "just-in-time" approach to client needs.
Understands the business	Knows what makes the business run as well as the key strategy. Is able to think strategically and leverage support for critical strategic issues. Supports managers in aligning the organization with the strategy.

Source: Foss et al. (2005).

The consulting process for the internal consultant is usually messy and organic; the steps are seldom linear, often overlap, or require cycling back to repeat or expand an earlier phase (see Figure 39-1). The consulting process does not begin with entry as it does for external consultants. It begins with the initial contact with the client and is heavily influenced by the consultant's reputation in the organization (to help prepare for the initial client meeting, see Tools 39-1, 39-2, and 39-3 on the accompanying CD-ROM). That reputation is as valuable as a popular product brand name, and many internal consultants use it successfully to market themselves within the organization. Internal consultants can help position their reputation by setting the stage at the time of hiring and negotiating their charter with their bosses and their most-senior potential clients. Successful movement through the consulting process is influenced continually by internal consultants' ability to manage relationships and the dynamics of living inside the organization. (For more on the eight phases of consulting, see the sidebar.)

In some cases, the best action might be to partner with an external consulting firm. If the internal practitioner makes a judgment that an external practitioner can help, it is often because the internal practitioner has already laid the groundwork with the organization and knows that the external initiative has greater likelihood of being successful. This work in the trenches is rarely acknowledged. Another frustration occurs when the external consultant or consulting firm proceeds to work directly with senior leaders or with HR staff without the involvement of the internal function. Managers often lack the ability to prepare the organization for the coming change initiative and frequently have

Figure 39-1. The Process of Consulting

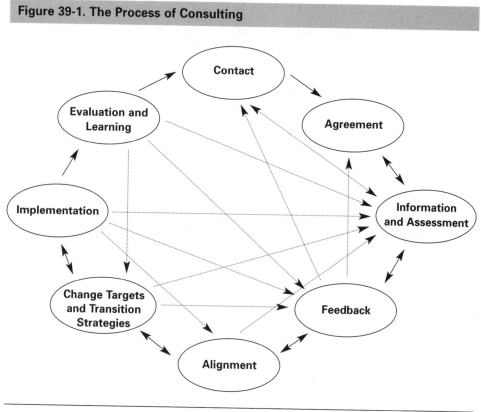

Source: Scott (2000).

difficulty guiding the work of the external practitioners. Failure to involve the internal consultant can result in less than optimal outcomes for the external consultant's intervention (Foss et al., 2005; Scott and Hascall, 2002, 2006; see Table 39-5).

Career

Although many consultants spend their careers both as externals and internals, it is possible to have an entire career as an internal consultant inside one or more organizations. We have discussed the many advantages of working inside an organization. Internal consultants can see changes become integrated in the organization, watch performance improve over time, feel a sense of satisfaction with their contribution, and experience the trust when new client leaders ask for help. There is reward from the development of long-term relationships, a sense of belonging and comfort as a member of a community

---

Eight Phases of the Consulting Process

- *Contact:* Seek an understanding of the client's organization or business need; lay the foundation of the consultant-client relationship.
- *Agreement:* Confirm the agreement on consultant and client roles, expectations, and the actions each will take. Define the need to be addressed and the goal or outcome to be achieved.
- *Information and assessment:* Gather information about the issue, the business, performance, and the organization. Assess or analyze the data and information collected. Gain an independent view and interpretation of the issues.
- *Feedback:* Provide the client with the information or data; seek acceptance or "ownership" of the data. Offer a consultant's analysis or interpretation.
- *Alignment:* Seek alignment with the client on the desired outcomes or future state and the approach to be used to achieve it.
- *Change targets and transition strategies:* Clarify which components of the system need to be changed, and identify necessary support and resources. Develop a transition strategy to navigate from the current state to the desired future.
- *Implementation:* Complete the project by providing guidance, coaching, facilitation, and leadership to implement the planned change.
- *Evaluation and learning:* Evaluate the success of the project with the client system by supporting the client's reflection and identification of learned skills, knowledge, and self-awareness. Explore enhanced knowledge, skills, and self-awareness.

Source: Scott (2000).

---

in which the people and the rules are known, and recognition that they are skilled professionals contributing to the organization. At the same time, all is not glamour and glory. There is a lot of hard work in the life of an internal practitioner. "Reputations must be earned, competencies must be shown, and trust must be established. The role can be rewarding, not because the internal practitioner always has the sterling answer, but because it is possible to be successful and deliver improvements in spite of the organizational system that may be arrayed against efforts to increase organizational effectiveness. Success as an internal is not just about competence; it is also about how the internal consultant fits into the system" (Foss et al., 2005).

Internal consultants are employees in the organization: They have both advantages and disadvantages. There may be opportunities to rise in the organization from an entry-level practitioner to a senior advisor to a mentor of other internal practitioners (see Table 39-6). Whether or not there are opportunities within the organization for this career path, almost all successful internal practitioners face the challenging opportunity of

Table 39-5. Internal–External Partnerships

Success Conditions

- Flexibility and open communication
- Sense of being in it together
- Opportunity to leverage cost, efficiencies, knowledge, and credibility
- Strengths of internal recognized and valued
- Internal is open to learning
- Insider knowledge is paired with outsider perspective and credibility
- Appreciation and understanding of cultural differences

Undermining Conditions

- Internals may not be in position to have organizational influence to lead a major change initiative.
- Senior management may not understand the value of the internal's organizational ties and thus fail to support the partnership.
- Externals ignore or go around the internal function promoting themselves solely to senior management.
- Internals left out of the contracting process may feel resentful, threatened, and marginalized, resulting in a lack of commitment.
- Externals are often seen as arrogant, exclusive, judgmental; in turn, internals are perceived as ineffective, incompetent, and "poor losers."
- Weak internal functions may be incapable of successfully leading change projects.

Source: Scott and Hascall (2002, 2006). John Wiley & Sons, © 2006. Used with permission.

whether to continue as an internal consultant or to accept a management role. The success and effectiveness of internal practitioners often leads to appreciation by senior leaders who may view them as "good management material." If the internal accepts this opportunity, however, and moves to operational management, this means the certain end of being a consultant in that organization (Foss et al., 2005).

"Last, it is important to consider the set of attitudes that a person must have to be an internal practitioner. The life of the internal is truly one of support. Often the internal does much work in the organization that is never recognized or acknowledged. The internal must be committed to successful outcomes and must be willing to step out of center stage if someone else in the organization is ready to champion necessary changes. The attitudes of humility, generosity of spirit, and a type of selflessness must exist in doing internal consulting work for the organization. If a practitioner has a need for the limelight, the internal role may not be the best career fit over the long term. [Table 39-7] contains ideas for how internal practitioners can thrive inside" (Foss et al., 2005).

Table 39-6. Stages of a Career in Internal Consulting

Student—Mastering a body of knowledge
Take basic courses specific to your field, such as

- Group dynamics
- Organization behavior
- Adult learning
- Individual and organization change
- Consulting process
- Systems thinking.

Apprentice—Applying basic knowledge, receiving specific feedback, and developing skills such as

- Facilitation
- Team development
- Interviewing
- Learning activity design
- Consulting
- Information and data analysis.

Practitioner—Increasing knowledge and skill base
Discover more and better ways to do things by

- Attending professional meetings, seminars, and conferences
- Reading professional journals and books
- Networking
- Specializing.

Coach and Mentor—Assisting others to develop professionally
Use coaching and counseling skills to develop others by

- Serving as role model and mentor
- Writing, presenting, speaking, training to help others learn skills, tools, and concepts.

Master—Leaving your mark and your legacy
Achieve peak performance by

- Becoming an inspiration and model of career success for others
- Becoming a leader in your field
- Creating a legacy through writing, speaking, and teaching.

Source: Scott (2000).

Table 39-7. Rules for Living Inside

- Know the business strategy, and identify needs and opportunities for which you can contribute to business results.
- Learn to manage the paradoxes. Operate at the margins, yet know the organization intimately; build strong relationships but confront with the truth; be congruent with the client organization but do not collude.
- Build and use the positive energy for change in the organization. Help clients see the "possible," create visions, and articulate their desires for the future to draw others to support and participate in the process.
- Develop broad support for projects by working with multiple levels of the organization, communicating, educating, modeling, listening, and facilitating.
- Seek to build relationships with key managers by finding ways to meet small but important needs; serving as a sounding board; or providing refreshing, candid perspectives.
- Coach clients to lead change, trust in self-organization, and communicate often.
- Seek agreements with client for the mutual exchange of feedback and the promotion of self-awareness and continuous learning.
- Develop competence and credibility by keeping agreements, being accountable for results, being authentic in relationships with others.
- Know the boundaries of your competence; avoid going out on "skinny branches."
- Develop the ability to initiate and build strong partnerships.
- Be a systems thinker; identify and support linkages and interconnections.
- Recognize and accept the client's readiness to take the risks of change.
- Improve continuously the internal-consulting craft, practice personal mastery as a lifelong journey, and stay grounded.

Source: Scott (2000).

Summary

There are many advantages of the internal consultant who uniquely benefits the organization on a continuing basis with deep and intimate knowledge of the organization and as a ready resource to management and staff. This insider knowledge makes internal practitioners valuable partners to external consultants. However, being internal challenges the neutral and objective role of the consultant and requires internals to manage a delicate balance of deep organizational knowledge while maintaining a marginal position in the organization.

Successful internal consultants cultivate trust and credibility as business partners to senior managers combined with demonstrated competence. Competence includes not only their professional expertise but the unique capabilities required as internal consultants. Knowledge of themselves, their clients, and the organization allows them to choose appropriate roles from traditional OD consulting, classic business consulting, or newly emerging roles. The professional committed to successful outcomes for the organization, willing to step out of the limelight, and humble and generous of spirit can find reward and make a significant contribution to the organization on the inside.

Parts of this chapter have been adapted from *Consulting on the Inside* (Scott, 2000) and from the work of a team of internal consultants who conducted a research project on internal consulting (Foss et al., 2005).

About the Author

Beverly Scott has served as a consultant to organizations for more than 30 years, bringing clarity, focus, integrity, and a sense of purpose to her work. She served for 15 years as the director of organization and management development for McKesson Corporation in San Francisco. She is the author of *Consulting on the Inside: An Internal Consultant's Guide to Living and Working Inside Organizations.* She is on the faculty of Organization Psychology at John F. Kennedy University. Her current consulting focuses on coaching and development of internal consultants. She has also served as chair of the OD Network board of trustees.

References

Block, Peter. 1981. *Flawless consulting: A guide to getting your expertise used.* San Diego: Pfeiffer.

Foss, Allan, David Lipsky, Allen Orr, Beverly Scott, Terrance Seamon, Julie Smendzuik-O'Brien, Anna Tavis, Dale Wissman, and Catherine Woods. 2005. Practicing internal OD. In *Practicing organization development: A guide for consultants,* eds., W.J. Rothwell and R. Sullivan. San Francisco: John Wiley & Sons.

French, Wendell L., and Ceci H. Bell Jr. 1999. *Organization development: Behavioral science interventions for organization development.* Saddle River, NJ: Prentice-Hall.

Lipsey, Joseph, and Beverly Scott. 2008. Consulting skills toolkit: Roles, available for members at www.odnetwork.org/resources/toolkit/consultingskills.php.

Marguilles, Newton. 1978. Perspectives on the marginality of the consultant's role. In *The cutting edge: Current theory and practice in organization development,* ed., W.W. Burke. La Jolla, CA: Pfeiffer.

Schein, Edgar H. 1988. *Process consultation: Its role in organization development.* 2nd ed. Saddle River, NJ: Prentice-Hall.

Scott, Beverly. 2000. *Consulting on the inside.* Alexandria, VA: ASTD Press.

Scott, Beverly, and Jane Hascall. 2002. Inside or outside: The partnerships of internal and external consultants. In *International conference readings book*, eds., N. Delener and C. Ghao. Rome: Global Business and Technology Association.

Scott, Beverly, and Jane Hascall. 2006. Inside or outside: The partnerships of internal and external consultants. In *The 2006 Pfeiffer annual, consulting*, ed., E. Biech. San Francisco: John Wiley & Sons/Pfeiffer.

For Further Reading

Bellman, Geoffrey M. 1992. *Getting things done when you are not in charge.* Fireside Edition. New York: Simon & Schuster.

Gebelein, Susan H. 1989, March. Profile of an internal consultant. *Training & Development*, 52-58.

Henning, Joel P. 1997. *The future of staff groups.* San Francisco: Berrett-Koehler.

Lacey, Miriam Y. 1995. Internal consulting: Perspectives on the process of planned change. *Journal of Organizational Change Management* 8(3): 77.

Ray, R. Glenn. 1997, July. Developing internal consultants. *Training & Development*, 30-34.

Schaffer, Robert H. 1997. *High impact consulting.* San Francisco: Jossey-Bass.

 **Chapter 40**

Consulting From the Outside

Geoff Bellman

In This Chapter

➢ Understand the importance of articulating your consulting style
➢ Learn ten steps for successful consulting

You create success for yourself and your clients through awareness of who you are and what you are doing. Making it in a crowded marketplace means being clear about how you consult and the skills you use to make a living and a life. Clients want to know why they should select you. And you need to be ready to help them understand what's unique about you; you want to help them choose a consultant they are willing to trust and take risks with—you hope that's you. Central to that is your consulting process—and that's what this chapter is about.

We consultants each cultivate our own consulting process. When a client asks, "What's your approach to consulting?" the correct answer is not, "Well, how do you want me to approach consulting?" Based on our experience and training, we should be able to tell a client what he or she can expect of us while we work together. Self-awareness, practice, and reflection allow us to speak confidently about how we prefer to work. My preferences are wrapped around the 10 steps in this chapter. As I write about how I consult, you can compare that with how you consult, clarifying your answer to the client's question above. Let's jump into my 10 steps and see how they fit with your consulting process. My process begins with the initial entry with a potential client and works through to the exit when the job is done.

The pages that follow elaborate on the 10 steps. Consider how this process relates to what you do and to your skills in performing each step. Consider these questions along the way:

- Which steps are particularly important to you in your work?
- Which steps are you most skillful in?
- Which do you need to learn most about?
- What is your own consulting process?

Step 1: Entry

The process usually begins with the client—and before you know about it. The client senses an important difference between what he or she has and what he or she wants. Clients think they might need some outside help. They remember you (because you've done such a good job of marketing yourself). They contact you because you might help them narrow the gap. Before you arrive for that first client meeting, think about the following points.

Identify the Problem

Clients usually call because they have a problem; they sometimes call because they have an opportunity. They have likely tried to resolve the problem on their own and were

---

The 10 Steps of Consulting

1. Entry
2. Contracting
3. Inquiry
4. Interpretation
5. Feedback
6. Alternatives
7. Decision
8. Action
9. Impact
10. Exit

---

unsuccessful. Clients often call long after the ideal intervention point has passed. We consultants usually hear about well-established, uncomfortable problems. We think to ourselves, "Why don't they call earlier?" Don't dwell on that; focus on the fact you are in their office now.

Get Consensus

Clients "know" what the problem is and what the solution is, too—that is why they called you. If you are a trainer, the client called because he or she thinks people lack ability and training will solve the problem. If you are a strategic planner, the client is without an effective plan and needs one. If you are a team builder, guess what? The client's team needs building. Any one of these solutions might be right, but usually the issue you agree to tackle is significantly different from the problem as it was first presented. A very important part of your job is to help the client (and others involved) understand and agree upon what the real issue is—as contrasted with the presenting issue. Respect the client's current expression of the problem. Respect his or her willingness to take action. And know that this is likely to change as you delve deeper into the project.

Begin where the client wants to begin—rather than where you would prefer to begin. He or she has a story to tell and wants to tell it. Listen to what the client says and the feelings that come with that. This is your starting point in understanding what is happening, and in your relationship with the client.

Specify Expectations

Establish your interest in helping the client. Make sincere statements that establish your willingness to take the next steps with him or her. Tell the client that this problem is interesting to you, that it is important, and that you would like to help. Offer comments on related experience you have had while being careful not to commit to exactly what will happen here. Also, talk about how you like to work with clients: how you engage with them, what you expect of them, what they can expect of you. Focus on the kind of results you hope to deliver.

Gather Preliminary Data

Ask for copies of related materials that you can read to help you understand the client's problem. Supplement what the client provides with a little online research of your own. Ask the client to arrange short meetings with a handful of trusted others who could add their perspectives. Set the date for your next meeting—and make it soon. Tell the client what you will bring him or her at that meeting: your updated impressions based on reading and interviews, and your proposed next steps.

❧ **Warren Bennis** ❧

Warren Bennis is an important figure in the behavioral science movement and is regarded as a pioneer in the field of leadership studies. He is distinguished professor of business administration at the University of Southern California and a founding chairman of The Leadership Institute at the University of Southern California.

Bennis began his groundbreaking work on leadership as one of Douglas McGregor's protégés, and he was greatly influenced by McGregor's interest in exploring and explaining the characteristics of effective leaders. Bennis was one of the first scholars to note the distinction between managing and leading, based on his observations that many organizations are managed well but have poor leaders. Bennis found that there is no one approach to becoming a successful leader, but after interviewing more than 90 top leaders in different fields, he identified some common characteristics or competencies among successful leaders:

- *The management of attention—the need for a vision to focus minds*
- *The management of meaning—the need to communicate the vision*
- *The management of trust—the need to be consistent and honest*
- *The management of self—the need to be aware of one's weaknesses.*

Bennis also acknowledged that successful leaders must be able to accept valid criticism and then decide whether it is best to change or to stick to their guns.

Later in his career Bennis began to study group dynamics, and he worried that his earlier work neglected the role that collaboration plays in the role of the successful individual leader. He now believes that leadership is increasingly becoming a shared task, which he has termed partnership instead of leadership.

In addition, Bennis served as an advisor to four presidents of the United States and has written voluminously on leadership; his book An Invented Life *(2004) was nominated for a Pulitzer Prize.*

Ask Questions

Before leaving, ask the client how he or she will know whether the project has been successful. Write down his or her response and save your notes for later assessment of the project. And ask the client how this meeting went: What worked? What didn't? What else does he or she want? The answers to these questions are your initial guides for how you work with this client.

In this entry step, you may find that your need to know more conflicts with the client's need for action soon. This is just the first of many times these conflicting needs meet. The two of you need to emerge from the entry meeting with each set of needs acknowledged and acted upon. You can aid this by agreeing to conduct your preliminary work—research and interviews—quickly. Respect the client's impatience now while the two of you figure out a way for you to find out more soon.

Step 2: Contracting

Using what you've learned during the entry step, draft a proposal for what you want to do with the client. During your next meeting, you expect to emerge with an agreement with the client on what you will offer to and expect of each other. Write down agreements so you have a record of what you decided; this is "the contract." Not a contract in the legal sense, but a record of what's agreed to at this stage, knowing that it will change many times along the way. The contract typically deals with questions such as:

- What is the work? The issue? The opportunity? The problem?
- What are the outcomes expected? By the client? By you?
- How will you approach the problem?
- What will you expect of the client?
- How will you gather information about what is going on? From whom? When?
- How will you and the client work with each other? Keep each other informed? Deal with issues? Support each other? Measure progress?
- What will this contract cost in energy, time, money, equipment, and materials?

Come to this meeting with a draft of your answers to these questions, knowing that you and the client will revise it. Suggest that the client come with his or her own notes. Assume that this agreement will be revised later as the work informs you. Unlike a legal contract, this consulting contract is expected to change; both client and consultant are expected to keep the contract up to date. Some specific suggestions for creating contracts are discussed below.

Take Notes
Make the contracting portion of your meeting more business-like, emphasizing mutual understanding, clarity, and agreement. Take good notes, knowing you will prepare a refined agreement from these notes.

Ask the Right Questions
Ask the client what he or she sees as the important questions that need answering. Recall what he or she said in your entry meeting. Get the current answers to the client's own questions. Weave your own questions around what the client offers. Make this conversation a real dialogue.

Set a date for your next meeting, and tell the client what you expect to deliver at that meeting. You really cannot complete the contracting meeting without having planned ahead into the next steps, inquiry and interpretation.

Refer to the Agreement

Follow this meeting with a memo that describes the main elements of your agreement. From this point forward, return to your agreement often. Keep it up to date as circumstance and progress inform your work. The contents of this agreement should be the basis for keeping your relationship with the client alive and your work on target.

I've detected an uncomfortable pattern in my own consulting: many of my problems with clients came through unclear contracting. I thought I was to do something different from what the client expected. Or, we thought we understood each other when we didn't. Or, I wanted to do something but wasn't clear with the client. When a project comes apart, I often find that my shabby contracting was the cause. Regularly check in with your clients on how their needs are being met.

Step 3: Inquiry

This step is all about intentional learning in the client organization. It is often labeled *data collection,* but I like *inquiry* better. Inquiry suggests an exploration, a genuine and positive curiosity, an openness to what is going on in this place. (Appreciative inquiry and its disciples would go further with this. See *The Change Handbook* in For Further Reading at the end of this chapter.)

You, with the support of your client, have to decide how you are going to learn more about the issue and what surrounds it. In large part, your inquiry will be directed toward people. You may learn from them by

- Watching people and interpreting what you see
- Reading about what has been happening around the organization
- Talking with and interviewing some individuals
- Gathering people in groups to talk with them—or have them talk with each other
- Asking people to complete questionnaires of your own or someone else's design
- Asking people to perform certain tasks to see what they do and how they do it.

Any of these methods and more can be appropriate; it just depends on the project's purposes and resources (time, money, energy, geography, culture). You can address people face to face, in groups, on the telephone, or online. You can do the inquiry yourself, or you can have people in the client organization do it.

The inquiry step involves deciding what you want to learn from whom, choosing methods for learning that, and entering the organization with your questions and methods. Here's what I think about as I inquire:

Consider Your Client

Whatever you decide to do must involve the client. You are planning to take his or her workers' time, you are making your project public, you are potentially putting the client at risk. The client must support this significant step.

Select Your Method of Inquiry

Draft your approach to inquiry while completing your draft of the agreement in the contracting step. Use the materials the client gave you and the few interviews you've had to develop your proposal to the client about how you will gather more information. Select inquiry methods that are easy to use and for the client to understand. If the client doesn't understand what you are doing, chances are he or she will not have faith in the data you eventually deliver.

Watch Out for Bias

Avoid gathering information in a way that confirms your assumptions. Imagine you were to ask middle managers, "What are your three biggest problems in working here?" They will answer, and you will leave the inquiry convinced that this organization has big problems among the management. But the question created the perception. Ask the same managers, "What are your three greatest joys in working here?" and quite a different bias would emerge. Your challenge is to inquire in a way that reflects what is really going on, rather than your bias.

Get People Talking

Gather information in a way that allows people to speak to what is happening at work, which is important to them and the organization. If you are a trainer, do not ask what kind of training they need. If you do, they will tell you, and you have misled yourself into thinking you have discovered something important. Not likely. Instead, ask what is happening at work and what should be happening. Or, ask what present performance is and what they think it should be. Get people to talk about what they know best: their work, their feelings, their performance, and their results.

Whom Do You Talk To?

Ideally, we would inquire of everyone who might be invested in the issue and its resolution. This ideal is usually too time consuming and expensive. But a practical application of the ideal would bias us toward including more rather than fewer people. The change that happens down the road will require the support of many people. And people are more likely to support change they participate in. Think about that as you decide whom to involve.

Do Not Collect Secrets

When you allow people to load you up with confidential data that you can't use, you are taking on a responsibility not worth carrying. Only collect data that you can use; don't gather information off the record. You can only help this client when you can use what you learn.

Be Transparent

Tell those you involve as much as you can about what you are doing and what you are going to do with what they have given to you. Tell them this before you collect data from them. When you are less than open, they will sense this and be more likely to withhold information from you.

Set Aside Biases

Avoid analyzing the data while you are collecting it. Doing so usually results in premature conclusions and affects the way you collect data from that point forward and biases your results. Wait until the interpretation step. You are biased; we all are. Give up the notion that you are an objective observer; you aren't. You cannot forget your biases, but you can put them aside during this inquiry. You want to ensure that you are really seeing what is going on in this organization; your biases won't help.

Step 4: Interpretation

There are two parts to analyzing the information you have collected: What does it say? and What does it mean? What's said is the more literal part; what's meant is more interpretive. Here are a few observations on how to sort reams of data when you have no established guide:

Find the New Order

Make sense of what's in front of you in a new way—that's what interpretation is about. How could all these data make sense in a way that would be useful to the organization?

That sense may emerge, or it may have to be imposed, or it may never come about (my lingering fear).

Sort Your Data

Sort the data at least three ways, withholding your commitment to any one of them. For example, you might sort the data by who said it, looking for patterns among the job titles or levels of those interviewed. And then you might sort again based on geographic location. Or shift. And then you might sort them by common issues. Don't finish this step too fast. Again, pay attention to your biases. It is safer to test them here than in the earlier step, but don't confine yourself to a one-bias analysis.

It's OK to Be Confused

Do not be afraid to get lost in the data; be willing to not understand what they mean. The client may have been struggling with this issue for years. Why should you immediately understand it? A natural part of the interpretation process is to be confused for a while; the data do not always make sense. As the saying goes, if you are not confused, then maybe you just don't understand. Being clear too early can mean that you are blind to what is really happening.

Sort, and Sort Again

If a clear sort of the information does not emerge, then force one. This can allow new ideas to emerge, perhaps another data sort will present itself. There are times when no significant patterns exist. Sometimes it means there was nothing to find; other times it means you need to ask other questions. What you know now usually contains clues of where to look next.

If you can, involve the client in this interpretation step. He or she can help your understanding of what the data mean. And his or her involvement in this analysis builds his or her commitment to act on its outcomes. If you want the client to believe your eventual recommendations, he or she needs to agree on the validity of the data you've collected and understand the way you interpreted them. The result of the inquiry and interpretation is a report containing

- An explanation of how the inquiry was done
- The kinds of people involved
- The data—what they say
- Interpretations that flow from the data.

All of this is essential to the next step.

Step 5: Feedback

This step has to do with taking what you've learned to the client, clarifying the data, and exploring interpretations. Meeting with your primary client and involved others is a focal point that is often challenging. People gather around your report to discuss important issues. Remember that those in the room had a hand in creating the issues that your report reveals. And the real issues revealed usually differ from the presenting issues the client originally called you about. Yes, this is a culminating, exciting, and tough step. Here are some tips that have helped me:

No Surprises

Meet with your primary client ahead of the larger meeting. Clients do not like public surprises. If you must surprise your client, do it in private. Review the report with him or her, get his or her reactions, tell him or her how you would like to put it before invested others. Decide on the client's role and your role in the meeting. Ask for leadership of the discussion of the report.

Share Your Report Ahead of Time

Plan time for individuals to absorb the report and figure out what it might mean. If it's a long report and a short meeting, you are unlikely to be successful in moving through to agreement and action. I've found it useful to get the report to people on the afternoon before the meeting, giving them time to read it but not enough time to gather and work on it.

The Client Owns the Data

In the meeting, seek the group's "ownership" of the data—meaning they believe that the data in the report are representative of the organization. Whether they agree with the data is quite a different point! When people challenge the data as false, invalid, or distorted, ask them for the data that are missing, and add them to what you have already collected. Be prepared to explain why you gathered the information you did and how you gathered it. People uncomfortable with the message often challenge the messenger. You need not defend the data because they are not yours; they come from the client and the client's people. And they need to "own" the data before they can act upon it.

Separate Data and Interpretations

If you can, divide your report into two parts: the sorted data and interpretations of the data. Give the client the data, gain his or her support and ownership of the data, then give him or her the interpretations. I know, usually the client wants the data and your interpretation together—along with your recommended actions. That seems efficient but reduces thinking, creativity, and ownership. Showing your interpretation before the client has made his or her own can both preclude his or her important analytical work and reduce his or her ownership of your interpretation.

After the client owns the data, help him or her move to interpret the data. Draw out the client's interpretation and weave in your own. Acknowledge that you made your analysis before having heard from him or her; let him or her know that what he or she has said has affected you. Build on the client's work.

Get the Client Involved

This feedback step may be the clients' first indication that they are not doing as well as they thought—and they are learning about it while in front of others. They may feel challenged, criticized, and defensive. Don't blame them for feeling that way, but don't let them be diverted from reaching ownership of the data, being involved in interpretation, and being engaged in alternatives and action.

This suggests a more "formal" presentation to the client group. Find out how they typically do this. What do they likely expect? Then do it better! Keep in mind the client's focus on action and results. Don't become too entranced with your methodology, wasting precious time on how you did this while the client waits to hear what you discovered. Prepare

- What you are going to say
- What you are going to show
- What you are not going to say, but are ready to talk about
- How you are going to engage them
- What outcomes you expect.

Step 6: Alternatives

Now that we agree on what the data say and what they mean, it's time to explore what we might possibly do about them. Slow down enough to consider the array of actions the client might take before deciding on one. (Most of my clients are more experienced in the second half of the 10-step process. Our more unique consulting skills come into play in the first five steps of the process.)

Develop Alternatives

Before meeting, anticipate the client group's interpretations and develop possible alternatives. You may never present these, but it is very useful to have thought about where the client might go with your report. It's generally better not to build the alternatives into your report because you may be moving the client toward action prematurely. Your advance thinking about alternatives allows you to ask questions and offer suggestions during the meeting that stimulate the clients to deal creatively with the report before them. Plan how you will involve them in developing their own alternatives. Do not pre-empt them, but do think ahead. Then, weave your alternatives in with those that come from the clients.

Design a piece of the meeting to develop alternatives. Choices made from among alternatives increase confidence because the deciders know they have deliberated. Their involvement results in more and better ideas without sacrificing any of the ideas you have developed.

Engage the Right People

Make sure you have the right people in the room to develop alternatives. They may be different people than those who agreed on the issue and decided to move ahead. Engage people who combine expertise with creativity, who are known for thinking outside the box, who are not stuck in the old system.

Our cultural bias toward action often means this alternatives step gets short changed. The result can be less creative solutions, less complete solutions, and less commitment.

Step 7: Decision

The decision, the choice, is usually bundled with alternatives. I create two steps here because they require different skills of you and of the client. Where creating alternatives involves an expansive reach outward, making a decision involves an analytical narrowing in.

For the decision to work when it is taken to action (in the next step), it's best to involve people who will be affected by the decision. Suggest to the client that he or she invite these kinds of people to the alternative-building and decision-making meeting:

- People with related and useful expertise
- People with necessary authority
- People affected by the decision
- People whose commitment is needed.

Consider All Alternatives Before Making a Decision

Try to keep the client group from making the decision until they have heard all the alternatives. Ideally, they will have complete and shared understanding of the data, the interpretation of the data, and the alternatives before the decision. This includes considering the consequences of each of the more viable alternatives.

Identify the Decision Makers

Involving people does not necessarily mean they make the decision together. They may act as listeners, advisors, or decision makers—or the boss can make the decision on his or her own if desired. Whatever the roles of all involved, make sure that they know their role in relation to the decision before the meeting, if possible.

Be Clear on What Is Being Decided

Make sure that people know what is being decided and the potential effect on them and the organization. They will have to live with this decision from day to day, and you want it to be well supported. If they choose a decision because it is sold to them, their implementation of it will be less than enthusiastic.

Identify Roles Clearly

After the decision, help the client lay out who will do what, where, and by when. Make this widely understood among those present. Have someone take note of this and get those notes out to all involved. Those specifics will inform what happens next in the action step.

During this step, you should be stepping back further. The client is moving beyond your report, taking his or her conclusions back to the organization. Where clients need to act, they should lead, you should not. Of course, when you have a role in the coming actions, you would lead within the confines of that role.

Step 8: Action

Many organizations are much better at action than they are at preparing for it. You've helped them prepare well so now they can act more wisely. Other organizations meet their first real test with this action step: until now, they haven't had to do anything substantive to change, and at this step you may detect resistance to change. Beginning to change the system can be threatening. Here are some ideas that help:

Maintain Momentum

Encourage immediate action, building on the momentum established in earlier steps. Resist the temptation to relax now that the client has decided to act. Very important work is about to begin; help it happen. All the good inquiry, interpretation, and planning will be lost if the momentum is not maintained. Momentum is precious; don't squander it!

Be Consistent with Plans

Participants involved in the last few steps of the process should see a direct, dynamic relationship between the action that is beginning and what they participated in earlier. Current action should be consistent with earlier plans and the underlying assumptions. For example, if earlier steps anticipated involving a wide array of people, that should be happening in this action step.

Help Key Leaders

Help the key leaders find and take specific, observable, immediate action that demonstrates change in line with the project's direction.

- What could key leaders do right now? They are the models others will look to.
- What could an individual employee do?
- How is the organization supporting action by all?
- What information or familiarization would move people into action more quickly?
- How could recent changes be communicated across the organization?
- How will the organization deal with the discomfort created by change?
- What could be done to reinforce individual and group initiative that supports the change?

Model Ideal Behavior

Carry out your part of the action promptly with no doubt that others will do their parts. Be a good and public example of support for the changes being implemented.

Be Supportive

Observe early actions closely; see them as a measure of commitment to and understanding of the project. Support and reinforce people who are trying new behaviors as a result of the changes being instituted. Even support changes that don't work that well; support the fact that they were tried.

Coach, but Don't Take Over

Find ways to coach and counsel your clients through their new actions rather than taking over and doing it for them. Avoid your tendency to "fill the breach" because you think they don't know how to do it, are neglecting it, or lack commitment. It's their organization, not yours. They live here; you don't. Certainly help, but they should be extending far more energy than you.

Expect Setbacks

Help your clients expect setbacks. Seldom do changes happen as expected; important change always encounters resistance. Expect that they will have problems. The more noble your aspirations, the more likely problems will occur. Anticipate those problems and develop contingency plans for dealing with them. Make "unexpected" problems "expected."

Be Encouraging

Encourage and lead meetings that help people review how they are progressing, accept their success and slippage, and figure out what they could do to build on their success.

All these ideas are ways of maintaining the project progress and priority through time. A most common difficulty with this step: Project initiators and leaders feel great about what they have started; they act as if change has been instituted and move on to new interests. They leave it to others to carry out the change; they shift their attention to more immediate priorities. I've seen more projects fail for this reason than any other.

Step 9: Impact

The breadth and depth of the impact of even a small change effort seeps out in directions too numerous and expensive to document. Nobody knows how much difference this change project made in any absolute ways. Yes, we might be able to quantify the time and money we put into it, but what about the energy? The commitment? The excitement? The emotional toll? All of the costs and benefits of the project cannot be assessed accurately.

When the project is successful, people celebrate that success, take credit for their accomplishment. When a project fails, participants often run for cover—including consultants. Most often, our results combine success and failure—hopefully a net gain, but not without some losses along the way. Assessing what has happened and who is responsible calls out a wide array of opinion and behavior, depending on the results achieved. Consultants are typically seen as responsible for work they helped guide but did not do. It comes with the territory.

These difficulties with determining impact should not outweigh the necessity of asking

- How have we done in relation to what we intended?
- What are we getting that we wanted? What are we not getting?
- How has the organization been affected?
- What have we learned along the way?

- How does what we did affect what we would do next time?
- How did our client-consultant relationship contribute to our results?

Do not wait until this ninth step to measure. Build in progress reviews that happen regularly during the project. For example, after reviewing the data coming from inquiry and interpretation, check with the client on how the project is going. Another example: When the client is planning actions, encourage him or her to build in meetings to assess the actions, to recognize successful actions, or to reinforce areas of weakness.

Initiate Progress Meetings

If you want regular progress reviews with your client, chances are, you will have to initiate the meetings. Most of my clients only initiate an evaluation, update, or progress review when they feel like they are trouble. You don't want to find out about problems that late. And there is a very positive side to regular reviews: you can look at the success you have had together. Success reinforces mutual commitment to the effort, it builds trust, and it's sure nice to be able to remind yourself of it when the bad times hit.

Check Yourself

Separate from the client; check with yourself to see that you are getting what you want out of this project. When there are other consultants involved, make sure that you check progress among yourselves. This will knit you closer, reveal results to celebrate, give recognition to key players, and often result in early identification of potential problems.

When people know that their work is being measured, they more likely deliver results aligned with the measures they perceive. Help people see this measurement as a sign that their work is valued. Others perform better to avoid looking bad or because they think they are being watched. If your project is important, the organization should know enough about the project to help it succeed.

Step 10: Exit

It is time to finish your work and leave—at least for now. This is more difficult than it might seem, especially with a very successful project. Exit means saying, "Our work together is ending; we have little more to do under our agreement. How might we best conclude this project?" Perhaps these ideas will help you decide what to do:

Close the Project

A summary report from you near project completion is one good way to acknowledge the work is coming to a close. The report helps both you and the client step back from the work and collect your thoughts before letting go. And it is also an opportunity to suggest getting together to close the project in person.

One of the primary ways that people build relationships is through working together. That's likely happened with you and your client, and perhaps with others in the organization. Considering this, there are better ways to leave than to just walk out the door. Exiting can often involve some combination of reflection, acknowledgement, and celebration of what you've done together, what you have gained through your work together, and how you feel about it. And sometimes refreshments and cake are involved.

Separate Celebration from Work

If you celebrate, separate that celebration from considerations of other work. A celebration is not time for analytical assessment of what you have done. That happens at another time. During the celebration, hold up what happened that was particularly valued and touched people at a more emotional level. This is more about heart than head.

Do not build on the emotion of the moment to propose more work, or accept work that the client puts forth while under the influence of the moment. Do that another time.

Don't Look to the Future

We consultants sometimes become financially dependent on a client. And we are tempted to make our clients dependent on us. Watch out for this temptation. You may end up doing work the client should be doing; you may recommend work that is a priority for you, but not for the client. In your long-term interest and in your client's immediate interest, finish this project well with few ties to the future.

Call to Say Hello

After you have exited a project that you valued, maintain regular, informal contact with the client. Do not call to pitch your work and talents. You don't need to do that; the client already knows your work. Just call to catch up with his or her life and remember the good work you did together. Sure, there will be an opportunities to check in on future work, but that is not the primary intent of these conversations.

Summary

There is an important underlying pattern to this 10-step process that we have not talked about. Think of it as a reaching out—as in stretching your arms and hands outward—and then a drawing in—as in bringing your hands together in front of you. In the reaching out phase, you gather information, you develop alternatives, you think creatively. What you gather in your reach feeds the bringing-together phase in which you analyze information, set priorities, decide action. This reaching out and gathering in process occurs all through the 10 steps:

- In the entry step, you and the client decide you should go out to see what else you can learn in a short while—that's the reaching out to gather information. You bring this information together in your proposal to the work in the contract.
- In the inquiry, you reach out to gather information from the larger organization. In interpretation and feedback, you pull information together for client consideration.
- In alternatives, you reach out for the possibilities. In decision and action, you narrow your options and reach out to act.
- In impact, you reach out for data on how the project is going; you pull them together to decide what actions to take.
- Even the exit step has this reaching out and drawing in aspect to it. You gather stories about what has happened from all involved, and use those to celebrate the ending of the work.

This reaching out and bringing together is not just a coincidence, it is the underlying rhythm. It feeds the life of the consulting process; it is as if the process lives by breathing out . . . then by breathing in.

About the Author

Geoff Bellman worked inside major corporations for 14 years before starting his own consulting firm. His external consulting has focused on renewing large, mature organizations. He has written five books about leadership, change, work, and life. His consulting and workshops have taken him to five continents. He serves as guest faculty for several graduate programs and is a charter member of the Woodlands Group, which has been meeting quarterly for 30 years, exploring individual, organizational, and societal change. He helped found the Community Consulting Partnership, which teaches consulting skills while providing free consultation to the not-for-profit community in Seattle, Washington.

For Further Reading

Bellman, Geoffrey. 2000. *The beauty of the beast: Breathing new life into organizations.* San Francisco: Berrett-Koehler.

Bellman, Geoffrey. 2002. *The consultant's calling: Bringing who you are to what you do.* 2d ed. San Francisco: Jossey-Bass.

Block, Peter. 2000. *Flawless consulting: A guide to getting your expertise used.* 2d ed. San Francisco: Jossey-Bass/Pfeiffer.

Hiebert, Murray, and Eilis Hiebert. 2005. *Powerful professionals: Leveraging your expertise with clients.* 3d ed. Calgary, Alberta, Canada: Recursion Press.

Holman, Peggy, Tom Devane, and Steven Cady. 2007. *The change handbook: The definitive resource on today's best methods for engaging whole systems.* 2d ed. San Francisco: Berrett-Koehler.

Schwarz, Roger M. 2002. *The skilled facilitator: Practical wisdom for developing effective groups.* 2d ed. San Francisco: Jossey-Bass/Pfeiffer.

Managing the Learning and Performance Function

Learning Linked to Business Results

Luminary Perspective

Daniel Ramelli

In This Chapter

> ➤ Understand the three critical dimensions of learning to drive competitive advantage

> ➤ Learn the importance of linking learning to business priorities

> ➤ Increase the effects of learning by using five strategic levers

---

After being in several great organizations and being responsible for learning and development, it's become apparent to me that there are three critical dimensions of learning and five strategic levers that chief learning officers (CLOs) should consider as they build their vision, strategy, and operating plans. The critical dimensions are the enterprise, the individual, and the leaders.

These three critical dimensions of learning are important to clearly understand the capability of the business to use learning to drive competitive advantage and operating capacity. Although each business has these three dimensions, CLOs need to understand the dimensions and how to use them together to build a learning culture.

The Enterprise Dimension—Fast Learning Is the Competitive Advantage

Most companies are in the midst of rapidly changing global competitive markets and are still determined to be great world class companies in the eyes of their stakeholders—customers, owners, employees, and their communities. They know this happens only if they deliver the best products, services, performance, results, and innovations in their industry on a sustainable basis.

Most companies know they can only be successful in the fiercely competitive markets they serve when talented individuals work together to deliver great business results and to find new ways to become best in class in delivering value. This means hiring and developing the best talent in the market—smart, capable, creative, and determined to win.

Two constants are that learning has to be linked to the business's priorities and that the learning model must work to be the fastest, most effective, and efficient learning method possible. This requires innovation, technology, experimentation, and some courage.

Companies don't have enough time and resources to misapply efforts in learning—they are fighting for survival in an intensely competitive marketplace. Great companies need a CLO who thinks like the CEO, chief operating officer, chief financial officer, and chief information officer—and maybe even like the board.

Great CLOs have a deep understanding of the business, customers, competitors, and operations and have identified the critical skills and capabilities required to win in the marketplace.

Learning was valued in the past because "if change is constant, learning must be continuous." We knew that even though we hired great talent, without learning our teams would become less contemporary and less competitive—so learning was an investment in keeping competitive and in driving innovative best practices.

Now as we are beginning to fully comprehend the faster pace of global competition we may need to upgrade our focus: "If change is accelerating, learning must be aligned, accessible, and agile." Our approach to enterprise learning must be 10 times better than before. The good news is that we hire smart techno-savvy people who are quick learners both in the classroom and on their computers. Now, new blended learning approaches using great classroom or webinar techniques can be coupled with low-cost e-learning approaches and can help us get to 10 times better sooner than we thought possible.

The Individual Dimension—The Self-Directed Learner

Individuals want to be successful and know that the more they improve and expand their skills and capabilities, the more they will be able to contribute value—and the more likely they will be recognized, rewarded, and advanced in their career.

Individuals need to take time to understand and assess their skills and capabilities. They should also reflect on their strengths and areas for improvement to create their short- and long-term development plans.

Smart employees know they should own and take the initiative to implement their development plans. In creating plans, they should consider undertaking challenging assignments, such as volunteering for special projects, working with different parts of the business, or partnering with experts. They should also focus on education and training that upgrades their professional and technical capabilities.

Really smart employees know they should discuss their development with their managers—to gain advice, coaching, and support. Really smart CLOs know they must provide the kind of real-time learning that the most competitive employees want—linked to key business priorities and best practices that build competitive capabilities or "hot skills." Training needs to be learner-centered, not instructor- or classroom-centered. As I watch both my daughters advance in their early careers, I am struck by how often on weekend afternoons they are in their office via technology getting work done or learning about new opportunities or best practices. They are both self-starters who are passionate about their work and are driven to be the best.

Great CLOs understand the employees, their work, their challenges, and their learning preferences, and identify the most effective ways to provide education and training that will drive competitive advantage.

The Leader Dimension—Nine Times the Learning Power with No Cost

Leaders and managers know that their team's capability will determine their personal level of success in obtaining critical business results. And they know that they themselves are responsible for the development of their team's skills, capability, and performance.

Smart leaders make sure they develop the right types of skills, capability, and teamwork for each member of their team. They take time in team meetings to make their decision-making approach visible. They make sure they discuss the pros and cons of different

---

✍ **Ken Blanchard** ✎

Ken Blanchard is a prominent speaker and author in the field of management. Blanchard has written or co-authored more than 30 books, including Leading at a Higher Level: Blanchard on Leadership, Creating High Performing Organizations *(2006), and* The One Minute Manager *(1981, with Spencer Johnson).*

Blanchard and Paul Hershey developed the situational leadership model, which helped managers analyze situations to determine the most effective style of management to use. The model describes four leadership styles, including delegating, directing, supporting, and coaching. To match the four leadership styles, Blanchard and Hershey described four development types for employees: low competence/low commitment, some competence/low commitment, high competence/variable commitment, and high competence/high commitment. The leadership style to use depends upon the type of employee with which the manager is dealing.

---

strategic and operating approaches. They will consider work assignments for individuals that broaden skill sets, partnering developing employees with experts on special business projects. They also recommend or approve appropriate education or training activities focused on business and professional development that will drive contribution and results.

Really smart leaders do this naturally—they develop team members in ways that are connected with and integrated into the way work gets done. They use work-related discussions about operations, project reviews, or progress reviews as a way to naturally coach and accelerate development. At the same time, they are focused on delivering business results. They use open two-way dialogue to understand and assess operating challenges and to get ideas and innovations on the table that can drive better performance.

Really smart CLOs know that 90 percent of learning in the workplace comes from challenging assignments and working with others, while 10 percent comes from organized learning offerings. Although that 10 percent is powerful, smart CLOs know how to enable and support the leaders who want to coach and develop their employees.

Great CLOs understand the leadership dimension and how to leverage it to get the full benefit of "leaders as teachers." Great CLOs know that by enabling leaders to be better coaches the business gets nine times the learning power at little or no cost.

This requires support on three different levels. First, all leadership courses have to start with the principle that leaders and the work environment they create are the biggest source of learning and development available—and leadership courses should help them become better coaches and mentors.

Next, all of the learning needs to be available to support quick learning opportunities that leaders can point out when coaching or mentoring—these can be e-tools or job aids geared to quick practical workplace application and improvements. This may feel like a wholesale rather than a retail effort—but deploying learning to where the work is done is learner centered and drives the right business-focused performance.

Finally, the enterprise has to rid itself of leaders who don't get it and are crippling the learning and development strategy of the enterprise. Developing others needs to be a valued and rewarded leadership competency. Senior leaders need to send home leaders who don't get it or won't develop their people.

If the World Is Flat, then Learning Must Be Fast, Focused, Fearless

Although understanding the dimensions of learning is critical, great CLOs know there are strategic levers that force the right movement and acceleration for learning in their organization. These levers are reasonably clear from my experience—five seem to stand out in terms of driving the right movement for the business cultures I have seen.

Managing the learning and performance function can increase its effect through the use of five strategic levers:

- Advocacy
- Alignment
- Action
- Agility
- Results.

Although I will use my AlliedSignal/Honeywell experiences for examples of these levers, the same strategic levers are at work in General Motors (GM) and Fannie Mae today. And although I didn't appreciate them fully in my early career, these levers were used by learning leaders in my experience in the U.S. Navy and at Coopers & Lybrand.

The art in our CLO science is to understand the dimensions of learning and work the strategic levers to execute your learning strategy quickly and effectively.

Advocacy—Leadership Advocacy

When I worked for Larry Bossidy at AlliedSignal/Honeywell, he often reminded the leaders that "at the end of the day you bet on people, not strategy." He spent a great deal of time on our talent reviews with his top leaders, Fred Poses (now chairman of American Standard) and Dan Burnham (former chairman of Raytheon). Together they would spend hundreds of hours a year assessing the top four levels of talent we had and deciding what key development actions should be taken to accelerate their growth and advancement. They were natural role models for our leaders on advocating the importance of learning and development in building a world-class business.

They and the rest of the leadership team had high expectations about all the aspects of development—challenging assignments, cross-functional and business rotations, the right leadership coaching and feedback, as well as the learning that had to be focused on critical business and leadership capabilities.

In 1997, I was asked to be the chief learning officer and vice president for organization and leadership development at AlliedSignal/Honeywell. I had already spent five years in the engineered materials operations working for Fred Poses deploying total quality, Six Sigma, and customer focus efforts that were connected to business operations and linked directly to business results. I worked with front-line leaders who needed improvements by their teams to make their numbers. Their feedback was immediate, candid, and connected to the customer. Because of that connection, their advocacy and input drove urgency in making everything we did improve effectively and quickly. Poses and his leadership team were terrific advocates for developing their talent, and he, as president of engineered materials, was personally involved in connecting the learning to the right processes and people to drive the right impact.

First and foremost, being able to create learning to address business priorities required me to learn the business, talk in business terms, and design learning that was focused on getting results that leadership valued. Engaging them in the learning efforts created real advocates that supported learning and development—because they knew it delivered better performance, results, and capability.

Alignment

There were very high expectations that focused, practical training could enable our talent to accelerate both their capability and contribution. Because I had access to the business's strategic and operating reviews, the performance priorities and gaps became apparent quickly. And because we were dealing with results that mattered, leaders were willing to be decisive about using focused training to achieve business priorities.

Bossidy required each business and every function to provide a learning plan when it submitted its operating plan for the next year. The learning plan was expected to show alignment to key actions to improve business-critical skill sets and to show the scope and funding the function would invest in its talent. He expected to see marketing training where growth was a key priority; and where cash flow was critical, he expected to see training focused on revenue and cash management.

Operating alignment was always connected through the human resource leader for the business or function. This connection is critical to HR strategic success and learning's contribution. HR leaders know what the business priorities are and where we should spend our efforts on learning and development. The same strong connection exists at GM and Fannie Mae. Sometimes the answer to a performance gap is recruiting or outsourcing; sometimes it's focused learning. HR knows strategically and operationally what the talent plan is and how learning can best enable the priorities. HR leadership can be terrific partners at keeping learning aligned on the right priorities.

Action and Application

AlliedSignal/Honeywell had already seen the benefit of the "action learning" of the total quality and Six Sigma efforts of driving specific operating results where training was focused on specific and valuable processes or transactions or activities. This General Electric technique of action learning was appealing to our business leaders because it was focused on application, improvement, and real business results. For example, we delivered $200 million of savings in the first year of Six Sigma. Once business leaders saw the value, the deployment efforts expanded and in the third year of Six Sigma, leaders committed enough black belts to deliver more than $450 million of savings to the corporation from these action-learning projects alone.

On a frequent basis Poses and Burnham were involved in encouraging and sponsoring operating teams to take on difficult improvements and would champion efforts focused on the customer, suppliers, product development, and operating excellence. They always expected real progress and results and had a great way of asking questions that were supportive, yet challenged teams to stretch for greater accomplishments. They engaged and empowered operating teams to be the benchmarks and the teams responded.

Agility

I have been through three turnarounds. Speed, agility, innovation, and perseverance separate the winners from the losers. Agility can be developed in the business, in the talent, and in how the learning efforts enable the business transformation. Having one favorite learning strategy seems to fail—being agile around how to deploy learning and how to build a natural learning culture seems to be the huge value CLOs can bring to the table.

"Train with the result in mind" is my advice. The question for you each day is, "How can you and your team deliver the right learning—quicker, better, faster, cheaper?" Business leaders expect us to deliver better than the old training departments. They want responsive, focused, results-oriented solutions—not expensive five-day programs from high-priced vendors.

Results

Without practical application and results, learning has no significant purpose in business! Not every course that learning delivers will yield headline-grabbing results, but all should help build meaningful capability and skills. Everywhere I have been, business leaders want to know the value of learning. Some leaders expect you to quote return-on-investment measures. I have had good success with simply telling stories about our business initiatives that used training to drive real business improvements. For example, Six Sigma savings were built up each year in engineered materials on 30 to 50 projects that saved $1 million to $5 million. The business leaders knew their stories because they personally presented the results to Bossidy each quarter at our operating reviews. At GM there were several learning efforts in sales, engineering, purchasing, and manufacturing that delivered huge savings—again the business leaders that championed the efforts knew the results and were the ones who advocated the case for learning that delivers results. Once leaders were reminded how applying new techniques improved business results—they became advocates with high expectations.

CLOs that know how to work the strategic levers will be successful in accelerating learning and in building competitive advantage for their businesses. They must build advocacy, create valuable alignment, drive for action or application, coach on agility, and focus on results. I have seen this work to drive performance, recover from setbacks, and to inspire a culture to be the best—the art is to stay connected to the heartbeat of the enterprise, the individual, and the leaders.

About the Author

Daniel "Donnee" Ramelli is Fannie Mae's vice president and chief learning officer and is responsible for leading the formulation, design, and implementation of individual learning strategies and programs to increase the contribution and performance of employees and advance Fannie Mae's goals. He defines the strategic learning initiatives and programs for Fannie Mae and leads the efforts to develop or procure business and professional learning programs.

Prior to joining Fannie Mae, he was president of General Motors University at the General Motors Corporation, where he was responsible for planning and implementing GM's global learning strategy.

Before that, he was vice president of learning and organization development for Allied Signal/Honeywell; vice president of quality/Six Sigma for Allied Signal, Engineered Materials; director of quality and productivity engagements for Coopers & Lybrand; and supply officer in the U.S. Navy. He has also served as a member of the ASTD Board of Directors.

Chapter 41

Managing Learning Like a Business

Howard Prager

When thinking about learning and development, we think about learning needs, learning outcomes, and results. But too often we don't think about learning from the standpoint of business needs, business outcomes, and business results. If we want a seat at the table, if we want to be taken seriously, we need to move from thinking learning to thinking business (and those who work for government and associations, this applies to you, too). That's what has gotten information technology into the mainstream and brought about the chief information officer (CIO)—they focused on how IT helps the organization meet its business needs. Chief financial officers (CFOs) don't talk about finance and accounting needs and outcomes, it's all business. Then why don't learning executives and chief learning officers (CLOs) talk about business first and learning second? In part it's because it's what we know, it's what we're comfortable with, and, after all, won't learning objectives help the business anyway? Usually, but only if learning objectives are tied specifically to organizational goals. And unless the chief executive officer is one of the rare breeds who is convinced that learning is instrumental, it doesn't matter!

So why manage learning like a business?

1. To become credible. You are in a business. Whether it's for-profit, nonprofit, or government, the principles of business still apply. Showing that you know, operate, and understand business means that other managers and leaders in the organization will feel more comfortable with you. They can talk to you because you know and understand their language, their needs, what life is really like, rather than talking only "training speak" and appearing to be a business bystander.

2. To demonstrate workplace learning and performance's (WLP's) direct contribution to financial performance. This cannot be stated strongly enough. What's frequently cut when business goes south? WLP. If you manage learning like a business, then you show that you know business principles by modeling the operations of a business. And you demonstrate the value of what you bring to the organization by measuring your results and sharing it with senior leaders in language they know—return-on-investment (ROI) using level 1–5 evaluations, success case methodology, and so forth. What's important to senior leadership should be important to you.

3. To show the full value of WLP. How is this different from measuring your contribution to the business? That has to do with savings and improved productivity and performance of the business. This is tied to adding value in other ways such as improving the readiness of the organization; implementing a change process; or maximizing the talent, knowledge, and effective use of human capital. Using metrics the organization watches, such as turnover, employee and customer satisfaction, improved performance, and cost savings, and sharing with senior leadership can help you demonstrate the added value that an aligned WLP department can have for the organization.

So what do you have to do? Understand and follow the four key functions of a business: strategy, marketing, finance, and operations.

Strategy

Strategy drives the direction a business is going in and what goals it has, and if you're managing learning like a business, it should drive your work, too. What is strategy? It's identifying the mission and vision of the organization, creating strategic goals, and translating the goals into action.

Often, strategy is set by the CEO and his or her executive team. Work in the nonprofit or government sector? Your organization must have a strategy too, although your strategy may be one of fulfilling your mission. Strategy asks: Where are we now? Where do we want to be? How can we get there?

There are three ways learning fits in:

- You develop a WLP strategy that is aligned with the CEO's strategic goals. By showing that the work WLP does helps the organization achieve its strategic goals, you will gain greater support for contributing to the success of the business.
- You develop a strategy aligned with your boss's goals (if not the CEO, often the chief human resources officer or CFO, or whomever you report to). By helping achieve your boss's goals (which should be aligned to the organizational goals), you are not only helping your department, you're showing interest in your boss's goals and providing him or her support.
- You develop a WLP strategy that shows how WLP helps the organization achieve its vision and mission. There's a saying from the total quality management days that if you're not meeting the needs of the customer, you need to meet the needs of those who do. In creating a WLP strategy that is aligned with the organizational strategy, you are contributing to the success of the business. You also show that your focus is not just on learning in and of itself, but learning with a purpose that's tied closely to the organization's needs.

There are several ways organizations look at strategy. To begin with, ask the following: Where are we now? Where are we going? Who are we? How will we get there? The answers to these questions are ones everyone in your organization should know, but should be especially known by WLP. Helping the organization to move in the right direction should be a key focus for you.

Then look at your department's strengths and weaknesses. What is your department's competitive advantage? (I hope it isn't "we're convenient" or "we're here anyway.") What focus do you want your department to have, and what do you do better than anyone else? It's a two-edged sword—you want to align yourself with the organization's goals, *and* you want to define what you want your department to be known for. These core strengths may include needs assessment, performance consulting, organizational consulting, organization development, instructional design, simulations, technical training, leadership training, evaluation, serving as a business consultant, executive development, and other capabilities.

Now examine the steps for creating a strategic framework, both from the organization's point of view and from WLP's.

Creating a strategic framework (see Figure 41-1) involves three primary tasks:

- Environmental analysis (SWOT—strengths, weaknesses, opportunities, and threats)
- Strategy formulation (vision, mission, and strategy)
- Implementation (cascading goals).

Environmental Analysis

Environmental analysis is often conducted using a SWOT analysis (see Figures 41-2 and 41-3). SWOT looks at both external factors and internal realities to identify areas and markets. Strengths and weaknesses look at internal factors. What are your strengths as a department? What are your weaknesses? Opportunities and threats look at external factors: What opportunities exist in the marketplace and with your customers? What threats are there (often competitive threats) that could affect you?

Because of the merging in a customer's mind of product and service, strength isn't necessarily a tangible product. At McDonald's, a strength is QSCV—quality, service, cleanliness, value. Whatever McDonald's you go to throughout the world, you're assured the

Figure 41-1. The Strategy Framework

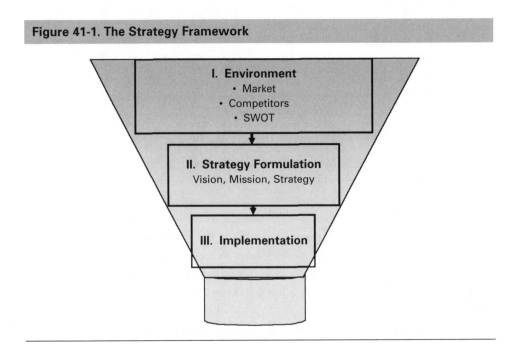

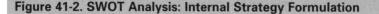

Figure 41-2. SWOT Analysis: Internal Strategy Formulation

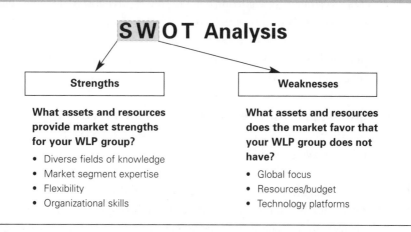

SWOT Analysis

Strengths	Weaknesses
What assets and resources provide market strengths for your WLP group?	**What assets and resources does the market favor that your WLP group does not have?**

- Diverse fields of knowledge
- Market segment expertise
- Flexibility
- Organizational skills

- Global focus
- Resources/budget
- Technology platforms

Figure 41-3. SWOT Analysis: External Environmental Factors

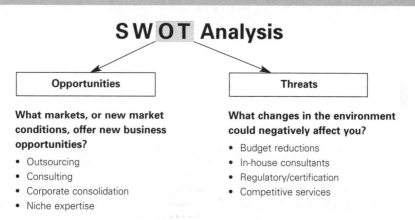

SWOT Analysis

Opportunities	Threats
What markets, or new market conditions, offer new business opportunities?	**What changes in the environment could negatively affect you?**

- Outsourcing
- Consulting
- Corporate consolidation
- Niche expertise

- Budget reductions
- In-house consultants
- Regulatory/certification
- Competitive services

same (or a very similar) experience. Opportunity for McDonald's may be finding markets where these qualities don't exist and entering that marketplace. In recent years, airports, museums, and toll road rest areas have all looked to recognized brand name fast food purveyors to meet the needs of their customers.

Weaknesses and threats have to do with vulnerabilities to your organization and where competitors may be poised to enter. A weakness can be a poor distribution system, manufacturing quality, or lack of speed or service. McDonald's strength and consistency can be a weakness to those who want a greater selection or local variety. A threat can be a local chain or restaurant that offers those advantages. A weakness of ASTD had been digitizing content. ASTD's investments in digitizing content to be searchable and retrievable online overcame this weakness. Had the association not done that, a competitor that offered electronic content could have beaten ASTD to the marketplace. A weakness in WLP may be having a finite budget and needing to decide which programs and projects to invest in to meet the organization's needs and goals.

Strategy Formulation—Create a Vision, Mission, and Strategy

Once you know who you are as an organization, the organization can begin to develop its vision, mission, and strategy (see Figure 41-4).

Vision. The vision is an idea or dream of the future, what the organization aspires to. For example, ASTD's vision is "To be a worldwide leader in workplace learning and performance." McDonald's is to be "The world's best quick service restaurant experience." What helps determine an organization's vision is an understanding of the organization's history and tradition, culture, core competencies, resources, management preferences, customer needs, and strengths and weaknesses versus other competitors. A vision is a compelling stretch goal, something people can get excited about.

Mission. A mission statement is a statement of an organization's purpose. It's a call to action consistent with the company's strategy. It needs to be short, actionable, measurable, memorable, and motivating. ASTD's mission is "Through workplace learning and

Figure 41-4. Vision, Mission, Strategy

Vision	Mission	Strategy
An idea or dream of the future unrealized	A daily call to action	A guideline to decision making
Descriptor of the future company success	Consistent with company vision and strategy	Consistent with company vision
May incorporate physical and value statements	Influenced by company values and competitive environment	Measurable!

performance, we create a world that works better." Merck's mission is "We are in the business of preserving and improving human life."

What is your organization's mission and vision? Is it first and foremost in your mind? Does your WLP department have a vision and mission? Do others know it? If not, create one and share it with others. Make sure it both ties into WLP's reason for being and helps the larger organization achieve its overall vision and mission.

Strategy. Strategy is a guideline for decision making. It's about choices—what to choose to do and what to choose not to do. It describes what the organization needs to do to achieve its goals. A strategy statement defines what markets the organization competes in, what specific goals and objectives it has, and what competitive advantage it may have.

For example, one of the key customer needs Lake Forest Corporate Education (LFCE) hears about is the need to develop leadership bench strength so that an organization can grow and expand and have the leadership necessary for growth and succession. From a strategic standpoint, meeting this need is an opportunity for LFCE to achieve its mission ("helping businesses advance their goals") by following one of its strategies (certificate programs).

Cascading Goals

Now that you've identified your areas of opportunity, your vision, your mission, and your strategy, it's time to make it operational. That happens through cascading goals. At the corporate level the mission, strategy, and goals are set. At the business unit or department level, you take the goals that are appropriate to your unit and identify the strategy and actions needed to achieve them, which in turn contributes to meeting the overall organizational goals. In this way, objectives and strategy cascade down from organization to department to group to individual, so that each person should know how he or she contributes to meeting the overall organization's goals.

Strategic Plan

ASTD BEST organizations, such as Caterpillar, prepare an annual learning and development plan (and later report) that provides data, details, and tie-in to the business. Think of this as an internal marketing plan and include these elements in your plan:

- Executive summary of the plan and recommendations
- Overview of WLP strategic plan (tied to strategic organizational goals)
- Situational analysis—what are the most pressing strategic needs of the organization that WLP can help address?

- Strategy—in what specific ways has WLP decided to address the situation?
- Objectives—what are the objectives for learning (and be sure to tie in all the way to the business goals)?
- Results—what are the desired results of the learning? (For reporting afterward, use Kirkpatrick's 4 levels, Phillips's ROI, Brinkerhoff's success case method—whichever method you choose—but be as measurable as you can be.)
- Budget—how much will it cost to achieve these results? What return do you anticipate? (Afterward, record actual costs and return so you can determine how accurate your estimate was.)
- Controls—how will you manage costs?
- Recommendations—what should this enable us to do? (Should the ongoing initiatives be continued?)

Think how powerful a plan and report like this could be, and how it could win over senior executives to the value of learning. Depending on the size and budget of the organization, this report could be more detailed or less, but don't skip it.

Marketing

The guru of marketing, Phil Kotler, describes the main task of an organization as to "determine the needs and wants of target markets and satisfy them through the design, communication and delivery of appropriate products and services" (Kotler and Keller, 2006).

Think Strategic Marketing

Marketing and strategy are closely related and use some of the same tools, such as a SWOT analysis. Organizations must invest in long-term, mutually satisfying customer relationships to keep their customer base. Why? First, it costs 10 times as much to get a new customer than to keep an existing one. Second, by understanding the needs of this customer base, organizations can plan better to meet those needs. Third, if you don't know what road to take, any road will do (but it may be long and bumpy). By knowing what your business is, who your customers are, and where your target market is, you will be better able to reach and keep the market you want to be in.

The marketing function helps an organization identify whether its emphasis and competitive advantage is in manufacturing/operations (Wal-Mart's operational excellence), product development (3M and Apple's innovative products), selling (push strategy such as generic and house brand products), or marketing (pull strategy, such as P&G). This in turn helps determine what marketing will emphasize.

ꔷ **Ron Zemke** ꔷ

Ron Zemke was a pioneer in creating the customer-service driven culture. In 1972, Zemke co-authored Service America! *with Karl Albrecht, a book that is credited with starting the customer service revolution. Zemke went on to create the* Knock Your Socks Off Service *series, writing that great customer service is reliable, responsive, reassuring, empathetic, and tangible. In 1972, Zemke founded Performance Research Associates (PRA), a consulting group that studies organizational effectiveness and productivity. He continued to research and write about service and co-authored with Tom Connellan a book about how to provide superior customer service on the web,* E-Service.

Zemke also developed a performance model together with Thomas Kramlinger. The figuring things out (FTO) model comprises six factors or categories of variables that have been found to affect performance:

- *Performer*
- *Objectives*
- *Expectations*
- *Rewards or punishments*
- *Feedback*
- *Support.*

What drives your organization? How do you find out? In part, look at where the budget goes. Look at who the CEO spends the most time with. Look at what your organization is best known for in the marketplace.

Study Customer Data

Marketing has many similarities to WLP. It is data driven using focus groups, interviews, surveys, and market research. Both have roots in the applied behavioral sciences. Both are inexact sciences and difficult to measure. But marketing is externally focused and totally business focused, asking how we can best reach our customers. What's of importance to them? What do they care about? What do they need?

Isn't that part of what WLP does with needs assessments? Too often we skip this phase because the organization says it knows what it needs. And we don't connect all the dots. We'll take assessment data and apply them to learning needs but forget to link them to business needs. Then we're happy if we can measure an improvement in learning (pre- or posttest) or application to the job (behavioral). But what about always connecting it to the business results desired? "These skills have improved 50 percent through learning, which enables people to work more quickly and effectively, while saving $3 for every $1 invested in learning." Communicating that line of sight shows that you are focused on organizational results, not just learning results.

Segmentation, Targeting, and Positioning

Segmentation, targeting, and positioning are at the heart of marketing strategy (see Figure 41-5). Segmenting can take various forms: geographic segments (learning via regional locations), demographics (programs to meet Boomer, Generation X, Generation Y, and Millennial needs), behavioral (based on learning styles), benefit (return-on-learning-investment), and level in the organization (executive, managerial, associate). Choosing the way you want to segment learning will help you meet the needs of different groups in your organization.

Targeting is selecting one or multiple market segments to pursue and develop. Executive development, supervisory development, employee development, technical training, and performance consulting are all options you may offer. Knowing what and who you are targeting will help keep your offerings focused on your audience needs.

Positioning is the act of designing and communicating a company's offering so that it occupies a distinctive place in the mind of the target market. How does your offering differ from that of others? Why should your organization work with you (internal) versus the multitude of external vendors that are available? What added value can you provide?

Figure 41-5. Segmentation Information

- **Geographic variables:**
  — Region
  — Size
  — Climate

- **Demographic variables:**
  — Age
  — Gender
  — Marital status
  — Family life stage
  — Family size
  — Income
  — Occupation
  — Education

- **Psychographic variables**
  — Values
  — Attitudes
  — Opinions
  — Personality

- **Behavioral variables:**
  — Benefit sought
  — Product usage rate
  — Brand loyalty
  — Product end use
  — Readiness-to-buy stage

After all, being internal you should know the organization the best—that should give you some leverage, if you've marketed WLP's capabilities effectively. "The end result of positioning is the successful creation of a customer-focused value proposition, a cogent reason why the target market should buy the product" (Kotler and Keller, 2006).

Using Marketing Every Day Internally

Remember the movie *Field of Dreams* and the famous line, "If you build it, he will come"? Maybe that works in the movies, but a business wouldn't last long if it just built it and put it out there. So typically a WLP department spends time on developing and delivering programs with little thought (or afterthought) as to how you internally market it to your audience. Spend some time identifying

- Who you should be marketing to
- How you can keep senior executives aware of your offerings
- How your offerings are tied in to achieving strategic business goals
- What results you have accomplished.

Branding

Branding is a way to ensure that your customers know who you are and what you can do. These four steps from the Nebraska ASTD chapter are good tips for developing an effective marketing plan:

1. *Determine benefit/value.* What do you offer and what is the benefit to your customers?
2. *Create objectives and strategy.* For each marketing objective, be sure to create a strategy to achieve that objective.
3. *Outline implementation into strategy.* Turn the strategy into action by creating specific action plans with accountability, budget, and resources.
4. *Review and evaluate success.* How do you know when you have succeeded? Have clear measures that tie back, as best you can, to your marketing initiatives.

Last, remember the strategic plan you put together? You can pull a lot of information from it for branding, as well as reporting results that use metrics.

Finance and Metrics

Setting specific, measurable goals and showing the results is the number one practice you can do to show that you are managing learning like a business. Whether it's tying into the business itself, reporting on productivity gains and cost savings, or detailing how you effectively manage the budget, demonstrating good financial acumen will allow other executives to see you, and WLP, as an important business function.

Understanding your organization's finances is critical to showing business acumen, and understanding your WLP finances is critical to managing learning like a business. Many nonfinancial people get nervous when the subject of finance and accounting is raised. If you can manage your household budget, you can manage the organizational budget. It just has more zeros.

It's also about showing how WLP is an investment rather than a pure expense. There are so many ways to show return-on-learning-investment today. Consider the following potential measures of WLP success: retained customers, retained employees, lower turnover, faster getting up-to-speed, higher satisfaction, increased productivity, cost containment, stronger negotiations, increased sales, improved communication, and greater team effectiveness. Whenever using estimates, be sure to be conservative, especially because WLP may not be the only reason for the cause-effect produced.

As you compute the return-on-learning-investment, be sure to look at the following:

- What are your fully loaded costs (overhead, salaries, and so forth)?
- What revenue do you generate (or indirectly help generate)?
- What is your financial value to the organization?

You should have top-of-mind answers to these questions and be sure to highlight them in your annual WLP report to the organization's senior leaders. Also, note that the best metrics are those already used by your organization—not by the WLP department—no matter how well grounded in finance.

Costs or Revenue

Understand where WLP is on the balance sheet. Are you a cost center (you don't generate revenue)? A profit center (you do generate revenue)? How do you allocate your services internally? Do you have a charge-back system? What costs do you include in charge backs—design and development, facilitation, salaries, food, and materials? Do you sell your products or services to others outside the organization? What's the basis of your costs?

Whatever your status, knowing the costs, expenses, and percentage of the corporate budget of WLP will allow you to make better internal decisions. Ask yourself: What's valued that we should do more of? What's not valued that we should reexamine or eliminate? Looking at the numbers gives you more questions to ask about your priorities, meeting the organization's goals, and the effect of WLP on the business.

Ratios That Matter

Companies use profitability ratios for determining how effectively they are (or are not) meeting their goals (see Figure 41-6). ROI is most common. But other ratios you may want to consider include return-on-assets (ROA) and return-on-equity (ROE).

Can you affect (positively, we hope) any of these business ratios with the work that you are doing? Do these give you any ideas for profitability ratios you may want to consider or create for WLP? Some that come to mind include return on classroom time, return on educational investment, times material reused, and accessibility to knowledge (think about the ways you can measure and show this metric and what it means in today's fast information environment), and costs versus departmental output and contribution.

Figure 41-6. Finance Metrics

Balance sheet accounts

1. Assets
   Things of value owned or controlled by the firm
2. Liabilities
   Debts and obligations owed to others
3. Equity
   Net worth of the firm's owners

Income statement accounts

4. Revenue
   Sales of goods and services, other income
5. Expenses
   Costs incurred by a firm in the creation of revenue

Common profitability ratios

Profit margin: Measure of net income produced by each dollar of sales

$$\frac{\text{NET INCOME}}{\text{NET SALES}}$$

Asset turnover: Measure of how efficiently assets are used to produce sales

$$\frac{\text{NET SALES}}{\text{AVERAGE TOTAL ASSETS}}$$

Return on equity: How well you manage your equity

$$\frac{\text{NET INCOME}}{\text{EQUITY}}$$

When LFCE measures a return-on-learning-investment, participants use their own formulas to demonstrate success, including estimating the percentage they thought was due to the training. Multiplying the two (savings or improvement times percentage due to training) provides a more conservative estimate of the return-on-learning-investment to present to management.

Balanced Scorecard

Take the most important of these financial measures and be sure to include them in a balanced scorecard (Kaplan and Norton, 2006). A balanced scorecard looks at achieving organizational goals through four key perspectives to show relative improvement. These areas include financial, customer, internal processes, learning and growth. Financial measures were just mentioned—what are the one, two, or three key financial measures that will show clearly how you are doing? Internal processes may include number of classes offered, participants enrolled, test scores, and so forth. Customer measures can include customer satisfaction, ability to apply learning effectively, and repeat customers. Learning and growth measures could show how learning affects organizational needs (percentage of project management professional certified managers, for example, for an engineering firm). Using a balanced scorecard helps you show senior leaders the value of WLP from multiple perspectives. As you choose the metrics to include in your scorecard, be sure to look for metrics that can affect the organization's mission, vision, and strategic plan.

Operations

Karl Albrecht (1993) talked about doing the right thing versus doing things right. Tying in and using skills from the first three functions mentioned—strategy, marketing, and finance—will help ensure you are doing the right things. Being operationally sound ensures you are also doing things right.

Continuous Improvement

In today's world, continuous improvement is often a mantra rather than a one-time program or fad. To manage learning like a business, constantly examine your processes and find ways to work more effectively and efficiently. Push down levels of responsibility so that senior people are used where they can add the most value. Upgrade the skills of frontline employees. A friend of mine runs a pediatric practice and when he or his colleagues are on call all night, a patient's call is first answered by a nurse practitioner who takes care of most everyday problems, saving the true emergencies for physicians (where their skills are needed most). This provides both a lower-cost first responder and saves the physicians for the cases where they can have the most effect.

Execution

Execution is also a key to successful operations. Develop standardized processes, forms, and procedures for working smarter. Using a consistent model and process will help you work faster and not miss any key steps before preparing materials for a customer so nothing slips through. Standardized forms can include anything from a needs assessment checklist to a production checklist to level 1 evaluation templates.

Clarify job skills and find tools to help expedite processes. What training does your staff need to work better? Would customer service training help in dealing with external customers? How would new software and technology training best be used? Be sure to clarify what you need to do and produce in-house versus what you can outsource. Will using an outsourced provider to print and deliver training materials save production time and shipping costs? Do you need to have graphic expertise in-house or can you bring in or outsource that work to a specialist? Do you create your own assessments or find ones available commercially you can use or customize? Do you hire external faculty to teach?

Cutting Back

Doing more with less is something many in business have come to abide by, and often is something WLP has to adjust to. Are you working in an efficient and effective manner? Technology makes that easier in some regard, but often creativity in coming up with a workable solution is just as important. Always look to see if you can do the same workload with less, or what percentage you can expand with existing capacity. That way you make the most of your resources, and when you need to decrease or increase headcount you can show what you have been able to accomplish and how the change will affect the work you can accomplish. Always be prepared to know what you can do with less. And if you have produced an annual WLP report with metrics, you may not be asked to cut back or may be able to cut back less severely.

Governance

All organizations have boards of directors to review plans, discuss strategy, and monitor results. Having an engaged, informed learning board that does these same things will ensure that you are managing learning like a business. Senior representatives from the various business units of your organization should be invited to form this council and regular meetings (usually quarterly) held to ensure that you are hearing the organization's needs and getting strong buy-in and support for your work from the organization. It also shows that you are holding yourself accountable to the needs of the organization.

Last, don't work in a vacuum. Call in help from other leaders in your organization you respect to brainstorm ways of creating operational efficiencies. Benchmark best practices with other WLP organizations. Adopt the ones that fit your needs and department. And continue to read the best of the business press to stay abreast of developments.

By paying attention to the organization's strategy, marketing, finance, and operations, and mimicking them in the WLP organization, you will more effectively manage WLP like a business and, in the process, run a more-respected and much-needed part of the organization.

About the Author

Howard Prager is a proven leader in business education with more than 25 years' experience in curriculum design, innovative learning solutions, and business performance consulting. He is accomplished at developing strategies, processes, and relationships that align with business purpose. He holds an executive position as director, Lake Forest Corporate Education, part of Lake Forest Graduate School of Management, working closely with senior management of *Fortune* 500 organizations. He was chairman of the ASTD national advisors for chapters (NAC) and was a member of the ASTD board of directors for 2003–2004. He is past president of the Chicagoland Chapter–ASTD. He is a sought-after speaker and author, presenting at many international conferences. He holds an MBA from the University of Michigan Ross School of Business and a BA from Northwestern University.

References

Albrecht, Karl. 1993. *The only thing that matters: Bringing the power of the customer into the center of your business.* New York: Harper Collins Business.

Kaplan, Robert S., and David P. Norton. 2006. *Using the balanced scorecard to create corporate synergies.* Boston: Harvard Business School Press.

Kotler, Phil, and Kevin Lane Keller. 2006. *Marketing management.* 12th ed. Upper Saddle River: Pearson Prentice Hall.

For Further Reading

Bossidy, Larry, and Ram Charan. 2002. *Execution: The discipline of getting things done.* New York: Crown Business.

Charan, Ram. 2001. *What the CEO wants you to know.* New York: Crown Business.

Israelite, Larry, ed. 2006. *Lies about learning.* Alexandria, VA: ASTD Press.

Prahalad, C.K., and Venkat Ramaswamy. 2004. *The future of competition: Co-creating unique value with customers.* Boston: Harvard Business School Press.

Thompson Jr., Arthur A. 2004. *Crafting and executing strategy: The quest for competitive advantage.* New York: McGraw-Hill.

Chapter 42

Tips for Outsourcing Success

Debbie Friedman

In This Chapter

- ➢ Determine what to outsource
- ➢ Select the right outsourcing partner and build relationships
- ➢ Build receptivity to outsourcing

O utsourcing in learning and development (L&D) is on the rise. Increases in organizational change have led to an increased demand on the L&D function. Today more than ever, line managers rely on L&D professionals to help provide the skills and knowledge needed for employees to execute their organization's strategies. At the same time, years of downsizing have left the L&D function with limited resources. As a result, L&D professionals regularly outsource initiatives to meet challenging deadlines and provide the level of sophistication in content and delivery methods their organizations require.

Given the cost of outsourcing, the stakes are high. Reputations are on the line. Success is based on the quality of the outsourcing decisions L&D professionals make and the kinds of partnerships they establish. This chapter provides tips to L&D professionals to help ensure the success of their outsourced initiatives.

Make Strategic Decisions About What to Outsource

A vice president of learning and development of a *Fortune* 500 company reflected on a recent experience:

> I was approached by senior management to facilitate their annual planning meeting. Although flattered, I didn't feel I had the expertise. Plus I wasn't sure that it was the best thing to take on from a political perspective. Fortunately, our president was open to an external, so I contacted an OD consultant I had worked with previously.

The comments of this learning professional point to some of the issues at play when deciding whether or not to outsource. Issues such as expertise, timing, cost, and the cultural and political ramifications of the decision are at stake when deciding whether or not to outsource.

Sometimes the decision to outsource is clear. You don't have the expertise or time. You have the budget, and your organization is open to outsourcing. However, there are times when the decision may not be so evident. You may want to go to the outside for political reasons, but not have the budget. You may think that an external provider could deliver a higher quality product, but your leadership may not value the expertise of consultants. Dilemmas such as these will need to be resolved by exploring the associated trade-offs and weighing the pluses and minuses of the various options.

The following questions will help you consider your options:

- Do I (my team) have the expertise or credibility to do the project or would an external provider be better equipped?
- Can internal resources meet the deadline, or, if not, is there time to find an external provider?
- Is the budget available?
- Is there some political or cultural sensitivity that would require either an internal or external resource?

Be Clear About Objectives

The old adage, "If you don't know where you're going, you'll never know if you have arrived" is true for outsourcing. Clear objectives pave the way to outsourcing success. They help you clarify your initiative to a potential outsourcing partner.

Learning professionals often use a request for proposal (RFP) when outsourcing, particularly when there is a competitive bidding process for the work. An RFP invites suppliers to submit proposals. It is a written document that outlines the services needed and requirements for selection.

Objectives form the basis of an RFP. In addition to objectives, an RFP also usually includes an overview of the organization, the background of the project, the target audience, a time line for the project, expectations for the proposal, and requirements for submission.

Your potential outsourcing partners will be better able to submit proposals that closely match your needs if objectives are clear. Clear objectives will help guide the design and development of the initiative and form the basis of your final evaluation.

Although you should be as clear as you can about your objectives before contacting external partners, be open to their counsel as you clarify objectives. One of the reasons to engage external consultants is to gain the benefit of their wisdom. Objective setting is a place where they can add value.

Select the Right Outsourcing Partners

In a telecommunications company, the head of L&D discussed her early experiences in outsourcing. She said, "In my first year heading the department, I engaged a consultant to help facilitate several senior leadership development programs. He was highly skilled, but unfortunately, not available for every program. He recommended two other consultants. I was under pressure, so I relied on his recommendation and engaged the two consultants. Midway through the first program, I had to ask the two consultants to leave. They were not a fit for our culture and had no credibility with participants. It was very unpleasant."

Once you have decided to engage external consultants or vendors, be sure to select the right partners. Consider the following:

- Do they have the required expertise?
- Is their pricing within budget?
- Will the proposed solution achieve the objectives?
- Do they have sufficient resources to achieve project objectives?
- Do they have a customer orientation?
- Are they a good fit for the culture?
- Do you think you can work effectively with them?
- Will they be true partners?

You may not be able to meet all your established criteria, so prioritize what is most important. Also consider the expertise of your team. Perhaps you will be able to fill certain gaps based on your team's strengths.

Negotiate a Fair Contract

A contract or letter of agreement between you and your consulting partners will help establish expectations for the project. It is an important step and a way to clarify issues before beginning the work. Taking time to negotiate a fair contract at the front end of a project can help you avoid conflict later on.

Contracts usually include a definition of the scope of work or services, fees, payment terms, how expenses will be handled, confidentiality, and ownership of materials. Depending on the complexity of the project, other issues such as cancellation of the project, insurance, unforeseen circumstances, and so forth may be included. (However, do not view this chapter as in any way providing legal counsel. An attorney should be involved when contracting to ensure that all legal issues are addressed appropriately and organization standards are met.)

One of the most important aspects of preparing a contract is negotiating a fair price. To help you prepare for the negotiation, gathering proposals from different outsourcing partners to become familiar with the potential range in pricing is helpful. Be sure you are comparing pricing for similar services. If you are new at negotiating, consulting with colleagues who are experienced and aware of typical consulting rates is a good idea. They can give you tips on how to negotiate. You may want to include your boss in the negotiations for additional support. In a true partnership, the internal learning professional pays a reasonable fee for the services, which allows the consultant or vendor to achieve the objectives and make a reasonable profit. Negotiating too sharp a price may limit the creativity of the external partner. The saying "You get what you pay for" certainly applies here.

Build Receptivity for the Initiative and the Outsourcing Partners

When you engage consultants and vendors, employees can feel threatened. A training executive commented on the first time he hired a consultant, "I could tell my staff was uncomfortable. I think they felt threatened; almost a feeling that if I was hiring an external consultant, maybe they would eventually lose their jobs. I probably should have spent more time with my team up front helping them understand why we needed the external perspective. They also could have been helpful in the vendor selection process. Fortunately, by the end of the project, they saw the benefit."

Often when outsourcing, internal L&D professionals look to external partners to make them successful. It is just as important for internal partners to take responsibility to make their external partners successful. Building receptivity for the project and the external provider by paving the way for them in the organization is a key to success. It is not uncommon for employees to feel threatened when consultants are hired or change is on the horizon. Working to minimize any sense of threat is important. In some organizations, key stakeholders help select the consultants and shape the project. Their involvement in the early stages of the project leads to greater support.

Consider the people in your organization who will be affected by the initiative and who will need to work with the external partner. These may include the project sponsor, subject matter experts, other learning professionals, the target audience, and their managers. Meet with them in advance of the launch of the project to help them understand who the consultants are, their background, why they were selected, the value they bring, and how they will work with your organization. Make sure people understand the value the consultants bring in terms of expertise, external perspectives, and ability to get the job done within the established time and budget constraints. It is also important to help all those involved understand the initiative. Be sure people understand the objectives, its link to strategy, timeframes, their role in the project, and any special requirements.

Orient Outsourcing Partners to the Organization

Another way to help externals succeed in your organization is to thoroughly orient them. You might think about them in the same way you think about new employees. A thorough orientation brings the consultant up to speed more quickly and helps him or her develop solutions that best meet the needs of your organization. Include a discussion of the following in your orientation:

- Business drivers of the initiative
- Objectives and how you plan to measure success
- Cultural and political issues that may affect the project
- Key stakeholders
- Roles and responsibilities
- How you will work together
- Timing and project milestones
- Potential landmines or obstacles
- Any other issues that you think will contribute to success.

L&D professionals typically use a kick-off meeting to begin to discuss these issues. By openly sharing this information, you are signaling your desire to build a strong partnership with your suppliers.

Make Project Management a Priority

Complex outsourced initiatives require rigorous project management to ensure the project stays on track and meets its stated objects. In the contracting phase, determine who will manage the project. It is not uncommon for there to be a project manager who represents the supplier or consulting firm and one who represents the client organization. Together they can build the project plan, allocate resources, and monitor progress over time. Strong project managers hold regular meetings to discuss the progress of the project, review the budget, anticipate obstacles, and confront issues that surface along the way. Regular communication is a key to success.

Maintain Good Communication

Strong partnerships develop when there is regular, authentic communication. A steady flow of communication should begin in the earliest stages of the partnership. Be available to potential consultants to answer questions they may have about your RFP. Keep them informed about your decision-making progress, letting them know as soon as possible if they have won the business. As soon as you make your decision, discuss next steps. Have an open dialogue as you jointly develop the contract. The more you clarify with each other at this stage, the smoother the relationship will be. Spend significant time in the early stages of the project getting to know each other and determining how you will work together. Communicate your desire to build a partnership and jointly discuss what it will take to make the project successful. Schedule regular check-in meetings to discuss progress and address any issues that may have surfaced. Important issues should be raised immediately.

Written communications are also important. Be sure someone on the team takes notes, recording decisions and open issues. These notes should be forwarded to the entire team after each meeting so that you can easily confirm your agreements. At each meeting review notes from previous meetings to be sure appropriate follow up has occurred. It is also a good practice to write a formal report at the end of the project. Record project successes and challenges. Identify lessons learned. These may be helpful, particularly if you work with the same outsourcing partner in the future.

Confront Conflict Quickly

The training director of a financial services firm contracted with an e-learning provider for a sales training program. The project had not gotten off to a good start because of conflicting information provided by subject matter experts. Because the early stages of the project had been difficult, in the first major review of the program, the training director was reluctant to express her concerns about the level of sophistication of the program. She alluded to the fact that the content was too simplistic, but the vendor did not leave the meeting with a clear understanding of what the training director expected to see different in the future. By not confronting the issue directly and early in the process, more extensive revisions were required later, deadlines slipped, and there were cost overruns.

It is not unusual to face conflict on a project. Differences need to be addressed and resolved as soon as they become evident. When conflict is surfaced early, it can usually be resolved more easily. More important, it helps the partnership flourish. A true partnership leads to stronger results.

Learn from Every Outsourced Initiative

Some of your greatest learning as an L&D professional will come from projects that you outsource. You can learn from the content of these projects as well as the process. Be sure to take advantage of this opportunity by building reflection time for you and the team into your project plans. At each major milestone, set aside time to discuss the project and the partnership. What is going well? What is not? What adjustments need to be made to ensure success? Record commitments. At the end of each phase, conduct similar meetings. Review previous commitments to make sure issues have been addressed. When a project is complete, conduct a more comprehensive review. Consider what you have learned and what you would do differently. Write a final project report. This report can be a good resource if you work on similar projects or engage the same external partners again in the future. Look for opportunities to learn. As you help build the capability of your organization through outsourced initiatives, you can build your own capability and that of your team.

About the Author

Debbie Friedman is author of *Demystifying Outsourcing: The Trainer's Guide to Working with Vendors and Consultants* (Pfeiffer, 2006). She is operating vice president at Macy's Inc. where she heads The Leadership Institute, an executive development function serving the top 2,000 executives. Macy's has been honored for two years as a Top 100 Company in Training and Development by *Training* magazine.

She held positions in sales and marketing education at AT&T and served as assistant director of career planning and placement at Xavier University. Friedman received a master's degree in education from Xavier University and a bachelor of arts from Stern College for Women, Yeshiva University.

For Further Reading

Anderson, Merrill C. 2000. Outsourcing as a strategic tool to enhance learning. In *Building learning capability through outsourcing*, ed., J. Phillips. Alexandria, VA: ASTD.

Block, Peter. 2000. *Flawless consulting*. 2d ed. San Francisco: Pfeiffer.

Friedman, Debbie. 2006. *Demystifying outsourcing: The trainer's guide to working with vendors and consultants*. San Francisco: Pfeiffer.

Maister, David H., Charles H. Green, and Robert M. Galford. 2000. *The trusted advisor*. New York: Touchstone/Simon & Schuster.

☙ Chapter 43

Using Technology to Manage Learning

Lance Dublin

In This Chapter

- ➤ Understand the evolving role of learning management technologies

- ➤ Learn some processes for selecting and implementing technologies

- ➤ Learn to incorporate technology into your organizational culture

---

We live in a world dominated by information, where knowledge is power and learning the means to survival. There is easy access to information across workers, customers, suppliers, partners, and competitors. This means that one of the last competitive differentiators a company can have is its ability to learn and have that learning affect performance at the employee, manager, executive, and organizational level.

> *"The ability to learn faster than your competitors may be the only sustainable competitive advantage in the future."*
>
> —Arie De Geus, head of planning for Royal Dutch/Shell (Senge, 1994)

Organizations are gearing up their learning to meet this challenge. They are working to make learning more personalized and customized, more tailored to the individual. And as a result they are supporting an ever-growing mix of activities and methods: formal as well as nonformal, instructor-led as well as self-paced, ad hoc as well as on-the-job. To gain the most benefit from this investment, it is necessary for organizations to manage these activities, which means capturing, compiling, leveraging, and reporting on all of these data and then turning those data into useful information. This is no easy task.

> *"Those companies that do the best job of empowering their workers*
> *through education and training are most likely to enjoy*
> *the highest levels of economic success."*
>
> —Steve Lynch (2006)

Most organizations lack a centralized repository—paper-based or technology-enabled—for learning content, records, tracking, and results; consistent and efficient delivery across business units and geographies; and the means to manage all of the details associated with delivering these learning activities. There is an absence of insight into the big picture, which leads to the duplication of effort, overspending, and inefficiencies, and often ends in uncertainty as to the effectiveness of the learning as well as its alignment with business goals.

All this explains the need for processes that help organizations select and implement effective learning management technologies and, more important, ensure that those technologies become incorporated into the organization's culture. This chapter explains the evolving role of learning management technologies, suggests processes for selecting and implementing the technologies, and presents some key factors involved in incorporating the technology into the everyday operations of the organization through change management and consumer marketing.

The Evolving Role of Technology

There are two aspects to using technology to manage learning. The first and most common is the use of technology to manage the learning function by enabling the planning, management, delivery, and tracking of both online learning and traditional classroom activities. The second is the use of technology to manage the creation, storage, reuse, and delivery of learning content.

Bottom line, learning is all about information regarding learners, activities, logistics, and content. And technology has long been a tool for managing information—its storage, manipulation and reporting, distribution, and creation. *Information technology* is the term popularized in the 1970s to best describe this marriage of computing and data.

Before the widespread application of information technologies, managing learning was most often referred to as training administration. It was a truly a nightmare of manual processes and paper to schedule classes, trainers, and facilities; to enroll and notify learners; to record training completion and test scores; to provide reports on learners and management; and the list goes on.

But as technology and information have become the very backbone of the modern organization, the focus is shifting to use information technologies not only to increase operational efficiencies but also to improve organizational effectiveness and generate true competitive advantage.

> *"The number one benefit of information technology is that it empowers people to do what they want to do. It lets people be creative. It lets people be productive. It lets people learn things they didn't think they could learn before, and so in a sense it is all about potential."*

—Steve Ballmer, CEO, Microsoft Corporation

Four Stages of Evolution

The automation of the process of instructor-led training to make it more efficient is an obvious first stage in an organization's use of technology to manage learning. Not surprisingly, these training management systems merely automate the administrative processes and eliminate some, but not all, of the paper.

Using information technology as a platform for e-learning is typically the second stage. At this stage, most organizations have as their goal saving money while making more learning available to more people. Off-the-shelf and custom e-learning courses can be implemented, as well as blended learning programs that combine online with instructor-led activities. There are three cautions at this stage. First, the demand for tailored online content can far outweigh the organization's capacity to develop or procure it. Second, organizations find that much of the generic online content they build or buy is not consumed. Third, the data show that although e-learning does reduce the cost per delivery of instructional hour, it may not save money overall due to the degree to which variable costs (for example, instructors) become fixed costs (for example, learning management systems [LMSs] and infrastructure) in organizations.

The third stage is implementing and managing the LMS as a corporate or enterprise-wide application. Organizations work to use the LMS to better align with the business goals and objectives. There is an increased focus on integrating with human resource and other business applications, consolidating the data, and using business analytics. In terms of content, the goal is to find ways to link learning activities to competencies and ensure the learning is job related and on demand (that is, just in time, just enough, just what's needed). And, in some cases, there is an acknowledgement that the traditional concept of courses, instructor-led or online, must be complemented with new learning modalities and approaches such as communities of practice, coaching, social networks, mobile learning, and other forms of online performance support.

The fourth stage in this evolution is integrating the full range of human resource development applications and processes within one application. The focus is on the strategic use of technology not just to manage learning but to manage the organization's greatest resource, its people. These stages of evolution are summed up in Figure 43-1.

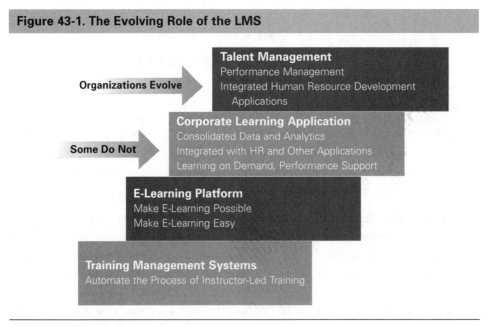

Figure 43-1. The Evolving Role of the LMS

Talent Management
Performance Management
Integrated Human Resource Development
Applications

Organizations Evolve

Corporate Learning Application
Consolidated Data and Analytics
Integrated with HR and Other Applications
Learning on Demand, Performance Support

Some Do Not

E-Learning Platform
Make E-Learning Possible
Make E-Learning Easy

Training Management Systems
Automate the Process of Instructor-Led Training

Source: Bersin & Associates (2007). Used with permission.

Systems That Support Learning and Performance

Another important view into using technology to manage learning puts the learner at the center. Figure 43-2 provides a way to look at the expanding capabilities and increasing importance of technology from this learner-centric view.

Figure 43-2. The Expanding Capabilities and Increasing Importance of Learning Management Systems

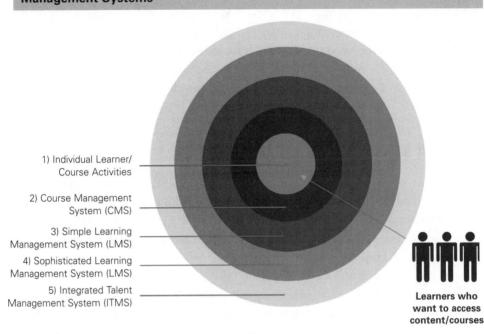

1) Individual Learner/
Course Activities

2) Course Management
System (CMS)

3) Simple Learning
Management System (LMS)

4) Sophisticated Learning
Management System (LMS)

5) Integrated Talent
Management System (ITMS)

**Learners who
want to access
content/courses**

Source: eLearning Guild Research (2007). Used with permission.

The innermost circle, level 1, represents content, courses, and information that a learner wants or needs to access. Level 2 represents a course management system (CMS) that provides publication of synchronous e-learning content, access to asynchronous e-learning courses, online simple assessment and testing, simple tracking, reporting, and measurement. Level 3 represents a simple LMS expanding on the CMS and offering additional functionalities and capabilities, often including managing scheduling of instructor-led training and classroom resources, registration, automated reporting and tracking, training histories, more sophisticated testing and assessment, and support for industry standards such as the Aviation Industry Computer-Based Committee (AICC) and Shareable Content Object Reference Model (SCORM).

The next level, level 4, represents a sophisticated LMS, which expands on the simple LMS and offers additional functionalities and capabilities, including but not limited to certification and regulatory compliance training and tracking, business analytics to support alignment of learning with strategic business objectives, ability to support complex business processes, skill-gap analysis, support for synchronous and blended learning, and integration with human resource enterprise resource program systems. The outermost circle, Level 5, represents an integrated talent management system (also called an enterprise talent management system or human capital management system), which includes everything in a sophisticated LMS plus recruiting management, performance management, compensation management, and succession planning and retention management. In many ways it is more of a sophisticated and highly functional HR system than an LMS—from hire to retire—recruiting, assessment, hiring, compensation and benefits, on-boarding, performance management, learning and development, and succession and retention.

The Full Scope of a Learning System

To meet the ever-changing business requirements and needs of an increasingly diverse and often dispersed learner population, organizations are looking for ways to leverage technology not only to deliver, manage, and report on learning activities but also to manage their creation. An LMS is a system that enables an organization to deliver, manage, track, record, and report on instructor-led and online learning activities. A learning content management system (LCMS) is a system that enables multiple developers to create learning content (for example, activities) and enables the organization to store, reuse, manage, and deliver learning content from a central repository or database (see Figure 43-3). These two systems are designed to work in concert, but an organization can choose to implement either one of them independently of the other. Figure 43-4 provides a very clear matrix to help illustrate the similarities and differences.

LMS Use, Benefits, Features, and Return-on-Investment

When looking at why organizations want to use learning management systems, there is a high degree of agreement across industries as well as small and large organizations. According to research conducted by Bersin & Associates (2006) and the eLearning Guild (2007), the top 10 reasons organizations typically use an LMS include

- Implement e-learning or manage and deploy e-learning
- Measure and report on training offerings and delivery or manage training administration
- Automate reporting and tracking or consolidate training information
- Ensure employee compliance with mandated training programs and regulatory agencies or meet regulatory compliance
- Manage instructor-led training logistics

Figure 43-3. Learning Systems Features

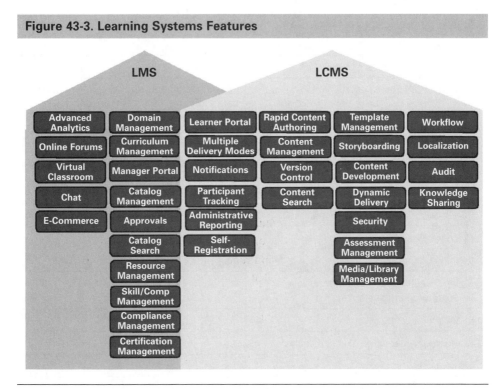

Source: Bersin & Associates (2006). Used with permission.

- Gain better access to and use of training data
- Align learning with strategic business initiatives or align training processes
- Centralize the learning or training function or reduce training costs
- Measure and report on business results of training
- Measure and report on the true costs of training.

The Bersin & Associates research shows that the top benefits organizations report include

- Track and report
- Facilitate e-learning strategy
- Manage enterprise-wide initiatives
- Improve efficiency
- Ensure regulatory compliance
- Reduce training costs.

Figure 43-4. Differences and Similarities Between LMSs and LCMSs

	LMS	LCMS
Primary target users	Training managers, instructors, administrators	Content developers, instructional designers, project managers
Provides primary management of…	Learners	Learning content
Management of classroom, instructor-led training	Yes (but not always)	No
Performance reporting of training results	Primary focus	Secondary focus
Learner collaboration	Yes	Yes
Keeping learner profile data	Yes	No
Sharing learner data with an enterprise resource program system	Yes	No
Event scheduling	Yes	No
Competency mapping—skill gap analysis	Yes	Yes (in some cases)
Content creation capabilities	No	Yes
Organizing reusable content	No	Yes
Creation of test questions and test administration	Yes	Yes
Dynamic pretesting and adaptive learning	No	Yes
Workflow tools to manage the content development process	No	Yes
Delivery of content by providing navigational controls and learner interface	No	Yes

Source: Brandon Hall Research (2006). Used with permission.

In terms of importance of specific features, the eLearning Guild research shows the most important features to be

- Tracking, reporting, and measurement
- Content delivery
- Asynchronous e-learning
- Training history

- Assessment and testing
- Blended learning.

The eLearning Guild research also showed the following return-on-investment (ROI) across large-, mid-, and small-size companies, as well as education and government organizations:

- Good return-on-investment: 20 percent–32.5 percent
- Modest return: 42 percent
- No return: 7 percent–10 percent
- Waste of time and money: 1 percent–4 percent
- Too early to tell: 16 percent–27 percent.

Selecting an LMS or an LCMS and Getting Started

The process of selecting an LMS or an LCMS is really no different than the one an organization uses for any other software application. The most typical steps are

1. Develop a business case to clearly state the business purpose(s).
2. Define requirements by gathering input from all people, departments, and units that will be involved to ensure the key functions are identified based on use cases specific to your organization. And determine "must have" and "high want" criteria.
3. Identify potential vendors by drawing on industry research and references.
4. Create and distribute a request for information (RFI) to narrow down the number of vendors.
5. Create and distribute a request for proposal (RFP) to make sure the vendors understand your requirements and can meet them.
6. Conduct reference checks by talking to current and former customers identified by the vendor and through professional networking.
7. Conduct on-site meetings to ensure vendors can demonstrate—in front of you— how their system will handle each use case.
8. Select the vendor that best demonstrates the ability to meet the requirements and alignment with your organizational culture.
9. Negotiate the contract with your selected vendor.
10. Begin the technical installation and application configuration phase.

Technical and Licensing Considerations

There are key technical and licensing areas that must be taken into consideration when selecting and implementing an LMS or LCMS. In determining which model is right for your organization, it is important to involve information technology professionals from the very start because there is no one-size-fits-all LMS or LCMS solution, and there are many choices. Ultimately, it is your organization's decision. And, equally important, once you have made the decision, you still want the flexibility to revisit it as your organization's needs change and grow; you don't want to be locked into what may have been the right choice at another time. Your LMS or LCMS should be flexible enough to scale to meet new business needs and support new and emerging learning modalities, technologies, and tools. And it should be based on standards so that you don't lose functionality and archival data if you do upgrade or change.

Hosting

The choices are to (1) host the LMS or LCMS internally within your organization, (2) host the LMS or LCMS through an external application services provider (ASP), or (3) outsource the LMS or LCMS to a third party. Each choice has its unique pros and cons.

Internal model. Organizations often select the internally hosted model for these reasons: less dependence on an outside company for an important business function, greater focus and more control, easier to budget for and procure as part of ongoing technology costs, and more confidence in their own security.

ASP model. Organizations often select the ASP model for these reasons: lower hardware, software, and licensing costs; continuous content and feature or functionality updates with no local impact; faster time to implementation; less internal technical support or development; one-call support; time and money savings as there is no need to buy the necessary hardware or to recruit IT staff for both content and site performance maintenance; and less risk. With an ASP you are buying a service, rather than a product.

Outsourcing model. Organizations often select this model because it reduces technology and operations costs in two areas:

- Implementation costs. Leveraging the outsourcer's IT investments and professional expertise saves both time and money. Implementations are simplified and streamlined because configuration options and customization options are typically limited.
- Operational costs. There can be dramatic cost savings based on the outsourcer's ability to pass on economies of scale and efficiencies of centralization to its customers. In addition, there can be cost savings associated with being able to reduce or not add on a dedicated technical staff.

Licensing

Basically, there are five licensing models to be considered:

- The software is purchased and installed and managed in-house.
- The company buys the software, but it is housed and managed remotely by a third party.
- Administrators, content builders, instructors, and learners access the system over the Internet through an ASP.
- The company buys the software and installs it on its own data platform, but the maintenance and upgrades are managed by the LMS vendor or another third party (for example, a system integrator).
- Some LMS or LCMS vendors operating their own enterprise systems offer to share access to their system; basically, the company leases "space" on the host data site.

Integration

Integration typically includes configuration and customization of the interface, fields, reporting, and data sets as well as the integration with existing applications and data systems.

Standards

The LMS or LCMS should comply with existing and emerging industry standards so that new online courses and other materials can be easily integrated. Two of the critical standards are the AICC and SCORM.

Security

Security is a priority in any application that handles information on individuals and proprietary content. And LMSs or LCMSs are no different.

Barriers to Success

As with any application of this type, there are barriers that must be overcome for an LMS or LCMS to be successfully implemented within your organization. The eLearning Guild (2007) and Bersin & Associates (2006) research reports showed the following barriers to success across large-, mid-, and small-size companies, as well as education and government organizations:

- Customization to meet business needs
- Cost
- Flexibility for future requirements
- IT support or IT issues and systems performance

- Legacy system integration
- Integration with other systems (content, HR, enterprise resource program) or content integration and integration with HR
- Ongoing administration.

Getting from Configuration to Incorporation

Successful organizations know from their experiences with other enterprise applications that thorough, up-front planning and a systematic approach help to avoid the "ready-fire-aim" and "rework—rework—rework" syndromes.

Stage 1: Installation and Configuration

In this stage you do whatever it takes to make sure your LMS really works when you are ready to put it to use. This means it is installed and technically working according to the specifications, configured for your organization based on your use requirements, fully tested in internal labs, and pilot tested in the field. It also means that the necessary management systems are in place and the roles, work flow, and business processes have been changed to manage and support its use—by learners, by their managers, and by the supporting organizations (for example, IT, HR, training).

Stage 2. Implementation

Following installation, you are now ready to focus on making sure your learners, their managers, and your organization know the context for the LMS or LCMS (that is, the business rationale, the anticipated business results); are aware of the features and functions, functionality, and benefits; and are able to actually use it as you have planned. This is the stage in which typically the majority of the communications and change management activities occur. Unfortunately, this is all too often where all these planned activities then also stop. This is a big mistake that is too often repeated.

Stage 3. Incorporation

Truly successful companies put as much time and attention into the completion of this third stage as they do into the other two combined. They don't leave this critical stage to chance. They recognize it is the difference between their LMS or LCMS being seen as just another application or embraced as a critical business system. In this stage you work to ensure your LMS or LCMS becomes fully incorporated into your organization through its structures, processes, and culture. Your goal is to make your LMS or LCMS an essential tool for the success of every employee and manager, core business process, and critical business initiative, and the organization as a whole. When the people in your organization refer to your LMS or LCMS as "just the way we do things around here," you know you have succeeded.

When All Is Said and Done, It's About People

"Our findings suggest that user commitment and motivation are critical not only for adoption of new information and communication technologies but also for their sustained use."

—Yogesh Malhotra, assistant professor of management information and decision sciences, Syracuse University Whitman School of Management, Syracuse, NY

—Dennis Galletta, professor of business administration, Fox School of Business and Management Temple University, Philadelphia, PA (Galletta and Malhotra, 2004)

An LMS or LCMS is a change. It is a change for employees, to frontline supervisors, to mid-managers, to senior management, and to all the supporting organizations. Even though the first stage may be as simple as delivering an e-learning course, it still is a change in the organization. Employees who are used to time away from their desks and work and spending time with colleagues and an instructor may resent having to learn "from a computer." Trainers who feel valued for their platform skills may feel threatened they will be replaced. Managers who have always controlled the access to training and information by knowing who was in what class and when may feel undermined when their employees can now access learning anytime and from anywhere. And often the organization as a whole is not aware, engaged, or supportive, nor understands why it should be.

But organizations do not change. People change—employees, managers, colleagues, partners, suppliers, customers—one at a time. By applying the discipline of change management you will increase your chances of success dramatically. Change management is the combination of processes, activities, and approaches that enable you to manage the people of the organization through the transition from the old way of doing things to the new way. Change management is about communication and exchange, dialogue and questions, leadership and support. Its focus is on attitudes and behaviors, and the objective is to win the battle for the hearts and minds of the people within your organization.

Another discipline that is important to apply is consumer marketing. The goal of consumer marketing is to attract and retain customers, and, at its best, it is an ongoing process that builds mutually satisfying long-term relationships. Building a brand and creating strong relationships are as important for your LMS or LCMS as they are for any successful consumer marketing program.

The success of the implementation of your LMS or LCMS requires that all of the people affected are informed and aware, involved and engaged. It also requires that the LMS or LCMS is integrated into the organization as a whole resulting in the organization's commitment to its ongoing success. Change implementation is a process-based, inclusive, and always two-way approach that draws upon both change management and consumer marketing principles and practices. It focuses not only on ensuring individuals think and act differently, but also on developing and reinforcing the necessary new individual and organizational attitudes and behaviors.

The I^3 Change Implementation model consists of three phases (see Figure 43-5) that form a never-ending cycle.

Phase 1. Inform—Generate Awareness

Through information and messaging activities, that is, marketing communications or *marcom* as it is known, employees, managers, and the organization are given simple and clear answers to the what, why, how, who, and when questions. And most important, in this phase, you begin to answer the what's in it for me question as well. The goal of this phase is to make sure the messages you want to be heard are heard, and that they are heard in ways that will be recognized, recalled, and remembered. Examples of specific activities during this phase might include newsletters, presentations, emails, webcasts, voicemails, documents, and speeches.

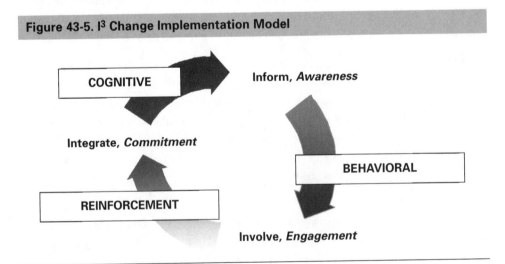

Figure 43-5. I^3 Change Implementation Model

Source: Lance Dublin, © 2007.

Phase 2. Involve—Generate Involvement

Just giving all the affected and involved individuals answers to these questions is not enough. For your LMS or LCMS to be successful, you must also change people's attitudes and behaviors. Behavioral change seldom happens based solely on someone passively receiving information or tokens. The key to this type of change is engaging everyone and paying particular attention to the key influencers within the organization. You want to provide a firsthand experience of your LMS or LCMS to give them a chance to take it for a test drive, ask questions, and form their own opinions. The goal of this phase is to have users internalize and personalize the benefits of the LMS or LCMS; to have it become theirs, not just yours. Specific activities during this phase might include videos, department meetings, lunchroom fairs, hallway expos, and traveling road shows.

Phase 3. Integrate—Generate Commitment

The long-term success of your LMS or LCMS depends on it becoming a recognized part of your organizational culture, fully integrated into the work-life of employees, supervisors, managers, and executives. In this stage, you want to identify the ongoing organizational processes and systems your LMS or LCMS can support as well as any critical business initiatives. The purpose is to ensure your LMS or LCMS brand becomes well accepted as the norm, critical to the success of individuals and the organization as a whole, and recognized as the platform of choice for ongoing learning and development. Specific activities during this phase might include integrating with the performance management process, supporting a new key business initiative, and launching and tracking all leadership development and management training.

Summary

To successfully use technology to manage learning you need to do more than purchase and install a learning management or learning content management system. Those applications are necessary, but just having them is not sufficient to ensure your success. Success comes from truly understanding the needs of your organization and the people within it (as well as partners, suppliers, and customers if appropriate) and making smart and informed decisions that are aligned with your organization's goals and objectives and fit your organization's culture.

About the Author

Lance Dublin is a management consultant, speaker, and author based in San Francisco, California, serving clients worldwide. His focus is organizational learning and change management. He specializes in strategy development, program design, and implementation for organizational learning programs and change initiatives. He has more than 30 years' experience in adult education and training, communication and change management, and organizational design and development.

He has worked across a wide range of industries, including financial services and insurance, technology and information services, pharmaceutical and health care, manufacturing and chemicals, oil and gas, telecommunications and communications, hospitality and food services, and nongovernmental agencies.

References

Ballmer, Steve. 2005, February 17. Alamo Area Community Information System (AACIS) Unlimited Potential Grant Announcement. San Antonio, TX.

Bersin & Associates. 2006. *High impact learning organization: What works in the management, operations, and governance of corporate training.* Oakland, CA: Bersin & Associates.

Bersin & Associates. 2007. *LMS 2008: Facts, practical analysis, trends, and vendor profiles.* Oakland, CA: Bersin & Associates.

Brandon Hall Research. 2006. *LCMS Knowledgebase 2006: A comparison of 30+ enterprise learning content management systems.* San Jose, CA: Brandon Hall Research.

eLearning Guild Research. 2007. *The eLearning Guild 360° report on learning management systems: The good, the bad, the ugly … and the truth.* Santa Rosa, CA: eLearning Guild.

Galletta, Dennis, and Yogesh Malhotra. 2004. Building systems that users want to use. *Communications of the ACM* 47(12): 88-99.

Lynch, Steve. 2006, September. The CLO's role: Balancing the learning mix in outsourced environments. *Chief Learning Officer.*

Senge, Peter. 1994. *The fifth discipline.* New York: Currency Doubleday.

For Further Reading

Cross, Jay, and Lance Dublin. 2002. *Implementing e-learning.* Alexandria, VA: ASTD Press.

Henderson, Allan J. 2002. *The e-learning question and answer book: A survival guide for trainers and business managers.* New York: AMACOM.

Langer, Arthur M. 2005. *IT and organizational learning: Managing change through technology and education.* London: Routledge.

Chapter 44

Intellectual Property:

Protect What Is Yours and Avoid Taking What Belongs to Someone Else

Linda Byars Swindling and Mark V.B. Partridge

In This Chapter

➢ Get a blueprint for converting your intellectual property into protected property

➢ Understand key intellectual property rights

➢ Learn to use legal rights to protect your intellectual property

➢ Avoid infringing on others' rights

Most learning professionals, whether working in large organizations, sole proprietorships, or any business entity in between, would agree they need to know the basics of human resource law to prevent discrimination or harassment while training or consulting. Most would agree they should know about the basics of contracts and entering agreements. Those smart learning professionals often speak with their internal legal counsel or their own attorney to review agreements they are drafting and signing. Many even want to understand liability, risk avoidance, and insurance when it comes to preventing property loss or injury. Remarkably, however, many learning professionals fail to invest the time in understanding their most important asset—their intellectual property.

What is intellectual property? *Wikipedia* defines intellectual property as "an umbrella term for various legal entitlements which attach to certain names, written and recorded media, and inventions."

More simply put, we are talking about the ideas, information, and innovations associated with your business. For most learning professionals who provide services, the biggest asset in your business is not composed of equipment, inventory, or employees, it is in your knowledge and expertise and how you deliver them. Therefore, protecting your asset or intellectual capital is critical for building and maintaining your business. For internal learning professionals, ensuring you have the proper ownership of materials and are properly using others' materials is paramount in protecting your organization and your own reputation.

Intellectual property exists when those intangible assets and intellectual capital of your business—your brand, content, data, information, website, innovations, systems, and methods—are converted into protected property. This protection occurs through the effect of certain legal rights—patent, trademark, copyright, and trade secret—collectively referred to as intellectual property rights. These legal rights are the tools that convert your intellectual capital into property that can be protected from infringement, sold and licensed for profit, and leveraged to increase the value of your business.

This chapter provides a blueprint for converting your intellectual capital into protected property, discusses the key intellectual property rights that shape success in your business, and shows how to use those legal tools to protect and enforce your rights in the critical assets. It also shows how to avoid infringing on the protected works of others.

Brands

Your brand is the ultimate symbol of your business. It represents who you are and how you perform business. It may be embodied in a name such as Ford or Disney, a symbol (the Nike Swoosh), a slogan ("you deserve a break today"), a sound (the Law and Order "thunk" "thunk"), a color (the color pink for Owens-Corning fiberglass), or any other device that identifies a particular source.

The primary legal tool to protect a brand is trademark law. Trademark law is designed to prevent confusion and mistake in the marketplace.

Creation of Rights

A trademark is entitled to protection when it is used in commerce and is distinctive of a particular source. In fact, *distinctiveness,* as a term of art, means the ability to serve as an indication of a particular source. Distinctive terms or devices—such as coined names like Exxon or Kodak or arbitrary names like Apple for computers or Camel for cigarettes—may be protected immediately upon use in commerce. Other terms—such as a surname like Ford or Disney, a descriptive term like *Sports Illustrated* magazine, or a geographic term like California Pizza Kitchen—can only be protected if they have been used enough so that they acquire a second meaning in the public mind associated with a particular source.

Rights in trademarks are not a monopoly. They cannot prevent all other businesses from using the name. The name must be associated with the particular goods or services involved. Marks used for unrelated goods or services may coexist without conflict. For example, Ritz hotels, Ritz crackers, and Ritz cameras. While all use the same name, each is distinctive for the products or services it represents.

The Benefits of Federal Registration

Trademark rights can be established based solely on use. However, federal registration has added benefits. For example, federal registration creates nationwide rights and creates notice of rights as a matter of law. This notice may discourage infringers.

Registration is obtained through the United States Patent and Trademark Office. Applications can be filed online at www.uspto.gov for a governmental filing fee of $325 (effective 2007). A valid application requires identification of the applicant, a drawing of the proposed mark, a description of the applicable goods or services, and a statement of current use or of a bona fide intention to use the mark in commerce.

The application process involves several steps:

Filing the application. Applications can be filed online. Required information includes identification of the applicant, description of the trademark, description of the goods or services, date of first use in commerce, or statement that applicant has a bona fide intent to use the mark in commerce.

Examination by a trademark office examiner. The trademark examiner reviews the application to determine if the information is complete and specific, that the mark is distinctive, and that it does not conflict with an existing application or registration.

Publication for opposition by others. If approved by the examiner, the application will be published to allow other parties to object if they believe they will be damaged by registration of the mark.

Final approval of application (if there is no successful opposition). If there is no opposition during publication, the application will be allowed for registration. If it was an application for a mark that is already in use, it will proceed directly to registration. If the application was based on an intent to use the mark, the applicant is required to file a statement of use before registration will issue.

Issuance of the registration certificate. When all the steps are cleared, the registration will finally issue. The entire process is likely to take 18 to 24 months or more, but the rights under the registration are based on the filing date.

Licensing and Assignment

Trademarks may be sold or licensed. Common examples include the licensing of university or sports logos for caps and apparel, or franchise names like McDonald's or Burger King. You might have seen a news story about the confiscation of sporting goods at a ballgame when the vendors did not have the license to use the team's registered logo. This violation of a trademark owner's rights is known as infringement.

Infringement

Trademark rights are infringed when a junior party uses an identical or confusingly similar mark for identical or related goods or services in a manner that is likely to cause confusion, mistake, or deception in the marketplace. The typical relief available in court is an order to prevent use of the infringing mark and an award of the actual damages caused by use of the mark. When a mark has been properly registered with the federal government those damages and relief may increase.

Content

Your content is key to conveying your knowledge and information to the world. For trainers, speakers, and consultants, content typically takes the form of books, articles, newsletters, workbooks, CD-ROMs, DVDs, media recordings, software, podcasts, and websites. Each of these may be a revenue source or a work distributed freely for promotional purposes. In either event, the author will want to control the use, receive credit, prevent unauthorized copying, and stop others from profiting improperly from using his or her material in undesirable ways. The principal tool for protecting content and transforming it into protected property is copyright law.

Copyright can create incredible value for you and your business. And misusing the copyrighted works of others can lead to disaster. In 1996, motivational speaker Anthony Robbins created a new financial course complete with a 300-page workbook. A jury found

Case Study

In 1985, L'Oréal determined that young people craved pink and blue hair. To meet the anticipated demand, L'Oréal created a line of hair cosmetics named Zazu. Apparently young people had better taste than expected. The product flopped, but not before spawning a federal lawsuit. The trial court awarded the plaintiff, the Zazu hair salon in Hinsdale, Illinois, more than $2 million in damages plus $76,000 in attorneys' fees. Obviously, a trademark can have incredible value, even to a small business.

Unfortunately, the story continues. L'Oréal appealed, claiming the hair salon had insufficient use to create nationwide rights. The appellate court agreed, taking away the award. The Hinsdale salon was left with nothing but a large bill for attorneys' fees. The story demonstrates the importance of small things. The Hinsdale salon had failed to seek trademark registration. If they had, at an expense of a few hundred dollars, the salon could have established nationwide rights that would have avoided this sad outcome.

As a learning professional, be careful that you have proper permission before creating posters, t-shirts, or training products displaying someone's brand. Also be careful about using the brands of others to attract traffic on the Internet. Certain fair uses of another's trademark are permissible, but the line between what is permitted and what is infringing can be hard to draw. When in doubt, consult a legal advisor. If you or your company has a brand, don't put your valuable rights at risk by failing to take appropriate action early to secure the intellectual property in your brand.

that two key passages in the workbook were copied from a book by Wade Cook, the author of the *Wall Street Money Machine*, and awarded Cook more than $650,000 in damages. Although the result may be extreme, this situation is not unusual. Think of how often some trainers borrow materials from another source. Many times there is no reference to the author. Other times, learning professionals forget where the materials originated. Some even begin to believe the materials are their own.

The Subjects of Copyright

Copyright protects original, tangible expression. Copyright does not protect concepts, ideas, or facts. This means that protection is available for the actual expression embodied in a work, such as an article, audio or video recording, or software program, but it is not available for ideas or concepts behind that tangible expression. Copyright protection also does not extend to short phrases such as simple trademarks or book titles.

Creating and Owning Copyright

Copyright exists from the moment of creation and belongs to the author of the work. Although beneficial for the reasons discussed later, copyright notice or registrations are not required to create a copyright in your content. As soon as original expression is set forth in a tangible form, such as a written document, photograph, or audio recording, the work is protected by copyright. For example, an original work of expression might be created by a trainer who sets forth ideas from a training session in a checklist, creates a written outline for a presentation, or records an audiotape of a training program. The copyright in that material extends to the original expression by the trainer and arises from the moment any of those works is created in a tangible medium. This same principle applies to a work that consists of an original arrangement of otherwise unoriginal material, such as the selection and arrangement of comments by others during a training session in a subsequent report. The original arrangement of those comments is protected by copyright, although the actual words taken from others are not original to the trainer.

Determining authorship is very important to your rights. If the work is created by an employee within the scope of his or her employment, usually the author or owner is the employer. But if you hire an outside vendor to create a work for you—a photographer, website designer, ghost writer—he or she owns the copyright in the work unless there is a written work-for-hire agreement or other written transfer of rights. If two people create a work together, they both own an undivided interest in the whole, unless there is a written agreement making other arrangements. Thus, if you are working with or relying on others to create work for you, it is critical that you have a clear understanding about ownership and the rights to use the work created.

If you are purchasing materials, make certain you understand the rights you are purchasing. Determine if you can reproduce the materials freely, if you or others can present the information without the creator's presence, or if the materials are developed for your organization alone. You don't want to pay a large sum to have materials developed for your team, only to find that the trainer plans to use the same course with your competitors.

If you are an outside vendor, it is now common practice for some companies to contract for all works created to become their property. Before you sign such an agreement, make sure you understand the rights you are giving and any limits on your ability to use the materials in the future. Those answers may determine how willing you are to do the work as well as the price you charge.

Exclusive Rights

Copyright provides the copyright owner a bundle of exclusive rights, including

- The right to make copies and reproductions
- The right to create modifications and derivative works
- The right to public performance or display.

The scope of rights includes the right to control copies that are identical as well as those that are substantially similar to the protected expression contained in the original. Substantial similarity is judged by whether or not the similarities would cause an ordinary observer to conclude that the infringing work was copied from the original.

Notice and Registration

As mentioned previously, you are not required to use a copyright notice or register your copyright to have rights. However, both provide important benefits and are simple and inexpensive to do.

A proper copyright notice includes a claim of copyright, the date of creation, and the name of the owner: © 2007 Jane Doe. One of the myths about copyright is that works can be freely copied if there is no copyright notice. This is false, but because it is commonly believed to be true, using a copyright notice can be very helpful to deter infringers. Copyright notice may also help you avoid claims of innocence if you are forced to take legal action against an infringer. In addition, a good practice is to include your contact information such as your phone number and website in case someone wants to contact

---

Useful Links

www.uspto.gov
United States Trademark Office. Search and register trademarks online.

www.copyright.gov
United States Copyright Office. Obtain forms and guidelines for copyright registration.

www.allwhois.com
Provides domain name registration records. Check ownership records for domain names.

www.wipo.int
World Intellectual Property Organization. File complaints against cybersquatters using infringing domain names.

www.aipla.org
American Intellectual Property Law Association. Locate attorneys who handle patent and other intellectual property matters.

www.inta.org
International Trademark Association. Trademark protection information.

www.bmi.com and www.ascap.com
Music licensing societies. Obtain permission for public performance of music to enhance seminars and training.

http://GuidingRights.blogcollective.com
The Guiding Rights Blog. Intellectual property information and articles by co-author Mark V.B. Partridge.

---

you about using your materials: © 2007 Jane Doe. All rights reserved. Doe & Associates. www.doeassociates.com; 972.555.1212.

Registration is also somewhat simple to obtain by submitting a two-page application form and specimen of the work to the United States Copyright Office. The current application fee is $45 (effective 2007). The process is explained at the Copyright Office website at www.copyright.gov.

Registration before an infringement occurs provides two key benefits. First, it is required to recover the statutory amount of damages specified in the Copyright Act, which is up to $150,000 per work infringed. Without prior registration, the copyright owner is limited to recovery of actual damages or profits. Second, registration prior to infringement permits the copyright owner to seek recovery of attorneys' fees from the infringement. Otherwise, the usual rule is that each party is responsible for its own attorneys' fees. Attorney fees in intellectual property litigation can be very high. A 2005 survey by the American Intellectual Property Law Association found that the average litigation cost for copyright infringement trials was more than $300,000 when less than $1 million was at stake, and went up dramatically from there.

The ability to recover statutory damages and attorneys' fees can be the difference in whether or not the copyright owner is able to protect his or her property. For example, a trainer finds that 10 of her articles have been used without her permission by a competitor in a book. The actual monetary damages are likely to be low (the royalty value of the articles or a portion of the royalties earned by the competitor from the book) and considerably less than the legal cost to pursue the claim. Although she has a claim, it could be financially unreasonable to pursue it. If, however, the trainer had registered her right before the infringement occurred, she would be in position to seek up to $150,000 per article and to recover the cost of pursuing the claim, obviously enough to justify the cost of registration and the legal action to protect her rights.

Fair Use

Fair use is an exception to the exclusive rights of the copyright owner, which permits another party to use the copyright holder's work for purposes such as commentary, news reporting, and education. Whether such use is permitted depends on consideration of four factors:

- The nature of the infringing work. Uses that transform the original into something new are more likely to be permitted. Noncommercial use is more likely to be permitted than a commercial use.

- The nature of the original work. Factual works receive less protection than expressive works such as poems or songs.
- The amount of the taking. The quality and quantity of the taking are important. Even a small taking may be an infringement if it is qualitatively important and "goes to the heart" of the original.
- The effect on the market for the original. An infringement is not likely to be permitted if it supplants market demand for the original.

Determining fair use in a particular case can be very difficult. Some examples of uses allowed as fair use include

- A hip-hop parody of Roy Orbison's song "Pretty Woman"
- The use of thumbnail copies of Grateful Dead posters in a history book about popular music culture
- A portion of a photograph used in a collage by the artist Robert Rauschenberg.

Uses that were not permitted include

- George Harrison's song "My Sweet Lord," which was found to be too similar to the song "He's So Fine"
- A parody about O.J. Simpson based on "The Cat in the Hat"
- Video clips of Elvis in a documentary.

When in doubt, the best course of action is to seek permission from the owner of the original or a noninfringement opinion from a qualified attorney. Also, the education exception is narrowly defined. For example, you cannot get around a copyright-protected piece by claiming it was for corporate education or education for a trade association program.

Obtain Permission for Use of Music for Seminars and Workshops

The situation: Music motivates, so Amway Corporation conventions and videos used to inspire its distributors featured popular songs by the likes of the Beatles, Michael Jackson, Whitney Houston, Gloria Estefan, and Michael Bolton—more than 100 songs in all.

The problem: Unfortunately, Amway and its agents failed to secure permission.

The result: A lawsuit in 1996 seeking more than $10 million in copyright damages.

The lesson: Public performance of music requires permission.

The cure: Obtain a license from a music licensing society, for example, BMI or ASCAP.

Online Protection

Online works are protected by copyright just as any other work of original expression. Special procedures are available, however, to help copyright owners stop unauthorized online use of copyrights works. The Digital Millennium Copyright Act (DMCA) creates a safe harbor for online service providers such as Google and You Tube who post content of others. If the copyright owner finds infringing works posted online, he or she may be able to submit a DMCA complaint to the service provider demanding that the work be taken down. If the service provider honors the demand, it will not be liable for copyright infringement. Because of this "safe harbor," most service providers have posted take-down procedures that comply with the DMCA. These procedures can be an inexpensive way to police copyrights online.

Domain Names

For many speakers and trainers or training companies, a website is an important market-ing and product delivery tool. Thus, domain names—the addresses for finding websites—have become critical business assets.

Rights in domain names are created by a contract with a domain name registrar, such as Verisign or GoDaddy. Domain names are typically renewed annually, so it is important to ensure that your registration information is up-to-date and results in the receipt of renew-al notices by someone who will respond. Otherwise, valuable domain names may lapse and be snapped up by others, a common occurrence afflicting small and large businesses alike. (This happened to Microsoft—twice!) Registration records can be checked for accuracy with the domain name registrar or at information sites such as www .allwhois.com or www.betterwhois.com.

The importance of domain names in the marketplace has inspired a new industry involv-ing the registration and use of domain names similar to the names of others. Bad faith use and registration of a domain name that is confusingly similar to another's trademark—cybersquatting—violates the domain name registration contract and the trademark laws in the United States. Victims of cybersquatting have several options for recovering the infringing domain name:

- A demand letter to the registrant of the domain name may result in a voluntary transfer of the domain name to resolve the dispute. Typically the registrant will want some payment to cover its expenses.
- A complaint may be filed under the Uniform Dispute Resolution Policy (UDRP) incorporated as part of the domain name registration contract. The UDRP is an

administrative procedure to resolve cybersquatting disputes without court action. The procedure is available for disputes on a global basis. Thus, a trainer located in the United States may use the procedure to challenge a domain name held by a registrant in China. There is no live hearing or trial. The dispute is decided based on written submissions by a neutral party appointed by the dispute resolution service provider. The only relief provided is a transfer or cancellation of the disputed domain name. More information is available from the United Nations' World Intellectual Property Organization, www.wipo.int.

- A lawsuit may be filed in the United States under the Anti-Cybersquatting Consumer Protection Act (ACPA), a provision contained in the U.S. Trademark Law. Litigating in federal court can be expensive and lengthy, but may be the right choice for extreme cases of cybersquatting, particularly when serial infringement is involved. The ACPA can result in recovery of attorneys' fees plus $100,000 per infringing domain name. The ACPA may also be used to recover domain names from distant cybersquatters if the relevant domain name registry is located in the United States, which is the case for .com, .net, and .org domain names.

Data and Information

A successful training business often rests on accumulated contact information about clients and prospects. Many training assignments may also involve access to client information that is subject to nondisclosure agreements. In other instances, training methods may be proprietary and only disclosed to clients under confidentiality agreements. Each of these situations involves data and information that may be protected under trade secret law.

A trade secret is any information that is (1) sufficiently secret to derive economic value, actual or potential, from not being generally known to other persons who can obtain economic value from its disclosure or use; and (2) the subject of efforts that are reasonable under the circumstances to maintain its secrecy or confidentiality. A trade secret can take any number of forms—a formula, a database, a customer list, blueprints, technical data, or a manufacturing process. One of the most famous trade secrets is the formula for Coca-Cola.

Trade secret law does not protect against the independent creation of the trade secret by a third party. Rather, it protects against the misappropriation or the unlawful taking of the trade secret by another. Generally, a court will find trade secret misappropriation in one of two circumstances, either (1) the trade secret was stolen from the company or obtained by improper means, or (2) a trade secret lawfully obtained was used or disclosed in violation of a confidential relationship. Damages may be awarded in trade secret cases, and in appropriate cases, a court may order the offending party to cease any further use or disclosure.

To determine if something is protectable as a trade secret, a court will typically look at whether the information is known outside the business, what safeguards are in place to protect its secrecy, how valuable it is to the business and its competitors, how difficult and expensive it was to develop the information, and how easy it would be to duplicate by lawful means.

Unlike trademark and copyright law discussed above, there is no agency that registers trade secrets. Ownership and protection is a function of the actions taken by the company to restrict access.

The owner of a trade secret must take affirmative action to protect a trade secret's confidentiality. It is important that employees who have access to a trade secret take steps to prevent its unauthorized disclosure, whether on the Internet, by word of mouth, or otherwise. All proprietary materials should be marked as such, denoting that they should be kept confidential and are considered proprietary. Access to the trade secret should be limited to those individuals with a need to know. Procedures for maintaining confidentiality should be implemented and enforced. If disclosure to employees and third parties is necessary, those who are granted access to trade secrets should execute nondisclosure and confidentiality agreements.

When you are hiring learning professionals, it is a good practice to make sure that they are not prevented from doing your work by a trade secret, noncompete, or nondisclosure agreement. Many organizations have begun asking whether an agreement would prevent the applicant from working with them. Some ask the applicant to sign a document that makes it clear that the hiring organization does not want the new employee to do anything that would violate a protective agreement or infringe on the rights of another company.

Systems and Methods

It is common to think of patents as applicable to technical inventions—a better mouse trap—and not applicable to the business of speakers, trainers, and consultants. In fact, the scope of patent protection is far broader and may cover systems and methods developed by learning professionals. For example, patents have recently been issued on tax preparation methods. It is easy to imagine how such protection could extend to training methods.

Important Checklists

Trademark Checklist

- Protects distinctive names, logos, designs, other devices designating source
- No protection for generic terms
- Rights arise from use
- Registration provides nationwide rights and enhanced damages
- Infringement based on likelihood of confusion

Copyright Checklist

- Protects original expression
- No protection for facts, concepts, or ideas
- Rights arise from creation
- Registration provides right to recover attorneys fees and statutory damages
- Infringement based on copying of protected expression

Patent Checklist

- Protects inventions and business methods
- Only available if invention is novel and nonobvious
- Rights arise only through registration
- Twenty-year term of protection
- Infringement based on a use within scope of claims covered by patent

Trade Secret Checklist

- Protects business secrets, information, and data
- Only available if information is maintained as a secret
- No registration
- Infringement based on misappropriation of secret information

---

A patent is a government grant of exclusive rights provided in exchange for disclosure of an invention. The grant involves the right to exclude others from making, using, selling, or offering to sell the invention for 20 years. After that, the invention enters the public domain.

The narrow view of patents being limited to technical inventions began to fade away about 10 years ago when the leading court responsible for patent claims acknowledged that "anything under the sun made by man is patentable." That court extended the protection of patent law to business methods, holding that any method or process that produces a "useful, concrete, and tangible result" is potentially protectable. Although this ruling has been controversial, numerous business methods have been patented, including Amazon.com's "one-click" method and the Netflix method of renting videos.

Four Key Ways to Use Intellectual Property to Make More Money

Intellectual property discussions often focus on legal rights: patents, trademarks, copyrights, trade secrets. These are important, of course, but they are merely legal tools for protecting key business assets. The starting point for learning professionals should be the underlying assets: information, innovation, content, brands, names, reputation, websites, and more. Applying intellectual property rights to these key assets can create value in four key ways.

Charge a Premium for Your Goods and Services

Consider generic cola versus Coca-Cola. Why is one worth more? Coca-Cola has used intellectual property to enhance the value of a simple commodity. It receives a premium because it has a secret formula and a distinctive, well-known brand. Generic cola has a formula, too, but it's not secret; it also has a name, but it is not distinctive. Anyone can make cola and use the cola name. Intellectual property keeps Coca-Cola from being copied. The formula is protected as a trade secret and the brand is protected as a trademark.

Earn Additional Revenue

Consider the average software developer versus Microsoft. The software developer is a knowledge worker paid for his or her labor. If the developer doesn't work, he or she can't make any money. Without his or her work, the developer's business has no value. Microsoft uses intellectual property to turn the product of many knowledge workers into property that can be licensed and sold. Once that is done, Microsoft can make money without further time and effort from the knowledge worker. Copyrights and patents are the intellectual property rights that keep others from copying Microsoft's products.

Increase Market Valuation

The value of a commodity business is typically the book value of its hard assets. The market value of an S&P 500 company is usually several times book value. The difference is largely the value of intellectual property. The same principal applies to learning professionals who can leverage intellectual property rights to increase business value beyond mere book value.

Create Marketable Assets

Markets exist for the resale of intellectual property rights. Brands and domain names can be sold or used as collateral for loans. David Bowie raised $57 million selling bonds backed by the royalties in his recordings. These financial strategies let intellectual property owners cash in on intellectual property assets.

For a business method to be patentable it must be novel (not in the prior art) and nonobvious (to someone skilled in the art in view of the prior art). In the United States, patent protection must be sought within one year of disclosure. The process of obtaining a patent can be complicated and expensive. A patent is best pursued with the help of an experienced patent attorney with knowledge about the subject matter of the patent. Qualified attorneys can be located through the American Intellectual Property Law Association in Washington, D.C., or through local patent law associations.

With all of the areas discussed above, it is always in your best interest to seek the advice of a competent attorney to help you understand what your rights are and how to avoid infringing on the rights of others. A learning professional's chief asset is intellectual capital. Protecting that property and having clarity around your use of others' property is an essential part of being a professional.

About the Authors

Before starting a training and speaking organization, Linda Byars Swindling practiced law for more than a decade and was a partner in Withrow, Fiscus, and Swindling. Coauthor of *The Consultant's Legal Guide* and creator of the popular *Passports to Success* series, she is known for positive influence strategies and negotiation results. She is a Certified Speaking Professional, an award-winning presenter, and an MPI Platinum speaker. She has served as a national director and an officer of the National Speakers Association. She is aligned with Vistage, the world's largest membership organization for chief executive officers, where she facilitates groups and coaches CEOs, presidents, and key executives.

Author, speaker, and attorney Mark V. B. Partridge is an internationally recognized expert in intellectual property law with more than 25 years of experience representing major corporations, business owners, and creative professionals. A Harvard Law School graduate, he is a partner with Pattishall, McAuliffe, a boutique law firm with a global practice helping businesses defend their brands, and the author of the book *Guiding Rights: Trademarks, Copyright and the Internet.* He is listed as one of the preeminent trademark attorneys in the world and named an Illinois Super Lawyer in intellectual property law. For more information, visit www.GuidingRights.com.

For Further Reading

Biech, Elaine, and Linda Byars Swindling. 2000. *The consultant's legal guide: A business of consulting resource.* San Francisco: Jossey-Bass/Pfeiffer.

Partridge, Mark V.B. 2003. *Guiding rights: Trademarks, copyright and the internet.* Lincoln, NE: iUniverse: Author.

Eyres, Patricia S. 1998. *The legal handbook for trainers, speakers, and consultants: The essential guide to keeping your company and clients out of court.* New York: McGraw-Hill.

Ward, Francine. 2007. *Staying legal: A guide to copyright and trademark use.* Alexandria, VA: ASTD Press.

Chapter 45

Preaching to the Choir: The Future of Integrated Talent Management

Kevin Oakes

In This Chapter

➤ Learn about research findings in the field of talent management

➤ Understand the effects of an aging U.S. workforce on the field

➤ Recognize the importance of effectively managing organizational talent

➤ Consider some talent management issues

"The killer app for the next decade is talent acquisition and retention."

—John Doerr, Partner, Kleiner, Perkins, Caufield & Byers

"There is no bigger problem in the global marketplace today than how to obtain, train, and retain knowledge workers."

—Michael Moe, Chairman & CEO, ThinkEquity Partners

These two quotes—from two respected individuals in the financial community—sum up many of the conversations taking place today concerning talent management. But if these statements get you excited, allow me to temper your enthusiasm—both of these quotes were uttered in the late 1990s just as the dot-com bubble was about to burst. Since then, the grand visions of a fully integrated set of human resource functions have yet to completely materialize (although as of this writing there is technically still time for Doerr's prediction to come true).

Lately though, the vision has come back in focus in a big way. And judging by the throngs of vendors who have recently reinvented themselves as integrated talent management providers, there's an abundance of rose-colored glasses in the industry.

Although there's a lot that's still blurry about the phrase *talent management,* one thing is very clear: it sure stirs up the emotions. Some long-time practitioners scoff at the term, regarding it as little more than a fuzzy, overhyped business buzzword for age-old concepts, such as leadership development or human resource (HR) management. Others see it as much more than that, identifying it as a term that represents an important paradigm shift in the way organizations acquire and manage their most valuable resources.

Research shows, however, that most people are at least slightly confused about what it is we're really talking about. In a recent study on the subject by the Institute for Corporate Productivity (i4cp, 2007), more than 75 percent of the respondents admitted they have no agreed-upon definition (see Table 45-1), even though two-thirds say that the phrase talent management is used to at least a moderate extent within their companies (see Table 45-2).

The perspective of the individual often changes the definition. Career recruiting specialists couch talent management in terms of selecting and assessing candidates. Leadership development professionals often view it as just another term for their profession. Technology vendors use it to mean having a full suite of applications.

Table 45-1. Talent Management Definitions

Does your organization have an agreed-on definition of talent management?	All Respondents (Percent)
Yes	24.7
No	75.3

Source: i4cp (2007). Used with permission.

Table 45-2. Talent Management Usage

To what degree is the phrase "talent management" used in your organization?	All Respondents (Percent)
Very little	17.2
Below moderate degree	16.1
Moderate degree	29.1
Above moderate degree	21.8
High degree	15.7

Source: i4cp (2007). Used with permission.

According to participants in i4cp's study, at least eight out of 10 respondents said the following were elements of talent management:

- Leadership development
- Career planning
- High-potential employee development
- Performance management
- Succession planning
- Learning and training
- Competency management
- Retention
- Professional development.

This string of functions has often been referred to as the "employee life cycle," or "cradle to grave" employment applications or the ability to "attain-train-retain" a workforce. Instead of talent management, other terms that have been loosely used to describe the entire process are *human capital management, employee relationship management,* or just *workforce management.*

Articles, research reports, and white papers on talent management appear everywhere. Here is a sure sign that we've reached saturation on the subject: the first *Talent Management for Dummies* book has been published (Wasdin and Docherty, 2007). Vendors are sponsoring webinars on this subject. Investors are (again) investing in the concept. And mergers and acquisitions are being contemplated to capitalize on this vision.

And it's an idea that didn't even originate in this decade.

✐ **Jim Kouzes** ✑

Jim Kouzes is an author, researcher, and expert on leadership. Kouzes is best known for authoring, with Barry Posner, the popular book The Leadership Challenge *(1987). The groundbreaking leadership model included in the book identified five fundamental practices for great leadership: challenging the process, inspiring a shared vision, enabling others to act, modeling the way, and encouraging the heart. Kouzes and Posner also created the Leadership Practices Inventory (LPI), a 360-degree assessment tool designed to develop leadership skills.*

The buzz is clearly back, but this time it extends beyond vendors and investors merely looking to profit from a new category of applications, or HR zealots. Long-time advocates will be encouraged that talent management is a top concern not just for HR professionals, but for organizational leaders as well. According to i4cp, seven in 10 respondents to a recent survey said talent management—as expected—is a priority for HR. What may surprise some is that a full six in 10 said it's also a priority for executives. Even more interesting: Among respondents from companies seen as top talent management performers, 82 percent said that executives view talent management as a priority, and 75 percent said the same about senior managers.

Clearly the promise of talent management has extended far beyond the audiences of the late 1990s. Why the renewed interest? Two main reasons:

- More technology vendors are proclaiming they can automate the entire process (either through integration of technologies or all-in-one offerings).
- More companies are ready to embrace the concept not only because of better integrated technologies, but more so because of the current and predicted shortage of available talent.

If talent management is going to live up to its promises, it's the second reason—corporate receptivity—that will be the catalyst.

The Reality of Silos

It was right after the dot-com crash when an overly anxious CEO of an HR technology company began pitching me hard on combining his company with the company I was running (a leading learning management system provider). He was not the first to approach me with the idea, but he was easily the most aggressive. His pitch: Together, we can be the only provider to offer end-to-end HR and learning products and services in the attain-train-retain continuum. *"Let's seize this opportunity now and drive the market!"* is the way he ended one memorable email.

The problem, as I unconvincingly kept describing to him, was that the potential buyers in corporations are in silos. There were very few—if any—companies in the marketplace that were positioned organizationally to take advantage of such a holistic solution. HR departments not only didn't traditionally work cooperatively, they often had underlying incentives to work against each other (fighting each other for budget dollars, attention within the company, a strategic seat with management, and so forth). In short, we can preach all we want, but there is no one choir ready to hear the message.

The preaching has begun again in earnest, but this time the choirs are certainly better prepared to hear the sermon. A big reason for this receptivity is the growing recognition of an upcoming worker shortage.

The War for Talent

There's a simple fact facing today's U.S. employers: baby boomers are beginning to retire, and the workforce is not being backfilled fast enough to meet demand. Depending on which census study you believe, there will be between a two and 10 million person worker shortage in the United States by 2010, with a shortage of as many as 40 million workers predicted by 2015.

Although this has been much discussed in the United States, the problem is not confined to North America alone. Japan and much of Europe's workforce are also projected to experience significant shrinkage, reducing by 1 percent per year over the next 10 years.

This phenomenon is not happening because the world's population is declining. In fact, the world's population is expected to double in the next 40 years. However, the greatest fertility will not be found in the countries commonly viewed as developed nations. Instead it will occur in those countries probably least able to support their existing populations. This means that corporations will be dipping into a nontraditional talent pool of workers and selecting from the traditional pool will become increasingly competitive. In a recent joint study by DDI and Monster (Howard, Erker, and Bruce, 2006, 2007), 73 percent of staffing managers (an overwhelming majority) reported that competition for talent had increased, and 79 percent expected the competition to only intensify going forward.

The i4cp study on the subject showed that many HR professionals think the talent shortage will get a lot worse (see Table 45-3). Nearly half of respondents said that it's quite or

Table 45-3. Ten Year Predictions (Percent)

To what degree do you think the following will be true in your organization in 10 years?	Not True at All	A Bit True	Moderately True	Quite True	Completely True	Quite or Completely
There is not enough talent.	19	12	20	27	21	48
Skilled workers retire.	17	17	25	24	17	31
Education system doesn't meet our needs.	31	24	24	14	6	20
We can't retain talent.	32	34	21	8	6	14
There's a lack of good programs and processes.	33	34	20	9	4	13
We don't have the right technology.	45	29	19	6	2	13
Talent management is a low priority.	66	13	10	5	6	11
We have a hard time integrating technology.	39	30	20	7	4	11
We can't attract talent.	39	28	23	8	3	11
We have poor development programs.	44	32	18	4	2	6
Outsourcing means we don't have to manage talent.	78	11	8	2	1	3

Source: i4cp (2007). Used with permission.

completely true that there won't be enough talent 10 years into the future, and nearly a third point to the retirement of skilled workers. In fact, census studies show that 43 percent of the U.S. civilian labor force is eligible to retire in the next decade, and some surveys indicate that *Fortune* 500 companies are expecting to lose 50 percent of their senior managers within the next five years.

There's also some pessimism about the education system to help replace departed talent. A fifth of respondents indicate that it's quite or completely true that the education system will not meet their organizations' needs in the future (which is actually not much different from those who think this is currently true).

Scarier than the forecast for worker shortages is the lack of preparation. Studies have shown that as many as 40 percent of *Fortune* 500 companies say that they have no formal succession plans for departing managers. When it comes to replacing these retirees from the outside, according to the DDI-Monster study, only 10 percent of hiring and staffing managers give themselves an *A* (9 or 10 on a 10-point scale) when rating their own companies' recruiting and selection effectiveness (Howard, Erker, and Bruce, 2006, 2007). Most gave themselves a *D* or a *C* (6 or a 7 on a 10-point scale).

Many corporate practitioners are looking at integrated talent management as the secret weapon in this war for talent. But although it's widely considered to be the biggest catalyst, an upcoming worker shortage isn't the only driver of talent management initiatives today. In its study, i4cp found a total of five primary drivers, and three of those five can be considered bottom-line business issues: the need to execute strategies, the need to stay competitive, and the need to serve customers (see Table 45-4).

The Bottom Line

Although all of this integration sounds sensible, many senior executives want to know one thing from human capital professionals: does it make a difference?

Effectively managing talent appears to be linked with better market performance, according to several sources:

- Better market performers—that is, those who reported success in the areas of revenue growth, market share, profitability, and customer satisfaction—tended to say they are better at talent management, according to i4cp. Whereas only about a third of all respondents gave their companies high grades for managing talent, nearly half (48 percent) of the best market performers rated their ability to manage talent as good or excellent.

Table 45-4. Drivers of Talent Management (Percent)

To what degree do the following factors drive the need to manage talent in your organization today?	Small Degree	Below-Average Degree	Average Degree	Above-Average Degree	High Degree	Above-Average and High Degree Combined
Need to execute strategies	5	5	31	35	23	58
Talent and skills shortages	7	9	27	31	26	57
Business competition	11	7	25	31	26	57
Retention and retention issues	11	10	22	32	24	56
Need for customer service	11	7	27	27	28	55
Need for innovation	12	7	29	29	22	51
Corporate culture	12	12	34	27	15	42
Cost of human capital	13	9	37	26	15	41
New technologies	24	8	34	21	14	35
Global marketplace	27	9	31	18	15	33
The flattening of organizations	27	17	34	17	6	33
Diverse workforce	21	12	35	24	8	32
Work/life balance issues	19	16	35	19	12	31
Compliance and regulatory issues	24	12	34	17	13	30
Outsourcing and/or offshoring	43	16	22	13	5	18

Source: i4cp (2007). Used with permission.

- Organizations seem to benefit from having an agreed-on definition of talent management. The best talent management performing organizations and the best market performing companies are more likely than average to say they have an agreed-on definition of "talent management" according to i4cp.

- "Talent will be the defining factor in the future success or failure of U.S. companies," according to a study from Spherion (2005), based on interviews with 502 senior HR executives and an online survey of nearly 3,000 U.S. workers. Spherion concluded that "workers may be the next great profit driver for U.S. industry."

- "There is a strong correlation between how having a talent mindset or focus impacts financial results," asserts *Human Resources Magazine* (Grossman, 2005), citing a study by Hewitt Associates, which links effective talent management (among other best practices) to higher revenue growth and lower recruitment costs, and another by Watson Wyatt (2001-2002) that links high scores in human capital practices that are part of talent management to high shareholder value.

- A focus on talent and a complementary corporate culture are among the practices that can lead to sustained organizational performance, according to the Amos Tuck School of Business of Dartmouth College (Joyce, 2005). Providing a performance-based environment in which employees thrive and the ability to attract, develop, and retain talented workers were among the practices identified as leading to success by researchers on a long-term study by a team of academics and practitioners that analyzed a decade of data from 200 firms.

Focus, Ownership, and Execution

When it comes to outperforming the market, applying talent management to a broader range of employees as opposed to just an elite group of employees seems to help. The best performing companies are considerably more likely than average to focus talent management on all jobs in their organizations, and they're considerably less likely than average to focus exclusively on senior executives or high-potential talent (see Table 45-5).

"The talent review process must extend down several levels in the organization to identify the real difference makers," states David Forman in an article in *Human Capital*, arguing that "an organization's real strength is in the 'deep pros' that make a discernible difference in the quality of products and services" (2006). The ability to find qualified employees for open positions is one of the many promises of an integrated talent management system. "Succession planning for the CEO is not sufficient," according to the article, which claims that effective talent management will also include talent reviews and succession planning that covers key positions several levels into the organizational structure.

Table 45-5. Talent Management Focus (Percent)

On which levels is talent management focused in your organization?	All Respondents	Best Market Performers	Best TM Performers
Senior executives only	13.1	6.8	3.9
High-potential talent only	20.3	20.4	9.8
All managers and professionals	17.6	17.3	27.5
Key positions throughout the organization	27.3	32.1	28.8
All jobs in the organization	15.3	19.8	25.5
Other (please specify)	6.5	3.7	4.6

Source: i4cp (2007). Used with permission.

Robin Athey (director of organizational performance at Deloitte Research) and Nick van Dam (global chief learning officer at Deloitte Touche Tohmatsu) agree that truly effective talent management should go deep into the organization. They advise talent management practitioners to "identify the segments of the workforce that drive their current and future growth. These are not just the stars, who are often the first to leave when other opportunities surface. Instead, they are the overlooked people who create the value that leads to growth—educators, researchers, customer service professionals—whoever does the work for which the market rewards innovation and differentiation" (Athey and van Dam, 2005). Failing to recognize the untapped skills of employees is an easy but crucial error. It's common for supervisors or executives to become set in a perception of the talents of those who work for them and later have difficulty perceiving growth or unacknowledged strengths in workers they have already mentally classified. *Wall Street Journal* columnist Carol Hymowitz warns that such pigeonholing is "one of the main causes of employee discontent and high turnover... rigid typecasting also discourages initiative and innovation" (2005). Managers must be careful to reassess their workers periodically and not to allow unfounded opinions to deprive the company of talent that should be developed.

Although there seems to be widespread acknowledgment that applying talent management deep into the organization is beneficial, there is no clear consensus on who is responsible for the ownership and execution of talent management initiatives. Among overall respondents to an i4cp survey, the "HR function generally" was seen as most often responsible for both the execution and the ownership of talent management.

Early Adopters

One company that has put some of the elements of integrated talent management into practice is Aetna. With more than 28,000 employees, Aetna is one of the nation's leaders in health care, dental, pharmacy, group life, disability, and long-term care insurance and employee benefits. Despite its leadership, at the beginning of this decade Aetna was experiencing several problems. Numerous service issues, alienated suppliers and customers, and a demoralized workforce were a little too common for the company at the time.

To combat this, Aetna implemented a corporate-wide business process that integrated corporate goal setting, operational goals, individual performance plans, and learning. The integrated approach was put into place to link learning more directly to strategy, thereby allowing for more focused development and a better return on Aetna's learning investment. The integrated approach included identifying the competencies and practices required to achieve the company's business strategy and then mapping learning content to those competencies. Aetna then built assessment instruments that allow the workforce to assess their skills against the required competencies. As a result, this approach allowed Aetna to deliver targeted, focused learning to build that competence.

Although Aetna primarily merged performance management with learning management, the company plans to link in the remainder of its human capital management functions. This includes leveraging existing systems such as the company's recruiting platform and adding compatible career planning, succession planning, and talent inventory functionality. Aetna credits the ability to effectively link learning and performance management as a big reason for the company's turnaround. However, despite the progress some companies like Aetna are making in this area, converging learning and HR functions, like performance management, is still very nascent.

However, respondents from the best market performers saw things a little differently. They selected "all managers" as most often responsible for the execution of talent (albeit by a slim margin), even while seeing HR as having ownership of talent management (see Table 45-6).

Several experts argue that, as technology comes together to provide a holistic solution, the learning management system is in a great position to be the focal point of an integrated system. But that viewpoint doesn't translate to the training function as an owner of talent management. However, when it comes to the common language that applications must use for talent management, the training function might be in the driver's seat.

A Shared Language

One of the commonalities in each of the applications viewed as part of an integrated talent management system is the use of competencies as a shared language. *Talent*

Table 45-6. Responsibility for Talent Management (Percent)

Who is responsible for the execution and ownership of talent management in your organization?	Human Resources Generally	Training Function	CEO	Executive Team	All Managers	All Employees	Other
All Respondents							
Execution of talent management	38	7	4	20	25	5	2
Ownership of talent management	37	4	9	23	19	5	3
Best Market Performers							
Execution of talent management	31	6	2	20	33	7	1
Ownership of talent management	36	4	6	20	23	7	3
Best Talent Management Performers							
Execution of talent management	31	3	3	21	31	10	2
Ownership of talent management	31	1	10	24	22	9	3

Source: i4cp (2007). Used with permission.

✌ **Jack Zenger** ✆

Jack Zenger is a pioneer in leadership training as well as a renowned author and speaker. He has co-authored numerous books on leadership, including The Handbook for Leaders: 24 Lessons for Extraordinary Leaders *(2004, with Joseph Folkman and John Zenger),* The Extraordinary Leader: Turning Good Managers into Great Leaders *(2002, with Joseph Folkman), and* Results-Based Leadership *(1999, with David Ulrich and Norman Smallwood). Zenger's research on leadership resulted in the identification of five clusters of leadership competencies, which include character, personal competence, interpersonal competence, driving for results, and leading change.*

Management for Dummies defines competencies as "directly observable behaviors, skills, abilities, talents, attitudes and other personal characteristics that are essential to successful job performance" (Wasdin and Docherty, 2007). With the need for alignment among HR functions such as selection and assessment, performance and learning, consistent competencies that serve as the basis for understanding what is expected in candidates and what is expected to be learned once they are in their role are important. But like talent management as a whole, competency models have yet to be widely instituted and it's definitions that get in the way. Most organizations have a hard time gaining agreement on common competencies across the enterprise, and in fact some of the early proponents of shared competencies have given up trying to achieve consensus.

Part of the problem is that competency models are often too complex. To work effectively, they typically need to be simple and integrated into the entire life cycle of the employee. When divisions and groups are allowed to use different models, managing competencies typically gets convoluted, and they lose adoption.

"Competency models have, in the past, been over-engineered and therefore complex to manage and maintain," agrees Gordon Bull, an ASTD board member and the former director of Global Learning Management at Vodafone, the world's largest wireless company. "I think there is merit in defining behavioral competencies that should apply across an organization. These can then be supplemented with functional, or job specific competencies, but without getting overly detailed or complex. Used throughout the employment cycle they can be useful guides and measures of performance and provide overall indications of the bench strength in the organization. Many tools used in recruitment can equally be used internally throughout an employee's life cycle" (Oakes, 2006).

Immature Technology

Although companies wrestle with the internal organizational issues to make talent management work, there is widespread recognition that the technology is still not where it needs to be to enable this. Although multiple vendors claim to have the full talent management suite of applications, the reality is that most are missing some core components, or have very immature offerings in certain areas.

Because of this, some potential buyers have become tired of waiting, opting to build a solution themselves. Although that usually is not recommended, for now the only viable off-the-shelf solutions involve integrating best-of-breed technologies. Anyone who has tried to connect different systems knows that integration is often fraught with multiple technical issues. In the case of talent management, integration problems are compounded by market issues such as competitive vendors being forced to work with each other, or required to map the business logic of their system with areas of human capital with which they have little experience. The bottom line is that, despite all the promise, the current state of integrated talent management is less than ideal, and the future is sure to contain many changes.

Continued Consolidation

For those who are tired of vendor consolidation, there is likely no relief on the horizon—it will continue to be a very active market for mergers and acquisitions. Gartner Group is one of many that are predicting consolidation to dominate the talent management landscape ahead. In a report on market conditions, the information technology consultancy predicted the industry will see multiple acquisitions, particularly among vendors from the performance management, succession planning, compensation management, recruitment, and learning domains. Maturity in certain segments—particularly the e-recruiting and learning management segments—causes many to predict, including Gartner, that vendors in these segments will drive consolidation (Gartner, 2006).

However, one of the hottest technology applications in the talent management suite is performance management. Although most companies have some sort of performance review process, a surprising number of organizations do not have an enterprise-wide performance management process in place, and even fewer have an automated process. This is quickly changing. Although performance management systems are much more immature than other components of a talent management suite, they are growing the fastest.

As with any large initiative, unless organizations have top-level buy-in, technical solutions will never succeed. An integrated talent management system contains many components that, by their nature, should support the key strategies, goals, and processes of management. Unfortunately, in many companies, human capital professionals are still not at the right strategic level to have the effect they would like. Before talent management can really take off and reach analysts' lofty predictions and vendors' rosy expectations, the reality is that executive support still has a long way to go. Despite the industry being rife with preachers clamoring to deliver the talent management sermon, there's obviously still a lot of missionary work left to do.

∽⌒

About the Author

Kevin Oakes is the CEO of the Institute for Corporate Productivity (i4cp) and is also currently a board member of SumTotal Systems. He was the 2006 chairman of ASTD and is a frequent speaker and author on workplace learning issues.

References

Athey, Robin, and Nick van Dam. 2005, October. Attracting top talent with performance management. *Workforce Performance Solutions,* 30-33.

Forman, David C. 2006, March/April. The missing ingredients: Leadership, talent development. *Human Capital,* 14.

Gartner. 2006. *Continued consolidation headlined in the human capital management software market in 2005.* Research report. Stamford, CT: Gartner.

Grossman, Robert J. 2005, March. The truth about the coming labor shortage. *HR Magazine,* available at http://www.shrm.org/hrmagazine/articles/0305/0305covstory.asp.

Howard, Ann, Scott Erker, and Neal Bruce. 2006, 2007. Slugging through the war for talent. *Monster Selection Forecast 2006, 2007,* available at http://intelligence.monster.com /12338_en-US_p1.asp.

Hymowitz, Carol. 2005, May 24. Bosses who pigeonhole workers waste talent, contribute to turnover. *Wall Street Journal Online,* available at http://www.wsj.com.

i4cp (Institute for Corporate Productivity). 2007. *Talent management survey 2007.* Seattle and St. Petersburg, FL: Institute for Corporate Productivity.

Joyce, William. 2005. What really works: Building the 4+2 organization. *Organizational Dynamics* 34(2): 118-129.

Oakes, Kevin. 2006, April. The emergence of talent management. *T+D,* 21-24.

Spherion. 2005. The great divide: The employer-worker disconnect. *Emerging workforce study,* available at http://www.spherion.com/downloads/Emerging_Workforce/The_Great_Divide-EW.pdf.

Wasdin, Marcus, and William Docherty. 2007. *Talent management for dummies.* Hoboken, NJ, and Mountain View, CA: John Wiley & Sons and SumTotal Systems.

Watson Wyatt. 2001-2002. *Watson Wyatt human capital index: Human capital as a lead indicator of shareholder value,* available at http://www.watsonwyatt.com/research/resrender.asp?id=W-488&page=1.

For Further Reading

Berger, Lance A., and Dorothy R. Berger. 2004. *The talent management handbook: Creating organizational excellence by identifying, developing, and promoting your best people.* New York: McGraw-Hill.

Jamrog, Jay. 2004. *The perfect storm.* Seattle and St. Petersburg, FL: Institute for Corporate Productivity.

Overholt, Alison. 2004, August. The labor shortage myth. *Fast Company,* available at http://www.fastcompany.com/magazine/85/essay.html.

Parsons, George D., and Richard T. Pascale. 2007, March 1. Crisis at the summit. *Harvard Business Review,* available at http://harvardbusinessonline.hbsp.harvard.edu/b01/en/common/item _detail.jhtml?id=R0703E&referral=2342.

Rothwell, William J. 2003. *The strategic development of talent.* Amherst, MA: HRD Press.

Rueff, Rusty, and Hank Stringer. 2006. *Talent force: A new manifesto for the human side of business.* Upper Saddle River, NJ: Prentice Hall.

Schaefer, Patricia. 2006. Baby-boomer-caused labor shortage: Ideological myth or future reality, available at http://www.businessknowhow.com/manage/labor-shortage.htm.

Schweyer, Allan. 2004. *Talent management systems: Best practices in technology solutions for recruitment, retention, and workforce planning.* New York: Wiley.

Sims, Doris, and Matthew Gay. 2006. *Building tomorrow's talent: A practitioner's guide to talent management and succession planning.* Bloomington, IN: AuthorHouse.

Thorne, Kaye, and Andy Pellant. 2007. *The essential guide to managing talent: How top companies recruit, train, and retain the best employees.* Philadelphia, PA: Kogan Page.

Section IX

The WLP Professional

Getting to Relevance

Luminary Perspective

Tony Bingham

In This Chapter

➢ Learn what it takes for organizations to gain
  and keep a competitive advantage

➢ Understand the pressures that organizations
  face today and how learning can help

➢ Know what is needed to prepare for the
  new roles of learning professionals

Employee training has spent many decades on the sidelines. In the past, organizational leaders regarded training as a nice thing to do for employees but not necessary for success. It was typically the first thing cut from budgets when times got tough and except for training in skills you could observe—like welding or taking an x-ray—many business leaders weren't sure what training could accomplish. The value of developing leaders or training managers to behave in certain ways was harder to demonstrate. Those subjects might be appropriate in business school, executives believed, but not in the workplace. Intangible assets, including what employees knew or how fast they learned new ways to think and behave, did not appear on balance sheets. Accountants and their bosses, for the most part, shrugged them off as unquantifiable and therefore of no relevance.

The driving force of the economy was not speed or brainpower: it was size.

But then the world changed. The economy became global. Technology, which had been a competitive advantage only for a few big companies with deep pockets, became affordable and widely available. Competition forced organizations to make process improvements, operate with less overhead, and become more efficient. Soon even those advantages became commodities. Today, even the smallest manufacturer understands lean production, and no organization can survive if it ignores its customers.

The 20th century is history, and a difficult era for business is, for the most part, behind us. Starting with a boom that few predicted, the previous decade ended with many of the world's greatest organizations struggling to stay alive. Many faltered and were eaten by competitors, or failed spectacularly like Enron and WorldCom. Some, such as the giant, 100-year-old Bethlehem Steel, went down in denial of what was happening around them. Early on Bethlehem Steel curtailed its research and development and failed to anticipate changes in its industry.

Many organizations are healthier now financially because of their commitment to cut costs and be more efficient, but these days, that is not enough. Those same companies may be risking their futures by ignoring the need to prepare for the next wave of change. To gain and keep competitive advantage, organizations must continually adapt and innovate, act fast, and learn even faster. What employees know today has a limited shelf life, and in a knowledge economy that is a liability. Leaders who fail to "right skill" their employees—repeatedly and strategically—risk the future success of their companies and perhaps even their survival.

Pressures Increasing

Many organizations find themselves ill-equipped to grow because the skills required to meet the demand for innovation and competitiveness are in short supply in the workplace and in the people entering the workplace from school. Table A shows perceived gaps in these skills.

In the global economy, companies can look for talent around the world, but even those workers who may be plentiful and cheap to employ now need to grow their skills. Companies in China and India—two fast-growing economies—are already finding that

Table A. Perceived Skill Gap

Skill Gap	Percent
Managerial and supervisory skills	55
Communication and interpersonal skills	51
Leadership and executive-level skills	45
Process and project management skills	27
Technical, IT, and systems skills	23
Customer service skills	20
Professional or industry-specific skills	19
Sales skills	17
Basic skills	11

Source: Davenport (2005).

a lack of managerial skills can hold back growth. A study by global human resource consulting firm DDI found that 47 percent of leaders in Chinese companies thought their organizations did a "poor" or "fair" job of leadership development (DDI, 2006).

According to the Conference Board, 40 percent of the U.S. workforce will be eligible for retirement by 2010 (Harmon, 2007). Adding to the pressure to find, keep, and develop the right brainpower is the departure from the workforce of millions of people nearing retirement age. Knowledge, skill, and experience are walking out the door of organizations around the world. At the United States Social Security Administration (SSA), more than half the managers will be eligible to retire by 2015. The agency is using communities of practice and building databases to help stem the tide of departing knowledge while also building the skills needed to achieve future goals (Harmon, 2007).

Organizations today realize that managing talent—their know-how—has the same importance as managing other aspects of performance, such as systems or processes. They feel the pressure to innovate, to drive learning throughout the organization, and to continually refresh what is truly their most important, competitive advantage—their people.

The net result for learning professionals is that they now contribute directly and measurably to the success of organizations. The relevance that eluded them when knowledge and skill were more static has arrived.

What CEOs Expect

Many CEOs today understand the value of learning and can articulate how it supports specific strategies. Bill Swanson, chairman and CEO of Raytheon, says, "When there's a gap, how do you fill it? Guess what? You have to learn. That's why learning is such an integral part of what we do. It's the only way to get from point A to point B" (Bingham and Galagan, 2007).

The expectations of CEOs are the same for learning as they are for any other function of the business. They expect learning and development to support the organization's strategies and to prepare employees to implement whatever new direction the company needs to take to survive and prosper.

Jim Owens, CEO of Caterpillar, explains the connection between learning and the company's strategy to become more customer-focused and grow the business: "One of the findings of a 1998 study was the need for Caterpillar to become a learning organization as part of its value chain. [The result was that] Caterpillar University was formed around a learning model based on three critical elements: a culture that supports learning, comprehensive knowledge sharing throughout the company and with our value chain partners, and the development of leadership that is very supportive of learning" (Bingham and Galagan, 2008).

CEOs expect accountability not only for training and development budgets but also for the outcome of learning initiatives. Organizations today use a much broader set of metrics than in the past to account for the effect of learning. CEOs are less likely to pay attention to the number of people trained than to what they accomplish as a result of the training. CEOs look for indicators such as increased sales, or greater depth in the leadership ranks, or widespread understanding of crucial new goals to tell them that learning is taking place at an acceptable level or speed. Often they themselves take part in developing employees. At Becton Dickenson, for example, CEO Ed Ludwig models the norm of leader as teacher. How better to assure that learning is relevant than to have the CEO take part as a teacher?

Today's CEOs have their eyes on the future, knowing that an organization is only as quick to act as its workforce is quick to learn. In industry after industry, companies are adjusting to new realities stemming from factors as diverse as rising fuel costs, health-conscious customers, and even the weather, which has grown more unpredictable with global warming. They look to their talent managers to make sure that the organization has the skills it needs now and in the future. To enter a new market or turn a company around requires the most efficient, effective, and productivity-oriented learning initiatives that a company can muster.

The Link Between Training and Corporate Communications

In many companies facing change at the strategic level, communication and training are closely linked at a high level. Cisco is a good example. After years of remarkable growth on a global scale, the company hit a wall, but instead of cutting back on training, they refashioned it. CEO John Chambers said at the time, "I really do believe in the productivity and customer satisfaction that will come from the training."

Cisco introduced large-scale e-learning—it was one of the first major companies to take this step—and tied learning closely to corporate communications. Tom Kelly, who was then vice president of the Internet Learning Solutions Group, explained, "The thing that has changed the most is that the e-learning tools and technologies are the way John [Chambers] and the rest of the executives interact, communicate, and inform."

When equipment manufacturer John Deere & Company was shifting its focus to growing the business and needed to roll out a new global performance management system to support the change, CEO Bob Lane said, "We needed extensive education and communication before implementation."

When Federated Department Stores acquired its rival, The May Company, and changed the name of all its stores to Macy's, CEO Terry Lundgren faced a huge communication challenge:

> We knew that we had to be very clear about what our new culture was going to be like. And the only way to do that was to over-communicate to make the strategy clear. We communicated who we were and what we were about, and we gave people the choice to be part of the new culture, knowing that it was probably going to be different than in the past.
>
> My role with regard to employee learning is really about communication. It starts with me.
>
> Even with 850 stores and nearly 200,000 employees, I believe that you can definitely get people to feel like they're in the know, they have a voice, and that you're listening. I think that company size is no longer a reason for not being able to execute a broad and effective communications strategy.

Source: Bingham and Galagan (2007).

The Emerging Role of the Learning Professional

With relevance for workplace learning have come new roles for learning professionals. A leading new role is to be a true business partner who helps shape strategy, communicates key messages, and produces results that support key goals. In contrast to the past when the training function was buried deep in the organization, learning professionals today operate at the executive level with roles that stretch from identifying core competencies for the whole organization to finding and developing its talent at all levels.

In the CEO's Own Words

"I feel that the greatest opportunities for us relate directly to our ability to learn. The world is moving very fast, especially the world of medicine. To keep doing what worked in the past is potentially a formula for disaster for us. So our ability to recognize new patterns and adapt quickly, to take advantage of situations as they occur, and to respond to them better than others becomes more important all the time. Our ability to learn fast, implement, and execute directly correlates to our long-term success."

—*Mike Mussallem, CEO and Chairman, Edwards Lifesciences*

"Ensuring that Caterpillar has the talented, knowledgeable, and engaged people required to produce the world's best machines, engines, and services is a never-ending job. Almost all jobs today—regardless of industry—require more and different skills than the jobs of yesterday. We must make sure that our employees have the knowledge and skills to succeed in the 21st century workforce."

—*Jim Owens, CEO, Caterpillar*

"The kinds of challenges we face have necessitated change and that as much as anything has revealed a very dramatic need for learning. I think that learning is, in essence, allowing people to think differently, and clearly that's what confronts us at Southwest Airlines.

"As we've tried to change Southwest Airlines to react to new realities, it has revealed deficiencies in ourselves that we needed to address. It has been clear that the company strategically needed to make some changes and that was very clearly linked to a need for education and leadership development."

—*Gary Kelly, CEO, Southwest Airlines*

Source: Bingham and Galagan (2007).

Change management has been part of the learning professional's toolkit for decades but that skill takes on new importance in today's fast-moving economy where agility can mean the difference between mere survival and great success. Today the organization development expert is expected to help lead change with the highest stakes.

Preparing for New Roles

Learning professionals have always come from a great variety of backgrounds including education, psychology, engineering, communications, and operations, to name just a few. Whatever their academic preparation or work experience, they need to be masters of the core competencies laid out in the ASTD Competency Model and certified by the ASTD Certification Institute with the Certified Professional in Learning and Performance

(CPLP) credential through a process that includes a knowledge test and a review of a work product. To play the role of learning leader also requires business acumen, strategic thinking, and the ability to drive results.

In 2007, the Wharton-Penn School of Graduate Education added an executive program in work-based learning, intended for people en route to the executive level of the learning profession. The requirements include successful completion of the CPLP certification.

Excelling in the Role

ASTD has reviewed the learning activities of more than 300 companies that have applied for the BEST Award, an honor that recognizes excellence in learning's effect on business success. Those that win BEST Awards excel in these areas:

- Demonstrating the connection between learning and organizational strategy.
- Articulating the value of learning and its effect on the bottom line. They understand the value of learning and protect the investment, even when times are tough.
- Ensuring that the company's leaders are involved in teaching others.
- Sharing a sense of urgency about developing a competitive workforce and keeping enough talent in the pipeline.
- Understanding learning's role as a leader of talent management—especially in recruitment, development, and retention.

There has never been a better time to be in the learning profession because, finally, relevance is assured. More and more organizations—including their leaders—get the importance of employee learning. Other organizations are aware of the need for workforce development but may not know what to do about it. Either of these situations represents an opportunity for the prepared learning professional. Do not waste it.

About the Author

As the world's largest association dedicated to workplace learning and performance professionals, the American Society for Training & Development (ASTD) is at the forefront of trends in learning and workforce development. Led by president and CEO Tony Bingham, ASTD offers programs and services to help members and practitioners improve individual and organizational performance through learning.

Together with the board of directors and supported by a staff of more than 100 and a wide volunteer network, he is focused on helping members build their business acumen, understand the profession's role in narrowing skills gaps, connect their work to the strategic priorities of business, and help their organizations leverage talent.

With broad-based business, financial, operational, and technical management expertise, Bingham joined ASTD in 2001 as the chief operating officer and as chief information officer. He became president and CEO in February 2004.

References

Bingham, Tony. 2007. Real value. *Learning Executive Magazine.* Premier Issue: 4.

Bingham, Tony, and Pat Galagan. 2007. *A view from the top: How CEOs link learning to corporate strategy.* Alexandria, VA: ASTD Press.

Bingham, Tony, and Pat Galagan. 2008, January. Learning is a powerful tool. *T+D,* 30-37.

Davenport, Rex. 2005, March. Eliminate the skills gap. *T+D,* 26.

DDI (Development Dimensions International). 2006. *Leadership in China: Keeping pace with a growing economy,* available at http://www.ddiworld.com/pdf/ddi_leadershipinchina_rr.pdf.

Harmon, Wayne. 2007. Riding the retirement wave. *Learning Executive Magazine.* Premier Issue: 36.

For Further Reading

ASTD Public Policy Council. 2006. Bridging the skills gap: How the skills shortage threatens growth and competitiveness...and what to do about it. White paper. Alexandria, VA: ASTD.

Chapter 46

Competencies: The Foundation of Our Profession

Richard S. Wellins and William J. Rothwell

In This Chapter

➢ Learn what competencies are and why they are important

➢ Get an overview of ASTD's most recent competency model

➢ Learn how to apply competency models to benefit you as an individual as well as to support your organization

---

ASTD has historically taken the lead to define the field and pinpoint the roles, competencies, work outputs, and quality standards necessary for success in the field. That historic role has been demonstrated through a series of ASTD-sponsored competency studies. But why are competency studies important? What really drives successful performance as a workplace performance and learning (WLP) professional? And how can we really use our competencies to make a difference? This chapter examines these and related questions.

What Are Roles, Competencies, and Work Outputs?

People are hired into jobs or positions. Often, a job description outlines what they are to do; a job specification describes the education, experience, or other requirements necessary to qualify for the job. Although job descriptions may briefly summarize what people do, they do not tell the whole story. How people approach their jobs is a question of *role*, the part played by an individual. Roles in our field might include trainer, instructional designer, or e-learning expert. A single person may play multiple roles.

Competencies are the characteristics associated with adequate or excellent performance. Competencies are in people, not in jobs. They may be demonstrated through behavior, skills, or knowledge. Competencies are typically measured by *behavioral indicators*.

Work outputs are the results of work efforts. They are the outcomes of demonstrated competencies and the behaviors associated with them. Work outputs themselves may be assessed through *quality indicators*. For our profession, work outputs might include a new training system, a return-on-investment evaluation, or delivered classes.

Why Are Competency Studies of the Field Important?

Competency studies provide a foundation for recruiting, selecting, developing, appraising, managing, rewarding, and counseling those who work in the field. In that sense, the application of a competency study is no different than it is for applications to other fields.

Competency studies are also important because they provide a foundation for preparing aspiring practitioners to enter the field through planned professional development experiences—such as college degrees or professional certification. College degrees should be based on employer expectations, and, as we will see, competency models provide a basis for identifying what employers expect of successful applicants. They become the basis for preparing people to enter the field, transfer into the field, qualify for the field, or advance in the field.

A Brief History of Competency Studies of the Field

Substantial attention has been devoted to the competencies appropriate for successful performance in our field. ASTD has sponsored, in all, six previous competency studies of the field (see sidebars for brief descriptions of each):

- A *Study of Professional Training and Development Roles and Competencies* (Pinto and Walker, 1978)

- *Models for Excellence* (McLagan, 1983)
- *Models for HRD Practice* (McLagan, 1989)
- *ASTD Models for Human Performance Improvement* (Rothwell, 1996, 2000)
- *ASTD Models for Learning Technologies* (Piskurich and Sanders, 1998)
- *ASTD Models for Workplace Learning and Performance* (Rothwell, Sanders, and Soper, 1999).

The most recent study, *ASTD Competency Study: Mapping the Future*, was released in 2004 and is the basis for this chapter. It is the most comprehensive of the efforts to date, involving more than 2,000 practitioners and experts across multiple disciplines around the world. It was considered pivotal not only because it is flexible enough to reflect our ever-changing profession, but because it was designed to serve as a foundation on which a certification process could be built.

1978: A Study of Professional Training and Development Roles and Competencies

A Study of Professional Training and Development Roles and Competencies was the first empirical study of the training and development field sponsored by ASTD in 1978. The project was led by Patrick Pinto and James Walker. Based on the results of a survey of 3,000 training and development professionals, it identified and categorized 14 major training and development activities:

- Analyzing and diagnosing needs
- Determining appropriate training approaches
- Designing and developing programs
- Developing material resources
- Managing internal resources
- Managing external resources
- Developing and counseling individuals
- Preparing job- or performance-related training
- Conducting classroom training
- Developing groups and organizations
- Conducting research on training
- Managing working relationships with managers and clients
- Managing the training and development function
- Managing professional self-development.

The study linked 104 related, minor activities to these 14 major activities.

The New Competency Model: An Overview

A visual representation of the 2004 ASTD competency model is shown in Figure 46-1. Some quick highlights:

- The model was purposely designed to cover a wide range of roles typically held by WLP professionals.
- The competencies in the model are largely unique to our profession. No other profession can claim this model as representative of their roles.
- The value of the model is in the details of the report *ASTD Competency Model: Mapping the Future*, which contains extensive descriptions of each competency beyond the scope of this chapter (Bernthal et al., 2004).

1983: Models for Excellence

Models for Excellence, the second ASTD-sponsored competency study, was published in 1983. The project was led by Patricia McLagan. It identified 15 key roles or functions. Also identified were 31 competency or knowledge areas and 102 work outputs (results) of the application of the competencies. The training and development roles identified in the study were

- Evaluator
- Group facilitator
- Individual development counselor
- Instructional writer
- Instructor
- Manager of training and development
- Marketer
- Media specialist
- Needs analyst
- Program administrator
- Program designer
- Strategist
- Task analyst
- Theoretician
- Transfer agent.

Competencies identified in the study included adult learning understanding, audiovisual skill, career development knowledge, competency identification skill, computer competence, cost-benefit analysis skill, counseling skill, data reduction skill, delegation skill, facilities skill, feedback skill, futuring skill, group process skill, industry understanding, intellectual versatility, library skills, model building skill, negotiation skill, objectives preparation skill, organization behavior understanding, organization understanding, performance observation skill, personnel and human resource field understanding, presentation skills, questioning skill, records management skill, relationship versatility, research skills, training and development field understanding, training and development techniques understanding, and writing skills.

Figure 46-1. 2004 ASTD Competency Model

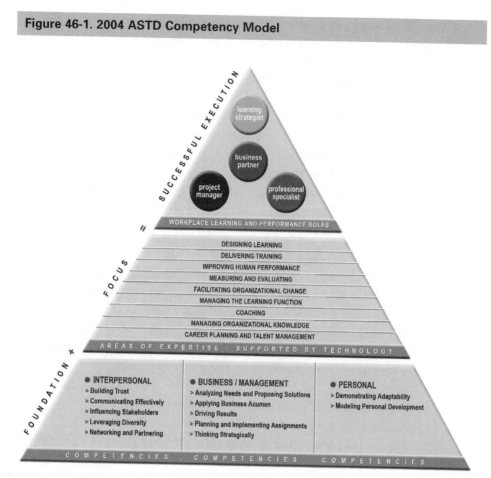

Source: Bernthal et al. (2004).

The new competency model includes three layers: foundational competencies, areas of professional expertise, and roles.

Foundational Competencies

Foundational competencies are linked to successful performance in the WLP field. Those competencies are desirable regardless of an individual's area of expertise or role. The model divides the foundational competencies into three clusters: interpersonal, business and management, and personal.

Interpersonal competencies. The first cluster focuses on the human touch and includes

- **Building trust**—interacting with others in a way that gives them confidence in one's intentions and those of the organization.

- **Communicating effectively**—expressing thoughts, feelings, and ideas in a clear, concise, and compelling manner in both individual and group situations; listening to others; adjusting style to capture the attention of the audience.
- **Influencing stakeholders**—gaining commitment to solutions that will improve individual, team, and organizational performance.
- **Leveraging diversity**—appreciating and leveraging the capabilities, insights, and ideas of all individuals; working effectively with individuals with diverse styles, abilities, and motivations.
- **Networking and partnering**—developing and using a network of collaborative relationships with internal and external contacts to leverage WLP strategies.

Business and management competencies. The second cluster focuses on using good business judgment and skills and includes

- **Analyzing needs and proposing solutions**—identifying and understanding business issues and client needs, problems, and opportunities; taking action that is consistent with available facts, constraints, and consequences.
- **Applying business acumen**—understanding the organization's business model and financial goals; using economic, financial, and organizational data to build and document the business case for investing in WLP solutions.
- **Driving results**—identifying opportunities for improvement and setting well-defined goals related to learning and performance solutions; orchestrating efforts and measuring progress.
- **Planning and implementing assignments**—developing action plans, obtaining resources, and completing assignments in a timely manner.
- **Thinking strategically**—understanding internal and external factors that affect learning and performance in organizations; keeping abreast of trends and anticipating opportunities to add value to the business.

1989: Models for HRD Practice

Models for HRD Practice focused on human resource development (HRD) and thus provided a broader focus than earlier competency studies of the field (McLagan, 1989). HRD integrated training and development, organization development, and career development to improve individual, group, and organizational effectiveness. The study results relied on more than 800 experts in the HRD field. The results were published in multiple volumes.

HRD was placed in the larger context of human resources, because other human resource areas were likely to influence and, in turn, be influenced by HRD efforts. *Models for HRD Practice* listed 11 HRD roles, 35 competencies, and 74 work outputs.

1996: ASTD Models for Human Performance Improvement

ASTD Models for Human Performance Improvement, released in 1996 and again in 2000, was a research-based study of the human performance improvement (HPI) process (Rothwell, 1996, 2000).

The study defined HPI as a systematic process of discovering, analyzing, closing, and evaluating important gaps in human performance. HPI does not favor a single solution to a performance problem—such as training, organization development, or career development—but emphasized finding the root causes of human performance problems before pinpointing appropriate ways to close the gaps by addressing the root causes. *ASTD Models for Human Performance Improvement* also listed 38 competencies and 95 terminal and enabling outputs linked to the work of HPI practitioners.

Personal competencies. The third cluster focuses on personal growth and includes

- **Demonstrating adaptability**—maintaining effectiveness when experiencing major changes in work tasks, the work environment, or conditions affecting the organization; remaining open to new people, thoughts, and approaches.
- **Modeling personal development**—actively identifying new areas for one's own personal learning; regularly creating and taking advantage of learning opportunities.

Areas of Expertise

In the second tier of the pyramid are the areas of expertise. AOEs are the specific technical and professional skills and knowledge areas required for success in the WLP field. The nine AOEs described in the model are specialized areas that build and rely upon the focused application of the foundational competencies. Thus, they are located in the middle tier of the overall model.

- **Career planning and talent management**—ensuring that employees have the right skills to meet the strategic challenges of the organization; ensuring alignment of individual career planning and organization talent management processes to achieve an optimal match between individual and organizational needs.

1998: ASTD Models for Learning Technologies

ASTD Models for Learning Technologies examined how changing technology affected the roles of HRD professionals (Piskurich and Sanders, 1998). Its focus was thus narrower than its predecessors. It examined only how traditional HRD roles, competencies, and outputs are influenced by new, emerging, and cutting-edge technologies for instruction.

- **Coaching**—using an interactive process to help individuals and organizations develop more rapidly and produce more satisfying results.
- **Delivering training**—delivering learning solutions in a manner that both engages the learner and produces desired outcomes.
- **Designing learning**—designing, creating, and developing learning solutions to meet needs; analyzing and selecting the most appropriate strategy, methodologies, and technologies to maximize the learning experience and effect.
- **Facilitating organizational change**—leading, managing, and facilitating change within organizations.
- **Improving human performance**—applying a systematic process of discovering and analyzing human performance gaps; planning for future improvements in human performance; designing and developing cost-effective and ethically justifiable solutions to close performance gaps.
- **Managing organizational knowledge**—serving as a catalyst and visionary for knowledge sharing; developing and championing a plan for transforming the organization into a knowledge-creating and -sharing entity.
- **Managing the learning function**—providing leadership in developing human capital to execute the organization's strategy; planning, organizing, monitoring, and adjusting activities associated with the administration of workplace learning and performance.
- **Measuring and evaluating**—gathering data to answer specific questions regarding the value or impact of learning and performance solutions; leveraging findings to increase effectiveness and provide recommendations for change.

1999: ASTD Models for Workplace Learning and Performance

ASTD Models for Workplace Learning and Performance examined the roles, competencies, and work outputs of WLP professionals (Rothwell, Sanders, and Soper, 1999). WLP became the new name for the field formerly called training, HRD, and performance improvement. *ASTD Models for Workplace Learning and Performance* lists seven roles of WLP professionals:

- Manager
- Analyst
- Intervention selector
- Intervention designer and developer
- Intervention implementer
- Change leader
- Evaluator.

It also lists 52 competencies for WLP professionals.

Roles

Roles are broad areas of responsibility within WLP that require a select combination of competencies and AOEs to perform effectively. The four roles sit at the top of Figure 46-1. Roles are not the same as job titles; they are much more fluid depending on the work or project. For the WLP professional, playing different roles is analogous to maintaining a collection of hats: when the situation calls for it, the practitioner takes off one hat and dons another.

- **Learning strategist**—determines how WLP improvement can best be leveraged to achieve long-term business success and add value to meet organizational needs; leads in the planning and implementation of learning and performance improvement strategies that support the organization's strategic direction and that are based on an analysis of the effectiveness of existing learning and performance improvement strategies.
- **Business partner**—applies business and industry knowledge to partner with the client in identifying workplace performance improvement opportunities; evaluates possible solutions and recommends solutions that will have a positive effect on performance; gains client agreement and commitment to the proposed solutions and collaboratively develops an overall implementation strategy that includes evaluating the effect on business performance improvement strategies.
- **Project manager**—plans, resources, and monitors the effective delivery of learning and performance solutions in a way that supports the overall business venture; communicates purpose, ensures effective execution of an implementation plan, removes barriers, ensures adequate support, and follows up.
- **Professional specialist**—designs, develops, delivers, or evaluates learning and performance solutions. Maintains and applies an in-depth working knowledge in any one or more of the WLP specialty areas of expertise, including career planning and talent management, coaching, delivering training, designing learning, facilitating organizational change, improving human performance, managing organizational knowledge, managing the learning function, and measuring and evaluating.

Analyzing the Model: Key to Success

As WLP professionals, we, more than anyone, can point to dozens of carefully constructed competency models that we ask others in our organizations to use. The benefit of any competency model lays not in a pretty picture or debating if it is 95 or 100 percent accurate, but in its use. In fact, if you closely examine the previous competency studies described in this chapter, more has remained the same than has changed. There are two general categories of model application: the individual and the organization. Let's start with the former, using the model to guide your own professional development.

Individual Application

The ASTD competency model describes what it takes for you, as an individual contributor and as a WLP professional, to achieve career success. It is a foundation on which you can build career plans and develop yourself in your chosen path.

The model provides the means to create a common language that you can use to discuss what it is your organization needs from workplace learning and performance. It also answers this question: what competencies should individuals possess to be successful in the field? It provides a clear picture of success so you can compare your performance against a set of valid descriptors.

You may, however, begin with some reflection on what it will take for you to be successful in the field and in your organization in the future. A good strategy for you to follow is to think about yourself in relation to the competencies outlined in the study and answer the following questions:

- Which competencies are likely to be most important in my current job?
- Which competencies will become more important in the future?
- How do I stack up against the competencies in terms of my performance?

There are many ways to carry out that assessment process, informally or formally. An informal method uses competencies as a foundation to prompt self-reflection and guide career conversations with your mentors or supervisors. A more formal method relies on such organized approaches to assessing individual competencies as 360-degree assessments, assessment centers, and work samples. The results of such assessments will indicate which strengths you should be leveraging and areas in which you need further professional development.

Once identified, strengths and development needs can be documented and used to form the basis of your own individual development plan. A well-prepared IDP can help you leverage your strengths and focus your developmental priorities. The plan can also facilitate accountability by clarifying what learning strategies you will use, when you will learn, what support you will need, and how your results can be measured. Your development needs can be met through many learning approaches, including training, education, rotational experience, mentoring, coaching, organized work assignments, e-learning experiences, and many other learning-oriented solutions.

Individuals may also use a competency model as a foundation for documenting their own accomplishments. Increasingly, employers want to see evidence of achievement, such as work samples, and not just evidence of education or experience. To that end, a competency model provides a basis for organizing resumés, focusing discussions about past experience, and assembling relevant work samples.

The model can also be used as the basis for professional certification. Formal certification as a WLP professional can help fuel personal development and career growth, as well as enhance the image of the profession. In 2006, the ASTD Certification Institute launched its formal process for certification in our field, which is summarized in the accompanying sidebar.

In summary, a strong assessment and development process based on the new competencies can be used across a variety of professional scenarios. It can be valuable for those who are preparing to enter this occupation, those who are making the transition from another occupation into this one, those who wish to advance professionally, and those who just want to build their competencies to preserve their current status in light of dynamically changing conditions.

Answering the following questions will give you a head start in using the competencies to drive your professional success:

- What are your career goals over the short term (one to two years) and long term (three to five years)?
- What competencies are already your strengths? How do you know?
- What competencies do you need to possess for future success in your current job and in your current organization? How do you know that they are important?
- What competencies will you need to acquire or build to achieve your short-term (one- to two-year) career goals? What competencies will you need to acquire or

---

ASTD Professional Certification

ASTD relied on data from the 2004 competency study to help shape the Certified Professional in Learning and Performance (CPLP) certification program. Nearly 2,000 professionals provided a profile of what it meant to be successful in their organizations and in the WLP field. Unlike years past, the WLP professionals were called upon to perform a wide range of roles that extended beyond classroom training and instructional design. They needed to be performance consultants, coaches, and talent managers and have numerous other skills under their belts. Additionally, both employers and practitioners indicated that it was not enough to have knowledge alone. To be a true professional, individuals needed to be able to apply that knowledge and demonstrate their skills.

As a result, the CPLP certification program was designed to be broad-based and included two exams. The first exam tests knowledge and covers all nine areas of expertise. The nine areas are weighted differently, based on the relative importance ratings for each area. The second exam is known as the work product submission and requires a demonstration of skill by submitting a sample of project work and responding to essay questions. The individual must pass both exams to become CPLP certified.

---

build to achieve your long-term (three- to five-year) career goals? How do you know they are important?

- How can you build these competencies?
- How can you measure your progress in building your competencies?
- What mentors or career sponsors might be helpful to you in your quest to build your competencies in WLP?

Organizational Applications

As we know, competency models can serve as an integrative framework for an organization's entire talent system to ensure harmony and consistency across the many facets of human resource activities that affect human performance.

Figure 46-2 shows how various talent systems (for example, selection, promotion, training and development, career planning, succession planning, and performance management) can be aligned around competencies.

Figure 46-2. Alignment of Competencies and Human Resource Functions

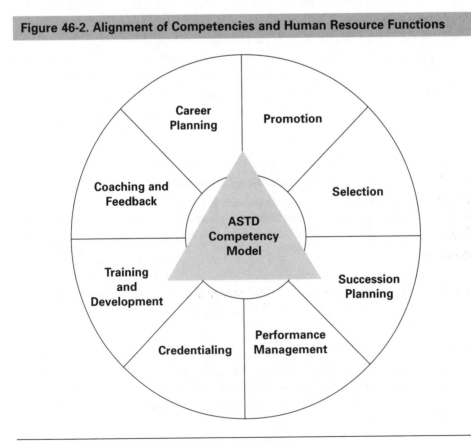

Here are some ways an organization can use the new model, properly adapted to its unique corporate culture, to enhance the effectiveness of its WLP professionals.

Plan for future talent requirements. Start by using the model to determine which roles, areas of expertise, and competencies are likely to be the most critical for the organization three to five years out. By comparing the collective capabilities of your current WLP team against the competencies in the model, your organization can pinpoint the overall strengths and gaps. You can then plan to fill the gaps through professional development or future hiring or promotion decisions as needed.

Identify (or clarify) work expectations. Both the competencies and areas of expertise can be used as the basis for job descriptions and setting behavioral expectations as part of a sound performance management process. The most effective performance management process uses both quantitative goals (addresses "what") and behavioral competencies (addresses "how").

Provide a common language for discussing individual performance and providing feedback on that performance. The model can be useful for coaching WLP professionals on a day-to-day basis and assessing their performance as part of a formal mid-year and year-end appraisal process. Behavioral data around each of the competencies can, and should, be collected on an ongoing basis to enhance the specificity and effectiveness of feedback.

Recruit and select new talent. The competencies and AOEs can provide the basis of a selection or promotion system. Up front, they can be used to calibrate candidate expectations by providing a "realistic preview" of what skills are required for success. The competencies can then be used as a basis for generating interview guides, testing and assessment tools, and as the criteria for final hiring or promotion decisions in organizations.

Pinpoint professional development and career growth needs. Training and development experiences should target the skills, knowledge, and abilities required for successful job performance. The competencies can be used as the basic content for individual and group "needs analysis," enabling organizations to target appropriate solutions to individual or team needs. In addition, the model can be helpful as a career development tool, expanding the depth and breadth of your WLP capabilities. The areas of expertise and roles components of the model can be particularly useful in deciding on stretch assignments and projects.

Calibrate expectations of your clients. A unique use of the model would be to provide a rich source of information for those who use WLP services but are unclear about what to really expect in an engagement. It can not only "educate" clients but also become the foundation on which to establish mutual expectations—and to determine our value.

The Future

As WLP professionals we have an obligation to our profession and our organizations to *practice what we preach!* The 2004 ASTD competency model gives us an opportunity to do just that. By using the model to its fullest extent in the months and years to come, we not only grow as professionals and provide more value to our organizations and clients, but we serve as models demonstrating how competencies can be used effectively.

At the risk of being trite, we live in a world of accelerated change. These changes will affect not only our organizations, but also our profession. The model is not meant to be static, but dynamic: like just about everything else, it will change and morph over time. In fact, at ASTD's 2007 International Conference, further research discussions were taking place to determine if and how the model may need to be "tweaked"—just 36 months after its initial release.

In the meantime, no time is better than right now. At no period in our history has the quality of talent meant more to the success of organizations. Furthermore, at no time in the history of our profession have we been poised to make immeasurable and personally satisfying contributions to the organizations we work with—and more important, to the lives of the millions of people who benefit from the roles we play.

About the Authors

Richard S. Wellins is a senior vice president with Development Dimensions International (DDI), a global human resource consulting firm in Pittsburgh, Pennsylvania. He is the author of four books and more than 20 articles on teams, leadership, and competency-based assessment. He served as the overall project sponsor for the *ASTD 2004 Competency Study: Mapping the Future.*

William J. Rothwell is professor in charge of workforce education and development in the department of Learning and Performance Systems on the University Park campus of the Pennsylvania State University, where he leads a graduate specialization in workplace learning and performance. He is also president of Rothwell and Associates (see www.rothwell-associates.com), specializing in train-the-trainer services.

References

Bernthal, Paul R., Karen Colteryahn, Patty Davis, Jennifer Naughton, William J. Rothwell, and Rich Wellins. 2004. *ASTD 2004 competency study: Mapping the future.* Alexandria, VA: ASTD Press.

McLagan, Patricia A. 1983. *Models for excellence.* Alexandria, VA: ASTD.

McLagan, Patricia A. 1989. *Models for HRD practice.* 4 vols. Alexandria, VA: ASTD.

Pinto, Patrick, and James Walker. 1978. *A study of professional training and development roles and competencies.* Madison, WI: ASTD.

Piskurich, George M., and Ethan S. Sanders. 1998. *ASTD models for learning technologies: Roles, competencies, and outputs.* Alexandria, VA: ASTD.

Rothwell, William J. 1996. *ASTD models for human performance improvement.* Alexandria, VA: ASTD.

Rothwell, William J., ed. 2000. *ASTD models for human performance.* 2d ed. Alexandria, VA: ASTD Press.

Rothwell, William J., Ethan S. Sanders, and Jeffery G. Soper. 1999. *ASTD models for workplace learning and performance: Roles, competencies, and outputs.* Alexandria, VA: ASTD Press.

For Further Reading

Competency Modeling—General

Brown, Tim. 2006. Stop competency blunders. *T+D* 60(1): 20, 22.

Dubois, David. 1993. *Competency-based performance improvement: A strategy for organizational change.* Amherst, MA: HRD Press.

Dubois, David, ed. 1998. *The competency casebook.* Amherst, MA: HRD Press.

Dubois, David, and William J. Rothwell. 2000. *The competency toolkit.* Amherst, MA: HRD Press.

Dubois, David, and William J. Rothwell. 2004. Competency-based or a traditional approach to training? *T+D* 58(4): 46-57.

Dubois, David, and William J. Rothwell. 2004. *Competency-based human resource management.* Palo Alto, CA: Davies-Black.

Green, Paul. 1998. *Building robust competencies: Linking human resource systems to organizational strategies.* San Francisco: Jossey-Bass.

Langdon, Danny, and Kathleen Whiteside. 2004. Bringing sense to competency definition and attainment. *Performance Improvement* 43(7): 10-15.

Lucia, Antoinette, and Richard Lepsinger. 1999. *The art and science of competency models: Pinpointing critical success factors in organizations.* San Francisco: Pfeiffer.

Spencer, Lyle, and Signe Spencer. 1993. *Competence at work: Models for superior performance.* New York: John Wiley & Sons.

Thompsen, J. 2006. Aligning content strategies with workforce competencies. *Chief Learning Officer* 5(54): 58.

Certification

ASTD Press. 2006. *The ASTD learning system.* Alexandria, VA.

Davenport, Rex. 2006. Credentialing: It matters to you; it matters to the profession. *T+D* 60(5): 60-61.

Dolezalek, Holly. 2004. Certifiably trained. *Training* 41(7): 22-28.

Hale, Judith. 1999. *Performance-based certification: How to design a valid, defensible, and cost effective program.* San Francisco: Pfeiffer.

Laff, Michael. 2007. The certified coach: A brand you should be able to trust. *T+D* 61(4): 38-41.

Mulkey, Jamie, and Jennifer Naughton. 2005. Dispelling the myths of certification. *T+D* 59(1): 20-26.

Salopek, Jennifer. 2006. Certification: A new industry trend. *T+D* 60(2): 24-25.

Weinstein, Margery. 2007. Business driven. *Training* 44(2): 40, 42, 44, 46.

White, Alicia. 2002. Building an internal certification program. *Infoline* No. 250203. Alexandria, VA: ASTD Press.

 **Chapter 47**

Careers in Workplace Learning and Performance

William J. Rothwell

In This Chapter

- ➤ Learn to plan your career in workplace learning and performance

- ➤ Investigate a wide selection of career moves

Workplace learning and performance (WLP) professionals help other people to develop their potential. But it is reasonable to expect that those who perform WLP work should be able to recognize and develop their own potential and improve their own performance. Unfortunately, however, that is not always the case. Sometimes the development of learning and performance staff members is forgotten amid efforts focused on developing others. This chapter describes one way to conceptualize career development for WLP professionals. It offers guidance on career planning in WLP. If WLP practitioners cannot manage their own careers, then it seems that they lose moral authority to advise others on how to do so.

Career planning is a process, and it is a subset of the larger issue of life planning. It is not a sequence of random job movements, driven by capricious, short-term efforts to bid up wages or by accident alone. Prudent practitioners do not jump from one opportunity to another with little regard to how these opportunities might affect them professionally.

Savvy WLP practitioners investigate careers in WLP, clarify career goals and objectives based on advice and careful reflection, assess individual strengths and weaknesses, prepare a career plan that lays out a path to follow, and implement the plan but modify it over time based on experience.

Investigating Careers in WLP

Investigate careers in WLP by gathering information from as many good sources as possible. Bring an open mind to that investigation. It is, in fact, difficult to investigate anything without knowing the facts and hearing the perceptions of other people with more experience. Explore opportunities in the field by surfing the web for information, reading books about the field, and talking to experienced practitioners as well as those who have just a little more experience than you have. Attend chapter meetings of relevant associations such as ASTD and set out to gain experience through planned internships or through unpaid volunteer work. Finally, draw conclusions from your investigations—and discuss them with others—so you will have a realistic assessment about what it takes to enter the WLP field, progress successfully in it, and (if necessary) move out of it.

Surprisingly little information is available in any one place about careers in the field. It will take some persistence to find out what you want to know. One place to start is on the ASTD website (www.astd.org), which contains some information about careers and educational opportunities in the field.

WLP Titles and Roles

Although WLP is different from human resource (HR) work, many WLP departments are organizationally positioned within HR departments. It is worth examining what is known about HR to gain perspective on WLP. Consider what the U.S. government indicates in *The Occupational Outlook Handbook* (Bureau of Labor Statistics, U.S. Department of Labor, 2007):

- Attracting the most qualified employees and matching them to the jobs for which they are best suited is significant for the success of any organization. However, many enterprises are too large to permit close contact between top management and employees. Human resources, training, and labor relations managers and specialists provide this connection.
- *Training and development managers and specialists* conduct and supervise training and development programs for employees.
- *Training managers* provide worker training either in the classroom or onsite. This includes setting up teaching materials prior to the class, involving the

class, and issuing completion certificates at the end of the class. They have the responsibility for the entire learning process and its environment to ensure that the course meets its objectives and is measured and evaluated to understand how learning affects business results.

- *Training specialists* plan, organize, and direct a wide range of training activities.
- *Trainers* respond to corporate and worker service requests. They consult with onsite supervisors regarding available performance improvement services and conduct orientation sessions and arrange on-the-job training for new employees. They help all employees maintain and improve their job skills and possibly prepare for jobs requiring greater skill. They help supervisors improve their interpersonal skills to deal effectively with employees. They may set up individualized training plans to strengthen an employee's existing skills or teach new ones.
- *Training specialists* in some companies set up leadership or executive development programs. These programs are designed to develop leaders to replace those leaving the organization and as part of a succession plan. Trainers also lead programs to assist employees with job transitions as a result of mergers and acquisitions, as well as technological changes. In government-supported training programs, training specialists function as case managers. They first assess the training needs of clients and then guide them through the most appropriate training method. After training, clients may either be referred to employer relations representatives or receive job placement assistance.

Education, Occupational Specialties, and Salaries

According to the U.S. government (Bureau of Labor Statistics, U.S. Department of Labor, 2007), the educational backgrounds of human resources, training, and labor relations managers and specialists vary considerably because of the diversity of duties and levels of responsibility. In filling entry-level jobs, many employers seek college graduates who have majored in human resources, human resources administration, or industrial and labor relations. Other employers look for college graduates with a technical or business background or a well-rounded liberal arts education.

Many colleges and universities have programs leading to a degree in personnel, human resources, or labor relations. Some offer degree programs in human resources administration or human resources management, training and development, or compensation and benefits. Depending on the school, courses leading to a career in human resources management may be found in departments of business administration, education, instructional technology, organizational development, human services, communication, or public administration, or within a separate human resources institution or department.

Human resources, training, and labor relations managers and specialists held about 820,000 jobs in 2004. Table 47-1 shows the distribution of jobs by occupational specialty.

Human resources, training, and labor relations managers and specialists were employed in practically every industry. About 21,000 specialists were self-employed, working as consultants to public and private employers. The private sector accounted for more than eight out of 10 salaried jobs, including

- 11 percent in administrative and support services
- 9 percent in professional, scientific, and technical services
- 9 percent in manufacturing
- 9 percent in health care and social assistance
- 9 percent in finance and insurance firms.

The U.S. government employed 17 percent of human resources managers and specialists. They handled the recruitment, interviewing, job classification, training, salary administration, benefits, employee relations, and other matters related to U.S. government employees.

The abundant supply of qualified college graduates and experienced workers should create keen competition for jobs. Overall employment of human resources, training, and labor relations managers and specialists is expected to grow faster than the average for all occupations through 2014. In addition to openings due to growth, many job openings will arise from the need to replace workers who transfer to other occupations or leave the labor force.

Table 47-1. Distribution of Jobs by Occupational Specialty

Occupational Specialty	Number of People
Training and development specialists	216,000
Employment, recruitment, and placement specialists	182,000
Human resources, training, and labor relations specialists, all other	166,000
Human resources managers	157,000
Compensation, benefits, and job analysis specialists	99,000
TOTAL	820,000

Source: Bureau of Labor Statistics, U.S. Department of Labor (2007).

Annual salary rates for human resources workers vary according to occupation, level of experience, training, location, and size of the firm, and whether they are union members (Bureau of Labor Statistics, U.S. Department of Labor, 2007). Median annual earnings of training and development specialists were $44,570 in May 2004. The middle 50 percent earned between $33,530 and $58,750. The lowest 10 percent earned less than $25,800, and the highest 10 percent earned more than $74,650. Table 47-2 lists the median annual earnings in the industries employing the largest numbers of training and development specialists for May 2004.

Finding a WLP Job

Think about the information presented above. Remember that the U.S. government groups WLP professionals with human resource professionals. There is an overlap, but WLP work focuses primarily on learning-oriented efforts to improve human performance. There is no one entry-level job into the WLP field; rather, there are many possible ports of entry.

Another way to explore career opportunities in WLP or related fields is to surf employment-related websites, read local newspapers, and find and examine WLP-related professional journals with care. Watch advertisements for positions in WLP over the course of several months. The job titles may vary, so it will be necessary to focus on descriptions of work duties. Common job titles listed may include trainers, staff development specialists, personnel trainers, job career counselors, employee development specialists, management development specialists, and organization development specialists. Note carefully the job requirements and, for the sake of future job hunting, also note the employers listing these openings. It is a good bet that an employer listing one WLP opening may also have others. Those employers may thus be good prospects to approach for other positions in WLP—or, at least for information about future prospects in the field.

Table 47-2. Median Annual Earnings of WLP Professionals

Management of companies and enterprises	$49,540
Insurance carriers	47,300
Local government	45,320
State government	41,770
Federal government	38,930

Source: Bureau of Labor Statistics, U.S. Department of Labor (2007).

In addition, explore career opportunities in the WLP field by subscribing to journals related to human resources management or WLP. If nothing else, go to the library to review them occasionally and skim such websites as www.astd.org, www.shrm.org, www.ispi.org, and www.ahrd.org. If you are seriously interested in a career in WLP, read these sites to gather career information about the field. Note also the names and website addresses of any specialized placement firms in WLP or human resources. It will be useful to keep track of this information if you ever plan to do a job search for a WLP position.

A third way you can explore career opportunities in WLP is by talking to people who are presently working in the field. Find them by contacting large local employers or attending meetings of a local chapter of ASTD or other professional associations. Once you have identified a few WLP professionals, call them or arrange to meet them. Plan to ask them some questions to help you in exploring opportunities in the WLP field. Here are a few:

- How did you first enter the field?
- How did you prepare yourself to enter the field?
- What did you do before you worked in WLP?
- What do you *like most* about working in WLP? Why?
- What do you *like least* about working in WLP? Why?
- What knowledge, skills, or previous experience would be helpful in your job that you do not presently possess?
- How could such knowledge, skills, or experience be acquired?
- What colleagues of yours would be particularly good for me to talk to about a career in WLP?
- What college courses, short seminars, or other learning experiences would be especially helpful to acquire the skills necessary to get a WLP job—or increase the chances of success after locating such a job?
- What books or references would you specifically recommend to someone interested in a WLP career?
- In what direction do you see your career headed? Why?
- Where do you feel the WLP field is headed, and what could potential job seekers do to prepare to take advantage of those opportunities?

If possible, meet several experienced WLP professionals with different job titles, working in different organizations and industries. Cultivate a network of these contacts over time. Meet them at local chapter meetings of ASTD, the International Society for Performance Improvement (ISPI), or the Society for Human Resource Management (SHRM).

Clarifying Career Goals and Objectives

Clarify career goals and objectives based on advice and on your own careful reflection. Reflect on your personal values and career or job preferences. Consider carefully what you really want—because you might just get it! Be sure to include realistic assessments about what you want to do, what you are best at doing, how you work best (alone or in groups), where you want to live, how you want to interact with others (virtually or inter-personally), and other such issues.

Assessing Individual Strengths and Weaknesses

A *career strength* contributes to realization of a career goal or preference; a *career weakness* impedes that realization. What do you do best? In what areas do you need improvement? Consider your answers carefully—and ask others who know you well to give you their thoughts, too.

One choice is to leverage your strengths. If you are good at teaching others, then consider training delivery. If you are good at writing, then consider work as an instructional designer. If you are good with computers, consider developing online instruction.

Focus particularly on your own vision of what an ideal job and an ideal career would be. What do you most want out of life and out of your career? Brainstorm the answer to that question carefully. How well prepared are you at this time to be hired for your dream job? How do you know how well prepared you are?

To help you assess your career strengths and weaknesses to identify areas for your future development, consider how well you are equipped to demonstrate the competencies associated with WLP work. Review the *ASTD Competency Study: Mapping the Future* (Bernthal et al., 2004) carefully to see how you rate compared with the full range of competencies essential for success in the field. Then draw your own conclusions by taking inventory of your career strengths and weaknesses.

Preparing a Career Plan

Develop a career plan in the form of an individual development plan (IDP) that sets forth career goals and objectives, ways to achieve them, milestones for achievement, and ways of evaluating success. Be sure to clarify exactly what competencies you need to acquire, strengthen, or otherwise develop and how you will do so. At best, an individual career plan should be a joint undertaking of individuals and their immediate supervisors.

Implementing and Modifying the Plan

To implement the individual career plan, take action to develop yourself. Seek work experiences, mentors, and places where you can build your competencies in line with your goals. Reflect on your milestones periodically and be willing to modify your expectations, time lines, or experiences based on your own reflections or on advice you receive from trustworthy mentors.

Choosing Your Career Path

Numerous career paths exist in WLP. To some extent they depend on how much education you have, because some opportunities—such as college teaching in WLP—will be available only with certain levels of education. But conceivably your career path could include any of the following, discussed in detail below.

Increasing the Scope of Your Present Job

One potential career move is to expand the range of competencies you use on the job. For example, you may opt for another WLP role or add competencies to what you already do. This choice is useful if you are feeling stale on the job and want to become revitalized. Of course, you may need to seek additional education and training to acquire needed competencies. In most cases, your supervisor must consent to, if not actually encourage, such development.

Decreasing the Scope of Your Present Job

Another potential career move is to reduce the scope but increase the depth of your present duties. For example, you may give up one or more roles but improve your facility with those you keep. This career choice is appropriate if the department is expanding (more people often means greater specialization), or if you are intensely interested in just one or two roles and their corresponding competencies.

Seeking Promotion in WLP

A traditional career aspiration is to move up the chain of command. Many WLP professionals begin as instructors or instructional designers or writers. In a large WLP department, the next step up is to supervisor of instructors in areas like professional, technical, or managerial training or as a unit chief responsible for media, instructional design, or evaluation. The final move is to manager of a WLP or training department. Variations in these career paths may depend on the nature of the industry or size of the organization.

Moving to a Larger Organization

Many WLP professionals begin in somewhat small organizations—including smaller banks, hospitals, government agencies, or manufacturing plants. As their competence increases, they may feel they are stagnating. One career move is to remain in the same industry but shift to a larger organization.

Moving to a Smaller Organization

Movement up the traditional chain of command is not always easy. People at the top tend to remain in their jobs longer than those at the middle or bottom—thus restricting the upward mobility of qualified people as they gain competence. This problem is expected to worsen in the United States, because the number of people in age groups customarily associated with middle and upper management jobs will increase as never before. Unfortunately, a corresponding increase in middle and upper-level jobs is not likely. In fact, just the reverse is true—organizations are reducing such jobs to improve communication and slash salary costs.

One alternative to traditional upward career movement is to shift from a larger to a smaller organization. The individual is usually "promoted" in the sense that the change often means a more impressive job title. For example, a technical trainer-instructor with 15 years' experience might be able to move to a smaller organization and be called director of training. In many cases it means changing to the role of generalist, who enacts several roles, rather than being a specialist, who concentrates on only one.

Moving from a Regional Office to Corporate Headquarters

In some organizations, trainers start out in field offices, where they run their own show and do everything in that location. Corporate-level WLP professionals or trainers, in contrast, may produce training materials and deliver specialized instruction—such as executive training. A career move from a regional to a corporate headquarters is a possibility if you want increased specialization.

Moving from Corporate Headquarters to a Regional Office

This is the reverse of the previous career move: a shift from corporate headquarters to a regional office. This change is desirable when you want greater autonomy and wish to become more of a generalist than specialist. It may also be a good idea from the organization's standpoint, because it will create a bridge for communication between corporate and regional offices.

Moving from a Line to Staff WLP Department

Large organizations sometimes maintain specialized WLP operations in line (operating) departments distinct from a more general but larger staff WLP department. For example, some firms split training for computer operators and programmers from training that serves the remainder of the organization. One possible career move is from one of these specialized WLP units, where technical skill is usually highly prized, to a central WLP department where instructional skill is often more important.

Moving from a Staff to Line WLP Department

Some WLP professionals begin in a large, central WLP staff department. There they learn how to design, deliver, and evaluate instruction. When they long for career movement and have specialized skills in some area other than WLP (for example, computer programming, marketing, production), they may want to consider moving into an operating department to head up specialized WLP units.

Moving Out of a Specialized WLP Job to One with Only Some WLP Components

Some jobs contain elements of WLP but are not focused on it in a specialized way. For example, some regional managers in retail focus their efforts on staff development or WLP. Similarly, some sales managers are really sales trainers. Their jobs include WLP but go beyond it in scope and responsibility.

Becoming a Full-Time or Part-Time WLP Consultant

Many people want to become WLP consultants after they have gained some experience in WLP. Clearly, the continuing trend toward organizational outsourcing has made this an appealing option. However, do not assume that you can get rich quick as a consultant—especially if your experience is limited. An advisable approach is to begin working under the mentorship of another consultant who is more seasoned and has already developed a client base. But, if you wish to move into consulting from a full-time WLP job, make sure that you have special expertise that you can market, that you have a network of professional contacts with whom to market your services, and that you have a sufficient war chest of funds to last you during the dry period that typically accompanies a move into consulting. To avoid problems with putting food on the table—and, more important, paying for costly health-care benefits by yourself—some consultants prefer to enter consulting gradually through part-time experience gained on vacation days from their "day jobs."

Moving Out of WLP Completely

Not everyone wants to make a lifelong career of WLP. In the past, few people even thought of WLP as a profession distinct from others. This view is changing but is not widely accepted by all managers or by all organizations.

One possibility is to try out work in WLP for a while. If it is not suitable, then shift to something else that is more to your liking.

Moving into Higher Management

In the past it was rare for personnel or WLP professionals to move up the ladder to higher management. Now, however, more of them are aspiring to such jobs.

A job in WLP tends to have high visibility—especially for classroom instructors and those involved in management training. Indeed, many firms rotate their highest potential talent through a tour of duty in the WLP department for just this reason. Although there is a potential for WLP professionals to move up the management ladder, those who want to do so should supplement their credentials and experience with those appropriate to new and more ambitious goals. Making friends with people who can help may also be important.

Working as a Temp or Contingent Work in WLP

One way to gain experience is to try to do temporary or contingent work in WLP. Ask to work as an intern, a temp, or a contingent worker for those who go on vacation or on leave. That way you can gain experience without the employer requiring too much commitment. But it is one way to gain experience.

Working Internationally

Many of the fastest growing markets in the world are in Asia. Cross-cultural experience is becoming important in a globalized world. Hence, it makes sense to consider spending time abroad. Gain experience there. Often, that is not as difficult as it might seem. In rapidly expanding markets, a little experience and a little education goes a long way.

Becoming a College Professor of WLP

Some WLP professionals think of moving into academia, for example, but teaching opportunities in higher education require research, writing, and publication in addition to mere teaching. Salaries are low—especially if the WLP program is organizationally positioned in a field outside of business. (Many of the best programs are in education.) Although tenure-track jobs in the academic world seem to be on a long-term decline due to cost cutting, they can still be found by those with a PhD, dedication, and sufficient publications to warrant consideration.

Becoming a Community College Training Expert

Community colleges are the chief outsourcing agent for business training in the United States. The money they receive from companies now exceeds the collective budgets of all internal training departments combined. Many opportunities exist as consultants to business through local community colleges. Although wages are not very attractive and turnover of staff can sometimes be high, work in a local business training center is a way to build experience and understanding of the field. Government funding for training often supports these community college–based efforts.

Taking a Leave of Absence from Your Job to Try Out Your Skills as a Full-Time Consultant in WLP

If you want to experiment with career options but hedge your bets with a day job to return to, consider taking a leave of absence from your job and trying it out as a full-time consultant. Although not all employers will permit a leave of absence, some will. Take advantage of it to try it out as a consultant.

Telecommuting or Working from Home

A growing industry exists in work from home. Some individuals make arrangements with their employers to telecommute. Others work full time from home on their own, often as instructional designers who prepare training materials or deliver online instruction. Consider that option if you are raising a family or simply want the convenience of avoiding to dress up for work each day.

Coming up with Your Own, Imaginative Option

The 19 career options listed above are not exhaustive. There are others. Some people create their own luck and their own opportunities by coming up with other options that leverage their own unique strengths.

Final Thoughts on Career Options

The skills of WLP are certainly transferrable to other fields. Instructors can become speakers and salespersons. Instructional writers can become technical writers, editors, or even reporters. Media specialists can use their talents in radio, television, computers, or in libraries. These are just a few examples. Of course, career moves of these kinds may require experience, education, and talents different from the typical skills picked up in WLP work. Additional education might be needed to qualify for such career moves.

Summary

WLP professionals should set a positive example and model the way by developing themselves and by managing their own careers assertively. To do so, WLP practitioners should investigate careers in WLP, clarify career goals and objectives based on advice and careful reflection, assess individual strengths and weaknesses, prepare a career plan that lays out a path to follow, and implement the plan but modify it over time based on experience.

∽

About the Author

William J. Rothwell is professor of workplace learning and performance at Pennsylvania State University. His graduate program is geared to prepare people for opportunities in the field of WLP. He is also president of Rothwell and Associates (www.rothwell-associates.com), a full-service consulting company in WLP. Before beginning his work at Penn State, he worked as a training director in a large insurance company and as a training director in a state government agency. He has authored, co-authored, edited, or co-edited more than 275 books and articles in the WLP field. A frequent speaker, he has visited China 40 times and often speaks on the Asian circuit. He is former director of the ASTD Global Network for China, an international advisor to the ASTD Global Network for Singapore, and has given keynote speeches at conferences on WLP in China, Dubai, Korea, Malaysia, the Philippines, Saudi Arabia, Taiwan, and Thailand.

References

Bernthal, Paul R., Karen Colteryahn, Patty Davis, Jennifer Naughton, William J. Rothwell, and Rich Wellins. 2004. *ASTD competency study: Mapping the future.* Alexandria, VA: ASTD Press.

Bureau of Labor Statistics, U.S. Department of Labor. 2007. Human resources, training, and labor relations managers and specialists. In *Occupational outlook handbook, 2006-07 edition,* available at www.bls.gov/oco/ocos021.htm.

For Further Reading

Gordon, Edward E., Catherine M. Petrini, and Ann P. Campagna. 1996. *Opportunities in training & development careers.* Lincolnwood, IL: VGM Career Books.

Rothwell, William J., and Henry J. Sredl. 2000. *The ASTD reference guide to workplace learning and performance.* 2 vols. Amherst, MA: HRD Press.

Walters, Lilly. 2003. *1,001 ways to make more money as a speaker, consultant or trainer: Plus 300 rainmaking strategies for dry times.* New York: McGraw-Hill.

✀ Chapter 48

Workplace Learning and Performance Certification

Jennifer A. Naughton

In This Chapter

- ➢ Learn about certification
- ➢ Understand what's involved in certification
- ➢ Learn why to get certified

"Why Certification? What's the big deal? It is a big deal."
—Elaine Biech (2005)

CareerJournal.com reports that 78,000 additional employees will enter the field of training and development between 2004 and 2014. With so many professionals entering the field, how can you demonstrate to hiring managers that you are a competent workplace learning and performance professional? What is available to help you to differentiate yourself from other candidates and to help employers in their search for new hires? The answer is certification!

Think about Microsoft's Certified Technology Specialist (MCTS). For years, the technology and software industries have been certifying people as a rite of passage. If a job candidate holds a certain credential, a hiring manager has confidence that the job applicant knows his or her stuff.

Why do such certifications exist? In a word, it's about credibility. When an industry is flooded with people, hiring managers have a supply problem. It becomes more difficult to decide whom to hire in a sea of resumés and applications. Certifications help to ensure that people have the needed expertise to be successful and that they can do what they claim they can do.

How can certification help you? This chapter describes the value and benefits of certification. It introduces the ASTD Certification Institute's certification for the workplace learning and performance field called the Certified Professional in Learning and Performance (CPLP), describes the requirements, and explains its significance to the field of training.

What Is Certification?

Certification is a voluntary process whereby a professional institution, such as an association like ASTD, grants a credential to those individuals who have met certain standards. Certified individuals earn the right to use program initials on their business cards to mark their accomplishment. For instance, a Certified Public Accountant can use the CPA designation after they successfully complete program requirements.

Many people in the training field are very familiar with certificate programs, but less familiar with certification programs. The terms *certificate* and *certification* are often used interchangeably, but they have very different meanings. What's the difference? In general, certificate programs focus on learning and acquiring skills. Certification programs focus on testing and validating skills. Both types of programs issue certificates, but only a certification program requires you to pass a test of some kind. Unfortunately, the lack of agreement and inconsistent application of these two terms really muddies the water when it comes to understanding what is what.

Why a Workplace Learning and Performance Certification Program Now?

ASTD embarked on launching a certification program for the training profession as a result of overwhelming member demand. Ninety percent of the nearly 2,000 academics, practitioners, employers, and leaders in the profession surveyed reported that an ASTD certification would provide much-needed benefits to the field. That was the consensus within ASTD's leadership as well. ASTD's leadership thought that certification would encourage professional development and provide a way for professionals to prove their worth. What's not to like about that?

Another reason ASTD built a certification program for the field is because of the value it brings to the profession itself. To do so, ASTD created the Certification Institute as the entity responsible for managing professional certification. Credentialing benefits the profession by creating standards and raising the bar and, perhaps most notably, by elevating and increasing the recognition of the learning and performance profession altogether.

What's the Value?

There are many ways that certifications can offer value to individuals, employers, and the profession:

- *Individuals.* Individuals seek to become certified because it adds to their credibility. It can also provide them with greater opportunities for employment, promotion, and increased earning potential. It also encourages them to stay current in their field. Sometimes, certification is even preferred for a given job. Table 48-1 provides more of the major certification benefits for candidates and employers.
- *Organizations and employers.* Organizations and employers use certification as a data point when evaluating job and promotion candidates. Organizations want to validate that a workforce is qualified, and certification provides one way of doing this through rigorous testing.
- *The profession.* The profession also benefits from certification. According to the U.S. Department of Labor, there are several criteria that characterize a profession. One criterion is that the profession must have a credentialing body. That's how you know the profession has really arrived.

Practicing professionals in the world of training can relate to why certification is a big deal. It's familiar territory to them. Developing people and ensuring that they can demonstrate the skills needed for success is what professionals in this field do each and every day.

Introducing the CPLP

Let's shift gears and focus on one credential in particular: the Certified Professional in Learning and Performance. The CPLP is a broad-based credential designed by the ASTD Certification Institute exclusively for the workplace learning and performance profession and is based on the ASTD Competency Model.

How is the competency model linked to certification? The answer is pretty simple. The ASTD Competency Model (covered in chapter 46 of this handbook) identifies the skills, knowledge, and specific behaviors needed for success. In broader terms, it identifies what people across the field need to know and do collectively for success.

Table 48-1. Certification Benefits

Candidates	Employers
• Quest for knowledge and personal satisfaction • Sense of achievement and knowledge verification • Desire to challenge oneself • Enhanced self-image • Acceptance by peers and colleagues • Competitive edge when seeking a job • Job promotion • Higher compensation	• Improved quality of products and services • Improved corporate image • Increased competitive advantage • Improved operating efficiency • Increased employee productivity • Increased profitability

Source: Knapp and Knapp (ASAE and the Center for Association Leadership, 2002). *The Business of Certification*. Used with permission.

The model essentially answers the "what to certify" question. The CPLP is based on the nine areas of expertise identified in the model as the specific technical and professional skills and knowledge required for success in workplace learning and performance. Standards are built later to answer the question "how well does one have to perform?" In combination, these drive the test requirements. When the individual passes these requirements, that person obtains the right to use the credential.

CPLP Testing

There are three testing requirements or steps to earning the CPLP, as outlined in Figure 48-1 and Table 48-2.

CPLP Recertification

There is one requirement to staying CPLP certified, detailed in Table 48-3.

Is Certification Right for You?

Understanding your career goals is important before embarking on the certification journey. Just as training is not the solution for everything, neither is the CPLP. What are the career goals that the CPLP can help satisfy? The CPLP is ideal for expanding or proving your skills and qualifications across the broader learning and performance field. It also can help you update or refresh your technical knowledge or give your career a boost.

Which is better: certifications or certificates? A degree or a certification? Determining whether or not to pursue a degree, a certificate, or certification is tricky. The reasons why

Figure 48-1. CPLP Steps

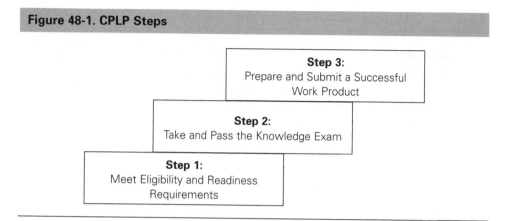

Step 3:
Prepare and Submit a Successful
Work Product

Step 2:
Take and Pass the Knowledge Exam

Step 1:
Meet Eligibility and Readiness
Requirements

individuals seek out one versus another are not always clear, so here are some points to consider:

- **A degree** is typically awarded upon completion of a program that covers general theory associated with a particular field.
- **A certificate** is awarded upon completion of a course or program that focuses on learning and acquiring a somewhat narrow set of skills. Some certificate programs have assessments, and some do not.
- **Certification** focuses on testing and verifying skills. There is usually an eligibility requirement and not everyone passes. There is generally a recertification component to ensure continuous learning.

Table 48-2. CPLP Testing Requirements

Requirement	Description
Experience	Candidates must provide evidence that they have a minimum of three years of related experience or equivalent, but five or more years is preferable.
Knowledge	Candidates must pass the knowledge exam. The knowledge exam has 150 multiple choice questions covering nine areas of expertise as defined by the ASTD Competency Model. The test is computer-based and delivered at a testing center.
Performance	Candidates must pass the work product submission. Candidates are asked to supply a project from their work history that illustrates how they put their knowledge into action. Candidates submit a sample of recent project work and responses to essay questions for a single area of expertise. Not all areas of expertise are available at present. Check with CPLP program representatives for updates.

Table 48-3. CPLP Recertification Requirement

Requirement	Description
Lifelong Learning	CPLP credential holders must satisfy recertification point requirements every three years to maintain their certification status. Points earned must relate to the profession and can be earned in a variety of ways, such as • Workshops • Conferences • Volunteer roles • Leadership roles • Research and publishing

The best choice depends on your goals and objectives, and what your employer needs. Sometimes one or a combination of options is the best solution. Ultimately, the ideal path depends on your given situation as well as the amount of time, energy, and money you have to spend on its pursuit. Use Tool 48-1 on the accompanying CD-ROM to help you assess whether you are ready to seek certification.

How Do You Prepare?

There are myriad ways to prepare for the CPLP certification exams. The method you choose will depend on your time, budget, and learning preferences. Some suggestions include

- **Self-study.** Study alone using your own library or purchased learning resources.
- **Study buddy.** Pair up with others who have different strengths, and you will broaden your areas of expertise. Plus, it can be more fun than studying alone.
- **Group study.** Join a study group to help divide the labor and build esprit de corps. Your local ASTD chapter may be able to guide you toward an existing study group.
- **CPLP Prep Workshops.** ASTD offers two-day workshops that help participants prepare for the exams and the work product submission.

Certification Life Cycle

You may have already guessed by now that certification has a larger significance than just passing a test at a single point in time. It is part of the professional development life cycle. As Elaine Biech explains in *Training for Dummies*,

You begin by assessing and building competencies to become certified. To ensure that you stay current, you develop a lifelong learning strategy.

ASTD's leadership in the training field goes hand in hand with its leadership in developing certification for the broader profession and the continuous learning that's needed to keep skills relevant. In fact, learning is at the core of ASTD's mission and vision. Part of that responsibility includes providing ongoing education and assessment to help keep the profession current.

Failing to keep current can rob an individual of early warning signs that problems may lie ahead. If the demand for some of your skills is starting to increase, you may miss a valuable opportunity to make a course correction.

What are your responsibilities as a member of the profession for keeping current? Keeping your certification status current through renewal indicates that you are up-to-date on industry standards. Lifelong learning and its importance is a popular concept these days. But the real challenge is not just talking about it, but doing it and also serving as a model for others (2005).

For More Information

For more information about ASTD Certification Institute's CPLP program, including testing locations and fees, dates and times, and exam details, go to www.astd.org/content /ASTDcertification.

It's Up To You

In closing, Biech notes that

Your career depends on your continued ability to reinvent yourself and add value. Use both the ASTD Competency Model and professional Certification Program as a means to establish the value connection from where you are to where you want to go. Certification is one of those small steps in your career that can make a huge difference. Achieving certification in your field can be an adventure, and one of those life experiences you should not pass up (2005).

About the Author

Jennifer A. Naughton is director of credentialing for ASTD's Certification Institute. She developed the Certified Professional in Learning and Performance (CPLP) credentialing program after managing the ASTD Competency Study initiative. She has 15 years of human resource consulting expertise that includes testing, designing training, and human resource strategy. Before she came to ASTD, she was an associate at Booz Allen Hamilton and a research scientist for the Human Resources Research Organization (HumRRO). Naughton holds a master's degree in human resource development from George Washington University and is a recognized Senior Professional of Human Resources (SPHR).

Reference

Biech, Elaine. 2005. Trainer certification. In *Training for dummies*. Hoboken, NJ: John Wiley & Sons.

For Further Reading

Bernthal, Paul R., Karen Colteryahn, Patty Davis, Jennifer Naughton, William J. Rothwell, and Rich Wellins. 2004. *ASTD 2004 competency study: Mapping the future*. Alexandria, VA: ASTD Press.

Knapp, Lenora, and Joan Knapp. 2002. *The business of certification: A comprehensive guide to developing a successful program*. Washington, D.C.: ASAE.

Mitchell, Jennifer, ed. 2006. *Navigating the CPLP. A guide to ASTD professional certification*. Alexandria, VA: ASTD.

Mulkey, Jamie, and Jennifer A. Naughton. 2005. Dispelling the myths of certification. *T+D* 58(1): 20-29.

Ethics for Workplace Learning and Performance Professionals

Tora Estep

In This Chapter

> ➤ Learn why ethics matter

> ➤ Understand common components in ethics codes for the profession

> ➤ Discover ways to build effective ethics programs in organizations

---

Ethical people are a pain in the butt. They insist on getting permission to use materials that are not their own, adding money and time to editorial and design processes. They won't provide access to data if they have promised that the data will remain confidential. They blow the whistle if an organization is involved in shady accounting practices. They insist on complying with the law, even if it means the organization may lose employees who are illegal. In short, they can slow or even halt organizational processes and procedures that might be very lucrative or just plain easy.

But being a pain in the butt is a good thing. It's good because you avoid your picture in handcuffs splashed all over the papers—remember Kenneth Lay and Jeffrey Skilling of Enron and Bernard Ebbers of MCI/WorldCom—or billion-dollar writedowns as in more recent media stories regarding major banks and subprime mortgages.

And it's good for more than just avoiding negative consequences: Harned, Seligson, and Baviskar (2005) report that overall employee satisfaction increases by 36 percentage points when people are held accountable for their actions. People are also more likely to report misconduct when they see it. Furthermore, ethical behavior leads to greater profits and business stability. In their 2003 report, *Does Business Ethics Pay?*, Simon Webley and Elise More found that organizations with an accessible ethical code generate more economic-added value and more market-added value than organizations that lack codes. They also found that ethical organizations tend to have a more stable price-earnings ratio, which means they tend to be more secure investments in the long term. Building on this study, Ugoji, Dando, and Moir (2007) found that organizations that apply their ethical codes by providing training to reinforce them do better than organizations that simply have codes that are published but not applied.

Simply put, ethics matter. They matter to organizations, and they matter to workplace learning and performance (WLP) professionals, who have a dual responsibility in this area. Professionals in the WLP field are responsible for their personal ethical behavior as well as for helping the organizations they serve become more ethical. This chapter will discuss both of those dimensions; but first, let's talk a little about what ethics are.

What Are Ethics?

Some confusion exists around the term *ethics* and related terms such as *values, morals,* and *compliance,* in part because the concepts can be very fluid, overlapping, and interconnected. However, this fluidity is not necessarily a negative. It allows the freedom to explore these ideas and continually refine them. It also creates an imperative to revisit these ideas from time to time to ensure that they align with current realities and remain relevant in daily practice. One example of how concepts of values and ethics can evolve is the treatment of women and minorities in the workplace, which has changed over time from being a nonissue to being an issue of compliance with civil rights laws to becoming widely recognized as the right thing to do.

The term *ethics* has several definitions. Johnson (2004) lists several examples:

- The set of core values (whether individual or organizational) used to make decisions and take action
- The study of what is good and right and how people make the decision to do what is good and right
- A set of principles used to make decisions and take action based on core values
- Decisions, behaviors, and choices that reflect personal or organizational values.

For the purposes of this chapter, we'll refer to ethics as a set of principles or standards that define good conduct. This definition refers not only to legal behaviors but also to right behaviors. For example, it may be legal to break confidentiality regarding collection of data, but it is not ethically right.

Codes of ethics or *codes of conduct* are synonymous terms that "refer to documents that convey organizational values and a stated commitment to upholding them. They are used as central guides for employees to support day-to-day decisions. They often clarify the organization's mission and values and may contain references to available resources related to ethics" (Johnson, 2004).

Values, which are a component of ethics, are the core beliefs that people have about what is good or bad, what matters, and how they should treat other people. Some examples of individual values are honesty, loyalty, trustworthiness, and balance between work and family. Organizational values can include service, quality, profit, safety, and respect. *Morals* are a class of values that relate specifically to right and wrong. They are often based in religious or philosophical ideals and thus have powerful meaning for individuals.

Compliance refers to behavior that conforms to rules, policies, or laws. Compliance differs from ethical behavior in that the former follows the letter of the law, whereas the latter follows the spirit of the law. Ethical behavior tends to be more aspirational in nature, which means that it is reaching for a higher ideal rather than simply obeying the rules.

Ethics for the WLP Professional

Because workplace learning and performance deals with people in situations in which they can be very vulnerable, such as training, change or transition, and other job-related issues, ethics are particularly important for WLP professionals. Most associations and societies for the WLP profession have stated codes of ethics (see the sidebars throughout this chapter for examples). Although distinct differences exist among these codes that reflect the unique needs of their constituencies, certain common themes emerge, such as professionalism, professional development, integrity, use of information and research, rights and dignity of people, compliance with pertinent laws, and conflicts of interest. Let's look at these elements more closely.

Professionalism

In one form or another, guidelines for professional behavior exist in all these codes of ethics. One component of professional behavior is competence, which involves striving to provide clients—be they organizations, learners in a classroom, or other groups—with the

---
◼

The ASTD Code of Ethics

The ASTD Code of Ethics provides guidance to individuals to be self-managed workplace learning and performance professionals. Clients and employers should expect the highest possible standards of personal integrity, professional competence, sound judgment, and discretion. Developed by the profession for the profession, the Code of Ethics is the public declaration of workplace learning and performance professionals' obligations to themselves, their profession, and society.

Workforce learning and performance professionals will strive to

- Recognize the rights and dignities of each individual
- Develop human potential
- Provide employer, clients, and learners with the highest-level quality education, training, and development
- Comply with all copyright laws and the laws and regulations governing their position
- Keep informed of pertinent knowledge and competence in the workplace learning and performance field
- Maintain confidentiality and integrity in the practice of the profession
- Support peers and avoid conduct that impedes their practicing of their profession
- Conduct themselves in an ethical and honest manner
- Improve the public understanding of workplace learning and performance
- Fairly and accurately represent their workplace learning and performance credentials, qualifications, experience, and ability
- Contribute to the continuing growth of the profession.

◼
---

highest-quality services possible. Therefore, WLP professionals must commit to providing only those services for which they are qualified through education or experience. Furthermore, they must avoid misrepresenting their qualifications when taking on projects, bidding for contracts, or working with consulting clients.

In addition to this fundamental focus on providing quality and adding value, guidelines exist for professional conduct. For example, in coaching, these guidelines include setting boundaries in the coaching relationship; establishing upfront, clear agreements regarding outcomes and confidentiality; and encouraging clients to seek other professional help (including another coach) if appropriate. More generally, professional conduct also involves supporting peers, avoiding behavior that negatively affects perceptions of the field, clarifying roles and expectations, and adapting methods to the needs of the client.

Professional Development

The concept of competence leads naturally to an emphasis on professional development. To ensure that they continue to provide the highest-quality services, WLP professionals undertake professional development activities, such as training, certification, and extensive reading. These activities enable them to keep up with developments in their fields and thus serve their clients' needs better.

Integrity

One way to define integrity is "making decisions that are consistent with each other and with one's values" (Johnson, 2004). Basically, integrity means honesty and fairness. More specifically, it means representing qualifications accurately, surfacing factors that may compromise objectivity, taking responsibility only for the results that are directly attributable to your work, and being accountable for mistakes.

Use of Information and Research

WLP work exposes professionals to a lot of information, some of it confidential, proprietary, potentially damaging, or simply private. This places WLP professionals in a position of trust. To maintain that trust as well as the credibility of the profession, ethical codes tend to emphasize the appropriate use of information, providing guidelines for protecting information; maintaining confidentiality; getting permission to use information; and getting up-front agreements regarding the use and reporting of data, such as those gathered from research and analysis.

Not only the use of data, but also the collection of data is governed by ethics. To ensure that data are accurate and cover only what is necessary for a WLP professional to be able to do his or her job, ethical guidelines govern data collection methods, appropriate analysis of data, reporting of data, and so forth. For example, the Academy of Human Resource Develoment's (AHRD) standards specify that reports and statements be "based on information and techniques that are sufficient to provide appropriate substantiation for their findings" (1999). Other specifications included in the AHRD standards are to conduct research that meets with recognized standards of competence and ethics, use subject matter experts and review boards, and protect research subjects.

Rights and Dignity of People

Respecting the rights and dignity of others is another important feature of most ethical codes, and this is especially true in a profession as people-centric as workplace learning and performance. This tenet takes the form of recognizing people's rights to privacy, confidentiality, self-determination, and autonomy. Furthermore, WLP professionals should strive to eliminate biases based on ethnicity, age, sexual orientation, gender, socioeconomic status, disabilities, and nationality from their work as well as from their behavior toward people. Other key points are treating people fairly and equitably and avoiding participating in or condoning discriminatory practices.

■

AHRD Standards on Ethics and Integrity

In 1999, the Academy of Human Resource Development (AHRD) published a comprehensive document that provides guidelines for ethical behavior in the WLP profession. The general principles that it lays down refer to

- Competence
- Integrity
- Professional responsibility
- Respect for people's rights and dignity
- Concern for others' welfare
- Social responsibility.

The standards provide explicit language governing how a WLP professional should behave in specific situations. Some examples include compliance with law and standards; reporting of research and evaluation results; protection of confidentiality; and accuracy, objectivity, and professionalism in programs. These standards are organized under the following major headings:

- General standards
- Research and evaluation
- Advertising and other public statements
- Publication of work
- Privacy and confidentiality
- Teaching and facilitating
- Resolution of ethical issues and violations.

Source: AHRD (1999).

■

Compliance

Compliance with existing laws and regulations is often considered a given in ethics. Nonetheless, considering the legal dilemmas organizations can get into (sometimes with disastrous consequences), some organizations include it in their ethical codes. *Managing the Learning Function,* module six of the *ASTD Learning System,* describes the laws that most frequently affect WLP professionals:

- **Employment law:** Regulations of the U.S. Equal Employment Opportunity Commission (EEOC) govern hiring, promoting, and discharging employees as well as relate to training situations.
- **Civil rights:** Section 201 of the Civil Rights Act of 1964 guarantees equal access to any place of public accommodation, regardless of race, color, religion, and national origin; the American with Disabilities Act of 1990 prohibits discrimination based on disability.
- **Workplace safety:** In 1970, the U.S. Congress passed the Occupational Health and Safety Act (OSHA) to protect workers from hazardous worksites. This

legislation affects learning and performance because training is often required to inform workers about the dangers of worksites.

- **Securities and financial reporting:** As a result of the accounting scandals of the early 2000s, the Sarbanes-Oxley Act of 2002 "was passed to protect investors from fraudulent accounting activities by improving the accuracy and accountability of corporate disclosures" (ASTD, 2006). Because the law requires organizations to document that their controls are sufficient, learning and performance professionals are affected as a result of training requirements.

- **Intellectual property:** Intellectual property—especially copyright law—is probably the area of the law that most affects WLP professionals because so much of their work involves creating and using content (ASTD, 2006).

Conflicts of Interest

A final theme that is common to most ethical codes concerns conflicts of interest. According to Johnson (2004), a "conflict of interest is a situation in which an individual has a vested interest in the outcome of a decision but tries to influence the decision-making process as if he or she did not." Some guidelines for avoiding conflicts of interest include refraining from using information received through relationships with clients for personal gain or from the appearance of doing so, disclosing potential conflicts of interest to stakeholders, and working with stakeholders to resolve such situations to the benefit of the stakeholder.

Organizational Ethics Programs

Now that we have looked at some of the ethical codes that apply directly to WLP professionals, let's take a look at their second area of responsibility regarding ethics: that is, helping the organizations that they serve to develop effective ethics programs to enable them to avoid the repercussions of ethical and legal lapses and to reap the benefits of improved employee satisfaction and morale, increased profits, and more stability.

How do you create an effective ethics program in an organization? Research regarding organizational ethics programs reveals that simply creating a code of ethics is not enough. In 2003, the Institute of Business Ethics published research that indicated that organizations with codes of ethics financially outperformed those that did not (Webley and More, 2003). However, by 2005, most organizations had created codes of ethics, making codes a less clear indicator of ethical behavior in organizations. To determine if there was a difference between organizations that simply created a public statement about their ethics and those that lived their ethics through training programs and other means, Ugoji, Dando, and Moir (2007) followed up on the earlier research, this time differentiating between two categories: *corporate-revealed ethics* and *corporate-applied ethics*. They found that organizations that applied ethics "showed a significantly greater positive relationship between provision of training for business ethics (Corporate-Applied Ethics) and financial performance compared to those which only disclosed ethical values and their financial performance."

Applying ethics means building an ethical culture, which includes important tasks such as starting from the top, creating a code of ethics, using hiring and training, creating a reporting mechanism, making ethical behavior a part of people's performance reviews, and using ethical models for decision making. Let's look at each of these more closely.

Start from the Top

Most experts agree that no "corporate ethics training program—or values statement—will be successful without the involvement and modeling of leadership" (Salopek, 2001). According to the 2005 National Business Ethics Survey (NBES), employees are 50 percentage points less likely to witness ethical misconduct in their organizations where the leadership displays certain ethics-related actions (Harned, Seligson, and Baviskar, 2005).

Where ethics codes and programs exist but leaders fail to act in accordance with those standards, however, the program will be perceived as a sham and will not be effective. Enron is a potent example of this point. Enron had a "highly developed code of ethics, but it was ignored by the company's leadership, whose unethical behavior eventually led to the company's precipitous bankruptcy" (Hatcher, 2003).

Although it's important for leaders to insist on ethical behaviors in their organizations, simply telling people to behave ethically is insufficient. Leaders have to model ethical behavior, showing their employees from day to day what it looks like. This both raises the program's credibility—thus making employees more likely to follow suit—and shows them how it's done. One example of a successful leadership behavior related to ethics involves making "evident the ethical components of [leaders'] decisions, even going so far as to explain the thought process behind certain difficult decisions" (Salopek, 2001). Other effective behaviors include having regular conversations about ethics with employees, communicating in a truthful and transparent way, and avoiding pressuring employees to act unethically (Thibodeau, 2006).

Create an Ethical Code

Codes alone are not sufficient to make an organization ethical, but they are an important first step. In developing a code of ethics, organizations must first identify relevant laws,

---

**SHRM Code of Ethical and Professional Standards
in Human Resource Management**

The Society for Human Resource Management's (SHRM) ethical code provides guidelines in these areas:

- Professional responsibility
- Professional development
- Ethical leadership
- Fairness and justice
- Conflicts of interest
- Use of information.

For each of these areas, the code explains the core principle for the area, describes the intent behind the principle, and provides specific guidelines for behaviors that align with the code. For example, in the area of ethical leadership, the core principle indicates that human resource professionals need to act as role models for ethical behavior. The intent behind this principle is to set standards for others as well as to increase credibility for the human resource profession as a whole. Finally, it describes some examples of behaviors that human resource professionals should espouse in support of the principle, such as acting ethically, questioning decisions to ensure they are ethical, consulting experts in cases where ethics may be in question, and supporting others in their attempts to become ethical leaders.

Source: SHRM (2007).

---

rules, regulations, principles, and best practices. And more important, they must identify their values, for example, honesty, trust, quality, and so forth. According to Hatcher (2003), "these values originate from the industry, the company, the culture, and employees and can be operationalized in a clear code of ethics."

Hatcher (2003) also provides some important resources that provide standards for developing a corporate code of ethics:

- Social Accountability International's SA 8000
- Institute for Social and Ethical Accountability's AA 1000
- International Organization for Standardization's ISO 14000 Environmental Management Standards
- Open Compliance and Ethics Group Project.

Use Hiring and Training to Build an Ethical Culture

A code of ethics can be thought of as the skeleton of an ethics program. It's a very important structural component, but without muscle, blood, and a beating heart, there's no life to it. There are several things that organizations can do to bring life to an ethics program, including using hiring and training. Hatcher (2003) cites a survey by the National Association of Colleges and Employers that found that "an organization's integrity and ethical business practices are the most important criteria for potential employees in choosing an employer." To attract top talent, organizations need to make their ethics culture a visible part of their recruitment and hiring activities.

Furthermore, training programs need to use company-specific business situations to make ethics relevant. According to Thibodeau (2006), "dialogue about ethical decisions in the context of real situations is more pertinent and memorable." In addition, dialogue about ethics can't be a single event. To be meaningful, discussions about ethical dilemmas and decision making have to take place regularly.

To help staff really understand what ethics look like in action, leaders and managers can provide real-life examples of ethical dilemmas and decision making to engage employees in discussions about ethics. According to David Gebler, president and founder of the Working Values Group, experiential or scenario-based ethics training is most effective because it allows employees to speak openly about real situations, without making them feel vulnerable because it isn't about them personally (Salopek, 2001). Scenarios allow participants to

- Examine behaviors in the context of the organization's values, the effect on its stakeholders, and the law
- Explore different ways of dealing with a situation and what the different outcomes might be
- Identify how the situation may have violated the organization's ethics
- Identify ways to avoid such situations.

The outcomes of scenario-based training include providing employees with methods to explore and evaluate different solutions to ethical dilemmas that they face in their own work and to understand the principles behind organizational policies.

Create a Reporting Mechanism

Another way to bring life to an organization's ethics program is to provide avenues for people to get advice for their own ethical situations and to report wrongdoing that they witness. Some ways of doing this include creating an ethics office, establishing an ombudsman, or setting up a hotline. Another way to do this is to encourage managers to make it safe for employees to come and talk about ethics. Making discussions about ethics a normal part of business operation will strengthen the ethical culture (Thibodeau, 2006).

ICF Code of Ethics

The International Coach Federation (ICF) provides a four-part ethical code. Part 1 explains the ICF's philosophy of coaching, describing the coaching client as someone who is an expert in his or her life and work and is "creative, resourceful, and whole." Part 1 also indicates the responsibilities of coaches.

Part 2 provides the ICF's definition of coaching: "Professional coaching is an ongoing professional relationship that helps people produce extraordinary results in their lives, careers, businesses or organizations. Through the process of coaching, clients deepen their learning, improve their performance, and enhance their quality of life." In addition, the definition describes the relationship and interaction between the coach and the client.

Standards of ethical conduct make up part 3 of the ICF Code of Ethics. These are divided into four areas: professional conduct at large, professional conduct with clients, confidentiality or privacy, and conflicts of interest. Examples of the statements contained in this section are "I will be aware of any issues that may potentially lead to the misuse of my influence by recognizing the nature of coaching and the way in which it may affect the lives of others" and "I will respect the confidentiality of my client's information, except as otherwise authorized by my client, or required by law."

Finally, part 4 presents the ICF pledge of ethics, in which the coach vows to abide by the code, to treat people with respect, and to act as a model for the standards set down in the code. The coach is also held accountable to the ICF for his or her ethical behavior and risks loss of ICF membership or credentials if he or she breaches the code.

Source: ICF (2005).

Make Ethical Behavior Part of Employees' Performance

Hatcher (2003) notes that one of the arguments against ethics programs is that you can't mandate values, because people come to organizations with their values systems already in place. Although it is true that you can't change people's core values by instituting an organizational code, organizations can create expectations about how employees will behave in compliance with their codes of conduct. One way to do this is through training. Another is by making ethical behavior a part of employee performance reviews.

Thibodeau (2006) notes that the difficulty in doing this lies in making ethics observable or measurable. To do so, managers need to identify specific behaviors that exemplify ethics. It's not enough to simply state, for example, that you want employees to be honest; honesty has to be defined and given a face. Continuing with the example of honesty, it may not be enough to say that honesty means telling the truth when asked a direct question. It may also mean communicating feelings even when they run counter to the perceived opinion of the group or a superior (Asacker, 2004). Many disciplines that offer

---

ISPI Code of Ethics

Signing a statement to behave in ways that align with the six principles of the code of ethics is a stipulation of the International Society for Performance Improvement (ISPI) certification. The six principles of ISPI's code of ethics are

- Add value
- Validated practice
- Collaboration
- Continuous improvement
- Integrity
- Uphold confidentiality.

For each of these principles, the code presents a set of specific guidelines that govern the behavior of human performance professionals.

The code of ethics also provides a statement of expectations that describes the objectives of the work of a performance professional:

- Supply organizations with the skills, knowledge, and attitudes required to accomplish needed results
- Help create knowledge that leads to results that meet performance criteria
- Use systematic, conscientious research to get that knowledge
- Get the results the client wants.

Source: ISPI (2002).

---

codes of ethics also offer specific examples of compliance, including several of the codes related to the WLP field discussed in the sidebars. These examples can be a starting point for defining specific behaviors that show an adherence to ethics.

Use Ethical Models for Decision Making

Ethics most frequently come into play in decision making. Using a model to guide decision making toward ethical outcomes can be very helpful. Darraugh (1991) offers three models for ethical decision making: a utilitarian system, a "models" method, and a personal system.

*A **utilitarian system.*** A utilitarian system refers to the ethic of utility, which indicates that the "right" action is the one that provides the most good for the greatest number of people. The steps in this system are as follows:

- Determine what is required by gathering the facts about the action being requested.
- Examine the possible consequences of the request.

■ Assess the consequences by using these criteria: Does the action provide the greatest benefit to all stakeholders? Does it value all the stakeholders? Does it fit my personal sense of values? If the answer to any of these questions is "no," then it's appropriate to not proceed with the action.

A "models" method. In *Models for HRD Practice,* Patricia McLagan provides a method for resolving ethical conflicts, which consists of these four steps:

■ Identify the ethical dilemma involved.

■ Identify the goals a solution would achieve. These should be broken out into individual or group rights and expectations; professional, legal, and moral requirements; and the employee's own values.

■ Identify the consequences of the possible solution—both positive and negative—on individuals, the organization, and the profession. Consequences that are harmful, illegal, or immoral, or that violate agreements, promises, or organizational or professional standards should not be tolerated.

■ Determine the right course of action. Would the employee be willing to publicize the decision or action to fellow professionals (McLagan, 1989)?

A personal system. Pat Amend in *Working Woman* magazine suggests that the following broad action plan is the "right way to deal with ethical dilemmas":

■ Make sure there is a conflict. Make sure you have all the facts.

■ Decide how much you are willing to risk. How serious is this situation?

■ Make your move. Tell your boss you are uncomfortable with the action or situation.

■ If there's trouble, get help. Talk to the ethics office or a human resource professional.

■ Consider a job change. If your values and those of your organization clash too much, you may want to consider getting a new job (Amend, 1988).

Committing to Ethical Practices

For WLP professionals, a commitment to ethics involves upholding principles stated in any one of the codes of ethics that have been published for the profession. As mentioned earlier, although these codes have differences among them, they hold several principles in common: professionalism, professional development, integrity, appropriate and ethical use of information, respect for people, compliance with the law, and the avoidance of conflicts of interest. These codes all apply to WLP professionals in their individual pursuit of ethical practice. The other half of a WLP professional's responsibility lies in enabling the organizations he or she works for to create ethical cultures by making ethical codes into living, breathing institutions.

One thing to remember about ethical behavior is that it is often inconvenient. It can slow the process of decision making and the pace at which projects are completed. It can mean that people may not always get what they want. And it can entail great personal risk.

However, on an individual level, committing to ethical practices means that WLP professionals can look themselves in the mirror and take pride in what they do and how they do it. On an organizational level, it can mean happier, more engaged employees; a good reputation and increased brand value; greater stability; and increased long-term profits—all good reasons for an increased focus on ethics. But perhaps the best reason is also the simplest: it is the right thing to do.

The section "Use Ethical Models for Decision Making" is adapted from "Ethics for Business," edited by Barbara Darraugh (1991).

❧

About the Author

Tora Estep is a senior associate editor at ASTD, where she has been a staff editor and writer for more than five years. She edited *Infoline,* ASTD's monthly publication dedicated to training workplace learning and performance professionals in a wide variety of topics and wrote several issues, including "Be a Better Manager," "Meetings That Work!," "Basics of Stand-Up Training," and "Managing Difficult Participants." She has also contributed several articles to *T+D* and was part of the editorial and writing team that produced the *ASTD Learning System,* a 10-volume study guide for practitioners preparing to take the CPLP knowledge exam. Prior to ASTD, she worked as an editor for International Communications Inc., editing books and magazines for the World Bank, the International Development Bank, the U.S. Southern Command, and others.

References

AHRD (Academy of Human Resource Development). 1999. Standards on ethics and integrity, available at http://www.ahrd.org/.

Amend, Pat. 1988, December. The right way to deal with ethical dilemmas. *Working woman,* 19.

Asacker, Tom. 2004. Ethics in the workplace: Start with honesty. *T+D* 58(8): 42-44.

ASTD (American Society for Training and Development). 2006. *Managing the learning function.* Module 6 of the *ASTD Learning System.* Alexandria, VA: ASTD Press.

Darraugh, Barbara, ed. 1991. Ethics for business. *Infoline,* 250103 (out of print). Alexandria, VA: ASTD.

Harned, Patricia J., Amber Levanon Seligson, and Siddhartha Baviskar. 2005. *National business ethics survey: How employees view ethics in their organizations 1994-2005.* Washington, D.C.: Ethics Resource Center.

Hatcher, Tim. 2003. New world ethics. *T+D* 57(8): 42-47.

ICF (International Coach Federation). 2005. The ICF code of ethics, available at http://www .coachfederation.org/ICF/For+Current+Members/Ethical+Guidelines/Code+of+Ethics/.

ISPI (International Society for Performance Improvement). 2002. Code of ethics, available at http://www.ispi.org/.

Johnson, Jennie. 2004. Ethics for trainers. *Infoline* 250406. Alexandria, VA: ASTD Press.

McLagan, Patricia. 1989. *Models for HRD practice.* Alexandria, VA: ASTD.

Salopek, Jennifer J. 2001. Do the right thing. *T+D* 55(7): 39-44.

SHRM (Society for Human Resource Management). 2007. SHRM code of ethical and professional standards in human resource management, available at http://www.shrm.org/ethics/code-of-ethics.asp.

Thibodeau, Jan. 2006. Course and discourse. *T+D* 60(8): 12-13.

Ugoji, Kaodi, Nicole Dando, and Lance Moir. 2007. *Does business ethics pay?—Revisited.* London: Institute of Business Ethics.

Webley, Simon, and Elise More. 2003. *Does business ethics pay?* London: Institute of Business Ethics.

℘ Appendix A

Glossary

A

Accelerated learning: A process that results in long-term retention by the learner. This is accomplished by honoring the different learning preferences of each individual learner and using experiential learning exercises (such as role plays, mnemonics, props, and music).

Active learning: A wide variety of strategies in which learners are engaged mentally, physically, and emotionally so that what is learned is acquired largely through their own activity instead of frontal teaching.

Active listening: A form of listening that differentiates between the cognitive and emotional content of the message and communicates these to the speaker. An active listener makes inferences regarding feelings expressed by the speaker while listening and reflects these back for verification (Reynolds, 1993).

ADDIE: An instructional systems development model that comprises five phases:

- **Analysis** is the examination of the training required and generally answers the who, what, where, when, why, and by whom questions to prepare for the design phase.
- **Design** is the planning stage to formulate a plan, or outline, and learning objectives for the training.
- **Development** is the phase in which training materials and content are selected and developed based on learning objectives.
- **Implementation** is when the course is taught and delivered.
- **Evaluation** is the ongoing process of scrutiny to measure and constantly improve instructional efforts during and following implementation. This last phase provides data that is incorporated into the analysis phase.

Adult learning theory: A term that encompasses the collective theories and principles of how adults learn and acquire knowledge. Popularized by Malcolm Knowles, adult learning theory provides the foundation that WLP professionals need. (See also *Andragogy.*)

Affective learning: Acquisition of knowledge based on Benjamin Bloom's taxonomy in which he identified three learning domains: cognitive (knowledge), affective (attitude), and psychomotor (skills). This taxonomy or classification of the processes of thinking and learning provides the framework for the creation of instructional strategies, materials, and activities used to improve individual workplace learning and performance. Affective refers to the learners' outlook or mindset.

After action review (AAR): Intense follow-up sessions used to better understand what happened in an event and what should have happened. Feedback in AARs can include raw material, such as recorded plays and timelines; analysis (what happened and why at a thematic level); coaching on how to get better results next time; evaluation (how ready the player is to handle a more complex situation); and even game elements like a high score or rewards and recognition to spur competition and replay or redo.

Analysis: The breaking up and examining of parts of a whole. In workplace learning and performance, these are some common analyses:

- **Gap analysis** identifies the discrepancy between the desired and actual performance or results.
- **Root cause analysis** identifies the true cause(s) of the gap between desired and actual knowledge, skills, and performance.
- **Job analysis** identifies all duties and responsibilities and the respective tasks done on a daily, weekly, monthly, or yearly basis that make up a single job function or role.
- **Needs analysis** is the process of collecting and synthesizing data to identify how training can help an organization reach its goals.
- **Task analysis** is the process of identifying the specific steps required to correctly perform a step within a job.

Andragogy: The adult learning theory popularized by Malcolm Knowles. Andragogy (from the Greek meaning "adult learning") is based on five key principles that influence how adults learn: self-concept, prior experience, readiness to learn, orientation to learning, and motivation to learn. (See also *Adult learning theory.*)

Appreciative coaching: A process of discovery centered on a topic that is based on Appreciative Inquiry Theory. Through positively focused inquiry, the coach can be a catalyst for retelling stories, reinterpreting reality, and creating a dream for a different future. This act of telling a new story in and of itself begins the process of change. To accomplish this coaching process, the coach follows a cycle with four distinct parts: discovery, dream, design, and destiny.

Appreciative Inquiry (AI) Theory: An approach to large-scale organizational change that involves the analysis of positive and successful (rather than negative or failing) operations. The AI 4-D cycle (discovery, dream, design, and destiny) includes identifying areas for improvement, analyzing previous successes, searching for solutions, and developing an action plan.

Assessment: The process used to systematically appraise a learner's skill or knowledge level.

ASTD Certification Institute (ASTD CI): The independent body that establishes standards and issues credentials for the workplace learning and performance profession.

ASTD HPI model: A results-based, systematic process used to identify performance problems, analyze root causes, select and design performance solutions, manage solutions in the workplace, measure results, and continually improve employees' performance within an organization.

Asynchronous learning: A type of just-in-time, on-demand learning that includes self-paced computer-based training (CBT), using CD-ROMs, or, more frequently, recorded synchronous e-learning events, such as webinars. Learners are hearing, observing, and applying the instruction at different times, not synchronously.

Authoring tools: Special software programs that allow a content expert to interact with the computer in everyday language to help develop computer-based training (CBT) courseware.

Aviation Industry CBT Committee (AICC): An international association of technology-based training professionals. The AICC develops guidelines for the aviation industry on the development, delivery, and evaluation of computer-based training (CBT) and related training technologies.

B

Balanced scorecard: A model for measuring effectiveness from four business perspectives: the customer perspective, the innovation and learning perspective, the internal business perspective, and the financial perspective.

Bandwidth: The speed at which information is transferred via modem or other network-access device to Internet users. The greater the bandwidth, the more quickly the data (audio, video, text, and so forth) reach the user.

Behavior: The activity or task that produces an accomplishment.

Behavioral coaching: The underlying assumption of behavioral coaching that human beings respond to stimuli, sustain behaviors that are pleasurable, and cease behaviors that produce pain. People's actions represent a continuous process of selecting among alternatives that bring rewards or punishment. The role of the coach is to create a clear understanding for the employee of the performance that is expected, the rewards that will come from satisfactory achievement, and the penalties that will come with failure to achieve.

Behaviorism: The learning theory usually associated with psychologist and author B.F. Skinner that applies to psychology focused on observable and measurable behavioral change and that stresses the role of the environment as a determinant of behavior.

Benchmarking: An evaluation of one's own practices and comparison with another company's. Benchmarking is frequently used in the quality process (Reynolds, 1993).

Blended learning: The combination of multiple approaches to learning. In the strictest sense, blended learning refers to any time that two methods of delivery of instruction are used. A typical example of this would be a combination of e-learning and in-person, instructor-led training sessions.

Blog: Short for weblog, an online journal or diary containing a chronological log of thoughts and ideas that is regularly updated and published on a webpage.

Bloom's taxonomy: Benjamin Bloom's classification of three learning domains: cognitive, psychomotor (behavioral), and affective; sometimes referred to as KSAs (knowledge, skills, and attitude). This taxonomy or classification of the processes of thinking and learning provides the framework for the creation of instructional strategies, materials, and activities used to improve individual workplace learning and performance.

Branching story: An educational simulation genre in which students make a series of multiple-choice decisions to progress through and affect an event (or story).

Browser: A software application that displays webpages, originally written in the text-based HTML language, in a user-friendly graphical format.

Business analysis: The process of identifying and clarifying primary organizational goals, targets, or needs.

C

Career development: A planned, structured process of interaction between a representative of the organization and the individual. Career development enables employees to grow within an organization and results in their optimal utilization (Reynolds, 1993).

Cause-and-effect analysis: An analytical tool that reveals the root causes of problems by displaying the relationships between the reasons or sources and the result. It may demonstrate that the root cause originates far from where the problem occurs.

Certification: The awarding of a credential that acknowledges that an individual has demonstrated proof of a minimum level of knowledge or competence, as defined by a professional standards organization. Professional certification can be used as verification of an individual's skills and knowledge.

Challenge and rescue: Instructional strategies that are designed to engage learners, avoid passive information presentations, and individualize learning experiences by putting authentic challenges first and presenting information only to rescue learners who need or request help.

Change agent: The person responsible for facilitating, coordinating, and implementing a change effort within an organization. The person who intentionally or indirectly causes or accelerates an organizational, social, cultural, or behavioral change.

Change leader: The person responsible for developing, leading, and supporting a change effort within an organization.

Change management: A process whereby organizations and individuals proactively plan for and adapt to change (Reynolds, 1993).

Chunk: A discrete portion of content, often consisting of several learning objects grouped together as a way to improve learner comprehension and retention. A trainer should break down and group, or chunk, larger pieces of information into smaller, easier-to-process components.

Coaching: A process in which a person, or coach, provides a worker or workers with constructive advice and feedback with the goal of improving performance. (See also *Mentoring*, which focuses on career development and advancement.)

Codec: A device used for video teleconferencing. A camera's video signal is fed into an electronic box called a codec (short for coder/decoder). The codec converts the audiovisual signals into digital information. The information is then sent, over high-capacity phone lines, to remote sites. Once the remote sites have received the digital information, the codec at each site converts the digital signal back to a signal that can be displayed on a television monitor.

Coding: In computer programming, the arrangement of information for storage or input in which letters, digits, and so forth correspond to binary numbers; also the set of instructions in the program.

Cognitive: The mental process of knowing something through perception, reasoning, or intuition.

Cognitive learning (or cognitivism): A "tell" approach to learning based on the theory that learning occurs through exposure to logically presented information, usually involving lecture. It can also include diagrams, videos, films, panels, class presentations, interviews with subject matter experts (SMEs), readings, debates, and class studies.

Community of practice (CoP): A group of people who share a common interest in an area of competence and are willing to share the experiences of their practice with one another.

Competency: Observable behavior that is based on specific knowledge, skills, and attitudes that relate to performance.

Computer-based training (CBT): An umbrella term for the use of computers in both instruction and management of the teaching and learning process. Computer-assisted instruction (CAI) and computer-managed instruction (CMI) are included under the heading of CBT. Some people use the terms CBT and CAI interchangeably.

Conative (conation, conative): The aspect of mental or behavioral processes that are directed toward action or change and include impulse and desire, volition, and striving.

Concept: A group or category of examples with a set of common identifying attributes and a label (concept name). Examples of concepts can be physical objects, or abstractions. You manipulate examples of a concept, so you can identify, classify, generate, group, or synthesize examples of a concept.

Conditions of learning: Robert Gagné's theory of nine instructional events that help ensure learning occurs. The nine events are

1. Gain the learners' attention.
2. Share the objectives of the session.
3. Ask learners to recall prior learning.
4. Deliver content.

5. Use methods to enhance understanding (for example, case studies or graphs).
6. Provide an opportunity to practice.
7. Provide feedback.
8. Assess performance.
9. Provide job aids or references to ensure transfer to the job.

Consultant: A person who provides needed information, help, and perspective. Consultants may be employees of an organization (internal) or under contract with the organization (external) because of competence, status, reputation, or experience. Strictly, this term should not be used to describe a person from outside the organization who only provides instruction (Reynolds, 1993).

Content-centric design: A paradigm that concentrates on content and its presentation; the counterpoint to individualization or learner-centric design.

Correlation: A measure of the relationship between or among two or more variables; if one changes, the other is likely to make a corresponding change. If such a change moves the variables in the same direction, it is a positive correlation; if the change moves the variables in opposite directions, it is a negative correlation.

Cost-benefit analysis: A method of evaluating the implications of alternative human resource development plans. Cost-benefit analysis determines whether a project will save an amount equal to or greater than its cost and lost opportunities. A technique for assessing the relationship between results of outcomes of human resource development programs and the cost required to produce them (Reynolds, 1993).

CPLP (Certified Professional in Learning and Performance): A professional credential offered by the ASTD Certification Institute (ASTD CI) to workplace learning and performance professionals.

Credentialing: A process that grants recognition and a credential upon a person, organization, program, product, or service after certain criteria have been met and verified. Examples of credentialing programs include certification, accreditation, and licensure.

Criterion reference: A system of training developed by Robert Mager in which results are measured by the learner's ability to meet specified performance objectives (criteria) upon completion.

Criterion validity: The extent to which an assessment can predict or agree with external constructs. Criterion validity is determined by looking at the correlation between the instrument and the criterion measure.

D

Data: Items of information, facts, or statistics organized for analysis.

Data collection: A frequently used term in the WLP profession that refers to the gathering and compiling of all data that are used for analysis. Some examples of data collection methods or tools are examination of in-house and external written sources, questionnaires, interviews, observation of trainees or jobholders, and experiments of training approaches.

Declarative knowledge: The facts, concepts (categories), and principles (if...then relationships) that people use to make sense out of the world.

Design matrix: A framework or skeleton for a course that is used to visualize a course or session. It enables course designers to take a broad view of what to accomplish and how to meet the learning outcomes. The design matrix consists of four parts: duration, content or learning points, methods or activities, and materials or aids. It is used to identify and sequence content subtopics, estimate the amount of time devoted to each subtopic, consider the methods to communicate the content, and identify potential training materials and aids.

Development: Learning or other types of activities that prepare a person for additional job responsibilities and enable him or her to gain knowledge or skills. It may also refer to the creation of training materials or courses. (See also *ADDIE.*)

Distance learning: An educational situation in which the instructor and learners are separated by time, location, or both. Education or training courses are delivered to remote locations via synchronous or asynchronous means of instruction.

Domains of learning: The three domains into which instructional activities can be placed. They include cognitive, psychomotor, and affective (Reynolds, 1993). (See also *Bloom's taxonomy.*)

E

Effect size: A way of quantifying the difference between two groups using standard deviation. For example, if one group (the treatment group) has had an experimental treatment and the other (the control group) has not, the effect size is a measure of the difference between the two groups.

E-learning: A term that covers a wide set of applications and processes, such as web-based learning, computer-based learning, virtual classrooms, and digital collaboration. Delivery of content may take place via the Internet, intranet or extranet (local area network [LAN] or wide area network [WAN]), audio- and videotape, satellite broadcast, interactive television, CD-ROM, and more.

Emotional intelligence: A form of intelligence as defined by Howard Gardner's multiple intelligence theory. It refers to an ability to accurately identify and understand one's own emotional reactions and those of others and is related to personal qualities, such as self-confidence and motivation. The emotional intelligence theory was developed by Daniel Goleman in the 1990s and popularized in his book *Emotional Intelligence.*

Evaluation: A multi-level, systematic method used for gathering information about the effectiveness and impact of training programs. Results of the measurements can be used to improve the program, determine whether learning objectives have been achieved, and assess the value of the training to the organization. These are Donald Kirkpatrick's four levels of evaluation and Jack Phillips's fifth level of evaluation:

- **Level 1** measures reaction and planned action. Level 1 evaluation instruments are often referred to as "smile sheets" and indicate how well the training was received by participants—did they like the trainer, did they like the content, did they like the method of training, and so forth. It also indicates how participants plan to apply what they have learned during training.
- **Level 2** measures learning. It provides indicators of an employee's knowledge, skills, and abilities related to job requirements. It also provides information to enable employees to assess whether they have the knowledge of work policies and procedures that will enable them to perform their duties. It may be completed using a self-assessment, test, or observation.
- **Level 3** measures on-the-job application. This is a higher level of evaluation that determines whether or not the skills and knowledge have transferred to the job and whether or not an employee's performance has changed as a result of training.
- **Level 4** measures business impact. Accountability for training is measured against business needs such as efficiency, customer needs, ability to establish priorities, changes in profits or sales, savings, and so forth. These results may be reflected in reports, performance, and budget.
- **Level 5** measures return-on-investment (ROI) and is another level of evaluation that compares the monetary benefits of training programs with the program costs. It is usually presented as a percentage or cost-benefit ratio.

Executive coaching: A form of coaching for executives. Coaches who work at the executive level need a broad understanding of business principles as well as a firm grounding in personal and organization development.

Exemplar: A term used by Thomas Gilbert, Joe Harless, and other performance pathfinders that refers to an employee who is an outstanding performer in at least one area. Some approaches also refer to this as a key performer. The purposes of studying an exemplar are to better understand the tasks, identify possible root causes, and determine quick ways to improve performance for others (by copying elements from the exemplar).

Experiential learning: A form of learning that occurs when a learner participates in an activity, reviews the activity, identifies useful knowledge or skills that were gained, and transfers the result to the workplace.

Experiential learning activities: Inductive learning through a five-stage cycle: experiencing (complete an activity), publishing (share observations of what happened), processing (interpret why the activity unfolded as it did), generalizing (connect what happened to real life), and applying (plan for change or next steps) the content learned in the activity to real life.

Explicit knowledge: A type of knowledge that includes information that has been documented or can be shared with someone. (See also *Formal knowledge.*)

Extant data: A category of data that comprises existing records, reports, and information that may be available inside or outside the organization. Examples include job descriptions, competency models, benchmarking reports, annual reports, financial statements, strategic plans, mission statements, staffing statistics, climate surveys, 360-degree feedback, performance appraisals, grievances, turnover rates, absenteeism, suggestion box feedback, accident statistics, and so forth.

External consultant: An individual who is hired from outside an organization to assist a client achieve a stated outcome. The assistance can come in the form of information, recommendations, or hands-on work.

Extrinsic feedback: A judgment (for example, correct or incorrect) that does not demonstrate the consequences of a learner's response.

F

Facilitation: The practice of guiding or making learning easier, both in content and in application of the content to the job.

Fact: Information that is recalled and used exactly as it was learned, without any transformation. People *state* facts.

Focus group: A facilitator-led group of participants that is convened for a specific purpose, usually related to gathering information about an organizational challenge, problem, or opportunity. Focus groups may meet only once or continually, depending on their character (Reynolds, 1993).

Forcefield analysis: A diagnostic tool developed by Kurt Lewin to assess two types of forces related to introducing change in organizations: driving and restraining. Driving forces are those that help implement the change, whereas restraining forces are those that prevent the change.

Formal knowledge: Information that can be documented in some manner and made available to various publics in the form of publications, patents, reports, and so forth. (See also *Explicit knowledge.*)

Formative evaluation: The evaluation of material conducted during its early developmental stages for the purpose of revising materials before widespread use. Formative evaluation is conducted during the development phase of ISD (Reynolds, 1993).

Front-end analysis: A term credited to Joe Harless that refers to performance analysis. Typically, performance analysis includes carrying out a business analysis (or identifying key organizational priorities); identifying performance gaps (expressed in terms of accomplishments or outcomes, not behavior); completing a task analysis, which identifies what performers do to achieve the outcome; performing a cause analysis; and usually identifying a key performer or exemplar.

G

Game elements: Techniques that motivate people to want to engage in an experience, outside of any intrinsic motivation. Game elements include fantasy, whimsy, competition, beauty, and a great story.

Goal: An end state or condition toward which human effort is directed.

H

Hard data: Objective and measurable quantitative measures that can be stated in terms of frequency, percentage, proportion, or time.

Herrmann Brain Dominance Instrument (HBDI): A method of personality testing developed by W.E. (Ned) Herrmann that classifies individuals' preferred approach to thinking into four different modes based on brain function: left brain, cerebral; left brain, limbic; right brain, limbic; right brain, cerebral. (See also *Learning style.*)

HTML (Hypertext Markup Language): The programming language used to create documents for display on the web.

Human performance improvement (HPI): A term originally coined by ASTD that refers to a systematic, systemic, results-based approach to helping organizations achieve their goals through people. HPI is about the process used to identify a potential solution. Thus, any solution that happens to work that does not use a systematic, systemic approach to analysis is not performance based. (See also *Human performance technology [HPT]* and *Performance consulting.*)

Human performance technology (HPT): A term originally coined by Thomas Gilbert in the early 1960s that refers to the systematic, systemic, results-based approach to helping organizations achieve their goals through people. The word *human* indicates a focus on people (rather than financial or computer ability). *Performance* deals with results or accomplishments. *Technology* refers to a body of knowledge and practice. It is important to note that HPT is about the process used to identify a potential solution. Thus, any solution that happens to work that does not use a systematic, systemic approach to analysis is not performance based. (See also *Human performance improvement [HPI]* and *Performance consulting.*)

I

Independent variable: The factor that influences the dependent variable. For example, age, seniority, gender, shift, level of education, and so on may all be factors (independent variables) that influence a person's performance (the dependent variable).

Individualization (or individualized instruction): The attempt to optimize instructional effectiveness by accommodating differences that exist among learners, such as ability, readiness, reading speed, and learning style. (See also *Learner-centric design.*)

Information: Raw data (facts, figures, ideas) that have been transformed through organization or reduction. When experience and understanding are added to information a person is said to have knowledge.

Instruction: Information that is taught. When a learning need requires instruction, training is provided. Instruction can be delivered via classroom, e-learning, and on-the-job training.

Instructional development:

1. The process of producing learning activities.
2. Related to the development phase of instructional systems development (ISD). (See also *ADDIE* and *Instructional systems development [ISD].*)

3. Loosely, a synonym for instructional design. Some practitioners prefer to use one of these terms, while other practitioners strictly use the other term (Reynolds, 1993).

Instructional strategies: The mechanisms through which instruction is presented (sometimes called presentation tactics or techniques).

Instructional system: An organized and arranged collection of instructional resources that, when combined, achieves the goal of addressing and providing appropriate training solutions.

Instructional systems development (ISD): A system approach to analyzing, designing, developing, implementing, and evaluating any instructional experience based on the belief that training is most effective when it gives learners a clear statement of what they must be able to do as a result of training and how their performance will be evaluated (sometimes also referred to as instructional systems design). (See also *ADDIE* and *Instructional development.*)

Intellectual capital: The sum total of all the knowledge assets that a company uses to accomplish its mission.

Interactive spreadsheets: An educational simulation genre in which learners typically try to affect three or four critical metrics (or variables, such as market share or profitability) indirectly by allocating finite resources along competing categories over a series of turns or intervals.

Internal consultant: A consultant who is paid as an employee by the client system (Reynolds, 1993).

International Coach Federation (ICF): A nonprofit, individual membership organization formed by professionals worldwide who practice business and personal coaching.

Interval variables: Factors that enable rank ordering of items measured and quantifying and comparing the sizes of differences between items.

Intervention: Another name for a solution or set of solutions, usually a combination of tools and techniques that clearly and directly relate to solving a performance gap or implementing an organizational change.

Interview: A meeting between an individual and one or more interviewers held for the purpose of collecting information, usually by verbal question and answer.

Intrinsic feedback: Feedback that demonstrates the consequences of the learner's response.

J

Job aid: Any device, simple or complex, that an employee uses on the job to perform reliably. Job aids reduce the amount of information the performer must recall or retain to successfully carry out a task and are usually employed to increase the likelihood of high-fidelity performance. The classic example of a job aid is the pilot's checklist. Job aids are usually not intended to instruct (Reynolds, 1993).

Job analysis: Analysis to identify all duties and responsibilities and the respective tasks performed on a daily, weekly, monthly, or yearly basis that make up a single job function or role (Reynolds, 1993).

Just-in-time training: Training that provides learning when it is actually needed and used on the job (Reynolds, 1993).

K

Knowledge: The cognitive abilities a performer needs to be able to complete a job that involve the development of intellectual skills.

Knowledge management: The explicit and systematic management of intellectual capital and organizational knowledge as well as the associated processes of creating, gathering, organizing, disseminating, leveraging, and using intellectual capital for the purposes of improvement of the organization and the individual.

Knowledge mapping: A process that connects information, educational expertise, and practical application of people in the organization for the purposes of sharing and access.

Kolb's Learning Style Inventory: An inventory, developed by David Kolb, of four learning styles or modes (concrete experience, reflective observation, abstract conceptualization, and active experimentation) and people's orientation to them. Kolb categorizes learners as convergers, divergers, assimilators, or accommodators. (See also *Learning style.*)

KSA: An abbreviation with two definitions:

- Knowledge (cognitive), skills (psychomotor), and attitudes (affective) are the three objective domains of learning defined by Benjamin Bloom's taxonomy in the 1950s.
- Knowledge, skills, and ability are also referred to as KSAs and are used by federal and private hiring agencies to determine the attributes or qualities an employee possesses for a particular job.

L

Leadership: The active process through which an individual seeks to identify courses of action and to guide and stimulate the actions of others toward goals desired by the leader. Leadership may be exhibited by any person at any level, with or without formal authority. It compares with management, which may or may not be accompanied by leadership and is applied from a position of formal authority (Reynolds, 1993).

Learner-centric design: An instructional design paradigm that focuses on optimal learning experiences (rather than content presentation).

Learning: The process of gaining knowledge, understanding, or skill by study, instruction, or experience.

Learning content management system (LCMS): A software system (or set of applications) used to manage the content (that is, computer files, image media, audio files, electronic documents, and web content) used in the development of online and instructor-led courses and to make it available to multiple authors.

Learning management system (LMS): A software system used for managing, administering, tracking, and reporting on instructor-led and online courses and other learning activities.

Learning objective: A statement that establishes a measurable behavioral outcome, used as an advanced organizer to indicate how the learner's acquisition of skills and knowledge is being measured.

Learning objects: Self-contained chunks of instructional material generally considered reusable in LCMSs. They typically include three components: a performance goal, the necessary learning content to reach that goal, and some form of evaluation to measure whether or not the goal was achieved.

Learning style: A description of a person's approach to learning that involves the way he or she behaves, feels, and processes information. (See also *Herrmann Brain Dominance Instrument [HBDI]*, *Kolb's Learning Style Inventory*, *Multiple Intelligence Theory*, and *VAK Model.*)

Likert scale: A type of instrument commonly constructed and used to measure opinion. It is characterized by requiring the participant to answer questions by selecting from among choices that range from strongly agree to strongly disagree (Reynolds, 1993).

M

Management development: The various human resource development activities to assist managers in acquiring or enhancing the knowledge, skills, and values needed to be effective in their current and future managerial or supervisory leadership roles. Management development usually includes activities for employees down to first-level supervisors, for example, time management sessions. This term is sometimes preferred over management training for prestige reasons (Reynolds, 1993).

Maslow's Hierarchy of Needs: A model of human motivation developed by Abraham Maslow and introduced in 1954 in his book *Motivation and Personality.* Maslow contended that people have complex needs that they strive to fulfill and that change and evolve over time. He categorized these needs as physiological, safety or security, social or belongingness, esteem, and self-actualization, with the basic needs having to be satisfied before an individual can focus on growth.

Measures of central tendency: The three averages: mean (the average of a group of numbers), median (the middle value of a distribution where half the scores are above the median and half are below), and mode (the most frequently occurring value in a group of numbers).

Mentoring: The career development practice of using a more experienced individual tutor or group to share wisdom and expertise with a protégé over a specific period of time. There are three types of mentoring commonly used: one-on-one, group, and virtual. (See also *Coaching.*)

Metrics: Numerical attributes that are used as the basis for judging productivity, proficiency, performance, and worth.

Mnemonic: A device, formula, or rhyme used as an aid to enhance or develop memory.

Motivation theory: A theory based on the idea that by creating the right environment for people to work in, they will be motivated to grow and become connected to that environment. This theory is important to coaching.

Multiple Intelligence Theory: A theory, popularized by Howard Gardner in *Frames of Mind* (1985), that describes how intelligences reflect the ways people prefer to process information. Gardner claims that most people are comfortable in three to four of these intelligences and avoid the others. For example, for learners who are not comfortable working with others, doing group case studies may interfere with their ability to process new material.

N

Neurolinguistic programming (NLP): A style of communication and behavior change management that is based on observations and analyses of unconscious physical behaviors that identify patterns of feeling and thought.

Nominal data: Numbers or variables used to classify a system, such as digits in a telephone number or numbers on a football player's jersey.

Normal distribution: A particular way in which observations tend to pile up around a particular value rather than be spread evenly across a range of values. It refers statistically to a bell-shaped curve that gives the distribution of probability associated with the different values of a variation.

Norm-referenced test: A test that measures a person's knowledge or skill relative to scores of other learners in the same group. Norm-referenced tests are useful for sorting people into groups. Grading "on a curve" involves norm-referenced measurement because an individual's grade depends on the position on the curve (performance of other students). Generally, norm-referenced tests are not appropriate in workplace learning and performance and should not be used to evaluate either the learners or the instruction if there are explicitly stated objectives (Reynolds, 1993).

O

Objectives: An end toward which efforts are directed. Also, an interim or enabling state or condition that, when combined with other objectives, leads to a goal. The following are some examples of particular types of objectives:

- **Affective** objectives are learning objectives that specify the acquisition of particular attitudes, values, or feelings.
- **Behavioral** objectives specify the particular new behavior that an individual should be able to perform after training.
- **Learning** objectives are clear, measurable statements of performance (knowledge or skill) that is desired after the training has been conducted.

Observation: A training activity in which participants are directed to observe an event and asked to share their reflections, reactions, or insights. Observation is also a method for data collection.

Online learning: An all-encompassing term that refers to any learning done with a computer.

On-the-job training (OJT): Often called the most common training method. The worker or learner usually performs under the supervision of someone else already qualified to do the job. OJT provides observation with guided practice in a practical situation, while learners engage in productive work (Reynolds, 1993).

Ontological coaching: An approach to coaching that seeks to alter the way of being that the client experiences in relation to a situation. The expectation is that the new, altered way of being will make possible behaviors that result in learning, growth, and resolution of a given situation.

Ordinal data: Numbers or variables that allow ranking order of importance from highest to lowest.

Ordinal variables: Factors that make it possible to rank order items measured in terms of which has less and which has more of the quality represented by the variable.

Organization development (OD): The process of developing an organization to be more effective in achieving it business goals. OD uses planned projects to develop the systems, structures, and processes within the organization needed to improve effectiveness.

Outlier: A data point that's far removed in value from others in a data set.

P

Pedagogical elements: Techniques that surround an experience, ensuring that a participant's time is spent productively. In simulations, pedagogical elements can include in-game tips or directions, graphs, highlights, forced moments of reflection, bread crumbs, coach or facilitator, background material, and after action reviews. Pedagogical elements in real life range from speedometers and caller identification to the advice of mentors.

Pedagogy: The function or work of learning where the focus is on what the instructor does as opposed to what the participants do; usually refers to teaching children.

Performance: A combination of the accomplishments produced by people on the job and the behaviors used to achieve these accomplishments.

Performance analysis: A form of analysis that measures the gap between an individual's, group of individuals', or an organization's desired and actual performance.

Performance consultant: A term popularized by Dana and Jim Robinson. The Robinsons support the concept of both partnering with clients and also adopting a consultative approach in addressing performance problems.

Performance consulting: A process in which clients and WLP professionals partner to achieve the strategic outcome of enhanced workplace performance in support of business needs.

Podcast: A method of publishing audio files to the Internet that allows users to subscribe and receive new files automatically via an RSS feed. The term derives from Apple's *iPod* and the word *broadcasting*.

Practiceware: The educational simulation genre that encourages participants to repeat actions in high-fidelity, real-time, often 3D situations until the skill becomes natural in the real world.

Principle: An *if...then* relationship that is typically expressed as a prediction or an explanation of why something has occurred.

Procedural knowledge: The sequence of decisions and actions a person performs to achieve a goal. Procedures vary from well-structured (algorithmic) to ill-structured. People perform procedures, or solve problems by doing procedures that they recall or formulate.

Process consulting: A consulting approach that relies on the intuitive awareness of the consultant who attends to and observes the emotional, nonverbal, perceptual, and spatial aspects of human behavior. Process consultants help the client understand what is happening, identify solutions, and transfer skills to the client to manage the ongoing process. Their focus is on the energy of the client system and a heightened awareness of the dynamics in the group or organization.

Program evaluation: An assessment of the effect of a training program on learning.

Project management: The processes involved in planning, organizing, directing, and controlling resources for a finite period of time to complete specific goals and objectives.

Q

Qualitative analysis: An examination of participants' opinions, behaviors, and attributes that is often descriptive.

Qualitative data: Information that can be difficult to measure or express in numbers.

R

Random assignment: The process of arbitrarily assigning a sample to different groups or treatments in the study.

Random sampling: A selection process for a sample in which every person in the population has an equal chance of being chosen. Choosing every tenth person from an alphabetical list of names, for example, creates a random sample.

Random selection: The process of drawing the sample of people for a study from a population.

Rapid instructional design (RID): A collection of strategies for quickly producing instructional packages to enable a group of learners to achieve a set of specific instructional objectives.

Reliability: The ability to achieve consistent results from a measurement over time.

Return-on-investment (ROI): A ratio of the benefit or profit received from a given investment to the cost of the investment itself. It constitutes accountability for training programs.

S

Script: A program or set of instructions that are not carried out by the computer processor but by another program. Code is interpreted at run time rather than being stored in executable format.

Self-directed learning (SDL): Individualized, or self-paced, learning that generally refers to programs that use a variety of delivery media, ranging from print products to web-based systems. It can also refer to less formal types of learning, such as team learning, knowledge management systems, and self-development programs.

Sharable Content Object Reference Model (SCORM): A model that defines a web-based learning "Content Aggregation Model" and "Run-Time Environment" for learning objects. SCORM is a collection of specifications adapted from multiple sources to provide a comprehensive suite of e-learning capabilities that enable interoperability, accessibility, and reusability of web-based learning content.

Simulation: A broad genre of experiences, including games for entertainment and immersive learning simulations for formal learning programs. Simulations use simulation elements to model and present situations, including actions, reflected in the interface; how the actions then affect relevant systems; and how those systems produce feedback and results. The simulation elements are mixed with game elements to make it engaging and pedagogical elements (including coaching) to make it effective and organized into tasks and levels to create incrementally challenging practice environments, leveraging linear content.

Six Sigma: A process-improvement strategy and measure of quality that strives for near perfection. Six Sigma is a disciplined, data-driven methodology for eliminating defects (driving toward six standard deviations between the mean and the nearest specification limit) in a process. The fundamental objective of the Six Sigma methodology is the implementation of a measurement-based strategy that focuses on process improvement and variation reduction through the application to projects.

Skills: The physical movement, coordination, and use of motor skills needed to accomplish a task.

Soft data: Qualitative measures that are more intangible, anecdotal, personal, and subjective, such as opinions, attitudes, assumptions, feelings, values, and desires. Qualitative data can't be objectified, and that characteristic makes this type of data valuable.

Standard deviation: A commonly used measure or indicator of the amount of variability of scores from the mean. The standard deviation is often used in formulas for advanced or inferential statistics.

Statistic: A number that summarizes data collected from a sample.

Strategic planning: The formulation, development, implementation, and evaluation of how an organization will reach its objectives.

Strengths, weaknesses, opportunities, and threats (SWOT) analysis: An analysis tool used in strategic planning to establish environmental factors within and outside an organization.

Subjective-centered instruction: A pedagogy-based instructional approach. Subject-centered instruction focuses on what will be taught as opposed to learner-related characteristics.

Subject matter expert (SME): A person with extensive knowledge and skills in a particular subject area.

Survey: A written, electronic, or verbal instrument used to collect information.

Synchronous e-learning: Learning that takes place over the Internet in which the trainer and the learners interact via the web in real time. Another name for this type of learning is webinar. Typically it involves the trainer presenting through either a teleconference phone call, or web-based audio or voice over Internet protocol (VOIP) supported by a slideshow presentation that the learners can view at the same time. Learners can also ask questions or provide comments through the phone line, or through a chat feature.

Synchronous learning: Instruction that is led by a facilitator in real time. Examples of synchronous interactions include traditional trainer-led classrooms, conference calls, instant messages, video conferences, whiteboard sessions, and synchronous online classrooms or classroom software.

Systems: A combination of parts forming a complex that when put in action produces results.

Systems thinking: A conceptual framework that encompasses considering the whole, making patterns (and ways to change them) more understandable.

T

Tacit knowledge: A type of knowledge that refers to personal knowledge in a person's head; knowing how to do something based on experience.

Thinking styles: A concept that relates to the patterns and preferences that emerge in the way people process information.

Total quality management (TQM): A continuous improvement methodology for every process, supported by management to improve customer satisfaction. TQM includes every employee using tools, data, and teamwork. W. Edwards Deming brought this concept to Japan and the United States, asserting that every function in the organization is responsible for quality (Reynolds, 1993).

Trainer: A person who helps individuals improve performance by teaching, instructing, or facilitating learning.

Training aids or materials: Items such as assessment instruments, videos or CD-ROMs, transparencies, slides, computer-generated visual aids, audiotapes, games, and evaluation tools that are used to assist in the instruction and learning process.

Training needs assessment: The process of collecting and synthesizing data to identify how training can help an organization reach its goals.

Transfer of learning: The process of learning delivery, retention, and implementation back on the job.

V

VAK Model: A model that describes the way that individuals learn and retain information. Some people learn primarily through one learning style, others through a combination of the three: visual (learners need pictures, diagrams, and other visuals), audio (learners need to hear information), and kinesthetic (learners need hands-on learning).

Validity: A measurement concept that indicates that an instrument measures what it is intended to measure.

Variance: A measure of how spread out a distribution is. It's calculated as the average squared deviation of each number from the mean of a data set.

Virtual lab: The educational simulation genre in which participants engage a virtual product, structured by tasks and levels, to learn about (or to demonstrate competency in) using some real-world item.

W

Web-based training (WBT): Delivery of educational content via a web browser over the public Internet, a private intranet, or an extranet. WBT often provides links to other learning resources such as references, email, bulletin boards, and discussion groups. WBT also may include a facilitator who can provide course guidelines, manage discussion boards, deliver lectures, and so forth. When used with a facilitator, WBT offers some advantages of instructor-led training, while retaining the advantages of computer-based training (CBT).

Whole Brain Thinking: The awareness of one's own thinking style and the thinking styles of others combined with the ability to act outside of one's preferred thinking style. Developed by Ned Herrmann using his own brain research as well as other studies, the model presents four patterns that emerge in terms of how the brain perceives and processes information. The Whole Brain Model emerged as a validated description of the four different preference modes, dividing the brain into four separate quadrants. Each quadrant is different and of equal importance. These are the specializations of the four quadrants:

- Quadrant A specializes in logical, analytical, quantitative, fact-based thinking.
- Quadrant B focuses on details and specializes in planning, organizing, and sequencing information.
- Quadrant C places a priority on feelings and the interpersonal, emotional, and kinesthetic aspects of a situation.
- Quadrant D synthesizes and integrates information and is more intuitive and holistic in its thinking.

WIIFM (What's in it for me?): A common statement used by trainers to ensure that learners need to know how the content will benefit them.

Wiki: A collaborative website with content that can be modified by users. A wiki allows anyone using a web browser to edit, delete, or modify information on the site, including the work of other authors. *Wiki wiki* means "quickly" in the Hawaiian language.

Workplace learning and performance (WLP): The professions of training, performance improvement, learning, development, and workplace education. It often is colloquially referred to as training or training and development.

Workforce planning: The process and activities that ensure that an organization can meet its goals and objectives within a changing business environment by ensuring the right numbers of the right kinds of people are available at the right times and in the right place.

WYSIWYG (What you see is what you get): An acronym that is pronounced *wizzy-wig*. WYSIWYG applications don't always display code; instead they provide a working area where text and graphics are placed on the screen.

X

XML (Extensible Markup Language): The webpage coding language that allows site designers to program their own markup commands, which can then be used as if they were standard HTML commands.

Reference

Reynolds, Angus. 1993. *The Trainer's Dictionary.* Amherst, MA: HRD Press. Used with permission. All rights reserved.

✎ Appendix B

Using the CD-ROM

Insert the CD-ROM and locate the file *How to Use This CD.doc.*

Contents of the CD-ROM

The CD-ROM that accompanies this *Handbook* contains three types of files:

- Adobe.pdf documents
- Microsoft Word documents
- Microsoft Excel documents.

Computer Requirements

To read or print the .pdf files on the CD-ROM, you must have Adobe Acrobat Reader software installed on your system. The program can be downloaded free of cost from the Adobe website, www.adobe.com.

To use or adapt the contents of the Microsoft Word or Excel files on the CD-ROM, you must have Microsoft Word and Excel software installed on your system.

Tools on the CD-ROM

Chapter 4—Performance Consulting: A Process to Ensure Skill Becomes Performance

- Tool 4-1. Sample Questions to Explore Manager Requests

Chapter 8—Selecting Solutions to Improve Workplace Performance

- Tool 8-1. Front-End Analysis Synthesis Tool
- Tool 8-2. Performance Intervention Selection Rating

Chapter 33—Bottom Line Measures in the ASTD WLP Scorecard

- Tool 33-1. ASTD WLP Scorecard—A Guide for Users
- Tool 33-2. ASTD WLP Scorecard Worksheets

Chapter 35—Organizational Culture

- Tool 35-1. Worksheet to Determine Activities to Build a Learning Culture

Chapter 39—Consulting on the Inside

- Tool 39-1. Preparing for the First Client Meeting
- Tool 39-2. A Readiness Checklist
- Tool 39-3. Potential Questions for Client Contact Meeting

Chapter 48—Workplace Learning and Performance Certification

- Tool 48-1. Certification Self-Assessment

~ About the Editor

Elaine Biech is the president and managing principal of ebb associates inc, an organizational development firm that helps organizations work through large-scale change. She has been in the training and consulting field for 30 years, working with many leading business, government, and nonprofit organizations. She specializes in helping people work as teams to maximize their effectiveness. Customizing all her work for individual clients, she conducts strategic planning sessions and implements organization-wide systems for initiatives such as improving quality, reengineering operational processes, and mentoring.

Biech has written or edited more than four dozen books and articles, including *Thriving Through Change*, 2007; *The Business of Consulting*, 2nd edition, 2007; *90 World-Class Activities by 90 World-Class Trainers*, 2007; the nine-volume set of ASTD *Certification Study Guides*, 2006; "12 Habits of Successful Trainers," ASTD *Infoline*, 2005; *The ASTD Infoline Dictionary of Basic Trainer Terms*, 2005; *Training for Dummies*, 2005; *Marketing Your Consulting Services*, 2003; *The Consultant's Quick Start Guide*, 2001; *The Pfeiffer Book of Successful Team-Building Tools*, 2001; *The Consultant's Legal Guide*, 2000; *Interpersonal Skills: Understanding Your Impact on Others*, 1996; *Building High Performance*, 1998; and *The ASTD Sourcebook: Creativity and Innovation— Widen Your Spectrum*, 1996. Since 1998, she has served as the consulting editor of both the *Pfeiffer Annual for Consultants* and *Pfeiffer Annual for Trainers*. Her books have been translated into Chinese, German, and Dutch. In addition, she has made presentations at many national and international conferences and has been featured in dozens of publications, including the *Wall Street Journal*, *Harvard Management Update*, *Washington Post*, and *Fortune*.

Biech received her B.S. from the University of Wisconsin–Superior in business and education consulting, and her M.S. in human resource development. She is active at the national level of ASTD, serving on the National Conference Design Committee in 1990, as a member of the National ASTD Board of Directors, and as ASTD's secretary from 1991 to 1994. She initiated and chaired the ASTD Consultant's Day for seven years and was the International Conference Design chair in 2000. In addition to her work with ASTD, she has served on the Independent Consultants Association's Advisory Committee and on the Instructional Systems Association Board of Directors. She was the recipient of the 1992 National ASTD Torch Award, 2004 ASTD Volunteer-Staff Partnership Award, and the 2006 ASTD Gordon M. Bliss Memorial Award. She was selected for the 1995 Wisconsin Women Entrepreneur's Mentor Award. In 2001, she received the Instructional Systems Association's highest award, the ISA Spirit Award. She can be reached at ebboffice@aol.com or at www.ebbweb.com.

℘ About the American Society for Training & Development

The ASTD Mission:
Through exceptional learning and performance, we create a world that works better.

The American Society for Training & Development provides world-class professional development opportunities, content, networking, and resources for workplace learning and performance professionals. Dedicated to helping members increase their relevance, enhance their skills, and align learning to business results, ASTD sets the standard for best practices within the profession.

The society is recognized for shaping global discussions on workforce development and providing the tools to demonstrate the impact of learning on the organizational bottom line. ASTD represents the profession's interests to corporate executives, policy makers, academic leaders, small business owners, and consultants through world-class content, convening opportunities, professional development, and awards and recognition.

Professional Development

- Certificate programs
- Conferences and workshops
- Online learning
- Certified Professional in Learning and Performance (CPLP) certification through the ASTD Certification Institute
- Career Center and Job Bank

Resources

- *T+D* (*Training + Development*) magazine
- ASTD Press

- Industry newsletters
- Research and benchmarking
- Representation to policy makers

Networking

- Local chapters
- Online communities
- ASTD Connect
- Benchmarking Forum
- Learning Executives Network

Awards and Best Practices

- ASTD BEST Awards
- Excellence in Practice Awards
- E-Learning Courseware Certification (ECC) through the ASTD Certification Institute

Learn more about ASTD at www.astd.org.
1.800.628.2783 (U.S.) or 1.703.683.8100
customercare@astd.org

℘ Index

Index